JON BALSBARK.

Sent to me by Tony Lane in exchange -
copy of my new YOUP book John Calvin as 16th Prophet
It arrived on Feb 14, 2014.

Tributes

TO
JOHN
CALVIN

The Calvin 500 Series

Tributes

TO

JOHN

CALVIN

A CELEBRATION OF HIS QUINCENTENARY

EDITED BY

DAVID W. HALL

P&R
PUBLISHING
P.O. BOX 817 • PHILLIPSBURG • NEW JERSEY 08865-0817

Library of Congress Cataloging-in-Publication Data
Tributes to John Calvin : a celebration of his quincentenary / edited by David W. Hall.
    p. cm. -- (The Calvin 500 series)
" ... conferences were sponsored during 2009 ... the papers that were presented in Calvin's own quarters July 6-9, 2009 ... the chapters comprising this book were presented at (or written by presenters of) Calvin 500 at the Auditoire in Geneva's Old Town"--Pref.
  Includes bibliographical references and index.
  ISBN 978-1-59638-096-7 (cloth)
  1. Calvin, Jean, 1509-1564--Congresses. I. Hall, David W., 1955-
BX9418.T75 2010
284'.2092--dc22

                          2009050166

To Ann,

The greatest woman in history,
without whom this and many other projects, volumes, and ministries
would never have occurred.
Thank you for everything.

Contents

     Theory?   504
     BRUCE L. McCORMACK

23. See You in Heaven: Calvin's View of Life, Death, and
     Eternal Life   530
     HERMAN J. SELDERHUIS

     Appendix: Original Schedule of Calvin500 Tribute Conference   547
     Index of Scripture   551
     Index of Subjects and Names   553
     Contributors   567

FOREWORD

Of this I am quite certain: no one would be more surprised by the continuing interest in John Calvin than John Calvin himself. And yet an entire academic industry has arisen around Calvin, and the five hundredth anniversary of his birth has become the occasion for celebrations, commemorations, and scholarly symposia all over the world.

Half a millennium after his birth, John Calvin continues to attract both interest and controversy. In recent years, both *Christianity Today*, the flagship periodical of American evangelicalism, and the *Christian Century*, the venerable masthead of Protestant liberalism, have run cover stories on the rise of "the new Calvinists." College students and young adults are observed wearing T-shirts emblazoned with the image of John Calvin, even as secular historians and sociologists debate Calvin's legacy and the lasting nature of his influence.

For some, Calvin represents a long-abandoned era of Protestant orthodoxy. Speak the name of John Calvin at one of America's great research universities and you are likely to conjure up the image associated with intellectual intolerance and repression. To others, Calvin remains a heroic figure, who represents the humble but tenacious commitment to the reform of the church by the Word of God. While some attempt to dismiss Calvin as a fanatic, others look to Calvin for his exemplary faithfulness.

In the end, it is the friends of Calvin who will have the last word. These friends are represented by those who gathered in Geneva in 2009 for a Calvin500 conference that considered Calvin in terms of his times, his thought, and his legacy. Along with many others, I am encouraged by the publication of this book that brings together these worthy essays and papers.

Why would the five hundredth anniversary of the Genevan Reformer be the occasion for commemorative events, the release of significant new books, and a growing industry in Calvin studies? The answer is actually quite simple. Half a millennium after Calvin's birth, his theological contribution appears more, rather than less, important than it appeared in his own day. The passage of five centuries has not dimmed interest in John Calvin—it has fueled a desire to see Calvin's commitment to the reform of the church embraced and carried on by a new generation of believers.

As the chapters in this book make clear, John Calvin was a multifaceted personality possessed of manifold gifts. God invested this man with extraordinary intelligence, theological courage, unquestioned tenacity, and a deep love for the church. While secular academics consider Calvin in terms of his cultural influence in the shaping of Western civilization, the scholars who gathered in Geneva were primarily concerned with Calvin the churchman, theologian, and pastor.

Calvin's lasting legacy is grounded in his remarkable ministry as a Reformer, theologian, preacher, biblical scholar, and devoted follower of the Lord Jesus Christ. As a Reformer, Calvin is primarily associated with his sacrificial commitment to the reform of the church in Geneva. Nevertheless, Calvin's reformation had an impact far beyond Geneva, even in his own day. Five hundred years later, it is no accident that so many churches and denominations look to John Calvin and his ministry for foundational grounding and identity. It is also no accident that a generation of young evangelicals looks hungrily to Calvin and the Reformation in Geneva as an example of what can happen when the gospel and the Word of God are recovered in the life of a Christian congregation.

The chapters in this volume also reveal the lasting legacy of John Calvin as theologian. The Reformation in Geneva was grounded in Calvin's brilliant and biblical theology that was itself grounded in the Word of God. In a very real sense, it can be argued that Calvin gave birth to both biblical and systematic theology in a Protestant context. His *Institutes of the Christian Religion* represents a theological and dogmatic achievement virtually unmatched in subsequent centuries. To a generation starving on a diet of contemporary evangelical superficiality, Calvin inspires as an exemplary Christian theologian, matching passion to intellect and comprehensiveness to biblical faithfulness.

Of course, Calvin continues to inspire preachers, and his own ministry of preaching stands as one of the great achievements not only of the Reformation, but of all Christian history. In essence, Calvin's singular aim was that the church of God would be properly fed by the Word of God and thus protected from all error. Calvin understood himself first and foremost as both a preacher and a professor of sacred Scripture. As a true doctor of the church, Calvin dedicated his life to the relentless preaching of the Word of God and to the training of those called by God to take up this task. Calvin's legacy of biblical exposition stands as a monumental achievement. Can anyone imagine that the sermons of any preacher alive today will be more widely disseminated in print five hundred years from now than in the present?

Calvin's influence as a scholar of the Bible and a student of Scripture continues both to instruct and to inspire a generation separated from Calvin by time, but united with Calvin in calling. His faithful, meticulous, and doxological exegesis continues to inform the interpretation of Scripture and to inspire the faithful and reverent study of the Bible as the Word of God.

Of course, there were not multiple John Calvins—only one man who, by the providence of God, was used as a human agent of a Reformation that continues in the hearts of God's people today. The gathering of scholars in Geneva in 2009 was not occasioned by merely antiquarian interests, but by a sense of Calvin's continuing relevance. He is indeed a figure of history who must necessarily appear somewhat remote from us. We would all desire to know more of Calvin the man. As Yale historian Bruce Gordon recently commented, "John Calvin as a child does not come easily to the eye." Nevertheless, we are the inheritors of a historical legacy and the possessors of a vast library of worthy works both by and about John Calvin. Thus, the five hundredth anniversary of John Calvin's birth is more than adequate justification for works such as this volume and many others that will surely follow. The scholars who contribute to this volume are united in the judgment that Calvin's legacy is of vital importance to our own times, our own thought, and our own churches. Readers of this volume will gain access to a conversation that may have appeared out of place in twenty-first-century Geneva and would no doubt have perplexed the great Genevan Reformer, but should bring great encouragement to the people of God.

Semper Reformanda!

R. Albert Mohler Jr., President,
The Southern Baptist Theological Seminary

PREFACE

The essays in this collection provide a celebratory tribute to one of the most influential human beings in history. They are intended to illumine the many contributions of John Calvin, and this volume is a gift to his honored memory. As attested by the many gathered to commemorate the quincentenary of Calvin's birth (July 10, 1509), it is a remarkable fact, in itself, that a French religious leader originally from a tiny village is still remembered half a millennium later. But that so many, from such far-reaching corners, did so in 2009 is, frankly, more surprising than our original and fondest hopes.

An earlier commentator described one by-product of such commemorations as the resultant liberation from the narrow constraints of the immediate present. If later participants have the opportunity to "ascend some eminence which commands a view of ways long since trodden, and then, from what is taught in the review, learn to forecast the ever-widening way of the future . . . [then we may] catch the spirit of the great historic eras which have been potent in shaping the institutions of our own times." "It is only," wrote Moses Hoge, "when we can transport ourselves to the distant past and evoke from its obscurity the forms of its heroic men; it is only when we acquaint ourselves with the errors they combated, the difficulties they surmounted, the hardships they endured, that we can fully comprehend the character of the men who thus toiled and suffered, or appreciate the value."[1]

One of the other benefits of periodic commemorations is the leveling of the ideological ground that no longer surrenders automatic superiority to the new, the recent, or the novel. In fact, such

---

1. Moses D. Hoge, *Memorial Volume of the Westminster Assembly, 1647–1897*, ed. Francis Beattie et al. (Richmond, VA: Presbyterian Committee of Publication, 1897), 189.

commemorations frequently leave us with more admiration of our parents than we previously had.

G. K. Chesterton perceptively lamented the infatuation with novelty of thought, warning that if past virtues were not championed, they would inevitably deteriorate as a result of adverse conditions. He understood that if things are simply left alone, those are abandoned to a torrent of change:

> If you leave a white post alone it will soon be a black post. If you particularly want it to be white you must be always painting it again; that is, you must be always having a revolution. Briefly, if you want the old white post you must have a new white post. But this which is true even of inanimate things is in a quite special and terrible sense true of all human things. An almost unnatural vigilance is really required of the citizen because of the horrible rapidity with which human institutions grow old. It is the custom in passing romance and journalism to talk of men suffering under old tyrannies. But, as a fact, men have almost always suffered under new tyrannies; under tyrannies that had been public liberties hardly twenty years before.[2]

Our motive for this commemoration took such counsel seriously. Such an assessment of the utility of commemoration was also well summarized years ago for a different commemoration by William Symington, who noted that the tendency to reflect on past events "springs from a law of our nature." Although aware that such commemorations could be abused, nevertheless he averred:

> Matters of great and permanent utility, the due consideration of which is fitted to exert a continued beneficial influence on society, are thus held forth to the view of the community, and prevented from passing into oblivion. The very act of reminiscence itself is calculated to call into operation, and consequently to improve by exercising, some of the higher moral principles of the heart, such as gratitude for benefits received, veneration for departed worth, and imitation of praiseworthy excellence.[3]

2. G. K. Chesterton, *Orthodoxy* (London: Lane, 1909), 210–11.
3. William Symington, *Commemoration of the Bicentenary of the Westminster Assembly of Divines* (Glasgow: D. Bryck and W. Blackwood, 1843), 31–32.

Thus, from the outset of our commemoration, we were grateful for those who had gone ahead of us, and we believe we may still learn from them. Moreover, the proper purpose of such an anniversary is neither boasting nor a triumphalism that would have embarrassed our honoree. Rather, our commemoration sought to be a means of humble review with a purpose to stimulate, reflect, celebrate, unify, and educate.

An earlier Swiss historian, J. H. Merle D'Aubigne, provided helpful advice for our perspective in this endeavor when he wrote: "We entertain no blind admiration. . . . We acknowledge that, sharing in the faults of his century or rather of ten centuries, [Calvin] believed that whatever infringed on the respect due to God ought to be punished by the civil power, quite as much as anything that might be injurious to the honor or life of man. We deplore this error." But D'Aubigne also continued to note: "How can anyone study with discernment the reformer's letters and other writings, and not recognize in him one of the noblest intelligences, one of the most elevated minds, one of the most affectionate hearts, and in short, one of those true Christian souls who unreservedly devote themselves to duty?"[4]

A perspective that values the past "protects us from confounding the errors and vices which are the true poison of society with its pleasant food, and the wholesome and necessary medicine with its poison. It teaches us," as Robert Dabney observed well, "to distrust the temporary and specious prosperity or gain which attends immorality and error, and tells us, with solemn and monitory voice, to remember, amidst all the clash of unthinking applause, that 'the lip of truth shall be established forever, but a lying tongue is but for a moment.' "[5]

In the earliest planning discussions for Calvin500, one of the *desiderata* was to provide a sympathetic (but not uncritical) academic forum to discuss the influence of John Calvin. Many fine conferences were sponsored during 2009 toward that end, and the papers that were presented in Calvin's own quarters on July 6–9, 2009, which are included in this volume, represent one of the more extensive efforts to bolster scholarly discussion

4. J. H. Merle D'Aubigne, *The History of the Reformation in Europe in the Time of Calvin* (New York: Robert Carter and Brothers, 1863–1879), 3.vi–vii.

5. Robert L. Dabney, *Lectures and Discussions* (Edinburgh: Banner of Truth, 1982), 3:17.

of John Calvin during the quincentenary. The chapters constituting this book were presented at (or written by presenters of) Calvin500 at the Auditoire in Geneva's Old Town. We have sought to share with our readers the fullest version of those presentations.

Of course, previous Calvin celebrations did similarly. Philip Vollmer compiled a set of essays at the four hundredth anniversary of Calvin's birth in 1909, as did the Southern Presbyterian church meeting that year in Savannah, Georgia (the original twelve essays of the *Calvin Memorial Addresses: Celebrating the 400th Anniversary of Calvin's Birth*, edited by B. B. Warfield, Thomas Cary Johnson, James Orr, and R. A. Webb, were reissued this year). Four outstanding 1909 lectures were featured by the *Princeton Theological Review* in 1909 (recently republished as *Calvin and the Reformation: Four Studies by Bavinck, Doumergue, Lang & Warfield*, edited by William Park Armstrong), and numerous other commemorative events were held early in the twentieth century, including the beginning of the Reformation Wall in the *Parc des Bastions* in Geneva in 1909.

Interestingly, few anthologies were compiled for the 450th anniversary of Calvin's birth—perhaps accounted for jointly by the low ebb of popularity of Calvin in that period and by the fact that celebrations are normally made at century marks instead of half-century ones. Of course, the largest monument to Calvin's honor in 1959 was the work and almost completion of Ford Lewis Battles's edition of *The Institutes of the Christian Religion*, published in 1960. In terms of sheer volume, however, this publication and others compiled for the quincentenary constitute the largest single year of literary commentary on Calvin in history.[6]

The presenters herein are some of the finest living Calvin scholars who contributed to that body of literature. They represent different continents, different religious communities, different eras, different specialties, and differing perspectives. All, however, honestly seek to deal with the texts, the times, the topics, or the contributions of John Calvin. Some may find it refreshing, too, that this faculty does not begin with an ax to grind or

6. As this volume was being completed, an ambitious ninety-seven-volume digitized set was released by http://www.Calvin500.com, including forty-six volumes of Calvin's commentaries, nine different editions of the *Institutes*, four volumes of Calvin's letters, eight volumes of Calvin's shorter treatises, ten biographies, and twenty works on Calvinism.

an attempt to discredit Calvin while denying him the opportunity to defend himself.

The result is both an introduction to a living and lively tradition and an exhibition of some of these scholars at the apogee of their professions. Each chapter could well spawn its own dissertations, monographs, and symposia; each will certainly engender discussion.

The arrangement of chapters is altered from the order of original presentation in Geneva, and the program is included in an appendix at the rear of this volume for historical and informational purposes. Notwithstanding, I thought it would be instructive to compile the sections around essays that set the context for Calvin (Part 1), or elaborated on some topic (Part 2), or discussed continuing relevance (Part 3).

Obviously, not all readers will agree with each essay; neither do all essayists herein agree on everything. Yet a worthy production is found in this collection, which gives friends and foes of Calvinism alike a glimpse into the state of Calvinism in our day—at least a snapshot of those who profess to identify largely with Calvin. No attempt has been made to alter the substance of any essay to fit an enforced mold; each author was free to use his or her sources, expertise, and pen as he or she saw fit. At the conclusion, when the papers were presented, a stunning assortment was delivered.

Although many tributes will be published in this eventful cycle, we trust that this one will contribute to the modern understanding of Calvin's life and work. It certainly has enough expertise from this group of all-stars to do so, since some of the finest scholars of Calvin's work are gathered between these covers.

We thank all the authors, their families, and their supporting institutions for their contribution to this project. I also wish to express a deep debt of gratitude to two excellent editors, John J. Hughes and Karen Magnuson, for their superb craftsmanship, which has greatly improved this work. The sacrifice of these writers and editors, combined with an informed willingness to edify the church, is surely a compliment to the Tributee. If Calvin is not somewhere smiling at his descendants for at least a minute or two over this momentary unity and potent witness, surely Theodore Beza must be.

All the authors have been a pleasure to consult with, and the work of each of them certainly stands on its own. Accordingly, we wish to dedicate this volume to our children—biological, adopted, peda-gogical, ecclesiological, or literary—in hopes that the robust faith that animated John Calvin and his children will so move our own children for centuries to come. SDG.

ABBREVIATIONS

CD	Karl Barth, *Church Dogmatics*, ed. G. W. Bromiley and T. F. Torrance (Edinburgh: T&T Clark, 1975)
CO	John Calvin, *Ioannis Calvini opera quae supersunt omnia*, ed. Guilielmus Baum, Eduardus Cunitz, and Eduardus Reuss, 59 vols., *Corpus Reformatorum* series, vols. 29–87 (Brunswick: C. A. Schwetschke and Son, 1863–1900)
Comm.	*Commentary*, from CO
CR	*Corpus Reformatorum*
CTJ	*Calvin Theological Journal*
ESV	English Standard Version
ET	English translation
Institutes	John Calvin, *Institutes of the Christian Religion*, various editions
JETS	*Journal of the Evangelical Theological Society*
KJV	King James Version
NASB	New American Standard Bible
OS	John Calvin, *Joannis Calvini, Opera selecta*, ed. Petrus Barth and Guilelmus Niessel, 5 vols. (Munich: Christoph Kaiser, 1926–54)
R. Consist.	Robert M. Kingdon et al., eds., *Registres du Consistoire de Genève au temps de Calvin*, 21 vols. (Geneva: Droz, 1996–)
RR	La Revue Reformée

RSV	Revised Standard Version
SC	*Supplementa Calviniana*
SRR	*Supplément a la Revue Reformée*
Serm.	*Sermon,* from CO
WCF	Westminster Confession of Faith
WLC	Westminster Larger Catechism
WSC	Westminster Shorter Catechism
WTJ	*Westminster Theological Journal*

PART I

CALVIN'S TIMES

I

CALVIN'S CHILDREN

WILLIAM A. MCCOMISH

This essay concerns the spread of John Calvin's ideas in the world. It is not based on a narrow study of a particular aspect of Calvin's life or work but rather provides a wide-ranging survey of Calvinist influence on the development of modern civilization. I am profoundly grateful to Dr. David Hall for his invitation to be a keynote speaker at the Calvin500 celebrations. I am deeply aware of the honor that he has shown me, and I believe that this invitation, and this essay that I now present to you, represents an "action de grace" or thanksgiving. It is also a confession of my faith, and it is a conviction statement. If it were not for Calvin and his successors, I would not be what I am. If it were not for Calvin and his successors—whom I have chosen to call his "children"—the modern world would be a much more primitive and barbarous place than it is. If we look only at the sixteenth century and look only at Geneva or at theology, then we are lost in a time warp and will never know who we are or from where we have come.

We are gathered here today on sacred ground—not that Calvinists have sacred ground, but we are here where it all began and in buildings that are powerful symbols for us all. My time frame is five hundred years and my field the whole world. In this conference we are aware of the great Latin motto of Geneva, *Post tenebras lux*, "Light comes after darkness," but I would like to place this article under the magnificent motto of my old and battered home city of Belfast in Northern Ireland, *Pro tanto quid retribuamus*, "For what we have received let us be truly thankful."

It is not enough to regard Calvinism as a purely academic theological system. From its beginnings in Geneva it had a strong practical application in human life in the real world. Calvin, I believe, was the greatest Christian theologian since St. Paul, and his work has ensured that for five centuries his followers have benefited from a vision of Jesus Christ that is more true, more accurate, and more clear than any other. But this revolutionary mind-set has not been confined to academic theologians. The kind of responsible middle-class people who accepted Calvinism then went out into the world with a living faith to serve their Master, Jesus Christ, in the world. I am reminded of the great question of Isaiah 53:1: "Who hath believed our report? and to whom is the arm of the LORD revealed?" (KJV).

Calvinists have lived in many countries and worked in many areas. The Calvinist principle of individual responsibility has led to wave after wave of Presbyterians turning their faith into practice in many different fields—and I will cite examples such as those of banking, politics, business, political thought and democracy, human rights, education, and Bible translation, printing, distribution, and reading. This is the topic of my present essay, which is also very personal. It is my own selection of a very few iconic women and men who, I believe, carry the heritage of Calvin's work in Geneva. In a very modest way I am following Theodore Beza when he wrote his *Icones* of 1580.[1] Some of my choices may surprise you, and fraternally, I suggest that creating your own list to celebrate Calvin500 would be a worthy exercise.

---

1. Theodore Beza, *Icones id est verae imagines virorum doctrina simul et pietate illustrum . . . quibus adiectae sunt nonnullae picturae quas Emblemata vocant* (Geneva, 1580).

Presbyterians, Calvinists, are not called to celebrate their own vision of the past. Rather, we are called to strive for God's kingdom in our own place and in our own time. But it is part of the pleasure of this fifth centenary to look back and not only to draw strength from the past but to gather strength to face an uncertain future. It is not my intention to produce a panegyric of Calvinist history, and this is my first caveat: Calvinists have made plenty of mistakes. Do we not, after all, believe that we are fallen, imperfect creatures that can be saved only by the grace of God? Yet one major feature of Calvinism has been the evolution of our practice, and we will see how the application of Calvinist faith to resistance theory or to human rights has changed over the centuries. This is normal and admirable. It must not be thought that Calvinism has always spoken with one voice; it has always been plural. It is an old joke, but a truth, that where you have three Presbyterians, you have five points of view! This is not a weakness but a strength. Calvinism and Presbyterianism are not authoritarian systems in which clone-like sectarians endlessly repeat a truth that they have been taught by their guru. Calvinists have seized a theological truth, and this truth has set them free to use their individual responsibility to apply a multitude of attitudes and solutions to the problems and challenges of the world.

My second caveat is to point out that although I believe Calvinism to be the primary force for progress in human society, I do not do so in any sectarian way. We are not alone in doing good and improving the lives of people. Who can ignore the work of the Quakers, the Methodists, and the Catholics, as well as secular groups and other faith families?

My third caveat is to state clearly that this essay is by no means exhaustive. Millions of women and men have lived lives far from the limelight but have put their faith into practice in modest, limited circumstances known perhaps only to themselves and to God. Calvinism at its best is a mass movement, not an elitist one. To concentrate on a few interesting people is not to decry or to diminish the rest. All, in Calvinism, are equal in the sight of God. I must add that one major difficulty for me in writing this essay is that there is simply too much to say. There are too many people to whom I would like to introduce you! We are in very good company.

3

Beginnings

The history of Calvinism really begins with the cataclysmic plague of the fourteenth century—the Black Death that wiped out a third, a half, perhaps two-thirds of the population of Europe. All figures are inaccurate, since there were so many dead that they could be neither counted nor buried. What is clear is that the Black Death spelled the end of the feudal system in western Europe. The system that had developed (after the fall of the late Roman empire) of the illiterate lord in his castle and the illiterate serfs laboring in the fields broke down for good. The towns sprang up, and a new, literate middle class came into being: the merchant, the trader, the industrialist, the banker. For the first time in a thousand years, literacy was not confined to the church. A literate, secular middle class now took life and religion seriously, wanted to read the Bible, hear intelligent sermons, and take part in the government of the church, as well as to have responsibilities in business and government. It was this new, urban middle class that became Protestant, in Hamburg, Zurich, Venice, and Amsterdam; in Edinburgh, Lausanne, Philadelphia, and Debrecen; and in Geneva—which is the perfect example because in 1536 the new middle-class citizens overturned an aristocratic civil government and Roman ecclesiastical government to take control of both themselves.

The Bible

Calvinists were not the first or the only translators of the Bible. The fourth-century *Biblia Vulgata* of Jerome contained many errors, but had been used for centuries. The wave of Greek-speaking scholars who came to western Europe in the mid-fifteenth century following the fall of Constantinople to the Turks stimulated the rediscovery of Greek texts in Renaissance Italy, notably at Florence and Ferrara. Theologians produced Greek New Testaments that were the basis of Protestant biblical scholarship. Erasmus's Greek New Testament was published in 1516 and was contemporary with the *Complutensian Polyglot* of the Spanish Cardinal Ximenes of 1522, published after twenty years of labor. Calvinist seminaries, including the Genevan Academy (founded by Calvin in 1559), taught from the Greek text. Theodore Beza published his Greek New Testament in 1565.[2]

The method of teaching was to develop propositions from the text that were formed into commonplaces and theses that were then developed into doctrines. This propositional form of revelation was controlled by a Melanchthonian hierarchy in the use of the books of the Bible. Calvin and others taught that if the Epistle to the Romans were properly understood, it would enable understanding of the whole Bible. The first and fourth Gospels were next in the order of authority, with the rest of the New Testament following, and the Old Testament following after that.

Comprehension of the biblical text was essential to the Calvinists for two reasons. The first was that Calvin and his associates understood clearly that the education of the clergy was essential to the Reformation's survival. In an increasingly educated secular world, people would listen only to properly trained ministers. The Genevan Academy attracted hundreds of young men from all over Europe and sent them out to preach the Word. Preaching was popular and an essential part of the life of the Calvinists—as it is today. The second reason was that private Bible study, alone or in the family circle, was encouraged and indeed required. Thus, translations were necessary as furnishings for church and home. The Calvinists became the greatest preachers and biblical translators in history. Bibles in French, English, and Italian were translated in Geneva. Calvin's own cousin Olivetan published a French translation in 1535. It was in Geneva that Robert Estienne, one of Calvin's followers, first divided the Bible into chapter and verse in his 1551 New Testament. Many other translations followed: an Irish version by 1602 and a Lithuanian version by 1662,[3] as well as Dutch (authorized by the Synod of Dort), Hungarian, Spanish, Polish, German—many in several versions, but all inspired by the Calvinist hunger to know and to practice the will of God. The vast

2. For all editions of the Bible, the best source is still the classic Thomas H. Darlow and Horace F. Moule, *Historical Catalogue of the Printed Editions of Holy Scripture* (London: Bible House, British and Foreign Bible Society, 1905–11). A good recent book on Beza is A. Dufour, *Théodore de Bèze Poète et théologien* (Geneva: Droz, 2006).

3. Stanislaus Kot, *La Réforme dans le Grand-Duché de Lithuanie* (Brussels, 1953); Henry Hall, *An Account of the Translation of the Bible into the Lithuanian Tongue* (Oxford, 1659); R. Steele, "Materials for the History of the Lithuanian Bible," *The Library*, January 1907.

amount of work involved in the making of these translations will never be known, but we can glean some idea of their success by looking briefly at two Bibles.

The Geneva English Bible was published by a group of exiles fleeing the persecution of the Catholic Mary Tudor in 1560. It is popularly known as the "Breeches" Bible because in Genesis 3:7 Adam and Eve made themselves breeches to cover their nakedness. But for fifty years it was the standard Bible in English and was reprinted some 160 times, making it one of the best sellers of all time. Its influence on the Protestant mind-set of the British is incalculable, especially when we realize that it was not simply the text that was reproduced but vast numbers of marginal notes inspired by Calvin, Beza, and Olivetan. James VI and I, who did not much like Presbyterians, wrote that the notes were "very partial, untrue, seditious, and savouring too much of dangerous and traitorous conceits,"[4] which is high praise indeed!

Another Bible with a specifically Genevan origin was that of Giovanni Diodati, a professor in the Genevan Academy and a delegate to the Synod of Dort. Diodati rapidly translated the New Testament into Italian in 1607 to support a Protestant conspiracy to take control of the Venetian Republic, where there were many Protestants among the ruling classes. Unfortunately, the conspiracy failed, but the Diodati Bible remained the standard translation used by Italian Protestants until our own day.[5]

These are only two Bibles; each Bible has its history. The outlines of the history of the Breeches and the Diodati Bibles are woefully inadequate, but I hope they begin to show the determination of those whom I have chosen to call "Calvin's children."

The reading and the preaching of the Word[6] was at the center of all Calvinist worship, life, and work. It is still our specificity. The serious-

4. An interesting discussion of preaching in seventeenth-century England, which underlines the importance of the Geneva Bible, is to be found in Christopher Hill, *Society and Puritanism in Pre-Revolutionary England* (London: Panther Books, 1964).

5. William A. McComish, *The Epigones* (Allison Park, PA: Pickwick Publications, 1989).

6. See the answer to question 89 of the WSC: "The Spirit of God maketh the reading, but especially the preaching of the Word, an effectual means of convincing and converting sinners, and of building them up in holiness and comfort, through faith, unto salvation."

ness and skill of those involved in this effort make it a summit of human achievement. And it is from this achievement that all else follows.

Political Thought

Calvin was a practical man in a real situation. He was not simply an academic theorist meditating in his office on the state of the world. Calvin dealt with the real problems of the real city of Geneva at many levels, not only theologically but practically, in matters as diverse as economics and education. We will discuss these matters later on, but what I want to consider now is Calvin's attitude to political power, comprising his thoughts on resistance against tyrants and democracy.

Democracy and Resistance

I have no doubt that Calvin was a democrat. Democracy is no one thing but has an infinite number of applications and functions. But in the basic sense that Calvin opposed autocratic government in the church and in the state and believed in the rule of the majority and the right of protest, he was a democrat. We can see this very simply in the archetypal Calvinist institution of the Company of Pastors. The executive function of the group is exercised by the whole group in discussion and not by a bishop, and one member of the group is equal to another. All power ultimately comes from God. This is as true, of course, in secular as in ecclesiastical matters. Calvin in his *Institutes* praises the work of the Genevan *Petit conseil*, where responsibility is shared by a number of people.[7] He wrote that a system composed of a mixture of aristocracy (not hereditary aristocracy but rather the body of believers) and democracy is the ideal.[8] But Calvin was faced with the harsh political realities of sixteenth-century Europe. His reading of Scripture led him, like Martin Luther, to state that kings were to be obeyed and that even bad magistrates were to be obeyed.

7. Classic study of Calvin's political thought in J. W. Allen, *A History of Political Thought in the Sixteenth Century* (London: Methuen, 1928 [and many reprints]).

8. John Calvin, *Institutes of the Christian Religion*, ed. John T. McNeill, trans. Ford Lewis Battles (London: SCM Press, 1961), 4.20.8.

But what should be done in a situation of intolerable injustice—for instance, when members of the true church were being persecuted? How was tyranny to be resisted? Calvin, from the more-or-less secure city of Geneva, where secular and religious governments were fused in the Supreme Council, suggested that it was the Christian duty of elected magistrates to resist tyranny. But what if you were a Scot, a Dutchman, or a persecuted French Protestant? Calvin's doctrine of opposition to tyranny was essentially passive and based on medieval political thought as expressed in the editions of the *Institutes* printed in 1539, 1543, and 1550. But in the 1559 edition he seems to suggest for the first time that the elect have a right to rebel if an ungodly tyrant orders them to break God's law.[9] This idea is repeated in a stronger form in a 1561 writing on Daniel. This was the period when the political and religious struggle was coming to a head in Scotland and the wars of religion were beginning in France. An evolution from Calvin's own doctrine began in his own lifetime as the Scotsman John Knox used his Calvinist faith to resist autocratic and, as he saw it, ungodly government. Scotland, with the encouragement of Knox, was the first country where the Calvinists were strong enough to rise against government, closely followed by the French Huguenots[10] and the Dutch Protestants[11] in 1566.

This right of rebellion, or resistance theory, became typical of Calvinists after 1560. One original aim in each case was to install some form of theocentric model after the Genevan experiment. The idea of the ideal state was one in which the ruler would protect and promote the true church. The magnificent final passage in the anonymous 1578 French Protestant work *Vindiciae contra tyrannos*[12] illustrates the political ideal for sixteenth-century Calvinists: "Piety bids us maintain the Law and the Church of God; justice demands that we bind the hands of the

9. Ibid., 4.20.3–7. See also T. H. L. Parker, *John Calvin* (London: Dent, 1975), passim.

10. Allen, *A History of Political Thought in the Sixteenth Century*, pt. 2. See also John Bowle, *Western Political Thought* (London: Methuen, 1947 [and reprints]).

11. Much material, but read Johan H. Huizinga's long essay "Dutch Civilisation in the Seventeenth Century," in *Dutch Civilisation in the Seventeenth Century, and Other Essays* (London: Collins, 1968).

12. Anonymous, *Vindiciae contra tyrannos, sive de principis in populum populique in principem legitima potestate, Stephano Junio Bruto Celia auctore* (Bâle, 1579 [Latin]; 1581 [French]).

tyrant who would destroy all right and all good government: charity requires that we lend a hand to lift up the fallen. Those who make no account of these things would drive piety, justice and charity from the world." Government is concerned not only with religion but also with justice and with welfare.

These were very advanced ideas for the time, as they still are in many countries. Too much may be made of the difference between Calvin and the Calvinists in the matter of political thought. They were in different situations, and ideas were evolving. The basic principle is that tyranny is not the will of God, who will himself judge the tyrant, and that the godly have the duty to resist by passive or active means. Many Protestants had to live as minorities in Roman Catholic or Muslim countries in either western or eastern Europe, and from these communities comes the idea of demanding freedom of conscience and the rights of minorities, law being applied to protect the rights of the individual as well as the community. This was the real beginning of the secular concept of human rights.[13] A clear thread can be traced from the sixteenth-century Calvinists to the modern concepts of democracy with their protection of minority rights. It is no surprise to note that Jean-Jacques Rousseau, who promulgated the idea that government is a social contract between ruler and ruled, was baptized in St. Pierre Cathedral or that the father of American democratic theory, James Madison (1751–1836), who argued for the rights of minorities and individuals to protect them from tyranny in his great papers in *The Federalist*, was a Presbyterian.[14]

Let me now introduce you to a few more of Calvin's children who have striven for human rights, liberty, democracy, and justice in many lands. They have not struggled alone but are an essential group in the establishment of a just and democratic world. I believe that they are the *sine qua non*, the group without which there would have been nothing. I cannot see democracy arising from any other European or Asiatic faith family without these impulses.

13. Bowle, *Western Political Thought*, bk. 3, chap. 2.
14. *The Federalist* papers date from 1787 to 1788. Madison, fourth president of the United States, 1751–1836, wrote about a third of them. They are the basis for American pluralist republican democracy.

Education

I have already noted that a literate population is an essential element for the Calvinist. This leads us to two further developments: (1) the education of children, and (2) the freedom of the press. When the citizens of Geneva adopted the reform of the church in 1536, they also adopted measures to educate children and care for the poor. Literacy was vital for the industrial and commercial society then developing. In Calvin's time, the college was founded for youth, and this right of education was not confined to the children of the rich; the children of the poor were to be taught and prepared for useful trades—education was not to be bought.[15] The Genevan Academy was founded in 1559 (now the University of Geneva) for the training of ministers.

This Calvinist concern for education became typical of Reformed bodies everywhere—for example, the founding of Princeton by American Presbyterians and the work of the Czech Calvinist Comenius (1592–1670), one of the first believers in universal education, an idea that he expounded in his *Didactica magna*. Comenius, who was asked to be the first president of Harvard, also published the *Orbis Pictus*, a kind of illustrated children's encyclopedia that was the first-ever picture book for children. It is not surprising, either, that the library of the University of Oxford was founded by Sir Thomas Bodley (1545–1613), the Geneva-educated son of one of the translators of the English "Breeches" Bible.

Freedom of the Press

The freedom of the press, which is an essential component of democracy, has no greater exponent than the Calvinist English poet and statesman John Milton (1608–74). In his *Areopagitica*[16] he thunders against censorship: "When complaints are freely heard, deeply considered, and

---

15. There are many recent works on life in Calvin's Geneva, but it is still worth reading the section in Richard Henry Tawney, *Religion and the Rise of Capitalism* (London: Penguin, 1926 [and reprints]).

16. John Milton, *Areopagitica: A Speech of Mr John Milton for the Liberty of Unlicensed Printing to the Parliament of England* (1644). Milton, now remembered as a poet, was foreign secretary to Cromwell's government.

speedily reformed, then is the utmost bound of civil liberty attained" and "Where there is much desire to learn, there of necessity will be much arguing, much writing, many opinions; for opinion in good men is but knowledge in the making." Once again I must leave aside a vast amount of material on the relationship between Calvin's children and the freedom of the press, but I wish to mention the role of the Scottish Presbyterian Lord Reith[17] (1889–1971), the founder of the independent British Broadcasting Corporation (the BBC), who courageously defended the independence of that organization against Winston Churchill during the Second World War when Churchill wanted the BBC to become an instrument of government propaganda.

Human Rights, Justice, and Democracy

The number of Calvin's children who have worked for human rights, justice, and democracy is not to be numbered in hundreds or thousands, but in millions, many of them known only to God. Many are unexpected figures, such as the Marquis of Montrose, a Presbyterian elder, who fought brilliantly for Charles I in the seventeenth-century English Civil War. He was a poet and a soldier, but it was he who warned the king not to aim at "absoluteness," since Charles I believed in the divine right of kings and was no democrat.[18]

The United States was also founded on a revolt against tyranny largely carried out by Calvin's children, in no small amount by Irish Presbyterians who had been forced to cross the Atlantic because of religious persecution. The Declaration of Independence is in the handwriting of Charles Thompson, an Irish Presbyterian. It was printed by a second Irish Presbyterian, John Dunlap; it was first read in public by John Nixon; and it was first signed by John Hancock (and subsequently signed by seven others, William Whipple, Robert Payne, Thomas McKean, Thomas Nelson, Matthew Thornton, George Taylor, and Edward Rutledge).[19] Thus, eleven Irish Presbyterians in

17. Ian McIntyre, *The Expense of Glory: A Life of John Reith* (New York: HarperCollins, 1995).
18. John Buchan, *Montrose* (London: Oxford University Press, 1928 [and reprints]).
19. William F. Marshall, *Ulster Sails West* (Belfast: Quota Press, 1943).

11

all were a dominant force in the establishment of American independence. Although the Geneva of Calvin and Beza was not a particularly liberal environment as seen from the twenty-first century rather than the brutal sixteenth, the ideas to which it gave rise have changed the face of the world.

This love of liberty has not diminished with the passing years. In the Second World War, the elderly and aristocratic president of the French Reformed Church, Marc Boegner (1881–1970),[20] denounced the treatment of the Jews, political prisoners, and imprisoned Protestant ministers to the heads of the Nazi puppet government in France, Petain and Laval—not by letter or by declaration but by personal interviews in which his courage put him in great danger. It was typical of the man that he later denounced French brutality in Algeria during the independence struggle in that country. Another figure from the same period was Willem Visser't Hooft (1900–1985), the Dutch Protestant founder of the World Council of Churches, who was very active in the resistance movement against the occupation of Holland.[21] Notably, a plaque in St. Pierre commemorates the first ecumenical service in western Europe after the war, in 1946. The preacher was the famous German pastor Martin Niemöller, just released from one of Hitler's concentration camps.

More Opponents of Tyranny

The turbulent years since 1945 have produced many opponents of tyranny inspired by Genevan ideals. "Sam" Ratulangi (1890–1949), Indonesian national independence hero and fervent Protestant, was a doctor of science from Switzerland. He returned to his country and obliged the colonial government to abolish forced labor in his home province of Minahasa. Involved in the independence movement, he died in a prison camp.[22]

20. There is a biography on the Web site of the Académie française. See also his own works *L'Evangile et le racisme* (Paris, 1939) and *Le Problème de l'unité chretienne* (Paris: Je sers, 1947), among others.

21. Willem A. Visser't Hooft, *Memoirs*, 2nd ed. (Geneva: WCC Publications, 1987).

22. Samuel Ratulangi, *Indonesia in den Pacific* (Surabaya 1937); C. P. F. Luhulima, *Ekonomi Politik Asia Pacifik* (Jakarta, 2004). See also the article on Ratulangi as national independence hero, "Dr G.S.S.Y. Ratulangi 1890–1949," available on the Web site of the Information Department of the Republic of Indonesia.

Dr. Chun Ming Kao, the general secretary of the Presbyterian Church of Taiwan, spent seven years in prison for refusing to give the names of his friends after the Kaohsiung incident of 1979 when a Human Rights Day rally was brutally dispersed by the then military government of that island.[23] The brothers Allen and John Foster Dulles, both Presbyterian elders, served their country in the Cold War, Allen as head of the CIA and John Foster as Secretary of State (1953–59), when it was believed that democracy was in great danger. John Foster was very active in the church, a founder of the Federal Council of Churches and the World Council of Churches.[24]

General Fidel Ramos (born 1928) of the Philippines, another Protestant, became president of his country. When the vast People Power Revolution broke out to oust Ferdinand Marcos in 1986, Ramos not only refused to use the army to crush the demonstrators for democracy, but went over to their side. As president he did much to bring in protection for Philippine migrant workers, of whom there are millions throughout the world.[25] Byers Naudé (1915–2004) was a distinguished minister of the South African Dutch Reformed Church. From a very conservative background he came to feel a tension between his Christian, Calvinist faith and the political reality of his country. He resigned from his post after the Sharpeville Massacre of 1960 and denounced apartheid, saying that he believed the authority of God came before the authority of man. He was one of the leaders who advocated civil rights for all and democracy, and one of those who negotiated the ending of the apartheid system. He was nominated for a Nobel Peace Prize.[26]

Individual Responsibility

The Calvinist teaching of individual responsibility has inexorably led Calvinists to promote and defend human rights. This has been, and in many cases still is, a long, slow process. In the seventeenth century,

23. C. M. Kao, *The Path to the Cross* (Taipei, 2001). See also his speech to the General Council of the World Council of Reformed Churches at Seoul 1989, "The Lord Turned My Grief to Joy."

24. Richard H. Immerman, *John Foster Dulles: Piety, Pragmatism, and Power in U.S. Foreign Policy* (Lanham, MD: SR Books, 1998).

25. Bryan Johnson, *Four Days of Courage* (New York: Free Press, 1987).

26. B. Lugan, *Ces français qui ont fait l'Afrique du Sud*; International Commission of Jurists, *The Trial of Byers Naudé* (Geneva, 1975) (Nobel Peace Prize nominations).

Dutch Protestants could see no incompatibility between their faith and the slave trade, and there is at least one Dutch Protestant church beside a slave dungeon on the coast of Ghana. The human nature of black people was not universally accepted. But by the eighteenth century, much had changed, and an Irish Presbyterian, Thomas McCabe, was able to prevent the setting up of a slave-trade company in Belfast.[27]

In the nineteenth century, the Scottish explorer and Presbyterian missionary David Livingstone[28] was a well-known opponent of the slave trade, while in the United States, another Presbyterian, this time of Irish extraction, Horace Greeley[29] (1811–82), founder of the *New York Tribune*, was also an opponent of slavery. He fought the Fugitive Slave Law of 1850 and condemned other social evils, such as drink, gambling, and prostitution. Another group that became Protestant in the tens of thousands in the twentieth century and who were not, at one time, considered human beings were Europe's Gypsies. Hundreds of thousands of them were gassed in Hitler's concentration camps, and it was in these frightful places that Protestant pastors, imprisoned with them, spoke of the love of God. In their surprise and joy at this good news, they converted, and thousands of Gypsies are now members of the Evangelical Reformed Church of France.

Humanitarianism

The nineteenth and the twentieth centuries have seen many of Calvin's children striving for peace, justice, and humanitarianism. Henry Dunant[30]

27. Robert M. Young, *Historical Notices of Old Belfast and Its Vicinity* (Whitefish, MT: Kessinger Publishing, 2007).

28. The Livingstone archives are in the library of the University of Glasgow. Lionized by Victorian society, Livingstone was a failure as a missionary but very influential in the matter of the slave trade. For a general history that includes much Reformed and Presbyterian material, see Stephen Neill, *A History of Christian Missions* (New York: Penguin Books, 1964).

29. See Horace Greeley, *The American Conflict* (Chicago: G. & C. W. Sherwood, 1864–66), and *Recollections of a Busy Life* (New York: J. B. Ford & Co., 1868); see also Glyndon G. Van Dusen, *Horace Greeley: Nineteenth-Century Crusader* (Philadelphia: University of Pennsylvania Press, 1953).

30. See Dunant's own book on the Battle of Solferino, the publications of the International Red Cross, and the Henry Dunant Institute, in Geneva. There is a museum at Heiden, in Switzerland.

(1828–1910) was the founder of the International Red Cross (he also founded the YMCA!). The Red Cross is the archetypal Genevan Protestant institution: efficient, dedicated, and neutral. In the mid-nineteenth century the first modern wars were fought with machine guns and barbed wire. Dunant decided to take action after seeing the slaughter at the battle of Solferino in Italy. The organization was set up in Geneva in the year that the battle of Shiloh was fought in the American Civil War. The International Red Cross is a secular organization that employs people without any religious discrimination, but it retains close personal and financial links to the French-language Protestantism of Switzerland. Many young Protestant Swiss work for this organization. This has always been the case. They are far too many to discuss here, but one representative figure might be Dr. Marcel Junod[31] (1904–61). Born into a family of Protestant ministers in Neuchâtel, he was the first foreign doctor to go to Hiroshima after the nuclear attack. Thanks to the International Red Cross, he arrived with several tons of medical supplies.

Woodrow Wilson[32] (1856–1924), another child of a Presbyterian minister, was instrumental in setting up the League of Nations after the First World War, in the hope that it might prevent future armed conflicts. It was a noble endeavor that foundered in the rising fascist movements of the thirties. But Wilson revealed his roots when he located its headquarters in Geneva, now the European center of the United Nations and some two hundred other international organizations.

Dunant and Wilson are well-known historical figures, but as I have said before, there is a vast cloud of Calvinist witnesses, some little known.

Let me conclude this long section by drawing your attention to an American Presbyterian missionary in China, Wilson Plumer Mills. He was in Nanking (Nanjing) when it was taken and sacked by the Japanese in 1937. Some two hundred fifty thousand to three hundred fifty thousand people were killed and at least eighty thousand women raped, many in frightful circumstances. Mills was instrumental in setting

---

31. P. Junod, *Le troisième combattant* (1947; repr., ICRC, 1989); *Témoin d'Hiroshima* (Jussy, 2004).

32. There is a standard biography of Wilson in several volumes by Arthur Stanley Link. Wilson's *Messages and Papers* have been published, and there is a Woodrow Wilson Presidential Library.

up a safety zone for civilians in the city, a zone that eventually held two hundred thousand people and offered some security in the midst of rape, arson, torture, massacre, and pillage.[33] Calvin's children have gone far, and accomplished much.

All Areas of Human Endeavor

Calvin's children have been active in all fields of human endeavor. I have no time to treat all aspects in this chapter, which features little about preaching or missionary work, about church organization and history, about science, medicine, women's issues, or philosophy. That all these aspects merit attention is evident. In astronomy, for instance, it is fascinating to note that the library of the Genevan Academy contained modern works on astronomy at a time when the Roman Catholics were silencing Galileo and the Lutherans persecuting Kepler.[34]

I wish to draw your attention to one subject that is frequently mentioned as a Calvinist specificity: finance and economics. Since Max Weber's *Die Protestantische Ethik* in 1903, and R. H. Tawney's *Religion and the Rise of Capitalism* in 1926,[35] it has been accepted that there is a strong link between the Genevan Reformation and the beginning of modern capitalism. There is no reason to doubt this. Calvinism is the only major faith that grew in the early modern period of European history, when the industrialists, traders, and bankers were beginning to take control of the cities. Calvin himself had no very developed economic system to offer, but in practice his city protected the poor and was suspicious of excessive wealth.

What was really revolutionary was Calvin's attitude to credit. The practice of lending money for a rate of interest no more bothered Calvin

33. Iris Chang, *The Rape of Nanking: The Forgotten Holocaust of World War II* (New York: Penguin Books, 1998). See also the published diaries of John Rabe, *The Good German of Nanking*, ed. E. Wickert, trans. J. E. Woods (New York: Little, Brown and Company, 1998).

34. McComish, *The Epigones*, 209ff.

35. See note 15. Max Weber, "Die Protestantische Ethik und der Geist des Kapitalismus," in *Archiv für Socialwissenschaft und Sozialpolitik* 20 (1905); E. Troeltsch, *Die Sociallehren der christlichen Kirchen* (1911).

than would the hire of a house or a field for rent. But this practice was revolutionary at the time. The lending of money for interest, called usury, was denounced by the Roman Catholic Church at several councils, one of which ordered the exclusion from the sacraments for usurers, claimed that their wills were invalid, and forbade their burial in sacred ground. There must have been a limited application of these rules as well as a lot of hypocrisy—even Notre Dame in Paris was built in this way. Once again it was a matter of bad Bible translation based on one of the many mistranslations of the Vulgate, in this case a text from St. Luke. Yet Aristotle was also quoted as being against usury, and Thomas Aquinas wrote against it. Calvin could find nothing against it in Scripture. He never mentions the subject in the *Institutes*.[36] The Jews were allowed to take interest payments from the time of the Lateran Council in 1215, and the early Protestants did so without any problem. This was one reason why the Protestants controlled the financing of the printing industry. Among Calvin's followers were book publishers such as Estienne, and Protestant works were printed and sold in vastly greater numbers than those of their opponents.

Usury also led to a great development of banking. In the Renaissance, the Italian city-states were Europe's bankers. Then the bishop of the important banking city of Lucca converted to Protestantism and, in turn, converted the leading banking families. Peter Martyr Vermigli (1500–1562) was a notable theologian, and his "Commonplaces" were an important source for Calvin's *Institutes*.[37] These Luccan families came to Geneva and founded the Genevan banking industry. Many of their descendants are still among us, and they have produced many theologians—Turrettini, Diodati, Micheli, Burlamachi, Calandrini—to be joined by other Italian Protestants from farther south, the Fatio family and the Lombards. They were joined by French Huguenot bankers in 1685, when Louis XIV

36. See note 8. William A. McComish, "Between Greed and Charity: A Religious Perspective on Our Relationship with Money," *Revue Economique et Sociale* (Lausanne) vol. 66, décembre 2008.

37. See the McNeill/Battles edition of the *Institutes*. They trace more than four hundred correlations between Vermigli and Calvin's text. A current edition of his works is forthcoming. There are biographies by Schlosser (1809) and Schmidt (1858). See article in the *Dictionary of National Biography*. See also the Peter Martyr library at Truman State University Press.

revoked the Edict of Nantes and the best part of the French Protestants chose exile rather than conversion.

It was often said that the Genevan bankers were not necessarily more competent than others, but that they were more honest. In the light of recent financial scandal, I believe that we should encourage a swift return to the Calvinist virtues of thrift, integrity, and hard work. There are so many Protestant bankers in the history of Europe and America that it is hard to single one out, but I might mention Andrew W. Mellon[38] (1855–1937), the forty-ninth Secretary of the Treasury of the United States, the owner of his own bank from the age of twenty-seven, and the founder of Gulf Oil and ALCOA. He gave away vast sums of money for charity and his art collection to create the National Gallery in Washington, DC.

Women

This chapter has concentrated on men, and it would be false to imagine that Protestant women have been anything other than equal partners in the struggle to reveal Christ to the world. Not enough of them have been celebrated in this article, but I would like to mention two courageous women whose faith, integrity, and courage are typical of millions of their sisters and should be an inspiration to millions of others.

It sometimes surprises visitors to discover a Portuguese chapel in St. Pierre Cathedral, but this chapel was the tomb of Princess Emilie of Nassau (1569–1629), daughter of William the Silent, who married a Portuguese prince. Refusing to renounce her Protestant faith, she deserted her husband and went into exile in Geneva, preferring uncertainty to wealth and comfort.[39]

One French Protestant heroine is Marie Durand, whose brother was a minister. Arrested for her faith at the age of fifteen in 1730, she was imprisoned in the Tower of Constance at Aigues Mortes in the south of

---

38. See his own *Taxation: The People's Business* (New York: Macmillan, 1924) and the biography by David Cannadine, *Mellon: An American Life* (New York: Vintage, 2008). The Andrew W. Mellon Foundation and the U.S. Treasury archives are also worth exploring.

39. M. F. Alves de Azevedo, *Suiçasimbolo de civilizaçao progresso e cultura* (Lisbon, 1970); C. V. Wedgwood, *William the Silent* (New Haven: Yale University Press, 1944).

France. She needed to say only one word, to abjure her Protestant faith, but this she refused to do, and so she remained in the tower for thirty-seven years. The word *resister*, which she carved into the stone of her prison, gave a particular meaning to the word *resistance* as it related to the French *resistance* to the German occupation of their country.[40]

Conclusion

I am now coming toward the end of this essay. I have used the terms *Reformed, Calvinist,* and *Presbyterian* as alternatives. Yet not all of Calvin's children would have used any of these terms about themselves. The modern world owes such a vast debt to Calvin and his children that the influence is pervasive and universal. Some Calvinists have even belonged to other faith families. An Archbishop of Canterbury, George Abbot[41] (1562–1633), sent a delegation to the Synod of Dort, which had no delegation from the Presbyterian Church of Scotland. Another is Cyril Lucaris,[42] Patriarch of Constantinople, who published Calvinist confessions of faith in 1633 and 1645!

Calvin's children can be counted in millions, and they have changed the world. They have been an influence for good, and they have evolved with their times. It is immensely important to tell the world who we are and from where we come, and to teach our own people so that they may become more confident in facing the future, sure in the knowledge of Calvinist honesty, courage, integrity, faith, and devotion in the past.

The history of Calvinism is not only a history of theology and religious institutions. It is above all a history of the transformation of people's lives, faith, and behavior. It is people's history. It is time that this great story was told to all our own people—and to the world. The lives of Calvin's

40. *Bulletin de la Société de l'histoire du Protestantisme français,* passim, but especially the 1968 anniversary edition. See also the Web site of the Musée du desert.
41. Paul A. Welsby, *George Abbot, the Unwanted Archbishop* (London: SPCK, 1962); Richard A. Christophers, *George Abbot, Archbishop of Canterbury, 1562–1633: A Bibliography* (Charlottesville, VA: University Press of Virginia, 1966).
42. These confessions of faith have caused concern among Orthodox Church theologians. See Sir Steven Runciman, *The Great Church in Captivity* (Cambridge: Cambridge University Press, 1986).

children have been transformed by their faith—and these transformed lives have changed the world.

Epilogue

It is possible that the Reformed Ecumenical Council and the World Alliance of Reformed Churches will unite at Grand Rapids in 2010. It is my hope and prayer that all bodies constituting Calvin's children will join to form one vast movement, to promote Jesus Christ in this world. Yes, I know that we are very different, but I believe that we are more like each other than we are like anyone else.

Let us thank God for the life and work of John Calvin.
I thank God that I am one of his children.
As he wrote himself at the end of the *Institutes*—God be praised!

2

CALVIN AND ECCLESIASTICAL DISCIPLINE

ROBERT M. KINGDON[1]

Of all the major sixteenth-century Reformers, John Calvin was the one who most insisted on the use of ecclesiastical discipline. Only the Anabaptists attached as much importance to the use of discipline, and they rarely obtained the support of a government that could have made this effective for a whole community. Before accepting the invitation to leave Strasbourg and return to Geneva in 1541, Calvin had insisted on the establishment of discipline

1. Dr. Kingdon was one of the first scholars to accept our invitation to speak at Calvin500. Unfortunately, he had a debilitating stroke in 2008 and was not able to present a paper in person. But his family provided us with a copy of this essay, which first appeared in *Bulletin de la Societe de l'histoire du Protestantisme Francais* 155 (Janvier–Fevrier–Mars 2009): 117–26. A former understudy and associate, Dr. William McComish, graciously and expertly read this essay at our conference. The translation printed here was provided by David W. Hall with initial technical assistance from the Rev. Joel Smit. Carolyn McComish further edited this translation. I thank each of these. DWH.

by the authorities; having trained as a lawyer at university, he was able to write the *Ecclesiastical Ordinances* of Geneva himself. These ultimately created a new court, the Consistory, charged with maintaining discipline. From the outset, he was a very active member, assisting in almost all of the Consistory's weekly sessions. The meetings lasted for several hours each Thursday, and it is estimated that 5 to 7 percent of the adult population was summoned before them each year. Calvin also insisted that the *Seigneurie* grant the Consistory the right to reinforce its judgments with excommunication. This request caused serious rifts within Genevan society during the 1550s, and Calvin threatened to leave Geneva for good if the Council did not confirm the principle that the Consistory had the right to excommunicate without reference to the civil authorities.

The use of discipline with the right of excommunication by the Roman church was fairly widespread in Europe before the Reformation. But it was disliked by the first Protestants, who saw it as an abuse that had to be removed. To my knowledge, one of the most striking examples of this abuse was pointed to by Lucien Febvre in his article "Un 'abus' et son climat social: L'excommunication pour dettes en Franche-Comté."[2] In sixteenth-century Franche-Comté, many of the contracts for monetary loans depended on the authority of the ecclesiastical courts of the Roman church. If a debtor could not discharge his debt according to the terms of the contract, the creditor could ask for his excommunication. And if a debtor died excommunicated, his heirs were obliged to pay the debt so that the priests of the parish could go ahead and bury him.

Confronted with such abuses, Martin Luther, Huldrych Zwingli, and the first Protestants questioned the authority of those ecclesiastical courts and the validity of the sanctions that they imposed. In their opinion, the application of laws on human behavior should be entrusted to the state courts and to civil justice. This refusal to entrust the clergy with the authority to punish worldly misdemeanors corresponded well with the central teaching of these Protestants: that justification comes from faith alone, and good works are not necessary to salvation.

2. In Lucien Febvre, *Au cœur religieux du XVIe siècle* (Paris: Sepven, 1957), 225–50.

For example, Nicolas von Amsdorf, one of the most devoted of Luther's first disciples, left a booklet with this title: *Dass die Propositio (Gute werck sind zur Seligkeit schedlich) ein rechte ware Christliche Propositio sey durch den heïligen Pauluni und Lutherum gelert und gepredigt* (1559).[3] From it one can conclude that his disciples had not really understood the global-ity of Luther's teaching, which had in fact insisted that faith should be expressed in charity. Indeed, some of these first Protestants were tempted by the antinomian heresy, which denied the need to obey human laws. From Rome's point of view, the repudiation among Protestants of canoni-cal laws on fasts, the celebration of festivals, and so forth was a veritable antinomianism, causing the very foundations of morality to be shaken.

Some Lutherans insisted on the control of the behavior of the faithful. In particular Martin Bucer, the Strasbourg Reformer, wanted to establish ecclesiastical discipline, probably inspired by the need to take up the chal-lenge resulting from the number of Anabaptists within the urban popula-tion. Bucer, however, could not persuade the city government to enforce his proposal, partly because the government did not want to give validity to the ideas of the Anabaptists. In the end, the government allowed Bucer to establish Christian associations (*Christliche Gemeinschaften*) among the members of any parish who voluntarily accepted the idea to practice disci-pline among themselves, albeit with no governmental authority enforcing this discipline.[4] Between his stays in Geneva, Calvin spent a few years in Strasbourg as the pastor of a congregation of French refugees. This was undoubtedly the period in which he became convinced of the need to introduce discipline into all Christian communities. One thing is sure: this idea played an essential part in the development of his thinking on his return to Geneva.

We are well informed of the activity of the Consistory of Geneva, thanks to the well-preserved registers of the epoch, now in Geneva's State Archives. This rich, detailed resource has been little exploited because the handwriting of the secretaries makes deciphering the registers difficult.

3. Robert Kolb, *Nicholas von Amsdorf, 1483–1565* (Nieuwkoop: B. de Graaf, 1978), 159–60n52.

4. Amy Nelson Burnett, *The Yoke of Christ: Martin Bucer and Christian Discipline*, vol. 26 of *Sixteenth Century Studies and Essays* (Kirksville, MO: Sixteenth Century Journal Publishers, 1994), 180–87.

To facilitate the consultation of this resource, and in order to make a draft transcription of the twenty-one volumes written during Calvin's ministry, I organized a research team with sufficient expertise in the French paleography of the time. We are now annotating and editing the transcriptions. These volumes reveal enthralling information on the daily life and beliefs of the Genevans of the time.

The Consistory is primarily recognized now as having been a matrimonial court. It assumed the functions of the bishop's curia, while also monitoring social mores, previously overseen by the municipal courts before the Reformation. The Consistory thus adjudicated many of the issues relating to the validity of marriage promises. There were also petitions for divorce (for adultery or desertion) with permission to remarry—an innovation of the Calvinist reform. We have already published two books on the work of the Consistory in these matters.[5] I now want to underline the fact that the Consistory worked in many other areas to try to establish discipline within the community.

During the early years, the Consistory endeavored to eliminate "papist" (Catholic) beliefs and practices and to firmly entrench Reformed duties and practices in the hearts of the Genevans. "How do you pray?" was often the first question to those summoned before the Consistory. Even if they had been summoned for a completely different reason (for example, fornication, disputes, or drunkenness), they often had to start by reciting their prayers. They frequently answered in Latin with an *Ave Maria* or *Pater Noster*, sometimes with much pride. None of these responses pleased the Consistory. If they recited an *Ave Maria*, the retort was that it was completely useless to pray to the Virgin or other saints—one must always pray to God directly, and to him only. If they prayed in Latin, they were told that it was useless to recite rote prayers in a liturgical language that they did not understand. The Consistory insisted that Genevans recite the Lord's Prayer and the creed in their native tongue and that they understand their meaning. If they were unable, they were ordered to learn to pray correctly. They were some-

5. John Witte Jr. and Robert M. Kingdon, *Sex, Marriage, and Family in John Calvin's Geneva*, vol. 1, *Courtship, Engagement and Marriage* (Grand Rapids: Eerdmans, 2005); Robert M. Kingdon, *Adultery and Divorce in Calvin's Geneva* (Cambridge, MA: Harvard University Press, 1995).

times sent to catechism classes, held in each parish church at midday on a Sunday. These courses were above all intended for children preparing for their first communion, but they were also used to teach adults to pray correctly. The Consistory may have even engaged a child to teach an adult.[6]

With the advent of the Reformation, the faithful were obliged to pray aloud together during worship, led by the pastor. One was not allowed to murmur his prayers in a corner during the service. Worship was centered on the sermon, and communion was celebrated only four times a year. Thus, it was very different from a Catholic service based on the Mass, and often without a sermon. While the pastor preached, the faithful had to listen without being distracted by private prayer. Many either did not understand this change or simply refused to obey. The ladies most of all, and doubtless those of a certain age, persisted in muttering prayers under the preacher's nose. The Reformed liturgy did not, however, leave room for such practices. The ladies were often summoned before the Consistory and accused of muttering during worship. The Consistory had to explain that they must listen to the sermon in silence in order to understand it.[7]

In Geneva it was understood that everyone should attend the preaching of the sermon at least once on Sunday and preferably also on Wednesday. People were often summoned before the Consistory if they were absent from sermons. Those in need of spiritual teaching were often requested to be present at the preaching several times a week. On the other hand, attending Catholic Masses was strictly prohibited. For Protestant theologians, the Mass was a "papist" abomination, a sort of idolatry, during which the participants were invited to adore things made by human hands, whether pieces of bread or cups of wine. Several members of the older clergy chose to accept the Reformation and to live in Geneva. The *Seigneurie* allowed them to continue receiving the income of their benefices

---

6. It was Jacques Emyn who suggested that a small child teach him (*R. Consist.*, 1.18–19 [March 23, 1542]). It is not known whether Emyn's education was finally entrusted to a small child or not.

7. Robert M. Kingdon, "Worship in Geneva before and after the Reformation," in *Worship in Medieval and Early Modern Europe*, ed. Karin Maag and John D. Witvliet (Notre Dame, IN: Notre Dame University Press, 2004), 41–60.

for the rest of their lives, with the condition that they never celebrate a Mass again. Initially, some former priests contravened the rule, which could earn them a short stay in prison.[8] For those Genevans who wished, however, it was quite easy to attend a Mass. The city was surrounded by villages that remained faithful to Catholicism and to the former bishop of Geneva. Some of these villages were so close that they could easily be reached on foot. Now they are the suburbs or districts of the current city of Geneva, such as Carouge. The Genevans who visited these villages often attended Mass because of local friendships or family. Sometimes it was because they were not convinced of the truth of Protestantism and effectively remained Catholic. One lady, for example, heard Mass once a year.[9] The Consistory often summoned such people to persuade them to repudiate these practices, sometimes without success.

But it was not only the Mass that the Consistory sought to prohibit in Geneva. There were many other devotional practices that the Consistory wanted to eliminate. A particularly touching example is that of a certain Tevene Peronet. Her husband was very sick, and she was in despair. Of her own volition, she decided to get hold of a votive candle. She bought a pound of wax in a neighboring village, undoubtedly for a significant sum, because wax was a luxury at the time. She used the wax to make a candle. But despite her efforts, her husband died. She excused herself to the Consistory, assuring them that she had been poorly instructed and that she prayed only to the Lord, never to the Virgin Mary. The Consistory discovered that Mrs. Peronet could recite the Lord's Prayer, but not the confession of faith, which they enjoined her to learn. This was a case in which the Consistory tried to act in a pastoral way. It is difficult to know, however, whether this course of action really helped the poor widow. She may have ended up believing that candles were useless in procuring health or salvation, but did she find another more efficient means of consolation?[10]

8. Gabriella Cahier-Buccelli, "Dans l'ombre de la Réforme: les membres de l'ancien clergé demeurés à Genève, 1536–1558," *Bulletin de la Societé d'Histoire et d'Archéologie de Genève*, 18.2 (1987): 367–88.

9. *R. Consist.*, 1.23–24 (March 30, 1542) (the case of Jeanne Pertemps).

10. Ibid., 1.277–78 (November 29, 1543); ibid., 1.284n.

These attempts to entrench a Protestant mentality and to remove the vestiges of Catholicism were frequent during the first years of the Consistory's work. Thereafter they became increasingly rare, without disappearing completely during the period that concerns us. Perhaps most Genevans converted heart and soul to the Reformation. At the least, Genevans learned what they had to say and do in public, and what should be done only in private.

Thereafter the Consistory was occupied more and more frequently with disputes. There were family quarrels between parents and children, brothers and sisters. There were business disputes between competitors. There were disputes between districts and neighbors. The Consistory became a sort of reconciliation agency. In certain matters, it even replaced the courts of justice. This function of the Consistory increased in importance with the passing of years—from Calvin's death at the end of the sixteenth century and over the following centuries. Currently, a team in Geneva is thoroughly researching this phenomenon.[11]

The Genevan Consistory was a type of county court. It heard cases of all kinds, but it had limited means to force people to follow its rulings. Each case started with the announcement of the reason for which a person had been summoned, often followed by his answer, sometimes confirmed and sometimes contradicted by witnesses' statements. Finally, there was either an "admonition" or a "remonstrance," made by one of the pastors of the Consistory. These were generally made by Calvin himself. After his death, his colleague Nicolas Colladon wrote in his *Life of Calvin* that Calvin had pronounced all the reprimands and remonstrances.[12] We found some exceptions, but it seems that Calvin actually announced the majority of these interventions. He was always the most active member of the Consistory, but he never presided over the meetings. That was the task of a *syndic*—one of the four magistrates, elected annually, at the head of the Genevan government. Sometimes a pure-stock Genevan wished to answer only the questions raised by the syndic.[13] But in general, we have the impression that it was Calvin who dominated the discussion.

11. The team is directed by Christian Grosse of the University of Geneva.
12. CO, 21.66.
13. See, for example, *R. Consist.*, 3.10, concerning François Favre.

If the Consistory determined that a case should be examined more carefully, it could always return it to the *Petit Conseil* (Small Council) of the city. This was indeed the usual practice whenever the Consistory believed that the accused needed further correction, which apparently occurred fairly often, especially once the Consistory was well established in the city. The meetings of the Consistory normally took place on Thursday, and the Council looked at cases referred from the Consistory on Monday. In the Council registers, also preserved in the State Archives of Geneva, we find official reports of the referrals from the Consistory almost every Monday. The Council would decide either to discuss the case at once or to bring the accused to face criminal trial. The Council could also drop the case entirely, if it thought an additional investigation was unnecessary.

The Consistory could also apply another means of punishment, the most controversial of the epoch: excommunication. If a sinner committed a very serious fault or was particularly unrepentant, the Consistory could simply announce that he could no longer receive communion until he sincerely repented. This threat was very serious, much more so than nowadays. Effectively, an excommunicated person lost not only the right to receive the sacrament but also the privilege of taking part in other ecclesial rites. For example, he could not become a godfather at a baptism. At the time, to be a godfather was a great honor and one that established and maintained friendships and commerce. He could not participate in a marriage service in a church, which was the only means to marry at the time. He would be scorned by friends, neighbors, and even members of his own family. Hence, almost all those excommunicated by the Consistory tried to be restored before the next communion was celebrated. There was only one way to do this: appear before the Consistory. One had to show true and sincere repentance in order to obtain the Consistory's permission to receive the Lord's Supper. Some sought to appeal to the Council, in theory sovereign in all matters. The pastors categorically resisted such appeals. In the famous case of the excommunication of Philibert Berthelier, Calvin himself affirmed that he would give his own life rather than accept that the Council reverse the excommunication pronounced by the Consistory. The other pastors then went before the Council and said that they preferred to die or be exiled rather than administer communion to Berthelier. The Council finally went back on its position.[14]

Many other Protestants of the time were opposed to such use of excommunication, in which they saw the continuation of an intolerable abuse by the bishops of the Roman church. The most serious reservations were expressed in Zurich. Heinrich Bullinger, the head of the company of pastors in Zurich, affirmed that he did not believe he had the right of excommunication. If Jesus Christ himself, he said, gave communion to Judas Iscariot during the first Holy Supper, knowing full well that Judas would betray him a few hours later, how could a pastor refuse to give communion to whomever wished to receive it?[15] Calvin and the Genevans were obliged to take account of the opinions of the church in Zurich. The Reformation could never have been established in Geneva without the military support of the government of Bern, a Zwinglian state closely linked to Zurich and its theologians. And faced with the threats from Savoy, Geneva continued to need the goodwill of Bern and the other Zwinglian states in the Swiss Confederation. After long discussions, the theologians decided to maintain their own ideas on this subject. The Genevans thus continued to employ excommunication by the Consistory. For its part, Zurich (company of pastors) continued to deny pastors the authority to excommunicate, allowing only the government the sporadic use of excommunication. Finally, all parties promised not to openly criticize.

Nowadays, I suspect that most people would not wish to live under such a severe regime as that established by Calvin and the Consistory. But there are reasons to believe that most Genevans and many of their contemporaries accepted this way of life, sometimes even with enthusiasm. Following the crisis of 1555, between the partisans of discipline by the Consistory and its opponents under the syndic and captain general, Ami Perrin, the partisans of discipline obtained a decisive victory. With ease, they seized power within the councils, and for good measure they drove the heads of the opposition party out of the city, as well as many of their partisans. A year later, John Knox, the future Scots Reformer, wrote his

14. R.C. 47, f. 145, 147v (September 2, 7, 1553). See also Amedée Roget, *Histoire du peuple de Genève* (Genève: Jullien, 1870–87), 4:64–71.

15. Philip Benedict, *Christ's Churches Purely Reformed: A Social History of Calvinism* (New Haven: Yale University Press, 2002), 54.

famous letter to Anne Locke, an English friend, in which he claimed "to find in Geneva the best school of Christ since the time of the apostles." He added that he had heard the doctrine well preached in other places, but that he had never seen elsewhere such a pure lifestyle and religion so well embedded.[16]

Recently, in carefully studying Calvin's followers in Geneva, I was astonished to find among them some Anabaptists. One in particular, named Jacques Mérauld, was a religious refugee from Lyon. He was accused of the Anabaptist heresy. This was in 1537, one year after the seizure of the German town of Münster by a group of Anabaptists, whose revolt was ferociously repressed by a mostly Catholic army. This affair shocked the urban authorities of central Europe. It was also one year after Calvin arrived in Geneva the first time—as a public lecturer, not then as a leading pastor. The reports of Mérauld's criminal trial are preserved in the State Archives of Geneva. Evidence proves that he was indeed an Anabaptist, that he believed firmly in the baptism of adult believers, and that he rejected the baptism of newborn babies. The official reports show that Mérauld formulated severe criticisms against the first Protestant pastors of Geneva. He found them to be bad preachers—not as good as the Catholic priests that they replaced. He was especially shocked that these pastors gave the Lord's Supper even to the most hardened sinners. He regarded this practice as a scandal. The Consistory decided to have him lodge with a pastor called Antoine Froment, so that he could be taught the truth. After a few days, Froment reported that he could not support this arrangement because he found Mérauld to be insane. Other arrangements had to be made.

But it is the continuation of Mérauld's career that astonishes me. He remained in Geneva. In 1540, he received a license to teach mathematics and Scripture in schools. The following year, an investigation was opened over the permission given to this Anabaptist to teach the children in a public school of the city, the Collège de Rive. But he was found to be a good teacher and allowed to continue his work. Three years later, he was granted a more suitable room for his teaching. In 1550, he was officially

---

16. Knox to Locke, December 9, 1556, in John Knox, *Works*, ed. David Laing (Edinburgh: T. G. Stevenson, 1854–64), 4:240.

accepted as a resident of the city. In 1557, he and his son were also accepted into the bourgeoisie of the city. Later, he apparently lived for some time in the general hospital of the city, a charitable institution directed by deacons, to assist orphans and the elderly infirm. One always needed a teacher in this institution to teach the orphans. It is probable that in 1563 Merauld returned to Lyon, and became secretary of the Reformed Consistory of the town.[17]

It is evident that Mérauld had become a good Calvinist, a faithful and active member of the Reformed church. I do not find any sign to explain this conversion. But to me it seems quite probable that Mérauld, having become acquainted with the teaching and practice of Calvin, decided to abandon his ideas on the sacraments in order to live according to the discipline of the church. I am convinced that this is what persuaded other Anabaptists, in Strasbourg as well as in Geneva, to follow Calvin. Even Calvin's wife was the widow of a converted Anabaptist in Strasbourg.[18] Calvin won them over by discipline.

There were great debates during the sixteenth century on the *notae* or marks of the true church of Christ. Each church tried to establish its position as the one true church by showing that only it had these marks. Catholics tended to have rather long lists; Protestants, on the other hand, had rather short lists. Cardinal Bellarmin, for example, in his *Controversiae*, offered a list of fifteen marks explained in great detail, which were in striking contrast to the Protestant teaching on this subject. The true church, he said, was to bear the name of Catholic, to have an uninterrupted history since the time of the apostles, to be dispersed everywhere in the world, to be directed by a succession of bishops located in the city of Rome since the apostles, to produce saints and to show miracles as evidence of its holiness, to teach the true apostolic doctrines, to have a prophetic light, and so on.[19]

17. For an account that documents the career of Mérauld, see Robert M. Kingdon, "Anabaptists in Calvin's Geneva," in *Wege der Neuzeit: Festschrift fur Heinz Schilling sum 65. Beburtstag*, ed. Stefan Ehrenpreis et al. (Berlin: Duncker & Humblot, 2007), 120–24. Information on the criminal action is in the State Archives of Geneva, P.C., 2ᵉ sér. no. 385, September 11–14, 1537. The other information is in the *Registers of the Conseil* and the *Registers of the Consistory*.

18. On the wife of Calvin, see Willem Balke, *Calvin and the Anabaptist Radicals* (Grand Rapids: Eerdmans, 1981; repr., Eugene, OR: Wipf & Stock, 1999), 133ff.

19. Roberto Bellarmino, *Opera Omnia*, vol. 2, ed. Justin Fèvre (Paris: Louis Vivès, 1870; repr., Frankfurt: Minerva, 1965), *Controversiarum de Conciliis*, lib. 4.301–407.

On the other hand, most Protestants considered only two marks essential to the true church: they concerned the preaching of the true doctrine and the correct celebration of the sacraments. If a group could offer these two things, it was a true church, even if it had been recently established, and even if it were limited to a restricted territory. Such is the stated formula found in the Augsburg Confession, which summarized the most important Lutheran doctrines. The formula found in Calvin's *Institutes*, the most important summary of the Calvinist doctrines, is this: "But every where we see the word of God is purely preached and heard, and the Sacraments are administered according to the institution of God, there it is never necessary to doubt that there the Church exists."[20]

But at the beginning of the Reformation, Protestant theologians wanted to add a third mark to this list, judged essential to distinguish the true church of God. This third mark was discipline. Most theologians sided with Calvin on other doctrinal questions of the time, but some were Lutherans. A striking example was Peter Martyr Vermigli, the eminent theologian who had taught theology beside Bucer in Strasbourg and in England. Vermigli finished his career in Zurich at the side of Bullinger. On at least two occasions in his biblical commentaries he put forward the formula of three marks, and these two comments could also be found in *Loci Communes*, which were elaborated after his death by his disciples and thereafter became one of the most important summaries of Reformed thought at the time, often used with Calvin's *Institutes*.[21] Vermigli never became the head of a church, as Bullinger and Calvin did, but remained a professor of theology during his entire career. Thus he never had the occasion to draw up a disciplinary code.

The contrast between Calvin and Vermigli is curious. Vermigli insisted on discipline in his theology but never tried to implement it. On the other hand, Calvin, who so furiously fought for discipline during his career in Geneva, never pleaded in favor of discipline in his theology. If I were to explain this phenomenon, I might suggest that Calvin did not want to

20. *Institutes*, 4.1.9.

21. See Robert M. Kingdon, "Peter Martyr Vermigli and the Marks of the True Church," in *Continuity and Discontinuity in Church History: Essays Presented to George Huntston Williams*, ed. F. Forrester Church and Timothy George (Leiden: Brill, 1979), 198–214.

disturb his theological allies, especially those in Zurich, with whom he always had to demonstrate much tact.

Nonetheless, in following years, the disciples of Calvin often added discipline as a third mark of a true church in the official summaries of their beliefs. This was the case in particular in the confessions adopted by the Reformed churches of Scotland, the Netherlands, and elsewhere. One can conclude that discipline, as practiced by Calvin, even if it was not contained in his principal teaching, became essential for all Reformed believers who followed his ideas.[22]

22. I am indebted to Thomas Lambert, who has helped me much in the preparation of this text, and Genevieve Dorais, who helped to correct my French.

3

CALVIN THE LAWYER

JOHN WITTE JR.

F or all his fame as a theologian and biblical commentator, John
Calvin was first and foremost a jurist. He studied law in Bourges
and Orléans, taking his licentiate (roughly a master's degree)
around 1531. He was pursuing advanced studies in law and related humanist subjects in Paris before having to flee the city and abandon his studies.[1]
Calvin's first introduction to theology, his 1536 *Institutes of the Christian
Religion*, was named after the standard introduction to law in his day, the
Institutes of Justinian. His first major reforms in Geneva were new laws—
the 1541 Ecclesiastical Ordinances, the 1542 Edict of the Lieutenant, and
the 1543 Ordinances on Offices and Officers, constitutional laws that
together defined the new structure, power, and relations of church and
state in Protestant Geneva. He drafted major new ordinances thereafter
on marriage, children, social welfare, public morality, education, and other

1. Josef Bohatec, *Calvin und das Recht* (Graz: H. Boehlaus, 1934); Basil Hall, "John
Calvin, the Jurisconsults, and the *Ius Civile*," in *Studies in Church History*, ed. G. J. Cumming
(Leiden: Brill, 1966), 202–16.

topics—more than a hundred new ordinances all told.[2] He left outlines of comprehensive new codes of civil and criminal law and procedure and fragments of new laws on property, inheritance, and commerce.[3] He left dozens of formal legal opinions (*consilia*) that gave crisp answers to specific legal questions and hundreds of private letters that dispensed legal advice and discussed legal topics with leading lawyers.[4] He sat as a judge in thousands of cases that came before the Consistory of Geneva during his lifetime.[5] And Calvin dealt with many intricate legal and political questions in his *Institutes*, commentaries, lectures, and sermons.

Calvin's attention to both theology and law would become a trademark of early modern Calvinism. Theologians and jurists together formed the leadership of many Reformed communities in the sixteenth to eighteenth centuries. For every new Calvinist catechism there was a new Calvinist code of law, for every fresh confession of faith a new charter of rights. Early modern Calvinists believed in law—as a deterrent against sin, an inducement to grace, a teacher of Christian virtue. Early modern Calvinists also believed in liberty—structuring their churches and states alike to minimize the sins of their rulers and to maximize the liberties of their subjects.

It is this legal side of Calvin's Reformation that I would like to probe a bit in this chapter. I focus on two main dialectics at work in Calvin's thought—the first balancing liberty and law, the second balancing church and state. These two dialectics intersected. For Calvin it was the responsi-

2. See Emile Rivoire and Victor van Berchem, eds., *Les sources du droit du canton de Genève*, 4 vols. (Arau: H. R. Sauerländer, 1927–1935), partially translated in John Witte Jr. and Robert M. Kingdon, *Sex, Marriage, and Family in John Calvin's Geneva*, 3 vols. (Grand Rapids: Eerdmans, 2005–) (hereafter *SMF*).

3. CO, 10/1.125–46.

4. For *consilia*, see ibid., 10/1.153–266, translated as *Calvin's Ecclesiastical Advice*, trans. Mary Beaty and Benjamin Farley (Louisville: Westminster/John Knox Press, 1991). For correspondence, see CO, 1–9, with partial translations in *Letters of John Calvin*, ed. Jules Bonnet, trans. D. Constable and M. R. Gilchrist, 4 vols., repr. ed. (New York: Burt Franklin, 1972), and in *SMF*. See especially Calvin's many exchanges with Theodore Beza, Germain Colladon, Hugo Donnellus, Guillaume Farel, François Hotman, Carolus Molinaeus, and Pierre Viret on technical legal and political questions.

5. See Jean-François Bergier and Robert M. Kingdon, eds., *Registres de la compagnie des pasteurs de Genève au temps de Calvin*, 2 vols. (Geneva: Droz, 1964); Robert M. Kingdon, ed., *Registres du Consistoire de Genève au Temps de Calvin*, 21 vols. (Geneva: Droz, 1996–).

bility of the church and state, separately and together, to protect and promote the law and liberty of Geneva. And in turn, it was Geneva's commitment to the rule of law and regime of liberty that allowed church and state to separate yet cooperate in the governance of a Christian republic.

Liberties and Rights

We begin with John Calvin the lawyer—more particularly, John Calvin the human-rights lawyer. Calvin learned a lot about rights (*iura*) and liberties (*libertates*) from the Roman civil law and the Catholic canon law that he studied as a young French law student in the 1520s.[6] He learned more from the many Lutheran Reformation ordinances and legal textbooks that he read as a new convert to the Protestant cause in the early 1530s.[7] It is thus no surprise that Calvin opened his first major theological publication, the 1536 edition of the *Institutes of the Christian Religion*, with a loud Luther-like call for freedom: freedom of conscience, freedom of exercise, freedom of assembly, freedom of worship, freedom of the church, and attendant public, penal, and procedural rights for church members. Calvin's opening dedication of his *Institutes* to King Francis I was, in reality, a cleverly drafted lawyer's brief on behalf of Protestants who were being persecuted by church and state authorities alike.

Only one paragraph after his glowing tribute to this "most mighty, illustrious and glorious" monarch of France, Calvin launched into his legal argument. He cleverly singled out those abuses of Protestants that defied widely recognized rights and freedoms of his day, particularly criminal procedural rights.[8] Calvin protested the widespread and unchecked instances of "perjury," "lying slanders," "wicked accusations," and the "fury

6. On rights in civil law and canon law, see Brian Tierney, *The Idea of Natural Rights: Studies in Natural Rights, Natural Law, and Church Law, 1150–1625* (Grand Rapids: Eerdmans, 2001); John Witte Jr., *The Reformation of Rights: Law, Religion, and Human Rights in Early Modern Calvinism* (Cambridge: Cambridge University Press, 2007) (hereafter RR). For Calvin's exposure to this, see Josef Bohatec, *Budé und Calvin: Studien zur Gedankwelt des französischen Frühhumanismus* (Graz: H. Böhlaus Nachf, 1950).

7. See my *Law and Protestantism: The Legal Teachings of the Lutheran Reformation* (Cambridge: Cambridge University Press, 2002).

8. On these, see John H. Langbein, *Prosecuting Crime in the Renaissance: England, Germany, France* (Cambridge, MA: Harvard University Press, 1974); Adhemar Esmein, *A

of evil men" that conspired to incite "public hatred" and "open violence" against believers. He protested that "the case" of the Protestants had "been handled with no order of law and with violent heat rather than judicial gravity." He protested various forms of false imprisonment and abuses of prisoners: "Some of us are shackled with irons, some beaten with rods, some led about as laughing stocks, some proscribed, some most savagely tortured, some forced to flee." He protested the many procedural inequities: Protestants were "fraudulently and undeservedly charged with treason and villainy." They were convicted for capital offenses, "without confession or sure testimony." "Bloody sentences are meted out against this doctrine without a hearing." He protested the bias of judges and the partiality of judicial proceedings: "Those who sit in judgment . . . pronounce as sentences the prejudices which they have brought from home." He protested the intrusions on the church's freedoms of assembly and speech: "The poor little church has either been wasted with cruel slaughter or banished into exile, or so overwhelmed by threats and fears that it dare not even open its mouth." All these offenses stood diametrically opposed to basic political freedoms recognized at the time both in the Empire and in France. "A very great question is at stake," Calvin declared to King Francis: "how God's glory may be kept safe on earth, how God's truth may retain its place of honor, how Christ's kingdom may be kept in good repair among us."[9]

Later on in his same 1536 *Institutes*, Calvin called for the freedom not just of Protestants, but of all peaceable believers, including Catholics, Jews, and Muslims. He denounced the forced baptisms, inquisitions, crusades, and other forms of religious persecution practiced by the medieval church and state:

> We ought to strive by whatever means we can, whether by exhortation and teaching or by mercy and gentleness, or by our own prayers to God, that they may turn to a more virtuous life and may return to the society and unity of the church. And not only are excommunicants to be so

History of Continental Criminal Procedure with Special Reference to France, repr. ed. (South Hackensack, NJ: Rothman Reprints, 1968).

9. *Ioannis Calvini Institutio Religionis Christianae* (Basel, 1536), translated as John Calvin, *Institutes of the Christian Religion*, trans. Ford Lewis Battles, rev. ed. (Grand Rapids: Eerdmans, 1986), dedicatory epistle.

treated, but also Turks and Saracens, and other enemies of religion. Far be it from us to approve those methods by which many until now have tried to force them to our faith, when they forbid them the use of fire and water and the common elements, when they deny them to all offices of humanity, when they pursue them with sword and arms.[10]

Over the next twenty-five years, Calvin continued to build his case for freedom. His touchstone was the Bible, especially those many passages on freedom in the letters of St. Paul: "For freedom Christ has set us free" (Gal. 5:1);[11] "You were called to freedom" (Gal. 5:13); "Where the Spirit of the Lord is, there is freedom" (2 Cor. 3:17); "For the law of the Spirit of life in Christ Jesus has set [you] free from the law of sin and death" (Rom. 8:2); "You will know the truth, and the truth will make you free" (John 8:32); "You will be free indeed" (John 8:36); you all have been given "the law of liberty" (James 2:12) in Christ, "the glorious liberty of the children of God" (Rom. 8:21).

Calvin's lectures, sermons, and commentaries on these biblical passages on liberty fill scores of pages of his collected writings. "There is nothing more desirable than liberty," he wrote. Liberty is "an inestimable good," "a singular benefit and treasure that cannot be prized enough," something that is worth "more than half of life." "How great a benefit liberty is, when God has bestowed it on someone." Calvin emphasized the importance of political suffrage and the franchise in the political community. The "right to vote," he once said, is the "best way to preserve liberty." "Let those whom God has given liberty and the franchise use it." "The reason why tyrannies have come into the world, why people everywhere have lost their liberty . . . is that people who had elections abused the privilege." "There is no kind of government more salutary than one in which liberty is properly exercised with becoming moderation and properly constituted on a durable basis."[12]

In his later years, Calvin also began to speak at times about the subjective "rights" (*iura, droits*) of individuals, in addition to their "liber-

10. Ibid., 2.28.
11. All quotations from the Bible in this chapter are from the RSV.
12. *Institutes* (1559), 3.19.1–8, 14; *Serm.*, Gen. 39:11; *Serm.*, 1 Sam. 8, 17; *Comm.*, Harm. Law Deut. 15:1–11; 17:14–18; 24:7; *Serm.*, Deut. 16:18–19; 18:14–18; *Institutes* (1543), 20.7.

ties" or "freedoms" (*libertates, libertés*). Sometimes he used such general phrases as "the common rights of mankind" (*iura commune hominum*), the "natural rights" (*iura naturali*) of persons, the "rights of a common nature" (*communis naturae iura*), and "the equal rights and liberties" (*pari iura et libertates*) of all.[13] Usually he referenced more specific subjective rights. He spoke, for example, about the "rights of Christian liberty," the "rights of citizenship" in the kingdom of God or in heavenly Jerusalem, and (one of his favorite expressions) the "right of adoption" that Christians enjoy as new sons and daughters of God and brothers and sisters in Christ. He referenced "the right to inhabit," "the right to dwell in," and "the right and privilege to claim the territory" that Yahweh gave to the chosen people of Israel. He mentioned "Paul's rights of Roman citizenship." He spoke frequently, as a student of Roman law would, about property rights: "the right to land" and other property, "the right to enjoy and use what one possesses," the "right to recover" and the "right to have restored" lost or stolen property; the "right to compensation" for work; the right "to sell," "to bequeath," and to "inherit" property, particularly in accordance with the "natural rights of primogeniture." He spoke of the "right to bury" one's parents and other relatives. He also spoke frequently of the "marital" or "conjugal" rights of husband and wife, and the "sacred," "natural," and "common" "rights" of parents over their children—in particular, the "right" and "authority" of a father to "name his child," "to raise the child," and to set the child up in marriage. He spoke in passing about the "sacred right of hospitality" of the sojourner, the "right of asylum" or of "sanctuary" for those in flight, the "right of redemption" during the Year of Jubilee, and the "natural rights" and "just rights" of the poor, the needy, the orphans, and the widows.[14] Rights talk became increasingly common currency in Calvin's Geneva—and even more so in early modern Calvinist communities thereafter. It is telling that, by 1640, Calvinists had defined, defended, and died for every one of the rights that would ultimately appear in the American Bill of Rights of 1791.

13. *Comm.*, Gen. 4:13; *Comm.*, Harm. Law Num. 3:5–10, 18–22; Deut. 5:19; *Comm.*, Ps. 7:6–8; *Lect.*, Jer. 22:1–3; 22:13–14; *Lect.*, Ezek. 8:17; *Comm.*, 1 Cor. 7:37.

14. For detailed citations of these terms in Calvin's writings, see *RR*, 57–58, and my *God's Joust, God's Justice: Law and Religion in the Western Tradition* (Grand Rapids: Eerdmans, 2006), 31–48.

Laws and the Limits of Liberty

But Calvinist rights talk was never divorced from duties talk. The whole point of having rights and liberties, Calvin insisted, was to enable a person to discharge the duties and responsibilities of the faith. As Calvin put it: "We obtain liberty in order that we may more promptly and more readily obey God in all things" spiritual and temporal.[15] Freedoms and commandments, rights and duties belong together in Calvin's formulation, balancing and bolstering each other. Subjective-rights claims must always be grounded in an objective-rights order.

Calvin spent a great deal of time defining this rights order. Sometimes he described this as a natural order, an order of nature, or an order of creation. Sometimes he used more anthropological language: our human conscience, the inner voice, our natural sense of right and wrong. More often, he described it as a divine, spiritual, moral, or natural law. What he basically meant by this unsystematized gaggle of terms is that set of norms that transcend and legitimize the positive laws of human authorities. God, he believed, has written this natural law on the hearts and consciences of all persons, rewritten it in the pages of Scripture, and summarized it in the Decalogue or Ten Commandments.

Calvin and his followers often used the Decalogue to define the natural rights of each person. The First Table of the Decalogue, Calvin said, prescribes natural duties that each person owes to God: the duty to honor God and God's name, to observe the Sabbath day of rest and holy worship, to avoid false gods and false swearing. The Second Table prescribes natural duties that each person owes to neighbors: to honor one's parents and other authorities, not to kill, not to commit adultery, not to steal, not to bear false witness, not to covet. Each person's natural duties toward God in the First Table can be recast as that person's natural religious rights: the right to honor God and God's name, the right to rest and worship on one's Sabbath, the right to be free from false gods and false oaths. Religious rights, said Calvin, are "inherent human rights," "part of our human nature," which church, state, and neighbor alike must respect. Our religious rights are also extensions of God's divine rights: the "eternal right of God

15. *Comm.*, 1 Peter 2:16; *Institutes* (1559), 3.17.1–2; 3.19.14–16; 4.10.5.

40

himself, to be properly worshipped and glorified," as Calvin put it.[16] Each person's natural duties toward a neighbor in the Second Table, in turn, can be cast as a neighbor's natural rights to have those duties discharged. One person's duties not to kill, to commit adultery, to steal, and to bear false witness thus give rise to another person's rights to life, property, fidelity, and reputation. Calvin hinted strongly in this direction in his many writings on the Decalogue. His followers spun out elaborate Decalogue-based theories of rights with this basic argument—beginning with Christopher Goodman and Theodore Beza in the 1550s and 1560s.[17]

For Calvin, the Decalogue and other natural-law formulae proved useful not only to define and ground each person's natural rights and liberties, but also to delimit and direct these rights and liberties to the loving service of God, neighbor, and self. Calvin, in fact, developed an innovative theory of what he called "the uses" of the natural or moral law for individuals and communities. He had already introduced this uses-of-the-law theory in his 1536 *Institutes*,[18] but he expanded it greatly in his later writings, especially as he wrestled with the many provisions of the Torah, and the treatment of the law in Paul's letters to the Romans and Galatians. The uses-of-the-law theory addresses what the law of God is really good for in this new dispensation of grace. Law is no longer a pathway of salvation; after Christ, salvation comes only through faith in God's grace. Should the law be discarded by Christians as useless? No, said Calvin. The law of God remains useful in governing our individual and collective lives and guiding the exercise and enjoyment of our liberties. Calvin distinguished three such uses.

First, God uses the moral law civilly—to restrain the sinfulness of nonbelievers, those who have not accepted his grace. "The law is like a halter," Calvin wrote, "to check the raging and otherwise limitlessly ranging lusts of the flesh. . . . Hindered by fright or shame, sinners dare neither execute what they have conceived in their minds, nor openly breathe forth the rage of their lust." The moral law imposes upon them a "constrained and forced righteousness" or a "civil righteousness." Although their consciences

16. *Lect.*, Dan. 6:22; *Serm.*, 2 Sam. 1:1–4.
17. See *RR*, 121–41.
18. *Institutes* (1536), 1.33; see also *Calvin's Commentary on Seneca's De Clementia*, trans. Ford Lewis Battles and A. M. Hugo (Leiden: Brill, 1969), 1.2.2; 1.22.1.

are "untouched by any care for what is just and right," the very threat of
divine punishment compels sinners to obey the basic duties of the moral
law—to fear God, to rest on the Sabbath, to avoid blasphemy, idolatry, and
profanity, to obey authorities, to respect their neighbor's person, property,
and relationships, to remain sexually continent, to speak truthfully of
themselves and their neighbors.[19]

God coerces sinful consciences to adopt such "civil righteousness" in
order to preserve a measure of order and liberty in the sin-ridden earthly
kingdom. "Unless there is some restraint, the condition of wild beasts
would be better and more desirable than ours," Calvin wrote. Persons
need the God-given constraints of conscience in order to survive in "a
public community." "Liberty would always bring ruin with it, if it were
not bridled by the moderation" born of the moral law. And again: "We can
be truly and genuinely happy not only when liberty is granted to us, but
also when God prescribes a certain rule and arranges for a certain public
order among us so that there may be no confusion."[20]

Second, God uses the moral law theologically—to condemn all persons in their consciences and to compel them to seek his liberating grace.
By setting forth a model of perfect righteousness, the moral law "warns,
informs, convicts, and lastly condemns every man of his own unrighteous-
ness." The moral law thereby punctures his vanity, diminishes his pride,
and drives him to despair. Such despair, Calvin believed, is a necessary
precondition for the sinner to seek God's help and to have faith in God's
grace. "It is as if someone's face were all marked up so that everybody who
saw him might laugh at him. Yet he himself is completely unaware of his
condition. But if they bring him a mirror, he will be ashamed of himself,
and will hide and wash himself when he sees how filthy he is." The moral
law is that mirror. It drives persons to seek the cleansing "spiritual liberty"
that is available to them through faith in God's grace—the liberty of
conscience from the condemnation of the moral law.[21]

Third, God uses the moral law educationally—to teach believers, those
who have accepted his grace, the means and measures of sanctification. "We

19. *Institutes* (1559), 2.7.10; 2.8.6–10; 4.20.3.
20. *Lect.*, Jer. 30:9; *Institutes* (1559), 2.7.10.
21. *Institutes* (1559), 2.7.6–9; 3.19.3–6; *Comm.*, Gal. 5:13; *Comm.*, Gal. 3:19; *Serm.*,
Deut. 5:23–27.

are not our own," Calvin wrote, quoting St. Paul. "The faithful are not given liberty to do whatever seems good to them and that each one follow his own appetite." Even the most devout saints, though free from the condemnation of the moral law, still need to follow the commandments "to learn more thoroughly . . . the Lord's will [and] to be aroused to obedience." The law teaches them not only the "civil righteousness" that is common to all persons, but also the "spiritual righteousness" that is becoming of sanctified Christians. As a teacher, the law not only coerces them against violence and violation, but also cultivates in them charity and love. It not only punishes harmful acts of murder, theft, and fornication, but also prohibits evil thoughts of hatred, covetousness, and lust. Such habits of "spiritual righteousness" are to imbue all aspects of the life of the believer—spiritual and temporal, ecclesiastical and political, private and public. Calvin stressed that Christians must take their faith and conscience directly into public life as "ambassadors and stewards of the treasure of salvation, of the covenant of God . . . of the secrets of God." By so doing, not only do they allow God's glory and image, but they also induce its sinful citizens to seek God's grace.[22]

The natural or moral law, as Calvin described it, thus provides two tracks of moral norms—"civil norms," which are common to all persons, and "spiritual norms," which are distinctly Christian. These norms, in turn, give rise to two tracks of morality—a simple morality of duty demanded of all persons regardless of their faith, and a higher morality of aspiration demanded of believers in order to reflect their faith. This two-track system of morality corresponds roughly to the proper division of jurisdiction between church and state, as Calvin saw it. It is the state's responsibility to enforce mandatory civil norms, to help achieve at minimum the civil use of the law. It is the church's responsibility to teach aspirational spiritual norms, to help achieve all three uses of the law.

Law, Liberty, and the State

Calvin based this division of legal labor on an innovative theory of church and state. Both the church and the state are separate legal entities,

22. *Serm.*, Deut. 5:4–7, 22; *Institutes* (1559), 2.7.12; 2.8.6; 2.8.51; 3.3.9; 3.6.1; 3.17.5–6; *Comm.*, 1 Peter 1:14.

Calvin argued. Each institution has its own forms of organization and order, its own norms of discipline and rule. Each must issue positive human laws on the basis of God's natural law and in extension and application of these enduring moral norms. Each must play a distinctive role in the enforcement of godly government and discipline in the community, and in the achievement of the "uses" of God's law. Each provides "external means or aids through which God invites us into communion with Christ, and keeps us there."[23]

Calvin described the political rulers and laws of the earthly kingdom in largely general and homiletic terms, following Protestant conventions of his day. God has appointed political rulers to be his "vice-regents," "vicars," and "ministers" in the earthly kingdom. Indeed, wrote Calvin, citing Psalm 82:6, "those who serve as magistrates are called 'gods.'" They are vested with God's authority and majesty. They are "called" to an office that is "not only holy and lawful before God, but also the most sacred and by far the most honorable of all callings in the whole life of mortal men." They are commanded to embrace and exemplify clemency, integrity, honesty, mercy, humanity, humility, grace, innocence, continence, and a host of other godly virtues.[24]

Political rulers must govern the earthly kingdom by written positive laws, not by personal fiat. Their laws must encompass the biblical principles of love of God and neighbor, but they must not embrace biblical laws per se. Instead, "equity alone must be the goal and rule and limit of all laws," a term that Calvin used both in the classic Aristotelian sense of correcting defects in individual rules if they work injustice in a particular case, and in his own sense of adjusting each legal system to the changing circumstances and needs of the local community. Through such written, equitable laws, political rulers must serve to promote peace and order in the earthly kingdom, to punish crime and civil wrongdoing, to protect persons in their lives and properties, "to ensure that men may carry on blameless intercourse among themselves" in the spirit of "civil righteousness."[25]

23. *Institutes* (1559), subtitle of bk. 4.
24. Ibid., 6.33–35; 6.39; *Geneva Catechism* (1536), item 21 on "Magistrates."
25. *Institutes* (1536), 1.33; 6.36–37; 6.48–49; *Institutes* (1559), 4.20.

Calvin was more innovative in arguing that the structure of political governments must be "self-limiting" so that "rulers are check-mated by their own officers" and offices. Such inherent political restraints rarely exist in a monarchy, Calvin believed, for monarchs, too, often lack self-discipline and self-control, and betray too little appetite for justice, prudence, and Christian virtue. "If one could uncover the hearts of monarchs," Calvin wrote late in his life, "he would hardly find one in a hundred who does not likewise despise everything divine." Thus, "it is safer and more tolerable that government be in the hands of a number of persons who help each other," such as prevails in an aristocracy, or even better in "a [mixed] system comprised of aristocracy, tempered by democracy." What Calvin had in mind was rule by the "best characters," by the spiritual and moral elite, who were elected to their offices by the people. Mere division of political authority, however, was an insufficient safeguard against political tyranny. Calvin thus encouraged all magistrates to govern through local agencies, to adhere to precedent and written rules, to divide their power among various self-checking branches and officials, to stand periodically for elections, and to hold regular popular meetings in order to give account of themselves and to give air to popular concerns.[26]

The purpose of political government and law is, in essence, to help God achieve the civil use of the moral law—to cultivate civil restraint and civil righteousness in all persons, if necessary through the coercive power of the sword. Calvin described this function in various ways. Magistrates are "ordained protectors and vindicators of public innocence, modesty, decency, and tranquility; their sole endeavor should be to provide for the common safety and peace of all." Magistrates have as their "appointed end" "to adjust our life to the society of men, to form our social behavior to civil righteousness, to reconcile us one with another, and to promote general peace and tranquility."[27] Calvin made clear that the magistrate's cultivation of the civil use of the law was inherently limited:

> It is true that when magistrates create laws, their manner is different from God's. But then their purpose has to do only with the way we govern

26. *Serm.*, 2 Sam. 1–4; *Serm.*, Job 10:16–17; 19:26–29; 34:138; *Serm.*, Deut. 17:16–20; 18:14–18; *Institutes* (1559), 4.20.9–11, 31; *Comm.*, Rom. 13:1–10.
27. *Institutes* (1559), 4.20.2, 9.

ourselves with respect to the external civil order to the end that no one might be violated and each might have his rights [protected] and have peace and concord among men. That is their intention when they create laws. And why? [Because] they are mortal men; they cannot reform inner and hidden affections. That belongs to God.[28]

The best means for the magistrate to help cultivate the civil use of the moral law, said Calvin, is through direct enforcement of the provisions and principles of the Decalogue. The magistrate is the "custodian of both tables" of the Decalogue, said Calvin.[29] He is responsible to govern both the relationships between persons and God, based on the First Table of the Decalogue, and the multiple relationships among persons, based on the Second Table. Thus the magistrate is to promulgate laws against Sabbath-breaking, blasphemy, heresy, "idolatry, sacrilege against God's name, against his truth, and other public offenses against religion" that violate the principles of the First Table. He is "to defend the worship of God, and to execute vengeance upon those who profanely despise it, and on those who endeavor . . . to adulterate the true doctrine by their errors." The magistrate is also to promulgate laws against homicide, theft, adultery, perjury, inchoate crimes, and other forms of immorality that violate the principles of the Second Table. By so doing, the magistrate coerces all persons, regardless of their faith, to respect and maintain the "civil righteousness" or "public morality" dictated by God's moral law.[30]

Calvin was convinced that, through this exercise of godly moral authority, the state magistrate enhances the ambit of liberty. By teaching each person the rudiments of Christian morality, even if by force, the magistrate enables those who later accept Christ to be "partially broken in . . . not utterly untutored and uninitiated in Christian discipline" and discipleship. By upholding minimal standards of Christian morality, the magistrate protects the "public manifestation of religion" and provides a public and peaceful space for Christianity and the church to flourish. By purging the community of overt heretics, idolaters, and blasphemers, the magistrate

28. *Serm.*, Deut. 5:17.

29. *Institutes* (1559), 4.20.9. See also ibid., 2.8.11–12; *Comm.*, Harm. Law Deut. 10:12–13; Deut. 6:5; 19:18.

30. *Institutes* (1559), 4.20.3; *Lect.*, Dan. 4:1–3.

protects the godly character of the community and the sanctity of the church and its members. Individual Christians and the church as a whole thus enjoy greater freedom to exercise the Christian faith.[31]

Calvin did not enhance the magistrate's civil jurisdiction over religious and moral matters without establishing safeguards. First, magistrates were not "to make laws ... concerning religion and the worship of God."[32] They were only to enforce God's law on religion and worship, especially as it was set forth in the First Table of the Decalogue and interpreted by the church authorities.

Second, Christian subjects were to resist magistrates who prescribed religious and moral duties that directly contravened the First Table of the Decalogue. "Earthly princes lay aside all their power when they rise up against God," Calvin wrote. "We ought rather to spit on their heads than to obey them when they are so restive and wish to rob God of his rights."[33] To be sure, said Calvin,

> we must obey our princes who are set over us. Even though they torture us bodily and use tyranny and cruelty toward us, it is necessary to bear all this, as St. Paul says. But when they rise against God they must be put down, and held of no more account than worn-out shoes. . . . When princes forbid the service and worship of God, when they command their subjects to pollute themselves with idolatry and want them to consent to and participate in all the abominations that are contrary to the service of God, they are not worthy to be regarded as princes or to have any authority attributed to them. And why? Because there is only one foundation of all the power of princes—that God has set them in their places. When they wish to tear God from his throne, can they be respected?[34]

"While we are commanded to be obedient to our superiors," Calvin continued, "the exception still remains that this must not detract from

31. *Institutes* (1559), 2.8.10; 4.20.3.
32. Ibid., 4.20.3.
33. *Lect.*, Dan. 6:22. See also discussion of the "rights of God" to have the duties of the First Table discharged in *Comm.*, Harm. Law Ex. 1:15–22; 10:21–29; 12:4–14; 20:1–6, 23:13, 20–23, 25–31; 28:1–43; 33:1–23; Num. 31:1–54; Deut. 5:8–10; 13:12–17; 17:12–13; 21:23; 23:9–14.
34. *Lect.*, Dan. 6:22.

any of those prerogatives which belong to God, which have already been treated in the First Table. For we know that the service by which God is worshipped must precede everything else." For a Christian in good conscience "to resist tyrannical edicts and commandments which forbid us to give due honor to Christ and due worship to God" is not to be "rebellious against kings, for they be not so exalted, that they may go about like giants to pull God out of his seat and throne."[35]

Third, magistrates were not to trespass or abridge the God-given rights and liberties of their subjects. To the contrary, said Calvin, "God empowered the magistrate to protect the rights of everyone" and called him to "pass uniform and consistent laws" to ensure that "no one suffered violations of his persons or property." It was "nefarious perfidy," Calvin repeated in his 1559 *Institutes*, for magistrates "to violently fall upon and assault the lowly common folk" and "dishonestly betray the freedom of the people, of which they know that they have been appointed protectors by God's ordinance."[36]

Fourth, magistrates were not to enforce God's laws indiscriminately. "We must not always reckon as contentious the man who does not acquiesce in our decisions, or who ventures to contradict us," said Calvin. "We must exercise moderation; so as not instantly to declare every man to be a 'heretic' who does not agree with our opinion. There are some matters on which Christians may differ from each other, without being divided into sects."[37]

Finally, magistrates were always to enforce God's laws equitably. They must seek to adjust their punishments to the capacities of each subject and the dangers of that person's crime. "All teachers have ... a rule here which they are to follow ... modestly and kindly to accommodate themselves to the capacities of the ignorant and the unlearned."[38]

This is what he [Isaiah] means by the metaphor of the bruised reed, that he does not wish to break off and altogether crush these who are

35. *Comm.*, Harm. Law Deut. 5:16; *Comm.*, Acts 5:29; 17:7; *Serm.*, 1 Sam. 26:22–25. For other texts and context, see *RR*, 48–55, 114–17.
36. *Serm.*, Deut. 25:1–4; *Institutes* (1559), 4.20.31; *Serm.*, 1 Sam. 8:11–22.
37. *Serm.*, 1 Cor. 11:6; *Comm.*, Titus 3:10.
38. *Comm.*, Rom. 1:14.

half-broken, but, on the contrary, to lift up and support them, so as to
maintain and strengthen all that is good in them. We must neither crush
the minds of the weak by excessive severity, nor encourage by our smooth
language anything that is evil. But those who boldly and obstinately resist
... must be broken and crushed.[39]

Law, Liberty, and the Church

Although God has vested in the state the coercive power of the sword,
Calvin argued, God has vested in the church the spiritual power of the
Word. God calls the members of the church to be his priests and prophets—to preach the gospel, to administer the sacraments, to teach the
young, to gather the saints, to care for the needy, to communicate God's
Word and will throughout the world. The church is to be a beacon of
light and truth, a bastion of ministry and mission. Just as pious Christians
must take their faith into the world to reflect God's image and glory, so
the church must take its ministry into the world to project God's message
and majesty for all persons to behold.[40]

God has established his church with a distinct and independent polity,
Calvin argued. The church's responsibilities must be divided among multiple offices and officers. Ministers are to preach the Word and administer
the sacraments. Doctors are to catechize the young and to educate the
parishioners. Elders are to maintain discipline and order and adjudicate
disputes. Deacons are to control church finances and to coordinate the
church's care for the poor and needy. Each of these church officials, Calvin
believed, is to be elected to his office by fellow communicant members of
the congregation. Each is subject to the limitation of his own office, and
the supervision of his fellow officers. Each is to participate in periodic
congregational meetings that allow members to assess their performance
and to debate matters of doctrine and discipline.[41]

God has vested in this church polity three forms of legal power (*potes-
tas*), said Calvin. First, the church holds *doctrinal power*, the "authority to lay

39. *Lect.*, Isa. 42:3. One person whom Calvin did "crush" was Michael Servetus. See
detailed sources and discussion of this infamous episode in *RR*, 67–70, 89–102.
40. *Institutes* (1559), 4.1.1–17; *Serm.*, Deut. 5:22.
41. *Institutes* (1559), 4.3; Ecclesiastical Ordinances (1541), in *CO*, 10/1.15–30.

down articles of faith, and the authority to explain them." Included herein is the power to set forth its own confessions, creeds, catechisms, and other authoritative distillations of the Christian faith, and to expound them freely from the pulpit and the lectern. Second, the church holds *legislative power*, the power to promulgate for itself "a well-ordered constitution" that ensures (1) "proper order and organization," "safety and security" in the church's administration of its affairs; and (2) "proper decency" and "becoming dignity" in the church's worship, liturgy, and ritual. "When churches are deprived of . . . the laws that conduce to these things," said Calvin, "their very sinews disintegrate, and they are wholly deformed and scattered. Paul's injunction that 'all things must be done decently and in good order' can be met only if order itself and decorum are established through the addition of observances that form a bond of union." Third, and "most importantly," said Calvin, the church has *jurisdictional power*, the power to enforce laws that help to maintain discipline and to prevent scandal among its members.[42]

The church's jurisdiction, which is rooted in the power of the keys, must remain "wholly spiritual" in character, Calvin insisted. Its disciplinary rules must be "founded upon God's authority, drawn from Scripture, and, therefore, wholly divine." Its sanctions must be limited to admonition, instruction, and, in severe cases, the ban and excommunication—with civil and criminal penalties left for the magistrate to consider and deliver. Its administration must always be "moderate and mild," and left "not to the decision of one man but to a lawful assembly"—ideally a Consistory court, with proper procedures and proper deference to the rule of law.[43]

The Consistory was a unique institution created by Calvin, and it would become one of the signature institutions of early modern Calvinism. In Calvin's Geneva, the Consistory was a hybrid of church-state authority. It was made up of two dozen men who sat on two benches. On one bench sat all the ordained pastors of the city, headed by Calvin as their moderator. On the other sat twelve elected lay commissioners called "elders." The Consistory met once a week in sessions that before long stretched

42. *Institutes* (1559), 4.1.5; 4.8.1; 4.10.27–38; 4.11.1; see further *De Scandalis*, in CO, 8.1–84.
43. *Institutes* (1559), 4.10.5, 30; 4.11.1–6; 4.12.1–4, 8–11; CO, 10/1.207–8, 210–11.

out for several hours. The Consistory participated in the enforcement of the city's laws governing spiritual and civil life. Fully two-thirds of the Consistory caseload in Calvin's day dealt with issues of sex, marriage, and family. Fornication and adultery, disputed engagements, family quarrels, and domestic abuse were the most common issues.

Cases came before the Consistory in a variety of ways. Sometimes they came on the initiative of an individual who sought relief. A jilted fiancée who wanted to have her engagement contract enforced or her dowry returned. A man who claimed that his wife was cheating on him and wanted a divorce. A woman who limped into court with blackened eyes and broken teeth, asking for protection from her abusive husband. A son whose parents threatened to disinherit him unless he married a woman he did not want. A poor person who felt unjustly banned from the local hospital and wanted a bed. A businessman who felt his partner had embezzled his funds. A renter whose landlord refused to fix the window. In these cases, which numbered in the hundreds each year, the Consistory acted as a mediator, seeking to resolve each dispute amicably among the parties, and referring suspected criminal activity such as battery, adultery, and embezzlement to the Council for criminal investigation and possible prosecution.

Other cases began on the initiative of a government official. Sometimes they alerted the Consistory to a serious need such as poverty, sickness, unemployment, loneliness, or neglect that the Consistory could address. More often, the complaint was about some moral irregularity— nonattendance or disruptiveness at worship services, failure to pay tithes, suspicion of polygamy, concubinage, or prostitution, public drunkenness, mixed public bathing, nonmarital cohabitation, wild or blasphemous songs, obscene speech, plays, or publications, a raucous party or wedding featuring dancing and debauchery. Occasionally more serious offenses such as rape, battery, sodomy, kidnapping, mayhem, torture, and homicide were also reported, although most of these cases went directly to the Council. In all these cases, the Consistory served more as a grand jury and preliminary hearings court. The Consistory had wide subpoena power to summon and investigate parties, witnesses, and documents. A complicated case could go on intermittently for months, sometimes a

51

year or two. The Consistory would compile a detailed record and then reach a decision. Roughly half the cases each year were disposed of by use of spiritual sanctions alone—a private confession followed by a "remonstrance," a public confession or reparation before the congregation, a temporary ban from communion to induce remorse and confession. Here the Consistory resolved to achieve the theological and educational uses of the law. If the members of the Consistory found an individual to be guilty of particularly offensive behavior, or to be unduly recalcitrant or resistant to remorse, confession, and reparation, they would send that person to the Council for criminal punishment or civil redress. Here the Consistory resolved to achieve at least the civil use of the law. In many of these cases, particularly the complicated ones, Calvin's legal skills shone through. His advice usually carried the Consistory, and he was usually tapped to issue the remonstrances, to draft the complex orders, to write *consilia* for further guidance, and to report on serious legal cases to the Council.

Despite the Consistory's cooperation in achieving these uses of the law, Calvin insisted on a basic separation of church and state, even quoting Ephesians 2:14 to call for a "wall of separation" between the two. "There is a great difference and unlikeness between the ecclesiastical and civil power" of the church and state, said Calvin. "A distinction should always be observed between these two clearly distinct areas of responsibility, the civil and the ecclesiastical." The church has no authority to punish crime, to remedy civil wrongs, to collect taxes, to make war, or to meddle in the internal affairs of the state. The state, in turn, has no authority to preach the Word, to administer the sacraments, to enforce spiritual discipline, to collect tithes, to interfere with church property, to appoint or remove clergy, to obstruct bans or excommunications, or to meddle in the internal affairs of a congregation. When church officials operate as members of civil society, they must submit to the civil and criminal law of the state; they cannot claim civil immunities, tax exemptions, or privileges of forum. When state officials operate as members of the church, they must submit to the constitution and discipline of the church: they cannot insist on royal prerogatives or sovereign immunities. To permit any such interference or immunity between church and state, said Calvin, would "unwisely mingle these two [institutions] which have a completely different nature."[44]

Calvin's principle of separation of church and state bore little resemblance, however, to modern American understandings of "a high and impregnable" wall between church and state.[45] Despite his early flirtations with the radical political implications of Luther's two-kingdoms theory, Calvin ultimately did not contemplate a "secular society" with a plurality of absolutely separated religious and political officials within it. Nor did he contemplate a neutral state that shows no preference among competing concepts of the spiritual and moral good. For Calvin, each community is to be a unitary Christian society, a miniature *corpus Christianum* under God's sovereignty and law. Within this unitary society, the church and the state stand as coordinate powers. Both are ordained by God to help achieve a godly order and discipline in the community, a successful realization of all three uses of the moral law. Such conjoined responsibilities inevitably require church and state, clergy and magistracy to aid and accommodate each other on a variety of levels. These institutions and officials, said Calvin, "are not contraries, like water and fire, but things conjoined." "The spiritual polity, though distinct from the civil polity, does not hinder or threaten it but rather greatly helps and furthers it." In turn, "the civil government has as its appointed end . . . to cherish and protect the outward worship of God, to defend sound doctrine of piety and the position of the church . . . and a public manifestation of religion."[46]

Summary and Conclusions

Let's step back now to survey briefly what enduring legal and theological contributions Calvin made to the Western tradition of law, politics, and society. Calvin's theory of Christian liberty provided the cornerstone for the constitutional protections of liberty of conscience and free exercise of religion advocated by later Protestants in France,

44. *Institutes* (1559), 3.19.15; 4.11.3–16; 4.20.1–4; *Consilia*, CO, 10/1.215–17, 223–24; Ecclesiastical Ordinances (1541), CO, 10/1.15–30.
45. *Everson v. Bd. of Education*, 330 U.S. 1, 18 (1947).
46. *Serm.*, 1 Sam. 11:6–10; *Institutes* (1559), 4.11.1; 4.20.2–3.

the Netherlands, England, Scotland, and America. His theory of moral laws and duties inspired a whole range of later Calvinist natural-law and natural-rights theories. His references to "the common rights of mankind," "the rights of our common human nature," and "the equal rights and liberties" of all provided normative traction for the later development of a robust Calvinist theory and law of public, private, penal, and procedural rights for all peaceable persons. His theory of coequal and cooperative clerics and magistrates provided a strong foundation for later constitutional protections of both separation and accommodation of church and state. His theory of the moral responsibilities of both church and state to the community lay at the heart of later theories of social pluralism and civic republicanism.

One of Calvin's most original and lasting contributions to the Western rights tradition lay in his restructuring of the liberty and order of the church. Calvin combined ingeniously within his ecclesiology the principles of rule of law, democracy, and liberty.

First, Calvin urged respect for the rule of law within the church. He devised laws that defined the church's doctrines and disciplinary standards, the rights and duties of its officers and parishioners, the procedures for legislation and adjudication. The church was thereby protected from the intrusions of state law and the sinful vicissitudes of its members. Church officials were limited in their discretion. Parishioners understood their duties. When new rules were issued, they were discussed, promulgated, and well known. Issues that were ripe for review were resolved by proper tribunals. Parties that had cases to be heard exhausted their remedies at church law. Disgruntled individuals and families that departed from the church left their private pews and personal properties behind them. Dissenting congregations that seceded from the fold left their properties in the hands of the corporate body. To be sure, this principle of the rule of law within the church was an ideal that too often was breached, in Calvin's day and in succeeding generations. Yet the principle helped to guarantee order, organization, and orthodoxy within the Reformed church.

Second, Calvin urged respect for the democratic process within the church. Pastors, elders, teachers, and deacons were to be elected to their offices by communicant members of the congregation. Congregations periodically held collective meetings to assess the performance of their church officers, to discuss new initiatives within their bodies, and to debate controversies that had arisen. Delegates to church synods and councils were to be elected by their peers. Council meetings were to be open to the public and to give standing to parishioners to press their claims. Implicit in this democratic process was a willingness to entertain changes in doctrine, liturgy, and polity, to accommodate new visions and insights, and to spurn ideas and institutions whose utility and veracity were no longer tenable. To be sure, this principle did not always insulate the church from a belligerent dogmatism in Calvin's day or in the generations to follow. Yet the principle helped to guarantee constant reflection, renewal, and reform within the church—*ecclesia reformata semper reformanda*, a reformed church dedicated to perpetual reformation.

Third, Calvin urged respect for liberty within the church. Christian believers were to be free to enter and leave the church, free to partake of the church's offices and services without fear of bodily coercion and persecution, free to assemble, worship, pray, and partake of the sacraments without fear of political reprisal, free to elect their ministers, elders, deacons, and teachers, free to debate and deliberate matters of faith and discipline, free to pursue discretionary matters of faith, the adiaphora, without undue laws and structures. To be sure, this principle, too, was an ideal that Calvin and his followers compromised, particularly in their sometimes undue empowerment of the Consistory and their brutality toward persistent dissenters such as Michael Servetus. Yet the principle helped to guarantee constant action, adherence, and agitation for reform by individual members of the church.

It was Calvin's genius to integrate these three cardinal principles into a new ecclesiology. Democratic processes prevented the rule-of-law principle from promoting an ossified and outmoded orthodoxy. The rule of law prevented the democratic principle from promoting a faith swayed by fleeting fashions and public opinions. Individual liberty kept both corporate rule and democratic principles from tyrannizing ecclesiastical minorities. Together, these principles allowed the church to strike a unique perpetual balance between law and liberty, structure and spirit, order and innovation, dogma and adiaphora. And together they helped to render the pluriform Calvinist church remarkably resilient over the centuries in numerous countries and cultures.

This integrated theory of the church had obvious implications for the theory of the state. Calvin hinted broadly in his writings that a similar combination of rule of law, democratic process, and individual liberty might serve the state equally well. What Calvin adumbrated, his followers elaborated. In the course of the next two centuries, European and American Calvinists wove Calvin's core insights into the nature of corporate rule into a robust constitutional theory of republican government, which rested on the pillars of rule of law, democratic processes, and individual liberty.

A second major contribution that Calvin and his followers made to the Western tradition was their healthy respect for human sinfulness, and the need to protect institutions of authority from becoming abusive. Calvinists worked particularly hard to ensure that the powerful offices of church and state were not converted into instruments of self-gain and self-promotion. They emphasized the need for popular election of ministers and magistrates, limited tenures and rotations of ecclesiastical and political office, separation of church and state, separation of powers within church and state, checks and balances between and among each of these powers, federalist layers of authority with shared and severable sovereignty, open meetings in congregations and towns, codified canons and laws, transparent proceedings and records within consistories, courts, and councils. And if none of these constitutional safeguards worked, later Calvinists called for resistance, revolt, and even regicide against tyrants. Calvinists were in the vanguard of the great democratic revolutions of France, Holland, England, and America fought in the later sixteenth to later eighteenth centuries.

A third and final major contribution that Calvinists made to the Western tradition was their integrative theory of rights. Early modern Calvinists insisted that freedoms and commandments, rights and duties belong together. To speak of one without the other is ultimately destructive. Rights without duties to guide them quickly become claims of self-indulgence. Duties without rights to exercise them quickly become sources of deep guilt.

Early modern Calvinists further insisted that religious rights and civil rights must go together. Already in Calvin's day, the Reformers discovered that proper protection of religious rights required protection of several correlative rights as well, particularly as Calvinists found themselves repressed and persecuted as minorities. The rights of the individual to religious conscience and exercise required attendant rights to assemble, speak, worship, evangelize, educate, parent, travel, and more on the basis of their beliefs. The rights of the religious group to worship and govern itself as an ecclesiastical polity required attendant rights to legal personality, corporate property, collective worship, organized charity, parochial education, freedom of press, freedom of contract, freedom of association, and more. For early modern Calvinists, religious rights and civil rights were fundamentally interdependent.

And early modern Calvinists insisted that human rights are ultimately dependent on religious norms and narratives. Calvin and his immediate followers, as we saw, used the Decalogue to ground their theories of religious and civil rights. This would remain a perennial argument. Later Calvinists grounded their theories of rights in other familiar doctrinal heads, including the doctrine of the Trinity and the creation. Some human rights, they argued, are temporal expressions of what Calvin had called the "eternal rights of God." These are the rights of God the Father, who created humans in his own image and commanded them to worship him properly and to obey his law fully. They are the rights of God the Son, who embodied himself in the church and demanded the free and full exercise of this body on earth. And they are the rights of God the Holy Spirit, who is "poured out upon all flesh" and governs the consciences of all persons in their pursuit of happiness and holiness.

Human rights are in no small part the rights of persons to do their duties as image-bearers of the Father, as prophets, priests, and kings of Christ, as agents, apostles, and ambassadors of the Holy Spirit. As image-bearers of God, persons are given natural law, reason, and will to operate as responsible creatures with choices and accountability. They are given the natural duty and right to reflect God's glory and majesty in the world, to represent God's sovereign interests in church, state, and society alike. As prophets, priests, and kings of God, persons have the spiritual duty and right to speak and to prophesy, to worship and to pastor, to rule and to govern on God's behalf. As apostles and ambassadors of God, persons have the Christian duty and right to "make disciples of all nations" by Word and sacrament, by instruction and example, by charity and discipline.

Further rights structures fall under the doctrine of creation. Calvinists saw in the story of God's creation and division of each creature "after its own kind" an original warrant for pluralism. This was not just the plurality of responsibilities that God gave Adam and Eve to name the many creatures, to eat of one tree but not another, to "be fruitful and multiply" themselves into new forms, to dress and keep the garden of Paradise in various ways. Calvinists eventually imputed to the order of creation structural or social pluralism—the basic division of divine authority and responsibility in the structures of family, church, and state. They also imputed to the order of creation a legal or normative pluralism—the basic division of laws and orders governing all persons' relationships to God above them, to persons beside them, and to nature below them. They even imputed to the order of creation a confessional or religious pluralism—the reality that God in his sovereignty can "walk and talk" with each and every human being as he once did with Adam and Eve in Paradise, and that each person draws his or her own conclusions of faith from these divine encounters. It was the need to respect and protect God's sovereign relationship with each and every human being that eventually led Calvinists to embrace the freedom of every peaceable believer in God.

4

CALVIN THE FRENCHMAN

HENRI A. G. BLOCHER

The Reformer of Geneva": one often encounters this title when John (Je[h]an) Calvin is referred to.[1] Obvious and innocent? It may give rise to the temptation into which even the *Encyclopaedia Britannica* could fall: that of labeling Calvin a "Swiss divine and reformer."[2] At least three considerations warn against such easy language. Geneva did not become "Swiss," part of the Helvetic Confederation, until 1815! In Calvin's time it was an independent city, although the treaty with Bern, of mutual assistance and recognition (*combourgeoisie*), proved essential for its survival. In the strictest sense, Calvin was not the *Reformer* of Geneva: the city had broken away from Roman Catholicism before Calvin arrived there for the first time. Under the influence of François Lambert's preaching, and above all Guillaume Farel's, the final,

---

1. To give just one prestigious example: Ford Lewis Battles, ed. and trans., *The Piety of John Calvin: An Anthology Illustrative of the Spirituality of the Reformer of Geneva* (1973; repr., Phillipsburg, NJ: P&R Publishing, 2009).

2. *Encyclopaedia Britannica*, 1961 ed., s.v. "Calvin, John," 4:630b.

solemn decision was made on May 21, 1536; Farel was *the* Reformer, and for many years the warmer partisans of the Reformation in Geneva were called *Guillermins*, that is, followers of Guillaume (Farel). Furthermore, if Calvin devoted most of his life to the establishment of a truly Reformed faith and discipline in Geneva, which he did call his *bonne ville*,[3] "good city," and which he made into the "Protestant Rome" for the whole world, he did not receive Genevan citizenship (*bourgeoisie*) until less than five years before his death! In the minutes of the Council, he is *ille Gallus*: "that Frenchman."

The Frenchman in Calvin is worthy of some close attention. Although his natural and cultural identity may not constitute the main dimension of his personality and the main factor in his historical role, it may highlight aspects that would otherwise remain in the shadows. It may help to discern the ways in which these aspects are interconnected and rooted in the sixteenth-century context. I propose first to recall some facts, drawing the contours of Calvin's "Frenchness," and then to inquire about the possible correspondences between specifically French traits and the physiognomy of his thought and lifework.

Calvin, French Indeed

Je(h)an Calvin was born a French child in the province of Picardy, which belonged to the kingdom of France (Noyon, July 10, 1509), of French parents, Gérard Cauvin and Jeanne née Lefranc. His father's name, Cauvin, sounds as a common name among the people (meaning "bald" originally);[4] in humanist fashion, our Reformer latinized it into *Calvinus*, and sometimes played with the letters of this name, using anagrams: Lucanius in Basel, when he rented a room in Mrs. Klein's pension, Alcuinus on the title page of some editions of the *Institutes*. Alcuinus was the name of Charlemagne's English theologian who had, with amazing courage, chided the emperor when he compelled the defeated Saxons to undergo

---

3. He used as his pseudonym "J. de Bonneville" in his June 7, 1553, letter to Madame de Cany, in *Lettres françaises de Jean Calvin*, ed. Jules Bonnet (Paris: Meyrueis, 1854), 1:394.

4. It is a variant form of the name from which *chauvinism* is derived.

Christian baptism (death or baptism!).[5] After early years in his native city, under the influence of Catholic piety (his mother is supposed to have been a devout worshiper) and exposed to the echo of church affairs that his father handled on behalf of the cathedral canons, the promising boy pursued "normal" studies in famous French university towns—Paris, Orléans, Bourges, Paris again. One must not be misled by the special use of the word *nations* in universities: it could bear a more restricted, merely regional meaning, so that four groups of students had been distinguished as "nations": of France, Picardy, Normandy, and Germany. While in Orléans, where the number of such "nations" had grown to ten,[6] Calvin was elected by his fellow students *procureur* of the Picardy nation (something like caretaker of the interests of the group): this does not take anything away from his possession of the French nationality in the usual sense.[7] A product of the French university system of the time, Calvin was a Frenchman both by birth and by education.

France, then, although its territory was only two-thirds of its present extension, had the largest population in Europe: from 15 to 16 million people, compared with only 3 million for England (12 million for all German-speaking areas, 10 million for Italy and for Spain with Portugal).[8] It was the most unified among the big countries, the achievement of a

5. Alcuin(us) boldly claimed: "It cannot be approved that the body should receive the sacrament of baptism if the soul has not previously accepted the truth of Faith," as quoted in Philippe Wolff, *Histoire de la pensée européenne: I. L'Eveil intellectuel de l'Europe*, Points Histoire (Paris: Seuil, 1971), 32. Unless otherwise indicated, all quotations from non-English sources are my translation.

6. According to Jean Cadier, *Calvin, l'homme que Dieu a dompté* (Geneva: Labor & Fides, 1958), 20.

7. In assemblies, distinct groups could also be formed according to "nations" in the broader sense. "The councils of Pisa (1409) and Constance (1414–18)," Carl Mirbt writes, "contrary to the Curia's intention, divided themselves into 'nations,' each consisting of the bishops, abbots, and prelates of the national Church, the delegates from the princes, and the doctors in theology and canon law, and each constituting an independent college with defined spheres of activity officially recognized as representative of the ecclesiastical and civil interests of its respective people. *There was thus a German, an English, a French, an Italian, and finally also a Spanish nation . . .*" ("Concordats and Delimiting Bulls," in *The New Schaff-Herzog Encyclopedia of Religious Knowledge*, ed. Samuel M. Jackson [New York/London: Funk & Wagnalls, 1909], 3:211a [emphasis added]).

8. I borrow these rough but eloquent figures from Pierre Janton, *Jean Calvin, ministre de la Parole, 1509–1564*, Histoire (Paris: Cerf, 2008), 8.

monarchy whose power had been steadily growing for generations: a stark contrast with Germany and Italy.[9] The Renaissance was in full bloom, one century later than in Italy. The weight of the Catholic Church was enormous; France, "the eldest daughter of the Church," was the country with thirty-six thousand church spires,[10] but also with a strong tradition of a relative independence from Rome. Gallicanism, as it is called and as it had been expressed in the "Pragmatic Sanction" of Bourges (1438), had led to decades of acute tensions between France and the Holy See. This had just been solved, through mutual concessions, by the Bologna Concordat concluded in 1516 by Francis I and Leo X: the king wielded considerable authority over the church of France, inclusive of the right to appoint bishops and abbots. One can muse on the consequences of this settlement: if the pope had refused to grant the king of France power over the church, would Francis I have divorced from Rome, in the English way of Henry VIII? At times, Calvin's policy gives the impression that he entertained hopes that a Gallican church might be freed from popish rule, with royal consent, after the Anglican pattern.

Calvin the Frenchman is heir to the earlier "reformist" evangelical movement in France. He was the second-generation Reformer: his work can be interpreted as a synthesis of the deep religious legacy of the German-speaking revolutionaries (Luther indeed, but also Bucer and even Zwingli) and of the trends set in motion by Erasmus that had gained much ground in France. Calvin, an Erasmus consumed by a Luther-like passion! Calvin, a Luther disciplined with Erasmian and French moderation, nuances, and philological rigor! One can see a beautiful symbol of the continuity in the meeting, at the Nérac court in April 1534, between the young Calvin and the old scholar Jacques Lefèvre d'Etaples, also from Picardy (Faber Stapulensis). Soon after his conversion, whereby God had "tamed his heart into teachability," Calvin, not yet twenty-five, received, as it were, the testament of the almost octogenarian celebrity who best

9. Pierre Chaunu, *Le Temps des Réformes: Histoire religieuse et système de civilisation: La crise de la chrétienté, l'éclatement (1250–1550)*, Le Monde sans frontière (Paris: Fayard, 1975), 489, underlines the similarity, in this regard, of England and France, the two kingdoms with a powerful structure of state control. The smaller size and insular character of England, however, created other conditions.

10. Janton, *Jean Calvin*, 8.

represented the French evangelical movement, who had already discovered and expounded the message of justification by faith in his commentaries on the Psalms (1509) and the Epistle to the Romans (1512), and had just published the whole Bible translated into French (from the Vulgate)! (Because documents are scarce, we are left to imagine what took place between the two men.) One can also mention Calvin's indirect relationship with Guillaume Budé, who was responsible for the founding by Francis I of the royal college that later became the "Collège de France": the widow of Budé (who himself may have died as a secret evangelical, and in any case, was sympathetic to the new approach) and his daughter and three sons moved to Geneva; Calvin had encouraged that move and was able to welcome them.[11]

The view that one can speak of an independent, indigenous Reformation in France has been ably refuted and cannot be maintained.[12] But this is no excuse for underestimating what took place before Calvin was converted. Of Erasmian influence and Lefèvre's scholarly output, one can say that they planted seeds and prepared the ground for the Protestant Reformation; these beginnings were not radical and did not draw ecclesiological consequences. Of the development in the 1520s, one must acknowledge that the leaven came from Luther (in Calvin's own training the German Lutheran Melchior Wolmar, who taught him Greek in Bourges, had a significant part). Evangelicals were stigmatized as "Lutherans." Yet this branch of the European Reformation (not another Reformation) retained its own flavor, with an emphasis on the study of texts, on simplicity in style, and on inwardness as essential in the Christian life. This also Calvin inherited when he joined the evangelical party. Pierre Chaunu's powerful simplification does not miss the mark: Luther's Reformation, which succeeded in the northern and eastern part of Germanic Europe, focused on salvation and left the rest relatively untouched (*adiaphora*). It had to, since it was chosen for the

11. See his 1546 letter in *Lettres françaises*, 1:180–85, and others.
12. Lucien Febvre, "Une question mal posée: Les origines de la Réforme française et le problème des causes de la Réforme," in *Au cœur religieux du XVIᵉ siècle*, Bibliothèque générale de l'Ecole des Hautes Etudes en Sciences Sociales (1929; repr., Paris: Livre de poche biblio/essais, 1984), 7–95; Emile-G. Léonard, "Les Origines de la Réforme en France," *Revue de Théologie et d'Action Evangéliques* 3.4 (October 1943): 291–309.

masses by princes and institutional authorities. What Chaunu calls the "humanist Reformation" really affected the cultural elite—mostly the upper middle class—and was more interested in consequences of gospel truth for the form of Christian and church life. It was concerned with purification of mores and worship, and it spread in the Western part (with the "hybrid" case of England) and aroused strong traditionalist reactions that Luther's Reformation had avoided. Calvin constructed the lasting expression, the "orthodoxy," of this humanist Reformation.[13] And to a large extent, he could do so as a Frenchman.

Lest misleading connotations attach to the word *humanist*, one should remember the ardent commitment of the French evangelicals' pure biblical faith (they were also called *bibliens*): they resisted unto blood adverse pressures under Francis I and Henri II—under atrocious tortures, they sealed their witness with the sacrifice of their lives. Calvin's references to their martyrdom show that he was deeply impressed. Before he was burned at the stake in Metz, the young wool-carder Jean Leclerc was branded as a heretic with red-hot iron in Meaux, his hometown (1524); his mother, among the crowd, shouted to him: "Praise to Jesus and his ensigns!"[14] Was there ever, under heaven, a more glorious cry of motherhood? The constancy of the martyrs moved even their bitter enemies. Florimond de Raemond, whose book is full of slander against Calvin, cannot help reporting:

> Stakes were lit everywhere. On the one hand, laws just and severe constrained the people to abide by their duty, but on the other, many were astonished by the stubborn resolve of those who were dragged to the gibbets, who would rather give up their lives than their courage. They were beholding frail females seek torments to prove their faith and, going to death, only call out "Christ, the Savior," sing out some psalm; young virgins walk to the place of torture more cheerfully than they would have to the nuptial couch; men rejoice at the sight of the frightening preparations and tools of death made ready for them, and half-burned and roasted, consider from the stakes, with unconquerable courage, the wounds made by the tongs, wear a blithesome face

13. Chaunu, *Le Temps des Réformes*, 486–88, 492ff., 498–500, 523.
14. *Vive Jésus et ses enseignes!* It is difficult to render *Vive* here (ordinarily "Long live").

between the executioners' hooks, be like rocks against the waves of pain, in short: gaily die . . .[15]

This Christianity was no syrupy humanism. Although part of the evangelical movement, well represented by its high protector, the sister of Francis I, the "Marguerite des Marguerites," duchess of Angoulême, Alençon, and later Queen of Navarre, mixed with it some sweet mystical streaks and tolerated teachers whom Calvin considered as dangerous libertines,[16] the core was solidly biblical. Erasmus mocks the French refugees with this doggerel: "These five words are never off their lips: Gospel, Word of God, Faith, Christ, Holy Spirit."[17] Of such was Calvin the Frenchman.

The third subset of historical facts that show the importance of Calvin's French identity relate to his interest in French affairs and personal investments on behalf of his French brothers and sisters.

It starts with the writing of the *Institutes of the Christian Religion,* soon after he had escaped the threat of arrest (and what usually followed) in the kingdom of France. As he found himself in safer Basel, he felt impelled by solidarity and *loyalty* toward his fellow evangelicals in France to write in defense of their faith and character. They were falsely accused of being seditious (with the Münster disaster still fresh in the memories of all governments and peace-loving bourgeois), of introducing novelties, of destroying the sacraments. The *Institutes* offers a rebuttal of these charges in the form of a positive exposition of evangelical beliefs. Calvin, in his famous introductory epistle, dedicates the work to the king of France, Francis I, and immediately declares his intention "to serve, by means of this work of mine, *our* French."[18] To prevent the suspicion that he is moved by self-interest, he plainly states that he is not asking for permission to

---

15. Quoted in Emile-G. Léonard, *Histoire générale du protestantisme: I: La Réformation* (Paris: Presses Universitaires de France, 1961), 1:271. His note 2 adds another quotation from Raemond, concerning the martyr's death of Anne du Bourg, a councillor in Paris Parliament: "His preaching from the gibbet and the stake had worse effects than a hundred [Protestant] ministers would have obtained."

16. See Calvin to the Queen, April 28, 1545, in *Lettres françaises*, 1:111–17.

17. In a letter, quoted in Léonard, *Histoire générale du protestantisme*, 1:271.

18. My emphasis (and translation). Page i (implicit numbering) in the 1565 French edition I am consulting (a beautiful volume, 683 numbered pages followed by detailed indexes, no publisher's name [probably precautionary], but with the date and the place, "Lyon" [Lyons]).

go back to France: as an exile he is not overwhelmed with grief, but he protests that he feels "the proper human affection" for his native land.[19] There may be an implicit theological justification of his exile in the argument he draws a little later from Psalm 45:11 (English versions, v. 10): "the obedience of faith must be so ordered that it causes us to forget our people and our father's house."[20] If Calvin felt the need for a justification, it testifies to his sense of obligation toward his own nation!

Calvin was also a man of letters in the epistolary sense! Among the thousands he wrote, a significant proportion is addressed to correspondents in France. Among them, one can signal the prisoners who were soon to undergo martyrdom: he comforts them with warm sympathy but also exhorts them in virile fashion, with the authority of God's Word, to remain steadfast to the end. "In his attitude towards prisoners and martyrs," Richard Stauffer affirmed, "the Reformer gave the full measure of his humaneness"; he summarizes: "without sparing his efforts, whenever he could, to deliver them, he was able to make them ready for the specious questionings of the inquisitors, to strengthen them in their painful imprisonments, to assure them, in the face of a dreadful death, that heavenly bliss was awaiting them."[21] Others are sent to leaders of the Protestant party, such as the Admiral de Coligny: Calvin gathers information, devises strategies. Others are sent to churches, in France (e.g., Paris, Angers, Poitiers, Aix), or refugee churches in London, Frankfurt, Wesel: he provides guidelines, tries to quieten quarrels, warns against doctrinal deviations, recommends ministers; he fulfills the role of a pastor of pastors. When the first (risky) synod was held in Paris (1559), he provided a full draft of the confession of faith that the synod was to adopt, *Confessio gallicana*, later known (from 1572) as "Confession de La Rochelle": apart from changes at the beginning, it follows Calvin's proposal rather closely.[22] Undoubtedly, Calvin reckoned that he was assigned a special responsibility for the church in France.

19. Ibid., ii.

20. Ibid., v.

21. *L'Humanité de Calvin*, Cahiers théologiques (Neuchâtel: Delachaux & Niestlé, 1964), 60.

22. Léonard, *Histoire générale du protestantisme*, 2:102, writes that the changes were "considerable and, theologically, very serious (*très graves*)," contrary to the "propitiatory" terms of the pastor's (Morel's) letter to Calvin. With most, I differ with Léonard's judgment in this

Two aspects of Calvin's active involvement in French church affairs call for a brief complement. Calvin was extremely concerned about a temptation he considered deadly to the evangelical cause in France and wrote repeatedly against the "Nicodemites." Just as Nicodemus came to Christ "by night," presumably to avoid being seen by "the Jews," and therefore remained a secret disciple until the cross, many evangelicals imagined that they could be inwardly at peace with God, through faith in Christ, free from superstition, and still attend Mass, still remain outwardly Roman Catholic. Elements of Erasmian evangelicalism and some Lutheran emphases converged to authorize this wonderful way of escaping the vicious persecution that was raging (for oneself and for one's family): the devaluation of externals (they do not matter in the soul's intimate relationship with God), the liberation from the necessity of "works," and probably the Constantinian conviction that the whole people is a *corpus christianum*, with princes called to guide their peoples also in spiritual matters (when princes are misled, the faithful Christian is to bow down under his or her God-given authority and simply pray for a change in leadership).

Calvin realized that such a compromise would entail the absorption of the clear gospel witness by the Catholic system. He preached the cost of discipleship, the way of the cross, total commitment as the only proper response to the grace of Christ, who had unreservedly given himself on our behalf. He denounced, in tones that seem to have grown more and more strident through the years, the idolatry of the Mass and other aspects of Roman worship, along with the resulting pollution contracted by participants. He probably started writing on the topic in 1536, while in Ferrare (where Renée de France, who had been married to the Duke of Ferrare, was won over to the faith of the Reformation, and Calvin later wrote to this princess several letters of spiritual direction); he published amplified versions in 1543, 1550, and 1552, in 1544 his *Excuse à Messieurs les nicodémites*, and still later, in 1554, a French version of a treatise on ecclesiastical benefits.[23] Calvin's fight against the cautious dissimulation of their real faith by many French evangelicals was combined with his attacks against other and more theological forms of compromise: against efforts

---

regard, which may have been influenced by a touch of Barthianism and also by Léonard's frequently expressed antipathy toward Calvin.

23. See Janton, *Jean Calvin*, 109–11, 204–7.

at minimizing differences and relativizing doctrinal issues, and therefore irenic policies that implied concessions. Calvin considered the *mediating* course taken by the "moyenneurs" as a betrayal of the gospel. In his *True Way to Reform the Christian Church and to Solve the Matters in Dispute*, he clearly identifies his opponents:

> This disputation is not directed to the Turks, or to the Jews, who wish the name of Christ were totally abolished, nor to forthright and honest papists who ask that we renounce entirely the truth, but to those who build I don't know which kind of a made-up concord. They leave us one half of Jesus Christ, in such a fashion that there is no part of Christ's doctrine which escapes being obscured and smeared by some lie of theirs. And to disguise such a wickedness, they call it Reformation. By slyly drawing us away from the one who is the author of peace, they promise us peace better to embaboon us (*pour nous embabouiner*).[24]

Since the conditions that prevailed in France (the importance of the evangelical party, but also the power of the state and the fierceness of persecution) made the temptation of compromise especially strong there, Calvin's fight against it is one aspect of his French involvement.

The second aspect that deserves signaling relates to church polity. The spontaneous tendency among the newly formed churches in France appears to have been *congregational*.[25] Calvin and his agents countered this tendency and were able to establish the presbyterian-synodal system of government.[26] Calvin's temperament and interpretation of biblical data (with the weight of Old Testament models in his ecclesiology) inclined him in this direction; he probably also realized that more autonomous congregations would more easily yield to surrounding pressures and adopt mediating views and less doctrinal forms of evangelicalism. Pierre de la Ramée (latinized: Ramus), who was, in Léonard's estimation, the greatest sixteenth-century philosopher and the influential founder of a

---

24. "La Vraye Façon de reformer l'Eglise Chrestienne, & d'appointer les differens qui sont en icelle," in *Recueil des opuscules, c'est à dire des Petits traictez de M. Iean Calvin* (Geneva: Baptiste Pinereul, 1566), 1043.

25. Léonard, *Histoire générale du protestantisme*, 2:84, 91–93.

26. Ibid., 2:115–23. Jean Morelli de Villiers was the champion of more democratic procedures.

new binary logic, lent his prestige to the congregationalist preference and actively promoted it, but since he did not join the Protestant camp until 1561, he was in conflict with Theodore Beza rather than with Calvin himself.[27] All the same, the polity choice was first Calvin's, and it determined the system that prevailed in France and does so to this day.

How French Is Calvin's Thought and Action?

If John Calvin was not only born a Frenchman but educated as such, indebted to previous Reformation beginnings in France, and highly conscious of special responsibilities toward his fellow countrymen, does his Frenchness show in the shape of his theology and the way he acted? May we spot typical French traits? May we detect noteworthy correspondences with the French spirit, soul,[28] or temperament, with the French manner, mind, or genius? This would raise the recognition of Calvin as a Frenchman from the level of contingent fact to that of meaning; it would add some intelligence of historical development and throw some light on the cultural incarnation of truth. It is worth trying.

Exploring such possible correspondences is beset by grave difficulties. The idea that any given nation may be ascribed a soul or spirit is highly questionable. Even the presence of "typical" traits is difficult to establish: as soon as one claims to have found one, myriads of exceptions and counterexamples may be brought to the table. The relevant data are so abundant and multifarious that a scientific treatment would be long and costly; and then, scientific method, with its bent toward the quantitative, could be suspected of missing what is more essential. I am inclined to follow George Devereux as he affirms a "psychological Newton law" that operates in every culture: for all *manifest* tendency there is a hidden one that goes against it.[29] We have grown wary of stereotypes that our

27. Ibid., 2:119–22. Ramus sought the support of Heinrich Bullinger (Zurich) and mixed with his congregationalism a dose of Erastianism (giving civil authorities extended rights in religious affairs). Beza opposed both.

28. Cf. Reuben Saillens, *The Soul of France* (London: Morgan & Scott, 1917).

29. I commented on the analysis of Devereux, the prestigious ethno-psychiatrist and thinker, in my articles "Invoquer la culture," *Théologie Évangélique* 2.2 (2003): 160, and "Discerner au sein de la culture," *Théologie Évangélique* 4.2 (2005): 50–51, quoting from the French

ancestors received as self-evident! We realize that some stereotypes have completely changed from one generation to another. A nineteenth-century *History of the Reformation* offers an amusing instance that is directly relevant to our search: the French author of the book exclaims: "Luther is so French!" and seems to interpret Calvin's character as far less French than Luther's, acting as a counterbalance to restrain the unruly passion of the French![30] He chooses to ignore Luther's self-conscious expression of the German genius, and depends on a stereotype of the French as exuberant revolutionaries, which he embraces enthusiastically as most of us would no longer.

Yet people remain attracted to stereotypes: stereotypes meet a need, and nobody can truly escape from them; they must at least retain a modicum of truth. If they are lenses through which we perceive a nation's disposition and life, they must not be totally unfit for that role. It will not be unreasonable, therefore, for us to make a wager and to use some stereotypes, especially those authorized by the opinion of notable representatives of French tradition (or foreign observers) and rather widespread feeling. The method cannot claim scientific rigor: it is intuitive and impressionistic, but not worthless for that. Since the contours of self-interpretation are often drawn by means of contrast and antithesis, stereotypes of the differences between the French and other nations are significant: if the "others" fail to recognize themselves, it is of little moment, for the stereotypes should count as self-description.

The French traits that are relevant to our inquiry are those that belong to Calvin's historical situation. The hypothesis that the spirit of France remained self-identical through many centuries is too precarious for us to turn it into a presupposition of our search. Traits of modern Frenchness that were imprinted, it seems, by events that occurred after Calvin's time must be ruled out of court. This prevents us from using André Glucksmann's brilliant essay *Descartes, c'est la France*, which demonstrates in the case of Descartes the kind of correspondence that we wish to explore in

translations of his books, first published in America (*Essais d'ethnopsychiatrie générale* and *De l'angoisse à la méthode dans les sciences du comportement*).

30. N. A. François Puaux, *Histoire de la Réformation française* (Paris/Geneva: Grassart/Béroud, 1857), 1:162.

the case of Calvin.[31] The key element in his perceptive reconstruction (which offers forceful evidence that changes the image of Descartes that most people harbor, without having read much of him!) is the trauma in French memory of the wars of religion;[32] this explains best the French "exception." But this happened *after* Calvin. Continuity through many generations need not be denied; some elements from other epochs may be significant for our inquiry, but we should use them only with reserve and caution.

In correspondences, matters are so intricate that it is difficult to tell on which side one should locate the cause and on which side the effects. In order to appreciate how French was Calvin's thought and action, we will take into account both his contributions to French culture that henceforth shaped French sensitivities, dispositions, intellectual style, and so on, and what Calvin owed his mother-community and context. Shaping, he was shaped, and as he was shaped, he shaped. Attention is drawn to the presence of likeness and kinship with little interest in causal direction.

Clarity

The greatest consensus would probably obtain concerning this first trait: clarity. Would anyone deny the champion-title to Calvin in this respect (leaving out, for some, the doctrine of the Lord's Supper)? Zwingli had not used circumlocutions,[33] but Calvin achieved a new pedagogical perspicuity on a much fuller presentation of Christian doctrine.[34] The

31. *Descartes, c'est la France*, Livre de poche (Paris: Flammarion, 1987).

32. France is the only country where the Reformation was so successful (up to a third of the population, at least in cities and among opinion-makers), and where it was nearly stamped out by persecution.

33. Zwingli's "swan song," which Bullinger published after the Reformer's death (1536), bore the title *Christianae Fidei a H. Zwinglio praedicate brevis et clara Expositio;* "brief and clear" sounds Calvinian before Calvin! Luther himself appealed to the *helle und klare Worte*, "lucid and clear words," of Scripture, but while he was an amazing communicator whom the common people heard gladly, his theologizing is too paradoxical for clarity. Aiming at clarity is in tune with biblical emphases (against scholastic abstraction and mystical seduction), with such a statement as that of Isaiah 45:19: the Lord repudiates secrecy, dark sayings, vertiginous chaos (*tôhû*), and affirms what is right and authentic (*tsedeq, méshàrîm*).

34. Anthony N. S. Lane aptly summarizes what must be said: "The durability of his contribution is both due to the skill with which he created the synthesis and [due] to the 'lucid brevity' with which he expressed it" ("Calvin, John [1509–64]," in *The Dictionary of*

expert on Calvin's rhetoric, Olivier Millet, highlights his clarification of issues: Calvin thereby accomplished an unprecedented prowess.[35] Millet stressed it in a recent lecture and answered a question concerning Calvin and poetry (Calvin wrote a little poetry, versified a few psalms, but did not persevere and humbly decided that more gifted poets should take over, at first Clément Marot and later Theodore Beza): clarity and poetry are not convergent pursuits.[36] Calvin preferred clarity.

How French! The French are wont to repeat Antoine de Rivarol's judgment: "What is unclear is not French."[37] The contrast is strongest with Teutonic depth—rather obscure depth in the stereotype. The saying goes (in France) that German philosophers wait until their works have been translated into French to read them and then to be able to understand themselves! If we accept the thought that it is not easy to wed clarity and poetry, we may observe that important poetic genres have not found supremely glorious poets to illustrate them in France. It is already true of lyrics, which the French always fear will lose them in sentimental haze, and of epic poetry: Voltaire's attempt (*la Franciade*) is a typical French failure; Victor Hugo is an epic poet, but the French almost feel a kind of shame when they hear his verse—just a bit too sonorous to be perfectly French.[38] Exceptions, however, could be found in the sixteenth century: Ronsard (a vicious enemy of the Reformed) and Joachim du Bellay in the lyrical vein, Guillaume du Bartas and Agrippa d'Aubigné for epic power. So the question arises: could we see an *effect* of Calvin's clarity, and of the mark it left on the French spirit, if their kind of inspiration tended to dry up later? Of course, others came along,

---

Historical Theology, ed. Trevor A. Hart [Carlisle, PA/Grand Rapids: Paternoster/Eerdmans, 2000], 100b).

35. *Calvin et la dynamique de la parole*, Bibliothèque littéraire de la Renaissance (Paris: Slatkine, 1992).

36. The lecture was given at Aix-en-Provence on February 20, 2009.

37. From his *Discours sur l'universalité de la langue française* (1784). The whole paragraph reads: "The distinguishing mark of our tongue is the order and construction of the sentence. This order must always be direct and, by necessity, clear. The French language, a unique privilege, is the only one which stayed faithful to direct order. Hence that admirable clarity, the everlasting basis of our tongue: what is unclear is not French." I quote, and translate, from Claude Gagnière, *Le Bouquin des citations* (Paris: R. Laffont, 1997), 217b.

38. One remembers and passes on Paul Valéry's answer: Who is the greatest French poet? "Victor Hugo, alas!"

among them one Monsieur Descartes, who also cared more obviously for clarity than for poetic feeling.

The French Language

The clarity of which the French are proud, the clarity Calvin attained in his exposition of the Reformation message, is to a great extent a matter of linguistic quality (this phrase referring not only to vocabulary and syntax, but also to the use of language).[39] The excellence of Calvin's prose has been widely acknowledged. Even Bossuet in his powerful attack against Protestantism—Bossuet, *the* orator of the classical age and who never fell into the temptation of sympathy—had to grant Calvin "the glory of having written as well as anyone did in his century."[40] If Calvin emulated Erasmus's elegance in Latin, it was his special investment if he took pains to translate scholarly treatises and discussions in limpid and juicy French. His taste for the national language is a remarkable feature of his lifework.

Again, how French! The shrewd literary critic Charles Dantzig writes: "A most French characteristic, perhaps a specifically French characteristic, is the amorous attention we give our mother tongue"; "the French are grammatical."[41] Napoleon is reported to have said: "France is the French language when it is well written."[42] I wonder whether in many other countries newspapers and magazines similarly offer regular rubrics discussing the propriety of words and phrases, warning against barbarisms, and, whatever their political line, fighting against the "franglais" contamination. Interestingly, this typical attitude dates back from Calvin's time! His former teacher Mathurin Cordier published in 1530 the substance of his lectures on corrupt turns to avoid (in Latin, by French writers).[43] Soon after, other books by Charles de Bovelles, d'Augereau, and Robert Estienne

---

39. For the French, generally, see Rivarol's statements in note 37 above.

40. *Histoire des variations des Eglises protestantes*, Classiques Garnier (Paris: Garnier, s.d. [orig. 1688]), 1:434 (bk. 9, chap. 81).

41. *Dictionnaire égoïste de la littérature française* (Paris: Grasset, 2005), 313, 314.

42. From Gagnière, *Le Bouquin des citations*, 219a.

43. *De corrupti sermonis apud Gallos emendatione*, reprinted nine times until 1536, according to Jacques Pannier, "Introduction," in *Jean Calvin: Institution de la religion chrestienne [1541]* (Paris: Société les Belles Lettres, 1936), 1:21.

himself appeared that dealt with proper usage in French.[44] In 1540, Etienne Dolet printed his reflections on translation and on finer points of French expression.[45] Continuity may be observed over five centuries.

As the foregoing references show, Calvin's effort to write fine French was influenced by his intellectual milieu. But it can be argued that the success of his effort was more importantly a *cause* of the lasting French concern for beautiful language. Calvin set an example. In a decisive pioneering way, he determined the shape of literary and scholarly French. This role has been recognized by authorities. Gustave Lanson wrote: "The French text of the *Institutes* is, together with Rabelais' book, the greatest monument of our prose in the first half of the sixteenth century"; Abel Lefranc hailed Calvin as "one of the most admirable writers in our tongue, the true creator of this French eloquence which all peoples of one accord proclaim to be the ornament and mark of our national genius."[46]

Calvin, indeed, deserves to be considered the Frenchman in his relationship to the French language.

Form: Logical Form

Investment in linguistic expression is one aspect of a more general disposition: a high valuation of form, which is also reflected in the search for well-ordered logical form. Lucien Febvre unhesitatingly affirmed: "Calvin had all the essential marks of the French genius. . . . Commanding, sovereign logic. A critical sense, both judicious and formidable. . . . His problem was to retain what is essential, and only what is essential, and to

---

44. Charles de Bovelles, from Amiens (Picardy!), *Liber de differentia vulgarium linguarum, et Gallici sermonis varietate* (1533), according to Michel de Toro, "Préface," in Adolphe V. Thomas, *Dictionnaire des difficultés de la langue française* (Paris: Larousse, 1971), v; d'Augereau, who was martyred as a heretic on Christmas Eve 1534, *Briefve doctrine pour bien et duement excripre selon la propriété du langage françois*, according to Pannier, "Introduction," 1:21; Robert Estienne, *De la manière de tourner en langue française les verbes actifs, etc.*, according to Pannier, "Introduction," 1:21.

45. *La manière de bien traduire d'une langue en autre, davantage de la ponctuation de la langue françoyse, plus les accents d'icelle*, according to Pannier, "Introduction," xxii. Lucien Febvre explored Dolet's relationship to the Reformation and suggested contacts with Calvin in his study "Un cas désespéré? Dolet propagateur de l'Evangile," in *Au cœur religieux*, 231–300.

46. Both quotations from *Nouvelles de la Cause* 28.279 (2d trim. 1964): 1 (references not given).

express it with precision, clarity, following good order and logic."[47] And on the same page, he immediately draws the contrast with German massive conglomeration and accumulation: he names Albrecht Dürer and Hans Baldung as powerful illustrations.

Most readers will grant that the description fits Calvin, although the character of Calvin's logic is a debated issue. His way of thinking is far removed, *toto coelo*, from the deductive logic of a self-contained system; his effort to espouse the "true and natural sense" of the various Scriptures, with their inner tensions, is constant, and the attempt to bring out coherence (based on the conviction that the Scriptures are the Word of God and that God cannot deny himself) represents a negotiation with the diversity among the data.[48] Hence the characterization of Calvin's thought as *complexio oppositorum*. Émile Doumergue goes even further and enthusiastically praises Calvin for having included contradictions—or, somewhat ambiguously, "contrarieties," the contradictions "of life."[49] This, I submit, amounts to a projection of romanticism, which is alien to Calvin's thought. Among doctors of the church, Calvin remains noteworthy for rigorous logic. One should simply remind oneself of his critique of the Lutheran idea of the omnipresence of Christ's body (in the *Institutes*, 4.17, the polemical treatises against Westphal and Heshusius)!

But how French is this? The difficulty on our way is that of determining whether such traits are really characteristic of "the French genius." Counterexamples come to mind: *la furia francese*, mob madness in revolutionary

47. "Une mise en place: Crayon de Jean Calvin," in *Au cœur religieux*, 340–41.

48. Again A. N. S. Lane offers a flawless summary: "Calvin aimed not to deduce doctrine from a controlling principle but simply to present in an orderly form the substance of the Christian faith as revealed in Scripture and, supremely, in Christ. Calvin was also not a systematic theologian in the sense of seeking after logical consistency as a primary goal. Where he discerns apparently contradictory themes in Scripture Calvin is happy to leave them in tension rather than to resolve them in a logical fashion" ("Calvin," 101b–102a).

49. *Le Caractère de Calvin* (Paris: Editions de Foi et Vie, 1921), esp. 46–49, 72–78, 81. He can write on one page: Calvin extends the lines he finds in religious experience; "he tries to make them converge towards a central point. But the effort fails. The most logical among logicians ends in the bankruptcy of logic. On all issues, his system ends in self-contradiction" (46). But then on the next page, Doumergue switches to the word *contrariété*, which he defines as *apparent* contradiction (47). This step back does not prevent him from opposing, in global fashion, the logic of concepts and the logic of life (48), for "life mocks formulas and systems" (81).

eruptions, the acute and voluptuous destruction of rationality among many late modern philosophers and artists. My proposal will not be unassailable, and it distinguishes between (1) the tendency to give more importance to form than most other peoples seem to do and (2) the predilection for critical reason.

It does appear that the French prize formal qualities to a degree that surprises other nations. The educational system trains gifted youths to write brilliant essays on topics they know next to nothing about. The substance of the argument is less important than the art of presentation. The form so attracts attention that the practical outcome goes out of sight; with benevolent irony, Henri-Frédéric Amiel (he was Swiss!) remarked in his diary: "[France] has always believed that when something has been said, it has been done."[50] The contrast is marked with Anglo-Saxon pragmatism, and generally empirical inclination. It may have started in the thirteenth century, with the more empirical bent of the University of Oxford, and the experimental research initiated by Roger Bacon—while the University of Paris majored on formal logic. The difference may be observed through the centuries, with the other Bacon, Sir Francis, as the counterpart of Descartes in the seventeenth century, and down to our own days.[51]

Apart from purely contingent factors (which also create traditions), one cause may be diagnosed: the constitutional diversity of the French population. France was the first "melting-pot" of the world: its geographical location, farthest west with the natural barriers of the sea and of the Pyrenees mountains, ensured that successive waves of invasion stopped there, and mixed. Already in the Neolithic age, the two Mediterranean and Danubian civilizations met and intermingled on that territory.[52] Historic France is born of the Celts, Romans, and Franks (who were "Germans"). Sociologists have shown that France has combined three different anthropological systems of family organization.[53] Polarization, at least at times,

50. Dated May 23, 1873, quoted in Robert Carlier et al., eds., *Dictionnaire des citations françaises* (Paris: Larousse, 1977), 13.
51. A friend of mine, who is an engineer with Michelin and works on both shores of the Atlantic, confided to me that the difference is quite obvious between American and French engineers in the same firm.
52. Pierre Chaunu, *Ce que je crois* (Paris: Grasset, 1982), 105.
53. Hervé Le Bras and Emmanuel Todd, *L'Invention de la France: Atlas anthropologique et politique*, Pluriel (Paris: le Livre de Poche, 1981).

turns diversity into division. The conflict of the "two Frances" has been dramatically real: it flared up with the eighteenth-century Revolution and was structurally important throughout the nineteenth century, with two intensely inimical memories of that Revolution; the two Frances were again at war with each other during the Dreyfus Affair, and also during World War II (for or against collaboration, for or against the Vichy regime, acknowledging Pétain or De Gaulle). I could not claim that there is nothing left of this trait, although we have probably entered a new configuration. The first certain manifestation of the conflict was precisely that of the Reformation, of which Calvin was a major protagonist, with one France in sympathy with the new face of religion and the other one enraged against it. More instinctively than reflectively, the French realized how the nation could survive: *The diversity had to be mastered.* To avoid a breakdown, a policy of unifying centralization was persistently carried out, and it could be carried out only *at the formal level.* Hence the weight of public administration in French life: its power, sometimes bordering on arrogance; its competence and lesser vulnerability to corruption (it seems) than in many other countries. The Roman legacy of *written* law (another difference from England) reinforced leanings toward abstract uniformity. As a matter of degree, of course, those leanings do characterize the French spirit.

There is a kinship between putting high value on form and trusting logic. Classical logic, at least, scrutinizes the form of arguments, while issues of content escape logic itself; they belong to premises, and therefore to conclusions: before-and-after logic. So the French, compared with other peoples, may be expected to privilege logical approaches—and bother less if they fail! But what about the critical cast? In a situation of potentially divisive diversity, or even of repressed conflict, reason will probably devote its powers to the refutation of rival views and verification of one's tenets: to the critical task. This may throw some light on the impression (quite subjective, I grant) that French thinkers have been more effective in criticism than they have in constructive metaphysics. Critical attention to form breeds the fear of ridicule: "France may be the only country," Paul Valéry suggested, "where ridicule played a historical role."[54]

54. Quoted in Gagnière, *Le Bouquin des citations*, 219b.

This simplified portrait of the French mind and sensitivity does not suit Calvin at every point, to be sure! Calvin, for instance, relied strongly on experience and took it into account—under biblical influence, perhaps—as Émile Doumergue emphasizes.[55] There are enough similarities, however, to lend credibility to Lucien Febvre's judgment: in the way Calvin took care of form and used logic, we recognize Calvin the Frenchman.

Universality

A strategy that imposes, in the name of logic or reason, a unity of form to heterogeneous agencies and situations quite naturally leads to universal claims. Using the word *general* as a quasi-synonym, the philosopher Henri Bergson so describes what he saw among his fellow countrymen: "The appetite for philosophy is universal: it tends to bring every discussion, even business discussion, on the level of ideas and principles ... The French soul goes straightaway to what is general."[56] The conviction is that the French civilization is deeply rooted in that French "soul," though in recent times, it hides under the guises of the defense of human rights (which, the French believe, originated in France), lest the charge of "ethnocentricity" become too obvious. Le Bras and Todd explain that because of the threat of inner diversity, "France needs the myth [of French universality] to be at ease."[57] The French feel overjoyed when they read this saying of President Thomas Jefferson: "Every man has two home-countries, his own, and France."[58]

It is therefore relevant to our inquiry when historians credit John Calvin with securing the universal impact of the Reformation. Luther's Reformation was so deliberately "German" that it succeeded, essentially, in the "Teutonic" area. Calvin's work exercised a major influence in a variety of cultural settings: not only in France and Switzerland, but also in western Germany (Palatinate), the Low Countries, Great Britain. "From Geneva," Timothy George reminds

55. *Le Caractère de Calvin*, 50–52. Doumergue exaggerates, as he often does, what is valid in his claims.
56. Quoted in Emile Saillens, *Toute la France: sa terre, son people, ses travaux, les oeuvres de son génie* (Paris: Larousse, 1925), 406 (reference not given).
57. *L'Invention de la France*, 80. They also conjecture that the final failure of the Reformation was caused by the advantage of Catholic universality (313).
58. Quoted in Saillens, *Toute la France*, 429. Unfortunately, I had to translate back from the French translation.

us, the insights of the Reformation as expounded by Calvin "took on a life of their own and developed into a new international theology, extending from Poland and Hungary in the East to the Netherlands, Scotland, England (Puritanism), and eventually to New England in the West."[59] Calvin's numerous letters to correspondents in almost all of Europe testify to the scope of the universal responsibility he felt was his. Referring to the dedicatory epistle to the Duke of Somerset, by which Calvin prefaced his commentary on Timothy (1548), Timothy George comments: "Here we see Calvin as the *episcopus* of Geneva looking beyond national boundaries and the particularities of his local situation in the interests of an ecumenical congregational reform."[60] He did not spare efforts to heal the divisions within the Reformation camp, and did not contradict in his behavior what he wrote to Archbishop Thomas Cranmer in 1552: "As the members are scattered, the body of the Church lies in lacerated state (*lacerum jaceat*). It affects me so much that, if someone saw that I could be useful, I would not hesitate to cross ten seas . . ."[61] At least with the Zurich church, his efforts were successful, and the *Consensus Tigurinus* was signed (1549): who can say how the Reformed churches would have fared had not this agreement been reached?

The universal influence of Calvin's ministry was not only the fruit of his pastoral and diplomatic efforts. His version of the doctrine of the Bible was able to appeal to all. "As he brought into full light [its principles] and bound them together in a well-ordered doctrine, Calvin provided the religious thought of the Reformation with the universal import which was implicit in that thought."[62] If Calvin is thus the best nominee for the title "universal Reformer," there is some correspondence with the common self-understanding of the French.

Measure

In Lucien Febvre's quotation (corresponding to note 45 above), one key word was omitted—on purpose, so that we may now bring it into focus:

59. *Theology of the Reformers* (Nashville: Broadman, 1988), 166.
60. Ibid., 236–37n126.
61. Quoted (from CO, 19.314) in Cadier, *Calvin, l'homme que Dieu a dompté*, 174.
62. Henri Bruston, "La Portée universelle de la pensée calviniste," *Revue de Théologie et d'Action Evangéliques* 3.4 (October 1943): 383 (the whole article is relevant [382–404]).

the word *measure* (*La mesure*). In Febvre's estimation, it is a typical trait, both of Calvin's character and thought and of "the French genius." The statement is likely to arouse some degree of skepticism, both as regards Calvin and as regards France; yet it should not be discarded too quickly.

Foreigners may be struck by instances of French immoderate actions or reactions (often associated with arrogance). The French, nevertheless, may point to a tradition that greatly values measure. It may take the form of Cartesian restraint (as interpreted by Glucksmann) or of Pascal's sense of a medium place for humankind halfway between the two infinites; it may take the form of bourgeois *mediocritas* in more modern times; it may take the form of the progressive, mildly modernistic form of Roman Catholic theology that was so influential in the Second Vatican Council. Even authors who cultivate the enormous, such as Rabelais, may do so with a second-degree intention: ultimately to insinuate the superiority of measure. I think French schoolchildren still learn the poem by the sixteenth-century poet Joachim du Bellay, who had been an ambassador in Rome and sings of his preference for the gentle measure of his native village (Liré, by the Loire River):

> I have rather the place which my fathers built
> Than the flashy front of Roman palaces,
> Rather than solid marble, slates ever so fragile,
> Rather than Latin Tiber, my Gallic Loire river,
> Rather my little Liré than Mount Palatine,
> Rather than sea breezes, Angevine gentleness.[63]

The value of measure helps to tolerate tensions, and it answers to the critical edge of the French use of reason. It contrasts, in French eyes, with the abyssal depth of German dreams, with the lightness of Italians,[64] with the Spaniards' hunger for the Absolute.

---

63. To be forgiven my foolish attempt to offer an English echo, I also give the French text of the poem (the last two stanzas of the sonnet): "Plus me plaist le séjour qu'ont basty mes ayeux, / Que des palais Romains le front audacieux, / Plus que le marbre dur me plaist l'ardoise fine: / Plus mon Loyre gaulois que le Tybre latin, / Plus mon petit Liré que le mont Palatin, / Et plus que l'air marin la douceur angevine."

64. V.-L. Bourrilly, "Humanisme et Réforme: la formation de Calvin," *Revue de Théologie et d'Action Évangéliques* 3.4 (October 1943): 276, notes a significant difference at the time of

Calvin valued measure. Paul Wernle's judgment penetrates to the heart: "In scarcely another of the Reformers is there to be seen such thoroughness, absoluteness. And yet what moderation, what real dread of every kind of excess . . . [!]"[65] This is manifest in his exegetical caution, but contrary to caricature, it also stamped his ethical teaching and exercise of discipline. Within the limits of proper measure, he commended aesthetic pleasure, and even sensuous delight.[66] According to Doumergue, he received into the fellowship of the church an Anabaptist believer (former Anabaptist, I would guess) who hesitated to affirm predestination, and it is well known that he had Melanchthon's *Loci communes* translated, and wrote a friendly preface, despite the German theologian's weakness on the same topic.[67] One can also interpret as true moderation the balance of Calvin's ecclesiology— a great subject! Calvin maintained to the end the thesis of the invisible church, whose membership is constituted only of regenerate believers, and finally only of all God's elect. But he also stressed the importance of the visible church, a divine institution; he labored and fought strenuously in order that due honor be rendered to the visible church, and came to use the language of motherhood for her God-given role. He tries to *measure* her prerogatives exactly: the visible church is important, yet it is fallible; it begets spiritual children only as the servant of the Word (*sealed* by the sacraments), whose office is *not* "to confer the benefits" of grace;[68] the visible church is a precious aid, not a subordinate "mediatrix."

Calvin's sense of the right measure is reflected in his attitude toward the Christian's intimate experience. Should one risk the word *mystical?* If it carries with it pantheistic overtones (as it does with most forms of mysticism), nothing could be further from Calvin's awareness of the

---

the Renaissance: Italian humanists rediscovered the *pagan* writers of antiquity; in France, Germany, and England, humanists also learned Hebrew and read the church fathers, and this added "gravity, seriousness, dignity" to their attitudes.

65. As quoted with approval in and translated (I suppose; there is no reference) by Benjamin B. Warfield in "John Calvin: The Man and His Work," originally published in *The Methodist Review* (1909), reprinted in the volume of Warfield's works *Calvin and Augustine*, ed. Samuel G. Craig (Philadelphia: Presbyterian and Reformed, 1971), 25.

66. Well demonstrated by Doumergue, *Le Caractère de Calvin*, 65–69.

67. Ibid., 76n3. Doumergue indicates 1520 for the Anabaptist's reception, obviously a typographical error.

68. *Institutes*, 4.14.14, 17.

distance between heaven and earth! If one alludes to specific procedures, steps in a planned itinerary to approach the divine, there is no trace of any interest in these on Calvin's part. Yet Ronald S. Wallace is not afraid of speaking of "a 'mystical' element in Calvin's experience and understanding of our knowledge of God."[69] After several telling quotations, he comments: "We have found a phraseology like that which Calvin uses to describe it [this aspect of our knowledge of God] often used by writers like Richard of St. Victor, Tauler, Bernard, Gregory Palamas, Thomas Merton, and we feel certain that if students of mysticism could overcome the prejudices which the current traditional picture of Calvin tends to create in our minds, then they might find something akin to themselves."[70] To believe in Christ means, in Calvin's words, "with ardent affection to hunger and thirst and sigh after him."[71] Émile Doumergue emphatically extols Calvin's "mysticism" and quotes from several passages that describe physical phenomena experienced in the most emotional moments of communion with God.[72] At the same time, the Word remains central and we do not hear of a *noche oscura*. Calvin was also critical of this typical expression of the late medieval mysticism of the Rhine regions, *Theologia deutsch* (whereas Luther had been enthusiastic when he had discovered it): Calvin warns against it in a letter to the French refugees' church in Frankfurt.[73] Despite Calvin's reserve, we may be sure that there was a strong existential, experiential, emotional component in his relationship with Christ, the union with whom is a central theme, maybe the central theme, of his preaching. For his personal seal, he chose a drawing illustrative of the sentence we find in a letter to Farel: "I offer my heart immolated as a sacrifice to the Lord."[74] This warmth, but not beyond measure, is not so far removed

69. "A Christian Theologian: Calvin's Approach to Theology," in *The Challenge of Evangelical Theology: Essays in Approach and Method*, ed. Nigel M. de S. Cameron (Edinburgh: Rutherford House Books, 1987), 126.

70. Ibid., 129.

71. *Institutes*, 4.14.8, as reproduced, in ET, by Wallace, "A Christian Theologian," 143.

72. *Le Caractère de Calvin*, 58–60, quoting from the commentary on Galatians 4:9, the *Institutes*, 3.20.33, and the CO, 29.284.

73. Letter dated February 23, 1559, in *Lettres françaises*, 2.259–60: although there are no obvious errors, Calvin writes, a deadly venom is hidden there.

74. Letter dated October 24, 1540. See Stauffer, *L'Humanité de Calvin*, 64 and n6.

from the "French school of spirituality" in the seventeenth century.[75] Such is the French measure.

Calvin the Frenchman did not suppress his Frenchness as he preached the Word, wrote theology, and organized the church; conversely, Calvin contributed to shaping the way the French, after him, have spoken, thought, felt, behaved—and approached God. But is this of any relevance, apart from mere historical curiosity, to non-French Christians today? If there is any grain of truth in the affirmation of a universal import of Calvin's work (and even in the French spirit?), the answer must be yes. Deep local roots enable the branches to overshadow a vaster territory and bear fruit all around.

One special word may be added for American readers. Over centuries, the relationship between France and the United States of America, the other "melting-pot" nation, has been quite special, and paradoxical: alternations of warm cooperation and rivalry, sympathy and misunderstandings, almost a love-hate relationship. Despite glaring differences, there have been striking resemblances, and a shrewd interpretation seems to be this: France and the United States have been (at times, at least) rivals *because they have much in common.*[76] Traits that other nations deride, or resent, in the French and in Americans are nearly the same! The same critical bent, the same claim to universality. In that perspective, Calvin the Frenchman should be considered by Americans as relevant indeed!

75. As Léonard observes, *Histoire générale du protestantisme*, 1:262 (naming St. François de Sales, Bérulle, St. Vincent de Paul).

76. So Bruno de Cessole in the newsmagazine *Valeurs Actuelles*, July 4, 2003, 57; also Jean Dutourd, *Le Vieil Homme et la France* (Paris: Flammarion, 1994).

5

CALVIN AND WOMEN: BETWEEN IRRITATION AND ADMIRATION

ISABELLE GRAESSLÉ

This subject will offer an opportunity to discover an unexpected John Calvin as well as impressive female characters, through their personalities, their writings, and their choices. Most of all, one will understand how all of these will intersect at the heart of one of the biggest changes to affect the Western world since its origin: the "invention of the individual."

According to historians,[1] the exact moment of the phenomenon changes, depending on region, social class, and intelligence. A certain consensus fixes the sixteenth century as the beginning of the process,

1. Jean-Marie Mayeur et al., eds., *Histoire du christianisme des origines à nos jours*, vol. 8, *Le temps des confessions (1530–1620/30)* (Paris: Desclée, 1992); E. William Monter, *Enforcing Morality in Early Modern Europe* (London: Variorum, 1987); Robert Muchembled, *L'orgasme et l'Occident. Une histoire du plaisir du XVIe siècle à nos jours* (Paris: Seuil, 2005); John Witte Jr. and Robert M. Kingdon, *Sex, Marriage, and Family in John Calvin's Geneva*, vol. 1, *Courtship, Engagement, and Marriage* (Grand Rapids: Eerdmans, 2005).

emphasized by the religious disruptions that would shake the European soil as earthquakes of anguish mixed with freedom.

The birth of the individual is a long process anyway, balancing between the testimony of one's own opinion (a quite modern notion—we tend to forget it in our culture, where it sounds self-evident) and the breaking of new ground in social and familial laws (a more aggressive way of affirming itself).

One can imagine how the process was even more difficult for the women of the century: how indeed was it possible for them to let their uniqueness, their vision, and their words be recognized, especially if they were poor and subjected to a society organized according to a strong patriarchal system? Another phenomenon increased these difficulties, since by the middle of the sixteenth century all the European states and religious institutions had started a vigorous recovery, controlling bodies and souls.

To summarize this introduction, let us remember these two factors concerning the changes in relationships between men and women in the sixteenth century: on one side, the emergence of an individual ego, and on the other side, the return of the individual and collective moral laws.

It is in the heart of this double phenomenon that John Calvin appears. He will follow both, trying to influence them according to his own theological preconceptions: with Calvin indeed, the individual cannot be the self-proclaimed center of the universe. If there is human recognition, Calvin will urge the person not to offend God but to hope for God's grace. Each believer belongs to Christ, and each one must glorify God through his or her life.

The reconsideration of moral behavior in Geneva (so important for Calvin's Reformation) appears to be a real *ecclesia nota*, a true mark of the church, which was understood as a place for preaching the Word, a place for celebrating the sacraments, and also a place of discipline—to educate or straighten human nature that is so easily inclined to sin. In this sense, the Calvinian ethics drive more toward exhortation than toward prescription: everything is more a question of measure and moderation than of interdiction. The pleasures of life are admitted, but not to excess.[2]

2. Robert M. Kingdon, "Calvin and the Establishment of Consistory Discipline in Geneva: The Institution and the Men Who Directed It," *Nederlands Archief voor Keerkgeschiedenes* 70

And it is in the heart of this double phenomenon that the women who will cross Calvin's path appear. Each of them embodies the rising of the individual by choosing this or that religious voice (the century of Reformation hates the halfhearted!).[3]

For some of these women, this affirmation of themselves will also combine a breaking—a verbal transgression most of the time—of the masculine order, understood as repressive.

In the sixteenth century, however, Protestant women belonged to the conjugal tie: a closed territory, limited mainly to giving birth and obeying.

Between obedience and transgression lies a small margin that let women exist by themselves in this century of Renaissance. Without being exhaustive, I would like to explore three circles of women in Calvin's entourage: first the familial milieu, then the "furious" ones, and finally the royals.

The Family of Calvin: The Mother, the Wife, and the Sinner

The Mother

Nobody knows much about Jeanne Le France, who died when Calvin was still a child. Calvin does tell about the pilgrimage he made with her, to kiss the body of St. Anne, the Virgin Mary's mother. The maternal figure symbolically appears as a woman submitted to the beliefs of an ancient time, a time of relics that the son would later ridicule in his famous treatises.

(1990): 158–72; Robert M. Kingdon, "A New View of Calvin in the Light of the Registers of the Geneva Consistory," in *Calvinus Sincerioris Religionis Vindex*, vol. 16 of Sixteenth Century Essays & Studies (1997), 21–33.

3. Charmarie Jenkins Blaisdell, "The Matrix of Reform: Women in the Lutheran and Calvinist Movements," in *Triumph over Silence: Women in the Protestant History*, ed. Richard L. Greaves (London: Greenwood Press, 1985), 13–44; John Lee Thompson, *John Calvin and the Daughters of Sarah* (Geneva: Droz, 1992); Jeffrey R. Watt, "Women and the Consistory in Calvin's Geneva," *Sixteenth Century Journal* 2.24 (1993): 429–39; Merry E. Wiesner, "Beyond Women and the Family: Towards a Gender Analysis of the Reformation," *Sixteenth Century Journal* 3.18 (1987): 311–21; Merry E. Wiesner, "The Reformation of the Women," *Archiv für Reformationsgeschichte*, special ed., *Die Reformation in Deutschland und Europa: Interpretationen und Debatten* (1993): 193–208.

The Wife

At the other side stands Idelette de Bure, a young woman from Flanders, who was a convert to Anabaptism, a more radical spirituality than the Reformed faith. Calvin met her during his Strasbourg exile, when she had become a widow. She is described as a pretty and educated woman in her thirties. She had two children from her first husband: a son and a daughter, Judith.

Apparently the meeting between Idelette and John was not as easy as I present it, since during these 1541–42 years, Calvin told his correspondents (especially Guillaume Farel) his worries about finding a wife:

> Remember well what I seek in this. I am not the foolish race of these lovers who, once taken by the beauty of a woman, cherish even her defects. The only beauty which is alluring to me is that of a woman chaste, obliging, modest, sparing, patient, who I then finally to hope to be attentive with my health.[4]

What comes out of these letters is the strong change between the first assumption of Calvin, searching for a companion, and the result of his marriage and honeymoon with Idelette: discovering the richness of a relationship of love and respect. Idelette indeed would be much more than a companion!

A little over two short years of happiness followed, punctuated with the trials of life and death. In July 1542, Idelette gave birth to a son, Jacques, who would not survive long. It is fascinating to read from Calvin's own pen the characteristic anxiety of a husband as his wife is in the middle of labor:

> In which great concern I wrote to you, this brother will say it to you. My wife has just been confined, not without running an immense danger, because its pregnancy had not arrived yet in the long term. That God protects us![5]

Beginning in 1549, Idelette was obliged to remain confined to bed, and it became obvious that she would not survive this new trial. She

---

4. Calvin to Farel, May 19, 1539, in Richard Stauffer, *L'humanité de Calvin*, Cahiers théologiques (Neuchâtel: Delachaux et Niestlé, 1964), 21.
5. Calvin to Pierre Viret, ibid., 26.

still worried about her two children, but Calvin promised to take care of them as if he were the father. She died on March 29 after having asked her husband and the beloved around her to pray for her. Modestly, Calvin wrote to his friends: "I am consumed by my sorrow." Contrary to the usual custom of the time, he would not marry again.

The Sinner

We also meet the "shamed" character—the most terrible figure for a Reformer who asked so much from his fellow citizens, who were forbidden to live scandalously, to sing saucy songs, and to engage in bawdiness and promiscuity. Calvin would find two of these shamed women on his journey: his daughter-in-law, Judith Stordeur, and his sister-in-law, Anne Le Fert, the wife of his brother, Antoine Calvin, who had followed him to Geneva.

In 1548, Calvin brought to the Consistory a rumor of adultery concerning Anne Le Fert. He earnestly asked the members to make no exception, even for somebody of his own family.[6]

We won't review all the details of this complicated story, except to refer to the procedure involved. Before any divorce, in order to reconcile, the couple underwent a type of ceremony—in this case, including a ritual of repentance for this woman who had been so careless in her behavior with a stranger (she was preparing him light suppers at 3 AM and receiving expensive gifts, as for example a symbolic ring). Farel came from Neuchâtel to lead the ceremony, since Calvin wanted, by duty, to be recused. Anne repented, the supposed lover was kept in prison for some weeks, and everything returned to normal.

In 1557, however, Antoine Calvin came back to the Consistory to denounce his wife, who was then left in prison and even tortured. She always denied having committed adultery. Banned from Geneva, divorced, obliged to abandon her children, she married again in Lausanne, aligning with her new husband and the "children of Geneva," the opponents of Calvin.

Facing a woman sinner, her infamy recognized or not, Calvin decided to try a marital reconciliation, an attempt to regain God's original intent.

6. Robert M. Kingdon, *Adultery and Divorce in Calvin's Geneva* (London and Cambridge, MA: Harvard University Press, 1995), 71–97.

But the adultery, considered as an offense made to God as to men, since the human body is nothing other than the temple of God (Calvin following here St. Paul), made the reconciliation more difficult. With his well-known irony, Calvin remained pessimistic toward the men and the women of his time. In his forty-second sermon on Ephesians, Calvin admitted:

> However when one looks at the friendship which the husbands carry to their wives, with large pains he finds one in one-hundred which did not want to leave it . . . The women also will have this lightness which they will want to be remarried thirty times a year. And from where does that proceed? It is because one does not look to God, who is author of the marriage.[7]

The "Furious"

In this century of ruptures, the Renaissance period opened real perspectives for educated women. Some took seriously the Reformed message of the "universal priesthood," understanding it as an authorization for anyone to become a minister of the Word. But the Reformation would urgently stop these expectations.

In his biblical commentaries as in his preaching, Calvin revealed himself as a man of his time: the fall, incited indeed by Eve, applies to human sin in general.[8] Women, indeed weaker and more easily influenced than men, still remained equal with men in their access to salvation.

Calvinian anthropology is therefore divided first according to a spiritual equality between men and women, second to a real juridical equality in the treatment of adultery and divorce, and finally to a biblical submission of women to their husbands.

One can find here the two elements of the medieval anthropology: subordination and equality. The question remains how these two elements are connected to each other and which one comes first.

7. André Biéler, *L'Homme et la femme dans la morale calviniste* (Geneva: Labor et Fides, 1963), 57.

8. Max Engammare, "Le Paradis à Genève: Comment Calvin prêchait-il la chute aux Genevois?" *Etudes Théologiques et Religieuses* 3.69 (1994): 329–47.

Another consequence of his Pauline reading is that Calvin forbade women from teaching, preaching, administering the sacraments, and taking part in ecclesial decisions. This prohibition, however, was followed by an indication in the *Institutes* that the silence of women (in the assemblies) belongs to the *adiaphora* (not ultimate things), which means that whether women are preaching or not is not fundamental to the salvation of humanity. Some historians have seen there a glimpse of a "feminist" Calvin. I prefer to consider this indication as a kind of good sense that he shows toward many other ethical questions.

With Calvin as a skilled interpreter of the Bible, there is the rule and the adaptation of the rule. There is the Pauline prohibition, and there are also the strong contrasting figures of Judith, Deborah, Miriam, and others.

In this context, how is Marie Dentière reconciled with a "furious figure"?[9] Marie Dentière, former abbess of Flandres, was married to the Reformer Antoine Froment (her second marriage), and arrived on the Geneva stage in 1535.

A furious woman, Marie Dentière? This educated woman read Latin, Greek, and Hebrew. She was a specialist of canon law. She authored one of the most vivid and spirited historical chronicles about Geneva's adopting the Reformation. She was a friend of Marguerite de Navarre, whom she made the godmother of one of her daughters.

At least, this was the description of Calvin to Farel as he told him of their argument in the streets of Geneva in September 1546: a woman who shouted "in all the shops, by all the avenues." A strong woman who argued against Calvin concerning his choice of the pastoral robes of his colleagues. Futile discussion? Maybe. The end of the adventure is interesting, as Calvin continued: "feeling put at the foot of the wall, it was rejected on complaints about our tyranny and that we do not allow each one to chatter without measurement." And he added, "I treated this woman as I was to do so."[10]

Beyond the question of the pastoral robes of Geneva, what was at stake here was free speech—a limited free speech, of course. A free speech

9. Isabelle Graesslé, "Vie et Légendes de Marie Dentière," *Bulletin du Centre Protestant d'Etudes* 1.55 (2003): 3–24.

10. Ibid., 8.

that Marie Dentière had already tried in her *Defense for Women* (already written seven years before), with a striking modernity, and of course with a frightening modernity, as she wrote: "Is there a Gospel for men and a Gospel for women?" The negative answer should authorize the boldness. But these bits of free speech would shortly be found dashed on the solid rocks of norms and interdictions.

One could also cite Benoîte Ameaux, a strange case of a woman victimized with a syndrome of affective fixation on Calvin,[11] or Françoise Favre, who dared to confront face to face the one who forbade her to dance furiously during clandestine balls.

Each of these speeches testifies of this "furious word," this "word of madness," as a way to escape a society that chained up these women in rebellion with values of oppression.

The Royals

In all the Calvinian correspondence, three figures play a distinct part: Marguerite de Navarre (1492–1549), who was quite open to the new "evangelical" ideas but who herself never turned to the Reformation. She was a powerful woman who influenced her brother, Francis I.

For Calvin, who tried to make some allies among the European nobility, the queen's aversion to all kinds of religious formalism was not a positive factor. This relationship brought him no satisfaction.

The daughter of Marguerite, Jeanne d'Albret (1528–72), queen of Navarra, in contrast to her mother, openly declared herself a believer in the Protestant faith in 1560. Her correspondence with Calvin reveals that she was helped by all the pastors sent by Calvin to Nerac once her Reformed confession was made public. Even Theodore of Beza would visit in the summer of 1560.

Finally, we turn to Renée de France (1510–75), daughter of Louis XII and of Anne of Brittany. Renée, Duchess of Ferrara, was from the first the ideal woman, sublimated, briefly encountered by the young Calvin

11. Kingdon, *Adultery and Divorce*, 31–70.

on a trip to Italy. Their printed correspondence exhibits a mutual esteem and sweet tenderness.[12]

I would like to end by referring to their correspondence, which reveals part of the multisided Calvinian personality. At the end of this short communication, John Calvin seems quite attached to the mentality of his time concerning human relationships, of a morality only turned to God (if there is a Calvinian litany, it is the one of continually "serving God"). But Calvin also seems, if not seduced, at least soothed by the women of his existence.

An Underrated Friendship: Jean Calvin and Renée of Ferrara

If the travel embarked on by the young Calvin and his friend Louis du Tillet in the spring of 1536 is frequently noted in biographies, if their quick departure from the court of Ferrara is also normally featured, so the correspondence that occurred between the duchess and the Reformer is also almost always listed.

But the meaning assigned to this exchange has differing interpretations: for the majority, Renée of Ferrara constitutes a reemerging correspondent on the long list of the epistolary addressees of Calvin, but she is not portrayed as more than a secondary political character.[13]

Coming back to this corpus, through a literary reading, another meaning reveals a unique correspondence, as well as an underappreciated side of the Reformer.

One can only be astonished indeed by the sweetness, comprehension, compliments, admiration, esteem, and respect that characterize these letters. The list of the affections that are contained in this correspondence is long—maybe too long for the Duke of Ferrara, who, by codicil, required his future widow to stop all contact with Geneva and its Reformation! Once the Duke was dead, Calvin urged Renée to abandon her vow: "as for

12. Charmarie Jenkins Blaisdell, "Renée de France between Reform and Counter-Reform," *Archiv für Reformationsgeschichte* 63 (1972): 196–225.

13. Charmarie Jenkins Blaisdell, "Calvin's Letters to Women: The Courting of Ladies in High Places," *Sixteenth Century Journal* 3.13 (1982): 67–84.

the oath that you were forced to make, as you failed and offended God by making it, do not be held to keep it, not more as one wish of superstition" (July 5, 1560).

Of course, the reasons for such a precaution were truly political in these times, when each segment of European territory could lead to an instance of war between Catholics and Protestants. But these words unveil several meanings, as jewels reflecting several colors, which mark the mutual affection that these two had for each other: "Madam, I humbly beg you to take in good portion the boldness which I had to write to you, estimating that it does not proceed so much of temerity than of pure and true affection to serve you in our Lord" (1541).[14]

To serve the duchess became part of the Reformer's task toward her: to teach her the subtleties of the new doctrine in a pedagogical way. To serve the duchess also meant providing pastoral support, even in tough times, such as September 1554, when Renée was separated from her children and confined to an obscure and watched residence.

She gave up, and renounced her Reformed commitments: she would confess to a priest and follow the Mass.

Calvin complained openly to Farel: "I receive a sad and very unquestionable news by misfortune of the duchess of Ferrare, overcome by the threats and fear and the opprobrium, it fell. Constancy is a quite rare virtue among the princes of this world" (between September 1554 and February 1555).[15]

But writing to Renée he had already forgiven, using the plural: "With the remainder, Madam, as our good God is always ready to receive us in mercy, and, when we fall, tightens the hand around us so that our falls are not mortal, please take again courage . . ." (February 2, 1555).[16]

In his last letters, Calvin worried; he wished to give her a souvenir, probably a golden coin: "I warn if I am bold: but because I wondered whether you had the similar one, I prevented myself until now, because there is only the innovation which gives him grace. Finally, I gave it to the carrier for you to show it and if it is for you new thing, then you may wish

14. Jules Bonnet, *Lettres de Jean Calvin* (Paris: Meyrueis, 1854), 1.43.
15. Ibid., 2.4n.
16. Ibid., 2.4.

to keep it. These are the most beautiful New Year's gifts that I can make you" (January 8, 1564).[17]

The answer of the duchess did not take long to arrive: "As for the present that you sent to me, I ensure you that I saw it and readily received and had never had one similar to it."[18]

The last letter, written on his deathbed (April 4, 1564), reassured Renée: even as the mother-in-law of the Duke of Guise, one of the most bloodthirsty enemies of the Protestant party, Calvin kept his admiration for her: "As for me, I testify to you that I am encouraged to have your virtues in greater admiration still."[19]

We know about a Calvin who was irascible, bitter, droll, cynical, but here appears the tender Calvin.

Finally, let us read Theodore of Beza, in his third biography of Calvin, from 1575, with more details than the former:

> Calvin was taken by the desire of visiting the Duchess of Ferrara, daughter of Louis the Twelve, king of France, whose piety was then well-known and in the same time, he wanted to greet Italy, as from away. He saw the princess and in the same time, as the situation was permitting it, he confirmed her in the true love of piety, so that since then, she loved him with a unique love; and now that she has survived him, she gives clear proof of her grateful recollection towards the deceased.[20]

The multisided personality of Calvin is worth uncovering in this commemoration.

---

17. Ibid., 2.549.
18. Ibid., 2.549n1.
19. Ibid., 2.549.
20. CO, 21.125.

6

PREACHING AS WORSHIP IN THE PULPIT OF JOHN CALVIN

HUGHES OLIPHANT OLD

For John Calvin, preaching has a strong doxological purpose.[1] In fact, this is one of the major features of Calvin's approach to preaching.[2] He sees it as worship every bit as much as the cel-

1. Calvin500 gives me another shot at the subject of preaching as worship in the pulpit of John Calvin. This chapter is a revision of a paper given at the International Calvin Colloquium in Seoul, Korea, in August 1998. It was previously published as Hughes Oliphant Old, "Preaching as Worship in the Pulpit of John Calvin," International Congress on Calvin Research, *Calvinus Evangelii Propugnator*, Seoul, Korea (August 1998): 7–14. This essay is also supplementary to the chapter on the preaching of Calvin in Hughes Oliphant Old, *The Reading and Preaching of the Scriptures in the Worship of the Christian Church*, vol. 4, *The Age of the Reformation* (Grand Rapids: Eerdmans, 2002), 90–134. Most recently, the subject has been treated in the Mullins Lectures at Southern Baptist Theological Seminary in Louisville, Kentucky, in March 2009. These lectures are available on the seminary's Web site.

2. On the preaching of Calvin, see the following: Pierre Marcel, "L'Actualité de la prédication," *RR* 7 (1951); Rodolphe Peter, "Jean Calvin Prédicateur," *Revue d'Histoire et de Philosophie religieuses* (1972); Rodolphe Peter, "Rhétorique et prédication selon Calvin,"

ebration of the sacraments and every bit as much as the service of prayer. Calvin thought of the reading and preaching of Scripture in the midst of the assembly of God's people as worship, and worship at its most profound. Sad to say, the liturgical renewal movement has been rather myopic in its approach to preaching. All too often, liturgical renewal has put its emphasis on anything else but preaching. Surely here is one place where Calvin's insights remain even today most prophetic.

For Calvin, worship in general is to serve God's glory.[3] How is it, then, that the reading and preaching of Scripture in particular serves God's glory? We can explore this question from several different perspectives. First of all, we can ask the question from the standpoint of worship as repentance or lamentation, that is, worship as turning to God in time of need. Second, we can consider it from an understanding of worship as delighting in the divine wisdom. Then, we can look at it from the standpoint of worship as participation in the covenant community. Finally, we might understand it as kerygma, the proclamation of the gospel. Other perspectives might be included, but these have a certain priority.[4]

Worship as Calling Out to God in Time of Need

Let us begin by asking how preaching is worship from the standpoint of the preaching of repentance. We need only look at the preaching of

Revue d'Histoire et de Philosophie religieuses (1975); Richard Stauffer, "Un Calvin méconnu; le prédicateur de Genève," *Bulletin de la Société de l'Histoire du Protestantisme française* (1977); Richard Stauffer, *Dieu, la creation et la providence dans la prédication de Calvin* (Bern: P. Lang, 1978); Pierre Marcel, "Une lecture non-Calviniste de Calvin," *SRR* 4 (1979); John H. Leith, "Calvin's Doctrine of the Proclamation of the Word and Its Significance for Today," in *John Calvin and the Church: A Prism of Reform*, ed. Timothy George (Louisville: Westminster/ John Knox Press, 1990), 206–29; Olivier Millet, *Calvin et la dynamique de la Parole. Essai de rhétorique réformé* (Paris: H. Champion, 1992); and T. H. L. Parker, *Calvin's Preaching* (Edinburgh: T&T Clark, 1992).

3. We find this stated quite straightforwardly in the introduction to the *Genevan Psalter*. "Comme c'est une chose bien requise en la Chrestienté, et des plus necessaires, que chascum fidele observe et entretienne la communion de l'Eglise en son endroit, frequentant les assemblees, qui se font, tant le Dimanche que les aultres iours, pour honnorer et servir Dieu ..." (OS, 2.12).

4. On other dimensions of worship, see my work on the theology of worship, Hughes Oliphant Old, *Themes and Variations for a Christian Doxology* (Grand Rapids: Eerdmans, 1992).

John the Baptist to discover that the preaching of repentance is essential to a well-balanced ministry of preaching. "Repent, for the kingdom of heaven is at hand" (Matt. 3:2).[5] This is an important element of Christian preaching. Behind John was the whole tradition of prophetic preaching. Calvin gave great attention to preaching through the Prophets. Especially memorable were his sermons on Amos, and again Calvin's sermons on Jeremiah are widely admired.[6]

The doxological dimension of the prophetic ministry is characteristic of biblical religion. God is holy, and therefore he demands holiness of his people. "Be ye therefore perfect, even as your Father which is in heaven is perfect" (Matt. 5:48 KJV). God's demand of holiness is but a logical reflection of his own holiness. We find this principle particularly in Calvin's sermons on Amos.

Calvin's recognition that repentance is essential to worship and the serving of God's glory is particularly clear from the prayer of confession that normally began the service of worship.

> Lord God, Father eternal and all powerful: we confess and recognize with all sincerity before your holy Majesty that we are poor sinners, conceived and born in iniquity and corruption, inclined to evil, incapable of any good. We transgress without end your holy commandments. We deserve, therefore, your just condemnation, ruin, and destruction.[7]

The obvious function of this prayer in the service of worship is to underline the humility and reverence that are essential to worship.

Besides this, much of our worship stems from our discovering our need. We lament before God our weakness, our failure, our poverty, and

---

5. All quotations from the Bible in this chapter are from the RSV, unless otherwise noted.

6. Cf. my study on Calvin and the prophetic criticism of worship. Hughes Oliphant Old, "Calvin's Theology of Worship: The Prophetic Criticism of Worship," *Calvin Studies III*, ed. John H. Leith, papers presented at the third Colloquium on Calvin Studies at Davidson College (Richmond: Union Theological Seminary in Virginia, 1986).

7. "Seigneur Dieu, Pere eternal et tout puissant: nous confessons et recongnoissons sans feinctise, devant ta saincte Maiesté, que nous sommes paovres pecheurs, conceuz et nez en iniquité et corruption: enclins à mal faire, inutiles à tout bien: et que de nostre vice, nous transgressons, sans fin et sans cesse, tes sainctz commandemens. Enquoy faisant, nous acquerons, par ton iuste Jugement, ruine et perdition, sur nous" (*OS*, 2.18).

our sickness. When we turn to God for our help and our salvation, therefore, we honor him.

The preaching of repentance is most clearly related to worship in that it is the first step in the celebration of baptism. Baptism is, after all, the initial act of worship. Preaching repentance ultimately issues in the offer of baptism to those who receive the preaching with faith. Preaching repentance is essential to worship because it is a necessary component of the sacrament of baptism. But let us turn now to a consideration of how preaching is worship from the standpoint of a wisdom theology.

Worship as Delight in Holy Wisdom

Biblical wisdom theology implies a distinct theology of worship that I have described elsewhere at some length.[8] A wisdom theology of worship understands that when God's Word is heard, God is glorified. In preaching God's Word, in studying God's Word, in hearing God's Word, and in meditating on God's Word, we glorify God. One place where we find this idea expounded with particular beauty is in Calvin's commentary on Psalm 19. Calvin delights in the heavenly bodies' preaching the glory of God.[9] Just as the day pours forth speech and the night declares knowledge, so God is glorified when his Word revives the soul, makes wise the simple, rejoices the heart, and enlightens the eyes (Ps. 19:1–8). Preaching displays the treasures of God's wisdom, that we might rejoice in them.

Throughout his commentary on this psalm, Calvin marvels at the wisdom of God as it is found in the starry heavens, to be sure, but also as it is found in the law of God, that is, in Scripture. "This psalm," Calvin says, "consists of two parts; in the first David celebrates the glory of God in his works; the second preaches the knowledge of God more fully reflected in his Word."[10] At one point Calvin even goes so far as to say that the heavens

8. See Old, *Themes and Variations for a Christian Doxology*, 63–89.
9. "Quod coelorum architectura, quasi lineatim ad regulam composite, longe lateque Dei gloriam praedicet." For the Latin text, see John Calvin, *Commentarii in librum psalmorum*, in *CR*, 59, cols. 194–207. The Psalms commentary is in volumes 59 and 60.
10. "Dixi iam huius Psalmi duas esse partes, quarum in priore Dei gloriam celebrat David ab operibus: in altera autem notitiam plenius in verbo relucentem praedicat" (ibid., 59, col. 194).

preach the glory of God. "David here metaphorically presents the splendor of the heavenly mechanism as a preacher expounding the glory of God."[11] The metaphor, of course, goes in both directions. Just as the starry night and the rising sun speak to us of God's glory, so the Scriptures preach the wisdom of God. In other words, Calvin sees an analogy between the way the heavens declare the glory of God and the way preaching declares the glory of God. That the purpose of preaching, in Calvin's estimation, is to proclaim the glory of God is surely most clear.

"The law of the LORD is perfect," our psalm continues (v. 7). It is perfect, Calvin comments, because it reveals God's wisdom. "The first commendation of the Law is that it is perfect or complete. By this David means that if a man is duly instructed in the law of God, he lacks nothing which is needed for perfect wisdom. . . . David, therefore, rightly claims this praise for the law of God, that it contains in it perfect and absolute wisdom."[12] Calvin is sensitive to the concerns of the wisdom school. Meditating on the wonder of the heavens and on the pages of Scripture, the one as the other, is presented to God as worship. "Let the words of my mouth and the meditation of my heart be acceptable in thy sight, O LORD, my rock and my redeemer" (Ps. 19:14). Such meditation brings us into God's presence. It is the essence of worship. "When we behold the heavens we cannot but be elevated, by the contemplation of them, to him who is their Creator."[13] Calvin's understanding of the place of the Word in worship has deep foundations in the wisdom theology of both the Old and the New Testaments. God is glorified when his Word is heard by his people and they are transformed into his image. Through the preaching of the gospel, God's people are transformed into the image of Christ.

Calvin's wisdom theology, like that of Augustine, is thoroughly Johannine. This is particularly clear from Calvin's commentary on the prologue

11. "Sed quum metaphorice coelestis machinae splendorum David hic instar doctoris de gloria Dei concionantem inducat" (ibid., 59, cols. 196–97).

12. "Prima legis commendatio est, quod sit integra vel perfecta: quo verbo significat David, si quis in lege Dei rite sit edoctus, ei ad perfectam sapientiam nihil defore. . . . Unde merito David laudem hanc vendicat legi, quod in se perfectam et absolutam sapientiam contineat" (ibid., 59, cols. 199–200).

13. "Fieri enim non potest quin od ipsum usque autorem nos attolat coelorum intuitus, ac mirabilis quae illic apparet distinctio, ornatus et splendor luculentum eius providentiae testimonium reddant" (ibid., 59, col. 195).

to the Gospel of John. There Calvin says that John calls the Son of God "the Word" because he is the eternal wisdom of God.[14] This statement tips us off to the fact that Calvin well understands the wisdom theology of the fourth Gospel. When God's people hear the Word and receive it by faith, they are saved from their sins and born into a new and eternal life, and being born from above and renewed by the Holy Spirit, they now worship God in spirit and truth (John 1:12; 3:5; 4:23). That Christian worship should be in spirit and in truth is fundamental to Calvin's understanding of worship.[15] Once one understands true worship as worship that is in spirit and in truth, then the central role of the reading and preaching of the Word of God becomes self-evident. If truth is essential to genuine worship, then teaching and preaching that truth is going to be at the center of worship. God is worshiped in spirit and in truth only if that worship is based on true faith, "which is necessarily born of the Word of God."[16] God is glorified simply in the proclamation of the Word, to be sure, but the Word has power to bring about what it says. The Word bears fruit, and this fruit magnifies God's glory.[17] Commenting on John 1:4, Calvin says, "It is God, therefore, who gives us life; but he does it by the eternal Word."[18] When God's people live together in holiness and praise God as the source of their life, then God's glory is magnified.

We find something similar in Calvin's sermon on Micah 4:1–4, a passage that speaks of the worship of the transformed Jerusalem.[19] In that day, the prophet tells us, all the peoples of the earth will go up to Jerusalem to learn of God's law. As Calvin understands it, this means that the reading and preaching of Scripture is to have a central place in the worship of the church. This reading and preaching is its primary responsibility.[20] In

14. "Quod sermonem vocat Dei filium, haec mihi simplex videtur esse ratio, quia primum aeterna sit Dei sapientia et voluntas, deinde expressa consilii eius effigies" (John Calvin, *Commentarius in Evangelium Ioannis*, in CR, 75, col. 1).

15. Elsewhere we have treated the subject of what this text may or may not say about the role of the Holy Spirit in our worship.

16. "Summa tamen huc redit, non rite coli Deum nisi ex fidei certitudine, quam ex Dei verbo gigni necesse est" (CR, 75, col. 87).

17. Ibid., 75, cols. 87–190.

18. "Deus ergo est qui nos vivificate: sed per aeternum sermonem" (ibid., 75, col. 5).

19. The sermons on Micah are found in SC.

20. SC, 5.130.

other words, Micah prophesied what John tells us is now being fulfilled. The worship that is in spirit and truth is actually being offered to God in the worship of the Christian church. In true Christian worship, all the peoples of the earth listen to the reading and the preaching of the Word of God.

This kind of worship, centered on the reading and preaching of the Word, is what God commanded of us in the First Table of the law.[21] The study of God's Word is the way we express our love for God. We do not make idols created by our own art and imagination, decorate them with precious stones and cloth of gold, carry them in procession, and burn incense before them. We listen to God's teaching. As is clear from Calvin's commentary on the fourth commandment found in book 2 of the *Institutes*, the reading, preaching, and meditating on the law was essential to the observance of the Sabbath.[22] For Calvin, the four commandments of the First Table of the law should order Christian worship even to this day.[23] These commandments should order Christian worship in their Christian form, to be sure, and that Christian form is the summary of the law that Jesus gave: The first and greatest commandment is that "thou shalt love the Lord thy God with all thy heart, and with all thy soul, and with all thy mind" (Matt. 22:37–38 KJV). It is in worship above all that we fulfill the first and greatest commandment. From the standpoint of a wisdom theology of worship, listening to the Word of our Lord is an expression of our love to him and a delighting in his love to us.

Worship as Participation in the Covenant Community

Now let us turn to look at this question from the standpoint of a covenantal theology of worship. How is it that the reading and preaching of the Scriptures is worship?

21. On the subject of the implications of the First Table of the law for Christian worship, see *Institutes*, 2.8.1–3. For the ET of Calvin's *Institutes*, see John Calvin, *Institutes of the Christian Religion*, ed. John T. McNeill, trans. Ford Lewis Battles, 2 vols. (Philadelphia: Westminster Press, 1960). For the Latin text, see *OS*, vols. 3–5.
22. *Institutes*, 2.8.28.
23. Ibid., 2.8.11.

A covenantal theology of worship understands worship in terms of the covenantal relationship between God and his people. It is in worship that the covenant is established, maintained, nourished, and renewed. In worship we experience God as our God and ourselves as his people.[24] In baptism we are introduced into the covenant community. In the reading and preaching of the Scriptures, as well as in the Lord's Supper, we are nourished in the covenant relationship. In the reading and preaching of Scripture we are taught the terms of the covenant and guided in the way of life lived by the covenant community. Through preaching, the traditions of the covenant people are passed on and God's mighty acts of salvation are recounted. In the celebration of the Supper we are nourished in the life of godliness. From the standpoint of a covenant theology, worship is a feast in this world and yet even more a foretaste of a heavenly feast. The Word proclaims the covenant and expounds it; the Supper seals it. In prayer again and again we exercise the bond of covenant love. We turn to God in our need because he is our God and we are his people. We call on him because of his covenant promises that he will hear our prayers when we offer them in Jesus' name. In the giving of alms we exercise the covenant responsibilities in a very practical way. Especially in the praises of the church, in the hymns and psalms, we experience the awe and the joy of the sacred relationship. We enter into his gates with thanksgiving and into his courts with praise (Ps. 100).

Let us look more closely at the function of the reading and preaching of the Scriptures in the covenantal assembly. We have said that the ministry of the Word nourishes the covenantal relationship. We find this especially in Calvin's commentary on the sixth chapter of the Gospel of John. There we read of how Jesus gave a sign of the deep spiritual significance of his teaching ministry by feeding a great multitude of people with five loaves of bread and two fishes. This sign shows that his teaching is of the very essence of his ministry. In the beginning of the chapter we read how a crowd gathered around Jesus as he taught. His teaching took place on a mountain in the wilderness, not unlike the teaching of Moses. For Calvin there is something providential about the fact that Jesus does this teaching and performs this miracle on a mountain in the desert. The preaching

24. Ibid., 4.14.13.

ministry of Jesus was, to be sure, far greater than the ministry of Moses, but the parallel is hard to miss. Just as Moses gathered the covenantal assembly before Sinai to present to them the law, so Jesus now gathered the crowds about him and preached to them the gospel. Just as Moses concluded the covenantal assembly with a sacred meal, so now Jesus fed the multitude. Jesus interpreted to them that meal in terms of the manna that the Father had given to Israel in the wilderness. Faithful Israel had always understood that the meaning of the manna was that man shall not live by bread alone but by every word that proceeds from the mouth of God (cf. Deut. 8:3; Matt. 4:4; and parallels). It is none other than God himself who is the source of our life. This is experienced when the people of God gather together and listen to God's Word. When this actually happens and God's people are nourished in holiness, then God is glorified.

For a covenantal theology of worship, the whole idea that worship is a means of grace is of major importance. To worship is first of all the serving of God's glory, but it is also a means of sanctifying his people. The most important way in which we glorify God is to reflect his glory, and the way in which we reflect his glory is to be holy as he is holy. This is a basic principle of the biblical understanding of worship. The most remarkable thing about God's glory is that it is a life-giving glory. God's glory is redemptive and sanctifying. When his glory is reflected, then his glory is magnified. For this reason, the faithful come together in solemn assembly to remember God's mighty acts of salvation in the past and to witness to God's saving glory in our own time. This magnifies God's glory.

In commenting on the text "I am the bread of life . . ." (John 6:35), Calvin asserts that "the teaching of the Gospel will be beneficial to all the godly, because none offers himself to Christ as a disciple who has not both perceived and experienced him to be a faithful and true teacher."[25] In other words, the true disciple is the one who devotes himself to the study of God's Word. It belongs to the devotion of the disciple to follow the teaching of the master, to listen to it, to learn it, and to practice it. If this is the case, then listening to the Word of God must be of the essence

25. "Unde sequitur salutarem fore omnibus piis evangelii doctrinam, quia nemo se Christo discipulum offert, qui non vicissim illum sentiat et experiatur fidum et probum doctorem" (CR, 75, col. 146).

of worship. A well-known leader of the liturgical renewal movement has charged classical Protestantism with not being so much interested in conducting worship for the glory of God as for the benefit of man. It is a false antithesis. God is never glorified quite so thoroughly as when his Word saves and sanctifies his people.

Referring to "It is written in the prophets, 'And they shall all be taught by God'" (John 6:45), Calvin points out that "it is not otherwise possible to restore the church than for God himself to become the teacher of the faithful. The sort of teaching of which the prophet speaks is not through the outward voice but the inner voice, that is, the secret operation of the Holy Spirit in the heart. In short, this is the teaching of God in our inmost hearts."[26] The reading and preaching of Scripture is worship because it is God's work. As I have elsewhere made the point at length, worship is the work of the Holy Spirit in the body of Christ to the glory of the Father. It is because Scripture is the Word of God that its reading and preaching is worship. The history of Christian worship shows again and again that when the church loses a sense of Scripture's being God's Word, its preaching loses force.

Continuing with the phrase "I am the bread of life," Calvin says, "For just as the eternal Word of God is the fountain of life, so Christ's flesh is the river to bring us this life which resides intrinsically, as the saying goes, in his divinity. In this sense it is called vivifying or life giving . . ."[27] The Word of God, incarnate in the person of Jesus, has given life to the world, once and for all, in all that he was and in all that he did and in all that he preached. When we in the church today preach the Word of God, Christ is present as a source of eternal life. When we pray in Christ's name, he is present with us. When we celebrate the sacraments, he is present even to the end of the age. The feeding of the multitude was a sign that the Word of God is a source of life, a source of holy life. It was a sign that Jesus gave

26. "Unde colligere promptum est, non alliter posse restitui ecclesiam, nisi Deus magistri partes suscipiens fideles ad se adducat. Docendi ratio de qua loquitur propheta non in externa tantum voce sita est, sed in arcana etiam spiritus sancti operatione. In summa, hoc Dei magisterium est interior cordis illuminatio" (ibid., 75, col. 149).

27. "Nam sicuti aeternus Dei sermo fons vitae est, ita caro eius veluti canalis vitam, quae intrinseca ut loquuntur in divinitate residet, ad nos diffundit. Atque hoc sensu dicitur vivifica" (ibid., 75, col. 152).

to make clear what worship really is, both in regard to preaching and in regard to the sacrament of communion. It is to enter into the house of the Father and to feast on his grace. When we enjoy the benefits of God's mighty acts of salvation in Christ, then God is glorified because it is he who is the source of our life.

Worship as Remembrance

There is another way of looking at this question of how preaching functions as worship. Calvin has a good sense of worship as *anamnesis*, that is, as remembrance. The ministry of the Word remembers and recounts the mighty acts of God for our salvation. We do this when we remember the Sabbath day. We sanctify the Sabbath by recounting the history of salvation. We meditate on God's mighty works of creation and redemption. Calvin makes this explicit in his remarks on the story of Jesus preaching in the synagogue. There Calvin says, concerning the worship of the synagogue, that however far from the truth the Jewish synagogue may have been, nevertheless the service of worship did preserve the public reading of the Scriptures followed by teachings and exhortations based on the passage read.[28] This shows us how the Sabbath should be kept. As Calvin sees it, God did not command the observance of the Sabbath simply to give us a day of idleness but rather to give us time to meditate on his works.[29]

This is also clear from Calvin's commentary on the fourth commandment.[30] As Calvin understands it, the purpose of the commandment to keep the Sabbath was in part that there be a specific time for the people of God to assemble, to hear the law, and to meditate on God's works. It is through this remembrance that God's people are to be exercised in piety.[31] Essential to preaching is the recounting of the mighty acts of God for our

28. John Calvin, *Harmonia ex tribus Euangelistis composita*, found in CR, 73. This passage is from CR, 73, col. 140.

29. Ibid., 73, col. 140.

30. This commentary is found in *Institutes*, 2.8.28–34.

31. "Diende statem diem esse voluit, quo ad legem audiendam et ceremonias peragendas convenirent, vel saltem quem operum suorem meditationi peculiariter darent: ut hac recordatione ad pietatem exercerentur" (ibid., 2.8.28).

salvation. It is a witnessing to what God has done. From the standpoint of covenant theology, worship is this recounting of the works of God for our salvation, and it is this that is worship at its most profound.

We are all well aware, of course, that there has been much criticism of the Sabbatarianism of Reformed worship. The truth is that this concern to fulfill the fourth commandment seriously is one of the richest theological facets of Calvin's understanding of worship. This is not merely a Judaistic tendency. Jesus had himself taught that our worship, as often as we celebrate it, is to be in remembrance of him (cf. 1 Cor. 11:24). Calvin had a profound understanding of what it meant to remember. The commandment tells us to remember the Sabbath day, to keep it holy. From the very beginning, the Sabbath was a day for remembering. It was a day for recounting the sacred history and repeating the sacred teachings. It was a day for reading over the law once more and discussing the interpretation of its statutes. It was a day for reading again the book of the covenant as Moses had read it when he came down from Mount Sinai or as Ezra had read it at the water gate in Jerusalem. For a covenantal theology, the remembering of the sacred traditions was central to worship. Here is the point I am trying to make: It was in that remembering that the Sabbath was sanctified.

Calvin obviously gives a centrality to the reading and preaching of Scripture in worship. The question usually asked is whether this centrality of the Word gave much place for anything else but preaching. To answer this question, we must look at the way in which preaching was positioned in the worship of the church of Geneva. In the introduction to the *Genevan Psalter* of 1542, Calvin tells us that three things should make up the service of worship: the preaching of God's Word, public and solemn prayers, and the administration of the sacraments.[32] Sometimes this list could be expanded to include psalms and hymns of praise, the reading of the law, the confession of sin, the reading of the gospel, the confession of faith, and the giving of alms.[33] Calvin very clearly sees more

32. "Or, il ya en somme trois choses, que nostre Seigneur nous a commandé d'observer en noz assemblees spirituelles. Assavoir, la predication de sa parolle: les oraisons publiques et solennelles: et l'administration des ses Sacrements" (OS, 2.13).
33. Ibid., 2.40–41. In regard to the giving of alms, it should be noted that while the worship of Geneva may not have included the giving of alms during Calvin's pastorate, the

to public worship than preaching. When seen in relation to these other things, the doxological character of preaching is particularly clear. First we must say something about the relation of the ministry of the Word to the ministry of prayer and then something about the relation of the ministry of the Word to the sacrament of communion.

For Calvin, prayer is the chief exercise of our religion. This famous statement makes sense above all when we understand prayer in a covenantal context. Prayer is an exercising of our faith. It turns to God in times of need; it lays hold of the rich promises of God and by faith holds onto these promises until they are fulfilled.

Calvin, following the custom that had developed in the Reformed churches of the upper Rhineland, prefaced the reading and preaching of the Scriptures with the prayer for illumination. We find the following rubric in the *Genevan Psalter* of 1542:

> Then the minister begins once more to pray, asking God for the grace of his Holy Spirit, that his Word be faithfully expounded to the honor of his name and the building up of the Church, and be received with the humility and obedience it deserves. The form is at the discretion of the minister.[34]

What is very clear from this prayer is that preaching is a work of God's grace among his people. We notice here that it is not only the preaching of the Word but the receiving of the preached Word that is worship. The whole congregation worships God by receiving his Word with humility and obedience. The ministry of the Word is not a solo sport, like a game of solitaire or playing tennis against the garage door. Preaching both honors God and builds up the church. It is, as prayer, and in fact as all worship, the work of the Holy Spirit in the body of Christ to the glory of the Father.

---

worship of the French congregation in Strasbourg did, during Calvin's pastorate, include the giving of alms as the congregation left the church. "Et les sainctes oblations et offrandes . . ." (ibid., 2.41).

34. "Cela faict, on chante en l'assemblee quelque Pseulme: puis le Ministre commence derechef à prier, pour demander à Dieu la grace de son sainct Esprit: afin, que sa parolle soit fidelement exposée à l'honneur de son Nom, et à l'edification de l'Eglise: et qu'elle soit receue en telle humilité et obeissance, qu'il appartient. La forme est à le discretion du Ministre" (ibid., 2.20).

Preaching builds up the church and brings blessings to God's people, all to the honor of his name. Here, indeed, it is very clearly stated that the purpose of our preaching is to glorify God, to bring honor to his name.

This prayer might be called the epiclesis of the sermon. It recognizes that just as it was through the inspiration of the Holy Spirit that the prophets and apostles proclaimed the Word of God and committed it to writing, so it must be by the inspiration of the same Holy Spirit that the minister of the Word expounds the Bible and the congregation receives it. This epiclesis defends the church against an *ex opera operandi* understanding of preaching. But on the other hand, it defends the church against a Pelagian understanding of preaching. It makes clear that preaching is in the end not merely a human work but, much more profoundly, a divine work. God does this work through his ministers, to be sure, but it is he who speaks.

As disciples, we are to listen to the Word of our Lord. As a Christian congregation, we are to receive God's Word with humility and obedience. We listen to the sermon because it is God's Word. This is the reverence and humility, the love and homage that we owe to him who has revealed himself to us as the Word. If God has revealed himself to us as the Word, then listening to that Word must be central to our worship.

The prayer for illumination makes something else clear: that God's Word is an answer to prayer. God's Word is his gracious gift to us in the time of our need. It is when we have discovered our alienation, our sin, and our frailty that we cry out to God for help, and he answers us by revealing his redemptive purpose, his saving power, and his will for our lives.

The prayer of confession stood at the beginning of the service in Geneva, and it was followed by the prayer for illumination. The prayers are closely related. The prayer of confession begins the service with a realistic expression of the frailty of the human condition.[35] With reverence the prayer calls on the Lord God, Father eternal and almighty, and confesses our weaknesses, our poverty, and our iniquity.[36] One approaches

35. Ibid., 2.18.

36. "Seigneur Dieu, Pere eternal et tout puissant: nous confessons et recongnoissons sans feinctise, devant ta saincte Maiesté, que nous sommes paovres pecheurs, conceuz et nez en iniquité et corruption: enclins à mal faire, inutiles à tout bien: et que de nostre vice, nous transgressons, sans fin et sans cesse tes sainctz commandemens" (ibid.).

the Word of God with humility and with a recognition of human need. Being assured that in Christ we are received by God, we then wait upon his Word.[37] Preaching is conceived in prayer.

Here, too, we recognize that Calvin is building on the older Reformers, especially on the order of worship that the Reformers of Strasbourg had developed. Calvin instituted the liturgical forms of Strasbourg with conviction and enthusiasm when he returned from exile. As he saw it, this was an order of service that was truly according to Scripture and after the example of the ancient church. The singing of the psalms, as Calvin saw it, played a major role in the worship of the church of Geneva.[38] The prayers and the singing of the psalms were fundamental to the liturgical order. That is made abundantly clear by the title of his book of worship, namely, *The Form of Prayers and Hymns Together with the Order for the Administration of the Sacraments.*[39] The singing of the psalms set the preaching in a context of praise and thanksgiving. This made especially clear the doxological intention of the preaching. Again, Calvin's sermons are best understood when they are seen in the liturgical position they held in the worship of Geneva.

If for Calvin God's Word is an answer to prayer, it is equally true for Calvin that God's Word calls us to prayer. Calvin's sermons invariably conclude by making clear the prayer concerns that the exposition of Scripture for that day had opened up to the church. A particularly rich collection of these prayers is found among Calvin's sermons on Jeremiah. Hundreds of these prayers have come down to us. Each of these prayers was offered at the conclusion of a sermon. It was followed then by the more general prayer of intercession for the needs of the church, for the leaders of the Christian community, for civil authorities, for pastors, for all peoples, for the spreading of the gospel to all parts of the earth, and for those suffering any kind of tribulation or affliction.[40] This prayer is a general prayer for the coming of the kingdom. The point of this prayer

---

37. Ibid., 2.19.

38. Ibid., 2.17.

39. *LA FORME DES PRIERES ET CHANTZ ECCLESIASTIQUES, avec la maniere d'administrer les sacremens et consacrer le mariage selon la coustume de l'Eglise ancienne* (ibid., 2.20–23).

40. Ibid.

seems to be that the reading and preaching of the Scriptures not only calls us to prayer but also illumines our prayer and directs our prayer. True Christian prayer is prayer that is according to God's Word. It is prayer that is in God's service. It is prayer for the doing of God's will on earth as in heaven. It is prayer that seeks first the kingdom of heaven and is confident that all these other things will be added unto us as well.

A strong covenantal understanding of prayer and preaching is at work here. Just as the children of Israel while slaves in Egypt cried to the Lord in their affliction and were delivered and then freed from Egypt and were claimed by God as his covenant people and therefore were given the law as a covenant responsibility, so we become Christians when in our sin and suffering we cry to God for help. He delivers us through the proclamation of the gospel of Christ, and unites us to himself in the new covenant. Through his Spirit he writes his law in our hearts and claims our service both in worship and in deeds of mercy to our neighbors. In worship we confess that we therefore belong to God. He is our God and we are his people. We witness to his saving grace toward us. A big part of preaching is witnessing, and this witness testifies to God's glory. From the standpoint of a covenantal theology, this is of the essence of worship. It is both a confession of our faith and a witness to our Savior.

When the preacher reads and expounds the Word of God, he does what he does in the service of God. He continues the work of Christ. But there is something else to be said: he expresses the faith of the congregation. He gives the witness of the faithful to the mighty acts of God that have brought us from sin to salvation, from futility to fulfillment, from death to life. In preaching, this witness is made before the Christian congregation as well as before the world. The sermon is at times a public witness that God has heard the cry of his people and given us the salvation for which we prayed. This witness is made that all might know that God, our God, is a God of salvation.

But there is more. Just as God gave to Israel the tabernacle in the wilderness so that his people might have access to him in prayer, so Christ gave to the people of the new covenant the promises of the gospel. He promises his presence when in his name we assemble for worship. He promises that if we pray in his name, the Father will hear our prayers. Even more, he gives us the responsibility of praying for the coming of the kingdom. The texts of the prayers as we find them both in the *Genevan Psalter* and in Calvin's prayers as they were recorded by the stenographers who took down Calvin's sermons are permeated with the covenantal understanding of the relation of the ministry of the Word to the ministry of prayer. For example, the prayer of intercession following the sermon begins:

> God all powerful, celestial Father, you have promised to hear our requests that we make in the name of your Son, JESUS Christ our greatly beloved Savior. We have been taught by his disciples that when we gather in his name as he has promised that he will be in the midst of us, and that he will be our intercessor, that we obtain all that we commonly request here on earth.[41]

The covenantal promises and covenantal responsibilities obviously play a strong role in this prayer. A covenantal understanding of worship recognizes that the gospel of grace calls us to service. In these prayers of intercession the church serves the neighbor in the bond of love and thereby serves the glory of God.

This dialectic between Word and prayer is of the essence of worship. The Word is an answer to prayer at the same time that prayer is an answer to the Word. The Word encourages prayer; it feeds prayer and directs prayer. Prayer plants the Word, roots it in our hearts, and brings it to flower and finally to fruit, and this fruit is well pleasing to God. When the Word bears fruit, God is worshiped in spirit and in truth.

Again it is in the way that Calvin relates the ministry of the Word to the celebration of the sacrament of communion that we see his covenantal understanding of the place of the Word in worship.[42] In the reading and preaching of the Scriptures we hear the proclamation of the gospel. We hear how God in Christ has reconciled us to himself and given to us the covenant of grace; in the sharing of the Lord's Supper, that covenant is

---

41. "DIEU tout puissant, Pere celeste, tu nous as promis de nous exaulcer en noz requestes, que nous te ferions au Nom de ton Filz JESUS Christ, bien-aimé, nostre Seigneur: et aussi nous sommes instruictz, par la doctrine de luy et de ses Apostres, de nous assembler en son Nom, avec promesses, qu'il sera au milieu de nous, et qu'il sera nostre Intercesseur envers toy, pour impetrer et obtenir toutes choses, dont nous consentirons sur la terre" (ibid., 2.20).

42. *Institutes*, 4.14.6. See also ibid., 4.17.1–2, 4, 38.

sealed.[43] While in the sermon the promises of the gospel are proclaimed to us, in the sacrament they are sealed to us.[44] The sacrament affirms the divine promises that have been preached as the signature authenticates a letter or as the seal makes valid a charter.[45]

Preaching is essential to the celebration of the sacrament. "Now, from the definition that I have set forth we understand that a sacrament is never without a preceding promise but is joined to it as a sort of appendix, with the purpose of confirming and sealing the promise itself, and of making it more evident to us and in a sense ratifying it."[46] The sacrament depends on the preaching of the covenant promises. A covenant is a promise of God, Calvin tells us. Sacraments are tokens or signs of these covenants. It is essential that the promises be announced, and their terms explained, before they can be sealed. Without this word preceding the sign, the sign has no meaning. Calvin says, "Yet when words precede, the laws of covenants are by such signs ratified, although they were first conceived, established, and decreed in words. The sacraments, therefore, are exercises which make us more certain of the trustworthiness of God's Word."[47]

The communion invocation of the *Genevan Psalter* of 1542 prays that in the sacrament we are about to celebrate our Lord Jesus would grant to us participation in his body and his blood. The prayer continues, asking that Christ unite us to himself in faith, that he live in us and guide us in a life of holiness and happiness from now unto all eternity. This prayer is clearly thought out in covenantal terms; it asks the Father "to make us participants in the new and eternal covenant, the covenant of grace."[48] For Calvin, the sacrament of communion is a covenant meal that seals the promises proclaimed in the preaching of the gospel. Without proclaim-

<hr>

43. Ibid., 4.17.1.
44. Ibid., 4.14.6.
45. Ibid., 4.17.4.
46. Ibid., 4.14.3.
47. Ibid., 4.14.6.
48. "C'est qu'en certaine Foy nous recevions son corps et son sang: voire luy tout entierement: comme luy estant vray Dieu et vray homme, est veritablement le sainct pain Celeste, pour nous vivifier: afin, que nous ne vivions plus en nousmesmes, et selon nostre nature, laquelle est toute corrumpue et vitieuse: mais, que luy vive en nous, pour nous conduire à la vie saincte, bien-heureuse et sempiternelle: par ainsi, que nous soyons faicts vrayement participans du nouveau et eternal Testament: assavoir l'alliance de grace" (OS, 2.25).

ing the promises of the gospel, there is not much point in observing the sacrament.[49] Preaching is essential to sacramental worship in particular, just as it is essential to worship in general.

Preaching is worship because it expresses the faith that enables us to enter into the covenant meal. The communion invocation prays, "Let us in firm faith receive his body and his blood."[50] Preaching is from faith to faith. Preaching expresses the faith of the congregation, and that expression of faith nourishes the faith of the congregation. It builds it up and magnifies it. Having heard the preaching, the congregation comes to the Supper in ever firmer faith and thereby celebrates the Supper to God's glory.

We find the same thing in the communion admonition that calls on the faithful to believe the promises that Jesus Christ gives with his own mouth that he truly wishes to make us participants in his body and his blood in such a way that he lives in us and we in him.[51] These are the covenant promises. The Admonition goes on to urge the faithful to be thankful for the infinite goodness of the Savior, who displays all the riches of his goodness at this table to be distributed to us. For in giving all this to us, he bears witness that all that he has is ours. And so let us receive this sacrament as a proof (*un gage*) that the power of this death and passion be imputed to us for our justification.[52] The sacraments are signs and seals of the covenant promises proclaimed in the gospel.[53] When the gospel is preached, then it is summed up and signed over by the sacraments.

Preaching is worship because it makes explicit the thanksgiving that is so central to the eucharistic meal. Preaching recounts the *Magnalia Dei*, the mighty acts of God. Elsewhere I have written about Calvin's preaching on the gospel accounts of the passion and resurrection before the celebration

---

49. *Institutes*, 4.17.39.

50. "C'est qu'en certaine Foy nous recevions son corps et son sang" (*OS*, 2.25).

51. "Premierement donques, croyons à ses promesses, que JESUS Christ, qui est la verité infallible, a prononcé de sa bouche; assavoir qu'il nous veult vrayement faire participans de son corps et de son sang: afin que nous le possedions entierement; en telle sorte, qu'il vive en nous et nous en luy" (ibid., 2.48).

52. "Ainsi, que nous ne soyons point ingratz à la bonté infinie de nostre Sauveur, lequel desploie toutes ses richesses et ses biens en ceste Table, pour nous le distribuer. Car, en se donnant à nous, il nous rend tesmoignage, que tout ce qu'il a, est nostre. Pourtant, recevons ce Sacrement comme un gage, que la vertu de sa mort et passion, nous est imputee à justice . . ." (ibid.).

53. *Institutes*, 4.14.5.

of the Easter Communion.[54] Calvin's preaching celebrated that for which the Eucharist gives thanks. Calvin's preaching was, as it were, his eucharistic prayer. To give thanks for God's saving acts is part of our covenant obligation. Because God has heard our cry for help and has answered our prayer, saving us from our sorrow, our sin, our misery, and our futility, we now owe him our thanksgiving. Having received God's salvation, we are obligated to offer to him the sacrifice of praise and thanksgiving. Our covenant obligation, as we find it in the communion invocation, is constantly to glorify God, to give thanks to him, and to magnify his name.[55]

Preaching is worship because it gives the witness that the congregation makes to God's mighty acts of salvation in Christ. It announces the Lord's death until he comes (1 Cor. 11:26). In his commentary on 1 Corinthians 11:26, Calvin makes very clear the importance of the Holy Supper as a profession of faith.[56] The communion invocation prays, "Grant to us, heavenly Father, to celebrate this day the memorial of your dear Son, to exercise ourselves in the recounting of his saving work, and to announce the benefits of his death."[57] This announcement or proclamation of God's saving acts is of the essence of the covenant memorial made in public worship. Worship witnesses to God's saving acts. It confesses to God that we owe our salvation to him, and it announces to the world the source of our life.

The prayer of thanksgiving that concludes the communion service once again makes clear the covenantal nature of the sacrament that has been celebrated. It gives thanks to the Father for having drawn us into the communion of his Son, our Lord Jesus Christ, and prays that all that has been displayed in the sacrament be written in our hearts, to the end that we live to

---

54. See Hughes Oliphant Old, "Calvin as Evangelist: A Study of the Reformer's Sermons in Preparation for the Christian Celebration of Passover," in *Calvin Studies VII*, ed. John H. Leith, papers presented at the seventh Colloquium on Calvin Studies at Davidson College (Davidson, NC: Colloquium on Calvin Studies, 1994), 51–60.

55. "Afin que incessament, nous te rendions gloire et actions de grace, et magnifions ton Nom" (*OS*, 2.25).

56. John Calvin, *Commentarius in Epistolam priorem ad Corinthios*, in CR, 77. This reference is from CR, 77, col. 490.

57. "Donne nous donques en ceste maniere, Pere celeste, de celebrer auiord'huy la memoire et recordation bien-heureuse de ton cher Filz, nous exerciter en icelle, et announcer la benefice de sa mort . . ." (*OS*, 2.25).

the glory of God and service to our neighbor.[58] The phrase "à l'exaltation de ta gloire," coming at the end of the service, is the key to the whole thing. All that has been done in the service of worship has been done to serve God's glory: the singing of the psalms, the offering of prayers, the celebration of the sacrament, and, to be sure, the reading and preaching of Scripture.

Worship as Kerygma

Finally, let us consider how preaching is worship from the standpoint of a kerygmatic theology of worship. It was really Jesus who most obviously opened up the kerygmatic theology of worship. At its center it was Jesus who set the example by his preaching the gospel, by his proclaiming the imminence of the kingdom of God. This was quite explicit when Jesus preached in the synagogue of Nazareth. He took his text from Isaiah:

The Spirit of the Lord GOD is upon me,
because the LORD has anointed me
to bring good tidings to the afflicted;
he has sent me to bind up the brokenhearted,
to proclaim liberty to the captives,
and the opening of the prison to those who are bound;
to proclaim the year of the LORD's favor. (Isa. 61:1–2)

Preaching as we have it in this text is kerygma, that is, the proclamation of the gospel. The word *kerygma*, or one of its cognate forms, appears several times in the Greek text. The point Jesus wanted to make was that he was even then fulfilling this passage from Isaiah in his preaching ministry.

58. "PERE celeste, nous te rendons louenges et graces eternelles, que tu nous as eslargy un tel bien, à nous paovres pecheurs, de nous avoir attiré en la communion de ton Filz JESUS Christ, nostre Seigneur, l'ayant livré, pour nous, à la mort, et le nous donnant en viande et nourriture de vie eternelle. Maintenant aussi octroye nous ce bien, de ne permettre, que iamais nous ne mettions en oubly ces choses; mais plustost les aiant imprimees en noz coeurs, nous croissions et augmentions assiduellment en la Foy, laquelle besogne en toutes bonnes oeuvres: et en ce faisant, ordonnions et poursuyvions toute nostre vie à l'exaltation de ta gloire, et edification de nostre prochain, par iceluy JESUS Christ ton Filz, qui en l'unité du sainct Esprit, vit et regne, avec toy Dieu eternellement, Amen" (ibid., 2.25–26).

Calvin in his commentary on this passage makes it very clear what he means by the preaching the church should normally provide. He wants preaching that witnesses to the grace of God, who will bring us out of ruin and death and will renew the church with spiritual power.[59] True preachers should be witnesses and ambassadors for our reconciliation with God.[60] Ministers of the gospel should perform their ministry by proclaiming peace to both those who are near and those who are far.[61] For Calvin, it is important to make clear that God himself empowers his servants with the gifts they need to perform their ministry. Jesus was anointed with the Holy Spirit in that he might fulfill the ministry to which the Father had appointed him, namely, to give good news to the poor.[62] Quite obviously, a Reformed ministry of the gospel is supposed to take the preaching ministry of Jesus as its pattern or example.

There is another aspect of the kerygmatic dimension of preaching as Calvin saw it, and that is the opening up of the gospel to the Gentiles. We find this particularly in Calvin's interpretation of the royal psalms, namely, Psalms 96 to 100. In these psalms we find the expectation that finally in the last days the Gentiles will come up to Jerusalem and worship the true God. Even the heathen will bend the knee to their true King. This will be the ultimate praise and adoration. Faithful Jews will extol the mighty works of God to the Gentiles and, wonder of wonders, the Gentiles will worship the true God (cf. Pss. 96:3, 10; 98:2; 100:1). These psalms indicate that the time will come, Calvin tells us, when God's rule over all the peoples of the earth will be far above all expectation.[63] This is put even more forcefully in Calvin's commentary on Micah 4:1–4 cited above. The stream of converted heathen making pilgrimage to Jerusalem will be the final and most eloquent homage to the universal authority of the God of Israel.[64]

From the psalms generally, it should be very clear that evangelism is a significant part of worship. There is, however, another place in the

---

59. John Calvin, *A Harmony of the Gospels Matthew, Mark and Luke*, ed. David W. Torrance and Thomas F. Torrance (Grand Rapids: Eerdmans, 1972), 147.

60. Ibid.

61. Ibid.

62. Ibid., 148.

63. *CR*, 60, col. 37.

64. *SC*, 5.130.

worship of Calvin's Geneva that we find this very powerfully expressed: in the long pastoral prayer that followed the sermon both at daily prayer and on the Lord's Day. We have already spoken of this passage, but it is sufficiently important to look at it once again. This prayer goes back to Bucer and the Reformed psalters of Strasbourg. Even more interestingly, we find very similar pastoral prayers far back in the history of the church. This prayer follows the admonition of the apostle Paul to Timothy to pray regularly for the pagan kings and all in authority, that we might live a peaceful and godly life (cf. 1 Tim. 2:1–8). We are specifically to pray for all men, not Jews only:

> First of all we have your commandment to pray for those whom you have established over us, Superiors and governors: after that for all the needs of your people as well as for all peoples . . . After that we pray to you, most benevolent God, most merciful Father, for all peoples generally. Since it is your will that you be recognized Savior of the world by the redemption accomplished by your Son JESUS Christ, that those who are still far away from a knowledge of you being in the shadows and captivity of error and ignorance might through the illumination of your Holy Spirit and the preaching of your Gospel be brought to salvation.[65]

The reason we are to pray for the Gentiles is that it is the will of God that the Gentiles and all kinds of godless people come to receive the gospel, too. The kerygmatic understanding of worship looks forward to the inclusion of all peoples in the worship of the kingdom of God.

It may have been a century after Calvin that the Westminster Assembly taught us that man's chief end is to glorify God, but when it comes to preaching, Calvin amply understood that concept at the inception of the Reformation. For the Reformer of Geneva, the whole purpose of preaching is to glorify God, to worship him in spirit and in truth.

---

65. "Premierement, nous avons ton commandement de prier pour ceulx que tu as constitué sur nous, Superieurs et gouverneurs: en apres, pour toutes les necessitez de ton peuple, et mesmes de tous les hommes. . . . Apres, nous te prions, Dieu tresbening et Pere misericordieux, pour tous hommes generallement, que comme tu veulx estre recongneu Saulveur de tout le monde, par la redemption faicte de ton Filz JESUS Christ, que ceulx qui sont encores estranges de sa congnoissance, estans en tenebres et captivité d'erreur et ignorance, par l'illumination de ton sainct Esprit, et la predication de ton Evangile" (*OS*, 2.20–22).

7

CALVIN THE LITURGIST[1]

TERRY L. JOHNSON

---

alvin the liturgist? In vain one may search for an article on the proposed subject. Volumes have been written on Calvin the theologian, Calvin the exegete, Calvin and the sacraments, Calvin the church leader, Calvin the dictator and tyrant, even Calvin's theology of worship. But Calvin the liturgist? Most of the standard works on John Calvin's thought fail to deal with his liturgical ideas in anything but the most cursory manner. These include biographies,[2] studies of Calvin and

---

1. The following material is adapted from a forthcoming publication by Terry L. Johnson, *Reformed Ministry in Worship: The Case for Its Historic Form*, reworked for this publication.

2. François Wendel, *Calvin: The Origins and Development of His Religious Thought*, trans. Philip Mairet (New York and Evanston: Harper & Row, 1950); T. H. L. Parker, *John Calvin* (Tring, Herts, UK: Lion Publishing, 1975); Alexandre Ganoczy, *The Young Calvin*, trans. David Foxgrover and Wade Provo (Philadelphia: Westminster Press, 1987); William J. Bouwsma, *John Calvin: A Sixteenth-Century Portrait* (New York and Oxford: Oxford University Press, 1988); and Alister McGrath, *A Life of John Calvin: A Study in the Shaping of Western Culture* (1990; repr., Cambridge, MA: Blackwell, 1995).

his thought,[3] and collections of essays about Calvin, his thought, and his influence.[4] At times the titles are promising. But time and again Calvin's liturgical work is either ignored or given only a superficial descriptive review without in-depth analysis or evaluation.

"It is common knowledge that Calvin and worship are incongruous topics," complains Elsie McKee of the liturgical "experts," "and that whatever the strengths of those who are predestined to the glory of God, they are hopeless failures when it comes to liturgy."[5] The best that

3. Georgia Harkness, *John Calvin: The Man and His Ethics* (New York: Henry Holt and Company, 1931); Abraham Kuyper, *Lectures on Calvinism* (1931; Grand Rapids: Eerdmans, 1983); A. Mitchell Hunter, *The Teaching of Calvin: A Modern Interpretation* (London: James Clarke & Co. Ltd., 1950); John T. McNeill, *The History and Character of Calvinism* (New York: Oxford University Press, 1954); Wilhelm Niesel, *The Theology of Calvin*, trans. Harold Knight (Philadelphia: Westminster Press, 1956); Ronald S. Wallace, *Calvin's Doctrine of the Word and Sacrament* (Grand Rapids: Eerdmans, 1957); E. William Monter, *Calvin's Geneva* (New York: John Wiley & Sons, 1967); Lucien Joseph Richard, *The Spirituality of John Calvin* (Atlanta: John Knox Press, 1974); Ford Lewis Battles, trans. and ed., *The Piety of John Calvin: An Anthology Illustrative of the Spirituality of the Reformer* (Grand Rapids: Baker, 1978); Ronald S. Wallace, *Calvin, Geneva and the Reformation: A Study of Calvin as Social Reformer, Churchman, Pastor and Theologian* (Grand Rapids: Baker, 1988); Wulfert de Greef, *The Writings of John Calvin: An Introductory Guide*, trans. Lyle D. Bierma (Grand Rapids: Baker, 1989); H. Henry Meeter, *The Basic Ideas of Calvinism*, 6th ed., rev. Paul A. Marshall (Grand Rapids: Baker, 1990); Richard A. Muller, *The Unaccommodated Calvin: Studies in the Foundation of a Theological Tradition* (New York: Oxford University Press, 2000); Richard A. Muller, *After Calvin: Studies in the Development of a Theological Tradition* (New York: Oxford University Press, 2003); Randal C. Zachman, *John Calvin as Teacher, Pastor, and Theologian: The Shape of His Writings and Thought* (Grand Rapids: Baker Academic, 2006).

4. *Calvin Memorial Addresses, Delivered before the General Assembly of the Presbyterian Church in the United States at Savannah, GA, May, 1909* (Richmond, VA: Presbyterian Committee of Publication, 1909); David E. Holwerda, ed., *Exploring the Heritage of John Calvin* (Grand Rapids: Baker, 1976); W. Stanford Reid, ed., *John Calvin: His Influence in the Western World* (Grand Rapids: Zondervan, 1982); Elsie Anne McKee and Brian G. Armstrong, eds., *Probing the Reformed Tradition: Historical Studies in Honor of Edward A. Dowey, Jr.* (Louisville: Westminster/John Knox Press, 1989); Donald K. McKim, ed., *The Cambridge Companion to John Calvin* (Cambridge: Cambridge University Press, 2004); Burk Parsons, ed., *John Calvin: A Heart for Devotion, Doctrine, and Doxology* (Lake Mary, FL: Reformation Trust, 2008); Randall C. Zachman, ed., *John Calvin and Roman Catholicism: Critique and Engagement, Then and Now* (Grand Rapids: Baker Academic, 2008).

5. Elsie Anne McKee, "Context, Contours, Contents: Towards a Description of Calvin's Understanding of Worship," in *Calvin Studies Society Papers 1995, 1997*, ed. David Foxgrover (Grand Rapids: CRC Product Services, 1998), quoted in John D. Witvliet, *Worship Seeking Understanding: Windows into Christian Practice* (Grand Rapids: Baker Academic, 2003), 127.

Calvin receives from the scholarly analysts is "polite indulgence," adds John Witvliet.[6]

This well-nigh universal assessment is ironic in that Calvin may rightly be regarded as among the most influential liturgists in the history of the church. His liturgical work, much like his theological work, honors the catholic tradition while synthesizing all that preceded him in the work of the Reformers. After Calvin, all subsequent developments in the Reformed tradition reflect his practice in worship, even if forms were altered in response to local circumstances. His form of worship "has had great influence on all succeeding Reformed liturgies," admits one authority.[7] From Calvin through the Westminster Assembly's *Directory* and into the present, one can clearly trace a commitment to Calvin's order and priorities. Worship moves in the Reformed order from praise, to confession of sin, to thanksgiving, to the means of grace (intercessory prayer, the reading and preaching of Scripture, and the administration of the sacraments), to blessing. The priorities are the *lectio continua* reading and preaching of Scripture, biblical psalmody and hymnody, a full diet of biblical prayer, and frequent administration of the Lord's Supper. Bruno Bürki, writing in *The Oxford History of Christian Worship*, concedes, somewhat apologetically, that the Genevan liturgy is "the durable model of worship for one of the great Christian families, the Reformed churches."[8]

Calvin's "Form" was quickly adopted and adapted by the French, Dutch, German, and other continental Reformed churches. Two editions of it, the French and the Dutch, were in use on Manhattan Island within a decade of the landing of the Pilgrim fathers.[9] Calvin has also had a decisive influence on the broader Reformed tradition, including

6. Witvliet, *Worship Seeking Understanding*, 127. That Calvin did not favor the use of the word *liturgy* may be a part of the problem. Then again, neither did any of the theologians of his day. See Hughes Oliphant Old, "Calvin's Theology of Worship," in Philip G. Ryken et al., eds., *Give Praise to God* (Phillipsburg, NJ: P&R Publishing, 2003).

7. J. G. Davies, *The New Westminster Dictionary of Liturgy and Worship* (Philadelphia: Westminster Press, 1986), 336.

8. Bruno Bürki, "The Reformed Tradition in Continental Europe: Switzerland, France, and Germany," in *The Oxford History of Christian Worship*, ed. Geoffrey Wainright and Karen B. Westerfield Tucker (Oxford: Oxford University Press, 2006), 443.

9. James Hastings Nichols, *Corporate Worship in the Reformed Tradition* (Philadelphia: Westminster Press, 1968), 82.

the Congregationalist, Baptist, Episcopal, and free-church traditions. Moreover, the Episcopal Church, in the Prayer Book of 1552, and even in its definitive 1662 form, borrows heavily from the example of Reformed Protestantism generally, and Calvin in particular. Low-church Protestantism maintained its commitment to the outlines of Genevan worship until swamped by revivalism in the late nineteenth century and the contemporary-worship movement in the late twentieth. Only in the post-American Civil War era did the commitment to the order and elements of Reformed worship begin to erode, and such things as the *lectio continua* and metrical psalm-singing begin to disappear. Even post-Vatican II Roman Catholicism owes considerable debt to Calvin and the Reformed tradition for its increased interest in congregational singing, vernacular Scripture reading, preaching, and expanded prayer-genres (e.g., invocation, intercession, illumination, congregational confession of sin, benediction).

Liturgical Movement

Calvin's liturgical work should be seen as the culmination of several decades of theologically driven liturgical reform. Perhaps we should speak more of Reformed liturgy than of Calvin the liturgist. The liturgical reforms of Reformed Protestantism began with Huldrych Zwingli's decision in January 1519 to preach through Matthew's Gospel ("the first liturgical reform of Protestantism," says Hughes Old).[10] The reform drew considerable inspiration from Martin Luther's *On the Babylonian Captivity of the Church*, published in October 1520.[11] It was given early and comprehensive defense in 1524 by Martin Bucer in his *Grund und Ursach* ("Ground and Reason").[12] It developed through the collegial interaction of a number of the sixteenth-century Reformers: those in Strasbourg

10. Hughes Oliphant Old, *The Reading and Preaching of the Scriptures in the Worship of the Christian Church*, vol. 4, *The Age of the Reformation* (Grand Rapids: Eerdmans, 2002), 46.

11. Martin Luther, "On the Babylonian Captivity of the Church," in *Three Treatises*, ed. James Atkinson (Philadelphia: Fortress Press, 1970).

12. Martin Bucer, *Grund und Ursach*. Text is found in Ottomar Frederick Cypris, "Basic Principles: Translation & Commentary of Martin Bucer's *Grund und Ursach*, 1524" (ThD diss., Union Theological Seminary of New York, 1971).

(Martin Bucer, Wolfgang Capito, Matthew Zell, Kaspur Hedio); in Basel (John Oecolampadius, Konrad Pellikan); in Zurich (Huldrych Zwingli, Heinrich Bullinger, Leo Jud); in other South German and Swiss cities; and of course, in Geneva (John Calvin, Guillaume Farel, Theodore Beza). The *Genevan Psalter* of 1542 and its *Form of Church Prayers* should be seen as the culmination of the efforts of numerous Reformers to forge a worship that was "according to Scripture." It was "the product of a community," says Hughes Old, an "inner church movement to reform the worship of the church."[13] Again, "it can be regarded as a good culmination of the Reformed liturgical revisions which preceded it and at the same time the archetype of Reformed worship which followed it."[14] It passed through many hands and through many cities. "It is in a very real sense the liturgy not of Calvin, not of Geneva, but the liturgy of the Reformed Church," concludes Old.[15]

The impact of the continental Reformers on the English and Scottish Reformers was considerable. This is particularly true of the influence of Bucer (1491–1551) and the Italian Reformer Peter Martyr (1499–1562) on Thomas Cranmer (1489–1556), Archbishop of Canterbury and primary author of the *Book of Common Prayer* (1549, 1552). The *Book of Common Prayer*—in its morning and evening prayer, with its confession of sin, absolution, Old Testament lesson, creed, intercessions, and psalm-singing; and in the communion service, the recitation of the Ten Commandments, exhortation, fencing of the table, invitation to the table, prayer of humble access, eucharistic prayer, post-communion thanksgiving, communion of both kinds, and weekly communion—is particularly noteworthy for its dependence on Reformed Protestantism's liturgical reforms.[16] Likewise, Calvin had a profound influence on John Knox (c. 1514–72), primary molder of the Scots Confession and *Book of Common Order* (1560) that structured

13. Hughes Oliphant Old, *The Patristic Roots of Reformed Worship* (Zurich: Theologischer Verlag, 1970), 95.

14. Ibid., 96.

15. Ibid., xiii.

16. See Nichols, *Corporate Worship in the Reformed Tradition*, 61–70; Charles W. Baird, *The Presbyterian Liturgies* (New York: M. W. Dodd, 1855; repr., Grand Rapids: Baker, 1957), 192–206.

Scottish worship along Genevan lines for nearly a hundred years. Even the Westminster divines, who knew well the work of the Reformers, their Anglican predecessors, and their Continental contemporaries, believed their *Directory for the Public Worship of God* (1645) was in strong continuity with the work of the first generation of English Reformers. "Were they now alive," the authors of the *Directory* insisted, "they would join with us in this work."[17]

Liturgical Theology

The liturgical reforms of Reformed Protestantism were never matters merely of taste, style, or personal preference. Rather, their reforms were driven by their concern that worship be conducted "according to Scripture." This led to careful exegetical work as well as extensive study of the church fathers and practices of the patristic church, the insights of which were valued as windows into the meaning of Scripture. Biblical and historical studies then led to theological reformulation, which in turn further highlighted the need for reform.

In other words, we may discern two lines of argumentation as the Reformers made their case. There was their exegetical work based on the New Testament descriptions of the preaching, praying, baptizing, and the breaking of bread of the apostolic church, including the narratives of the Last Supper (e.g., Acts 2:42; 1 Tim. 2:1ff.; 4:13; Matt. 26:28; John 6). There were also new theological insights into the doctrines of Scripture, the atonement, justification, and pneumatology that demanded changes in the practices of the church of that day.

What worship practices were in need of reform?

There was a broad consensus in Renaissance Christendom that the worship of the late medieval church was in need of reform. The ordinary services of the Lord's Day were conducted in Latin, an unknown tongue for most people. There was little or no preaching outside of the Sunday-afternoon "prone" service. Preaching at the end of the fifteenth century, says Bruno Bürki, liturgical scholar and pastor in the

17. Bard Thompson, *Liturgies of the Western Church* (Philadelphia: Fortress Press, 1961), 355.

Swiss Reformed Church, "was generally in a decadent state." It had lost touch with the biblical text and "was drowning in hagiographical tales and moral recommendations and took delight in artificial scholastic distinctions."[18] There was little prayer, and monastic choirs handled the singing. Scripture reading was by *lectio selecta*, the Old Testament was not read (not until Vatican II did the Old Testament begin to be read in the ordinary services of the Lord's Day in the Roman Catholic Church), and extracanonical readings (the lives of the saints, legends of their exploits, and so on) were common. The Eucharist was understood as a sacrificial Mass. The ministry was sacerdotal, the sacraments were said to operate *ex opera operato*, and the need of personal faith in Christ was diminished in favor of a doctrine of "implicit faith," trust in the church as teacher. The congregation was passive, the Mass unintelligible, and the cup withheld from the laity.

The Exegetical Case

The Reformers went "to the sources," *ad fontes*, with the zeal of Christian humanists. They devoured Scripture in the original languages as well as the freshly published works of the church fathers. Beginning with Acts 2:42, a text that, according to Elsie McKee, provided "the key Biblical paradigm for 'Calvinist' Reformed worship," they discerned a simplicity in the worship of the apostolic and post-apostolic church sadly lacking in medieval worship.[19] We may outline their findings based on their exegesis of Scripture and reading of the church fathers and documents of the early church, using the useful categories of elements, forms, and circumstances.[20]

18. Bürki, "The Reformed Tradition," 437.
19. McKee, "Context, Contours, Contents," 82.
20. Granted, these three categories did not seem to be specifically delineated until the Westminster Confession (1.6; 31.3, 5; 32.1), yet they are operative in the Reformed tradition from the beginning. See Terry L. Johnson, *Reformed Worship: Worship That Is according to Scripture: Revised & Expanded* (2000; Greenville, SC: Reformed Academic Press, 2003), 30–33; also T. David Gordon, "Some Answers to the Regulative Principle," *WTJ* 55 (1993): 321–29; and Rowland S. Ward, "The Directory for Public Worship," in Richard A. Muller and Rowland S. Ward, *Scripture and Worship: Biblical Interpretation and the Directory for Public Worship* (Phillipsburg, NJ: P&R Publishing, 2007), 101–9.

Regarding the Essential Elements of Worship

The Reformers found that the early church followed the pattern of the synagogue in reading the Scripture *lectio continua*, that is, sequential readings, picking up each week where one left off the previous week, with the exhortation or sermon arising out of the reading (Neh. 8:5–8ff.; Luke 4:16–27; Acts 13:14; 15:21; 1 Tim. 4:13; cf. Acts 5:42; 6:2, 4). The apostle Paul wrote, "Until I come, give attention to the public reading of Scripture, to exhortation and teaching" (1 Tim. 4:13).[21]

"The public reading" is literally "the reading." Apparently the practice of reading Scripture was widely known and could be referred to in this general way. "Exhortation and teaching" follow upon the reading. The Reformers further found *lectio continua* reading and preaching in the works of Origen (c. 185–c. 254), Augustine (343–430), Chrysostom (c. 347–407), Jerome (c. 343–420), and others.

They found a variety of types of prayer in Scripture and the fathers, including the invocation and praise (e.g., Pss. 145–150), confession of sin (Pss. 32; 51; Neh. 9; Dan. 9), intercession (fivefold based on 1 Timothy 2:1ff., the apostle Paul's prayers for sanctification in Ephesians 1, Philippians 1, and Colossians 1, and James's direction to pray for the sick in 5:14–15), thanksgiving (1 Tim. 2:1; Phil. 4:6; Pss. 65; 136), illumination (Eph. 1; Phil. 1; Col. 1), and benediction (e.g., Num. 6:24–26; 2 Cor. 13:14); and they found extemporaneous prayers in Justin Martyr's *First Apology* (AD 155), where Justin describes the presiding elder as praying "according to his ability," as does Hippolytus in the *Apostolic Tradition* (AD 217).

They found evidence of the early church singing psalms (e.g., Acts 4:24–26; Eph. 5:19; Col. 3:16; James 5:13) (primarily), and also hymns (e.g., Luke 1:46–55, 68–79; 2:29–32; Phil. 2:5–11; Col. 1:15–20). Pliny the Younger's letter to the emperor (AD 112) describes the early Christians' singing hymns to Christ. The church fathers, the Reformers found, were effusive in their zeal for psalm-singing, with Tertullian (c. 150–c. 225), Eusebius (c. 260–c. 320), Athanasius (c. 295–373),

---

21. All quotations from the Bible in this chapter are from the NASB.

Augustine, Jerome, Basil (c. 330–79), Ambrose (c. 339–97), and Chrysostom all providing testimony.[22]

The Reformers found that scriptural baptisms were simply washings (Acts 2:38; 8:38; 16:33), as were those described in the *Didache* (c. AD 80–110) and Justin Martyr's *First Apology* (c. AD 155). The apostle Paul identified baptism with circumcision (Col. 2:11), giving it a covenantal interpretation that, for the Reformers, answered the claims of the Anabaptists (Gen. 17:7; Acts 2:39; Rom. 4:11). Tertullian (c. 150–225) was first to use the Latin term *sacramentum*, meaning "sacrament" or "oath," indicating a covenantal understanding of baptism in the early church.

They reexamined the words of institution, particularly the words of consecration, "This is My body" and "This is My blood," and determined on exegetical grounds that they should be understood symbolically and metaphorically, as should the words of John 6. Building on this foundation, they denied any alteration in the substance of the bread and the wine, denied the doctrine of transubstantiation, and denied the sacrificial nature of the Eucharist. They found in Scripture a pattern of covenantal meals that finalize agreed-upon obligations between parties (Gen. 14:18; 18:1–8; 27:19; Ex. 12–13; 24), into which pattern Jesus deliberately placed his Supper (Matt. 26:28; Mark 14:24; Luke 22:20; cf. Heb. 9:20). The Supper, they argued, is simply that—a meal. The *Didache* (c. AD 80–110) and Justin Martyr's *First Apology* (c. 155) confirmed the simplicity and nonsacrificial nature of the early Eucharist. Augustine reemphasized the covenantal understanding of the Lord's Supper and gave to the sacraments their classical definition of *verba visibilia*, "visible words" or, more broadly, external visible signs of inward spiritual realities.

Regarding Forms

The Reformers found no written liturgies until the third century, no ritual or ceremony until the fourth century, no incense used until the fourth century, no visual art in worship until the third century, no devo-

---

22. See John McNaughter, *The Psalms in Christian Worship* (Pittsburgh: United Presbyterian Board of Publications, 1907; repr., Edmonton: Still Water Revival Books, 1992); John D. Witvliet, *The Biblical Psalms in Christian Worship: A Brief Introduction and Guide to Resources* (Grand Rapids: Eerdmans, 2007), for collections of these testimonies.

tional use of art until the sixth century, and no instrumental music until the tenth century.

Regarding Circumstances

They found no altars until the fourth century, simple church buildings (often house churches), no developed church calendar until after the fourth century, and an emphasis on the Lord's Day as the day of the public assembly (Acts 20:7; 1 Cor. 16:2; Rev. 1:10). Worship on the first day of the week, Lord's Day worship, was confirmed by Pliny the Younger's letter (AD 110), Justin Martyr's *First Apology* (c. AD 155), the *Didache* (c. AD 80–110), and Tertullian.

Upon these exegetical and historical foundations the Reformers began to reform worship. They believed that they were recovering the simpler and more biblical worship of the apostolic and patristic eras, and sought to conform to the ancient pattern. The form of worship that Reformed Protestantism developed was and is profoundly biblical, taking seriously not only individual texts, but each of the genres of Scripture. It is rooted in the law of God, as Calvin demonstrates when he develops his theology of worship in the First Table of the law.[23] We offer three alternatives to the previous sentence: (1) it is highly sensitive to the prophetic tradition's critique of formalism and ritual in Israel and the neglect of the Word of God (e.g., Isaiah through Malachi), including the "former prophets" (Joshua through 2 Kings); (2) it is highly sensitive to the critique of the prophetic traditions (including the "former prophets" [Joshua through 2 Kings]) of formalism and ritual in Israel and the neglect of the Word of God; or (3) it is highly sensitive to the prophetic tradition's critique of formalism and ritual in Israel, and the neglect of the Word of God.[24] It has been deeply influenced by the Wisdom School and its bookish piety, a piety that delights in and meditates on the law of God "day and night" (Ps. 1:2ff.; cf. Ps. 119).[25] Its devotion to biblical poetry, seen in

23. *Institutes*, 2.7.11–34; see Old, "Calvin's Theology of Worship," 412–35.

24. See Hughes Oliphant Old, "John Calvin and the Prophetic Criticism of Worship," in *John Calvin and the Church: A Prism of Reform*, ed. Timothy George (Louisville: Westminster/John Knox Press, 1990), 230–46; see also Hughes Oliphant Old, "Prophetic Doxology," in *Themes and Variations for a Christian Doxology* (Grand Rapids: Eerdmans, 1992), 91–110.

25. See Hughes Oliphant Old, "Wisdom Doxology," in *Themes and Variations*, 63–89.

its commitment to metrical psalmody, takes second place to none. The New Testament genres of gospel, epistle, and apocalypse were all studied in detail. The Law and the Prophets, the wisdom literature and biblical poetry, the Gospels and Epistles—all have been thoroughly integrated into the practice of Reformed worship.

Theological Implications

But the Reformers' exegetical and historical insights into biblical worship practices were paralleled by new theological insights, which in turn solidified the call for liturgical reform. This second line of argumentation clinched the case for nothing less than a liturgical revolution, even if it was a restorative revolution. Specifically, the Reformers' insight into the completeness and finality of Christ's atonement, justification by grace through faith, the central role played by the Holy Spirit in the application of redemption, and the unrivaled authority of Scripture for all matters of faith and practice necessarily pushed the Reformation beyond the debates of the theologians to the worship practices of the parish church. The revival of preaching that accompanied the sixteenth-century reforms is well known. Less widely recognized are the other revolutionary liturgical changes that took place alongside of it. The Reformation brought about a:

+ Revolution in *reading Scripture*
+ Revolution in *praise*
+ Revolution in *prayer*
+ *Eucharistic* revolution

The Swiss Reformers, says Nicholas Wolterstorff, "had a new vision of what was to be done in the liturgy and how it is to be understood." They brought about, he says, "the most radical liturgical reform that the Christian church has ever known."[26] *Lectio selecta* readings gave way to *lectio continua*; festal or lectionary preaching gave way to expository preaching; limited, formal prayer gave way to a broader spectrum of prayer;

26. Nicholas Wolterstorff, "The Reformed Liturgy," in *Major Themes in the Reformed Tradition*, ed. D. K. McKim (Grand Rapids: Eerdmans, 1992), 277.

monastic choirs gave way to congregational singing of psalms and biblical hymns; the church calendar gave way to the Lord's Day; the Mass gave way to the Lord's Supper; the priestly ministry gave way to the pastoral and proclamational; and eventually, split chancel sanctuaries with central altars gave way to central pulpits and communion tables. Simple services of the Word read, preached, sung, prayed, and received (in the sacraments) replaced the ritual and ceremonial of medieval worship, as the Reformers sought to restore apostolic and patristic practice. The worship of Reformed Protestantism was never merely preliminaries and preaching. "We call the worship of God," says Calvin, "the beginning and foundation of righteousness."[27] Regrettably, the reform of worship as a central concern of the Reformation has been neglected by the historians, who have typically dwelt on its political, social, and theological aspects at the expense of the liturgical (excepting the eucharistic controversies).[28] We may summarize the interaction of the theological insights of the Reformation with the liturgical reforms that resulted, using the categories designated by the Reformation mottos.[29]

First, the principle of *sola Scriptura* led to the reduction of the liturgy. The Reformers believed that Scripture's own self-testimony is that Scripture alone is the final authority in all matters of faith and practice (e.g., Mark 7:1ff.; 2 Tim. 3:16–17). The principle of "Scripture alone" meant in the realm of worship that the church's services must be conducted "according to Scripture." "The Bible was at the heart of Zwingli's reformation," explains Zwingli scholar W. P. Stephens.[30] Virtually every page in

---

27. *Institutes*, 2.8.11.

28. Notable exceptions to this tendency have been Old, *Patristic Roots*, and Carlos Eire, *War against the Idols: The Reformation of Worship from Erasmus to Calvin* (Cambridge: Cambridge University Press, 1986). There is a great need for a comprehensive, chronological work that traces the interaction between the Reformation's fresh theological insights and the working out of the liturgical reforms that followed.

29. Eire, *War against the Idols*, argues that *sola fides*, *sola Scriptura*, and *soli Deo gloria* are the controlling principles of Calvinistic thought (2–7, 195–233). Alexandre Ganoczy, *The Young Calvin* (Edinburgh: T&T Clark, 1999), sees Calvin's theology as centered on the principles of *soli Deo gloria*, *solus Christus*, and *verbum Dei* (188–94). Eire also cites the German scholar Ernst Saxer, who sees Calvin's opposition to the Roman Catholic worship rooted in *sola fides* and *sola Scriptura* (Eire, *War against the Idols*, 198n12).

30. W. P. Stephens, *Zwingli: An Introduction to His Thought* (Oxford: Clarendon, 1992), 30, quoted in Begbie, *The Resounding Truth*, 114.

Bucer's *Grund und Ursach* (1524) records an appeal to Scripture in order
to justify the reforms of worship in Strasbourg. Bucer insists of their
reforms that "everything is based on the Scriptures."[31] Calvin is emphatic
that there is "nothing obscure, nothing ambiguous" in the warnings of
Deuteronomy 12:32 and Proverbs 30:6 not to "add to" or "take away"
anything from God's Word, "when the worship of the Lord and precepts
of salvation are concerned."[32] The church is forbidden "to burden consciences with new observances, or contaminate the worship of God with
our own inventions."[33] "I know how difficult it is to persuade the world
that God disapproves of all modes of worship not expressly sanctioned
by His word," Calvin laments in his 1543 treatise on "The Necessity of
Reforming the Church."[34] He calls "for the rejection of any mode of worship that is not sanctioned by the command of God."[35] This insistence was
maintained through Calvin and the Westminster divines and continues to
the present day.[36] The church, Reformed Protestantism has agreed, is to
do in worship only that which Scripture enjoins. Inherited practices that
could be biblically justified were maintained and typically transformed,
as in the cases of preaching, prayer, Scripture reading, singing, and the
administration of the sacraments. Extrabiblical ceremonies, rituals, signs,
images, symbols, decorations, and gestures were removed so as to allow
undistracted focus on the ministry of the Word and the God-ordained
signs of the Lord's Supper and baptism.

The principle that worship must be "according to Scripture" has sometimes been called the "regulative principle" and has distinguished Reformed
Protestantism from the less rigorous approach to the reform of worship
pursued by the Lutherans and Anglicans. As noted above, as the discussion
was refined over time, *elements*, which were carefully limited (Scripture
reading, sermon, prayer, sung praise, and the administration of the sacra-

31. Bucer, *Grund und Ursach*, 208; cf. 76, 174, 184, 185, 198, 204, etc.
32. *Institutes*, 4.10.17.
33. Ibid., 4.10.18.
34. John Calvin, "The Necessity of Reforming the Church," in *Selected Works of John Calvin: Tracts and Letters*, ed. Henry Beveridge, vol. 1, *Tracts*, pt. 1 (Grand Rapids: Baker, 1983), 128.
35. Ibid., 133.
36. E.g., *Institutes*, 2.8.17; "The Necessity of Reforming the Church," 133; WCF 21.1; WLC 108, 109; the work of modern authors such as John Leith, Hughes Old, and Robert Godfrey, among others.

ments, creeds), were distinguished from *forms* (types or shapes that the elements might take) and *circumstances* (lighting, seating, building, time, etc.), in which greater latitude was allowed.[37] Still, *sola Scriptura* meant in practice that the reform of worship was based on exhaustive biblical exegesis and careful theological formulation.

Second, the principle of *solus Christus* led to the reform of the Eucharist. Since the Reformers understood that Christ's atoning work was "finished" (John 19:30), that he died once for all time, and that his sacrifice was final and complete (Heb. 10:12; 1 Peter 3:18), the medieval *understanding* of the sacrament was transformed as well as the *manner* of its administration and the *identity* of the administrator. Luther began to work out these principles in his *On the Babylonian Captivity of the Church* in 1520. He termed the "most dangerous of all" of Rome's errors "the common belief that the mass is a sacrifice which is offered to God."[38] He urged the church to "put aside whatever has been added to its original simple institution by zeal and devotion of men: such things as vestments, ornaments, chants, prayers, organs, candles, and the whole pageantry of outward things."[39] In his *Formula Missae*, his first reform of the Mass (1523), he repudiates "all those things which smack of sacrifice" and retains only "those things which are pure and holy,"[40] though he later drew back from some of the implications of the new theology.

Bucer in *Grund und Ursach* (1524) and the whole Reformed tradition went much further than Luther proved willing to go. Bucer, like Luther, vehemently insists that "it is the most abominable, most poisonous and most harmful insult and slander of Jesus Christ our Lord and Saviour, to believe and to say that the priest in the Mass offers Him as a sacrifice."[41] He cites Hebrews 9:24–28; 10:12, 14; Isaiah 53:6–7, and a number of other basic texts, as he repeats eight times in twelve pages (in our translation) that Christ's sacrifice was "once-for-all."[42] Calvin speaks of the belief in the Mass as a sacrifice as "a most pestilential error" and "an unbearable

37. See Johnson, *Reformed Worship*, 30–32.
38. Luther, "Babylonian Captivity," 171.
39. Ibid., 153.
40. Thompson, *Liturgies*, 111; cf. Luther, "Babylonian Captivity," esp. 151–53.
41. Bucer, *Grund und Ursach*, 69.
42. Ibid., 80–92.

blasphemy." Indeed, "the cross of Christ is overthrown as soon as the altar is set up." Christ's sacrifice, Calvin says, citing John 19:30 and Hebrews 9:12, 26; 10:10, 14, 18, "was performed only once and all its force remains forever."[43] The finality of Christ's atonement is central to Reformed eucharistic theology. Writing a number of years later in the *Book of Common Prayer* (1547), Thomas Cranmer in his communion prayer of consecration underscores with dramatic redundancy the Reformed view:

> Almighty God our heavenly Father, which of Thy tender mercy did give thine only son Jesus Christ, to suffer death upon the cross for our redemption, who made there by his *one oblation of Himself once offered, a full, perfect and sufficient sacrifice, oblation, and satisfaction for the sins of the whole world.*[44]

Bucer explains at length that the language of sacrifice, as well as gestures, clerical clothing, sanctuary furnishings, and rituals that implied sacrifice, had to be removed from the administration of the Lord's Supper lest the external trappings of the Eucharist contradict the Reformed (i.e., biblical) theology of the Eucharist. The sacrifices that Christians offer, the Reformers argued, are sacrifices of praise offered on a spiritual altar in a spiritual house by a royal priesthood of all believers (1 Peter 2:5; cf. Pss. 50:12–15, 23; 116:17; Heb. 13:15). Whatever implied or suggested sacrifice had to be eliminated from the liturgy. Altars were replaced by tables, priestly vestments were replaced by simple robes, and the term *priest* was replaced by the term *pastor* or *minister*. These alterations were more than mere changes in terminology. The whole job description of the clergy changed as the implications of *solo Christo* began to be grasped. Calvin said, "The Lord has given us a table at which we may feast, not an altar on which a victim may be offered; He has not consecrated priests to sacrifice, but ministers to distribute a sacred 'feast.' "[45] That is to say, the Eucharist, Reformed Protestantism has understood, is *communal*, not mystical; is a *meal*, not a Mass; is a *supper*, not a sacrifice; is administered by a *pastor*, not a priest; is set out on a *table*, not an altar; and is served to those who are *seated*, not kneeling.

43. *Institutes*, 4.18.1–3.
44. Quoted in Thompson, *Liturgies*, 280 (emphasis added).
45. *Institutes*, 4.18.12.

Third, the principle of *sola fide* led to the reform of the reading and preaching of Scripture. The doctrine of justification by grace alone through faith alone in Christ alone apart from works also implied significant changes in the manner of worship. Since believers are justified by faith, and since justifying faith "comes from hearing, and hearing by the word of Christ" (Rom. 10:17), it became necessary for Scripture in the language of the people to have a prominent place in the worship of the church.[46] "The chief and greatest aim of any Service is to preach and teach God's word," said Luther in his introduction to his *Deutsche Messe* (1526).[47] Vernacular services replaced the Latin Mass; *lectio continua* reading and preaching (consecutive texts, picking up where one left off the previous time) replaced *lectio selecta* (texts selected according to the themes of the church calendar), or even extracanonical readings; congregational singing of vernacular psalms and biblical hymns replaced monastic choirs singing incoherent "versicles." The Reformers insisted that the reading, preaching, singing, and praying in worship had to be rich in scriptural context, that the people might be sanctified by the truth (John 17:17). "In contrast with either the Catholic or Lutheran church, Reformed worship was characterized by a particular single-minded focus on the sacred text of the Bible as preached, read, and sung," notes Reformation scholar Philip Benedict, "and by a zeal to eliminate all unscriptural elements from the liturgy."[48]

Fourth, the principle of *sola gratia* led to the reform of prayer. "Grace alone" was emphasized by the Reformers beyond "faith alone" in order to guard the gospel from any encroachments of works-based righteousness. The faith that saves is itself a "gift of God" (Eph. 2:8–9). Salvation is a product of the divine initiative beginning in eternity, accomplished in the person and work of Christ, and applied by the Holy Spirit. On this all the Reformers agreed. The agent of application, the One who initiates redemption in the believer's experience, is the Holy Spirit. Believers are

---

46. Luther, "Concerning the Ordering of Divine Worship in the Congregation," quoted in Thompson, *Liturgies*, 98.

47. Thompson, *Liturgies*, 129.

48. Philip Benedict, *Christ's Churches Purely Reformed: A Social History of Calvinism* (New Haven and London: Yale University Press, 2002), 490. Elsie McKee adds, "For Reformed Christians, as for Protestants generally, the exposition of the Biblical text, in the language of the people, became a central and necessary part of all right worship of God" ("Context, Contours, Contents," 82).

born again by the Holy Spirit (John 3:5–8), confess Jesus as Lord (and are justified) by the Holy Spirit (Rom. 10:9; 1 Cor. 12:3), receive the Spirit of adoption (Rom. 8:15), are sanctified by the Spirit (Gal. 5:22–23; 1 Peter 1:2), and are kept or preserved by the power of God the Holy Spirit (1 Peter 1:5). The application of the whole *ordo salutis* is a supernatural event. This understanding of the role of the Holy Spirit had a powerful impact on worship, leading to the above-mentioned "revolution in prayer" as dependence on God the Spirit came to be expressed through what Hughes Old has called "a full diet of prayer."[49] The invocation, the congregational confession of sin, the intercessions, the prayer of illumination, and the benediction were restored to the regular worship of the church. Moreover, the internal and spiritual dimension of worship came to take precedence over the external and formal, simplicity over elaborate and ostentatious ritual and ceremony.

Fifth, the principle of *soli Deo gloria* led to an insistence on reliance on the ordinary means of grace. Carlos Eire argues that in the late Middle Ages, access to divine power was sought through the cult of saints, relics, images, and pilgrimages. In Eire's terms, the transcendent was sought through the imminent, the heavenly through the earthly, and the spiritual through the material:

> Late medieval religion sought to grasp the transcendent by making it imminent: It was a religion that sought to embody itself in images, reduce the infinite to the finite, blend the holy and the profane, and disintegrate all mystery.[50]

The Reformers protested: *soli Deo gloria*—to which might be added, urges Eire, the principle *finitum non est capax infiniti*, "the finite cannot comprehend the infinite." John Leith explains that "Reformed theology has resisted every effort to get control of God, to fasten the infinite and indeterminate God to the finite and the determinate whether it be images, or the bread and wine of the sacraments, or the structures of the church."[51]

49. Old, *Worship*, 173.
50. Eire, *War against the Idols*, 11.
51. John H. Leith, *Introduction to the Reformed Tradition*, rev. ed. (Atlanta: John Knox Press, 1981), 74.

Negatively this meant the elimination of everything in the church's external devotion that implied magic or the domestication of God: Marian
devotion, the cult of saints, relics, images, pilgrimages, and the doctrine
of transubstantiation. Positively, it meant an internalizing of piety and a
simplified approach to God through the ordinary means of Word, sacraments, and prayer.

Soli Deo gloria effectively summarizes the Reformers' concerns even
as it elevates those concerns to the highest level. The reforms of worship
were necessary, the Reformers argued, because God is glorified when his
people worship "according to Scripture" and refuse to embrace human
novelties and innovations. God is glorified when the church's eucharistic
practices affirm the finality and sufficiency of Christ's atonement and in
no way imply the need for its perpetual supplementation. God is glorified in Word-filled worship services that underscore that justification is
by personal faith in Christ alone and not by implicit faith in the church
and her sacraments. God is glorified in prayer-saturated worship services
that demonstrate dependence on the Holy Spirit, rather than rituals and
ceremonies or, in our day, marketers, demographers, and entertainers.
Historic Reformed worship, by its content, form, order, furnishings, and
buildings, provides an unmistakable witness to the central truths of the
Christian faith: Scripture alone leads us to Christ alone, whom we receive
by faith alone, as initiated by God's grace alone, all to God's glory alone.

The liturgical reforms of Reformed Protestantism were revolutionary, and just as clearly the direct product of the critical exegetical insights
and theological reforms of the Reformed churches of which Calvin is the
culmination. The two lines of argument combined, the exegetical and the
theological, to make a powerful case for reform. "Far from being a minor
disagreement on ceremonies, the question of the right worship of God
was intrinsically related to the key theological concerns of Protestants:
Christ alone, faith alone, grace alone, Scripture alone," McKee maintains.[52]
Although Luther proved to be "very conservative" in liturgical matters, as
Bainton says, he wrote in *The Babylonian Captivity of the Church* of the
need (in light of Protestant doctrines) to "*alter almost the entire external
form of the churches and introduce, or rather reintroduce, a totally different kind*

52. McKee, "Context, Contours, Contents," 67.

of ceremonies."[53] Theological reform "demanded a reshaping of worship," Hughes Old has argued.[54] Reformed worship took the shape it did not because of the taste or cultural preferences or ethnicity of the Reformers, but because of the theology that lay behind it. Reformed worship gave expression to the convictions of Reformed theology. Another way of putting this is to say that one cannot understand Calvin the liturgist without first understanding Calvin the *exegete*, Calvin the *historian*, and Calvin the *theologian*. The Reformed churches purposefully designed worship services that were simple and spiritual and that consisted of rich and substantial Bible content expressed through the limited number of essential elements because that is what Reformed theology required:

+ Sequential expository preaching
+ *Lectio continua* Bible reading
+ Congregational psalmody and biblical hymnody
+ Scripture-rich prayers or invocation, confession, thanksgiving, illumination, intercession, and benediction
+ The regular administration of the sacraments of the Lord's Supper and baptism, understood covenantally
+ Use of creedal summaries of Christian teaching

A generation later the *Westminster Directory for the Public Worship of God* (1645) was produced by the Puritans of the Westminster Assembly.[55] The aim of the English Puritans, evident in both the Middleburg Liturgy (1586), the Westminster Assembly's *Directory*, and Baxter's Savoy Liturgy (1661), was to restructure the worship of the Church of England according to the pattern of the best Reformed churches abroad. "Puritan apologetics were filled with citations to the liturgical ideas of the Reformed divines," notes Thompson, who continues: "And the service-books themselves gave testimony, in title or preface, that a fellowship of worship ought to exist

53. Roland Bainton, *Here I Stand: A Life of Martin Luther* (New York: Abingdon-Cokesbury Press, 1950), 339 (emphasis added); see also Luther, "Babylonian Captivity," 152–53.

54. Old, *Reading and Preaching*, 4:74.

55. See bound with *Westminster Confession of Faith* (Glasgow: Free Presbyterian Publications, 1985), 369–94. See also Thompson, *Liturgies*, 311–74.

between 'the Godly at home' and 'the Reformed Churches abroad.' "[56] The oft-repeated notion that the English Puritans did not know the continental Reformed tradition cannot be sustained with any scholarly credibility. The Puritans generally, and the Westminster divines specifically, were in regular communication with the continental Reformed theologians and brought to their work a profound knowledge of biblical, patristic, medieval, and Reformation-era exegesis and practice.[57] The *Directory* was considerably freer in form than the Continental or Scottish liturgies. It recommended only the use of the Lord's Prayer and perhaps the Apostles' Creed as fixed or regular items in the order of service. Yet all the same elements may be identified.[58]

Since the time of the *Directory*, Reformed worship has sometimes made less use of fixed forms (e.g., seventeenth to mid-nineteenth centuries) and sometimes more (mid-nineteenth to mid-twentieth centuries). Yet the continuity seems clear enough. Still today, historic Reformed worship may or may not make limited use of fixed forms (e.g., Ten Commandments, Doxology, Gloria Patri, Apostles' Creed, written prayers), yet it still aims to be biblical in its elements and content and reflect the finality of Christ's completed work of atonement on the cross.[59]

56. Thompson, *Liturgies*, 319.

57. On the question of continuity between the Puritans and Calvin, as well as the exegetical background to their work, see Muller and Ward, *Scripture and Worship*. Behind this brief work stands Muller's four-volume *Post-Reformation Reformed Dogmatics: The Rise and Development of Reformed Orthodoxy, ca. 1520 to ca. 1725* (Grand Rapids: Baker Academic, 2003). Mueller destroys the "Calvin against the Calvinists" school of thought and demonstrates development with continuity within the Reformed tradition, not discontinuity and change as many have assumed without verification.

58. The authors of the *Directory* urge sequential expository preaching; *lectio continua* Bible reading (a chapter from each Testament); psalm-singing; Scripture-rich prayers: of praise, of confession of sin, of assurance of pardon, of intercession, and of illumination (all combined), of thanksgiving and consecration, and of benediction; "frequent" administration of sacraments of the Lord's Supper and baptism; and religious oaths or creeds (see also WCF 31.5 and 22.1).

59. Tim Keller and R. J. Gore Jr. both accuse traditionalists of "oversimplification" for asserting, as I do in the introduction to *Leading in Worship* (Oak Ridge, TN: Covenant Foundation, 1996), that there were four hundred years of consensus on what constituted Presbyterian worship (Keller, "Reformed Worship in the Global City," in *Worship by the Book*, ed. D. A. Carson [Grand Rapids: Zondervan, 2002], 199; Gore, *Covenantal Worship: Reconsidering the Puritan Regulative Principle* [Phillipsburg, NJ: P&R Publishing, 2002], 1). Given that I elaborate considerably on the breadth of diversity within which that consensus

Those who have insisted that no such thing as Reformed worship has ever existed, or that the Reformed faith is compatible with most any form (that is, style) of worship, typically fail to interact with the exegesis, the history, or the theology. Historic Reformed worship arises out of and is an expression of the Reformed faith. It is what it is because the convictions of Reformed Christianity are what they are. The case for its forms was powerful then and now, its norms compelling.

Liturgical Order

Calvin not only agreed with the broad liturgical implications of Protestant theology, but adopted the forms of his predecessors as well. Above all, it was Martin Bucer to whom Calvin was most indebted for his liturgical ideas.[60] Bürki calls Strasbourg "a cradle of the Reformed liturgy."[61] Calvin "made no serious departure from Bucer either in phrase or order," observes William D. Maxwell.[62] Calvin should be understood as a synthesizing rather than as a creative liturgist. He was able to glean the fruit of the previous twenty years of Protestant theological thought and liturgical activity and give it definitive form. As we have said, the *Genevan Psalter* of 1542 with its *Form of Prayers according to the Custom of the Ancient Church* is properly seen as both

---

has existed on pages 6–8 of the same work, this criticism seems unwarranted. Keller sees two distinct Reformed traditions: the Zwinglian/free church and the Calvinistic. Our point of difference would seem to be perspective. He sees discontinuity where I see continuity. The selection of Zwingli as a "founder" is curious. No one, after Bullinger, followed his example in eliminating singing from the church's worship. By the end of the sixteenth century, the Zwinglians were singing the psalms and had become part of the larger Reformed movement. There is no Zwinglian tradition of worship per se. See Jeremy S. Begbie, *Resounding Truth: Christian Wisdom in the World of Music* (Grand Rapids: Baker Academic, 2007), 118. Reformed people have differed some (though mainly as a matter of preference) on the use of fixed forms (e.g., Apostles' Creed, Lord's Prayer), over the use of hymns in addition to psalms, and over the use of musical instruments to accompany singing. Is this two traditions or one tradition within which there is a degree of diversity?

60. LindaJo H. McKim, "Reflections on Liturgy & Worship in the Reformed Tradition," in Donald K. McKim, *Major Themes in the Reformed Tradition* (Grand Rapids: Eerdmans, 1992), 305.

61. Bürki, "The Reformed Tradition," 443.

62. William D. Maxwell, *John Knox's Genevan Service Book, 1556* (Edinburgh: Oliver and Boyd, 1931), 23–24.

the culmination of all that preceded and the pattern for all that followed it. Consequently, Calvin is rightly seen as a liturgist of the highest order and greatest importance. Yet it must also be acknowledged that Calvin wrote very little on liturgy per se. He assembled the *Form of Prayers*. Yet he provided no extended defense of or even explanation of the Genevan order aside from the rather short "Preface" or "Foreword" to the *Psalter*,[63] and an even briefer description in the *Institutes*.[64] How is this to be explained? We may assume, given the importance of Bucer to Calvin's liturgical ideals, that Calvin agreed with the reasoning found in Bucer's *Grund und Ursach* (1524), his seminal defense of the reforms of worship in Strasbourg, and saw no need to repeat it. Bucer covers in detail Reformed Protestantism's concern for *lectio continua* reading and preaching of Scripture, biblical prayer, biblical hymnody, and a simple administration of the sacraments. This seems a safe assumption, given that Calvin also had firsthand experience of the order of service found in the *Strasbourg Psalter* of 1539, and largely based his Genevan order on it.

Ecclesiastical Context

For Calvin, worship is the church's worship, and worship is the context of the church's ministry. "God is pleased to gather his sons," says Calvin, into the bosom of the church, "that they may be nourished by his help and ministry."[65] Calvin understands the church to be the institution in which the saints are "nourished" by God's "help" and "ministry." He says:

> For there is no other way to enter into life unless this mother conceive us in her womb, give us birth, nourish us at her breast, and lastly, unless she keep us under her care and guidance until, putting off mortal flesh, we become like angels.[66]

63. John Calvin, "Foreword to the Psalter," in *John Calvin: Writings on Pastoral Piety*, ed. Elsie Anne McKee (New York: Paulist Press, 2001), 91–97. This may also be found at http://www.fpcr.org/blue_banner_articles/calvinps.htm; or Henry Beveridge, ed., "Form of Prayers," in *Selected Works of John Calvin*, 2:100–112.
64. *Institutes*, 4.17.43.
65. Ibid., 4.4.1.
66. Ibid., 4.1.4.

How does the church conceive, give birth, nourish, and keep her sons? Through her ministry of the Word and sacraments. The "marks" of the true church are simply these: "wherever we see the Word of God purely preached and heard, and the sacrament administered according to Christ's institution, there, it is not to be doubted, a church of God exists."[67] Worship, for Calvin, is central to the identity and mission of the church.

Elements

Calvin in his Foreword to the *Psalter* speaks of three elements commanded by God for spiritual assemblies: "the preaching of the word, the public and solemn prayers, and the administration of His sacraments."[68] His proof text? Acts 2:42, the "key biblical paradigm" for the Reformers. This was elaborated in terms of the following elements.

1. *Invocation.* The invocation, or call to worship, Psalm 124:8, was taken from Farel's *Neuchâtel Service Book* of 1533 as mediated to Calvin through Strasbourg. By the time of the *Genevan Psalter*, 1562, the call was preceded by the singing of a psalm.[69] It may be that it became customary from the earliest days in Reformed churches to sing psalms as the people gathered.[70]

2. *Prayers.* Calvin explains from Matthew 21:13 ("house of prayer") that "the chief part of [God's] worship lies in the office of prayer."[71] For Calvin, prayer is "the chief exercise of faith."[72] The primary prayers for the Genevan service—the prayer of confession, the prayer of illumination, the prayer of intercession, and the post-communion thanksgiving—were all borrowed from Strasbourg.[73] "As for the Sunday prayers,

67. Ibid., 4.1.9.
68. Calvin, "Foreword," in McKee, *Calvin: Writings on Pastoral Piety*, 92.
69. McKee, *Calvin: Writings on Pastoral Piety*, 100.
70. This has been suggested by Hughes Oliphant Old.
71. *Institutes*, 3.20.29.
72. Ibid., 3.20.1.
73. Old, *Patristic Roots*, 93.

I took the form of Strasbourg and borrowed the greater part of it," said Calvin.[74]

3. Lectio Continua *Reading and Preaching of Scripture.* This critical reform was instituted by Zwingli, followed by nearly all the other Reformers, and mediated to Calvin through Strasbourg. In *Grund und Ursach* and the *Strasbourg Psalter* of 1539, Bucer had insisted on *lectio continua* reading of Scripture in public worship. "As Calvin understands it," says Hughes Old, "the reading and preaching of Scripture is to have a central place in the worship of the church; it is its primary responsibility."[75] Moreover, reading and preaching are acts of worship. The proclamation of the gospel is "worship pleasing and precious to God," says Calvin.[76]

4. *Congregational Singing of Psalms.* Calvin recommended the singing of psalms in the first edition of the *Institutes* in 1536, again in the Articles placed before the Geneva Town Council in 1537,[77] and once more as a condition of his return to Geneva in 1541. Congregational singing had been overlooked by Zwingli in Zurich and Farel in Geneva prior to Calvin. Hymnody had become popular in Lutheran realms. A beginning to metrical psalmody had been made among the German-speaking congregations of Strasbourg, their 1539 *Psalter* having eighteen metrical psalms. But Louis Benson is surely right in saying that psalmody, the distinctive contribution of the Reformed churches to the church's songs, was "the conception of one man's mind and the enterprise of one man's will. . . . It was the element . . . for which he found least sympathy among his colleagues and least preparation among the people."[78] The 1542 *Genevan Psalter* included 30 psalm texts written by Clément Marot, the leading French poet of the day, as well as five additional psalm renderings by Calvin himself, several canticles, and Marot's metrical versions of the Lord's Prayer and Creed.[79] By 1562 the *Genevan Psalter* had

74. Thompson, *Liturgies*, 189. It may be that by "the Sunday prayers" Calvin means not just the prayers per se, but the whole Sunday service, *prayers* functioning as a synonym for *worship*.
75. Old, *Reading and Preaching*, 4:133.
76. Quoted in McKee, "Context, Contours, Contents," 83.
77. This may be found in J. K. S. Reid, trans. and ed., *Calvin: Theological Treatises*, vol. 22, Library of Christian Classics (Philadelphia: Westminster Press, 1954), 47–55.
78. Louis F. Benson, "John Calvin and the Psalmody of the Reformed Churches," *Journal of the Presbyterian Historical Society* 5.1–3 (March–September 1909): 4.
79. Ibid., 57.

been completed, and became, arguably, the most influential "hymnbook" ever written. Calvin's will and vision was the determining factor in the publishing of metrical versions of whole psalms and the whole *Psalter*.

5. *The Administration of the Lord's Supper*. The sacraments are for Calvin (as they were for Augustine before him) "visible words" to which doctrine must be joined lest they become merely an exterior spectacle.[80] Calvin's *Form* required that the words of institution be read and explanation given. "The sacrament requires preaching to beget faith," Calvin maintains.[81] Calvin followed the Strasbourg order with explanation, exhortation, creed, words of institution, distribution, thanksgiving, benediction. Calvin borrowed the *Sursum Corda* from Farel and introduced the "dismissal of the unrepentant." His program for weekly communion, proposed in the Articles of 1537, was rejected by the Geneva Town Council in favor of monthly communion in one of Geneva's three churches, that is, quarterly in each church. The *Institutes*, to the last edition, argue for weekly observance.[82] As late as 1561 Calvin declared, "Our custom is defective."[83] Calvin's service "remained an Ante-communion," says Thompson, truncated, "standing in anticipation of the Holy Supper."[84]

6. *Liturgical Use of the Ten Commandments*. Calvin followed the suggestion of Bucer in *Grund und Ursach*, singing the commandments after the prayer of confession in the *Form of Prayers* of 1545 (Strasbourg).[85] Also, Farel had used the Ten Commandments in *La Maniere et Fasson* (Neuchâtel, 1533) in connection with baptism. The Ten Commandments did not make it into the "Form of Prayers" of 1542 (Geneva), but they did become a feature of most subsequent Reformed liturgies.

Order

Calvin's order of service may be outlined as follows:

80. *Institutes*, 4.14.6.
81. Ibid., 4.14.4; see also 4.17.39.
82. Ibid., 4.17.44ff.
83. Thompson, *Liturgies*, 190.
84. Ibid.
85. Ibid., 191.

Ante-Communion	Communion
Psalm (sung)	Communion Exhortation (Geneva)
Call to Worship—Psalm 124:8	Creed (sung)
Confession of Sin	Prayer of Humble Access (Strasbourg)
Absolution (Strasbourg)	Lord's Prayer
Singing of the First Table of the Law (Strasbourg)	Words of Institution
Prayer of Commitment	Fencing of Table (Geneva)
Singing of the Second Table of the Law (Strasbourg)	Exhortation to Believe God's Promises
Psalm (sung)	*Sursum Corda*
Prayer for Illumination	Distribution of the Elements
Scripture Reading	Thanksgiving
Sermon	Psalm (Strasbourg)
Great Prayer and the Lord's Prayer	Benediction (Aaronic)
Psalm (sung)	

The movement of flow of the service is clear and, as we have mentioned, will prove influential. It moves from praise (metrical psalms and call) to the confession of sin (confession, absolution, law of God, commitment), to the means of grace (Scripture reading, sermon, prayer of intercession, sacraments), to thanksgiving (psalm, benediction). This is essentially the flow of the gospel, driven by the logic of the gospel, and is evident in virtually all the historic liturgies. It should be noted that Calvin favored a strong statement of absolution. In this he followed the pattern of Bucer's *Strasbourg Psalter* (1539), as well as John Oecolampadius's *Form & Manner* (1525), used in Basel.[86] The absolution was considered a novelty in Geneva

86. Thompson, *Liturgies*, 171, 213.

and was resisted. Calvin "yielded to their scruples," though the absolution was retained in the Strasbourg edition of the *Form of Prayers* (1545).[87] The Reformed tradition has tended to follow the Genevan practice, typically replacing a formal absolution with words of assurance, expressed either in the prayer itself or immediately following.[88]

We note as well what is missing. The various liturgical responses of the congregation in the medieval Mass (usually spoken by priests or monks) have been removed. The *sanctus* ("Holy, holy, holy Lord . . ."), *Kyrie eleison* ("Lord have mercy, Christ have mercy"), *Gloria* ("Glory to God in the highest . . ."), *Sursum corda* ("Lift up your hearts"), and other congregational responses (e.g., to the greeting, to Scripture readings) have been eliminated.[89] In the Reformed service the congregation responds by singing. The deletions were made by Farel in his order, *La Maniere et Fasson* of 1524, and by Bucer in the *Strasbourg Psalter* of 1526, and were never restored by Reformed Protestants.

Liturgical Ethos

We will now look at what we refer to as Calvin's liturgical ethos. Several key principles govern the tone of divine worship.

First, Calvin insists on *reverence* in worship. The tone of the prayers and songs and sermons in Geneva was sober, serious, and reverent. This can be illustrated by the language that he uses to describe the tunes that would be used in the singing of the psalms. The church's tunes, he says, should "be neither light nor frivolous, but have gravity and majesty, as St. Augustine says." Further, "There is a great difference between the music that one makes to entertain people at table and in their homes and psalms which are sung in the presence of God and his angels."[90] The melody, he says, should be "moderated" in order "to carry gravity and majesty appro-

---

87. Ibid., 191, 198.
88. E.g., Knox's *Form of Prayers* (1556), in Thompson, *Liturgies*, 297; Puritans' *Middleburg Liturgy* (1586), in Thompson, *Liturgies*, 323; *Book of Common Prayer* (1552), in Thompson, *Liturgies*, 278–79.
89. W. D. Maxwell comments on the Reformers' decision to eliminate the responses: "The responses of course had long ago disappeared from the people's usage, but now they were excised from the text" (in Davies, *Dictionary of Liturgy and Worship*, 458).
90. Calvin, "Foreword," 94.

priate to the subject and even to be suitable for singing in the church."[91] What was true of the church's song was to be true of the entire service. Reverence is Calvin's "first rule" of prayer, and he denounces "levity that marks an excess of frivolity utterly devoid of awe."[92] The people knelt for the confession of sin, the men with their heads uncovered.[93] Similarly, sermons were to be preached with dignity and humility.

Second, services of public worship should be conducted with *ritual simplicity*. Simplicity was the "hallmark of Calvin's liturgical policy," says Thompson.[94] All the "shadowy symbols of the old dispensation," all the "lifeless and theatrical trifles" of the medieval church, as Calvin called those things, and all external forms that encumbered spiritual worship were removed, that the Word might be heard unhindered.[95] Preaching was to be in a plain style. Ministers were to handle the Scripture with "modesty and reverence."[96] They "must not make a parade of rhetoric, only to gain esteem for themselves."[97] Public prayers were to be offered without "ostentation and chasing after paltry human glory."[98] Baptism was to be administered in simplicity, omitting the "theatrical pomp" of the medieval service with its candles, chrism, exsufflations, spittle, exorcisms, and so forth, "which dazzle the eyes of the simple and deadens their minds."[99] No other ceremonies were to be allowed to distract the elect from those few ceremonies (that is, baptism and the Eucharist) ordained by God. "Everywhere there is too much of processionals, ceremonies, and mimes," Calvin complains. "Indeed," he says, "the very ceremonies established by God cannot lift their head in such a great crowd, but lie as if crushed down."[100] Only as much ceremony was allowed as was necessary for the

91. Ibid.

92. *Institutes*, 3.20.4–5.

93. Baird, *Presbyterian Liturgies*, 27; McKee, *Calvin: Writings on Pastoral Piety*, 100; *Institutes*, 3.20.33.

94. Thompson, *Liturgies*, 194.

95. Ibid., 195; *Institutes*, 4.17.43.

96. From Calvin's commentary on Luke 4:16, quoted in Wallace, *Calvin's Doctrine of the Word and Sacrament*, 119.

97. John Calvin, "Letter CCXXIX—To the Protector Somerset," in Beveridge, *Selected Works of John Calvin*, 5:190.

98. *Institutes*, 3.30.30.

99. Ibid., 4.15.19.

100. Ibid., 4.18.20.

conducting of the service. In keeping with this, the churches of Geneva were stripped of their pictures, statues, and symbols; clergy traded their priestly vestments for black robes; altars were removed and replaced by plain communion tables; the various anointings and excommunications in connection with baptisms were eliminated; processionals, incense, and extraneous gestures and postures were abolished.

Likewise, the calendar was simplified. Saints' days were eliminated, and only the "Five Evangelical Feast Days" were retained: Christmas, Good Friday, Easter, Ascension Day, and Pentecost. Otherwise, the weekly Lord's Day was to be the primary holy day of the Christian community.

Simplicity was closely associated with spirituality. Focus was to be on the heart, not right formulas, right rituals, or right ceremonies. Prayers were to be offered with "a single and true affection that dwells in the secret place of the heart."[101] Singing was to "spring from deep feeling of heart" and with care "that our ears be not more attentive to the melody than our minds to the spiritual meaning of the words."[102] Simplicity facilitated the undistracted attention of the mind on God's Word, and undistracted devotion of the heart upon Christ.

Third, public worship was to be characterized by both *form* and *freedom*. Fixed forms were provided in order to guarantee a degree of uniformity among the churches and in order to provide what we would call quality control. Bucer, initially a champion of liturgical latitude, later was overtaken by his concern for greater uniformity. He denounced the "deplorable differences" of practice and "detestable changes" made in the name of Christian liberty.[103] He grew to have a greater appreciation for the church as a community of discipline as well as love, and for the ordained ministry as the distinctive channel through which the means of grace are exercised. "The prevailing opinion of Strasbourg, an opinion which the Reformed Church has often reaffirmed, is that liturgical reform is not to be left to the illumination of individual pastors, but rather is a concern of the Church as a whole," says Old.[104]

To the end of increased uniformity, Bucer produced his *Gesangbush* in 1541, replacing a variety of hymnbooks then in use in the church. Calvin, in

101. Ibid., 3.20.30.
102. Ibid., 3.20.31–32.
103. Thompson, *Liturgies*, 163.
104. Old, *Patristic Roots*, 82n1.

a letter to England's Protector Somerset, approves of the English liturgy's establishing for the prayers and the administration of the sacraments "a certain form from which the ministers not be allowed to vary." Prescribed forms may be provided, he said, "to help the simplicity and unskillfulness of some," and to provide the "consent and harmony of the churches one with another." Further, prescribed forms help restrain novelty. By their use "the capricious giddiness and levity of such as affect innovations may be prevented."[105]

Yet room was made for freedom in worship. The form of the prayer before the sermon, the prayer of illumination, was "left to the discretion of the Minister."[106] And the public prayers of the weekday services as well as the afternoon service of the Lord's Day were free. The minister was to use "such words in prayer as may seem to him good, suiting his prayer to the occasion, and the matter where he treats."[107] By doing so Calvin, according to nineteenth-century church historian Philip Schaff, "opened the inexhaustible fountain of free prayer in public worship, with its endless possibilities of application to varying circumstances and wants."[108]

Whatever restrictions he might contemplate in the liturgy, Calvin is adamant respecting freedom in preaching. He complains to England's Protector Somerset that "there is very little preaching of a lively kind in the kingdom, but that the greater part deliver it by way of reading a written discourse." Without discounting the possible abuse of fanatics, he insists that preachers be allowed to have "free course," and that their preaching "ought not to be lifeless but lively." He appeals to 1 Corinthians 14:24–25 and 2 Timothy 3:16–17 in proclaiming that "the Spirit of God ought to sound forth by their voice, so as to work with mighty energy." Whatever the dangers, nothing ought to be allowed "to hinder the Spirit of God from having liberty and free course." He feared that if ministers were tied down to books of homilies and written sermons, the Reformation would not make the progress in England that it would if "this powerful instrument of preaching be developed more and more."[109]

105. Calvin in Baird, *Presbyterian Liturgies*, 23.
106. Thompson, *Liturgies*, 199.
107. Baird, *Presbyterian Liturgies*, 24.
108. Philip Schaff, *History of the Christian Church*, vol. 8, *Modern Christianity: The Swiss Reformation* (1910; repr., Grand Rapids: Eerdmans, 1950), 371.
109. Calvin, "Letter to Protector Somerset," 190–92.

Baird sees the union of free prayer and prescribed forms as the "peculiar excellence of the Genevan worship."[110] The subsequent Reformed tradition moves in the direction of increasing latitude in worship, from Knox to the Westminster *Directory*, to the present, yet not always wisely. In this, as in so much else, Reformed Christians would do well to consider Calvin's liturgical wisdom today.

Liturgical Strengths

We may make several brief observations regarding the strengths of the Genevan service as we have understood it, with some attention to how those strengths might serve us today.

First, it is a God-centered service. No attempt is made to entertain the congregation with liturgical theater. Each element, and the service as a whole, is fixed on the central purpose of glorifying God. "The church today needs to listen anew to Calvin on worship," insists Robert Godfrey, "so that its worship will not be man-centered, but God-centered and God directed."[111] Church boards should ask themselves a very simple question: What should churchgoers be aiming at when they arrive at church each Sunday? What should their primary intention be? Should congregations function as a studio audience to provide the backdrop against which the unsaved get evangelized? Do we want them coming to hear a stimulating talk? Do we want them seeking an exciting experience? Do we want them coming as consumers in pursuit of spiritual entertainment? Or do we want them coming so that they might meet with the true and living God through his Word and Spirit, and present to him public praise, confession of sin, thanksgiving, and petitions offered in "spirit and truth" (John 4:7ff.), and with "reverence and awe" (Heb. 12:28)? Is it not obvious that if a worship service is a worship service, then all that takes place within that service must have a Godward devotional quality? God must be at the center of the whole. He must be the hub, and all else must revolve around him. What Hughes Old says of American Protestantism applies internationally:

110. Baird, *Presbyterian Liturgies*, 24; see also Thompson, *Liturgies*, 197.
111. Robert S. Godfrey, "Calvin & the Worship of God," in *The Worship of God: Reformed Concepts of Biblical Worship* (Fearn, Ross-shire, UK: Christian Focus, 2005), 49.

The greatest single contribution which the Reformed liturgical heritage can make to contemporary American Protestantism is its sense of the majesty and sovereignty of God, its sense of reverence, of simple dignity, its conviction that worship must above all serve the praise of God.[112]

Second, the service has a gospel-structured order. That is to say, it centers on Christ and redemption. The worshiper is led from praise to confession of sin to the assurance of pardon to the application of the means of grace for sanctification, including the remembrance of Christ's death in the Lord's Supper. "While all true worship is God-centered," says former Fuller Seminary professor Robert Shaper, "Christian worship is no less Christ-centered."[113] Christ is "the central focus of all authentic Christian worship," say Plantinga and Rozeboom.[114] Participants in the Genevan order reexperience the gospel each time the church assembles. Many leading churchmen today are eager that their ministries be "gospel-driven" and "grace-centered." We are urged by many to "preach the gospel to ourselves" regularly. What better way to do so than to practice historic Reformed worship, in which the gospel is preached before the sermon even begins? Some advocates of contemporary worship have disparagingly referred to this gospel structure as a "re-enactment of redemption."[115] Tim Keller, on the other hand, sees "Gospel re-enactment" as a strength of historic Reformed worship.[116] Sean Michael Lucas, in his popular introduction to Presbyterianism, *On Being Presbyterian*, entitles his chapter on public worship "Gospel-Driven Presbyterian Worship."[117] "The very movement of worship," he says, "re-presents

112. Hughes Oliphant Old, *Worship That Is Reformed according to Scripture* (1984; repr., Louisville: Westminster/John Knox Press, 2004), 176–77.

113. Quoted in Carson, *Worship*, 26.

114. Cornelius Plantinga Jr. and Sue A. Rozeboom, *Discerning the Spirits: A Guide for Thinking about Christian Worship Today*, Calvin Institute of Christian Worship Liturgical Studies Series (Grand Rapids: Eerdmans, 2003), 154.

115. John Frame, for example, has not been too keen on the idea. He thinks that because "redemption is in the past," a "re-enactment liturgy" obscures the fact that our sins are already forgiven. Thankfully, he does see "a place in worship for asking God's forgiveness of our continuing sins for the sake of Christ" (John M. Frame, *Worship in Spirit and Truth* [Phillipsburg, NJ: P&R Publishing, 1995], 68). Since he does, he really shouldn't be too troubled by the fact that *some might* draw the wrong conclusion at a historic Reformed worship service.

116. Keller, "Reformed Worship," in *Worship by the Book*, 214–17.

117. Sean Michael Lucas, *On Being Presbyterian: Our Beliefs, Practices, and Stories* (Phillipsburg, NJ: P&R Publishing, 2006), 115–31.

the gospel to us and recalls for us the hour we first believed."[118] There does seem to be a consistent way to approach God, to bridge the gulf between a holy God and fallen humanity, Old Testament and New Testament, which is fulfilled in Christ and experienced in public worship each time the assembly of believers convenes. Genevan worship honors this order.

Third, it is a Word-filled order. The Word provides the content for all the elements of the service. The language of Genevan worship is the language of Scripture, as it is read, preached, sung, and prayed, and the visible Word is administered in the Lord's Supper. R. Kent Hughes argues that we are witnessing today a "debiblicizing of corporate worship."[119] Much of the debate between traditional and contemporary worship viewpoints would end if Genevan principles were followed and all parties agreed to read substantial portions of Scripture (not just the bit to be preached), sing whole psalms and biblical hymns (and not just Scripture fragments, as in "Scripture songs"), preach sequentially and expositorily through books of the Bible (and not use texts as launching pads for topical sermons), add five to ten minutes of Bible-saturated prayer to their services, and administer the sacraments with thorough biblical explanation. Such a consensus would leave little left to debate. Regrettably, there seems to be little enthusiasm for these traditional Reformed practices today, or understanding of their roots in the apostolic church, in the patristic church, and in the liturgies of Reformed Protestantism. Ironically, voices from the old mainline Protestant denominations seem to understand the need for biblical content even as many evangelicals do not. "The native language of the church's worship is, and I think must be, biblical language," says Ronald P. Byars, professor emeritus of preaching and worship at Union Theological Seminary in Richmond, Virginia.[120] The church, he says, must "relearn the use of scriptural language, and use it boldly . . . as language that is indispensable to the worshiping assembly."[121]

Fourth, it is Spirit-dependent worship. By restoring the several prayer genres, especially the prayer of illumination, Genevan worship displays

118. Ibid., 125.
119. R. Kent Hughes, "Free-Church Worship," in *Worship by the Book*, 147.
120. Ronald P. Byars, *What Language Shall I Borrow? The Bible and Christian Worship* (Grand Rapids: Eerdmans, 2008), xvii.
121. Ibid., 7.

an understanding of the church's dependence on the Holy Spirit for life, acceptable worship, and fruitful ministry. "If there is one doctrine which is at the heart of Reformed worship," says Hughes Old, in his crucial study *The Patristic Roots of Reformed Worship*, "it is the doctrine of the Holy Spirit ... Worship is the manifestation of the creative and sanctifying presence of the Holy Spirit."[122] We would expect no less than this from Calvin, who has rightly been called "the theologian of the Holy Spirit."[123]

Fifth, the service is church-aware. Calvin and his successors were not Anabaptist revolutionaries. They were very concerned to maintain catholicity and promote the communion of the saints. They looked primarily to the patristic church for their inspiration. But they also honored medieval traditions. The Zurich and Strasbourg liturgies from which Calvin drew inspiration were both "derived from the mass."[124] The novelties of the medieval church were to be corrected, for sure. But all that safely could be retained was for the sake of ecclesiastical continuity. Moreover, the Genevan form is transferable. It is able to transcend ethnic, racial, generational, and cultural differences. It takes the communion of all the saints seriously. The Genevan liturgy and psalter were translated almost immediately upon publication into German, Dutch, Spanish, Italian, English, Hungarian, and other languages. The differences between Romantic, Germanic, Slavic, and Celtic cultures, for example, were not seen as barriers to implementing historic Reformed worship.[125] Could there have

---

122. Old, *Patristic Roots*, 341.

123. The attribution is that of B. B. Warfield. He explains:

In the same sense in which we may say that the doctrine of sin and grace dates from Augustine, the doctrine of satisfaction from Anselm, the doctrine of justification by faith from Luther, we must say that the doctrine of the work of the Holy Spirit is a gift from Calvin to the Church. It was he who first related the whole experience of salvation specifically to the working of the Holy Spirit, worked it out into its details, and contemplated its several steps and stages in orderly progress as the product of the Holy Spirit's specific work in applying salvation to the soul ... What Calvin did was, specifically, to replace the doctrine of the Church as sole source of assured knowledge of God and sole institute of salvation, by the Holy Spirit ... In his hands, for the first time in the history of the Church, the doctrine of the Holy Spirit comes to its rights.

B. B. Warfield, *Calvin and Augustine* (Philadelphia: Presbyterian and Reformed, 1980), 485–86.

124. Davies, *Dictionary of Liturgy and Worship*, 335; also McNeill, *Calvinism*, 150.

125. Those who respond, "Yes, but these are all European cultures" may not appreciate how different these cultures can be, exceeding, at times, the differences between races, genders, and generations.

been more unreceptive soil on which to plant Reformed faith and worship than violent, amoral, backward, illiterate, and clannish sixteenth-century Scotland? Yet it did flourish there and elsewhere without any particular attempt to contextualize or show sensitivity to cultural preferences. Reformed worship was theologically, not culturally, driven.

Genevan worship is both "transferable" and "flexible," as J. Ligon Duncan observes. "Reformed worship has worked and is working in every situation and culture where there is an historic Protestant church committed to scriptural principles of worship," he argues. Duncan provides global examples, from the Peruvian Andes, to West Philadelphia, to Dundee in Scotland, to Malawi in east Africa, to eastern Australia, to Japan, to Israel, among Baptists, Presbyterians, Congregationalists, and Anglicans. There are churches, Duncan says, "on six continents, first world and two-thirds world, ministering to every conceivable class of society[, that] are following in the train of historic Reformed Protestant worship."[126]

This kind of catholicity is possible when it is recognized that the church has its own biblical and organically developing liturgical culture through which its form of worship is expressed. Rather than dividing and excluding through new worship services that cater to popular styles and tastes, the Genevan ideal was for the church to maintain a significant measure of uniformity of worship, expressed in the forms of its own ecclesiastical heritage, through which the diversity of its peoples could unite. "Only a church which resists being merely of one generation [or ethnic culture, we would add] can be relevant to them all," Gene Veith reminds us.[127]

These features of Genevan worship are timeless. They have also, by and large, been compromised by today's church. Much that ails the church in our day might be cured by the restoration of the "form" of worship practiced by the ancient church and the historic Reformed churches, worship that is "according to Scripture."

126. J. Ligon Duncan, in *Give Praise to God*, 70–72.

127. Gene E. Veith, "Through Generations," *For the Life of the World* 2.1 (March 1998): 9.

8

CALVIN'S NEW TESTAMENT COMMENTARIES AND HIS WORK AS AN EXEGETE

GEORGE W. KNIGHT III

Lining the walls of a number of pastors' studies are the works of John Calvin, not only his famous *Institutes of the Christian Religion*, but also his commentaries on the Old and New Testaments. As one scans them to see how many he has produced, one is astonished to see that a great deal of the Old Testament is dealt with and almost all of the New Testament. There are Genesis (2 vols.), the Pentateuch (5 vols.), Joshua, Psalms (5 vols.), Isaiah (4 vols.), Jeremiah and Lamentations (5 vols.), Ezekiel (2 vols.), Daniel (2 vols.), and the Minor Prophets (5 vols.). Alongside of these Old Testament works are his commentaries on all the New Testament except 2 and 3 John and the book of Revelation, with the Synoptic Gospels being considered together in his *Harmony of the Evangelists*. With these New Testament books we are dealing with works that Calvin wrote as commentaries, whereas with the Old Testament works most of that which we have as commentaries are transcripts of expository lectures, except for Genesis and the Pentateuch (the books of Moses), Joshua, and the Psalms.

When we consider John Calvin as the New Testament commentator, we need to contemplate two matters: (1) the style of commentary writers who are his contemporaries, and (2) the production and significance of his *Institutes*. Calvin mentions a couple of his contemporaries in "The Epistle Dedicatory" addressed to Simon Grynaeus in the preface to his first commentary, namely, Romans. He had hoped that "by adopting a different plan, I should not expose myself to the invidious charge of rivalry."[1] His different plan is that of "*lucid brevity*,"[2] which he immediately characterizes as laying open "the mind of the writer whom he undertakes to explain" and not leading "away his readers from it." Thus Calvin goes on to say this about two of his contemporaries: "Since then the first [Melanchthon] has not explained every passage, and the other [Bucer] has handled every point more at large than it can be read in a short time, my design has not even the appearance of being an act of rivalship [rivalry]."[3] So Calvin writes with "lucid brevity" to tell us clearly what the writer means in what he writes. Moreover, he does so in distinction from the pattern that was common in his day.[4] Parker sums it up well when he says that Calvin possesses "the highest virtues of a commentator—deep penetration into the author's thought, a self-less faithfulness to his views, and clarity and force in expression."[5]

But Calvin also wrote with "lucid brevity" because he was working at the same time on his *Institutes of the Christian Religion*, and in the words of dedication to the reader he expressed how his commentaries and the *Institutes* relate to one another. He wrote:

1. John Calvin, *Commentaries on the Epistle of Paul the Apostle to the Romans*, trans. and ed. John Owen (1849; repr., Grand Rapids: Eerdmans, 1955), xxvi; also in *The Epistles of Paul the Apostle to the Romans and to the Thessalonians*, ed. David W. Torrance and Thomas F. Torrance, trans. Ross Mackenzie (Grand Rapids: Eerdmans, 1960), 3. Hereafter the page numbers of both translations will be given.
2. Calvin, *Romans*, xxiii and 1.
3. Ibid., xxvi and 3.
4. Cf. T. H. L. Parker, *Commentaries on the Epistle to the Romans 1532–1542* (Edinburgh: T&T Clark, 1986), 73–77.
5. Ibid., 77.

If, after this road has, as it were, been paved [that is, the *Institutes*], I shall publish any interpretations of Scripture, I shall always condense them, because I shall have no need to undertake long doctrinal discussions, and to digress into commonplaces. In this way the godly reader will be spared great annoyance and boredom, provided he approach Scripture armed with a knowledge of the present work, as a necessary tool. But because the program of this instruction is clearly mirrored in all my commentaries, I prefer to let the book itself declare its purpose rather than describe it in words.[6]

Not only does this statement of John Calvin reference commentaries in general, but the 1539 edition mentions his commentary on Romans in particular, and the dates of the *Institutes* and of his commentary on Romans also undergird his assertions ("The Epistle Dedicatory" to Simon Grynaeus is dated October 18, 1539, Strasbourg, even though Romans was not published until March 1540; and the first edition of Calvin's *Institutes* was published at Basel in 1536).[7]

So we have seen that both the style of his contemporaries (which he realizes does not capture the essence of the biblical writings and hence he wants to avoid this style) and his work on the *Institutes* (in which he can expound doctrine more fully from all biblical texts taken together) have brought Calvin to realize that the best way to write a commentary is with lucid brevity.

Although we know less about Calvin than we wished we knew, at least we gain some insights from the autobiographical comments he made in the "Author's Preface" to volume 1 of his *Commentary on the Book of Psalms*.[8] Calvin writes of God's giving him a sudden conversion.[9] Others began to come to him to learn about this gospel and the Scriptures, and he felt

6. Calvin, *Institutes of the Christian Religion*, ed. John T. McNeill, trans. and indexed Ford Lewis Battles (Philadelphia: Westminster Press, 1960), "John Calvin to the Reader" (1559), 1.4–5.

7. The contents of the 1539 "Epistle to the Readers" in ET is given in John Calvin, *Institutes of the Christian Religion*, trans. Henry Beveridge (Edinburgh: Calvin Translation Society, 1845; repr., Grand Rapids: Eerdmans, 1958), 1.20.

8. John Calvin, *Commentary on the Book of Psalms*, trans. James Anderson (Edinburgh: Calvin Translation Society, 1845), 1.40–49.

9. "God by a sudden conversion subdued and brought [Calvin's] mind to a teachable frame" so that he "thus received some taste and knowledge of true godliness" (xl). See the careful

so pressed that he felt he should leave France and go to Germany (and then later Basel), and thus he spent the next three years outside of France. During this time he resolved to produce the *Institutes* to help protect and defend those being persecuted and defamed. While on his way from Basel to Strasbourg, he spent one night in Geneva; while there, Guillaume Farel constrained him to stay in Geneva and help the Reformation in that city. (By this time, 1536, he had disentangled himself from the Roman Catholic Church.) By 1538, however, Calvin was asked to leave Geneva, and so he went on to Strasbourg, where he stayed and served until 1541, when he was asked to return to Geneva. He stayed and ministered in Geneva until his death on May 27, 1564.

Thus it was while Calvin was in Strasbourg that he published in 1540 his first New Testament commentary, the volume on Romans.[10] Calvin was only thirty years of age when the work was published in Basel in March of that year (having been born in Noyon, France, on July 10, 1509). The work was written in Latin (the language of the scholarly world at that time), as were the others, and sooner or later these works were translated into French. The first complete French translation for Romans appeared in 1550. The other commentaries appeared in the following order in Latin (unless indicated as being in French): 1 Corinthians appeared in 1546, 2 Corinthians in 1548, Galatians, Ephesians, Philippians, and Colossians in 1548 as well, 1 and 2 Thessalonians in 1551 in French, 1 and 2 Timothy in 1548, Titus in 1550 in French, Philemon in 1551 in French, Hebrews in 1549 and 1551, James in 1542 and 1550 in French, all of Paul's Epistles, Hebrews, and the Catholic Epistles except 2 and 3 John in 1551 and 1556, the Gospel of John in 1553, the Harmony of the Gospels (Matthew, Mark, and Luke) with John in 1555, Acts 1–13, volume 1 in 1552, and Acts 14–28, volume 2 in 1553. All the New Testament commentaries were written by 1555 and published by 1556. So from 1540 to 1556, a space of sixteen years, Calvin published commentaries on all the New Testament books (except 2 and 3 John and Revelation).

---

analysis of this sentence in its context by T. H. L. Parker, *John Calvin: A Biography*, app. 2, "Calvin's Conversion" (Philadelphia: Westminster Press, 1975), 162–65.

10. For the data on these matters, see T. H. L. Parker, *Calvin's New Testament Commentaries*, 2nd ed. (Louisville: Westminster/John Knox Press, 1993), 206–13, and Parker, *Commentaries on the Epistle to the Romans 1532–1542* (Edinburgh: T&T Clark, 1986), 71.

Furthermore, during this time, Calvin started work on some Old Testament commentaries as well (Isaiah and Genesis). This is a phenomenal achievement in and of itself, but even more so considering all his other responsibilities at the same time. Part of the explanation is the fact that secretaries were provided for Calvin, not when he was writing Romans, but in the years that followed.[11]

But the questions that must be asked now are why he began with the Pauline Epistles and especially Romans, and why he wrote on the Gospel of John before he wrote on what we now call the Synoptic Gospels. We find Calvin giving his own answer in the "Argument" that he presents to the readers in the beginning of Romans: "this can with truth be said of it, and it is what can never be sufficiently appreciated—that when any one gains a knowledge of this Epistle, he has an entrance opened to him to all the most hidden treasures of Scripture."[12] What did Calvin mean by this statement? Not that Romans had to be read and understood first before any other parts of the Scriptures could be understood. No, that would mean that the first readers of other parts of the New Testament could not have understood what they read. And we know that that is not true. He meant rather that:

> When once Romans has been grasped a certain point of view will have been gained which will then enable the reader to comprehend the intention of the rest of the Scripture. The consequence for the expositor is that a commentary on Romans will lay a solid foundation for the understanding of the genuine meaning of the rest of the New Testament and thus prepare for those expositions which are to follow. Hence Calvin did not write first on Romans because it happened to come first among the Epistles in the canonical order. Rather, he agreed

11. "It was due solely to his secretaries that he was able to write so many commentaries after 1549" (Parker, *Calvin's New Testament Commentaries*, 27). Nicolas Colladon, who knew Calvin intimately and is a primary source for his life, wrote a biography of Calvin as a preface to the Latin edition of Calvin's commentary on Joshua (1565). We quote Parker's ET of the words of Colladon as a further proof of the assertion given above about Calvin's use of secretaries and the help they provided to him in producing his commentaries: "At home he lay down on the bed fully clothed and pursued his labours on some book . . . This is how in the mornings he dictated the most of his books, when he could give his genius full flow" (quoted in Parker, *John Calvin: A Biography*, 104).
12. Calvin, *Romans*, xxix and 5.

with the canonical ordering which had decided that Romans should be placed first.[13]

Why then did Calvin write his commentary on John before he wrote the Harmony on the other three Gospels? Here again Calvin explains himself in the "Argument" that he gives to his readers at the beginning of his commentary on John. After explaining why all of them are called *Gospels* because they contain the account of the heart of the gospel in Jesus' work for us, he proceeds to distinguish John from the others in the following way:

> Yet there is also this difference between them, that the other three are more copious in their narrative of the life and death of Christ, but John dwells more largely on the doctrine by which the office of Christ, together with the power of his death and resurrection, is unfolded. They do not, indeed, omit the mention that Christ came to bring salvation to the world, to atone for the sins of the world by the sacrifice of his death, and, in short, to perform every thing that was required from the Mediator, (as John also devotes a portion of his work in historical details;) but the doctrine, which points out to us the power and benefit of the coming of Christ, is far more clearly exhibited by him than by the others ... On this account, I am accustomed to say that this Gospel is a key to open the door for understanding the rest; for whoever shall understand the power of Christ, as it is here strikingly portrayed, will afterwards read with advantage what the others relate about the Redeemer who was manifested.[14]

Thus in reading the Gospels a different order should be followed from that in which they are printed in our Bibles, namely, "that when we wish to read in Matthew and the others, that Christ was given to us by the Father, we should first learn from John the purpose for which he was manifested."[15] Calvin thus writes that John is the "key to open the door for understanding" the other Gospels, and thus he commends us to read John first before the other Gospels.

13. Parker, *Calvin's New Testament Commentaries*, 32.

14. John Calvin, *Commentary on the Gospel according to John*, trans. William Pringle (Edinburgh: Calvin Translation Society, 1846; repr., Grand Rapids: Eerdmans, 1949), 1.21–22.

15. Ibid., 22.

Calvin manifests his lucid brevity in the way he unfolds the argument of Romans. Listen to these excerpts of his writing as he guides us through the letter. Thus Calvin writes of Paul:

> Having begun with the proof of his Apostleship, he then comes to the Gospel with the view of recommending it; and as this necessarily draws with it the subject of faith, he glides into that, being led by the chain of words as by the hand: and thus he enters on the main subject of the whole Epistle—justification by faith; in treating which he is engaged to the end of the *fifth* chapter.
>
> The subject then of these chapters may be stated thus: that man's only righteousness is through the mercy of God in Christ, which being offered by the Gospel is apprehended by faith . . .
>
> Having wholly deprived all mankind of their confidence in their own virtue and of their boast of righteousness, and laid them prostrate by the severity of God's judgment, he returns to what he had before laid down as his subject—that we are justified by faith; and he explains what faith is, and how the righteousness of Christ is by [faith] attained to us.[16]

In this lucid brevity, for all his emphasis on the sovereignty of God, the keynote of Paul's teaching that we are justified by faith comes through very clearly—indeed, that the righteousness of Christ through the mercy of God offered in the gospel "is apprehended by faith" and "attained to us" by faith. Yes, that faith is given by God's gracious action on us, but it is the God-ordained way by which the gospel and its attendant blessings are received. Paul adds, Calvin writes, "that this righteousness is through God's bountiful goodness offered indiscriminately to all nations, but that it is only apprehended by those, whom the Lord through special favour illuminates."[17]

Calvin was bound to the text of the Scriptures, and would not accede to a view regarding its meaning even if a great number in the church seemed to be lined up on that side. This fidelity to the Scriptures is evidenced in his dealing with the authorship of Hebrews. He is quite convinced that it is canonical, but does not agree to its being written by the apostle Paul.

16. Calvin, *Romans*, xxix–xxxi and 5–6.
17. Ibid., xxxv; cf. also page 9 of the Torrances' edition.

He summarizes his views on the question in the "Argument" that he gives on the letter to the Hebrews for his readers:

> I, indeed, can adduce no reason to shew that Paul was its author.... But the manner of teaching, and the style, sufficiently shew that Paul was not the author; and the writer himself confesses in the second chapter that he was one of the disciples of the Apostles, which is wholly different from the way in which Paul spoke of himself.... There are other things which we shall notice in their proper places.[18]

In Calvin's comment on Hebrews 2:3b, "It was declared at first by the Lord, and it was attested to us by those who heard,"[19] he writes the following: "Moreover, this passage indicates that this epistle was not written by Paul; for he did not usually speak so humbly of himself, as to confess that he was one of the Apostles' disciples.... It then appears evident that it was not Paul who wrote that he had the Gospel by hearing and not by revelation."[20]

Calvin also believed that God had given a multiple presentation of the gospel and of the person and work of our Lord, and therefore to rightly understand the gospel in its completeness and Jesus Christ in his wholeness "it is beyond all dispute, that it is impossible to expound, in a proper and successful manner, any one of the Evangelists [Synoptic Gospels], without comparing him with the other two."[21] Thus to aid the preacher or teacher of these Synoptic Gospels, "I thought that it might prove to be a seasonable and useful abridgment of their labour, if I were to arrange the three histories in one unbroken chain, or in a single picture, in which the reader may perceive at a glance the resemblance or diversity that exists."[22]

18. John Calvin, *Commentaries on the Epistle to the Hebrews*, trans. John Owen (Edinburgh: Calvin Translation Society, 1855; repr., Grand Rapids: Eerdmans, 1949), xxvii.

19. All quotations from the Bible in this chapter are from the RSV, unless otherwise indicated.

20. Calvin, *Hebrews*, 54. The translator and editor of Hebrews has served readers well by giving in the footnotes his own argument for the Pauline authorship of the letter to the Hebrews, so that in one place both sides of the argument may be read. Because there is no explicit self-indication given in the letter, I have inclined to Calvin's position.

21. John Calvin, *Commentary on a Harmony of the Evangelists, Matthew, Mark, and Luke*, trans. William Pringle (Edinburgh: Calvin Translation Society, 1844; repr., Grand Rapids: Eerdmans, 1949), 1.xxxix.

22. Ibid., xl.

It is to be wished that the spirit of Calvin would more readily be found in those who preach on any one of the Synoptic Gospels, that the message of Jesus written by each, and not the theology of the Gospel writer, might be proclaimed from these texts aided by the insight provided by the others.

Calvin revised his commentaries on the New Testament in the years 1551 and 1556. In 1551 he revised his Pauline works (and Hebrews), and in 1556 he revised all the Epistles together. Then in 1557 he submitted to the printers a single-page list of eighteen errata that was not published until 1563.[23] Parker has edited the Romans and Hebrews commentaries for the new *opera omnia Calvini*, supplying valuable insight into Calvin's two editions on these two books.

The work on Romans was at first a small one of sixty-five thousand words. In 1551 it was expanded to seventy-seven thousand words. The final edition added the equivalent of about half the length of his first edition, that is, about thirty-one thousand words, to produce the 1556 edition of ninety-six thousand words. The work was altered in form but not in substance. Besides the various verbal changes and alterations, the most significant changes were the enlargement of his comments, especially on Romans 8:5–6.[24] We note the 1556 rewriting of the later part of the 1540 and 1551 statement concerning Romans 8:5, "For those who live according to the flesh set their minds on the things of the flesh, but those who live according to the Spirit set their minds on the things of the Spirit." We quote most of the rewriting as given by Parker:

> Now, in the second clause he exhorts believers to hope well if, raised up by the Spirit, they will lift their minds to the meditation and practice of righteousness. For wherever the Spirit reigns it is a sign of God's saving grace; just as God's grace has no place where the Spirit is extinct and the reign of the flesh flourishes. Moreover, what I have mentioned before I repeat briefly here: "in the flesh" or "according to the flesh" is equivalent to being empty of the gift of regeneration.[25]

23. I am indebted to Parker, *Calvin's New Testament Commentaries*, 36ff. and 210–11, for the facts given above and also in the following text above.
24. For the details, see Parker, *Calvin's New Testament Commentaries*, 52–56.
25. Ibid., 55.

The alterations to Calvin's commentary on Hebrews are very light, some pages showing no changes at all. "The longest addition is no more than six lines and there are only four others of more than two."[26] Parker gives us that longest change, but cites only the Latin form of the work to indicate where it is found in Calvin.[27] It is the greater part of the last paragraph of the comments dealing with Hebrews 6:17 ("So when God desired to show more convincingly to the heirs of the promise the unchangeable character of his purpose, he [guaranteed it] with an oath" [esv]).[28] I quote the change from the 1549 and 1551 editions with the addition of the 1556 edition as Parker presents it:

> 1549, 1551: lest any should doubt that this teaching comes from God's deep feeling. 1556 *adds*: But rather believers should, as soon as they hear the voice of the Gospel, be surely convinced that there is being proclaimed to them the secret counsel of God which was hidden in him; and hence that what he had decreed before the creation of the world concerning our salvation is made open.[29]

The New Testament commentaries of Calvin were translated into English by the Calvin Translation Society and published at Edinburgh in the 1840s and 1850s. This edition was reprinted by Eerdmans approximately a hundred years later in the 1940s and 1950s, and then reprinted again by Baker in 1979. *Calvin's New Testament Commentaries*, edited by David W. Torrance and Thomas F. Torrance and newly translated, were published by Eerdmans in 1959–72.

What can we learn in general from this survey of Calvin's New Testament commentaries? John Murray in giving "The Annual Lecture of The Evangelical Library, in London, 1964" summarizes this well in the three observations that he makes of "Calvin as Theologian and Expositor." First, "it is the biblically oriented and biblically conditioned way in which the biblical material is treated that makes Calvin's presentation abidingly and

---

26. Ibid., 56; for specific examples, see 57–59.
27. Parker cites the reference as CO, 55.79–80 (which is the *Opera Calvini* [CR edition]), in his *Calvin's New Testament Commentaries*, 58.
28. Calvin, *Hebrews*, 151.
29. Parker, *Calvin's New Testament Commentaries*, 58.

irresistibly relevant to the Scripture itself."[30] "The second factor that contributes to this permanent significance of Calvin's work is what becomes evident on cursory examination. . . . In exposition of Scripture there are few faults more exasperating than that of reciting a mass of opinions in which the aim of elucidating the text is lost sight of, and the mind of the reader is bewildered rather than instructed. It is to Calvin's own words we may turn to illustrate his determination to spare himself and his readers this liability."[31] Murray then adds, "Perhaps no statement respecting his method and aims excels that in his Epistle Dedicatory to the exposition of the twelve minor prophets, dated January 26, 1559."[32]

> If God has endued me with any aptness for the interpretation of Scripture, I am fully persuaded that I have faithfully and carefully endeavored to exclude from it all barren refinements, however plausible and fitted to please the ear, and to preserve genuine simplicity, adapted solidly to edify the children of God, who, being not content with the shell, wish to penetrate to the kernel.[33]

"A third factor . . . is that Calvin united in an eminent degree . . . piety and learning."[34] We find Calvin manifesting in the *Institutes* and in his commentaries that which he defined as "pure and real religion" in the early pages of the *Institutes* when he writes: "Here indeed is pure and genuine religion: faith so joined with an earnest fear of God that this fear also embraces willing reverence, and carries with it such legitimate worship as is prescribed in the law."[35] And Calvin demonstrated this most significantly in his motto that said that he offered his heart to God promptly and sincerely.

Ned B. Stonehouse and John Murray each wrote an Introduction to the reprinting of Hebrews and Romans by Eerdmans in the mid-1900s. In seeking to sum up the excellencies of Calvin as an exegete,

---

30. *Collected Writings of John Murray* (Edinburgh: Banner of Truth, 1976), 1:308.
31. Ibid., 1:308–9.
32. Ibid., 1:309.
33. John Calvin, *Commentaries on the Twelve Minor Prophets*, trans. John Owen (Edinburgh: Calvin Translation Society, 1846), 1.18–19.
34. Murray, *Collected Writings*, 1:311.
35. *Institutes*, 1.2.2; 1.43.

they both reached out and quoted another to express their own deep appreciation and esteem for all of Calvin's labors. Stonehouse quoted the distinguished German exegete, Professor F. A. G. Tholuck of Halle, saying that the evaluation was even more impressive because Tholuck was not a Calvinist. Stonehouse summarized Tholuck's evaluation in his own words: "Among the formal excellencies of Calvin's commentaries Tholuck singled out their elegance of diction, conciseness of expression, symmetry and freedom from immoderate digressions. On the material side he sums up their qualities in terms of doctrinal impartiality, exegetical tact ('which makes it even impossible for him to adopt forced interpretations'), his considerable and inobtrusive learning, and his deep Christian piety."[36] Murray in his Introduction to Romans cited Dean Farrar, who he also indicated "was very far from being a Calvinist," saying that Farrar "speaks of him as the greatest exegete of the Reformation." He quoted Farrar as follows: "The neatness, precision, and lucidity of his style, his classic training and wide knowledge, his methodical accuracy of procedure, his manly independence, his avoidance of needless and commonplace homiletics, his deep religious feeling, his careful attention to the entire scope and context of every passage, and the fact that he has commented on almost all the Bible, make him tower above the great majority of those who have written on Holy Scripture."[37]

What does a preacher get from Calvin today as an exegete of the Scriptures? Let's first of all mention some of his weak points: one doesn't get much in the way of a technical introduction, and relatively little of technical discussions, and he does not interact much with other commentators. Thus, if one puts his commentary on Romans alongside those of Moo, Murray, and Schreiner, one will not find the detail that they provide, and one should not expect to find those matters. But if one wants a com-

36. Calvin, *Hebrews*, ii of Stonehouse's "Introduction" (unnumbered). For this summary of Tholuck set in its larger context, see his article on "Calvin as an Interpreter of the Holy Scriptures" in ET as a dissertation in the back of John Calvin, *Commentaries on the Book of Joshua*, trans. Henry Beveridge (Edinburgh: Calvin Translation Society, 1854), 345–75.

37. Calvin, *Romans*, iii (in unnumbered section of Murray's "Introduction" to Romans, which quotes Farrar).

mentary like that which Tholuck and Farrar (and also Schaff[38]) describe as written by Calvin, written for preachers from a preacher/scholar who gets to the point of the text, grasps the text in its closest and largest context, knows that Christ is the central idea in all the Scriptures, and will virtually not allegorize at all, nor spiritualize from his own vantage point but only from that of the text, who does not speculate but gives sober exegesis of the text, then Calvin is the man for lucid brevity and decisive help even though he wrote the commentaries some 460 years ago.

38. Philip Schaff, "Calvin as a Commentator," *Presbyterian and Reformed Review* 3 (1892): 463, comments that Calvin "combined in a very rare degree all the essential qualifications of an exegete—grammatical knowledge, spiritual insight, acute perception, sound judgment, and practical tact."

9

CALVIN AND LUTHER: COMRADES IN CHRIST

JAMES EDWARD McGOLDRICK[1]

A Damaging Division

Following the death of Martin Luther in 1546, relations between the Lutheran and Reformed branches of Protestantism became tense and sometimes overtly hostile. This distressing development has continued into modern times, although in diminishing measure, as spokesmen for the two traditions at times misunderstand and therefore misrepresent each other.[2] Lack of understanding and appreciation in the latter part of the sixteenth century caused divisions at the very time the Protestant movement was in urgent need of unity, as it faced a resurgent Roman church inspired by Counter-Reformation zeal. Rather than presenting a united

1. Dr. McGoldrick prepared this article for Calvin500, but was providentially hindered from presenting it because of a family illness.
2. A staunchly orthodox Lutheran pastor once presented me with a tract that identified Luther's major opponents as the Romanists, the Radicals, and the Reformed.

front, however, Lutherans and Reformed engaged in mutual recriminations and thereby enlarged the distance between them.

A particularly emphatic expression of distrust occurred when Lutheran Prince Ludwig IV (r. 1576–83) in the German state of Palatine removed Reformed professors from the faculty at the University of Heidelberg and purged other Calvinists from various offices in his government. By that time French Protestants were enduring bloody persecution in the wake of the St. Bartholomew's Day Massacre of 1572, and consequently seeking support in other lands, especially in Germany, where Reformed churches had been growing. That very growth alarmed Lutheran rulers, who feared that it would disrupt the fragile Peace of Augsburg (1555), which had inaugurated a policy of toleration for the Catholic and Lutheran faiths alone. They perceived vigorous Calvinist missionary work in Germany as a threat to the peace.

In 1577 most German Lutherans subscribed to the Formula of Concord as a means to settle doctrinal disputes among themselves in an effort to achieve stability for their territorial churches. The Formula as adopted is confessional and apologetic and aimed, in part, at the Reformed churches, an intention that Calvinists in and outside of Germany were quick to discern. It is clear that some Lutheran leaders had, by that time, come to regard their Reformed counterparts as heretics, even though in 1540 John Calvin had signed the revision (*variata*) of the Augsburg Confession of Faith (1530), the initial Lutheran statement of doctrine.

Despite obvious Lutheran hostility toward them, some Reformed leaders worked to promote understanding as a means to obtain unity with the Lutherans. Perhaps no one was more energetic in this pursuit than Philippe du Plessis-Mornay (1549–1623), the most prominent and influential Huguenot at that time. This adviser to the king of Navarre, who would become French monarch Henry IV (r. 1589–1610), desired a comprehensive Protestant union of international scope, and to that end, he tried to convince the Lutherans that Reformed Protestants agreed with them in all essential matters. Mornay's efforts failed, as the Germans rebuffed his appeals by insisting on Huguenot subscription to the Formula of Concord as the price for their agreement. The formal Huguenot response appeared in A Harmony of the Confessions of the

Orthodox and Reformed Churches, the composition of which Calvin's successor Theodore Beza (1519–1605) was the supervisor. The Harmony includes the Augsburg Confession and the territorial confessions of Saxony and Würtemberg and affirms Reformed concurrence with them, while offering friendship to the Lutherans of Germany. The preface to the Harmony expresses a lament that other Protestant churches were not supporting their persecuted brethren in France, while urging the Lutherans to reconsider their disavowal of the Reformed faith. When Germany became engulfed in the Thirty Years' War (1618–48), Calvinists expressed sympathy for their "Lutheran brethren," but even that did not evoke a positive response.

Although the Formula of Concord accomplished much for Lutheran unity, it did so, in part, by depicting the Reformed churches as dangerous competitors, enemies rather than allies against Rome. Lutheran leaders continued to assail their Calvinist counterparts, especially Theodore Beza, for whom they expressed particular disdain. Reformed Protestants were, in that era, much more vigorous than the Lutherans in seeking unity.[3]

A Fraternity of Faith

Unfortunate divisions notwithstanding, in the early phase of the Reformation, relations between Lutherans and Reformed had been more cordial. Martin Luther and John Calvin held each other in high regard, and Calvin and Philipp Melanchthon (1497–1560) maintained a close personal friendship that endured in spite of disagreements between them. Twenty-five years older than Calvin, Luther welcomed the younger Reformer's efforts to promote a resurgence of biblical Christianity. Calvin, in turn, revered Luther as the pioneer of the Reformation to whom he owed a large debt. In a letter to Heinrich Bullinger (1504–75), chief pastor in Zurich, Calvin wrote at a time when the Wittenberg Reformer

3. For a concise and insightful treatment of these matters, see Robert D. Linder, "The French Calvinist Response to the Formula of Concord," *Journal of Ecumenical Studies* 19 (1982): 18–37, an essay from which I have borrowed extensively. See also Theodore G. Tappert et al., eds., *The Book of Concord* (Philadelphia: Fortress Press, 1959), 486.

had recently expressed disdain for other Protestants who did not endorse some of his ideas. Calvin's moderation contrasts sharply with Luther's invective. He wrote:

> Of this I do earnestly desire to put you in mind, that you would consider how eminent a man Luther is, with what strength of mind and resolute constancy, with how great skill, with what efficiency and power of doctrinal statement, he hath hitherto devoted his whole energy to overthrow the reign of Antichrist, and at the same time to diffuse far and near the doctrine of salvation.... Even though he were to call me a devil, I should still nonetheless hold him in such honor that I must acknowledge him to be an illustrious servant of God. But while he is endued with rare and excellent virtues, he labours at the same time under serious faults. Would that he had rather studied to curb this restless, uneasy temperament which is apt to boil over in every direction.[4]

It is worthy of note that this tribute to Luther appeared only two years before he died, a time when he had become irascible and therefore difficult to placate. Calvin nevertheless admonished Bullinger to "consider ... that you have to do with a most distinguished servant of Christ to whom we, all of us, are largely indebted." He urged Bullinger against disputing with Luther, for that would benefit only enemies of the Reformation.[5] Calvin, in fact, criticized other Reformers who did not share his admiration for Luther. It is no exaggeration to call John Calvin "Luther's best disciple,"[6] yet the Reformer of Geneva reserved the right to differ with his mentor and to express disapproval for some of Luther's actions, his bombastic and often acidic polemics especially. Calvin too engaged in strident polemics at times, but he was more reserved and temperate than Luther where other Protestants were concerned. Calvin perceived correctly that unrestrained attacks on fellow evangelicals would benefit no one but enemies of the Reformation.

4. Calvin to Bullinger, November 25, 1544, in *Selected Works of John Calvin: Tracts and Letters*, ed. Henry Beveridge and Jules Bonnet, 7 vols. (1858; repr., Grand Rapids: Baker, 1987), 4:433.

5. Ibid., 4:433–34.

6. David C. Steinmetz, "Luther and Calvin on Church and Tradition," *Michigan Germanic Studies* 10 (1984): 99.

Luther became aware of Calvin's work as a Reformer by 1539 when, in a letter to Martin Bucer (1491–1551), Reformer of Strasbourg, the Wittenberg professor expressed delight at reading one of Calvin's defenses against the papal church. The book Luther had in mind appears to have been the *Reply to Sadoleto*, which Calvin composed while in Strasbourg, after being forced to leave Geneva in 1538. The absence of Calvin from Geneva prompted Jacopo Cardinal Sadoleto (1477–1547) to appeal to the magistrates there to restore Catholicism in the city-state, and no one there was competent to answer the learned papal scholar, so the rulers turned to the Reformer they had recently banished. Calvin then produced an effective rebuttal, one that Luther applauded.[7]

A short time before Calvin's *Reply to Sadoleto* appeared, Luther had issued *On the Councils and the Church*, so he was pleased that Calvin too had assailed the claims of the papacy, thereby making himself an effective ally in the cause of reformation.[8] A comparison of these two treatises shows the great affinity between the authors. Both contended that they were not innovators, and both cited inconsistencies in conciliar pronouncements and referenced ancient fathers of the church in support of their doctrine, while they insisted on the supremacy of Scripture over councils and fathers.[9]

The two Reformers did not aspire to abolish traditions per se, only those that conflicted with Scripture. Calvin, in particular, contended that Protestants were not schismatics but true Catholics who loved the true church. To Sadoleto he explained, "With this church we deny that we have any disagreement. Nay, rather, as we revere her as our mother, so we desire to remain in her bosom."[10] Neither Luther nor Calvin was content to surrender the name *Catholic* to Rome.

7. Texts of Sadoleto's appeal and Calvin's response appear together in John C. Olin, ed., *John Calvin and Jacopo Sadoleto: A Reformation Debate* (1966; repr., Grand Rapids: Baker, 1976); Luther's letter of October 14, 1539 is in *Luther's Works*, vol. 50, ed. and trans. Gottfried G. Krodel (Philadelphia: Fortress Press, 1975), 187–91.

8. Martin Luther, "On the Councils and the Church," in *Luther's Works*, vol. 41, trans. Charles M. Jacobs and Eric W. Gritsch (Philadelphia: Fortress Press, 1966), 3–178.

9. Calvin, *Reply to Sadoleto*, 92; Steinmetz, "Luther and Calvin," 101–5.

10. Calvin, *Reply to Sadoleto*, 62.

Luther read Calvin's answer to Sadoleto while traveling to Weimar to meet Philipp Melanchthon. Luther's approval of Calvin's *Reply* appears also in a letter sent by Marcus Crodel, a teacher in Torgau, to Calvin on March 6, 1545.[11] Luther himself, writing to Martin Bucer in 1539, expressed satisfaction with Calvin's apologetic against Sadoleto.[12] About that same time (fall 1539), Melanchthon indicated that both Luther and Bucer rejoiced about Calvin's defense of the Reformation.[13]

Early in the development of Protestant thinking about the sacraments, Calvin had expressed reservations about Luther's doctrine of the real and bodily presence of Christ in the Lord's Supper, an issue about which Luther was especially sensitive. This might have led to a hostile relationship between the two leading Reformers, and Luther related to Bucer his wish that Calvin would reconsider his attitude toward the teaching at Wittenberg. That no animosity did develop is a tribute to the patience with which each treated the other, while the two theologians studied the matter and maintained a relationship of mutual respect. Complaints about Calvin's teaching on the Eucharist came more from Lutheran professors than from Luther himself.

A Costly Contention

By 1529, which was before John Calvin embraced the Protestant faith, diverse understandings of the Eucharist had become intense to the point that they threatened to divide the evangelicals at a time when the survival of the Reformation appeared to demand unity. To avoid a permanent rupture, Martin Luther met with Huldrych Zwingli (1484–1531), the original Reformer in Zurich, at Marburg Castle. The Swiss scholar had aroused Luther by advocating the view that the Lord's Supper is only a memorial meal, one in which there is no special presence of Christ. Broad agreement on other doctrines could not compensate for disagreement

11. B. A. Gerrish, *The Old Protestantism and the New* (London: T&T Clark, 1982), 285n31, quotes the full documentation.

12. Wilhelm H. Neuser, "Calvin and Luther," Hervormde Teologiese Studies 38 (1982): 90, quotes the text of Luther's letter.

13. Ibid., 90–91.

about this one, and when the colloquy disbanded, Luther and Zwingli separated, never to reunite. Thereafter Lutheran leaders came to regard Zwingli's view as the position of the Reformed churches at large, one they deemed no more acceptable than that of the detested Anabaptists. Lutherans did not, at that point, realize that Zwingli's doctrine would soon lose credibility among Reformed Christians, as Calvin's teaching superseded it.

Although Luther had expressed dismay about Calvin's rejection of his belief in the bodily presence of Christ in the Supper, he learned eventually that Calvin stood closer to his teaching than to that of Zwingli. By about 1533 Calvin had renounced the view of the elements in the Eucharist as "bare signs," the concept prevalent in Zurich. He found the concept of the real presence more convincing, although he did not endorse belief in a bodily presence. When this came to Luther's attention, he praised Calvin's view as contrasted with that of Zwingli and his disciples. In 1540 John Calvin set forth his understanding of this sacrament in a *Short Treatise on the Supper of Our Lord*, a work that a book merchant in Wittenberg brought to Luther's attention. That great Reformer read it with much interest and concluded that if the Zurichers had read it earlier, disputes about the sacrament could have been avoided.[14]

Luther had good reason to acknowledge Calvin's contribution, for it displays the Genevan Reformer's high regard for the sacraments that includes a categorical denial of a merely memorial significance assigned to the Supper. On the contrary, Calvin held that in the Eucharist believers receive nourishment for their souls, since the sacrament testifies to the finished work of Christ at Calvary and provides a means for continuing communion with the Savior. This assertion reflects its author's belief in the real but *spiritual* presence of Christ in the Supper.[15]

14. The text of Calvin's treatise is in Calvin, *Selected Works*, 2:163–98; see also Gerrish, *Old Protestantism and New*, 287n53.

15. John Calvin, *Institutes of the Christian Religion*, trans. and annotated Ford Lewis Battles (1975; repr., Grand Rapids: Eerdmans, 1989), 102–23. This is the first edition of the *Institutes* from 1536. Cf. the final edition of 1559: the Library of Christian Classics edition, ed. John T. McNeill, trans. Ford Lewis Battles (Lexington: Westminster/John Knox Press, 1960), 4.18.2–3. All subsequent references to the *Institutes* are from this edition.

Calvin adopted Luther's view of a sacrament as a sign that God has annexed to his gospel promises. The Reformer of Geneva may have read Luther's treatise *The Babylonian Captivity of the Church* (1520). Both theologians saw the sacraments as signs to confirm the Word of promise, whereas Zwingli, like the Anabaptists, regarded the sacraments as ways to confess the faith. Calvin seemed to combine the teachings of Luther and Zwingli when he defined a sacrament as "a testimony of divine grace toward us, confirmed by an outward sign, with mutual attestation of our piety toward him."[16] Since the sacraments proclaim the gospel, the Word of God makes them efficacious. The Supper confirms the gospel truth that Christ died for his people; as a pictorial representation of the atonement, it nourishes believers' souls.[17]

Exactly how this occurs, Calvin admitted, is a mystery beyond comprehension. He nevertheless insisted that the Holy Spirit makes Christ truly present to believers who commune with him, receiving his body and blood in the Supper. In these words the Reformer asserted:

> The substance of our doctrine is that the flesh of Christ is vivifying bread, because when we are united to it by faith, it nourishes and feeds our souls . . . in a spiritual manner only because the bond of this sacred union is the secret and incomprehensible virtue of the Holy Spirit.[18]

Abundant evidence shows that John Calvin believed in the real presence of Christ in the Eucharist and was therefore closer to the teaching of Luther than to that of Zwingli. While in Strasbourg (1538–41), he enjoyed fine relations with the Lutherans, perhaps because he, more than any other Protestant leader, maintained fidelity to Luther's position on almost all major doctrines. As pastor of a French refugee congregation in Strasbourg, Calvin ministered to people who espoused Luther's understanding of the gospel, and while in that position he joined with Martin Bucer and Philipp Melanchthon in

---

16. *Institutes*, 4.14.1. For a helpful analysis of Calvin's understanding of the sacraments, see B. A. Gerrish, *Grace and Gratitude* (1993; repr., Eugene, OR: Wipf and Stock, 2002).

17. *Institutes*, 4.18.1–3.

18. Calvin, *Selected Works*, 2:374.

representing the evangelical cause at colloquies with papal theologians. German Lutherans in attendance regarded him as one of their own persuasion. At one such meeting in Worms (1540), Calvin joined a delegation from the Lutheran state of Lueneberg. He had not gone to Worms to promote a sectarian position but to advocate the cause of reformation.[19]

With considerably more zeal than Luther displayed, Calvin earnestly sought the unity of the Protestant cause. This became especially evident as he demonstrated goodwill toward Lutherans suspicious of his sacramental theology. Even though his own doctrine of the real presence was not identical with the teaching at Wittenberg, both Luther and Melanchthon appreciated Calvin's contributions to the Reformation. Calvin hoped to obtain agreement between Wittenberg and the Swiss Protestants, but Luther showed little interest in that matter.

As an expression of sincere desire for evangelical unity, John Calvin endorsed the Augsburg Confession, the statement Melanchthon presented to Holy Roman Emperor Charles V (r. 1519–56) and the Imperial Diet in 1530. When, in 1536, Martin Luther and Martin Bucer agreed to the Wittenberg Concord, with its affirmation of the real presence within a sacramental union, Calvin rejoiced and subscribed. It is clear that he believed this was a sufficient basis to cement a bond among the Protestants of Wittenberg, the South German states, and the Swiss—a hope destined to be dashed by future disputes.

The death of Zwingli in 1531 seemed to open possibilities for improved pan-Protestant relations, but his successor Heinrich Bullinger was, at first, reluctant to concede anything to the Lutherans. Calvin, however, saw an opening to promote Protestant ecumenism and so moved to obtain an agreement between Zurich and Geneva, an effort that led to the Consensus of Zurich (1549). This drew Swiss Protestants together but made further progress with the Lutherans almost impossible. Calvin misunderstood the Lutherans by thinking the Consensus would convince them that Reformed Christians were sound in their doctrine of the Supper. Most Lutherans, however, regarded the agreement in Zurich as an

---

19. Excellent coverage of this matter appears in Willem Nijenhuis, *Ecclesia Reformata: Studies on the Reformation*, 2 vols. (Leiden: Brill, 1972), 1:97–114.

unwarranted compromise with Zwinglian doctrine. Thereafter Calvin lost all credibility with strict Lutherans. His vigorous affirmations of Luther's theology in general and his subscription to the Augsburg Confession availed little, and his hope that Melanchthon would endorse the Consensus of Zurich was disappointed. His Wittenberg friend refrained and began moving away from Luther's doctrine of the bondage of the will, much to Calvin's dismay.[20]

Luther had been dead three years when the Swiss concluded the Consensus, and Calvin keenly felt the loss, for he believed that all major assertions in the Augsburg Confession and the Consensus were harmonious. He thought, had Luther lived, agreement could have occurred. Instead, the heirs of Luther, minus Melanchthon, launched recurrent tirades against the Swiss, the doctrine of the Lord's Supper being the principal item of contention. Joachim Westphal (1510–74) became the major antagonist of the Reformed faith, as he spoke for a faction known as *gnesio-Lutherans*, that is, original Lutherans, defenders of true Lutheran doctrine.

Building on some items critical of the Swiss that Luther had written in 1544, Westphal, in 1552, began assailing the Reformed community in general and Calvin in particular. He realized that Calvin's view of the Eucharist had influenced Melanchthon and his followers, so purging the Lutheran churches of that doctrine was his passion. Melanchthon had aggravated the gnesio-Lutherans when, after Luther died, he began referring to Calvin as *the theologian*.

Calvin responded to Westphal's tirades, still trying to show that there was no fundamental disparity between the Augsburg Confession and the Consensus of Zurich, but to no avail. Calvin did hold that the Augsburg Confession was vague and imprecise in places, and he blamed that defect for some of the issues dividing evangelicals. He insisted nevertheless that the Lutheran and Reformed positions were compatible where cardinal doctrines of the faith were concerned, and he urged recognition of those principles as the basis for fellowship and unity. Because he cherished unity, Calvin warned against intemperate expressions, but Westphal would not be deterred by appeals for civility.

20. Ibid., 2:48–72.

Philipp Melanchthon's failure to support his efforts at conciliation was a particular disappointment for Calvin. The 1544 revision of the Augsburg Confession, known as the *Variata*, had pleased Calvin because he thought it expressed a view of the Eucharist much like his own. Melanchthon's timidity, when confronted with stern criticisms from gnesio-Lutherans, grieved his Swiss friend deeply. Calvin therefore expressed his dismay in a letter to Melanchthon dated August 27, 1554. It is irenic in tone and contains touching affirmations of affection while indicating its author's distress because of his friend's failure to declare his support against those who assailed the Reformed churches.[21]

Although Melanchthon hesitated to take a stand, Westphal's attacks continued and became increasingly vituperative. Calvin greatly lamented the estrangement from the Lutherans because of what he thought was a matter that did not warrant it.[22] Luther and Calvin had agreed that the Eucharist is a gift of grace, not just a means to profess faith, and together they maintained belief in the real presence of Christ, although they differed about the nature of that presence. To Westphal, earlier cordial relations between the two Reformers did not matter. He chose to indict Calvin and the Reformed churches because they denied the ubiquity of Christ's humanity, and because they insisted that only people with faith in the Savior receive the body and blood with the sacrament. All of Calvin's protestations notwithstanding, Westphal branded his doctrine of the Supper as Anabaptist, and the Formula of Concord decried the Reformed position even though Reformed statements of faith in that era incorporated some Lutheran elements.[23]

A Concord in Christ

Although lamentable divisions shattered Protestant unity, the essential concord between Martin Luther and John Calvin remains a matter

21. Calvin, *Selected Works*, 6:61–63.
22. *Institutes*, 4.17.33; Calvin, *Concerning Scandals*, trans. John Fraser (Grand Rapids: Eerdmans, 1978), 80–83.
23. Formula of Concord, no. 7 in *Book of Concord*, 481–86; Joseph N. Tylenda, "The Calvin-Westphal Exchange: The Genesis of Calvin's Treatises against Westphal," *CTJ* 9 (1974): 182–209, is a thorough treatment of this subject; Calvin's "Last Admonition to Joachim Westphal" appears in his *Selected Works: Tracts and Letters*, 2:346–494.

of record. Both Reformers subscribed heartily to the ancient ecumenical creeds and so regarded themselves and each other as exponents of the genuine Catholic faith. *Sola Scriptura*, the formal principle of the Reformation, was the foundation for all they believed and espoused, and both referred often to the writings of St. Augustine (354–430) to show that their doctrines were not innovations but reaffirmations of truth proclaimed tenaciously by that Doctor of Grace, as he had become known.

Because of his stature as the pioneer of the Reformation, Martin Luther received due applause for his courageous stand against false doctrine and in support of the gospel of grace. Early Protestant authors frequently hailed him as the restorer of real Christianity, even a prophet comparable to biblical spokesmen of God's Word. This understandable adulation no doubt encouraged such confidence in Luther's teaching that any deviation from it aroused profound suspicion among his disciples. Luther himself, however, did not expect absolute concurrence with his position, as his relations with Calvin attest. To move from a Lutheran to a Reformed affiliation was not necessarily to abandon the great theologian of Wittenberg.

The experience of Prince Frederick III (r. 1559–76), the ruler of Palatine, illustrates this well. When, in 1560, he adopted the Reformed faith, he denied having rejected the Augsburg Confession, and he continued to hail Luther, while arguing that some Lutherans had distorted that Reformer's teaching. The prince scolded people who assumed that Luther was immune to error. Reformed theologians from Palatine echoed their ruler's confidence in Luther but denied that he had brought the restoration of biblical Christianity to completion. When Hohenzollern Prince John Sigismund (r. 1608–20) embraced Calvinism, he allowed both evangelical churches to operate in Brandenburg, although he cherished the eventual triumph of the Reformed Church, a development that he believed would complete the work Luther had begun. Pastors and scholars who supported their princes' efforts regarded themselves as disciples of Luther carrying forward the reform he had initiated, and at times they accused Lutherans of adulterating their founder's actual teaching, as, they contended, the Formula of Concord had done. Along with Calvin, his heirs desired the preservation of Luther's achievements while avoiding excessive veneration that could thwart the consistent application of his principle *sola Scriptura*. They professed to continue the work of reformation without renouncing or underappreciating Luther's immense contributions. The Lutheran reaction was, one must regret, overwhelmingly negative, and often Calvinists encountered the complaint that they had deformed the principles of the Augsburg Confession.[24]

Whatever their heirs may have said about one another, Luther and Calvin must be regarded as comrades engaged in a common cause. When Calvin composed the first edition of the *Institutes of the Christian Religion* (1536), he followed Luther's Large Catechism, a Latin translation of which had appeared in 1529. When he explained his objections to the Roman Mass, the Reformer of Geneva drew from Luther's earlier polemic *The Babylonian Captivity of the Church* (1520). Both authors denied that the Mass is a means to secure forgiveness of sins, and both maintained that Christ is the perfect Priest and that no earthly professional priesthood continues, so the Mass insults the finished work of Christ. To Luther and Calvin, the Eucharist is a *sacrament*, not a *sacrifice*, and when Christians receive the sacrament, they do not do something for God, but God, in conferring his grace, does something for them. The only sacrifice remaining to be rendered is one of praise as an act of faith.[25]

Perhaps more than in any other area of doctrine, the Reformers of Wittenberg and Geneva stood together in their understanding of sin and salvation. They affirmed categorically the depravity of human nature because of the fall, and both rejected all synergistic and semi-Pelagian views of salvation. In dealing with the human condition, Luther and Calvin published major treatises that assert *sola gratia* in unequivocal terms. In 1525 Luther responded to Desiderius Erasmus (1466–1536), when that prince of humanists attacked him for contending that the sinfulness of mankind extends to a paralysis of the will. In *De Servo*

24. An excellent analysis of Lutheran-Reformed relations in Brandenburg comes from Bodo Nischan, "Reformation or Deformation? Lutheran and Reformed Views of Martin Luther," in *Pietas et Societas: New Trends in Reformation Social History*, ed. Kyle Sessions and Philip Bebb (Kirksville, MO: Sixteenth Century Journal Publishers, 1988), 203–15.

25. *Institutes*, 4.18.1–3; Luther, "The Babylonian Captivity of the Church," trans. A. T. W. Steinhauser, Frederick C. Ahrens, and Abdel R. Weitz, in *Luther's Works*, 36:66; cf. Herman J. Selderhuis, "Luther *Totus Noster est*: The Reception of Luther's Thought at the Heidelberg Theology Faculty," *Mid-America Journal of Theology* 17 (2006): 101–19.

Arbitrio Luther, in language more forceful than Calvin would use in addressing the same topic, contended that original sin has permeated every facet of human nature so that no faculty has escaped its debilitating effects, and that means the intellect and the will are in bondage to sin. The Wittenberg theologian rebutted Erasmus effectively and in the process produced the most emphatic and powerful exposition of that fundamental Christian doctrine. In doing this Luther inspired others to write in defense of *sola gratia* in general and divine sovereignty over salvation in particular.[26]

As Luther replied to Erasmus, so Calvin defended the same principle against Albertus Pighius (c. 1490–1542), a papal official who represented the Vatican at theological discussions with Protestant leaders at Worms and Regensburg in 1540 and 1541. Pighius showed inflexible opposition to evangelical teachings in such discussions, and thereafter he wrote polemics against them. Calvin, whom he appears to have met at Worms, became one of his targets, as the Catholic scholar defended papal authority against all its detractors. In accord with Christian tradition, Pighius acknowledged the reality of original sin but maintained that it did not produce the corruption of human nature, as Augustine and other early Catholic thinkers had claimed, and as all Protestant scholars insisted. His arguments in favor of free will eventually led Calvin, in 1543, to issue a rebuttal entitled *The Bondage and Liberation of the Will*. In refuting the charges of his critic, John Calvin aligned himself with Martin Luther, whose earlier work on the will he defended against the complaints of Pighius. The Reformer of Geneva cited his Wittenberg colleague as a most

> distinguished apostle of Christ whose labor and ministry have done most in these times to bring back the purity of the Gospel; . . . that teaching which is the chief issue in this controversy, we defend today just as it was put forward by Luther and others at the beginning.[27]

26. Martin Luther, The *Bondage of the Will*, trans. J. I. Packer and O. R. Johnston (Westwood, NJ: Fleming H. Revell, 1957). For an analysis of Luther's view, see James Edward McGoldrick, "Luther's Doctrine of Predestination," *Reformation and Revival* 8 (1999): 81–103.

27. John Calvin, *The Bondage and Liberation of the Will*, ed. A. N. S. Lane, trans. Graham I. Davies (1996; repr., Grand Rapids: Baker, 2002), 28–29. For additional evidence of Calvin's

In the course of his reply to Pighius, Calvin did not hesitate to identify himself as a Lutheran.

Closely connected with the doctrine of human depravity and the loss of genuine free will is the condition of human minds since the fall, the *noetic* effects of sin. In assessing this matter, Luther and Calvin concurred heartily. Luther's description is especially graphic and compelling:

> Sin has so blinded human nature that it no longer knows the Creator. . . . Man does not know even his own sin and thinks his blindness is the highest wisdom. If only Adam had not sinned, men would have recognized God in all creatures, would have loved and praised Him so that even in the smallest blossom they would have seen and pondered his power, grace, and wisdom. . . . These things [the beauties of nature] would have turned the mind of Adam and his kin to honor God and laud and praise Him and to enjoy His creatures with gratitude.[28]

Calvin's position on this subject is almost identical with that of Luther, as the following excerpt from the *Institutes* reveals:

> All parts of the soul were possessed by sin after Adam deserted the fountain of righteousness. For not only did a lower appetite seduce him, but unspeakable impiety occupied the very citadel of his mind, and pride penetrated to the depths of his heart . . . [so] none of the soul remains pure or untouched by that mortal disease; . . . the mind is given over to blindness and the heart to depravity.[29]

As one perceptive interpreter has remarked, when commenting about Luther's Large Catechism, "Calvin's understanding of man and his place in the world might almost be said to provide a theological exegesis of this matchless confession of Luther's faith."[30] That conclusion applies equally well when one compares the writings of these Reformers that

---

support for Luther, see Doede Nauta, "Calvin and Luther," *Free University Quarterly* 2 (1952–53): 1–17.

28. Quoted in translation by David Steinmetz, *Luther in Context* (Bloomington, IN: Indiana University Press, 1986), 24–25.

29. *Institutes*, 2.1.9.

30. Gerrish, *Old Protestantism and New*, 150.

pertain to the condition of human minds after the fall. Both scholars understood the noetic effects of sin and so cited the warped condition of the intellect as responsible for the way in which people deceive themselves about ultimate realities. So grave are the noetic effects of sin that humans are unable to perceive their own interests correctly. Lacking the proper knowledge of God, they fail to understand their own condition and, as a consequence, remain content with their own depravity and alienation from their Creator.[31]

In 1539, in a letter to Guillaume Farel, John Calvin reported receiving word from Philipp Melanchthon affirming that Luther and Johann Bugenhagen (1485–1556), a highly regarded scholar at the University of Wittenberg, wished him to extend warm greetings to Calvin. As Melanchthon stated, "Calvin has acquired great favor in their eyes."[32] Luther and Bugenhagen had good reason to express confidence in their French colleague, since they labored in the same cause, sought the same goals, and proclaimed the same message.

Although some scholars have magnified the differences between the Reformers of Wittenberg and Geneva, on all matters of cardinal importance the two agreed. Nowhere is this more evident than in their mutual understanding of justification *sola fide*, through faith alone. Luther considered this truth the article by which the church would stand or fall. In a doctrinal statement he prepared for the Smalkaldic League of Evangelical States in 1537, Luther wrote of justification *sola fide*:

> On this article rests all that we teach and practice.... Therefore, we must be ... certain and have no doubt about it. Otherwise all is lost, and the pope, the devil, and all our adversaries will gain the victory.[33]

Calvin readily concurred with Luther and considered the biblical doctrine of justification "the main hinge on which religion turns."[34] Both

31. Paul Helm, "John Calvin and the *Sensus Divinitatis* and the Noetic Effects of Sin," *International Journal for Philosophy of Religion* 43 (1998): 87–107, covers this matter well.
32. Calvin to Farel, November 4, 1539, in *Selected Works: Tracts and Letters*, 4:167.
33. Luther, "Smalkald Articles," in *Book of Concord*, 292.
34. *Institutes*, 3.11.1.

Reformers regarded this doctrine as indispensable to the gospel. In Calvin's words, it is "the foundation on which to establish ... salvation, on which to build piety toward God." Justification "consists in the remission of sins and the imputation of Christ's righteousness."[35] This concurs exactly with Luther's view of justification as a once-for-all adjudication of God by which he declares believing sinners righteous before the bar of his justice, as he imputes the perfect righteousness of Christ to them.[36] These Reformers maintained that theirs was the only understanding of justification that glorifies God, so they denounced the common scholastic teaching that asserted justification through faith plus works of merit. As Luther expressed this, "human nature, corrupt and blinded by the blemish of original sin, is not able to imagine or conceive of any justification above and beyond works."[37] In Calvin's view, the contention about justification then raging was "the principal point of contention we have with the papists."[38]

Neither Luther nor Calvin would have had any patience with modern interpreters who deny that justification necessarily includes the imputation of Christ's righteousness to needy sinners. Both Reformers identified *sola fide* as the heart of the gospel, and both scorned synergism and emphasized mankind's sinful inability to merit God's favor. In their view, imputed righteousness, received through faith, is the sole means of justification. As Luther stated this idea, justification "is accomplished by imputation on account of the faith by which I take hold of Christ."[39] Proclaiming this truth is the central feature of worship, so Lutheran and Reformed churches elevated their pulpits to show the supremacy of God's Word. God confers the gift of faith in conjunction with the

35. Ibid., 3.11.2.
36. Martin Luther, "The Disputation Concerning Justification 1536," trans. Lewis W. Spitz, in *Luther's Works* (Philadelphia: Muhlenberg Press, 1960), 34:151ff.
37. Ibid., 34:151.
38. *Institutes*, 3.19.11n14.
39. Martin Luther, "Lectures on Galatians 1535," trans. Jaroslav Pelikan, in *Luther's Works* (St. Louis: Concordia Publishing House, 1963), 26:232. To see how their doctrine of justification influenced the preaching of these great theologians, see David J. Lose, "Luther and Calvin on Preaching to the Human Condition," *Lutheran Quarterly* 10 (1996): 281–318; Mark Beach, "The Real Presence of Christ in the Preaching of the Gospel," *Mid-American Journal of Theology* 10 (1999): 77–134.

proclamation of his Word, so preaching is the essential outward means to impart inward grace.[40]

Rather than seeking nuances or differences in emphasis between Martin Luther and John Calvin on justification, it would be well to recognize their full concurrence about this truth. As one modern observer has appropriately remarked, "Reformation teaching spoke with one voice on justification. On nothing were all the reformers more agreed."[41]

Contrary to the contentions of Roman Catholic leaders in the sixteenth century and modern critics of *sola fide*, Luther and Calvin vigorously rejected the complaint that their teaching encouraged moral laxity and indifference toward good works. They concurred in declaring that the freedom that comes with the reception of Christ through justifying faith leads to genuine piety expressed in obedience to God's will. As Luther had affirmed in his treatise The *Freedom of a Christian* (1520),[42] Calvin declared that "those who seriously fear God will enjoy the incomparable benefit of this doctrine." This truth prompts believers "to zeal for holiness and innocence."[43] Like Luther, Calvin taught that freedom from the condemnation of the law obtained through justification leads to eager obedience to the will of God.

Conclusion

Much to the dismay of John Calvin, his affection for Martin Luther as a comrade in Christ and his adherence to almost all of the German Reformer's teaching did not prevent serious and sometimes acrimonious divisions among Protestants. Perhaps Calvin underestimated the significance of those few items of belief on which the theologians of Wittenberg and Geneva disagreed. The role of divine law in the Christian life, for example, became a subject of spirited debate between leaders of the two major branches of continental Protestantism, as did the permissibility to

40. Ibid., 117.
41. M. Eugene Osterhaven, *The Faith of the Church* (Grand Rapids: Eerdmans, 1982), 106.
42. Martin Luther, "The Freedom of a Christian," trans. W. A. Lambert and Harold J. Grimm, in *Luther's Works* (Philadelphia: Muhlenberg Press, 1957), 31:327–77.
43. *Institutes*, 3.19.2.

conduct religious ceremonies that Scripture does not mandate. In such matters Calvin was more tolerant than the Lutheran theologians who succeeded to leadership of their churches after Luther died. As was the case with differences about the Lord's Supper, contention became common and sometimes hostile as other issues appeared.

Calvin's concern for Protestant unity led him to decry disputes and the divisions they were producing, and once, in an expression of his chagrin, he wrote, "O God of grace, what pleasant sport and pastime do we afford to the papists, as if we hired ourselves to do their work."[44] To show the sincerity of his desire for unity, the Reformer tolerated Lutheran rites of which he did not approve, and he sought an international conference of Protestant leaders to seek accord on issues dividing them. To that end he solicited cooperation from Philipp Melanchthon, Heinrich Bullinger, and Anglican Archbishop Thomas Cranmer (1489–1556). Calvin proposed formulating a confession acceptable to all churches of the Reformation. It was a painful disappointment when the death of Protestant King Edward VI (r. 1547–53) and the subsequent execution of Archbishop Cranmer at the hands of Bloody Mary (r. 1553–58) ended prospects for such a conclave in England.[45]

Although some interpreters have cited the differing positions of Luther and Calvin on the role of divine law in the Christian life, there is reason to conclude that they have exaggerated the discrepancy between the Reformers' respective views.[46] The third or didactic use of God's moral law was of great importance to Calvin, less to Luther. The latter did not, however, want to discard the law. Rather, he held that in ideal circumstances Christians should not need the law because their love for God would prompt them to do his will without legal instructions. Luther knew, however, that circumstances in this sinful world are far from ideal, so believers need God's law after all. To assist them in understanding their moral obligations, he composed his Small and Large Catechisms, major portions of which expound the Ten Commandments. In practice, then, Luther did recognize the need for the law in Christian living, so there was

---

44. Calvin to Melanchthon, January 21, 1545, in *Selected Works: Tracts and Letters*, 4:438.

45. Calvin to Cranmer, April 1552, in ibid., 5:345–48.

46. See Lose, "Luther and Calvin on Preaching to the Human Condition."

no essential discrepancy between his view and that of Calvin, who gave the law greater prominence.[47] On the function of the law to expose and condemn sin and to restrain evildoers, so that civil society may endure, there was absolutely no difference in the teachings of these two Reformers. Luther and Calvin agreed that the law impels people to resort to the Christ of the gospel, which they do when by faith they obtain acceptance with God *sola gratia*. Both theologians denied that faith has an inherent power to justify. It is rather, as Calvin put it, "a kind of vessel" to receive the righteousness of Christ.[48]

Although Luther emphasized justification primarily and Calvin sanctification, they agreed about both phases of salvation. Luther faced legalists who extolled salvation by works of merit, while Calvin contended with antinomians who made the doctrine of grace an excuse for their libertine behavior. The diverse challenges in Germany and Switzerland led the Reformers to emphasize doctrines pertinent to those particular errors. Calvin, as a consequence, stressed the didactic use of the law as a means to promote sanctification, while Luther emphasized the role of the law that exposes sin and human helplessness to achieve salvation.

In addressing the human condition and mankind's urgent need for forgiveness and reconciliation with God, the Reformers of Wittenberg and Geneva were united in the conviction that God's Word and his Holy Spirit work together to bring lost sinners to Christ. Although Scripture is God's Word and therefore imbued with divine power and authority, only people regenerated by the Holy Spirit will accept it in faith and respond positively to its proclamations. Calvin expressed this well when he asserted that faith receives the truth of Scripture only when that is "both revealed to our minds and sealed upon our hearts through the Holy Spirit."[49] Luther was no less emphatic in maintaining the necessity for the Spirit's operation to make the Word efficacious.[50] There was no fundamental disagreement between these theologians concerning the

47. Luther, "Lectures on Galatians 1535," 222–25.
48. *Institutes*, 3.11.7.
49. Ibid., 3.2.7; Neuser, "Calvin and Luther," 96–99.
50. A thorough study of Luther's understanding about the relationship between the Word and the Spirit is the work of Regin Prenter, *Spiritus Creator*, trans. John M. Jensen (Philadelphia: Muhlenberg Press, 1953), esp. chap. 2.

relationship of the Word and the Spirit. Both men were able expositors of Scripture, men of articulate ability and literary skill, who relied on the Holy Spirit to make their ministry of the Word effective.

Martin Luther and John Calvin, the most influential theologians of the Reformation, were united in their love for the truth of *sola gratia*, *sola fide*. They knew themselves to be unworthy recipients of divine favor through sovereign election, and they were painfully aware of the continuing presence of sin in their own lives and in those of all other Christians. They therefore called for daily repentance because the goal of the Christian life is perfection to be achieved only in eternity. As Luther declared in the first of his Ninety-five Theses, "when our Lord and Master Jesus Christ said 'repent,' he willed that everyday in the life of a Christian be one of repentance."[51]

Although Luther and Calvin lived in different countries and spoke different languages, and had very different backgrounds, they, by God's grace, arrived at substantially the same understanding of the gospel. Disagreements between them were few, and when they did occur, they did not lead to ruptured relations. Mutual appreciation bound them together, as they labored for the cause of Christ, even though their systems of theology were not identical. The heirs of the Reformation, orthodox Lutherans and Calvinists, would do well to compare the works of their sixteenth-century mentors with a view toward realizing the immense body of doctrine they hold in common and to appreciate one another as Luther and Calvin did. Organic union between Lutherans and Calvinists may not be possible or even necessary, but the two bodies of Christians have good reason, as did the Reformers, to consider each other comrades in Christ.

---

51. Martin Luther, "The Ninety-five Theses," trans. C. M. Jacobs and Harold J. Grimm, in *Luther's Works*, 31:17. For an examination of Calvin's view of repentance, see T. H. L. Parker, *Calvin: An Introduction to His Thought* (Louisville: John Knox Press, 1995), 85–88.

PART 2

CALVIN'S TOPICS

10

THE CATHOLICITY OF
CALVIN'S THEOLOGY

DOUGLAS F. KELLY

W hat, if any, was the controlling center of the theology of
John Calvin? Was his thought the servant of any one major
principle? Did he seek to fit everything into some sort of
systematic schema? That will be the question we hope to answer here.

Under the influence of some of the nineteenth-century German historians of dogma, it was long popular to seek for one controlling idea in
Calvin's theology. Usually it was said to be predestination or the sovereignty of God, whereas the controlling principle of Martin Luther was
said to be the concept of justification by faith.[1] Thus, various magisterial

---

1. E.g., F. C. Baur, *Lehrbuch der christlichen Dogmengeschichte* (1847). Reinhold Seeberg,
however, rendered a much more balanced account of the fullness of Calvin's theology in his
Lehrbuch der Dogmengeschichte (Erlangen: A. Deicherische Verlagsbuchhandlung Wermer
Scholl, 1920), Band 4, 2 Halfte, 551–643. The same theological balance in his summary of
Calvin is the case with George Park Fisher of Yale in his *History of Christian Doctrine* (New
York: Charles Scribner's Sons, 1896), 298–309.

theologians were looked at more as philosophers than as theologians. They supposedly worked with one central concept, and organized their thought around it (as, for instance, Friedrich Schleiermacher's "feeling of dependence on God"). The central idea was a sort of Procrustean bed into which all the other material content had to be fitted, whether by stretching or cutting off (like the mythological monster who killed his guests in this gruesome fashion)!

But as early as 1919, the great Calvin scholar Paul Wernle redressed the balance by stating: "It cannot be over-emphasized: faith in predestination is a long way from being the centre of Calvinism; much rather is it the last consequence of faith in the grace of Christ in the presence of the enigmas of experience."[2] And in 1950, François Wendel, with careful scholarship, showed that predestination was not the controlling factor in Calvin's theology.[3]

After an adult lifetime of reading Calvin, I suggest that instead of some kind of philosophical or religious central principle, Calvin's theological work must finally be characterized as catholic. By *catholic* I simply mean that he was seeking to expound the fullness of the entire Word of God to his people (and to the reading public). To do so, one must appropriate the whole of Old Testament history, and see how it is summed up in Christ, Lord of all nations, and, through his gospel, offered to all of them. As Ford Lewis Battles said of Calvin, "his theology defies ultimate systematization: it is a salvation-history faith; it must be told as the story of Israel, narrowly begun in the Old Testament, but in Christ embracing all nations."[4]

If the observation is correct that Calvin's theology has no controlling or systematizing principle, then what was he doing in his huge corpus of writings? It seems to me that Calvin was primarily a biblical theologian, not a philosopher seeking to construct a new system of thought on any sort of central principle. He was first a Christian humanist (in the sixteenth-

2. Paul Wernle, *Der evangelische Glaube nach den Hauptschriften der Reformatoren*, vol. 3, *Johann Calvin* (Tübingen, 1919), 403.

3. François Wendel, *Calvin: Origins and Development of His Religious Thought*, trans. Philip Mairet (New York: Harper & Row, 1963), 263–84.

4. John Calvin, *Institutes of the Christian Religion*, 1536 ed., trans. and ann. Ford Lewis Battles (Atlanta: John Knox Press, 1975), 24.

century sense of that word), who desired the reform and renewal of the church in France. By age twenty-seven, he was called to a doctrinal (and then pastoral) ministry in the church in Geneva, which had opted for the Reformation in various actions between 1533 and 1536. Although Calvin was expelled from Geneva in 1538 for three years, until he accepted the invitation of the Town Councils to return as head pastor in 1541, he carried on his biblical studies, lecturing, writing, and above all preaching in Strasbourg, his place of exile. After his return to Geneva, he would continue in this primarily biblical and pastoral work with unremitting toil until the end of his days in 1564.

As we will see, through all these years of labor, Calvin's goal was the restoration of the church to its ancient catholic form. Before we look at how he accomplished this massive task, let us first consider the propriety of employing the word *catholic* to convey the sense of "fully biblical."

The Word *Catholic* as Totality of Scriptural Truth

Although the word *catholic* is not itself in the Bible (though the idea is), we find it employed in AD 325 in the Nicene Creed: "I believe in one holy, catholic and apostolic church." And nearly a century before that, it was used by St. Cyprian.[5] What did it mean?

Let us refer to some Reformed scholars in France and Switzerland, whose work shows that in its most basic meaning, *catholic* does not primarily denote a particular religious denomination (such as, most notably, *Roman Catholic Church*), but rather the wholeness and integrity of scriptural truth. Pierre Courthial, the French Reformed minister and scholar, and former dean of the Reformed Seminary at Aix-en-Provence, has explained this primary meaning of catholicity with clarity:

> *Catholic* does not refer simply and primarily to spatial and temporal universality. This expression refers above all to the confession by the Church of God of the integrality of the scriptural truth. For the Greek word *katholikos*, which signifies literally "according to the whole," speaks above everything else to a qualitative totality:

5. Cyprian, *On the Unity of the Catholic Church* (AD 251).

191

"according to the whole of normative revelation, which is for the Church, the Holy Scriptures."

To be *catholic* is to respect the inseparable whole of the text of Scripture, in the adoration of the One who is its primary and sovereign author. It is to refuse "to choose" some part of Scripture; it is to refuse heresy (in Greek, *airesis* means a choice; from the verb *airetizo*: in the aorist it is *heretisa*). Hence *sola scriptura* (meaning that the norm for the church is only Scripture) must be accompanied by *tota scriptura* (thus, the norm for the church is Scripture in its totality). The opposite word to *catholic* is *heretical*.[6]

Pierre Courthial drew upon the thought of Swiss Reformed scholar and pastor Richard Paquier, who in 1935 wrote *Vers la Catholicite Evangelique*.[7] Paquier stated:

To have the spirit of catholicity is to desire to be complete, and not unilateral; to live with an integral Christianity, and not a truncated one; a universal and not a sectarian one. To be catholic is to affirm God entirely, the Scriptures entirely, the church entirely, the "cosmos" entirely. It is to believe in God as transcendent *and* immanent, Principal *and* Energy, in God Three and One, Father, Son and Spirit. It is to confess Christ as God *and* man; not only as the prophet, or the priest; not exclusively as either man or God; not exclusively as either a moral example or the mystical indweller of the soul [of the redeemed]; not exclusively as either the Saviour or the Judge. It is to recognize the Old Testament *and* the New Testament, and the latter in its entirety: the synoptics and John, Paul and James. It is to be in communion with the Church of all ages, and not to begin the history of the church with the Reformation, or on the contrary, to stop the life of the church in its medieval period. It is to be in communion with the Church on earth *and* the Church in heaven, with the church triumphant as well as militant. It is to recognize in the sacraments and the worship the harmonious unity of spiritual and corporal reality, of nature and spirit, of this world

6. Pierre Courthial, *Le jour des petits recommencements* (Lausanne: L'Age d'Homme, 1998), 133.
7. Richard Paquier, *Vers la Catholicite Evangelique*, Cathier no. 6 (Lausanne: Eglise et Liturgie, 1935).

and the other one. *Catholicity is that attribute of Christianity that means complete, total, integral.*[8]

And yet many of you may be feeling that this definition of *catholic* is a very arcane one—or, even worse, a sort of sleight of hand to keep it from saying what everybody knows it really means: the Roman Catholic communion. If so, let me ask you to consider carefully how Pierre Courthial responds:

> For the umpteenth time, with strong determination, I must insist (in spite of the frequent confusion of our dictionaries and every-day usage) that to identify "catholic" with "Roman Catholic" is a grave error, and that to translate "catholic" by "universal" is another grave error, for it is a serious and unacceptable reductionism.
>
> The Greek word *katholikos* puts together the words *kata* (according to) and *'olos* (the whole). If, in a quantitative sense, catholic could mean as much universal (according to spatial wholeness) as well as perpetual (according to temporal wholeness), then to speak of the Catholic Church, for instance, or the Catholic Faith, would be thereby to speak of the universality of the Church or of the Faith; that is, of their perpetuity. But this is neither the most important issue, nor the most essential one.
>
> It is the qualitative sense which is the most primary, principial and profound. Certainly the qualitative sense of catholic carries along with it the quantitative characteristics of universal space and time, but its truest and foundational qualitative significance is ACCORDING TO THE WHOLE OF THE REVEALED TRUTH; "according to the whole" of the sacred text of the Covenant; the *Bible* of Israel *and* the written tradition of the *Apostles.*
>
> The Reformed confessors or reformed Catholics of the 16th and 17th centuries desired to be and understood themselves to be so thoroughly catholic...that the original 1566 French edition of the beautiful Second Helvetic Confession had the long title: "CONFESSION and simple exposition of the true Faith and *catholic* articles of the pure Christian religion, drawn up by common accord by the ministers of the Church of Jesus Christ, who are in Switzerland ... brought into light in order to witness to all the faithful that they persist in the unity of the true

8. Ibid., 8.

193

and ancient Catholic Church, and that they are not planters of any new or erroneous doctrine, and consequently that they also have nothing in common with either sects or heresies of whatever sort. Therefore they now publish this Confession of Faith with the express purpose that all men who fear God may be able to judge."[9]

Courthial goes on to note that the two central "catholic" dogmas held by all truly orthodox Christians of various denominations and continents are the Holy Trinity and the hypostatic union of the two natures in the one person of Christ, as these have been defined by the first six ecumenical (or "catholic") councils from the fourth to the seventh centuries.[10]

The great Dutch Calvinist theologian Herman Bavinck conveys essentially the same point about "catholicity" of the church:

And finally, there is the characteristic of catholicity or universality which belongs to the church. This characteristic appears by name first of all in a post-apostolic piece of writing, and the intention was to declare that, over against all kinds of heresy and schism the true church is the one which obeys the bishop and remains with the main body since the whole, universal church is the one in which Christ is. Later all kinds of other explanations were attached to the name; people came to understand by it that the church is spread out over the whole world, that from the beginning to the present day it includes all believers of all time, and that sharing as it does in all truth and grace, it is an adequate means of salvation for all. These explanations are not mistaken, if only in thinking of the church one does not think merely of one ecclesiastical organization, the Roman Catholic one, for example, but takes it to refer to the Christian church which reveals itself in all the churches together and in very differing degrees of purity and soundness. For that church is in very fact a catholic church.[11]

It is this conveying of the everlasting gospel to all people at all times that so motivated the sixteenth-century Reformation, which had caught

9. Pierre Courthial, *De Bible en Bible*, Messages (Lausanne: L'Age D'Homme, 2002), 12–13.

10. Ibid., 14.

11. Herman Bavinck, *Our Reasonable Faith: A Survey of Christian Doctrine*, trans. Henry Zylstra (Grand Rapids: Baker, 1977), 526.

a new vision of it as they were taken hold of by the Spirit of Christ, and in line with which they sought the renewing grace of God in their almost desperate study of his written Word. Luther's world-changing stand at the Diet of Worms ("I can do no other; my conscience is bound to the Word of God") as well as his almost liturgical response to Roman Catholic charges of heresy and novelty ("Es steht geschrieben") certainly prepared the way for Calvin to base all of his life and teaching on the Word of God written.

Calvin, both in his youth and in old age, believed that he would find the true catholic faith in its integrity and power in the whole of the Scriptures, and so he devoted his active and laborious life to study and to exposition of the whole Word of God written. By this way alone could a corrupted church be renewed, and so he gave himself wholeheartedly to this task.

Details of Calvin's Theological Catholicity

Let us examine how Calvin sought to work this out by considering three points: (1) the background of Calvin's catholicity; (2) how Calvin's catholicity led him into the Protestant Reformation; and (3) how Calvin expresses catholicity in his theology.

The Background of Calvin's Catholicity

All competent biographies of Calvin show that within a few years after he began his formal higher education in Paris (he arrived there at the College de la Marche in 1523 at age fourteen), he came into contact with the thinking and some of the personalities of the Christian humanist movement, led by such famous scholars as Erasmus and Lefevre d'Etaples. These scholars, who were part of the Christian side of the late Renaissance, followed Erasmus in his call to return *ad fontes*, and hence used the best resources of the Renaissance scholarship in studying the Old Testament in its original Hebrew and the New Testament in its original Greek, as well as a more pure Latinity, along with a careful sense of historical context and cultural development since the New Testament. At the time Calvin came into contact with them, these men—unlike Luther, who was on the European scene by 1520—stayed within the Roman Catholic Church, and were seeking to purify its corruption and superstition by taking it down to its original roots, especially in Holy Scripture and in the church fathers of the first five or six centuries.

It was from these reforming Catholic humanists of France (though Erasmus was all-European) that Calvin got his theological bearings by his late teens and early twenties. What started as a medieval scholastic education for the young John Calvin, especially at the College du Montaigu, soon turned into channels of the French Catholic humanism that was earnestly seeking to reform the church. These reformist contacts became important especially after Calvin began the study of law at the Universities of Bourges and Orléans (by 1528). During Calvin's second period of study in Paris (1531–33), he studied at the newly founded "Northern Renaissance"[12] College Royale, where he would have learned more of Erasmus and Lefevre from the royal readers, such as Guillaume Budé, Nicholas Cop, Pierre Danes, and Francois Vatable (whom the traditionalist, anti-reform scholastic theologians of the Sorbonne vainly hoped to put out of business).

During this second period in Paris, Calvin wrote his first book: a commentary on Seneca's *De Clementia*. Alexandre Ganoczy, a Roman Catholic theologian and a leading Calvin scholar, who assesses Calvin's work carefully and fairly, says about that first book: "It bears the mark of Erasmian moralism and exalts providence 'which excludes chance and directs princes.'"[13] François Wendel in his study of the young Calvin notes about this work: "Calvin's humanism is evident in his method properly so called. In his *Commentary* he shows a remarkable knowledge of classical antiquity and a hardly less accurate knowledge of the Fathers of the Church. St. Augustine, whose *City of God* he had lately read, is mentioned fifteen times. But Calvin had also read Erasmus, Budé, Laurent Valla and a number of other French and Italian humanists, of whom he did not spare his praises . . ."[14]

12. In the "Northern" European Renaissance, literary studies were based on classical sources, using Renaissance-type grammars, word lists, and so forth, but in a definitely Christian context, as contrasted with the rather more pagan context of the "Southern" (Italian) Renaissance.

13. Alexandre Ganoczy, *The Young Calvin*, trans. David Foxgrover and Wade Provo (Philadelphia: Westminster Press, 1987), 74.

14. Wendel, *Calvin: Origins and Development*, 31.

Wendel goes on to explain what he means by Calvin's Renaissance humanist methodology:

> Like Budé, Calvin begins with a rather long philological explanation, he appeals to grammar and logic, he points out the figures of rhetoric, draws upon his knowledge of antiquity to collect parallel quotations from other ancient writers . . . Calvin . . . after his conversion applied [this method] to the Scriptures themselves . . . True, Valla had already employed the humanist method in his *Annotations upon the New Testament* and Erasmus was following him along that path: but it was Calvin who first made it the very basis of his exegesis and in doing so founded the modern science of exegetics.[15]

The exact time of John Calvin's conversion from the scholarly humanist reformism of Erasmus, Lefevre, Bishop Briconnet, and others to what came to be called the Protestant Reformation (then usually termed *Lutheranism*) has been much disputed, and I will not enter into the debate. Certainly this "sudden conversion" (as Calvin speaks of it in his introduction to his *Commentary on the Psalms*) must have taken place either shortly before the rectoral address at the Sorbonne of his friend Nicholas Cop on November 1, 1533, or fairly soon thereafter. Some have thought that Calvin himself wrote this address, but this is probably not the case (although he copied it out by hand).

In this address on the eight beatitudes from the Gospel of Matthew, Cop affirms that "the Christian philosophy" is based on the belief that sins are forgiven by the grace of God alone, that Christ is the one intercessor before the Father. In the language of Luther, the gospel is opposed to the law, and God rewards the faithful "by grace alone" and not because of our merits. He attacks the hard-line theologians, "those corrupt sophists," and states: "we believe that man is justified by faith apart from the works of the law."

Alexandre Ganoczy comments:

> To the Catholic theologian of today, nothing would appear heterodox about the proclamation. The author certainly quotes entire passages of

15. Ibid.

Luther, but the passages contain what is essentially Catholic doctrine. J. Lortz, L. Bouyer, and Hans Kung have shown that "by faith alone," and above all "by grace alone" are not in themselves anti-Catholic principles; on the contrary, they can express authentic Catholic doctrine.[16]

Ganoczy accurately describes the fierce reaction of the Sorbonne theologians (who were backed by the police power of the French state):

> The speech set off a massive reaction by the Faculty, who were charged with defending Catholic dogma. Following his profession of reformist faith, an indictment for heresy was issued against Cop, and some of his friends were arrested. Calvin was one of Cop's friends . . . Colladon relates that as a friend of Cop, Calvin was also sought out. Calvin was warned of the danger in time and fled from his Paris dwelling. They searched his room and confiscated his papers and correspondence. It was the first time that the future reformer learned at his own expense the cost of persecution.[17]

How Calvin's Catholicity Led Him into the Protestant Reformation

Calvin knew and made use of Martin Luther's 1520 *Babylonian Captivity of the Church* (as in Calvin's first [1536] edition of the *Institutes of the Christian Religion*, particularly in the chapters on "The Five False Sacraments and on Christian Liberty"). *Babylonian Captivity* argues that medieval Romanism had departed from the true and original Catholic faith, and that reformation was necessary to return to the integrity of the Christian tradition on the basis of the teaching of the Holy Scriptures, which clearly negate "papist innovations." Ganoczy frequently points out that Calvin opposed "papistry," not true Catholicism:[18]

> How profoundly positive and sacred to the reformer was the adjective "catholic." The epithet "Protestant" is not found anywhere in his work in the confessional sense we use it today. In rare cases when Calvin uses it, he applies it to the group of *German* Lutherans who sided with the

16. Ganoczy, *The Young Calvin*, 82.
17. Ibid., 82–83.
18. Ibid., 9.

princes and the cities that protested against the religious policies of the
emperor, such as the Diet of Speyer in 1529. The context of these passages is not confessional but *political and religious*. Besides, the term that
is generally opposed to *protestantes* is never *catholici* but—and this is
significant—*pontifici*.[19]

Calvin's principle in terms of which he criticized the corrupt Roman
church of his time was to bring it under the light of the Holy Scriptures.
He was not like the still-popular stereotype of the narrow Protestant. That
is, he did *not* assume that nearly everything that had been believed and
practiced before 1517 was incorrect, and therefore needed to be written
off as "catholic" or papist. Ganoczy summarizes Calvin's real position:

> Calvin does not criticize "tradition" as much as "customs" and "constitu-
> tions" which are based only on their antiquity or on a human "consensus."
> The reformer demands that they be carefully examined to learn if they
> conform to the Word of God or not. This rule is valid for all doctrines
> and all ecclesiastical authorities; neither councils, pastors, nor popes are
> exempt from it.[20]

Or to put it another way:

> Calvin's plan for upholding "true religion" is quite clear. Both the faithful
> individual and the community should obediently submit to the "rules"
> of the Bible, return to and remain within its limits, content themselves
> with what is essential, and renounce all superfluous and superstitious
> extras in order to give themselves with fear and love to the worship of
> God in spirit and in truth.[21]

Calvin had as his criterion conformity with the Scriptures. Antiquity
alone was not enough. Nor was universality. Thus Calvin rejects much
traditional doctrine, because he judged that it lacked foundation in the
sacred texts. He scornfully labels as "novelties" those doctrines which
contradict the source of revelation and the teaching of the Fathers which

19. Ibid., 44.
20. Ibid., 192–93.
21. Ibid., 207.

are faithful to the Scriptures. Statements concerning the five "false sacra-ments" especially fall into this category.[22]

Thus, Calvin did not wish to reform the church because it was too catholic. On the contrary, he believed that it had profoundly departed from its true catholicity in the Middle Ages. It, in fact, was not catholic enough, because it had departed from the Scriptures and from the best in the church fathers.

This is made clear in his famous response to the Epistle of Cardinal Sadoleto, who had written to Geneva while Calvin was exiled to Stras-bourg (1538–41). The cardinal exhorted reformed Geneva to return to the Roman fold in order to avoid being schismatics and heretics. Calvin, from his enforced exile in Strasbourg, responded on behalf of the Geneva that had put him out. In doing so, he opposed the Word of God to "human inventions." "He gives a veritable summary of Luther's criticism of evil pastors, superstitions, the improper worship of saints, the sacrifice of the Mass, the sacrificial priesthood, and especially jus-tification by works."[23]

Calvin shows Sadoleto that it is the Reformers who wish to have the ancient Catholic Church restored:

> Not only do we agree more clearly with antiquity than all of you, but we ask for nothing else than that the ancient face of the Church may sometime be restored. . . . I beg you to consider and place before your eyes the ancient state of the Church as it was among the Greeks at the time of Chrysostom and Basil, and among the Latins at the time of Cyprian, Ambrose, and Augustine. . . . Then contemplate the ruins that remain about you.[24]

Calvin argues that "the pope and his faction" are themselves responsible for having ruined and "almost destroyed" the church.[25] Calvin concludes his answer to Sadoleto this way:

22. Ibid., 211–12.
23. Ibid., 256.
24. OS, 1.466.
25. Ibid.

And now, O Lord, what else remains for a miserable man like me, other than to offer to you for our defense a plea that you not call me to judgment for that horrible defection from your Word, from which you delivered me once and for all by your wonderful kindness.[26]

As Bernard Cottret shows:

Calvin describe[s] the true believer in Jesus Christ, pure and fearing God, who flees from Roman rites. He is a "Christian," pure and simple. Similarly, his adversary is not defined as "Catholic"; Calvin is content with the adjective "papal."[27]

In Calvin's thirty-eighth sermon on *The Harmony of the Three Gospels*, he expands this point:

We know that the Scriptures were villainously corrupted, and the Pharisees above all introduced the custom of glossing holy Scripture . . . And it was a principle in that sect, as it is today in the papacy, that one must not simply stop at the holy Scriptures but also have the tradition of the Fathers, and that all that was required for salvation was not in the Law or in the Prophets . . . In short, the corruption that existed in Judea and that reigned at the coming of our Lord Jesus Christ was entirely similar to that which exists today in the papacy. For what do we principally debate about with the papists? If they would grant us this article, that all our wisdom is contained in the holy Scriptures and that God taught us enough about his will there, and that it is not lawful to add or remove anything whatever, it is certain that we would soon settle all the differences by which the world is now so much troubled.[28]

How Calvin Expresses Catholicity in His Theology

In a word, Calvin believed that the corrupted papal church could be restored to its true catholic heritage only by a profound and fresh submission to the totality of the Word of God. He who as a young student in the late

26. Ibid., 1.486.
27. Bernard Cottret, *Calvin: A Biography*, trans. M. Wallace McDonald (Grand Rapids: Eerdmans, 2000), 286.
28. CO, 46, cols. 471–72.

French Renaissance had been so allured by the beauty of the rediscovered classical literary inheritance was now subject to a higher power, to a trans-forming Word that by means of the gospel had brought the true Catholic Church into being. That scriptural Word alone could now restore it.

Hence he writes in the *Institutes*:

> Now this power which is peculiar to Scripture is clear from the fact that of human writings, however artfully polished, there is none capable of affecting us at all comparably. Read Demosthenes or Cicero; read Plato, Aristotle or any other of that class. You will, I admit, feel wonderfully allured, delighted, moved, enchanted. But turn from them to the reading of the sacred volume and whether you will it or not, it will so powerfully affect you, so pierce your heart, so work its way into your very marrow, that compared with the impression so produced, the power of the orators and philosophers will almost disappear; making it clear that the Holy Scriptures breathe something divine, which lifts them far above all the gifts and graces of human industry.[29]

As Calvin understood the task lying before him, a corrupted church could be reconstructed into newness of life only by bringing it back to the wholeness of the Word of God. Ronald S. Wallace describes this superhuman task well:

> Calvin thought of himself in relation to the Church as an architect of reconstruction. In the letter dedicating his *Commentary on Isaiah* to King Edward VI he described the state of the Church. It had become like the ruined temple of God, utterly deformed, having lost all the glory of the early centuries of its life. But God had begun to raise it up so that men might begin again to see the beauty and glory of the former outline, and Calvin describes himself as one of the many inconsiderable persons selected by God "as architects to promote the work of pure doctrine" [C.L., October, 1541]. In his important letter to the King of Poland, he refers again to his call "to build up the Church now lying deformed among the ruins of Popery" [C.L. to King of Poland, 1554].[30]

29. *Institutes*, 1.8.1.
30. Ronald S. Wallace, *Calvin, Geneva, and the Reformation* (Edinburgh: Scottish Academic Press, 1988), 133–34.

This deformation of the church was not because it was catholic, but because the papacy had cut it off from the pure Scriptures. As Bouwsma states it (quoting Calvin's twelfth sermon on 2 Samuel): "The worst exercise of this [spiritual] tyranny, for Calvin, was the claim of the papacy to dominion over Scripture itself, a blasphemous and diabolical assertion that undermined confidence in the promise of the Gospel."[31] Bouwsma adds:

> The substitution of domination for learning in the church had trivialized the Gospel. Sermons, Calvin charged, consisted of "little but old wives' tales and fictions, all equally frivolous." The schools "resounded with brawling questions, but Scripture was seldom mentioned."[32]

In his chapter on "A Comparison of the False and the True Church" (4.2.1 of the 1559 edition of the *Institutes*), Calvin directly connects the existence of the true church with the listening to the voice of her shepherd through the Word of God:

> [We ought not to grant] ... that the church exists where God's Word is not found. For this is the abiding mark with which our Lord has sealed his own: "Everyone who is of the truth hears my voice" [John 18:37]. Likewise: "I am the Good Shepherd; I know my sheep, and they know me" [John 10:14]. "My sheep hear my voice, and I know them, and they follow me" [John 10:27].... Paul reminds us that the church was founded not upon men's judgments, not upon priesthoods, but upon the teaching of apostles and prophets [Eph. 2:20].... To sum up, since the Church is Christ's Kingdom, and he reigns by his Word alone, will it not be clear to any man that those are lying words [cf. Jer. 7:4] by which the Kingdom of Christ is imagined to exist apart from his scepter (that is, his most holy Word)?

Calvin then goes on to quote St. Cyprian, "who following Paul, derives the source of concord of the entire church from Christ's episcopate alone." Calvin summarizes Cyprian's teaching, which was as needed in the sixteenth century as ever: "We see how he continually calls us back to the

---

31. William J. Bouwsma, *John Calvin: A Sixteenth Century Portrait* (New York and Oxford: Oxford University Press, 1988), 60.
32. Ibid., 61, quoting *Institutes*, 3.5.1.

Head himself. Accordingly, Cyprian declares that heresies and schisms arise because men return not to the Source of truth, seek not the Head, keep not to the teaching of the Heavenly Master."[33]

Calvin believed that the Roman church of his time had lost its catholicity because the papal system had intruded its power structures between the people and the voice of the Lord speaking in Scripture. Thus he says: "The power of the church, therefore, is not infinite but subject to the Lord's Word and, as it were, enclosed within it."[34] He explains that "[the Lord] willed to have his Word set down and sealed in writing, that his priests might seek from it what to teach the people, and that every doctrine to be taught should conform to that rule. Therefore, after the law has been published, the priests are bidden to teach 'from the mouth of the Lord' [Mal. 2:7]. This means that they should teach nothing strange or foreign to that doctrine which God included in the law; indeed, it was unlawful for them to add to it or take away from it [Deut. 4:2; 13:1]."[35]

Later, in discussing "Councils and Their Authority," he writes:

> If one seeks in Scripture what the authority of councils is, there exists no clearer promise than in this statement of Christ's: "Where two or three are gathered together in my name, there I am in the midst of them" [Matt. 18:20] ... Christ promises nothing except to those who are gathered in his name ... I deny that they are gathered in his name who [cast] aside God's commandment that forbids anything to be added or taken away from his Word [Deut. 4:2; cf. Deut. 12:32; Prov. 30:6; Rev. 22:18–19] ... who, not content with the oracles of Scripture, that is, the sole rule of perfect wisdom, concoct some novelty out of their own heads.[36]

Calvin held that valid church councils (and he definitely held to the first four ecumenical councils as authoritative)[37] are to be followed on

33. *Institutes*, 4.2.6.
34. Ibid., 4.8.4.
35. Ibid., 4.8.6.
36. Ibid., 4.9.2.
37. As in his letter to Mme. de Beze of February 6 (probably 1562), quoted in *Calvin's Ecclesiastical Advice*, trans. Mary Beaty and Benjamin W. Farley (Edinburgh: T&T Clark,

these grounds: "Now it is Christ's right to preside over all councils and to have no man share his dignity. But I say that he presides only when the whole assembly is governed by his word and Spirit."[38] It will come as no surprise to students of Calvin's theology that he holds the risen Christ as still presiding over the affairs of his church on earth through his Word and Spirit. This is a worldview precisely the contrary to that of deism, which dualistically separates heaven and earth. It is, in fact, the worldview of passages such as Ephesians 4 and elsewhere.

All of these considerations prepare the way for us to survey Calvin's theological work. He was above all else a man of the Word, for he believed that only Christ, the head of the church, speaking in all of his Word, could cleanse and guide his church to be what he had raised her up to be: Christ's reflected light to the nations; the channel of living water and of the bread of life; the place of spiritual resurrection for the dead, where the sons and daughters of Adam are "born again, not of corruptible seed, but of incorruptible, by the word of God, which liveth and abideth for ever" (1 Peter 1:23).[39]

Calvin believed that the risen Christ speaks through his Word in transforming power, and so from his early doctrinal ministry, he understood himself to have been gifted and called to instruct students of the Bible in effectively discerning God's truth conveyed through it. This is evident in his famous *Prefatory Address to King Francis I of France* (which stood as the introduction to all editions of his *Institutes* from 1536 to 1559). He tells the king:

> My purpose was solely to transmit certain rudiments by which those who are touched with any zeal for religion might be shaped to true godliness. And I undertook this labor especially for our French countrymen, very many of who I knew to be hungering and thirsting for Christ . . . The book itself witnesses that this was my intention, adapted as it is to a simple and, you may say, elementary form of teaching . . .[40]

1991), 75. See also Anthony N. S. Lane, *John Calvin: Student of the Church Fathers* (Grand Rapids: Baker, 1999), 39–40.

38. *Institutes*, 4.9.1.

39. All quotations from the Bible in this chapter are from the KJV.

40. Ibid., "Prefatory Address" (Battles ed.), 9.

Wendel relays an even fuller explanation of Calvin's purposes in composing his *Institutes*, by quoting from the second [Latin] edition of 1539:

> My purpose has been so to prepare and instruct those who wish to give themselves to the study of theology that they may have easy access to the reading of the Holy Scriptures, make good progress in the understanding of it, and keep to the good and straight path without stumbling. For I think I have so understood the whole of the Christian religion in all its parts, and have summarized it in such order, that whoever has rightly understood the form of instruction that I have followed will easily be able to judge and resolve for himself what he should seek in the Scriptures and to what end he must relate the purpose of the same. And yet in sooth there is no need that in my *Commentaries*, where I expound the books of Holy Scripture, I should enter into long disputations upon the matters dealt with there, seeing that the present book is a general address in guidance of those who wish to be helped.[41]

Calvin's vision was that the fullness of the Scriptures is necessary to restore the church, and so he writes: "All things that pertain to Christianity are comprehended and prescribed in the Scriptures."[42] That is the case because through the Scriptures, Christ, the head of the church, directly speaks and reforms, as accompanied by his Holy Spirit. Ganoczy notes that Calvin "demands that every element in the practical organization of the life of the Church be in harmony with Scripture and manifest the absolute total dominion of Christ over his people."[43]

In the organization and content of the first edition of the *Institutes*, we find the young Calvin following a traditional catholic catechetical program. That is, it is largely based on Martin Luther's Small Catechism (1529), which had followed the ancient model of "teaching young Christians the elements of the Christian Faith. [It] commonly consisted of instruction on the Apostle's Creed, the Ten Commandments and the Lord's Prayer."[44]

41. Wendel, *Calvin: Origins and Development*, 146–47.
42. *OS*, 1.166.
43. Ganoczy, *The Young Calvin*, 222.
44. T. H. L. Parker, *Calvin: An Introduction to His Thought* (Louisville: Westminster/ John Knox Press, 1995), 4–5.

This arrangement was very traditional in the Western catholic tradition. Thomas Aquinas had followed it in his *Compendium of Theology* (1273), as had Augustine in his *Enchiridion* (421). Calvin in following this schema identifies himself with the best in the catholic tradition. To these, T. H. L. Parker notes, "was added in the Reformation period teaching on the Sacraments."[45] A final chapter was added by Calvin on Christian liberty, the authority of the church, and political authority. Thus we find six chapters in the 1536 edition:

I. Concerning the law, which expounds the Decalogue.

II. Concerning Faith, in which the Apostle's Creed is explained.

III. On Prayer, in which the Lord's Prayer is commented upon.

IV. Concerning the sacraments, in which Baptism and the Lord's Supper are dealt with.

V. Of the five other sacraments which are not really sacraments although they have hitherto commonly been considered such, and what they are.

VI. Concerning Christian liberty, of the power of the Church and civil government.[46]

Although Calvin in this first major theological work has clearly followed the traditional catechetical program, he is already going in a different direction from Luther on the "Law,"[47] and in his chapters on the "Sacraments" goes in a somewhat different direction from both Luther and Huldrych Zwingli (though he is closer to Luther). And as Battles points out, the chapter on "Faith" "affords the clue to Calvin's Christological differences from the Lutherans."[48] His chapter on the "Five False Sacraments" owes much to Luther's *Babylonian Captivity*, and it no less severely criticizes the innovations of medieval papistry, which led the church away from its original catholic tradition.

It is not possible in this essay to chart the growth and changes in arrangement and emphasis of the many editions of the *Institutes* that

45. Ibid.

46. Jean Cadier, *The Man God Mastered*, trans. O. R. Johnson (London: Inter-Varsity Fellowship, 1964), 65.

47. *Institutes* (Battles ed.), xliii.

48. Ibid., xlv.

occurred between the second edition in 1539 and the final one in 1559. The McNeill/Battles edition and English translation of that final Latin summary of Calvin's theology has superb notes and textual markings showing the development of the various stages of this incredibly influential work:

> By the time of the final, definitive edition of the *Institutes* (1559), the work had grown from a small to a very large book, and from six to eighty chapters. The organizing principle for this edition was simply the Apostle's Creed, and as it contains four major articles—God, Christ, Holy Spirit, Church—so Calvin divided the work into four corresponding books. He regarded this structure as especially adequate for the purpose of doctrinal instruction.[49]

Particularly book 4 (*The Church*) after establishing the highest view of the church as "our mother," whom it is necessary to have if God is our Father,[50] presents it as "catholic" or "universal" because there could not be two or three churches unless Christ be torn asunder (cf. 1 Cor. 1:13), which cannot happen.[51] Then Calvin devotes long passages to assailing the unbiblical innovations of the medieval papacy that obscured the gospel and took the church far from its original catholic foundation. This fourth book shows that it is Calvin's desire to call the Roman communion back to its catholicity, not to start a new denomination.

A careful reading of the recently transcribed and published *Registres du Consistoire de Genève au Temps de Calvin*[52] will demonstrate that the Consistory—the ruling body of pastors and lay elders in Geneva—sought to keep the population accountable for essential catholicity, not for a new denominational program or emphasis.[53] That is, the Consistory interrogated the many congregants who appeared before it on Thursday night

---

49. Hugh T. Kerr, ed., *Calvin's Institutes: A New Compend* (Louisville: Westminster/ John Knox Press, 1989), 11.

50. *Institutes*, 4.1.4.

51. Ibid., 4.1.2.

52. *R. Consist.*, vols. 1–3.

53. See Douglas F. Kelly, "Calvin Pasteur, presente par les process-verbaux du Consistoire de Geneve," chap. 3 of *L'Actualite de Jean Calvin 1509–2009*, ed. Jean-Marc Berthoud, Messages (Lausanne: L'Age D'Homme, 2009), 73–109.

in any given week about whether they knew the Lord's Prayer and the Apostles' Creed (or, frequently, *which parts of it*, if any, they could recite). In the three volumes of *Consistory Minutes* that I have studied so far, I find no cases of the Consistory's interrogating congregants on such issues as predestination and divine sovereignty.

In addition to his *Institutes*, which he kept revising for most of his professional life (from 1536 to 1559) and which was intended as a sort of primer to interpreting the Holy Scriptures, Calvin preached constantly, and published commentaries and homilies on most of the books of the entire Bible. In no other way could the church be reformed to its original catholicity than by submitting to the voice of her Lord speaking in all parts of his Word (which would provide wholeness or catholicity).

What did Calvin think his constant preaching of the Word would accomplish? T. H. L. Parker explains it well:

> "The Word of God" meant "the Word that God himself speaks." It was the Word of God that created the universe; that is, God spoke and what he said called into being that which had not been. It was by his Word that God in his free majesty encountered man. "The Word" was a synonym for the Son of God who became man and who lived among men as the living declaration of God's eternal will to man. "The Word" was also the creative utterance of the Word made flesh; his words brought Lazarus again from the dead; his words will judge men at the last day. But then, as the Reformers read the Acts of the Apostles and the epistles, they perceived that the preaching of the apostles and evangelists was also called "the Word of God" or "the Word of the Lord." So that it was necessary to regard the terms "gospel," "preaching" and "Word of God" as synonymous.[54]

Parker describes Calvin's laborious pulpit-work:

> He preached through whole books of the Bible . . . At first he preached, we must assume, twice on Sunday and once on every Monday, Wednesday, and Friday . . . In October 1549, however, sermons were ordered for every day and from now he usually preached on every day of alternate

54. T. H. L. Parker, *John Calvin* (Tring, Herts, UK: Lion Publishing, 1975), 106–7.

weeks as well as twice on Sunday. His custom was to expound the Old Testament on weekdays, the New on Sundays, although sometimes he gave up Sunday afternoon to psalms.[55]

David L. Puckett notes:

Although Calvin preached on most of the Old Testament, many of his sermons were lost in the early nineteenth century. Lost were the sermons on Judges, 1 Kings, much of Lamentations, almost all of the minor prophets, and substantial portions of the Psalms, Isaiah, Jeremiah, Ezekiel, and Daniel. Fortunately, in the case of Calvin's lectures at the academy, no such disaster occurred. All of his known lectures on the Old Testament are extant.[56]

In addition to his preaching, Calvin devoted much of his waking hours to the writing of commentaries on the various books of Holy Scripture. This too was a mode that the Lord could use to restore his church. Calvin composed commentaries on every book of the New Testament, except 2 and 3 John and Revelation.[57] As we have seen, it is probable that Calvin actually preached, lectured, or wrote on every book of the Old Testament, but to refer again to David L. Puckett: "In the Old Testament we are not so fortunate [as to the completeness of his New Testament work]. Missing are expositions of Proverbs, Ecclesiastes, Song, Judges, and 1 Kings."[58]

In other words, a study of his *Institutes* and *Commentaries*, not to mention his *Tracts and Treatises* and voluminous correspondence, will show us that John Calvin was not the man of one controlling idea by which he constructed a new religious synthesis. Not predestination, not divine sovereignty, not even the divine glory is the centerpiece of his theology. Of course, all of these concepts play a part—a very important one—in his thought. But none of them is either a central concept or a controlling idea.

55. Ibid., 108.
56. David L. Puckett, *John Calvin's Exegesis of the Old Testament* (Louisville: Westminster/John Knox Press, 1995), 147.
57. T. H. L. Parker, *Calvin's New Testament Commentaries* (Grand Rapids: Eerdmans, 1971), 25.
58. Puckett, *John Calvin's Exegesis*, 147.

He was the servant of the entire Word of God; thus, his thought was too broad and too vast to subsume it under any one theological category. He simply and painstakingly sought to exegete and to apply (that is, to bring out and make available) the life-transforming truths of God speaking in his Word. He did this in the interests of catholicity, for he believed that the fallen church of God could be restored to its catholic wholeness only by exposing it to the whole Word of God. That is why Calvin's theology was broadly and deeply biblical, without emphasizing one doctrine to the exclusion of the others. As we have already seen from Courthial, "To be *catholic* is to respect the inseparable whole of the text of Scripture ... It is to refuse 'to choose' some part of Scripture; it is to refuse heresy ..."[59]

Bringing every aspect of the church's faith and life back under the entirety of the Scriptures was necessary for her deliverance from the innovations of the papacy and the return to her ancient catholicity. Calvin made this point to Sadoleto:

> You know very well, Sadolet, and if you deny it I shall tell everyone that you have maliciously and cunningly hidden the fact, that not only do we agree more clearly with antiquity than all of you, but we ask for nothing else than that the ancient face of the Church may sometime be restored. Moreover, we want to reestablish completely that which was deformed and stained by unlearned men, after which it has been miserably torn apart and almost destroyed by the pope and his faction.[60]

No doubt it is for reasons of restoring ancient catholicity that Calvin so heavily depended on the fathers of the church. He sought to show that for the most part (though never completely and always imperfectly), the Greek and Latin fathers of the first five centuries, if correctly understood, would support the reforms called for in the sixteenth century, rather than backing the teaching, practices, and pretensions of the papacy. This was certainly the young Calvin's claim at the Disputation of Lausanne in October 1536, at which "Protestant" and Roman Catholic theologians debated in hopes of gaining the support of the Canton of Vaud. There, Calvin argued that the fathers had come far closer to supporting the Reformation than the

---

59. See above under the heading "The Word *Catholic* as Totality of Scriptural Truth."
60. *OS*, 1.466.

papacy. He did so by massive quotation from memory of precise passages of a number of fathers.

As Anthony N. S. Lane notes:

[Calvin] does not simply make remarks about [the fathers] or make sweeping claims about their teaching but he quotes them at length. The power of his memory is evidenced by the detail that he is able to include. As far as he is able from memory, he gives the source of his quotations, including such details as "in the 11th Homily about the middle" and "in Epistle 23 very near the end."[61]

After his remarkable citations from memory of many passages in the fathers (in "The Third Conclusion" of this famous Disputation), he challenges the Roman opponents:

Everyone can easily perceive with what rashness you reproach us as having the ancient doctors against us. If you had only read a few pages of their writings, you would not have been so brave in making such a judgment, not having even seen the covers of their books, as is indicated by what you have just said.[62]

Calvin went so far as to claim that "Augustinus . . . totus noster est."[63] In explaining, for one out of numerous instances, that affliction by the Lord is not a penalty, but fatherly chastisement to instruct us, Calvin states: "In this matter, Augustine is plainly on our side . . ."[64] Calvin cites Augustine as a witness to the necessity and doctrine of the Reformation scores upon scores of times.[65] As Lane summarizes:

Some 60 percent of Calvin's citations are taken from the Western fathers between Nicea and Chalcedon. The bulk of these citations come from

61. Anthony N. S. Lane, *John Calvin: Student of the Church Fathers* (Grand Rapids: Baker, 1999), 27.
62. John Calvin, "La Troisieme Conclusion," in *Les Actes de la Dispute de Lausanne 1536*, ed. Arthur Piaget (Neuchatel: Secretariat de L'Universite, 1928), 228–29.
63. CO, 8.266 (*De predestinatione*).
64. *Institutes*, 3.4.33.
65. See *Institutes* (Battles ed.), vol. 2, "Author and Source Index," 1592–1634, and R. J. Mooi, *Het Kerken Dogmahistorish Element in de Werken van Johannes Calvijn* (Wageningen: H. Veenman, 1962).

Augustine, who alone accounts for almost 45 per cent of the total. Jerome comes a poor second, though ahead of any other father, followed by Ambrose, Hilary and Leo. These fathers are cited for a wide range of topics.[66]

Although Anthony Lane rightly emphasizes the specific influence of particular church fathers on Calvin by means of collating how many times Calvin refers to them (and thus, the preponderance of influence is given to the Western Latin tradition), Thomas F. Torrance has argued for a considerable influence of general theological concepts of some of the Greek fathers on Calvin, even though he quotes them far less often. Torrance especially seeks to demonstrate the influence of Athanasius[67] and Gregory of Nazianzus[68] on his theology. Lane believes that Torrance has not proved his case.[69]

But none would deny that Calvin knows and uses church fathers of both East and West as he calls on his theological opponents in the Roman system to listen to the wholeness of Scripture and to listen to their own church fathers; if so, they could return to true and original catholicity, which they had lost in the high Middle Ages with the rise of the papacy. Yet as Lane correctly writes: "Did the true church cease to exist during the time of medieval darkness? Calvin would not admit that the church had ever ceased to exist. Christ has promised to be with his people to the end (Matthew 28:20) and this guarantees the perpetuity of the church."[70]

For all its deformation and corruption under the papacy, Calvin admitted that there were still "vestiges of the church" within the Roman communion.[71] "However, when we categorically deny to the papists the title of *the* church, we do not for this reason impugn the existence of churches among them . . . In them Christ lies hidden, half buried, the gospel overthrown, piety scattered, the worship of God nearly wiped out . . . I call them churches to the extent that the Lord wonderfully preserves in them

---

66. Lane, *Calvin: Student of the Church Fathers*, 42.

67. Thomas F. Torrance, "Calvin's Doctrine of the Trinity," in *Trinitarian Perspectives: Toward Doctrinal Agreement* (Edinburgh: T&T Clark, 1994), 178.

68. Ibid., 41–76.

69. Lane, *Calvin: Student of the Church Fathers*, 67–86.

70. Ibid., 46.

71. *Institutes*, 4.2.11.

a remnant of his people, however woefully dispersed and scattered, and to the extent that some marks of the church remain . . ."[72]

Calvin especially notes that "the Lord's covenant abode [among them] . . . When [the countries of Christianized Europe] were oppressed by the tyranny of Antichrist, the Lord used two means to keep his covenant inviolable. First, he maintained baptism there, a witness to this covenant; consecrated by his own mouth, it retains its force despite the impiety of men. Secondly, by his own providence he caused other vestiges to remain, that the church might not utterly die."[73]

Yet at the same time, his conviction that at least some true vestiges of the church remained among the papists did not mean that Calvin was willing for those who had recovered the gospel to remain in the Roman communion. In that regard, Calvin viewed the compromise of some Reformed Christians in France with deadly seriousness. In 1544 he wrote *The Excuse of John Calvin to the Nicodemites on the Complaint They Make about His Excessive Harshness*. For various reasons (largely fear), they continued to frequent the Mass, while claiming Reformed convictions.[74] He severely rebukes their compromise:

> What shall I say of those who, after having tasted the gift of God, instead of opposing this insufferable tyranny with all their force as they ought, conceal on the contrary, despite their real opinions, the sad state of the [persecuted] Church. Out of consideration for their reputation or for their wealth they suffer in silence those iniquitous judgments, and they would regard it as dishonour if they were to be the objects of the least suspicion.[75]

By exhorting the fearful French "Nicodemites" to cease attending papal ceremonies, he did not think that he was calling them out of the true Catholic Church. As strongly as Calvin called for Reformed believers in France by the 1540s to break with the papal Mass, still he did not understand himself to have willfully withdrawn from the corrupted remains of the Catholic Church in order to start a new denomination. Instead,

72. Ibid., 4.2.12.
73. Ibid., 4.2.11.
74. CO, 6.589–614.
75. Ibid., 6.598–600, quoted in Cadier, *The Man God Mastered*, 130–31.

Calvin thought that he was reforming and purifying the remnants of the church back to her original catholicity by recalling her to the voice of her Lord and Savior, speaking in the whole Word and dispensing His Spirit to accompany that Word. God's people who had been enlightened needed themselves to take a clear stand for the gospel truth, so that others might see the facts and do so as well. After having paraphrased Cyprian, Calvin concludes (to quote this significant phrase once more): "We see how [the Lord] continually calls us back to the Head himself."[76]

To be truly and fully catholic, that is to say, traditional Christian in the fullest sense of the term, one needs to be truly and passionately submitted to the whole Word of God in all its parts, for there one meets and is transformed by the God who speaks and changes his deformed image-bearers into the beauty of his own likeness, such as we have seen in Jesus Christ. Submission to all parts of the inspired Word transforms human personalities and institutions from brokenness and partial obedience and sectarianism into integral wholeness, or truest catholicity.

Before concluding, let me make a confession. If this essay dealt with the fullness of Calvin's catholicity of thought and full application of Holy Scripture, then, following the word of Richard Paquier, we would need to survey what *catholicity* meant for Calvin in regard to Christ's control of the entire cosmos. Calvin's comments (in his *Commentaries*) on Genesis 1, 2, and 9, Matthew 28, Romans 8:19–23, and 2 Corinthians 10:1–6 are relevant here.[77] We would not be far from what the Eastern Orthodox fathers meant by Christ as *Pantocrator*. Pierre Courthial discusses the biblical wholeness or catholicity of Calvin's theology as applied to the entire created order.[78] The Dutch Calvinist philosopher Herman Dooyeweerd discusses this issue in great detail in his writings on "cosmonomic spheres."[79] This would lead us into important issues

76. *Institutes*, 4.2.6.

77. Jean-Marc Berthoud, "Humanite de Jean Calvin," in *L'Actualite de Jean Calvin 1509–2009*, 29–67.

78. Pierre Courthial, "Une Vision Theocosmonomique," in *De Bible en Bible*, 154–99.

79. Herman Dooyeweerd, *A New Critique of Theoretical Thought*, trans. David H. Freeman, William S. Young, and H. de Jongste, 4 vols. (Philadelphia: Presbyterian and Reformed, 1953–58). See also Herman Dooyeweerd, *A Christian Theory of Social Institutions*, ed. John Witte, trans. Magnus Verbrugge (La Jolla, CA: Herman Dooyeweerd Foundation, 1986).

on the environment and much else, but that is a task for which I am unfortunately not equipped.[80]

In general, we can summarize the entire matter of Calvin's catholicity of theology by noting the connection in Psalm 19 between "The heavens declar[ing] the glory of God" (v. 1), and "The law of the LORD is perfect, converting the soul" (v. 7). The very One who was the agent of creation (John 1:3), and for whose pleasure "all things . . . were created" (Rev. 4:11), is the same One who redeemed it by his blood (Rev. 5:9). The incarnation, holy life, crucifixion, resurrection, and triumph of the eternal Christ are the reason and goal of creation itself, and the purpose and final hope of humankind. He is the One we meet throughout the Word, and to know him is life eternal (John 17:3), and the source of temporal and everlasting transformation (2 Cor. 3:18). To make some contribution to the attaining of this glorious goal for that "multitude that no man can number" was the heart and driving force of the theology of John Calvin.

80. Yet other Calvin scholars are already entering into this pressing subject, such as Calvin Beisner, who devotes a regularly updated Web site to it: "Cornwall Alliance for the Stewardship of Creation."

II

JOHN CALVIN ON SACRED AND SECULAR HISTORY

RICHARD BURNETT

J
ohn Calvin drew a fundamental distinction between sacred and secular history. He was not the first to do so, of course. Theologians from Augustine to Martin Luther had done so for more than a thousand years. Yet the prominence of this distinction in Calvin's work is without parallel among the sixteenth-century Reformers and perhaps without parallel in the history of the Christian church.[1] The phrases *secular history*

---

1. Augustine's *Civitas Dei* is often cited as a major source in the inauguration and establishment of this distinction. R. A. Marcus states: "We must begin an account of Augustine's views on human history with a distinction between 'sacred history' (*Heilsgeschichte*) and secular history. He does not often use such phrases, but the distinction is implicit in all his utterances" ("Augustine: Man in History and Society," in *The Cambridge History of Later Greek and Early Medieval Philosophy*, ed. A. H. Armstrong [London: Cambridge University Press, 1967], 406). See also R. A. Marcus, *Saeculum: History and Society in the Theology of St. Augustine* (Cambridge: Cambridge University Press, 1970), 1–21. Whereas the "distinction is implicit" for Augustine, it is abundantly explicit for Calvin, and far more so than in such Reformers as

and *sacred history* appear hundreds of times in Calvin's writings, especially in his commentaries. It is beyond the scope of this essay to provide an exhaustive discussion of these concepts in Calvin, but it is my aim to try to define them according to Calvin's use, to understand how they relate to each other, and to comprehend their role in Calvin's understanding of the exegetical task. Before pursuing these matters, however, I wish to begin with this question: Why did Calvin draw a distinction between sacred and secular history in the first place?

According to Alan Richardson's book *History Sacred and Profane,* Calvin had no other choice. He was a child of his times, and it never occurred to him to think otherwise. It never dawned on him to question the distinction. This "dual conception of history, which had been gradually evolving since the early Middle Ages, was the universally accepted way in which Christendom regarded the past."[2] Ever since Augustine, "the total of human historical knowledge could be divided into two quite distinct types, differing on account of the utterly disparate sources from which they came.""Sacred history was, of course, the history of the world as it was divinely ... disclosed in the Bible; this history was complete not only for all past time since the creation of the world, but also for all future time until its consummation in the Last Judgment.""Profane history, as contrasted with sacred history, was purely a human enterprise; there was therefore an absolute qualitative difference between sacred and profane history. The latter was held in low esteem by all except a handful of antiquaries and their circle of devotees."[3] Even in Calvin's day, Richardson claims, "profane history was not a source of assured knowledge; the partiality of historians and the unreliability of their evidence was a by-word amongst the men of reason," whereas sacred history was "immune from the critical judgment of reason."[4]

Richardson acknowledges that the strict dichotomy between sacred and secular history began to change somewhat with the Renaissance.

Luther, Philipp Melanchthon, and Huldrych Zwingli. I do not have the space in this essay to demonstrate that "the prominence of this distinction in Calvin's work is without parallel among the sixteenth-century Reformers and perhaps without parallel in the history of the Christian church," but I hope to address this topic in a forthcoming work.

2. Alan Richardson, *History Sacred and Profane* (Philadelphia: Westminster Press, 1964), 23.

3. Ibid., 25–26.

4. Ibid., 28.

Humanist scholarship, he admits, did "much to break down the old Augustinian view of the control of history by Providence, and to create a secular or nontheological attitude towards profane history; but it did not succeed in producing a convincingly accurate reconstruction of the past."[5] But of one thing Richardson is sure: *the Reformation did nothing to alter the prevailing view of sacred and secular history*, and the result was that it did not produce a theology that was really new when compared to what had preceded it. According to Richardson:

> The Reformation, which is to be regarded as an incident in mediaeval church history rather than as the beginning of a radically new period of theology, did not in any way change this situation: Calvin would have agreed with Aquinas in his conception of the nature and task of theology as the systematizing of the revealed truths of Holy Scripture. This is a profoundly unhistorical conception of the nature of divine revelation, since the effective medium of revelation is no longer history but a literary communication. This unhistorical attitude persisted until the religious upheaval ushered in by the Age of Reason, which marks the period of the real "waning of the Middle Ages."[6]

Historical Interest in Calvin's Humanistic Background

Did Calvin have a "profoundly unhistorical conception" of revelation, as Richardson claims? Is such an "unhistorical attitude" reflected in his approach to the Bible? Did humanists, generally, and Calvin, in particular, really care so little about "accurate reconstruction of the past," as Richardson claims? Josef Bohatec, Ford Lewis Battles, and, more recently, Irena Backus have shown that from early on Calvin was deeply committed to accurate reconstruction of the past.[7] The most influential teachers in the life of Calvin, a student of law, were on the cutting edge of transforming

5. Ibid., 30.
6. Ibid., 78–79.
7. Irena Backus, *Historical Method and Confessional Identity in the Era of the Reformation (1378–1615)* (Leiden: Brill, 2003); Ford Lewis Battles, "Calvin's Humanistic Education," in *Interpreting John Calvin*, ed. Robert Benedetto (Grand Rapids: Baker, 1996); Josef Bohatec, *Budé und Calvin: Studien zur Gedankenwelt des französichen Frühhumanismus* (Graz: Hermann Böhlaus, 1950). Translations are my own.

219

not only the study of law but also the entire medieval university by means of historical inquiry.[8] In the early Middle Ages, "law was taught under judicial rhetoric"; it was a "primarily literary or philosophical" field. After the middle of the thirteenth century, it was dominated by a method whereby glosses on a given Roman law were gathered from the history of its interpretation and then debated. Calvin was inculcated into this approach under the tutelage of Pierre de l'Estoile at the University of Orléans (1528–29).

But Calvin was introduced to a very different approach to the study of law when he and other friends moved to Bourges to sit under the renowned Milanese jurisconsult Andrea Alciati in the fall of 1529. "Alciati," Battles claims, "dealt a deathblow to the traditional school of the glossators who . . . had determined the character of legal education for a long time. By viewing Roman law within the larger context of Latin language, literature, and history, Alciati brought a new humanistic method" that transformed not only the study of law, but eventually other fields as well.[9] "Most striking . . . is the general impact of Alciati's search for principles in Roman history, his linking of legislation, customs, and institutions of the ancient classical world."[10]

This approach of taking the historical context of a document seriously, of considering its social, political, and cultural background, made a profound impact on Calvin. Guillaume Budé, for whom Calvin had more affection, deepened this "new learning." Bohatec argues that in an era when astrology, Fate, and "the wheel of Fortune" were still considered by many to be important factors in shaping history and politics, Budé played a decisive role in developing in Calvin a more Christian and scientific understanding of history.[11] Both Alciati and Budé were humanists at the forefront of revolutionizing the study of law, and their methods of historical investigation exercised enormous influence on Calvin and many other young scholars.[12] This is important, according to Battles,

8. Battles, "Calvin's Humanistic Education," 47.
9. Ibid., 56.
10. Ibid., 57.
11. Bohatec, Budé und Calvin, 263ff.
12. The nature of this "revolution" and its influence on Calvin can be overstated, but Michael L. Monheit provides a detailed analysis of it in "Guillaume Budé, Andrea Alciato,

because "the upheaval in legal instruction that occurred in the midst of Calvin's course of studies was as fateful for the shaping of his theology as any single aspect of his education."[13]

Not only was historical interest in the air during Calvin's studies, but it is also clearly manifest in his first book published in the spring of 1532. Erasmus had produced a new edition, first in 1515 and then a second in 1529, of *De Clementia*, a work by Seneca, the great Roman philosopher, dramatist, historian, and mentor of young Nero. As a budding scholar in search of a dissertation topic, Calvin took up Erasmus's public invitation to correct and supplement this work. Calvin hoped his *Commentary on Seneca's De Clementia* would establish his academic reputation, but it was hardly noticed by the guild. In fact, his efforts to promote it left him deeply in debt. Nevertheless, this work gives us insight into Calvin's gifts as a young scholar.

Some have exaggerated the classical competence of the young Calvin while others have understated it, but Battles's analysis of this question in his essay "The Sources of Calvin's Seneca Commentary" still seems the most measured.[14] Of the seventy-four Latin and twenty-two Greek authors Calvin cites, his knowledge of most of them is secondhand. And his knowledge of Greek at this stage was only rudimentary compared to his knowledge of Latin. But Calvin did have firsthand knowledge of a wide range of Latin literature: philosophers, poets, and especially historians. Battles states that in his Seneca commentary, "the historians are richly represented: not only had he read with some care the chief Latin writers (notably Suetonius, Tacitus, and Livy) but also the lesser [historians], and was to some extent familiar with the main Greek historians of Rome— Plutarch, Arrian, Herodian, Dio Cassius, and Dio Halicarnassus."[15] "To sketch the background of Seneca's essay on the political instruction of the young Nero, Calvin needed a clear conception not only of the early empire, but of the whole course of Roman history. Technical questions on the size

---

Pierre de l'Estoile: Renaissance Interpreters of Roman Law," *Journal of the History of Ideas* 58.1 (January 1997): 21–40.

13. Battles, "Calvin's Humanistic Education," 54.

14. Ford Lewis Battles, "The Sources of Calvin's Seneca Commentary," in *Interpreting John Calvin*, 65–85.

15. Ibid., 67.

of Roman legions, the population of imperial Rome, the political offices of Republic and Empire, and the social classes had to be answered."[16] He utilizes statistical material from the first century on Roman population and wealth to do so.[17]

Although dependent on Budé for much of this information, Calvin demonstrates that he is quite capable of independent research, perceptive criticisms, and, when necessary, going his own way and even critiquing his own mentors.[18] Above all, Calvin is aware that in order to deal with the genuine sense of Seneca's text, he must penetrate layers of interpretation— of classical authors, classical intermediaries, and humanist compilers.[19]

However one may assess Calvin's competence as a classical scholar, it seems difficult to deny that his Seneca commentary demonstrates serious historical interest. It typifies the humanist motto: *ad fontes*, a pursuit of history based not only on knowledge of primary sources but also on the context from which they arose. Erasmus, whom Calvin acknowledges as the greatest scholar of his day next to Budé, had insisted in his "Introduction to the Edition of the Greek New Testament" (1516) that the Bible be interpreted in light of a careful study of its historical and geographical context, its customs, institutions, and so on. When this occurs, according to Erasmus, "Then a marvelous light, and, I might say, life, is given to what is being read, which however, would be boring and dead if this knowledge, and as is so often the case, even a knowledge of the language is lacking."[20] It is precisely this approach that Calvin pursues in his Seneca commentary.

Battles concludes: "In the commentary can be seen the beginnings of Calvin the exegete. The same attention to the close study of the text will later mark Calvin's Christian writings. The tools of exegesis—grammatical and rhetorical analysis, a wide background in history, philosophy, literature, science, and other studies—characterize the young Calvin as they will more fully the later Calvin."[21] My point is that if it is true, as Richardson

16. Ibid., 71.
17. Ibid.
18. Ibid., 68ff.
19. Ibid., 79ff.
20. Quoted in Hans-Joachim Kraus, "Calvin's Exegetical Principles," trans. Keith Crim, *Interpretation: A Journal of Bible and Theology* 31.1 (January 1977): 14.
21. Battles, "The Sources of Calvin's Seneca Commentary," 84.

claims, that secular history "was held in low esteem by all except a handful of antiquaries and their circle of devotees," then it is not true, as Richardson claims, that Calvin should not be included in this circle. The evidence suggests that if he was not at the center, he was at least close to it.[22]

But something distinguishes Calvin from most humanists even in this period of his so-called "pagan apprenticeship."[23] Unlike most northern European humanists, Calvin refuses to Christianize his classical sources. He refuses, for example, to make Seneca into an "anonymous" or "latent Christian," as had been done so often throughout the Middle Ages and celebrated in such popular works as *The Golden Legend*.[24] Nor does he try to baptize Seneca's concepts of "mercy" or "justice" and palm them off as somehow proto- or crypto-Christian concepts.[25] This does not mean that Calvin does not have nice things to say about Seneca. On the contrary, he praises Seneca for several virtues: his erudition, his eloquence, and especially his ethics.[26] He even praises Seneca for his wide knowledge of history, though he also criticizes him for his occasional historical lapses. Yet even here he excuses Seneca because, Calvin says, history has different uses.[27]

22. "Calvin lived in an environment imbued with Christian humanism. He visited several friends (the de Hangest family, Olivétan, Cop, Daniel, Duchemin, and Wolmar) and was taught by several masters (Cordier, Alciati, Danés, Vatable) who were—at least in the beginning—followers of Erasmus and Lefèvre. Through contact with them he himself became a 'biblical' humanist, an advocate of the inner renewal of the Church by a return to its original sources" (Alexandre Ganoczy, *The Young Calvin*, trans. David Foxgrover and Wade Provo [Philadelphia: Westminster Press, 1987], 178).

23. Battles, "The Sources of Calvin's Seneca Commentary," 84.

24. Theologians as early as Tertullian had referred to Seneca as "our Seneca."

25. Indeed, Cornelius Augustijn claims on this basis that Calvin was not a true humanist. See "Calvin und der Humanismus," in *Calvinus Servus Christi*, ed. Wilhelm H. Neuser (Budapest: Presseabteilung des Raday Kollegiums, 1988), 127–42. In what sense Calvin ever was or remained a humanist is a debate among Calvin scholars. See, for example, William J. Bouwsma, *John Calvin: A Sixteenth Century Portrait* (Oxford: Oxford University Press, 1988), 86–127; Bernard Cottret, *Calvin: A Biography* (Grand Rapids: Eerdmans, 2000), 25–104, 330ff.; Alister E. McGrath, *A Life of John Calvin* (Oxford: Blackwell, 1990), 51–78. For a helpful summary, see Christoph Burger, "Calvin und die Humanisten," in *Calvin Handbuch*, ed. Herman J. Selderhuis (Tübingen: Mohr Siebeck, 2008), 137–43.

26. Battles, "The Sources of Calvin's Seneca Commentary," 75ff.

27. Battles quotes Calvin: "Yet to the philosophers and orators, whose job is not to weave lasting history, it is permitted to put to their own use matters of doubtful authenticity, as this passage demonstrates" (ibid., 75n67).

Battles finds it significant that Calvin refused to Christianize classical figures, to draw Christian analogies, or to allegorize their concepts in a Christian way, especially when compared to his contemporaries. "Most important of all," Battles says,

> Calvin never succumbs to the easy allegorical appropriation of things pagan to Christian truth that Budaeus already betrays in the *Annotationes* and *De Asse,* and was later much more explicitly to express in the *De Transitu.* Calvin remained true to the exacting philological discipline of the humanists without practicing their excesses. (This is perhaps because he first held his classicism free of Christian piety and made no hasty amalgam before his conversion.) He could not say with Erasmus, *O sancta Socrates, ora pro nobis*; he could not with Budaeus see Christ in the ancient god Hermes; he could not with Zwingli find a place in the Christian afterlife for ancient pagan worthies.[28]

Battles highlights this to demonstrate that Calvin was never an intellectual philistine. But he also wishes to say that Calvin's appreciation for classical learning did not diminish after his conversion. Certainly a time came when Calvin took "with uncompromising seriousness the superiority of the Bible over all mere human learning.... Yet despite Calvin's profound change of life, his deep study of classical antiquity left an indelible mark on all that he later wrote."[29] Evidence for this is not lacking. Battles cites two passages from the 1559 *Institutes* where knowledge of antiquity is extolled and readers are exhorted to receive it with gratitude, for "'Those men whom Scripture calls 'natural men' were, indeed, sharp and penetrating in their investigation of things below. Let us, accordingly, learn by their example how many gifts the Lord left to human nature even after it was despoiled of its true good."[30] Irena Backus has recently argued that there are more "links between pagan and Christian piety and moral values" in Calvin's mature thought than Battles and others claim.[31] This may

28. Ibid., 73–74. Of course, Battles could have included here the later Melanchthon!
29. Ibid., 74.
30. John Calvin, *Institutes of the Christian Religion,* trans. Ford Lewis Battles, ed. John T. McNeill (Philadelphia: Westminster Press, 1960), 2.2.15; CO, 2.199. The other passage Battles cites is 1.8.1; CO, 2.61–62.
31. Backus claims that Battles, Bohatec, Partee, et al., are mistaken to the extent that they emphasize "a split between Calvin the humanist as evidence in *De clementia* and

be so, but Battles' thesis (as even Backus seems to agree) still holds: "Conversion was to bring not an utter repudiation of Calvin's classical learning, but a transformation of it, tested by God's Word."[32]

My concern is not so much with how pagan concepts of piety or morals were transformed in Calvin but with how his concept of history was transformed. What role did secular history have in Calvin's thought after his conversion? How was it transformed in light of his theological program? Above all, and perhaps more important as we reflect on his legacy and that to which he dedicated most of his life, what role does it play in Calvin's exegesis? Obviously, a time came when Calvin drew a distinction between sacred and secular history. Battles says that this transformation in Calvin's thinking with regard to classical learning occurred by 1539, basing this claim on a passage from the 1539 *Institutes*.[33] It may have happened earlier.[34] But my question is not so much

---

Calvin the theologian" (Backus, *Historical Method and Confessional Identity*, 64).

32. Battles, "The Sources of Calvin's Seneca Commentary," 84–85. "The result was no loose allegorical binding together of classical and Christian; Calvin could not repeat Budaeus' confident assertion that Alexander worshiped Jesus Christ. Rather, the message of Seneca's *De Clementia*—that the mighty should rule with mercy, accountable to God—was recast in the passionate essays in Christian political teaching that introduce and conclude the *Institutio Christianae Religionis*" (85). The disagreement between Backus and Battles lies in the nature of this "transformation." Backus concludes: "We can say that Calvin was indeed not a humanist in the strict sense of the word. However, our examination of his philosophy of mind also shows that it makes no sense to say that Calvin saw no links between pagan and Christian piety and moral values. Calvin did see links and his thought *did not undergo a radical alteration* between the commentary on *De clementia* and his theological works. Where he differed from standard humanist practice was in the way he reworked those links" (Backus, *Historical Method and Confessional Identity*, 85 [emphasis added]). I think Backus understates the significance of this transformation, at least with respect to Calvin's understanding of history.

33. "As philosophers have fixed limits of the right and honorable, whence they derive individual duties and the whole company of virtues, so Scripture is not without its own order in this matter, but holds to a most beautiful dispensation, and one much more certain than all the philosophical ones. The only difference is that they, as they were ambitious men, diligently strove to attain an exquisite clarity of order to show the nimbleness of their wit. But the Spirit of God, because he taught without affectation, did not adhere so exactly or continuously to a methodical plan; yet when he lays one down anywhere he hints enough that it is not to be neglected by us" (*Institutes* [1539], 3.6–10, quoted in Battles, "The Sources of Calvin's Seneca Commentary," 67n13).

34. Ganoczy suggests on the basis of the *Psychopannychia* that although still not a "Protestant," such a transformation may have occurred in Calvin by 1534 (*The Young Calvin*, 178ff.). For a more extensive examination of this transformation, see George H. Travard, *The Starting Point of Calvin's Theology* (Grand Rapids: Eerdmans, 2000).

when it occurred, but *why* and *how* it occurred *with regard to his understanding of history.* That brings me back to my original question: Why did Calvin draw a distinction between sacred and secular history in the first place?

How Sacred History Differs from Secular History

Richardson claims that Calvin had no other choice. As a child of his times, he simply accepted it; he simply drew the same distinction that theologians had drawn for more than a millennium. And Calvin did draw this distinction. But the point I want to make is that he did so for different reasons, or at least for different reasons than Richardson gives. Calvin did not draw this distinction because of any sense of the intrinsic unreliability of secular historians or because he saw profane history as inherently corrupt, as Richardson claims. On the contrary, Calvin had great respect for secular history, just as he had great respect for mathematics, science, and all the liberal arts. That he sought to establish himself as a credible historian before he established himself as a credible theologian (and might otherwise have remained a historian) hardly makes sense if he held history in such "low esteem," as Richardson claims. The reason Calvin drew a fundamental distinction between sacred and pagan history is the same reason he refused the easy conversion of any pagan concept. It was not because he saw secular history as irrelevant or unrelated. It was because he came to see it as inherently different.

The difference, according to Calvin, is not that sacred history always provides *more* facts, details, or information than secular history or even *more accurate* facts, details, or information. Sometimes it does.[35] But

35. E.g., "But Isaiah presents lively descriptions, so as to place the actual events, as it were, before our eyes. Certainly Xenophon does not describe so historically the storming of the city; and this makes it evident that it was not natural sagacity, but heavenly inspiration, that taught Isaiah to describe so vividly events that were unknown" (Calvin, Isa. 21:5 [2:96]; CO, 36.357). Quotations from Calvin's Old Testament commentaries will rely on the English translations by the Calvin Translation Society edition of Calvin's commentaries. See *Commentaries of John Calvin,* 46 vols. (Edinburgh, 1843–55; repr., Grand Rapids: Eerdmans, 1948). Quotations from Calvin's New Testament commentaries will come from *Calvin's New Testament Commentaries,* ed. David W. Torrance and Thomas F. Torrance (Edinburgh, 1959–72; repr., Grand Rapids: Eerdmans, 1975). I will cite these commentaries by scriptural reference, volume, and page number.

sacred history sometimes *omits* facts, details, or information—some of which would be helpful in understanding biblical texts; Calvin provides many examples.[36] Indeed, Calvin says that sacred history sometimes omits information that is "highly worthy of observation."[37] Nor does sacred history differ from secular history in that it always provides a better, more accurate chronology of events. On the contrary, sacred history sometimes completely ignores chronological sequence. Calvin says repeatedly in his *Harmony of the Gospels* that the Evangelists did not pay much attention to times, dates, or the exact sequence of events: "They neglected the order of days and were content to put together the chief events in Christ's career as they saw them. . . . They freely confuse the miracles which occurred at much the same period and this we shall see clearly from a number of cases."[38] "Anyone who will consider how little care the evangelists bestowed on pointing out dates will not stumble at this diversity in the narrative."[39] And there are many instances in the Old Testament where the "historical connection is frequently disturbed, and that what was first in the order of time, comes last in the narrative."[40] Neither does sacred history differ from secular history primarily because the latter is derived from human value judgments based on probability whereas the former is "inspired." Calvin certainly believes sacred history to be "inspired."[41] But the means of transmission is not the primary distinction he draws between sacred and secular history.

The primary distinction Calvin draws is that sacred history has a different focus, a different subject matter, content, and theme. Calvin brings this out at various points in his commentary on the Psalms. Reflecting on Psalm 86:2, he says:

36. "The time this earthquake happened, sacred history does not mention. But Josephus says, that it was when Uzziah seized on the priestly office, and was smitten with leprosy" (Calvin, Amos 1:1 [2:150]; CO, 43.3). See also Calvin, Jer. 14:1 (2:202); CO, 38.178.

37. Calvin, Isa. 38:9 (3:163); CO, 36.653.

38. Calvin, Matt. 4:18 (1:155); CO, 45.148. See also Matt. 4:5; 8:27; 9:18; 27:51; Luke 4:5; 19:1, 39–49; 24:12; etc.

39. Calvin, Matt. 21:10ff. (2:1ff.); CO, 45.577ff.

40. Calvin, Isa. 36:2 (3:79); CO, 36.601. E.g., "Moses is frequently accustomed to place those things which have precedence in time in a different order" (Gen. 25:1 [2:33]; CO, 23.343). See also Jer. 35:1 (4:302); CO, 39.100.

41. Calvin, Ps. 57:1 (2:359); CO, 31.554; Ps. 60:1 (2:397); CO, 31.574; Ps. 134:1 (5:167); CO, 32.355.

> In reading profane history, we are disposed to marvel how it came to pass that God abandoned the honest, the grave, and the temperate, to the enraged passions of a wicked multitude; but there is no reason for wondering at this when we reflect that such persons, relying on their own strength and virtue, despised the grace of God with all the superciliousness of impiety. Making an idol of their own virtue they disdained to lift up their eyes to Him.[42]

In other words, "when bad things happen to good people" (or ostensibly good people), profane history does not know what to make of it. Its purview is limited to externals. It does not penetrate to the intentions of the heart or the secrets of the human spirit because it has no access, no true insight into how a man or woman stands before God. It makes no claim to his righteous judgments. This is a significant difference. Yet this is still not the most basic way of stating it.

In Psalm 107, where we read, "Some went down to the sea in ships, doing business on the great waters,"[43] Calvin describes the fundamental difference between sacred and secular history:

> True, indeed, the mariners imagine from certain phenomena, that a storm is approaching, but sudden changes proceed only from the secret appointment of God. Therefore, he gives not merely a historical narrative of the manner in which squalls and storms arise, but, assuming the character of a teacher, begins with the cause itself, and then directs to the imminent danger with which the tempest is fraught; or rather, portrays, as in a picture, the image of death, in order that the goodness of God may appear the more conspicuous when the tempest happily ceases without loss of life. . . . He makes the storm a calm. A profane author, in narrating the history of such an event, would have said, that the winds were hushed, and the raging billows were calmed; but the Spirit of God, by this change of the storm into a calm, places the providence of God as presiding over all; thereby meaning, that it was not by human agency that this violent commotion of the sea and wind, which threatened to subvert the frame of the world, was so suddenly stilled.[44]

42. Calvin, Ps. 86:2 (3:381–82); CO, 32.792.
43. All quotations from the Bible in this chapter are from the ESV.
44. Calvin, Ps. 107:23–32 (4:257–58); CO, 32.140ff.

The key phrase here is: "it was not by human agency that this violent commotion . . . was so suddenly stilled. . . . *He* makes the storm a calm." Divine agency is the fundamental difference between sacred and secular history. Moreover, divine agency, God's invisible hand in the affairs of men and nature, was not a category of explanation that fit within the causal nexus of an increasing number of scholars in Calvin's day.

Of course, most northern European humanists did not deny divine agency. But there has been considerable research on humanist historiography in recent decades, and however many exceptions or qualifications one may make, there is consensus that even if not as thoroughly secular as once thought, the Italian Renaissance represented at least the beginnings of the "negation of Christian transcendency."[45] Such a negation may have been slow in emerging as a direct attack on Christian faith, but this was the source of it.[46] In contrast to the explanation of medieval historians, divine providence was no longer the primary category of explanation, even among many "Christian humanists."[47] Gradually, a host of complex naturalistic causalities and horizontal relations began to take center stage and became, at least for some, their singular focus. Yet there were a growing number of skeptical

45. I owe the phrase "negation of Christian transcendency" to Stephen Edmondson, who, in his article "Christ and History: Hermeneutical Convergence in Calvin and Its Challenge to Biblical Theology," *Modern Theology* 21.1 (January 2005): 3–35, attributes it to Benedetto Croce, *History: Its Theory and Practice* (New York: Russell and Russell, 1960), 224.

46. Louis Dupré, *Passage to Modernity: An Essay in the Hermeneutics of Nature and Culture* (New Haven: Yale University Press, 1993). Dupré claims that the rise of modernity began in late medieval theology and the early Italian Renaissance with the "disintegration of the medieval synthesis" between nature and grace. With the shattering of this synthesis and an unprecedented emphasis on human creativity, a new naturalism was born that grew "unfettered" in the Enlightenment. "Calvin understood the religious problem of modernity because he experienced it within himself. Once converted, he single-mindedly focused on the issue that concerned religious humanists most seriously, namely, the radical incompleteness of a nature that requires a transcendent dimension yet somehow seems deprived of it" (209). One need not agree with all of Dupré's conclusions to appreciate his claim: "Calvin was fighting a battle with a Renaissance naturalism whose strong attraction he had experienced" (213).

47. "The ambiguity inherent in the term Christian humanism extends well beyond the limits admissible by a meaningful use of it. Some have granted the name Christian humanist to all writers who, in whatever capacity, shed light on the religious quality of Renaissance culture, including such dubious candidates as Rabelais" (ibid., 223; see further 223ff.).

humanists who did deny and even openly scorned divine agency as a means of explanation.[48] Calvin had been long aware of them, but when it was reported that such a group was making life difficult for "certain men of the Reformed Church, particularly the Franco-Gauls," Calvin determined that he would write a book, *De scandalis*, published in 1550, the title of which in English is *Concerning Scandals, which, in our day, frighten away a great many people, and are even the cause of alienating some from the pure doctrine of the gospel.*[49] Bohatec highlights the significance of this work in sharpening Calvin's position not only against skeptical humanists but also against other Christian humanists, including his own teacher, Budé.[50]

But what were these scandals that were "frighten[ing] away a great many people" and "alienating some from the pure doctrine of the gospel"? Calvin says that they are nothing new. Scandals have always been associated with the Christian faith, stumbling blocks, things that "seem to be contradictory to human reason and completely absurd."[51] And this should come as no surprise, since Christ himself is described as "a stone of stumbling, and a rock of offense" (1 Peter 2:8, quoting Isa. 8:14). This is not to say that the term *scandal* is proper to him or his gospel.[52] "However, because of

48. Max Gauna, *Upwellings: First Expressions of Unbelief in the Printed Literature of the French Renaissance* (London: Associated University Presses, 1992), 70–107. See also Battles, *Institutes*, 1.7.4n14; Wulfert de Greef, *The Writing of John Calvin, Expanded Edition: An Introductory Guide* (Louisville: Westminster/John Knox Press, 2008), 127–28.

49. See the "Introductory Note" by Peter Barth and Dora Scheuner and "Dedicatory Epistle to Laurent de Normandie," in John Calvin, *Concerning Scandals*, trans. John W. Fraser (Grand Rapids: Eerdmans, 1978), xi, 1–4.

50. Bohatec claims that Calvin directed this work to three different groups of humanists: (1) men such as Bunel, who were "not sworn enemies of the Gospel, but nevertheless have fallen from it because of their exaggerated self-consciousness and vain addiction to admiration"; (2) open despisers of religion, such as Agrippa von Nettesheim, Villanovanus, Dolet, Rabelais, Des Périers, and Govéan; and (3) "Christian humanists," such as Budé. See *Budé und Calvin*, 149ff. For a helpful analysis that develops Bohatec's discussion of the natural sciences and the liberal arts as it relates to *De scandalis*, see Thomas F. Torrance, *The Hermeneutics of John Calvin* (Edinburgh: Scottish Academic Press, 1988), 140ff.

51. Calvin, *Concerning Scandals*, 13; CO, 8.14. Calvin defines *scandala* as "obstacles of all kinds, whether they divert us from the right direction, or keep us back by being in the way, or provide means for making us fall" (Calvin, *Concerning Scandals*, 8; CO, 8.10).

52. "There is nothing more out of keeping with Christ or the gospel than the name 'scandal'" (Calvin, *Concerning Scandals*, 8; CO, 8.10).

the perversity of men," because "such ill will or badness is rooted in [fallen] human nature, so that what is accidental to Christ is just as normal as if it were of the very essence of his function,"[53] it is necessary to acknowledge the scandal of the gospel as such; and Calvin has little patience with those who do not, especially Christians who think their minds so redeemed that they are no longer obliged to regard the gospel as a scandal.[54] "The teaching of the gospel," Calvin says, "is constantly bound up with many scandals."[55] Indeed, it "contains many things which, according to human standards, are irrational in the extreme."[56]

And nowhere were such scandals being celebrated with more revelry in Calvin's day than among humanist skeptics in their reading of Scripture:

> I should be attempting something like emptying the sea if I wished to examine and enumerate one by one all the scandals which wretched men devise for their destruction out of the teaching of Scripture. For it is not simply a matter of their making blind assault if they run up against some difficulty, but, having freely given their minds to the matter, they become agitated by all the rough features, as if their one satisfaction in life lay in tormenting their mind with thorny questions. For they carefully note anything that shows the slightest sign of being irrational, and criticize it sharply, so as not to give the impression that they can be made

53. Calvin, *Concerning Scandals*, 9; CO, 8.10–11.

54. "I now come to those who at one time embraced the gospel of Christ, and do not reject it now but yet wish to have it without scandals. I am dealing with Christians. Do they want Christ free from every scandal? Let them invent a new Christ for themselves! For he can be no other Son of God than the one made known in the Scriptures. Or let them at least change men's natures and make the whole world different! We listen to what the Scriptures tell us. This situation applies not only to the person of Christ but also to the whole of doctrine. It is not something temporary, but something that will continue in existence as long as the doctrine will be taught. . . . What if they had been alive in the very first days of the gospel, when scandals of every kind were flowing in a constant stream from the gospel? How quick they would have been to put a lot of ground between themselves and Christ! . . . If they say that they would not have done that in those days, why then are they so fastidious today? Why do they not recognize that the same characteristics are also to be found in Christ now?" (Calvin, *Concerning Scandals*, 9–10; CO, 8.11).

55. Calvin, *Concerning Scandals*, 8; CO, 8.10.

56. "Quae humano iudicio valde sunt non absurda modo, sed etiam ridicula" (Calvin, *Concerning Scandals*, 12; CO, 8.13).

to believe all that easily. If there is also any appearance or disagreement and contradiction in several Scripture passages, they seize on it eagerly, and by collecting all the examples of that kind, they make a great fuss about their own shrewdness.[57]

Of course, the greatest scandal of the Christian faith is Jesus Christ himself. Calvin says: "The proclamation that the Son of God, who is eternal Life, has put on our flesh and become mortal man, that we have acquired life by his death, righteousness by his condemnation, salvation by his being made a curse, is so abhorrent to the common sense of men [*communi hominum sensu*] that the sharper a man's mind is, the quicker he will be in repudiating it."[58] But what does this have to do with sacred history?

It is that sacred history cannot be understood apart from this one great scandal: Jesus Christ. *There is nothing sacred about sacred history apart from him.* Indeed, *sacred* history is sacred *history* only because it is about him and the covenant fulfilled in him. Even the covenant cannot be understood apart from him, for although it is important to understand Christ in light of the covenant, the covenant cannot be understood at all apart from him, the Lord of the covenant.[59] If this one Lord, one truth, Jesus Christ, is not understood as such, then neither sacred history nor any of its truths can be understood. What Calvin says about Scripture applies equally to sacred history: "the Scriptures should be read with the aim [*scopus*] of finding Christ in them. Whoever turns aside from this object, even though he wears himself out all his life in learning, will never reach the knowledge of the truth."[60] As Bohatec puts it, for Calvin "the revelation of God in Christ is the meaning of history, or more precisely, Christ is the center of meaning within history."[61] Thus, sacred history differs from secular history because it acknowledges what secular history does not, namely, that standing at its living center and also as its presupposition and goal is the scandal of Jesus Christ, the Lord of history, in

57. Calvin, *Concerning Scandals*, 25; CO, 8.20–21.

58. Calvin, *Concerning Scandals*, 12 (translation slightly altered); CO, 8.13.

59. Edmondson puts it well: "Christ, as the Mediator of the Covenant, was the instrument by which it was founded, the end at which it aimed, and the substance of which it consisted" ("Christ and History: Hermeneutical Convergence in Calvin," 6).

60. Calvin, John 5:39 (1:139); CO, 47.125.

61. Bohatec, *Budé und Calvin*, 296.

whom time and eternity, divine and human agency, the vertical and the horizontal dimension meet hypostatically.

Therefore, because of its different content, presupposition, and goal, sacred history should not be judged by the same standards as secular history. Its standards of credulity and canons of explanation differ. Calvin makes this clear from the outset of his *Commentary on Genesis:* "The end to which the whole scope of the history tends is to this point, that the human race has been preserved by God in such a manner as to manifest his special care for his Church."[62] Later he adds: "So then, we must not judge of this history after our natural opinion: but we must weigh to what end and purpose it is here rehearsed . . ."[63] The scandal of divine agency, of God's grace and the invisible hand of his providential ordering, are necessary for understanding the sacred history of the gospel narratives. "Without this seasoning," Calvin says, "we shall never have any relish for this history."[64] Nowhere is this clearer than in the gospel accounts of the resurrection:

> Scorners will treat as a fairy tale [*puerile ludicrum*] what the Evangelists relate as history. What value will the tidings have, brought by poor frightened women and confirmed by disciples almost lifeless with fear? Why does Christ not rather set up shining trophies of his victory in the midst of the Temple and in the public places? Why does he not appear with terrible mien before Pilate? Why does he not also prove to the priests and the whole of Jerusalem that he had returned to life? Worldly men would scarcely admit that the witnesses he chose were adequate. I reply: Although in these beginnings his weakness could be despised, by God's wonderful providence all this was so governed . . .[65]

Neither were the prophets interested in relating "bare history," Calvin claims. The book of Jeremiah is a good example. That it begins with the cry "Behold" indicates to Calvin that "the prophet does not

62. Calvin, "Argument," *Genesis Comm.*, 64; CO, 23.11–12.
63. John Calvin, "Sermon on Gen. 25:29–34," in *Sermons on Election and Reprobation*, trans. John Field (Audubon, NJ: Old Paths Publications, 1996), 97; CO, 58.74–75.
64. Calvin, Luke 19:29–38 (2:291); CO, 45.570.
65. *Institutes*, 3.25.3; CO, 2.732.

speak as an historian . . . but performs the office of a teacher."[66] This is not to say that the prophet does not "narrate historically" many things.[67] The book of Jeremiah is full of "real history," "remarkable history," "a history worthy of being remembered, and very useful to us."[68] Indeed, sometimes it appears that Jeremiah undertakes "the office of an historian rather than that of a Prophet,"[69] but history as such is never the main thing. Doctrine trumps it every time. In fact, remarkably, Calvin cuts off his commentary on Jeremiah abruptly at chapter 51 because chapter 52 "contains history only as far as was necessary to understand what is here taught."[70] We see this priority in other prophetic books as well.[71]

Yet it is in his New Testament commentaries that Calvin is explicit about the reason for this priority. In Luke's prologue, for example, where "an orderly account" based on "eyewitness" testimony might seem to grant some standing to "bare history," Calvin says: "unless God's authority holds pride of place, faith will never be satisfied with the testimonies of men, but when the inward assurance of the Spirit has led the way, it may subsequently allow them some standing, in an historical knowledge of events."[72] And then Calvin gives us great insight into his understanding of history:

66. Calvin, Jer. 1:15 (1:55); CO, 37.487.

67. Calvin, Jer. 38:28 (4:421); CO, 39.10.

68. Calvin, Jer. 32:6–15 (4:165); CO, 39.10; Jer. 26:1 (3:305ff.); CO, 38.512ff.; Jer. 36:1 (4:325); CO, 39.15.

69. Calvin, Jer. 39:1 (4:421); CO, 39.180. See also Jer. 40:1–4 (4:441ff.); CO, 39.193ff.

70. Calvin, Jer. 51:60–64 (5:289–94); CO, 39.499–502. The fact that it "contains history only" leads Calvin to say: "We hence conclude that the last chapter is not included in the prophetic book of Jeremiah"; Calvin has an interesting take on the provenance of the book of Jeremiah. He argues that "the order of time in which the prophecies were written has not been retained" and "that Jeremiah did not write the book as it exists now, but that his discourses were collected and formed into a volume without regard to the order of time." This is not a problem for him, since: "In history the regular succession of days and years ought to be preserved, but in prophetic writing this is not so necessary" (Jer. 35:7 [4:302ff.]; CO, 39.100ff.).

71. E.g., "although Daniel narrates the history, it is our duty, as I have said to treat of things far more important; for God who had promised his people deliverance, was not stretching forth his hand in secret" (Calvin, Dan. 5:1 [1:309]; CO, 40.695). See also Isa. 23:9 (2:152); CO, 36.390; Joel preface (3:xv); CO, 42.515; Ps. 78:5 (3:231); CO, 31.723.

72. Calvin, Luke 1:1 (1:2); CO, 45.7.

I mean by an historical knowledge, one which we conceive from events which either we have seen ourselves or have heard from others. With the manifest works of God, we are as much to listen to eyewitnesses as to trust our experience. Besides, Luke is not dealing with private sources, but men who were ministers of the Word. He gives them a distinction that places them above the rank of human authority: he means, that they who gave him testimony on the Gospel had been divinely entrusted with the role of publishing it. Hence that security . . . which, unless it rests on God, will ever be disturbed.[73]

"It is not the intention of St. Luke," Calvin says, "simply to write a history of what happened."[74] "Those who simply know the bare history have not the Gospel, unless there is added a knowledge of the teaching, which reveals the fruit of the acts of Christ."[75] Calvin makes the same point in his commentary on John: "since the bare history would not be sufficient, and indeed, would be of no use for salvation, the Evangelists do not simply relate that Christ was born, and died, and conquered death, but also explain to what end He was born, and died, and rose again, and what benefit we derive from this."[76]

Like Luther, Melanchthon, and other Reformers, Calvin rejected the assumption that mere "historical faith" (*fides historica*) was truly faith even if it were only a so-called "unformed" or "implicit faith."[77] Calvin says that "many are dangerously deluded today in this respect . . . Indeed, most people, when they hear this term [*faith*], understand nothing deeper than a common assent to the gospel history."[78]

73. Calvin, Luke 1:1 (1:2–3); CO, 45.7.

74. Calvin, Sermon 2, "The Nativity of Jesus Christ," in *Sermons on the Deity of Christ,* trans. Leroy Nixon (Grand Rapids: Eerdmans, 1950), 45; CO, 46.957.

75. Calvin, Acts 1:1 (1:22); CO, 48.1 ("Hinc notandum est, qui nudam duntaxat historiae notitiam habent, evangelium minime tenere; nisi accedat doctrinae cognitio quae fructum gestorum Christi patefaciat.").

76. Calvin, *John Comm.,* "Theme" (1:5–6); CO, 47.vii–viii.

77. See *Institutes,* 3.2.1n3. "Accordingly, without the illumination of the Holy Spirit, the Word can do nothing. From this, also, it is clear that faith is much higher than human understanding. And it will not be enough for the mind to be illumined by the Spirit of God unless the heart is also strengthened and supported by his power. In this matter the Schoolmen go completely astray, who in considering faith identify it with a bare and simple assent arising out of knowledge, and leave out confidence and assurance of heart" (*Institutes,* 3.2.33; CO, 2.425–26).

78. *Institutes,* 3.2.1; CO, 2.398.

Of course, most people believe that there is a God, and they consider that the gospel history and the remaining parts of the Scripture are true. Such a judgment is on a par with the judgments we ordinarily make concerning those things which are either narrated as having once taken place, or which we have seen as eyewitnesses. There are, also, those who go beyond this, holding the Word of God to be an indisputable oracle; they do not utterly neglect his precepts, and are somewhat moved by his threats and promises. To such persons an ascription of faith is made, but by misapplication . . .[79]

The reason the apostles were not interested in narrating "bare history"[80] or fostering a mere historical faith, which is really not faith at all,[81] is that they were committed to narrating sacred history, history that pertains principally to our redemption in Christ. Even when Paul discusses the event of Christ's resurrection, he does not do so, Calvin observes, apart from "our redemption and salvation. For we must always remember this principle, that Scripture does not usually speak of these things as cold facts and mere matters of history [illis historice tantum ac frigide loqui], but makes indirect reference to their fruit."[82] There are "questionarians," however, Calvin says, who bring to Scripture all sorts of "foolish questions" of a speculative nature that "are held in high esteem by the schools of the Sorbonne." They "forget to gather fruit from the sacred histories and seize on the lineage of race and trifles of that kind, and weary themselves with them to no end."[83] They forget or have never known what sacred history is about.

Sacred history is, to be sure, nothing more, nothing less, and nothing other than "real history." It narrates what really happens in time and space, but not according to our general knowledge of time and space. Above all, sacred history is not knowable apart from the redemption of Christ. As far as Calvin is concerned, it is impossible to understand sacred history or its parts apart from this one whole, Jesus Christ, in whom "all things hold

79. Institutes, 3.2.9; CO, 2.405. See also Institutes, 3.2.1; CO, 2.398.
80. E.g., Calvin, Acts 1:3 (1:24); CO, 48.4; Acts 10:37 (2:310); CO, 48.245; Acts 17:3 (2:93); CO, 48.394.
81. Calvin, Rom. 10:9 (227); CO, 49.201.
82. Calvin, 2 Tim. 2:8 (309); CO, 52.363.
83. Calvin, Titus 3:9 (386); CO, 52.434.

together" (Col. 1:17). The truth at issue in sacred history, therefore, like the truth at issue in Holy Scripture, is one, which is why Calvin insists that "the Scriptures should be read with the aim of finding Christ in them. Whoever turns aside from this object, even though he wears himself out all his life in learning, will never reach the knowledge of the truth."[84]

This statement is misunderstood, however, if it is read to imply that Christological interpretation so dominates Calvin's exegesis that genuine historical interpretation of Scripture is rendered superfluous. That he does not find explicit reference to Christ on every page of the Old Testament, that he refuses to follow so much of the Christian interpretive tradition in assigning messianic interpretations to so many Old Testament passages but instead tries to read them in light of their historical context,[85] is testimony that this is not what reading Scriptures "with the aim of finding Christ in them" means to Calvin. Whether he always did justice in relating historical interpretation on the one hand and Christological interpretation on the other (or whether they are juxtaposed as such in Calvin) is another question and one that continues to be debated.[86] I agree with those who argue that there are not "two agendas" at work in Calvin's exegesis.[87] Calvin did not see Christological interpretation and historical interpretation as two separate tasks. But how Christological interpretation and historical interpretation relate in Calvin's exegesis seems to me to have a lot to do with how sacred and secular history relate in his theology. And that is the question to which we now turn.

How Sacred History Relates to Secular History

84. Calvin, John 5:39 (1:139); CO, 47.125.

85. David L. Puckett, *John Calvin's Exegesis of the Old Testament* (Louisville: Westminster/John Knox Press, 1995), passim.

86. E.g., Edmondson, "Christ and History: Hermeneutical Convergence in Calvin," passim.

87. Among those who argue that Calvin's approach is more bifurcated (with Christological or dogmatic interpretation ultimately triumphing over historical interpretation) are H. Jackson Fortsman and Emil Kraeling. Among those who argue that Calvin's approach is more unified are Stephen Edmondson, Hans-Joachim Kraus, David L. Puckett, and T. F. Torrance.

Calvin elaborates his understanding of the relationship between sacred and secular history most fully in his *Romans* commentary, his first commentary, published in 1540. In Romans 4:23–24, Paul writes: "But the words 'it was counted to him' were not written for his sake alone, but for ours also." Calvin comments:

> We are reminded in this passage of the duty of seeking profit from scriptural examples. The pagan writers have truly said that history is the teacher of life [*Historiam esse vitae magisterium*], but there is no one who makes sound progress in it as it is handed down to us by them. Scripture alone lays claim to an office of this kind. In the first place it prescribes general rules by which we may test all other history, so as to make it serve our advantage. In the second place, it clearly distinguishes what actions we ought to follow, and what to avoid. But as far as doctrine is concerned, which is its special province, it is alone in showing us the providence of God, His righteousness and goodness towards His people, and His judgments against the wicked.[88]

Calvin wrote in his Seneca commentary, "Hence for Cicero, history is life's schoolmistress; in her, as in a mirror, we see our own life. We discern with our eyes what we are to avoid, what to follow. But for those who are naturally upright no external examples are needed."[89] Calvin calls history the "instructress of life" and uses the image of history as "a mirror" many times throughout his writings.[90] Thus, he maintains the same conviction

88. Calvin, Rom. 4:23–24 (100–101); CO, 49.86. A similar statement appears in the "Argumentum" of Calvin's Acts commentary: "The highest praise for a history by secular writers is to call it an 'instructress of life'. If a narrative of events, which only gives guidance in connection with men's deeds, as to what ought to be avoided, and what followed, merits such a splendid description, what title will the sacred histories [*sacrae historiae*] deserve? For not only do they regulate the external life of man so that he may obtain commendation for virtue, but, what ought to be of more value to us, they also show that God has cared for His Church from the beginning, that always He stood by, a just vindicator, for those who turned to Him for support and protection, that He was gracious to, and easily moved by, miserable sinners. By instructing our faith in this way they raise us up higher than the heavens" (Calvin, "Argumentum," Acts of the Apostles [1:17]; CO, 48.vii).

89. Ford Lewis Battles, *Calvin's Commentary on Seneca's De Clementia* (Leiden: Brill, 1969), 51; CO, 5.26.

90. Calvin, Josh. 10:25 (1:160); CO, 25.503; Ezek. 16:6 (2:100); CO, 40.339; Mic. 1:1 (3:151); CO, 43.281; Acts 12:20 (1:345); CO, 48.273; Acts 16:11–12 (2:70–71); CO, 48.375;

he had during his "pagan apprenticeship." But as he continues to comment on Romans 4:23–24, we see how this conviction is heightened with respect to the sacred history of the Bible because:

> It is alone in showing us the providence of God, His righteousness and goodness towards His people, and His judgments against the wicked.... If, therefore, we would make a right and proper use of the sacred histories [*Proinde si pure ac pie sacras historias tractare libet*], we must remember that we ought to use them in such a way as to draw from them the fruit of sound doctrine. They instruct us how to form our life, how to strengthen our faith, and how we are to arouse the fear of the Lord. The example of the saints will be of assistance in the ordering of our lives, if we learn from them sobriety, chastity, love, patience, moderation, contempt for the world, and other virtues. The help of God, which was always available to them, will contribute to the confirmation of our faith, and His protection, and the fatherly care which He exercised over them, will afford us consolation in time of adversity.[91]

"Consolation in time of adversity" is one reason Calvin highlighted the significance of sacred history and constantly pointed his readers to it.[92] Joseph Haroutunian observes:

> A church under persecution was plagued with profound doubts. Excommunicated ex-Romanists, subject to enemy power, deprived of home and goods, in exile and at death's door, these poor people who lived in anxiety and despair, subject to miseries from which even the dregs and criminals of society were exempt, had nothing to sustain them except the promises of God. They were invited by Calvin to turn their eyes to Abraham and Moses and Noah and David, to the great deliverance of God, to the mysterious workings of his "secret

---

Acts 23:16 (2:239); CO, 48.513. See esp. Calvin, *Sermons on Job*, trans. Arthur Golding (London, 1574; repr., Carlisle, PA: Banner of Truth, 1993 [facsimile]), 1; CO, 33.22; 111; CO, 33.302; 143; CO, 33.385–86; etc.

91. Calvin, Rom. 4:23–24 (101); CO, 49.86.

92. E.g., "We very often find in the Sacred History that whatever happens proceeds from the Lord..." (*Institutes*, 1.18.1; CO, 2.168); "Indeed, the principal purpose of Biblical history is to teach that the Lord watches over the ways of the saints with such great diligence that they do not even stumble over a stone" (*Institutes*, 1.17.6; CO, 2.159).

purpose," to the manifestations of his wisdom and power, rooted, in his eternal purpose and his predestined end—all established in Jesus Christ crucified, risen, ascended, and at the right hand of God the Father Almighty.[93]

Yet we ought not miss the point on which Calvin's understanding of history turns: "The pagan writers have truly said that history is the teacher of life, *but there is no one who makes sound progress in it as it is handed down to us by them. Scripture alone lays claim to an office of this kind.*"[94] Secular history *as such* does none any good apart from the truth of Scripture.[95] Even sacred history *as such* does none any good apart from the doctrine taught in Scripture, which, Calvin says, "is its special province."[96] "If, therefore, we would make a right and proper use of the sacred histories, we must remember that we ought to use them in such a way as to draw from them the fruit of sound doctrine."[97] Not only does the truth or "fruit of sound doctrine" that Calvin instructs us to draw from sacred history provide an edifying aid to living the Christian life, but *"it prescribes general rules by which we may test all other history [generales praescribit regulas, ad quas unamquamque historiam exigamus]."*[98]

Calvin does not specify what these "rules" are, but surely they have to do with the operations of a divine agency for which secular writers have no category, with a vertical dimension for which secular history cannot account yet that stands at the very heart of sacred history. And how might such rules be used to "test all other history"? Surely by reminding us of the true presupposition and goal of all history, of its true meaning and purpose, and by calling into question any historiographical strictures that

93. Joseph Haroutunian, "Introduction" to *Calvin's Commentaries* (Philadelphia: Westminster Press, 1958), 42.

94. Calvin, Rom. 4:23 (100).

95. In his Seneca commentary Calvin did not challenge Cicero's claim, "History is life's schoolmistress. . . . *But for those who are naturally upright no external examples are needed.*" But here he is emphatic: "there is no one who makes sound progress in [history] as it is handed down to us by [pagan writers]."

96. Calvin, Rom. 4:23 (101).

97. Ibid.

98. Ibid.

would deny, limit, or minimize this vertical dimension that Calvin calls "the providence of God, His righteousness and goodness towards His people, and His judgments against the wicked."[99] Nevertheless, whatever Calvin means by "general rules by which we may test all other history," the point is that such rules come from sacred, not secular, history. It is not that we first learn from secular history how to understand sacred history. It is from sacred history that we learn how to understand secular history. The movement is from the particular to the universal, from biblical history to "all other history," from special hermeneutics to general hermeneutics.

The sequence of this movement is not arbitrary. It is definite and irreversible. It is not that secular history has nothing to contribute to our understanding of sacred history but that this sequence must not be confused. Calvin's talk about the *insufficiency* of bare history or statements such as "Those who simply know the bare history have not the Gospel, *unless there is added* a knowledge of the teaching, which reveals the fruit of the acts of Christ,"[100] might suggest that bare history, even though inadequate in itself, may still provide, with proper supplementation, a starting point for understanding the truth of the gospel or the "fruit of sound doctrine" at the heart of sacred history. But this is precisely what Calvin rejects. There is no way from secular history as such to sacred history. Those who think there is are "doing things backwards."[101]

Calvin makes this point throughout his commentaries, but he treats this question most systematically in the *Institutes*. The truth of Holy Scripture, the "fruit of sound doctrine" at the heart of sacred history by which we may test all other history, is not established from below but from above. It does not depend on "rational proofs," nor is it "sustained by external props," "human reasons, judgments, or conjectures"; rather, it stands or falls on "the secret testimony of the Spirit."[102]

99. Ibid.

100. Calvin, Acts 1:1 (1:22); CO, 48.1.

101. *Institutes*, 1.7.4; CO, 2.59.

102. *Institutes*, 1.7.4; CO, 2.59; *Institutes*, 1.8.1; CO, 2.61. "Let this point therefore stand: that those whom the Holy Spirit has inwardly taught [*quo Spiritus sanctus intus docuit*] truly rest upon Scripture [*solide acquiescere in Scriptura*], and that Scripture indeed is self-authenticated [*autopiston*]; hence, it is not right to subject it to proof and reasoning. And the certainty it deserves with us, it attains by the testimony of the Spirit [*Spiritus testimonio consequi*]. For even if it wins reverence for itself by its own majesty, it seriously

Unless this certainty, higher and stronger than any human judgment, be present, it will be vain to fortify the authority of Scripture by arguments, to establish it by common agreement of the church, or to confirm it with other helps. For unless this foundation is laid, its authority will always remain in doubt. Conversely, once we have embraced it devoutly as its dignity deserves, and have recognized it to be above the common sort of things, those arguments—not strong enough before to engraft and fix the certainty of Scripture in our minds—become very useful aids.[103]

Calvin does not deny the value of human reasoning or judgments, nor of human *historical* judgments. They can "become very useful aids." But he is unambiguous about *when* they can become useful aids:

There are other reasons, neither few nor weak, for which the dignity and majesty of Scripture are not only affirmed in godly hearts, but brilliantly vindicated against the wiles of its disparagers; yet of themselves these are not strong enough to provide a firm faith, *until* our Heavenly Father, revealing his majesty there, lifts reverence for Scripture beyond the realm of controversy. Therefore Scripture will ultimately suffice for a saving knowledge of God *only when* its certainty is founded upon the inward persuasion of the Holy Spirit. Indeed, these human testimonies which exist to confirm it will not be vain *if*, as *secondary aids* to our feebleness, they *follow* that chief and highest testimony. But those who wish to prove to unbelievers that Scripture is the Word of God are acting *foolishly*, for only by faith can this be known. Augustine therefore justly warns that

---

affects us only when it is sealed upon our hearts through the Spirit [*per Spiritum obsignata est cordibus nostris*]. Therefore, illumined by his power [*Illius ergo virtute illuminati*], we believe neither by our own nor by anyone else's judgment that Scripture is from God [*a Deo esse Scripturam*]; but above human judgment we affirm with utter certainty (just as if we were gazing upon the majesty of God himself) that it has flowed to us from the very mouth of God [*ab ipsissimo Dei ore*] by the ministry of men. We seek no proofs, no marks of genuineness upon which our judgment may lean; but we subject our judgment and wit to it as to a thing far beyond any guesswork! . . . Such, then, is a conviction that requires no reasons; such, a knowledge with which the best reason agrees—in which the mind truly reposes more securely and constantly than in any reasons; such, finally, a feeling that can be born only of heavenly revelation. I speak of nothing other than what each believer experiences within himself—though my words fall far beneath a just explanation of the matter" (*Institutes*, 1.7.5; CO, 2.60).

103. *Institutes*, 1.8.1; CO, 2.61.

godliness and peace of mind *ought to come first* if a man is to understand anything of such great matters.[104]

Where one starts mattered to Calvin. He was not a presuppositionless exegete. He did not believe that the Bible lends itself as a mere "storehouse of facts," certainly not "brute facts," for theological construal. Nor did he believe that "bare history" provides us with some sort of starting point for faith. As there is no way from reason to revelation, i.e., unaided reason, reason alone, or reason as such, so there is no way from secular to sacred history. To repeat: "Unless God's authority holds pride of place, faith will never be satisfied with the testimonies of men" (which is another way of saying "secular history"). "But," Calvin adds, "when the inward assurance of the Spirit has led the way, [faith] may *subsequently* allow them some standing, in an historical knowledge of events [*in historica rerum notitia*]."[105]

There is no way from secular history as such to sacred history, but there is a way from sacred to secular history and back again. Once secular history has been "tested" in light of the "rules" of sacred history and freed from unnecessary historiographical strictures, there is no reason why secular history cannot shed light on sacred history. Thus, there is a way from secular to sacred history. Once ordered, secular history can serve an important use. It can speak to sacred history, even teach and contribute something to it.

This is what Calvin is at pains to explain to those assailed by humanist skeptics in *Concerning Scandals*:

> For what would I be accomplishing were I to give a clear proof of the divinity of Christ to men like that? They will certainly fiercely reject anything I bring forward. What is more, the reason they reject the whole of Scripture is that whenever it does not happen to please them, they take up the attitude that it is absurd. Thus they appear to be intellectually superior in their own eyes only when they are laughing at our stupidity, because we accept with complete trust things that not only lack proof but are also incredible as far as human opinion goes. "Who

104. *Institutes*, 1.8.13; CO, 2.69 (emphasis added).
105. Calvin, Luke 1:1 (*Harmony*, 1.2); CO, 45.7.

is so ignorant," they ask, "as to allow himself to be persuaded about something for which he sees no reason?"[106]

Calvin says, "If I were to strive with such arguments as the human mind, acute as it is, can grasp, I should be exceedingly *inept*. For Paul acknowledges that our belief that Christ was God 'manifested in the flesh' (1 Tim. 3:16) is a mystery, far beyond the reach of all human perception."[107] Calvin appears to take the opposite tack in dealing with such critics in the 1559 *Institutes* when he says: "Although I do not excel either in great dexterity or eloquence, if I were struggling against the most crafty sort of despisers of God, who seek to appear shrewd and witty in disparaging Scripture, I am *confident* it would not be difficult for me to silence their clamorous voices."[108] Yet whether with confidence or ineptitude, it is clear in both texts that in arguing with such despisers all efforts are ultimately futile. In *Concerning Scandals*, Calvin continues: "What then? If they plead any incongruity as an excuse, it will certainly be disposed of easily and in such a way that they will be forced to keep silence, unless they have a mind to bluster in their impudence. However, I shall not be able to do so without making them think that we are more stupid than any idiots you care to mention, seeing that we depend upon Scripture alone for convincing people about such great matters."

Calvin has no remedy for those who have already made up their minds about the Bible and its "incongruities." "That is why," he says,

> I shall address myself to those who are indeed troubled by scandals of that kind, but who are still curable. To such people the only remedy I shall give is the one Paul prescribes, that they learn to become fools in this world in order to become capable of the heavenly wisdom (1 Cor. 3:18). By *"being fools"* we do not mean being stupid; nor do we direct those who are learned in the liberal sciences to jettison their knowledge, and those who are gifted with quickness of mind to become dull, as if a man cannot be a Christian unless he is more like a beast than a man. The profession of Christianity requires

106. Calvin, *Concerning Scandals*, 18; CO, 8.15–16.
107. Calvin, *Concerning Scandals*, 18; CO, 8.16 (emphasis added).
108. *Institutes*, 1.7.4; CO, 2.59 (emphasis added).

us to be immature, not in our thinking, but in malice (1 Cor. 14:20). But do not let anyone bring trust in his own mental resources or his learning into the school of Christ; do not let anyone be swollen with pride or full of distaste, and be so quick to reject what he is told, indeed even before he has sampled it. *Provided that we show ourselves to be teachable we shall not be aware of any obstacle here.*[109]

The school of Christ requires docility of mind, Calvin insists, but this does not mean we may despise knowledge gleaned from the liberal sciences: "we shall not be aware of any obstacle here." We have nothing to fear from secular history, if it is honest history. Of course, not all that passes for "history" is honest history. That is why it must be tested. But once tested, it can be a very useful aid.

Conclusion

I have claimed that Calvin did more than any other theologian in the sixteenth century to highlight the distinction between sacred and secular history. But my second claim is that no theologian did more to try to relate these concepts. I have sought to demonstrate how Calvin relates sacred and secular history but not yet how secular history can be of use, specifically. This must wait.

Therefore, to summarize: Calvin understood that the major difference between sacred and secular history is that whereas secular history was about many things (and not all things equally true), sacred history was about one thing, the truth, Jesus Christ, the source of all truth, in whose Spirit he promised to lead us (John 16:13), in whose light we see light (Ps. 36:9). Sacred history differs from secular history in that the truth to which it bears witness is one. Sacred history is thus unified to this extent, whereas secular history is incoherent and fragmented. But secular history can be healed of its incoherence and fragmentation and serve an important purpose. This does not mean that secular history can be of use to us only in distilled or diluted form. Nor does it mean that it will tell us only what we already know. No, contrary to Richard-

---

109. Calvin, *Concerning Scandals*, 18–19; CO, 8.16 (emphasis added).

son, that sacred history is unified does not mean that it is "complete" in every respect, and that it cannot learn from secular history. The Bible gives us what we need to know, but not all that is worth knowing. Yet secular history must be tested and, as I think Calvin would agree, tested according to what Erich Auerbach called the Bible's "tyrannical" claim to truth: "The world of the Scripture stories is not satisfied with claiming to be a historically true reality—it insists that it is the only real world, is destined for autocracy. All other scenes, issues, and ordinances have no right to appear independently of it, and it is promised that all of them, the history of all mankind, will be given their *due place* within its frame, [yet] will be subordinated to it."[110]

I do not claim that Calvin always "got it right" (nor would he), but his effort to give secular history its due place without losing his focus on the one truth of Holy Scripture is, I believe, his greatest contribution and most enduring legacy as an exegete in service of Christ's church.

---

110. Erich Auerbach, *Mimesis: The Representation of Reality in Western Literature*, trans. Willard R. Trask (Princeton: Princeton University Press, 1953), 14–15 (emphasis added).

12

CALVIN'S PRINCIPLE OF WORSHIP

R. SCOTT CLARK

One of John Calvin's earliest, most fundamental, and persistent concerns was the reformation of public worship according to the Word of God. In the 1536 edition of the *Institutes* he advocated liturgical reforms concerning prayer, the sermon, and the weekly administration of the Lord's Supper.[1] One of the first steps that he and the other ministers took toward the reorganization of the Genevan church was the reformation of worship. In January of 1537 he and the other ministers submitted to the Council the Articles Concerning the Organization of the Church and of Worship in Geneva.[2] In these articles Calvin and the ministers asked not only for weekly communion, the election of elders,

---

1. CO, 1.139–40. See also John Calvin, *Institutes of the Christian Religion*, trans. Ford Lewis Battles (Grand Rapids: Eerdmans, 1986), 122–23. See also Wulfert de Greef, *The Writings of John Calvin*, trans. Lyle D. Bierma (Grand Rapids: Baker, 1993), 126–27, and especially note 8 for a bibliography of important research on Calvin's liturgy.

2. See CO, 10.5–14; J. K. S. Reid, ed., *Calvin: Theological Treatises*, Library of Christian Classics (Philadelphia: Westminster Press, 1954), 47–55.

and the institution of church discipline, but also that the congregations should sing psalms as had been done in "the ancient Church and in the evidence of St. Paul himself."[3] That Calvin advocated sweeping reform of the Western liturgy is reasonably well known. What is not as often appreciated, however, is Calvin's theory of worship, i.e., the principle on which he attempted to effect those reforms.

It is interesting to observe the degree to which Calvin's principle of worship has been neglected.[4] This is exceedingly odd, since even a superficial reading of Calvin reveals a profound and passionate concern for the reformation of public worship. Calvin repeatedly articulated a clear principle on which reformation was to be conducted and around which worship was to be organized, and yet that principle has been overlooked.[5] This may be because it does not fit the dominant modern agendas.[6] Two examples must suffice. Leading up to the Confession of 1967, Calvin was read as the theologian of the existential encounter with the Word.[7] More recently, in our age of "Liquid Modernity," as Zygmunt Bauman has it,[8] Calvin has been read by Suzanne Selinger and William J. Bouwsma as an angst-ridden Modern.[9] Bernard Cottret, following Max Weber, describes Calvin (and his view of worship) as a "Modern" man disenchanted with the

---

3. *Calvin: Theological Treatises*, 53. "Laultre part est des pseaulmes, que nous desirons estre chantes en lesglise comme nous en auons lexemple en lesglise ancienne et mesme le tesmoignage de S. Paul, qui dict estre bon de chanter en la congregation de bouche et de cueur" (*CO*, 10.12).

4. François Wendel's otherwise excellent survey of Calvin's theology contains no discussion of Calvin's theology of worship. See his *Calvin: The Origin and Development of His Religious Thought*, trans. Philip Mairet (New York: Harper & Row, 1950). More recently Burk Parsons, ed., *John Calvin: A Heart for Devotion, Doctrine, and Doxology* (Lake Mary, FL: Reformation Trust, 2008), despite the promising title, contains no entry on Calvin's theology and practice of worship. In neither of these works does the word *worship* occur in the index.

5. See, e.g., Wendel, *Calvin: Origin and Development*, an otherwise excellent work that ignores Calvin's doctrine of worship.

6. On the effect of modern agendas on Calvin studies, see Richard A. Muller, *The Unaccommodated Calvin*, Oxford Studies in Historical Theology (New York and Oxford: Oxford University Press, 2000).

7. E.g., A. Dowey Edward, *Knowledge of God in Calvin's Theology*, 3rd ed. (Grand Rapids: Eerdmans, 1994).

8. Zygmunt Bauman, *Liquid Modernity* (2000; repr., Oxford: Polity/Blackwell, 2004).

9. Suzanne Selinger, *Calvin against Himself: An Inquiry in Intellectual History* (Hamden, CT: Archon, 1984); William J. Bouwsma, *John Calvin: A Sixteenth Century Portrait* (New York: Oxford University Press, 1988).

world.[10] In such a milieu Calvin's concern for the form of worship might seem superfluous. As a consequence of the dissonance between modern concerns and Calvin's, he is not always portrayed as teaching consistently that we glorify God by worshiping him only as he has commanded. When scholars do pay attention to Calvin's view of worship, some continue to give in to the temptation to set his theology of worship against the later Reformed tradition.[11] Other writers treat Calvin as if he were a forerunner of the mainline liturgical renewal movement.[12] In contrast, this essay sympathizes with the accounts of Calvin's principle of worship given by

10. Bernard Cottret, *Calvin: A Biography*, trans. M. Wallace McDonald (Grand Rapids: Eerdmans, 2000), 281.

11. See R. J. Gore Jr., *Covenantal Worship: Reconsidering the Puritan Regulative Principle* (Phillipsburg, NJ: P&R Publishing, 2003), 71–89. For a response to Gore's characterization of the regulative principle, see R. Scott Clark, *Recovering the Reformed Confession: Our Theology, Piety, and Practice* (Phillipsburg, NJ: P&R Publishing, 2008), 235–37, 241–42, 245–49, 263. Derek Thomas is right to criticize R. J. Gore's account of Calvin's theology of worship in R. J. Gore, "Renewing the Puritan Regulative Principle of Worship," *Presbyterion* 20 (1995): 46. Gore argues that Calvin taught "freedom to worship God in any manner warranted by Scripture." Such a view attributes to Calvin the very sort of subjectivism he opposed. For Calvin, it is not we who decide what God will accept, but rather God who has already decided what he will accept and how he will be approached and who has unequivocally revealed his will in Scripture. See Derek Thomas, "The Regulative Principle: Responding to Recent Criticism," in *Give Praise to God: A Vision for Reforming Worship: Celebrating the Legacy of James Montgomery Boice*, ed. Philip Graham Ryken et al. (Phillipsburg, NJ: P&R Publishing, 2003), 81–82.

12. E.g., Pamela Ann Moeller, *Calvin's Doxology: Worship in the 1559 Institutes with a View to Contemporary Worship Renewal*, vol. 44, Princeton Theological Monograph Series (Pittsburgh: Pickwick Publications, 1997). At one point Moeller imputes to Calvin a principle of worship closer to Luther than to Calvin. See also Hughes Oliphant Old, "John Calvin and the Prophetic Criticism of Worship," in *John Calvin and the Church*, ed. Timothy George (Louisville: Westminster/John Knox Press, 1990), 233–38. We should take exception to the claim (233) that Calvin was not opposed to the use of instruments in worship. The ground of the claim is that where Calvin should have mentioned such opposition, he did not. Of course, this is an argument from silence. Calvin opposed the use of instruments explicitly and implicitly. In his comments on Psalm 149:2, he wrote, "Musica instrumenta quorum meminit, ad tempus paedagogiae pertinent: ne stulta aemulatione in usum nostrum trahamus quod proprium fuit verteri populo." In his comments on Psalm 150:3, he characterized the use of musical instruments as being "usus viguit sub legali cultu" (CO, 32.438, 442). These two passages form an unequivocal rejection of the reinstitution of musical instruments in the new covenant on the basis that they were proper to the old covenant and improper to the new. The expression *stulte aemulatione* captures the animus of Calvin's rejection of musical instruments. Old's more recent exposition of Calvin's doctrine of worship is better but still incomplete and still written with the mainline liturgical renewal in view. See Hughes Oliphant Old, "Calvin's Theology of Worship," in *Give Praise to God*, 412–35.

Carlos M. N. Eire, W. Robert Godfrey, Derek Thomas, and Rowland Ward, among others.[13]

This essay argues that Calvin's principle of worship was that we must do in worship only that which God has commanded. It was essentially what has become known as the regulative principle of worship that was adopted and practiced by the English and European Reformed churches.[14] More significantly, it was essentially that contained in the Heidelberg Catechism, the *Directory for Publique Worship* (hereafter *DPW*), and the Westminster Standards.[15]

Public Worship and Piety

Because modern scholarship has often asked anachronistic questions about Calvin, such as whether he anticipated Friedrich Schleiermacher's subjectivism or Karl Barth's neo-orthodoxy, it has sometimes failed to ask the questions that Calvin himself was asking. Few topics, however, were as important to Calvin as the reformation of public worship. For Calvin, our piety, our growth in godliness, and our growth in the knowledge of God are the direct result principally of attendance to public worship, the preaching of the gospel, and the administration of the sacraments. "Clearly the first foundation of righteousness is the worship of God. When it is overturned, all the other members of righteousness, like a building torn apart, and in ruins, are wrecked and scattered."[16] There is no virtue in refraining from committing theft against one's fellows if "in the interim,

13. Carlos M. N. Eire, *War against the Idols: The Reformation of Worship from Erasmus to Calvin* (Cambridge: Cambridge University Press, 1986); W. Robert Godfrey, "Calvin, Worship, and the Sacraments," in *Theological Guide to Calvin's Institutes: Essays and Analysis*, ed. David W. Hall and Peter A. Lillback, The Calvin 500 Series (Phillipsburg, NJ: P&R Publishing, 2008), 368–89; Derek Thomas, "The Regulative Principle: Responding to Recent Criticism," in *Give Praise to God*, 74–84; Richard A. Muller and Rowland S. Ward, *Scripture and Worship: Biblical Interpretation and the Directory for Public Worship*, Westminster Assembly and the Reformed Faith (Phillipsburg, NJ: P&R Publishing, 2007), 98–106.

14. See Clark, *Recovering the Reformed Confession*, 228–91.

15. See Philip Schaff, ed., *The Creeds of Christendom*, 3 vols. (Grand Rapids: Baker, 1983), 3:343; *A Directory for Publique Worship of God* (London, 1644); WCF 21.1.

16. *Institutio Christianae Religionis* (Geneva, 1559), 2.8.11. "Primum sane iustitiae fundamentum, est Dei cultus: quo everso, reliqua omnia iustitiae membra, velut divulsi collapsique aedificii partes, lacera et dissipata sunt" (*OS*, 3.352.16–18).

through criminal sacrilege, you steal the majesty of God."[17] It is "meaning-less to speak of righteousness apart from religion."[18]

It seems sure that for Calvin to speak of *cultus Dei* in this context, even if these words had indirect reference to worship in the broader sense of one's general attitude toward God, the direct reference here is to the act of public worship. This is the highest and most significant expression of divine worship. It is fundamental because to violate God's canon for worship is spiritual theft. It robs God of that which is his by right. Calvin repeated his thesis again near the end of the section: "Therefore we call the worship of God the beginning and foundation of righteousness ..."[19] Whatever other external, civil virtues (e.g., continence or temperance) might exist, without true worship they are "empty and frivolous before God."[20] For Calvin, the congregation's approach to God in public worship was the beginning of Christian piety.

His view of human nature after the fall was another reason that this principle was so important to him. In contrast to the generally optimistic view of human nature that has prevailed in the modern period, Calvin understood the effect of the fall to be pervasive and corrosive of human inclinations. For Calvin, worship must follow an explicitly revealed divine norm because, *post lapsum*, the "perpetual disposition" of human beings is to be a "factory of idols."[21] "The mind begets an idol and the hand creates it."[22] Under his read-ing of redemptive history and "daily experience" (*quotidiana experientia*), our "carnal iniquity" is never satisfied until we find a representation of ourselves, which we then proceed to present to the world as if it were God.[23] The only antidote to idolatry is to worship God "simply as he commands[;] we do not obey him by mixing our inventions with his worship."[24]

17. "Si per sceleratum sacrilegium interim Dei maiestatem sua gloria spolias" (*OS*, 3.352.19–20).

18. "Frustra igitur sine religione venditatur iustitia" (ibid., 3.352.24).

19. "Principium ergo et fundamentum iustitiae vocamus Dei cultum . . ." (ibid., 3.352.16).

20. "Inane est ac frivolum coram Deo" (ibid., 3.352.29).

21. "Unde colligere licet, hominis ingenium perpetuam, ut ita loquar, esse idolorum fabricam" (ibid., 3.96.28–30; *Institutes*, 1.11.8).

22. "Mens igitur idolum gignit: manus parit" (*OS*, 3.97.11; *Institutes*, 1.11.8).

23. *OS*, 3.97.20–25; *Institutes*, 1.11.8.

24. "Illo colendo simpliciter quod mandat, nullas nostras inventiones miscendo sequimur" (*OS*, 5.186.33–34).

The Second Commandment in the 1540s

Throughout his career Calvin applied his understanding of human nature and his understanding of the second commandment to a variety of circumstances. In 1543, in response to a request from Martin Bucer (1491–1551), Calvin wrote a "Humble Exhortation" to Charles V and the Diet of Speyer.[25] He summarized the entire Protestant case in one sentence:

> If it is asked by what things chiefly the Christian religion should continue to stand among us and retain its truth, it is certain that these two things not only occupy the highest place but also all the remaining parts and even the whole strength of Christianity is comprehended under it: that God should be worshiped duly and that men should know from where our salvation is to be sought.[26]

Although the modern reader is not surprised by his mention of the ground of salvation, one might be surprised that the first thing he mentioned was "that God should be worshiped duly." The phrase "duly worshiped" meant more than mere solemnity. "Let us now define the legitimate worship of God. The principal foundation is to recognize him as he is, the only source of all virtue, righteousness, sanctity, wisdom, truth and thus to ascribe and attribute to him alone glory for all those goods, and to seek all things from him alone."[27] Prayer arises from a consciousness of these realities. This is "true sanctification of his name."[28]

25. *Supplex Exhortatio ad invictissimum caesarem carolum quintum* ([Geneva, 1543]; CO, 6.453–534). See also the ET in Henry Beveridge and Jules Bonnet, eds., *Selected Works of John Calvin: Tracts and Letters*, repr. ed., 7 vols. (Grand Rapids: Baker, 1983), 1:123–234 (hereafter *SW*). See also de Greef, *The Writings of John Calvin*, 160–61.

26. "Si quaeritur, quibus potissimum rebus stet christiana religio inter nos, suamque veritatem retineat, has duas non modo summum locum occupare certum est, sed reliquas etiam omnes partes, adeoque totam vim christianismi sub se comprehendere: ut rite colatur Deus, ut unde salus sibi petenda sit, noverint hominess" (CO, 6.459).

27. "Nunc cultum Dei legitimum definiamus. Huius vero praecipuum est fundamentum, eum sicuti est, omnis virtutis, iustitiae, sanctitatis, sapientiae, veritatis, potentiae, bonitatis, clementiae, vitae et salutis fontem unicum agnoscere, ideoque bonorum omnium gloriam illi adscribere in solidum, et tribuere quaerere in ipso solo omnia" (CO, 6.460).

28. "Haec est veia nominis eius sanctificatio" (ibid.).

Genuine worship is essential, and it is the Holy Spirit who produces self-denial and genuine adoration of God. The form of worship, however, was equally important for Calvin. As his petition continued, he pressed closer to the question of the reformation of public worship. "In these parts is contained the true and sincere worship of God, of which alone he approves, and in which he delights, which the Holy Spirit teaches in Scripture..."[29] This was always the pattern of true worship. Under Moses it was clothed in figures, but in the new covenant it is "*simplex.*"[30] Calvin appealed to and quoted John 4:23 as a proof. The substance has not changed, but the form has. Calvin wanted the emperor and the electors to understand that the "universal rule of pure worship" that he was about to articulate was no novelty.[31]

He distinguished between that which adheres to this "universal rule" and that which he described as "fictitious worship" (*fictios cultus*).[32] Nevertheless, he was quite conscious that he was articulating a principle that has been neither universally observed nor universally accepted, not even among his Protestant colleagues. "I know that this world is persuaded with difficulty that God disapproves of all worship except that instituted by his Word."[33] The inclination to do the very opposite is "embedded in all their bones or marrow."[34] Desiring God is not enough. True worship must take a certain form. For proof of this, Calvin quoted 1 Samuel 15:22 and Matthew 15:9.[35] When one approaches God in ways other than those commanded, one is adding (*additur*) to his Word, and any such addition is necessarily a lie (*mendacium*). More than that, it is "will worship" and "vanity" (*vanitatem*).[36] For Calvin, it was not a matter of deciding how we will approach God in worship but whether

29. "His partibus contineri verum sincerumque Dei cultum, quem solum probat, et quo delectatur, tum spiritus sanctus ubique in scripturis docet..." (ibid.).

30. Ibid.

31. "Porro, universalis est regula, quae purum Dei cultum a vitioso discernit: ne comminiscamur ipsi quod nobis visum fuerit, sed quid praescribat is, qui solus iubendi potestatem habet, spectemus" (ibid.).

32. Ibid., 6.461.

33. "Scio quam difficulter hoc persuadeatur mundo, improbari Dao cultus omnes praeter verbum suum institutos" (ibid.).

34. "In ossibus omnium defixa est, ac medullis" (ibid.).

35. Ibid.

36. Ibid. ἐθελοθρησκίᾳ occurs in Colossians 2:23.

we will submit to God's revealed will. "Wherever the judge has ruled, there is no more time for litigating."[37]

At stake here is the divine glory. The Roman church says that it intends to give glory to God, but in fact, it robs (*spoliant*) him of the greater part because it divides (*partiuntur*) among the saints that which is proper to God alone.[38] It transfers to creatures glory that belongs to God alone.[39] Calling on God is not sufficient. One must have confidence that God alone is our helper. The Roman piety does not rest on this confidence.[40] Instead of resting on the intercession of Christ for us, Rome invokes competing mediators.[41] It has become "a new Judaism" (*novum iudaismus*).[42] It has fundamentally misread the history of redemption and has reinstituted the very typological sacrifices and ceremonies that "God, clara voce, abrogated [*abrogaverat*]."[43]

There should be no question that, for Calvin, the doctrine of justification was the "axis of religion" (*cardinem religionis*).[44] The second animating concern of the *Supplex Exhortatio* took up that point. He also believed, however, just as fervently in the media (means) through which God operates, including worship. His concern for God's use of means in redeeming humans is evident in the title of book 3 of the *Institutes*: "Concerning the media of receiving Christ's grace . . ."[45] His concern for the correct use of means in the human response to divine salvation appears in the title of book 4 of the *Institutes*: "Concerning the external media or helps by which he calls us into the society of Christ and retains us in the same."[46]

37. "Ubi semel pronunciavit iudex, iam amplius litigandi non est" (*CO*, 6.461).
38. Ibid.
39. "Transferant ad creaturas" (ibid.).
40. The Council of Trent, session 6, on January 13, 1547, in canon 12 would pronounce an anathema upon anyone who says, "Fidem iustificantem nihil aliud esse quam fiduciam divinae misericordiae peccata remittentis propter Christum, vel eam fiduciam solam esse, qua iustificamur" (Heinrich Joseph Dominik Denzinger, ed., *Enchiridion Symbolorum*, 30th ed. [Freibourg: Herder, 1960], 296, 822).
41. *CO*, 6.462.
42. Ibid., 6.463.
43. Ibid.
44. "Religionis cardinem" (*OS*, 4.182.16).
45. "De modo percipiendae Christi gratiae . . ." (ibid., 4.1.3).
46. "De externis mediis vel adminiculis, quibus Deus in Christi societatem nos invitat, et in ea retinet" (ibid., 5.1.3–5).

His principle of worship brought Calvin into conflict with Rome. It also created tension with fellow evangelicals.[47] The 1548 Leipzig Interim highlighted this tension. It was a pragmatic response to the collapse of the Schmalkaldic Princes against Charles V. With respect to worship, the Interim rested on an expansive definition of *adiaphora*. It essentially froze the Reformation in place and forbade further reformation. The interim provoked a response not only from Lutheran theologians, e.g., Matthias Flaccius (1520–75), but also from Calvin, who in 1549 characterized the entire project as *The Adultero-German Interim*. To this critique he appended a treatise, *On the True Ground of Ecclesiastical Pacification and Reformation*.[48] As with the *Supplex Exhortatio*, his critique of the *Interim* was in two parts, in effect, justification and sanctification.[49] Under the second heading he addressed point by point those corruptions of Christian worship introduced during the Middle Ages.

In the much longer *Vera Ratio* he addressed the fundamentals behind his critique of the Roman sacerdotal system. The true ground of peace is genuine reformation according to the Word. Rome's problem was that she was not really interested in genuine peace and reformation. Whatever concessions she was offering now, as part of the interim, were mere strategies and stalling tactics.[50] Calvin once more surveyed the Protestant doctrine

47. "Calvin and company wanted to stay as close as possible to the biblical text and further chose to make exclusive use of the Psalms as the songbook given by God himself. The Germans, on the other hand, were as determined to be biblical but thought that this could also be achieved with biblically-based hymns" (Herman J. Selderhuis, *John Calvin: A Pilgrim's Life*, trans. Albert Gootjes [Downers Grove, IL: InterVarsity Press, 2009], 90).

48. *Interim adultero-Germanum, cui adiecta est vera Christianae pacificationis et ecclesiase reformandae ratio*, in CO, 7.545–674. The ETs are in *SW*, 3.190–358.

49. The bipartite structure of these two treatises reflects his commitment to the "duplex gratia Dei." See *Institutes*, 3.11.1. "Christum nobis Dei benignitate datum, fide a nobis apprehendi ac possideri, cujus participatione duplicem potissimum gratiam recipiamus; nempe ut ejus innocentia Deo reconciliati pro judice jam propitium habeamus in coelis patrem: deinde ut ejus spiritu sanctificati innocentiam puritatemque vitae meditemur" (*OS*, 4.182.4–8). See Cornelis P. Venema, *Accepted and Renewed in Christ* (Göttingen: Vandenhoek and Ruprecht, 2007); R. Scott Clark, *Caspar Olevian and the Substance of the Covenant: The Double Benefit of Christ*, Rutherford Studies in Historical Theology, repr. ed. (Grand Rapids: Reformation Heritage Books, 2008); R. Scott Clark, "The Benefits of Christ: Double Justification in Protestant Theology before the Westminster Assembly," in *The Faith Once Delivered: Essays in Honor of Dr. Wayne R. Spear*, ed. Anthony T. Selvaggio (Phillipsburg, NJ: P&R Publishing, 2007), 107–34.

50. CO, 7.592.

of justification (and assurance) *sola gratia et sola fide* before articulating his case for the reformation of worship.[51]

The second step toward the pacification and reformation of the church was the restoration of "true religion" (*vera religio*).[52] The worship of God comprehends and is premised on justification, but it would be preposterous to refuse to dispute how God is purely worshiped, since this is the means by which salvation is administered.[53] As in the *Supplex Exhortatio*, he surveyed the history of redemption to show that the contemporary corruption of worship was not unique to their time, concluding with a declaration: "Thus, all worship counterfeited against his command, he not only rejects as useless, but is plainly condemned."[54] To those who appealed to the example of David's dancing before the ark as a pattern for Christian worship, Calvin replied that this was nothing but a Roman trick, another way to establish "false worship" (*commentitos cultus*).[55] Even King David was subject to the second commandment, the *lex communis* that forbids any worship except that commanded by God himself. If he sinned, then he is no example. Nevertheless, Calvin did not concede that David had violated the second commandment. "It is well known that the ceremonies were an exercise of piety, not that we should reckon from the exercise itself but from the purpose of the exercise."[56] David "was led" to such exercises "by a peculiar prompting of the Spirit, which is always to be observed in the extraordinary acts of the saints."[57] In other words, David was a special player in the history of redemption. He acted according to the second commandment, but his dancing before the ark was extraordinary and not intended as a pattern for

51. That section concludes at ibid., 7.607.
52. Ibid.
53. "Sed disputare, quomodo salutem adipiscantur homines, quomodo autem rite colatur Deus tacere, nimis est praeposterum" (ibid.).
54. "Itaque omnes cultus, praeter mandatum suum confictos, non modo tanquam irritos respuit, sed plane damnat" (ibid., 7.608).
55. Ibid., 7.609.
56. "Satis scitur, caeremonias ita pietatis fuisse exercitia, ut non tam ex se, quam ex fine aestimarentur" (ibid.).
57. "Quanquam non dubium est, quin peculiari spiritus instinctu huc adductus fuerit: quod in extraordinariis sanctorum factis semper observandum est" (ibid.).

postcanonical worship services and certainly not new covenant worship services.

As in 1543, Calvin presented a binary choice. Either one obeys the clear revelation of God by offering "legitimate worship" (*legitimum cultum*) or one is guilty of "will worship."[58] For Calvin, it was not a matter of following Moses over Paul. His proof texts for this argument were Matthew 15:9 and Romans 12:1. Paul condemns (*damnat*) will worship just as plainly as Moses. The reasonable worship of which Paul spoke in Romans 12:1 was nothing less than "legitimate worship" or that which is "ad eius voluntatem."[59] It is not creatures but the Creator who defines "legitimate" or "reasonable" when it comes to worship. If we allow "works" not commanded by God to "sneak in" to the divine worship, "to become part of the divine worship and spiritual righteousness, the principal matter in religion is overturned."[60]

Just before the close of this argument, Calvin promised to return to the subject of "mediate works" (*de operibus mediis*).[61] He did so after surveying a series of Romish errors.[62] He listed a series of religious practices in worship, e.g., the folding of the hands, kneeling at the altar, kissing the altar, making the sign of the cross, elevating the host, and striking one's breast, among other things. These were said by some to be "indifferent" (*indifferens*). If so, why should the Reformed wish to forbid them? Calvin replied suggestively but cryptically that it is not right for a "performer on a stage" (*histrionem*) to arrogate to himself more gravity than a priest (*sacerdos*) has in "ratifying the covenant of God."[63] He summarized his objection by arguing that "they take to themselves too much license in external things."[64] Here Calvin was addressing the distinction between "externals and essentials," to which we now turn our attention.

---

58. Ibid, 7.610.
59. Ibid.
60. "Tantum ostendere volui, si absque Dei mandato suscepta a nobis opera in partem divini cultus spiritualisque iustitiae obrepant, quod in religione praecipuum est everti" (ibid.).
61. Ibid.
62. Ibid., 7.650.
63. "Verum, ut hoc subticeam, quam indignum est histrionem plus habere centuplo in scena gravitatis, quam in saciendo Dei et hominum foedere habeat sacerdos?" (ibid.).
64. "Sibi licentiae in rebus externis sumunt" (ibid.).

Pastoral Use of the Principle

In the major controversies over worship and ecclesiastical authority in Europe and England in the 1540s, Calvin, like other Reformed authors, articulated a distinct principle of worship on the basis of the primary and unique authority of Scripture. He did not regard his disagreement with Rome or even with fellow evangelicals as a matter of competing religious subjective experiences. Implicit in his polemic against idolatry generally and against the Roman corruption of worship in particular was his doctrine of the perspicuity of Scripture. God's Word is the "mark" (*notam*) by which "true worship is discerned from corrupt and vitiated worship."[65] God's moral will is so clearly revealed that one may see that "the whole form of worshiping God, which is used today in the world, is nothing more than mere corruption."[66]

Nevertheless, however clear Calvin's principle, its application to the Reformed churches in Europe was less obvious. In his correspondence one witnesses the struggle to translate the principle into praxis. Repeatedly in his letters he appealed to a distinction between externals or ceremonies on the one hand and essentials on the other. To complicate things a bit, however, it is not always clear what Calvin meant by the noun *ceremony*. Its meaning must be determined by its context. For example, his use of *externals* often reminds one of Martin Luther's use of the term against Andreas Karlstadt (1486–1541).[67] In other cases, his distinction between *externals* and *essentials* seems to have been the distinction made by later Reformed writers between *circumstances* and *elements*.

During his stay in Strasbourg he confided in a 1539 letter to Guillaume Farel (1489–1565) that "so intense is the desire of Bucer for spreading the gospel, that, content to have obtained those things which are most important, he is sometimes more lenient than is right in yielding those things which he considers less important, but which, nevertheless, have

---

65. "Quum autem verbum Dei notam esse dixerimus, quae verum eius cultum a vitioso pravoque discernat" (ibid., 6.463).

66. "Totam collendi Dei formam, quae hodie mundo est usitata, nihil quam meram esse corruptionem" (ibid., 6.464).

67. Eire, *War against the Idols*, 66–73.

their weight."[68] Calvin had to negotiate the narrows between principle and the necessity of a holy alliance with those who were less rigorous in their application of the principle or who, perhaps, did not share his principle. Again, writing to Farel about a month later, he observed that Bucer defended "Luther's ceremonies" not out of principle and would not "endeavor to introduce them." He assured Farel that Bucer was opposed to "the Latin chants" and that he "hated images." He was confident that Bucer would not restore these ceremonies once removed, and he sympathized with Bucer's concern to prevent a separation from Luther over the reformation of worship.[69]

Writing to Farel from Regensburg in 1541, just after the equivocal and largely failed colloquy,[70] he noted that there were *res medias* in worship that the Protestants had conceded. He did not indicate precisely what those were. Nevertheless, he stipulated some of the liturgical doctrines and practices on which all the Protestants agreed to be unacceptable: "Transubstantiation, reposition, circumgestation, and other superstitious forms of worship (*superstitiosi cultus*)." At the suggestion that the Protestants should accept these things, even Bucer (*Collega mea*) became indignant. They all agreed that transubstantiation was a *rem fictitiam* and that reposition and adoration were "idolatrous or at least dangerous and without the Word of God."[71]

In 1543, after an outbreak of the plague in Geneva, Calvin responded to a certain Monsieur Le Curé, a Roman Catholic lay critic of the Genevan Reformation. Calvin conceded that God was chastising Geneva by the plague, but he disagreed with Le Curé's analysis

68. "Tanto enim studio propagandi evangelii flagrat Bucerus, ut quae praecipua sunt contentus impetrasse, interdum sit aequo lenior in iis concedendis, quae minutula quidem ipse putat, sed habent tamen suum pondus" (*CO*, 10.328; *SW*, 4.125).

69. "Quod Bucerus, porro defendit Lutheri caeremonias, non ideo fit quod appetat, aut invehere eas moliatur. Cantum latinum adduci nullo modo potest ut probet: ab imaginibus abhorret. Alia partim contemnit, partim non curat. Sed non est timendum ut quae semel abrogata sunt, rursus postliminio reducat. Tantum non patitur, ut ob externas illas observatiunculas a Luthero disiungamur. Nec sane iustas esse puto dissidii causas" (*CO*, 10.341; *SW*, 4.137).

70. On the negotiations at Regensburg, see Clark, "The Benefits of Christ," 110–16.

71. "Iussi sumus omnest ordine dicere sententias: fuit una omnium vox, transsubstantionem rem esse fictitiam, repositionem supersitiosam, idolatricam esse adorarationem, vel saltem perciulosam, quum sine verbo Dei" (*CO*, 11.215; *SW*, 4.261).

of providence. Whereas Le Curé interpreted the plague to mean that God was unhappy with the Genevan Reformation, Calvin argued that it was that the Reformation had not gone far enough: "You drive us back to the means which rather serve to provoke and inflame" God's wrath even more.[72] He identified two things that "specially provoke the wrath of God," the first of which is idolatry and superstition.[73] He accused Roman Catholics of adoring "stone and wood," of invoking the dead, and of serving God "by ceremonies foolishly invented without the authority of his word."[74] Specifically he attacked "silly baptismal ceremonies" that have been "invented by men." Rome had likewise corrupted the Supper by turning it into a sacrifice.[75] Le Curé would have had Geneva go back to the very thing that provoked God's wrath in the first place. Calvin's answer was further reformation. He could not see how "candles and torches" or "reliquaries of the dead . . . comport with Christianity."[76]

In 1551, dedicating his (1550) commentary on the "*Epistolas Canonicas*" to that young Josiah, King Edward VI, and aware of the complexities of the on-again/off-again Reformation of the English church, he spoke directly to "choses indifferentes" that might be allowed in worship.[77] He exhorted Edward to follow the rule that "sobriety and measure" be observed so that the "light of the gospel" should not be obscured by the "shadows of the law" (*les umbres de la loy*).[78] The medieval church was, as it were, the old covenant, the period of types and shadows, and the Reformation was the new. Among the "manifest abuses" (*des abus manifestes*) that "cannot be endured" were "prayers for the souls of the departed" (*prier pour les ames des trespassez*) and to the saints.[79]

In his attempt to mediate the dispute between the Anglicans and Genevanists, if we may, in exile at Frankfurt in 1555, Calvin found it necessary to castigate both parties for failing to live together as fellow

72. *SW*, 4.370.
73. Ibid., 4.365.
74. Ibid., 4.366.
75. Ibid., 4.369.
76. Ibid., 4.370.
77. CO, 14.39. See de Greef, *The Writings of John Calvin*, 99.
78. "*La clarte de levangile*" (CO, 14.39).
79. Ibid., 14.40.

Englishmen in exile.[80] With respect to "externals," he remonstrated first with some of those who identified with the Genevan party, who seemed to find leisure (*otio*) to agitate for a particular *precandi forma* and for certain ceremonies.[81] His approach was to show (*praebeo*) himself to be "easy" (*facilem*) and "flexible" (*flexibilem*) "in rebus mediis ut sunt externi ritus."[82] This language might surprise the modern reader who knows Calvin primarily as the stern "accusative case," and certainly there were limits to his easiness and flexibility in the application of the principle of worship. He drew the line at capitulating to those who were more inflexible than he. Some things in the Anglican liturgy, as used in Frankfurt and as described to Calvin, which were "tolerable trifles" (*tolerabiles ineptias*). However tolerable, they were not preferable because the liturgy did not possess the "desired purity."[83]

The question was not whether there should be further reformation but what strategy should be employed to reach that end. Calvin took issue with those who were demanding to "correct the defect *statim die*." Unless there was "manifest impiety" (*manifesta impietas*), prudence required that one bear with such infirmities "for a time" (*ad tempus*).[84] The Anglican liturgy should be regarded as a starting place for further reformation.[85] The goal was to arrive at a liturgy that was "uncommon and pure" (*limatius ac purius*).[86] Lest anyone think Calvin was indifferent even to these impurities or that he was willing that Christians should endure them for long, he made it clear that he could not understand how people were able to tolerate such "papisticae reliquae."[87] Such things should have been removed long ago, and a fresh start in Frankfurt presented an opportunity to be rid of them.

Calvin's practical adaptability to exigent circumstances did not mean a change in his views. This is evident from his June 17, 1555 sermon on

---

80. *CO*, 15.393–94; *SW*, 6.117–19.
81. *CO*, 15.394.
82. Ibid.
83. "Non fuisse eam purtitatem, quae optanda fuerat" (ibid.).
84. Ibid.
85. "Sic ergo a talibus redimentis incipere licuit" (ibid.).
86. Ibid.
87. Ibid.

Deuteronomy 5:8–10.[88] There he reiterated his conviction that the effect of sin is so vitiating and fallen humans are so inclined to idolatry that unless God threatens them with the severest punishments, we are prone to "imagine of God all that is contrary to his majesty."[89] Our sinful inclinations do not end with gross idolatry. They extend to "our good intentions" (*nos bonnes intentions*),[90] because by them we excuse idolatry. Men always justify their idolatry on the basis of the intended good effect, namely, greater devotion (*plus grande devotion*) within worshipers.[91] For Calvin, however, these good intentions are nothing more than mere "pretext" (*couleur*) for idolatry. God has condemned those who allow themselves to be governed "by their opinion" (*par leur cuider*) rather than by the objective revelation of the divine will.[92] In this sermon, it is not difficult to hear echoes of the controversies in which he had been enmeshed throughout his ministry in Geneva, in Wesel a year earlier, and in Frankfurt just six months prior.

We gain an even clearer picture of how Calvin intended his principle of worship to be applied in a 1554 letter written on behalf of the ministers of Geneva to the "Brothers in Wesel."[93] He agreed that they had good reason to be concerned about the form of the administration of the sacraments.[94] The "commandment of God" ought to be our sole rule in worship.[95] Any mixture of human invention is nothing but a corruption. If the pastors and elders were fulfilling their duty, things such as "meaningless religious ceremonies" (*menuz fatras*) and the "residue of papist superstitions," which obscure the gospel, would have been "exterminated" (*dexterminer*).[96] The

88. Ibid., 26.258–70. A contemporary ET of this sermon is in John Calvin, *John Calvin's Sermons on the Ten Commandments*, trans. Benjamin W. Farley (Grand Rapids: Baker, 1980), 65–80. See also John Calvin, *The Sermons of M. John Calvin upon the Fifth Booke of Moses Called Deuteronomie* (London, 1583; repr., Edinburgh: Banner of Truth, 1987), 187–93.

89. Calvin, *Sermons on the Ten Commandments*, 65. "Ou autrement leur vanité les transportera pour imaginer de Dieu tout le contrraire de ce qui convient à sa maieste" (*CO*, 26.258).

90. *CO*, 26.258.

91. Ibid.

92. Ibid.

93. Ibid., 15.78–81; *SW*, 6.29–32.

94. "Quant a la forme duser des Sacremens, ce nest pas sans cause que vons en avez quelque doubte et scruple" (*CO*, 15.79).

95. "Duquel lordonnance nous doibt estre pour reigle unique" (ibid.).

96. "Un residu des supersititons papales" (ibid.).

question was not whether lighted candles (*chandelles allumees*) and figured bread (*pain figuré*) in the Supper should be tolerated but whose office it was to correct such abuses.[97] It is not the vocation of the laity to correct abuses. That office belongs to the ministers and elders. Calvin insisted that his scruples against direct democratic cult reform were not to be taken as indifference toward corruption. In fact, such things are not indifferent, and he would not tolerate their introduction.

Once again, the question was not the principle or even the goal but the strategy to be employed in reaching the goal of a worship service conformed to God's Word. Were one in a situation in which such things (e.g., "dune chandlle ou dune chasuble") already existed, one ought not to separate himself from the body of the church ("separer du corps de lEglise") and deprive (*priver*) himself of the use of the Supper (*la Cene*) because of them.[98] It is lawful for God's children to submit to things of which they do not approve. The stronger should, for a time, bear with these imperfections for the sake of the weaker brothers so as not to scandalize the body and damage the establishment of the French church there. Where there is no "prejudice to the confession of our faith," then those who are more mature should accommodate those who are less so.[99] The unity of the church should not be damaged by "grande rigeur ou chagrin."[100] Whatever concessions might be necessary regarding ceremonies, doctrine is not to be compromised.

Calvin's Practice of Worship

When Calvin counseled patience, he knew whereof he spoke. His own reformation of the Genevan worship services was frustrated on at least two counts. First, he was never able to achieve his goal of weekly communion; second, the City Council also denied him the right to pronounce

97. Ibid.

98. Ibid., 15.79–80.

99. "De prejudice a la confession de nostre foi" (ibid., 15.80).

100. Ibid. By 1568 there was a growing Reformed presence in Wesel. Alistair Duke describes the process as a movement from "clandestine Bible-reading societies" to "Reformed congregations" (Alistair Duke, *Reformation and Revolt in the Low Countries* [London: Hambledon Press, 1990], 286).

the absolution in the service. Nevertheless, he did achieve much of what he hoped.

We can understand Calvin's goals only if we grasp from where the Genevan Reformation began under Farel. According to Herman A. J. Wegman, by the sixteenth century, the "essential elements" of the Roman Mass were "the service of the word and the service of the table." He admits, however, that the table "was no longer a table in fact but an altar" and that the service of the Word was in "unintelligible Latin."[101] The Roman service, as Calvin knew it, was organized around the sacrifice of the Mass. As Hubert Jedin wrote, "all the reformers had denied the sacrificial character of the Mass, and its abolition had always been the decisive step toward separation. For the Catholic Church the Mass is the center of the mystery of salvation, latreutic and Eucharistic but also propitiatory, a commemoration but also a rendering present of the sacrifice of the cross."[102] Jedin continued to argue that the Tridentine doctrine of the propitiatory eucharistic sacrifice of the transubstantiated host does not injure the uniqueness of the cross, but the Reformers, including Calvin, certainly did not see it that way. As W. Robert Godfrey summarizes:

> In practice Calvin purified church buildings by removing all religious images and symbols, including the cross. He made the reading and preaching of the Bible in the language of the people central to worship. He eliminated rites and ceremonies that were without biblical warrant. He removed musical instruments and introduced the singing of the Psalms by the congregation. He restored the Word of God, the gospel of Christ, and a profound sense of meeting with God to the center of worship.[103]

As Wulfert de Greef has observed, Calvin adapted the Strasbourg Liturgy, and he began setting the psalms to verse, beginning with Psalm 46 and incorporating settings of psalms by Guillaume Farel and Clément

101. Herman A. J. Wegman, *Christian Worship in East and West: A Study Guide to Liturgical History*, trans. Gordon W. Lathrop (New York: Pueblo Publishing, 1993), 229.
102. *New Catholic Encyclopedia*, 2nd ed., Hubert Jedin, s.v. "Trent, Council Of."
103. W. Robert Godfrey, "Calvin, Worship, and the Sacraments," in *Theological Guide to Calvin's Institutes: Essays and Analysis*, ed. David W. Hall and Peter A. Lillback, The Calvin 500 Series (Phillipsburg, NJ: P&R Publishing, 2008), 369.

Marot (1496–1544). He also versified the Song of Simeon and the Decalogue for use in worship.[104]

The only noncanonical text he used in public worship was the Apostles' Creed. It seems difficult to give an airtight explanation as to how Calvin himself related the use of the Creed to his principle of worship, but in the absence of Calvin's own explanation, one may speculate that at least two factors may have influenced him. First, even though it was well known in the sixteenth century that the Creed was not actually the direct product of the apostles, it retained a quasi-canonical quality. Second, the pedagogical attractiveness of the Creed and its functionality for expressing the catholicity of the Reformed faith must have been compelling.[105]

As a consequence of the restoration of Scripture as the unique norm by which all acts of worship are judged, through the application of the principle that only those things are to be done in worship that are commanded by God, and by distinguishing between those things that are essential to worship (i.e., Word, sacrament, and prayer) and circumstances (e.g., time and place),[106] Calvin led a profound reformation of worship in Geneva that reverberated within the Reformed churches in Europe and Britain and eventually in the New World for almost two centuries afterward.

A second outstanding characteristic of Calvin's Strasbourg and Genevan liturgies is their dialogical organization. *Dialogical* means that, for Calvin, God speaks to his people through the ministry of the Word and the people respond to that Word with God's own Word. The service began with the votum, a recitation by the minister of Psalm 124:8. It moved to the confession of sin. In Strasbourg, Calvin concluded the confession of sin with the absolution. This pattern helps to provide context for Calvin's practice of singing principally the psalms in worship.[107] To these words, the

---

104. De Greef, *The Writings of John Calvin*, 128.

105. For more on the role of the Creed in Reformed theology in the period, see Clark, *Caspar Olevian*, 85–91.

106. De Greef, *The Writings of John Calvin*, 129.

107. In the absence of any clear evidence of the use in public worship, in Geneva or Strasbourg, of the hymn "I Greet Thee, Who My Sure Redeemer Art," the claim by the editor in a footnote to the publication of Ford Lewis Battles's translation of Calvin's June 10, 1543 "Epistre au Lectur," in "The Form of Prayers and Songs of the Church, 1542, Letter to the Reader," in *CTJ* 15 (1980): 160, that the hymn was intended for public worship may be questioned. The epistle as it appears in *OS*, 2.12–18, does not contain the hymn, nor

congregation responded by singing the Decalogue in the *tertius usus legis*.[108] The minister prayed, and the congregation responded with a psalm.[109]

If the eucharistic sacrifice was central to the Roman Mass, the central liturgical act in the Genevan liturgy was the preaching of the Word. In the service of the Word, the minister prayed for illumination, the text was read, and the sermon was preached. The sermon was followed by the pastoral prayer. Calvin administered the Holy Supper monthly in St. Pierre, as permitted by the Council.[110] Afterward the minister gave thanks. To the gospel of the Supper, the congregation responded with a psalm. With the concluding benediction, Calvin's liturgy ended as it began, with the divine Word to the people.

Calvin and the Calvinists on Worship

There were differences between Calvin's practice and that of his students and of some wings of the Reformed tradition after Calvin. The seventeenth-century Scottish Presbyterian and commissioner to the Westminster Assembly George Gillespie (1613–48) was correct in his judgment that Calvin tolerated existing customs, to the extent he did, as a form of temporary conservative pragmatism in order to see congregations through a transitional period in the hope of a more complete reformation of worship according to the Word.[111]

does it appear in *La Forme des Prieres Ecclesiastiques* (ibid., 18–58). In the epistle, Calvin spoke only of the singing of psalms in worship (e.g., "Letter to the Reader," 163). Further, he explicitly distinguished between the music "that one makes to give joy to men at table . . . and the Psalms, which are sung in the church in the presence of God and his angels" (163). He concluded his thoughts on this topic by saying that "no one can sing things worthy of God unless he has received them from him. . . . We will not find better songs nor ones more appropriate for this purpose than the Psalms of David, which the Holy Spirit has spoken to him and made. Therefore, when we sing them, we are certain that God has put the words in our mouth as if they themselves sang in us to exalt his glory" (164).

108. The 1537 Genevan church order stipulated that only canonical psalms be sung, but the liturgy came to include the First Table of the Decalogue and then, in 1545, the Second Table. The two tables were separated by a prayer for obedience. See de Greef, *The Writings of John Calvin*, 129–31.

109. See de Greef, *The Writings of John Calvin*, 129–31. See also Bard Thompson, ed., *Liturgies of the Western Church*, repr. ed. (Philadelphia: Fortress Press, 1980), 185–224.

110. Clark, *Recovering the Reformed Confession*, 281–84n206.

111. George Gillespie, *A Dispute against the English Popish Ceremonies Obtruded on the Church of Scotland*, 2nd ed. (Dallas: Naphtali Press, 1993), 49–53.

There are three things to consider in assessing the relations between Calvin and the later Reformed tradition on worship. First, in the Heidelberg Catechism and the Westminster Standards, the Reformed churches articulated the same principle of worship. The language of Heidelberg Catechism Q. 96, "That we in nowise make any image of God, nor worship him in any other way than he has commanded in his Word," might have been taken verbatim from Calvin.[112] Both Zacharias Ursinus (1534–83), the primary author of the catechism, and Caspar Olevianus (1536–87), a coauthor of the catechism, studied in Geneva under Calvin. The latter made a synopsis of the *Institutes* and lectured through them annually in Heidelberg. These men had opportunity not only to hear Calvin's principle of worship but to see it in practice; they taught it in their lectures, and it was expressed in church order and practice of the palatinate churches.[113] This same principle and practice of worship was transmitted to the Westminster divines. Calvin was obviously influential on the divines, but his theology, including his principle of worship, was also mediated to the divines through a variety of sources, including the Heidelberg Catechism and Ursinus's lectures on the catechism.[114]

Second, the discontinuity that existed was a matter of time, place, and possibility. When Calvin counseled piously pragmatic patience to Wesel or Frankfurt, or even to John Knox or John Hooper,[115] he never counseled compromise of the principle itself, which he regarded as divinely revealed. In most of those places where the worship was not fully Reformed, Calvin's counsel was always given with the understanding that, when circumstances permitted, a more complete reformation would be undertaken.

112. Schaff, *The Creeds of Christendom*, 3:343.

113. See Clark, *Caspar Olevian*, 32–33, 43. See also Zacharias Ursinus, *Corpus Doctrinae Ecclesiarum a Papatu Romano Reformatarum* (Hanover, 1634), 528–47. Ursinus's vocabulary in the exposition of Q. 96 of the catechism was nearly identical to Calvin's, including, for example, the invocation of "will worship" and Calvin's expression *cultus fictitius* (528).

114. See R. Scott Clark and Joel R. Beeke, "Ursinus, Oxford and the Westminster Divines," in *The Westminster Confession into the 21st Century: Essays in Remembrance of the 350th Anniversary of the Publication of the Westminster Confession of Faith*, ed. J. Ligon Duncan (Fearn, Ross-shire, UK: Mentor, 2003), 2:1–32.

115. CO, 14.74–75. Calvin supported Hooper's resistance to "pileo et veste linea" in principle and, in practice, to his being anointed. See also John H. Primus, *The Vestments Controversy: An Historical Study of the Earliest Tensions within the Church of England in the Reigns of Edward VI and Elizabeth* (Kampen: J. H. Kok, 1960), 63n30.

Third, if we consider the approach of the *DPW*, adopted by the Westminster Assembly in 1644, the circumstances, however chaotic, were considerably different from Calvin's. Eighty years is a long time. By the time the divines adopted the *DPW*, the theology, piety, and practice of Reformed worship was rather more settled than it had been in the mid-sixteenth century. The Reformed literature that existed by that point was more developed than existed even at Calvin's death. One has only to look at the sorts of volumes produced by Reformed writers addressing the very same kinds of questions that Calvin faced and that were faced by the Reformed churches after Calvin to see how much development occurred. Consider the literature produced by the controversy between William Ames (1576–1633) and Thomas Morton (1564–1659; Bishop of Litchfield and Coventry) and that produced by the controversy with John Burgess (1563–1635) over the principle and practice of worship from 1622 through 1633.[116] Although it is not well known now, Ames's massive *Fresh Suit against Human Ceremonies in Gods Worship* (1633), written against his former father-in-law, Burgess, was an extensive restatement and application of the same principle articulated by Calvin sixty years prior.[117] Just four years after Ames's treatise appeared, George Gillespie (1613–48) published *A Dispute against the English Popish Ceremonies Obtruded on the Church of Scotland* (1637).[118] By the time the *DPW* appeared, the struggle over the principle and practice of worship was a century old. In that time arguments had been refined and clarified and greater precision had been achieved than was possible in Calvin's time and circumstance.

The Reformed churches from the late sixteenth century through the middle of the seventeenth century were not trying to hold together the same sort of fragile, transconfessional, Protestant alliance that

116. On the background to Ames's work, see Keith L. Sprunger, *The Learned Doctor William Ames: Dutch Backgrounds of English and American Puritanism* (Urbana, IL: University of Illinois Press, 1972), 188–91, 230–46. Ames's application of the principle of worship may be seen in his exposition of Heidelberg Catechism Lord's Day 45 in William Ames, *A Sketch of the Christian's Catechism*, trans. Todd Rester, vol. 1, *Classic Reformed Theology* (Grand Rapids: Reformation Heritage Books, 2008), 161–64.

117. On Burgess, see *The Dictionary of National Biography*, s.v. "Burgess, John (1653–35)."

118. On Gillespie, see William S. Barker, *Puritan Profiles: 54 Influential Puritans at the Time When the Westminster Confession Was Written* (Fearn, Ross-shire, UK: Mentor, 1996), 110–12.

Calvin attempted to maintain. By the time the *DPW* appeared, confessional lines were well established.

Conclusions

Throughout his career, Calvin articulated a clear, simple principle of public worship: only that may be done which must be done, and what must be done is that which is commanded by the Word. He applied this principle by making distinctions between that which is essential to the faith and that which is not, between that which is a matter of confession and that which is a matter of preference. He was pastoral and realistic in his application of the principle. Without compromising his principle or his confession, he counseled patience and graciousness in the implementation of the principle.

Calvin understood the need to be as "easy and flexible" as possible, within the parameters of principle, in order to keep together a coalition that, in his mind, at least in the 1530s and 1540s, included Luther, Bucer, the Anglicans, and others who did not share his understanding of the implications of the second commandment for public worship. His willingness to postpone implementation of the principle also reveals how highly he valued the visible unity of the church. As long as what was congregated was actually a church, as long as it had the marks, then it had for him the authority of divine institution. All these considerations remind us that Calvin was a relatively conservative reformer of the Reformation he inherited and not a radical individualist. Nevertheless, the principle that he articulated repeatedly throughout his career in multiple literary genres (e.g., biblical commentaries, sermons, and theological treatises) remained remarkably stable. It was that principle which was taken up by his students in the Palatinate, at Franecker, at Leiden, at the Synod of Dort, and at the Westminster Assembly.

13

CALVIN'S DOCTRINE OF ASSURANCE REVISITED

ANTHONY N. S. LANE

I n 1979 I published an article entitled "Calvin's Doctrine of Assurance."[1] Since then, there have been many publications on the topic. This essay is a revision of the previous one, taking account of subsequent scholarship and also mildly revising the original conclusions in places.[2]

There has been some confusion about John Calvin's doctrine of assurance. It has often been misrepresented, especially in the popular

1. "Calvin's Doctrine of Assurance," *Vox Evangelica* 11 (1979): 32–54.
2. I am grateful to Robert Letham for reading a draft of this essay and making some helpful comments about English Calvinism especially. I am also grateful to Randall Zachman for reading a draft and making some helpful comments, especially on its relation to his *The Assurance of Faith: Conscience in the Theology of Martin Luther and John Calvin* (Minneapolis: Fortress Press, 1992). I regret that pressures of time have not enabled me to interact with that work as much as I would have liked. If I had had more time (and space!), I would also have explored more fully Calvin's teaching in his sermons and the question of the development of his teaching through time, especially between the first two editions of the *Institutes*. On the latter point, cf. note 151 below.

idea that he taught that no one can be certain of his or her own salvation.[3] Errors have also arisen from fathering onto Calvin the ideas of later generations of Calvinists.[4]

The Necessity of Assurance

Calvin's theology is popularly seen as cold and remorseless. This fallacy is encouraged by the belief that he did not consider assurance of personal salvation to be possible. In fact, the very reverse is true: Calvin taught that assurance, far from being impossible, is an essential ingredient of salvation. Paul "declares that those who doubt their possession of Christ and their membership in His Body are reprobates."[5] Calvin, in his commentary on Galatians, argued that the confidence there described is so important that "where the pledge of the divine love towards us is wanting, there is assuredly no faith."[6] For Calvin it was not possible to partake of salvation without being sure of it. This is because saving faith is seen as faith in God's mercy to *me*. "Now we shall possess a right definition of faith if we call it a firm and certain knowledge of God's benevolence *toward us*, founded upon the truth of the freely given promise in Christ, both revealed to our minds and sealed upon our hearts through the Holy Spirit."[7]

3. Cf. Benjamin Charles Milner, *Calvin's Doctrine of the Church* (Leiden: Brill, 1970), 62–65, where an element of uncertainty foreign to Calvin's teaching is introduced.

4. Arthur S. Yates, *The Doctrine of Assurance* (London: Epworth, 1952), 169–70, appears to attribute to Calvin a "Calvinistic system" that is in fact far removed from his thought. Elsewhere (168) he quotes, as if it were from Calvin, part of the 1548 *Interim* of Charles V, which Calvin is attacking.

5. *Comm.*, 2 Cor. 13:5. Quotations from the commentaries are taken from the Oliver and Boyd series of translations where these are available and elsewhere from the nineteenth-century Calvin Translation Society editions. Quotations from the commentaries and treatises have been checked against CO. This series is slowly being replaced by the *Ioannis Calvini Opera Omnia denuo recognita* . . . (Geneva: Droz, 1992–).

6. *Comm.*, Gal. 4:6.

7. *Institutes*, 3.2.7. Quotations from the *Institutes* are all taken from John Calvin, *Institutes of the Christian Religion*, ed. John T. McNeill and Ford Lewis Battles, Library of Christian Classics, vols. 20–21 (London: SCM and Philadelphia: Westminster Press, 1960) and have been checked against OS. In this and all subsequent quotations from Calvin, the emphases are mine.

Briefly, he alone is truly a believer who, convinced by a firm conviction that God is a kindly, and well-disposed Father *toward him*, promises himself all things on the basis of his generosity; who, relying upon the promises of divine benevolence toward him, lays hold on an undoubted expectation of salvation. . . . No one hopes well in the Lord except him who confidently glories in the inheritance of the Heavenly Kingdom. . . . We cannot otherwise well comprehend the goodness of God unless we gather from it the fruit of great assurance.[8]

It is clear that Calvin allowed no dichotomy between saving faith and the assurance or confidence that one is forgiven. Saving faith is not an abstract general belief in the divine mercy without an application of it to oneself. In the Scriptures, faith includes a full assurance and confidence in the divine favor and salvation. Indeed, Calvin argued that the word *faith* (*fides*) is often used as equivalent to *confidence* (*fiducia*).[9] To separate faith and confidence is like separating the sun from its light and heat. Confidence can be distinguished from faith in that it fluctuates according to the degree of faith, but it will always be found in some measure where there is true faith.[10] That confidence or the assurance of salvation was for Calvin an integral part of faith and not an optional extra, as can be seen especially from his commentary on 1 John 5:13. The author says that he is writing "to you who believe in the name of the Son of God, that you may know that you have eternal life." It would be easy to conclude from this that faith does not of necessity involve the knowledge or assurance that one has eternal life. But Calvin understood John to be urging his readers to believe more firmly and *thus* to enjoy a full assurance of eternal life. Any uncertainty is to be ascribed to the remnants of unbelief in us and to the weakness of our faith. Confidence is but faith writ large.

---

8. *Institutes*, 3.2.16; cf. *Comm.*, Rom. 8:14, 16; *Antidote to the Council of Trent*, antidote to chap. 9 of the *Decree concerning Justification* (hereafter *Antidote*, chap. 9, etc.), 125–27. Page numbers refer to the translation in *Selected Works of John Calvin*, ed. Henry Beveridge, *Tracts*, vol. 3 (Edinburgh: Calvin Translation Society, 1851; repr., Grand Rapids: Baker, 1983). Calvin treats the preface as chapter 1 and thus numbers the chapters one too high. Chapter numbers have been corrected in these footnotes.

9. *Institutes*, 3.2.15.

10. *Comm.*, Eph. 3:12; cf. *Comm.*, Col. 2:2. Cf. the section on "Justification by Faith" below on the relation between faith and confidence.

Calvin appears to be inconsistent concerning the possibility of doubt. He repeatedly asserted that faith leaves no room for doubt. "They are ignorant of the whole nature of faith who mingle doubt with it."[11] But at the same time he recognized that this does not seem to accord with the experience of believers. "Surely, while we teach that faith ought to be certain and assured, we cannot imagine any certainty that is not tinged with doubt, or any assurance that is not assailed by some anxiety. On the other hand, we say that believers are in perpetual conflict with their own unbelief. Far, indeed, are we from putting their consciences in any peaceful repose, undisturbed by any tumult at all."[12]

The contradiction is only apparent. When rejecting the possibility of doubt, Calvin was opposing those (Roman Catholics) who defined *faith* in such a way that it does not include the confidence that God is gracious to me, both now and for eternity. But this does not mean that Christians have no doubts. Such doubts as they experience arise not from the nature of faith itself but from the constant struggle within them between faith and unbelief. Faith has to struggle against the doubts of the flesh. Furthermore, there are degrees of faith. Faith is weak and needs to increase and be strengthened. Our faith is imperfect in that our knowledge is partial and incomplete. But despite these difficulties, true faith is never extinguished. Believers never "fall away and depart from the certain assurance received from God's mercy."[13] Joel Beeke correctly notes that "the smallest germ of faith contains assurance in its very essence, even when the believer is not always able to grasp this assurance due to weakness in being conscious of his faith." There is in believers a seed of faith planted by the Spirit that cannot perish.[14]

It is not only sinful unbelief that tempers confidence. There is a reverential fear and trembling that establishes faith and is necessary to prevent

11. *Antidote*, chap. 9 (126), cf. notes 213, 226 below; *Institutes*, 3.2.7, 24; *Comm.*, John 3:33; *Comm.*, Eph. 1:13; *Comm.*, 1 John 5:6.

12. *Institutes*, 3.2.17.

13. Ibid.; cf. *Institutes*, 3.2.4, 15, 17–21, 24, 37; *Comm.*, Gen. 32:6; *Comm.*, Mark 9:24; *Comm.*, Acts 17:11; *Comm.*, Rom. 4:19; 8:35; *Comm.*, 1 John 5:13. Cf. Cornelis Graafland, *De Zekerheid van het Geloof* (Wageningen: H. Veenman & Zonen, 1961), 29–32; Walter E. Stuermann, *A Critical Study of Calvin's Concept of Faith* (Tulsa, OK: University of Tulsa, 1952), 112–16, 236–43.

14. Joel R. Beeke, *Assurance of Faith: Calvin, English Puritanism, and the Dutch Second Reformation* (New York: Peter Lang, 1991), 60–61. The quotation is in italics in the original.

presumption. When believers see the examples of divine vengeance on the ungodly, they are to abandon all arrogance and rash confidence and to keep watch in dependence on God. But the rejection of a vain confidence does not mean the end of all grounds of assurance or confidence in the mercy of God. Confident faith is to accompany a religious fear or reverence. Such a fear makes a person cautious but not despondent.[15]

Calvin was aware of the pastoral problem of believers with weak assurance, but he did not conclude that faith and assurance should be separated. Assurance is not a second stage in the Christian life, subsequent to and distinct from faith—as was taught in the following century by at least some English Calvinists, leaving its mark on the Westminster Confession.[16] Beeke recognizes that for Calvin, assurance is of the essence of faith.[17] He also, correctly, recognizes that Calvin qualifies this and does not imagine that Christians never have any doubts.[18] But he takes this second point further than does Calvin. He takes Calvin's statement that "faith ought to be certain and assured"[19] as if this implied that faith should, but might not, give assurance, and proceeds to quote with approval Paul Helm's remarkable claim that Calvin's definition of *faith* is merely "a *recommendation* about how his readers ought habitually and properly to think of faith."[20] In that passage, however, Calvin is not questioning the fact that faith implies assurance but rather reaffirming that in the believer faith has to struggle against doubt. Beeke goes on to conclude that the teaching of Calvin and of the Westminster Confession, where faith and assurance are separated, reflects different concerns and views the two as ultimately complementary rather than contradictory. But there is more to the difference than that, and Beeke proceeds to cite with approval the statement that Calvin does not distinguish between a "refuge-taking faith" (i.e., saving faith) and an "assured faith." Assurance belongs to faith from

15. *Institutes*, 3.2.22–23; cf. 1.2.2; 3.2.8, 12, 26–27; 3.3.15; *Comm.*, Phil. 2:12–13; *Antidote*, chap. 13 (137). Cf. Stuermann, *Critical Study*, 243–50. Cf. section on "Perseverance and Temporary Faith" below.

16. Cf. section on "Westminster Confession" below.

17. Beeke, *Assurance of Faith*, 47–51.

18. Ibid., 51–54.

19. *Institutes*, 3.2.17 ("fidem docemus esse debere certam ac securam").

20. Beeke, *Assurance of Faith*, 51–52, 55, quoting Paul Helm, *Calvin and the Calvinists* (Edinburgh: Banner of Truth, 1982), 26 (emphasis added).

the beginning.[21] It is hard to see how this does not contradict the belief that assurance is something subsequent to and distinct from faith.

At this point we need to note a common fallacy. A number of authors, including me in the original version of this essay, have fallen into the trap of treating later Calvinists as "followers" of Calvin who at this or that point have altered, betrayed, or perverted his teaching. This is to misread the situation. Calvin was a second-generation Reformed theologian, but because he stands head and shoulders above his colleagues, the tradition has come to be named after him. It must not be forgotten that there was already a Reformed tradition (more precisely, Reformed *traditions*) while Calvin was still being taken to venerate the relics at Ourscamp. Later Reformed theologians may be judged according to their faithfulness to the Reformed tradition, although they saw themselves as above all being faithful to Scripture, but they made no claims to be followers of any one Reformed theologian, and to judge them by that criterion is unreasonable. On our present topic there was already variety in the Reformed tradition prior to Calvin. Seventeenth-century English Calvinism was also diverse and was influenced by more than one strand of this tradition. Where English Calvinists differed from Calvin, it was because they stood in a different strand of that tradition, not because they "departed from" Calvin or "betrayed" him.[22]

The Grounds of Assurance

What is the ground of assurance for Calvin? Here it is important to distinguish between the primary ground, that on which faith must rest for assurance, and other secondary grounds that can confirm and

---

21. Beeke, *Assurance of Faith*, 62–63, citing Graafland, *Zekerheid*, 40–41.

22. This point is well demonstrated by Robert W. A. Letham in his "Saving Faith and Assurance in Reformed Theology: Zwingli to the Synod of Dort," 2 vols. (PhD thesis, Aberdeen University, 1979). This is scheduled to be published by Rutherford House Publications in Edinburgh at some point in the indeterminate future. The Introduction (1–14) gives the main thrust of the thesis; chapter 3.2 (114–41) expounds Calvin. Endnotes appear in volume 2. A useful summary of part of Letham's thesis is to be found in his "Faith and Assurance in Early Calvinism: A Model of Continuity and Discontinuity," in *Later Calvinism: International Perspectives*, ed. W. F. Graham (Kirksville, MO: Sixteenth Century Journal Publishers, 1994), 355–84.

strengthen this confidence. We will examine the latter first, before ending with the former.

Predestination[23]

Some have seen Calvin's doctrine of predestination as the enemy of assurance, and it is certainly true that in the seventeenth century, predestination caused many to doubt their salvation.[24] Calvin was aware of this possibility and guarded against it. We can be tempted to doubt our election and to seek assurance in the wrong way. The wrong way is to ask the question "am I elect?" and to seek the answer by speculation concerning the divine will, concerning God's decrees. Whoever tries this "tangles himself in innumerable and inextricable snares; then he buries himself in an abyss of sightless darkness."[25]

> Consequently, if we fear shipwreck, we must carefully avoid this rock, against which no one is ever dashed without destruction....Those engulf themselves in a deadly abyss who, to make their election more certain, investigate God's eternal plan apart from his Word.[26]

To speculate directly about one's election is presumption and folly, since God has never published a list of the elect. No earthly library contains the Book of Life. Faith and assurance must rest not on what God has not chosen to reveal but on what he has revealed—Christ and the gospel.[27] "If Pighius asks how I know I am elect, I answer that Christ is more than a thousand testimonies to me."[28] It is only in Christ that we are elect and pleasing to God, and so it is to him that we must turn. "We have a suf-

---

23. Cf. Fred H. Klooster, *Calvin's Doctrine of Predestination*, 2nd ed. (Grand Rapids: Baker, 1977), 48–54.

24. Yates, *Doctrine of Assurance*, 167, argues that Calvin made predestination the ultimate ground of certainty. He concludes that for Calvin it was not possible to be fully certain.

25. *Institutes*, 3.24.4; cf. *Antidote*, chap. 12 (135).

26. *Institutes*, 3.24.4; cf. *Comm.*, John 6:40; *Comm.*, Rom. 11:33–34; *Comm.*, 2 Thess. 2:13; *Comm.*, 1 Peter 1:2.

27. *Institutes*, 3.24.4–5; cf. *Concerning the Eternal Predestination of God*, trans. John K. S. Reid (London: James Clarke, 1961) (hereafter *Predestination*), 8.4 (113). Internal references (8.4, etc.) are the translator's and are not part of the original.

28. *Predestination*, 8.7 (130).

ficiently clear and firm testimony that we have been inscribed in the book of life if we are in communion with Christ."[29] In other words, assurance of salvation teaches us that we are elect, not vice versa. Here, as elsewhere, the order of being and the order of knowing are reversed. Our election precedes and is the cause of our experiencing salvation, but it is through knowing ourselves as God's children that we come to realize that he has chosen us. "It is [God's] will that we be content with his promises, and not inquire elsewhere whether he will be disposed to hear us."[30]

But predestination is not simply a potential cause of shipwreck. It is also an aid to assurance, and Calvin can even claim that we have no other sure ground of confidence and that predestination is the best confirmation of our faith, from which we reap rich fruits of consolation.[31] This is because election teaches us that salvation is all of grace—that is, that it depends not on our merit but on God's will.[32] To believers who are *already* persuaded of their election and salvation, this is a great comfort. Because their salvation is totally the work of God, they can rest assured that God will complete that which he has begun.[33] Election reminds believers that their salvation is ultimately dependent not on their own will and efforts but on God's purposes, and that it is therefore as secure and immovable as God's eternal election.

Works

Many Christians seek assurance from their good works, from the fruit of the Holy Spirit in their lives.[34] Calvin firmly opposed any such attempt

29. *Institutes*, 3.24.5; cf. note 58 below.
30. *Institutes*, 3.24.5.
31. Ibid., 3.21.1; 3.24.4, 9.
32. Ibid., 3.21.1; 3.24.2; *Predestination*, 2 (56).
33. *Institutes*, 3.21.1; 3.24.4–6; *Predestination*, 2 (57); *Antidote*, chap. 12 (135–36). Cf. section on "Perseverance and Temporary Faith" below.
34. For this section, cf. Wilhelm Niesel, "Syllogismus practicus?" in *Aus Theologie und Geschichte der Reformierten Kirche (Festgabe für E. F. Karl Müller)* (Neukirchen: K. Moers, 1933), 158–79; Wilhelm Niesel, *The Theology of Calvin* (London: Lutterworth, 1956), 169–81; CD, 2.2:333–40; G. C. Berkouwer, *Divine Election* (Grand Rapids: Eerdmans, 1960), 287–90; Graafland, *Zekerheid*, 48–51; G. Oorthuys, "De Beteekenis van het Nieuwe Leven voor de Zekerheid des Geloofs, volgens Calvijns Institutie," *Onder Eigen Vaandel* 13 (1938): 246–69; Beeke, *Assurance of Faith*, 72–78. Zachman, *The Assurance of Faith*, part 2, emphasizes the role of a good conscience as a supplementary testimony to one's salvation.

to base our assurance on something within ourselves. He observed that our works and the state of our hearts always fall short of perfection. "For there is nowhere that fear which is able to establish full assurance. And the saints are conscious of possessing only such an integrity as intermingled with many vestiges of the flesh."[35] Any attempt to base assurance on such works is doomed to failure, since the tender conscience will soon see the inadequacy of the foundation. The result of relying on our works is that our "conscience feels more fear and consternation than assurance."[36] If we maintain assurance on such a basis, it shows that we do not recognize our own imperfection and opens the door to self-trust.

But the New Testament clearly teaches that holiness is a test of the genuineness of our faith. Calvin openly acknowledged this, both in his comments on such passages and in his *Institutes*.[37] Our lives can be a proof to us that we are elect. "One argument whereby we may prove that we are truly elected by God and not called in vain is that our profession of faith should find its response in a good conscience and an upright life." But if the faithful may use this argument, it is only "in such a way that they place their sure foundations elsewhere."[38] The argument from works may never be the *primary* ground of our confidence. This must be "God's goodness," "God's mercy," "God's clemency," "the free promise of justification," "the certainty of the promise," "Christ's grace."[39]

> We only know that we are God's children by His sealing His free adoption on our hearts by His Spirit and by our receiving by faith the sure pledge of it offered in Christ. Therefore, love is an accessory or inferior aid, a prop to our faith, not the foundation on which it rests.[40]

Calvin recognized that our works can strengthen or confirm our confidence, as evidences of God's work in us, and that they are a test of

35. *Institutes*, 3.14.19.
36. Ibid., 3.14.20.
37. Ibid., 3.14.18–19; 3.20.10; *Comm.*, Ps. 106:12; *Comm.*, Rom. 8:9; *Comm.*, 1 John 2:3; 3:7, 24.
38. *Comm.*, 2 Peter 1:10–11.
39. *Institutes*, 3.14.18–19; 3.20.10; *Comm.*, Isa. 33:2; *Comm.*, 1 Cor. 10:12; *Comm.*, Heb. 11:6; *Comm.*, 1 John 2:3; 3:14.
40. *Comm.*, 1 John 3:19; cf. *Institutes*, 3.2.38; *Comm.*, Josh. 3:10; *Comm.*, Isa. 5:19.

the genuineness of faith. But once they become the primary ground of assurance, a *de facto* justification by works has been introduced that will lead either to despair or to a false self-confidence. Calvin acknowledges that "newness of life, as the effect of divine adoption, serves to confirm confidence; but as a secondary support, whereas we must be founded on grace alone."[41] It is important to understand what is meant by secondary support. It is not that Christ shows us the basis for salvation and that works then demonstrate to us that we have attained that salvation, with works functioning as the second stage of a process. Rather, Christ and the gospel show us that we in particular are accepted by God, and this assurance or conviction is then strengthened when it is confirmed by further evidence.

The Sacraments[42]

Martin Luther famously combatted the temptation to doubt by reminding himself that he had been baptized—*baptizatus sum*. He did not, of course, believe that all who are baptized will be saved, but recalling our baptism reminds us of God's promises.[43] Calvin also understood the sacraments to strengthen our faith and our assurance. The promises of God are found in his Word and visibly presented to us in the sacraments, God's visible words. Thus the sacraments strengthen our assurance by confirming God's promises to us.[44] Through the memory of our baptism, "we may always be sure and confident of the forgiveness of sins." This is not because of baptism itself but because it fastens our minds on Christ alone.[45] The Lord's Supper, likewise, serves to assure us of the forgiveness of sins and eternal life.[46] Calvin also acknowledged a role for private confession to one's pastor, which can strengthen a weak assurance.[47]

41. *Comm.*, 1 John 4:17.
42. Cf. Beeke, *Assurance of Faith*, 59–60; M. Charles Bell, *Calvin and Scottish Theology: The Doctrine of Assurance* (Edinburgh: Handsel Press, 1985), 27–28.
43. Cf. the Large Catechism, in the Fourth Part, on Baptism, for this approach.
44. *Institutes*, 4.14.3. This is not to imply that Calvin confined the sacraments to a merely didactic role.
45. Ibid., 4.15.1–3.
46. Ibid., 4.17.1–5.
47. Ibid., 3.4.12–14.

The sacraments have this role, but of course, they are not the primary ground of assurance. Their role is to point us to the promises of God:

> We have determined, therefore, that sacraments are truly named the testimonies of God's grace and are like seals of the good will that he feels toward us, which by attesting that good will to us, sustain, nourish, confirm, and increase our faith.[48]

The Holy Spirit

For Calvin, the Holy Spirit plays a major role in assurance. The outworking of the Spirit in our lives and in our good works is a secondary aid to assurance.[49] The Spirit is the seal and pledge of our adoption and assures us that we are God's children.[50] The Spirit is also given as the earnest of eternal life and assures us of our election.[51] Without the Holy Spirit as a witness in our hearts, we falsely assume the name of *Christian*.[52]

The Holy Spirit is a witness to us of our election. But it is important to be clear how this happens. The Holy Spirit seals our adoption by confirming to us the promises of the Word.[53] It is not that the Holy Spirit gives us a private revelation that we are God's children.[54] This would be

---

48. Ibid., 4.14.7.

49. Cf. section on "Works" above. It is going too far to state that "Christ in and through His Spirit is the ground of our faith" (Cornelis Graafland, "'Waarheid in het Binnenste': Geloofszekerheid bij Calvijn en de Nadere Reformatie," in *Een Vaste Burcht voor de Kerk der Eeuwen*, ed. Klaas Exalto [Kampen: J. H. Kok, 1989], 60, quoted in Beeke, *Assurance of Faith*, 69). The ground for faith is God's promises in Christ. The Spirit has an important role in our appropriation of them, but it is not the Spirit that died for us and is our Savior. It is more accurate to state that "personal assurance is never to be divorced from the election of the Father, the redemption of the Son, the application of the Spirit, and the instrumental means of saving faith" (Beeke, *Assurance of Faith*, 68). This statement does not claim that these are all *grounds* of assurance.

50. *Institutes*, 2.8.8, 11–12; 3.24.1; *Comm.*, John 6:40; *Comm.*, Rom. 8:15–16; *Comm.*, 1 Cor. 2:12; *Comm.*, Gal. 4:6; *Comm.*, Eph. 1:13; 4:30; *Comm.*, 2 Thess. 2:13; *Comm.*, Heb. 6:4–5; 10:29; *Comm.*, 1 John 2:19; 3:19; *Antidote*, chap. 12 (136).

51. *Institutes*, 3.2.41; 3.24.1–2; *Comm.*, Rom. 8:15–16; 11:34; *Comm.*, 1 Cor. 1:9; *Comm.*, Heb. 6:4–5; *Comm.*, 1 Peter 1:2.

52. *Institutes*, 3.2.39; *Comm.*, 2 Cor. 1:21–22; cf. *Comm.*, Eph. 3:19.

53. *Institutes*, 3.1.4; 3.2.36; *Comm.*, Rom. 8:15; *Comm.*, 1 Cor. 1:6; 2:11; *Comm.*, 2 Cor. 1:21–22; 5:5; *Comm.*, Eph. 1:13–14; *Comm.*, 2 Thess. 2:13; *Comm.*, Heb. 6:4–5.

54. Cf. note 215 below for Calvin's opposition to basing assurance on private revelation. Cf. Beeke, *Assurance of Faith*, 70–71.

to fall into the error of seeking assurance by asking whether we are elect, of prying into God's secret will.[55] It is not that the gospel makes general promises and that the Holy Spirit informs us that these relate to us. This would be to divide the Spirit from the Word, which Calvin strongly condemns.[56] The Holy Spirit confirms our adoption by testifying to us concerning the truth of God's promises, by assuring us of the truth of the gospel.[57] The testimony of the Spirit is not to be separated from the testimony of the Word.

Faith

How do Christians know that God is their gracious Father? By believing the gospel. The evidence of our election is God's effectual calling of us, issuing in our faith.[58] It might therefore appear that for Calvin the ground of assurance is our faith. But this would be seriously to distort his teaching.[59] It would be to suggest that assurance is after all based on something *in ourselves*, which Calvin denied. "If you contemplate yourself, that is sure damnation."[60] It would be to make faith the condition of salvation in the sense of something that we must do in order to achieve salvation. This Calvin also denied.[61] Assurance would not be secure if it were based on our faith, since our faith is always such that we need to pray, "Lord, help our unbelief."[62] "Unbelief is, in all men, always mixed with faith."[63] To base assurance on our faith opens the door to introspection and leads to agonizing doubts concerning the genuineness of our faith. This danger is all the more acute because of the phenomenon of "temporary faith,"[64] which can only serve to undermine an assurance based on my possession of faith.

55. Cf. section on "Predestination" above.

56. *Institutes*, 1.9; *Comm.*, Acts 16:14. Cf. Graafland, *Zekerheid*, 37–39.

57. Cf. *Institutes*, 1.7 on the inner witness of the Holy Spirit. Cf. Stuermann, *Critical Study*, 65, 70, 101–2, 148–51.

58. *Institutes*, 3.21.7; 3.24.2; *Comm.*, John 6:40; *Comm.*, Rom. 8:33; 10:17; *Comm.*, Phil. 1:6; *Comm.*, 2 Thess. 2:13; *Comm.*, Heb. 6:4–5; *Comm.*, 1 Peter 1:2.

59. Milner, *Calvin's Doctrine*, 60–62, interprets Calvin this way.

60. *Institutes*, 3.2.24; cf. 3.24.5; *Comm.*, 1 Cor. 1:9; *Comm.*, 2 Peter 1:10–11.

61. Cf. section on "Justification by Faith" below.

62. John Calvin, *A Short Treatise on the Lord's Supper*, 26, in *Selected Works of John Calvin*, ed. Henry Beveridge, *Tracts*, vol. 2 (Edinburgh: Calvin Translation Society, 1849; repr., Grand Rapids: Baker, 1983), 177–78; cf. *Comm.*, Mark 9:24.

63. *Institutes*, 3.2.4. Cf. section on "The Necessity of Assurance" above.

64. Cf. section on "Perseverance and Temporary Faith" below.

Christit

Christ

For Calvin, the ground of assurance does not lie within ourselves. It is not our faith or our works or our experience of the Holy Spirit. These can play a secondary role as a confirmation of or an aid to our assurance. But the primary ground of assurance is objective. It is the gospel, the mercy of God, the free promise of justification in Christ.[65] I know that God is my gracious Father because of his love for me, shown in Christ and declared in his Word. The ground of assurance lies not within ourselves but rather in the promises of God in Christ. "Confidence of salvation is founded upon Christ and rests on the promises of the gospel."[66]

> But if we have been chosen in [Christ], we shall not find assurance of our election in ourselves; and not even in God the Father, if we conceive him as severed from his Son. Christ, then, is the mirror wherein we must, and without self-deception may, contemplate our own election.[67]

The ground of assurance cannot be distinguished from the ground of faith itself—Christ and the promises of God. This follows because, for Calvin, assurance is not a second stage subsequent to faith but is simply faith itself writ large. Since saving faith is not simply faith in the promises of God *in general* but faith that they apply *to me*,[68] faith in itself includes assurance.

It might appear that Calvin has performed a sleight of hand. Since there is no salvation for those who do not believe, as Calvin clearly held, our salvation must depend on our having believed, which makes faith the ground of our assurance. But this does not follow, for two reasons. First, assurance does not follow from faith as a second stage, as a logical deduction from the fact of my faith. If, as some later Calvinists have held, assurance of salvation is a logical consequence of the fact of my having believed, it does follow that faith is the ground of assurance. But for Calvin,

65. Cf. note 39 above. Cf. *Comm.*, John 3:16, 36. Cf. Zachman, *The Assurance of Faith*, 180: "Faith has as its object Jesus Christ himself, as he offers himself to us in the preaching of the gospel and the administration of the sacraments, illumined by the testimony of the Holy Spirit."
66. *Predestination*, 2 (56).
67. *Institutes*, 3.24.5; cf. *Predestination*, 8.4, 6 (113, 127).
68. Cf. sections on "The Necessity of Assurance" above and "Justification by Faith" below.

faith and assurance are not separated in this way.[69] Second, it is true that there is no salvation without faith, but Calvin did not allow that faith is a *condition* of salvation.[70] It is not faith that saves but Christ, and assurance, like faith, looks away from ourselves to Christ alone.

Assurance in Relation to Other Doctrines

The Knowledge of God

Dr. William H. Chalker, in his important thesis on the relation between Calvin and later English Calvinism, seeks to relate Calvin's doctrine of assurance to his other doctrines. He correctly notes that for Calvin, unlike much of later Calvinism, assurance was no problem.[71] He also shows how assurance is grounded on Christ, on God's promise, and not on our act of faith.[72] But he seeks to relate this to Calvin's doctrine of the knowledge of God in a way that is open to question:

> We know God as our gracious Father when we see him in Jesus Christ through the witness of the Spirit, *and we do not know God until then.* Christ does not reconcile us to a God whom we previously knew to be angry with us. Rather he reveals to us the God who is already reconciled to us. Christ does not reveal to us additional information about a God whom we already know through natural revelation. He reveals to us the one true God.[73]

This means that there *cannot* be any difficulty with assurance because one cannot know the true God except as one's personal Savior. There is no

69. Cf. ibid.

70. Cf. section on "Justification by Faith" below.

71. William H. Chalker, "Calvin and Some Seventeenth-Century English Calvinists" (PhD thesis, Duke University, 1961), 59–62, 64. Chalker's thesis has been considered at some length because he is an extreme representative of one school of interpretation of Calvin and because the issues that he raises are vital for a correct interpretation of Calvin's doctrine of assurance. Chalker has been criticized for not recognizing the variety of views found among seventeenth-century English Calvinists.

72. Ibid., 14, 61–62, 64–66, 76–77.

73. Ibid., 37 (his emphasis).

possibility of knowing him as wrathful toward oneself and no possibility
for one who knows him of not being saved. The English Calvinists asked
themselves the wrong question: "How can a man, who presumably knows
himself to be a sinner worthy of eternal damnation, determine whether
or not he has the good fortune of being one of God's elect?"[74]

This argument is attractive because it offers a clear explanation of why
Calvin saw no difficulty in assurance while many Calvinists in the following
century had such problems. But it is less than clear that the explanation
offered by Chalker is truly grounded in the teaching of Calvin, and one
may perhaps be permitted to speculate that twentieth-century Basel has
influenced his interpretation as much as sixteenth-century Geneva. His
case depends entirely on two claims, which must be examined.

First, he claims that for Calvin there is no knowledge of God that
is not saving. To prove this, he argues that for Calvin there is no true
natural knowledge of God and that humanity's natural "knowledge" of
God is no preparation for a true knowledge of God.[75] But he has to
admit that "Calvin, unaware of the importance that this subject would
assume in following centuries, never totally avoided ambiguity respecting
it. Although he uses the strongest language to indicate that the natural
knowledge is perverted, he yet leaves cause for some to infer that the
discontinuity between the natural knowledge and the specially-revealed
knowledge is not total or absolute."[76] But even if we were to concede
this point to Chalker, his first claim is far from proved. Granted that
the gospel does not reveal to us a God already known from nature, it
does not follow that the gospel does not reconcile us to a God already
known from *revelation* to be wrathful toward us. But Chalker will not
allow this: "Any 'God' who is known but not as redeemer is an idol."[77]
"A God who is not known to be propitious toward us is not the God of
whom he [Calvin] is writing."[78] The English Calvinists are chided for
teaching that it is possible to know God before faith, to know Christ as

74. Ibid., 52.
75. Ibid., 18–28.
76. Ibid., 24. This has, of course, been an area of controversy since the famous Barth-
Brunner debate, but it need not concern us here.
77. Ibid., 13.
78. Ibid., 14.

the Redeemer of believers but not of oneself.[79] This involves separating the knowledge of God and faith in such a way that "assurance becomes a problem which faith solves." For Calvin, this is not so because "all the true knowledge which we have of God is in faith—all knowledge of God is knowledge of our salvation." For the English Calvinists, faith "became the means of appropriating a salvation previously known to be available," the fulfilling of "a certain part of a previously understood bargain."[80] But for Calvin:

> Because God is known in Christ alone, there is no knowledge of God as only a righteous judge, no knowledge of ourselves as only helpless sinners, no knowledge of Christ as other than *our* Saviour, no knowledge of a promise of salvation which is conditional. In short, outside of faith there is no possibility of raising the question of assurance in a way which would be meaningful to Christian theology.[81]

"To know God in Christ is to know him not as a *possible* savior, but as one's own savior."[82] If Chalker is correct, it is transparently clear why assurance could never be a problem for Calvin. But it is dubious whether in fact this interpretation can be upheld.

Chalker's thesis is based on a confusion of the different possible meanings of *faith* and *knowledge*. Calvin denied that the word *faith* meant mere intellectual assent but did not deny that such an assent exists. There are some who "[hold] the Word of God to be an indisputable oracle" but do not have true saving faith. Scripture may refer to this as faith, as with Simon Magus, "but this shadow or image of faith, as it is of no importance, does not deserve to be called faith."[83] There is also the phenomenon of "temporary faith."[84] The reprobate can for a time have a false faith that to others is indistinguishable from true faith and that they themselves believe to be genuine. Those with mere intellectual assent or a temporary faith

79. Ibid., 57–58.
80. Ibid., 64–65.
81. Ibid., 66 (his emphasis).
82. Ibid., 82 (his emphasis).
83. *Institutes*, 3.2.9–10. Chalker alludes to mere assent ("Calvin," 58–59) but does not seem to recognize its implications in the present context.
84. Cf. section on "Perseverance and Temporary Faith" below.

clearly have some grasp of the content of the gospel.[85] It can be granted that for Calvin such people have no *true* faith or knowledge of God. But this does not alter the fact that they can know of the existence of salvation without experiencing it, of Christ as a *possible* Savior but not as their own Savior. Since Calvin repeatedly chided his Roman opponents for just that,[86] it can hardly be denied that such knowledge is possible. Clearly it is possible, for Calvin, to know enough *about* the gospel to pose the question of assurance. Certainly Calvin held that this ought not to happen and would not happen if the nature of faith was correctly understood. But that it did happen was indisputable. If for Calvin, unlike the English Calvinists, assurance was no problem, this is not, as Chalker maintains, because doubting one's salvation was *impossible*.

The same observation applies to Chalker's claim that for Calvin "there is no real knowledge of election, except in faith,"[87] so that "there is never such a thing as the knowledge of one's own reprobation, or even of the *possibility* of one's own reprobation."[88] Calvin seems to imply that certain (rare) individuals did know of their own reprobation—or at least of the virtual certainty of it.[89] It would also seem to be inevitable that those who treat the Bible as an infallible oracle could come to know of election without having true faith. When Calvin says that unbelievers will jeer at the doctrine,[90] he is commenting on the reception it was receiving from his opponents, not making a dogmatic assertion about the possibility of unbelievers' ever accepting it, as Chalker implies. It is true that Calvin warned his readers against seeking assurance by asking whether they are elect,[91] but this is different from saying that only the elect can accept the doctrine of election. The fact that it is possible to seek assurance by specu-

85. Cf. section on "Justification by Faith" below for a more precise analysis of how much the reprobate can know of Christ and the gospel.

86. Cf. notes 213, 226 below.

87. Chalker, "Calvin," 68; cf. 67, 74.

88. Ibid., 82 (emphasis added). Clearly, it is not normally possible to know in this life that one is reprobate, not because one cannot know oneself as lost (Chalker's claim) but because no one can know before death whether he or she will turn and be saved.

89. *Comm.*, Matt. 27:3; *Comm.*, Heb. 12:17.

90. *Institutes*, 3.21.4, cited by Chalker, "Calvin," 68. The other reference that he gives in this context is misquoted.

91. As Chalker argues ("Calvin," 71–73). Cf. section on "Predestination" above.

lating about one's election and thus to suffer shipwreck[92] would seem to suggest that the reprobate can indeed know of predestination and suffer ruin as a result. "Am I elect?" may be an illegitimate question for Calvin; it is clearly not an impossible question.

The second of Chalker's claims is closely related to the first. He argues that we cannot know our lost condition and the wrath of God prior to our knowledge of God as Savior. He argues that for Calvin there is no true knowledge of oneself apart from knowledge of God.[93] This is certainly true,[94] but it does not necessarily follow that this knowledge of God is a knowledge of him *as Savior*. The passages cited by Chalker base our self-knowledge on a knowledge of God's *justice*.[95] This conflicts with his oft-repeated assertion that "all negative statements [in Calvin] concerning man's ability before God are *always* made on the basis of an understanding of God's great work for man in Jesus Christ, never on the basis of an independent appraisal of man."[96] If "independent appraisal" means an appraisal independent of God's revelation, then the second half of the statement is true; but if, as the context demands, it means independent of the revelation of God *as Savior*, it is not true. It is true that the knowledge of God's grace shows us the extent of human sinfulness. It is not true that for Calvin this is the *only* way in which we can know our sinfulness, as Chalker argues. He shows how Calvin explains original sin in the light of Christ's righteousness given to us, but goes beyond Calvin in asserting that he (Calvin) "implies that those who do not know Christ will not understand it."[97] It is significant that he has to admit that there are "difficulties," "for in spite of his continual assertions that man judges himself correctly only in the light of his knowledge of the Triune God, it is evident that at

92. *Institutes*, 3.24.4. Cf. section on "Predestination" above.
93. Chalker, "Calvin," 39–43, 52.
94. *Institutes*, 1.1.
95. Ibid., 2.1.2–3; 3.12.1–2, 4. The very title of 3.12 illustrates this.
96. Chalker, "Calvin," 17–18 (emphasis added); cf. 41, 43–48, 52. Chalker appeals to Thomas F. Torrance, at this point, but Torrance's position in fact undermines Chalker's case. He argues that from the dogmatic point of view, Calvin sees the fall and human sinfulness as a corollary of grace and salvation, but that from a didactic point of view, it is possible through the law alone to come to an awareness of sin (*Calvin's Doctrine of Man* [London: Lutterworth, 1949], 16–20). Clearly, this destroys Chalker's case.
97. Chalker, "Calvin," 44, citing *Institutes*, 2.1.6.

times Calvin speaks of what seems to be true self-knowledge prior to the knowledge of grace."[98] But there is no difficulty, since true self-knowledge comes from a knowledge of God, not necessarily of grace. The assumption that causes Chalker his difficulty is the assumption that for Calvin there is no nonsaving knowledge of God and that it is not possible to know God's justice without his grace. But this he has failed to demonstrate, and if we drop the assumption, the "difficulties" vanish.

Calvin himself describes the path to faith in terms that contradict Chalker's case. He outlines for Cardinal Sadolet the pattern of the 1538 catechism:

> First, we bid a man begin by examining himself, and this not in a super-ficial and perfunctory manner, but to present his conscience before the tribunal of God and, when sufficiently convinced of his iniquity, to reflect on the strictness of the sentence pronounced upon all sinners. Thus con-founded and stricken with misery, he is prostrated and humbled before God; and, throwing away all self-confidence, he groans as though given up to final perdition. Then we show that the only haven of safety is in the mercy of God as manifested in Christ, in whom every part of our salvation is completed.[99]

Again, in his treatise *Concerning Scandals*, Calvin urges the hard of heart to look within in order to discern their wretchedness. When they are aware of the judgment that they face as sinners, they will no longer be scandalized by the cross of Christ.[100]

In his treatise on *The Necessity of Reforming the Church*, Calvin speaks clearly of three stages in the knowledge of our salvation. The first stage is to become aware of our individual wretchedness, by contemplating our depravity and the sins we have committed. We then rise to the second stage,

98. Chalker, "Calvin," 48–49, citing *Institutes*, 2.7.9, 11; 3.18.9.

99. *Reply to Sadolet*, in *Calvin: Theological Treatises*, ed. J. K. S. Reid, Library of Christian Classics, vol. 22 (London: SCM and Philadelphia: Westminster Press, 1954), 234–35. For the catechism, cf. Ira John Hesselink, *Calvin's First Catechism: A Commentary* (Louisville: Westminster/John Knox Press, 1997). The relevant sections for the self-examination are 6, 7, and 11.

100. John Calvin, *Concerning Scandals*, trans. John W. Fraser (Edinburgh: Saint Andrew Press, 1978), 20–21.

which is to turn to Christ, having been humbled by the awareness of our sin. From there we rise to the third stage, which is to rest in Christ with firm and solid confidence, with the assurance that Christ is so completely ours that in him we possess righteousness and life.[101]

Clearly, according to Calvin in these three examples, people are expected "first" to become aware of their lost state before God, and "then" to discover that salvation is found in Christ. Not only can people know their lost condition prior to knowing God as Savior, but here at least Calvin advocates that order of events.[102]

The role of the law is crucial for Chalker's case. Does the law reveal human sinfulness independently of the gospel? Can people from the law come to a knowledge of God as righteous and themselves as sinful, without and prior to a knowledge of God as Savior and themselves as redeemed? Clearly, Chalker's case requires a firm negative answer to both questions. Equally clearly, Calvin's answer to both is *Yes*, as Chalker is virtually forced to admit.[103] He acknowledges that the first use of the law for Calvin is "to admonish, convince, and convict us of sin, in order that we will see and come to the mercy of God in Christ."[104] He seeks to blunt the force of this by arguing:

> The proper use of the law, then, never allows it to be a separate and independent source of knowledge about ourselves. The God whose righteousness is revealed in the law cannot be properly separated from the God who is merciful to those whom the law condemns.[105]

This is true but does not alter the fact that people *may* attain to a knowledge of themselves as sinful through the law *prior* to their knowledge

101. *Selected Works of John Calvin*, ed. Henry Beveridge, *Tracts*, vol. 1 (Edinburgh: Calvin Translation Society, 1844; repr., Grand Rapids: Baker, 1983), 133–34.

102. Zachman, *The Assurance of Faith*, 150–58, argues that by the time of the 1559 *Institutes*, Calvin has moved away from the Lutheran law-gospel framework. In the light of *Institutes*, 2.7.6–9; 2.8.3, one might question whether he has totally abandoned it. Even if Zachman is correct, that does not mean that it is impossible for anyone to have an awareness of being lost, as Chalker argues.

103. Chalker, "Calvin," 46–48; cf. 41.

104. Ibid., 46, citing *Institutes*, 2.7.6–9. Cf. *Institutes*, 2.8.3; 3.3.7; *Comm.*, John 3:36.

105. Chalker, "Calvin," 47.

of God as gracious in Christ. Chalker also shows how Calvin did not advocate minute self-examination before the law and discourages morbid introspection.[106] Again, this is true but does not affect the point at issue. It is clear why Chalker has "difficulties" with Calvin. The difficulties arise not from any ambiguity in Calvin himself but from the incompatibility of Chalker's case and Calvin's teaching. His concluding comment on the "difficulties" is significant:

> It seems to be entirely unjustified to conclude, on the basis of these and similar passages, that if we are to follow Calvin, we must treat Christ as the answer to a preconceived question or the solution to an independently known problem. Calvin says many things clearly which rule out the possibility of seeing an independent anthropology in his theology.[107]

That there is no anthropology independent of revelation is one thing; that there is no anthropology independent of soteriology is another.

Chalker's case rests on certain points that go beyond Calvin's teaching, namely, that for Calvin there is no knowledge of God that is not saving and that people cannot come to self-knowledge, to a knowledge of their lost condition, through the law prior to their knowledge of salvation. It is significant that these claims are not supported with firm evidence from Calvin,[108] that Chalker himself is forced to acknowledge "difficulties," and that passages in Calvin seem clearly to refute them.

If this conclusion is correct, Chalker is wrong in his analysis of the difference between Calvin and the English Calvinists. If it is possible for people to have a nonsaving knowledge of God, to know their own sinfulness without having experienced salvation, the question of assurance

---

106. Ibid., 47–48.

107. Ibid., 49–50. He proceeds to argue that the fear of the reprobate is different from the fear of the elect, that genuine hatred of sin leads on to Christ, and that we cannot prepare ourselves for faith (50–52). All this is true, but does not affect the point at issue.

108. Some of Chalker's key references to Calvin do not bear out the point that he is seeking to make. On page 31 he claims, on the basis of *Institutes*, 1.7.5, that only the elect know God *the Creator*, by faith. But Calvin states that it is only the elect who have true faith, not that only they know God the Creator.

remains. Chalker is not fair in blaming the seventeenth-century Calvinists for posing the following "absurd question":

> How can a man, who presumably knows himself to be a sinner worthy of eternal damnation, determine whether or not he has the good fortune of being one of God's elect? For Calvin, such a man would not so know himself unless he were elect. Calvin had the good sense to throw such questions out of court.[109]

Calvin's doctrine of assurance is different from that of the English Calvinists not because he abolished the question but because he gave a different answer. How his answer differs can be seen from the examination of assurance in the context of justification by faith.

Justification by Faith

Assurance is closely related to justification by faith. It is because of the promise of free justification in Christ that we can have assurance. Assurance, like faith, is based on the promises of God in the gospel. Assurance is simply a natural outworking of justification by faith, since faith is faith that God is merciful to *me*. Thus Calvin criticized Rome as much for basing assurance on works as for basing justification on them.[110] Indeed, he argued that to base assurance on works is to undermine justification by faith, since it causes us to place our whole trust in ourselves.[111] If assurance rests on works, the outcome is that we look within, to our sanctification, for the basis of our confidence and that this can undermine assurance as effectively as the doctrine of justification by works.[112]

Calvin had to face the fact that the New Testament in places appears to base our assurance on our good works, on the fruit of the Spirit in our lives.[113] His treatment of such passages is similar to his treatment of passages that seem to teach that our good works are meritorious or can justify us. Calvin met these with his doctrine of double justification.

109. Ibid., 52–53; cf. 41.
110. Cf. section on "The Council of Trent" below.
111. *Antidote*, chap. 16 (146).
112. Cf. section on "Works" above.
113. Cf. ibid.

God accepts our persons as righteous in his sight because of the righteousness of Christ. But he goes further and accepts our works also, on the basis of Christ:

> Therefore, as we ourselves, when we have been engrafted in Christ, are righteous in God's sight because our iniquities are covered by Christ's sinlessness, so our works are righteous and are thus regarded because whatever fault is otherwise in them is buried in Christ's purity, and is not charged to our account.[114]

It can be said that Calvin likewise has a doctrine of "double assurance" to accommodate the biblical teaching on assurance through works. Our primary ground of assurance is Christ, the gospel. But the contemplation of our works, of the fruit of the Spirit in our lives, can serve as an aid, as a strengthening of our confidence. As with double justification, at least part of Calvin's aim is to accommodate "awkward" biblical passages that do not immediately accord with his teaching.[115] The supplementary role of works can also be compared to the role of "proofs" in convincing us of the divine authority of Scripture. Without the inner witness of the Spirit, we cannot discern the authority of Scripture; but once we have received this witness, the proofs can be a useful help, confirming our faith.[116]

If assurance is related to justification by faith, it might appear that our assurance is based on our faith, on our having fulfilled the condition of justification. But Calvin rejected any such suggestion and denied that faith is a condition of salvation.[117] Chalker rightly points to this fact, and it could appear that this vindicates his thesis. If salvation is unconditional, if faith "*apprehends* a free promise rather than *appropriates* a conditional one,"[118] then it would appear that the conclusions of the last section are

---

114. *Institutes*, 3.17.10; cf. 3.17.5–10. Cf. Ronald S. Wallace, *Calvin's Doctrine of the Christian Life* (Edinburgh and London: Oliver and Boyd, 1959), 302–3; François Wendel, *Calvin* (London: Collins, 1963), 260–62.

115. The teaching on the role of works in the *Institutes* (3.14.18–20) comes in the context of answering Roman objections. Calvin's aim was primarily to minimize the role of works, not to exalt it.

116. Ibid., 1.8.1, 13. Cf. 1.7. Barth also draws this comparison in CD, 2.2:334.

117. *Institutes*, 3.2.29. Strictly speaking, it is *works* as a condition that Calvin is rejecting.

118. Chalker, "Calvin," 77 (his emphasis); cf. 62–63.

mistaken. If the promise is unconditional, there can be no knowledge of it as something that does not apply to oneself, no possibility of knowing oneself to be lost. This, according to Chalker, is why for Calvin, unlike the English Calvinists, there was no problem of assurance.

> For Calvin, faith is not giving assent to doctrine in order thereby to be justified. Rather faith is the genuine—existential, if you please—apprehension that we *are* justified by the work of Christ.[119]

By contrast, some of the English Calvinists see in Christ "a conditional covenant or promise: God promises mercy to those who will have faith in Christ." The result is that "faith for them ceases to be the knowledge of God's unconditional promise, and becomes the fulfilment of the human obligation in an independently known conditional covenant."[120] It follows that:

> For assurance of his salvation, then, a person looked within himself to see if he possessed "faith," his end of the bargain, and to see if he was performing good works, the evidence of faith. . . . Assurance was based not on *what faith knows*, but on the fact that the person possessed something called faith, which fulfilled a covenant obligation.[121]

In order to see why Chalker's thesis is not correct, it is necessary to distinguish between three different senses in which it could be said that faith is the condition of salvation. In the first place, it could mean that faith is something that we do, independently of God, to appropriate salvation. God provides the possibility of salvation and leaves it to people to decide for themselves whether or not to avail themselves of this possibility. Clearly, neither Calvin nor the English Calvinists believed faith to be the condition of salvation in this sense, since they held that faith is the gift of God, wrought by the Holy Spirit.

In the second place, it could mean that faith is the distinguishing mark of the people of God, that without faith there is no salvation. Calvin, like

119. Ibid., 59 (his emphasis).
120. Ibid., 57.
121. Ibid., 60.

the English Calvinists, believed that in this sense faith *is* the condition of salvation. Faith does not simply recognize that we are already justified. Before we believe, we are *not* justified. Faith is the instrumental cause of justification.[122] It is by means of faith that we possess Christ and obtain salvation through him.[123] Eternal life is the reward of willing submission to Christ.[124] Christ is offered to all in the gospel, but not all embrace this offer by faith.[125] Faith is the mark that distinguishes between the children of God and the reprobate.[126] Faith is the condition of salvation in that without faith there is no salvation.

There remains a third sense in which faith could be seen as a condition of salvation, and here Calvin differs from the English Calvinists, *as portrayed by Chalker*. Although for the latter faith is something active that people perform to fulfill a condition,[127] for Calvin faith is passively receiving a free gift. Faith is not a meritorious condition nor a work deserving of a reward. Faith comes to Christ empty-handed, bringing nothing of its own but simply receiving Christ and his righteousness.[128] To say that the gospel is conditional upon faith is simply to say that it is conditional upon Christ. Faith does not fulfill a condition in the sense of performing something that God requires of us before he will bestow his salvation upon us. Faith is simply laying hold of Christ, who is freely offered to us. Faith is the condition of salvation only in that receiving Christ is the condition of salvation.

The promise of the gospel is free in the sense that it is free for the taking, not that it applies irrespective of acceptance. The promise

---

122. *Institutes*, 3.11.7; 3.14.17, 21.

123. Ibid., 3.1.1; 3.2.1, 13, 30; 3.3.1; 3.11.7; *Comm.*, Gen. 15:6; *Comm.*, John 1:12; 3:16, 36; 6:29; *Comm.*, Rom. 4:12; *Comm.*, Heb. 11:6.

124. *Comm.*, John 5:24. Calvin's more precise teaching is that faith is "a passive work . . . to which no reward can be paid" (*Comm.*, John 6:29; cf. *Comm.*, Gen. 15:6). Cf. the following paragraph and note 128.

125. *Institutes*, 3.1.1; *Comm.*, Matt. 15:13; *Comm.*, Luke 1:45; *Comm.*, John 1:12; 3:36; *Comm.*, Rom. 10:10; *Comm.*, Phil. 2:12–13.

126. *Institutes*, 3.2.13, 30.

127. Chalker, "Calvin," 57, 59–60, 127–39. Robert Letham has pointed out to me that on this matter Calvin's views are strongly represented in the minutes of the Westminster Assembly.

128. *Institutes*, 3.11.7; 3.13.5; *Comm.*, Hab. 2:4; *Comm.*, John 6:29; *Comm.*, Rom. 3:27; *Comm.*, Eph. 2:8; *Antidote*, chap. 8 (125).

is unconditional and gratuitous because faith is simply laying hold
of it and accepting it, not performing a condition that is required.
The gospel is unconditional in that it is the offer of a gift that needs
only to be accepted. But this concept of faith as the acceptance of the
gospel offer might appear to be contradicted by Calvin's concept of
faith as knowledge. He defined *faith* as "a firm and certain *knowledge*
of God's benevolence toward us" and "the knowledge of God and
Christ."[129] Chalker relies heavily on this definition in his thesis. As
faith is knowledge, it is the awareness that one is justified, not the
appropriation of justification.[130] Faith is not the human response to
an already-known conditional promise but is simply coming to know
the promise.[131] The English Calvinists perverted Calvin, he claims,
by seeing faith as man's act of appropriation of an already-known
conditional promise.

In order to understand Calvin's concept of faith as knowledge, it is
first necessary to examine his anthropology and in particular his view of
the heart. Calvin divided the soul into two:

> Thus let us, therefore, hold—as indeed is suitable to our present purpose—
> that the human soul consists of two faculties, understanding and will. Let
> the office, moreover, of understanding be to distinguish between objects,
> as each seems worthy of approval or disapproval; while that of the will,
> to choose and follow what the understanding pronounces good, but to
> reject and flee what it disapproves.[132]

Calvin taught the primacy of the intellect or understanding over the will
in that the will follows the mind. "The understanding is, as it were, the
leader and governor of the soul; ... the will is always mindful of the bid-
ding of the understanding, and in its own desires awaits the judgment
of the understanding."[133] But this should not be taken to mean that the

129. *Institutes*, 3.2.7, 3; cf. 3.2.2, 8, 12, 14–16, 19; *Comm.*, Isa. 52:15; *Comm.*, John
17:3, 8; *Comm.*, Eph. 3:19; *Comm.*, Phil. 3:10; *Comm.*, 2 Tim. 1:12.
130. Chalker, "Calvin," 77; cf. 37.
131. Ibid., 57, 59, 65.
132. *Institutes*, 1.15.7.
133. Ibid. The older Beveridge translation misleadingly states that "the will always follows
[the intellect's] beck," suggesting that the will cannot go against it.

will is totally dependent on the mind. Adam fell by the choice of his will even though his mind and will were upright.[134] The will is not totally determined by the mind.

The soul possesses no faculty that cannot be referred either to the intellect or to the will.[135] To which does the heart belong? Calvin's use of *heart* is inconsistent, and he sometimes uses it of the mind, especially when commenting on passages of Scripture that do so.[136] But normally the heart is contrasted to the mind and can be seen as an aspect of the will.[137]

For Calvin faith is knowledge, but this does not mean that it is confined to the mind.[138] Faith is knowledge as opposed to the Roman idea of "implicit faith," which is to submit one's convictions to the teaching of the church, without necessarily knowing what that teaching includes. Against this idea Calvin emphasizes the intellectual content of faith.[139] But faith is not to be seen as merely intellectual assent.[140] It is more than an acceptance of the

134. Ibid., 1.15.8.
135. Ibid., 1.15.7.
136. *Comm.*, Deut. 29:4; *Comm.*, John 12:40; *Comm.*, Acts 16:14. In these passages Calvin acknowledges that Scripture sometimes uses *heart* for *mind*. But he implies that its usual meaning in Scripture is the seat of the affections (*Comm.*, Deut. 29:4, cf. *Comm.*, John 12:40), and himself contrasts the affections of the heart and the understanding of the mind (*Comm.*, Acts 16:14). Calvin is not consistent in his use of *heart*. He can refer to the *understanding* of the heart (*Comm.*, Isa. 43:10). But it is going too far simply to state that "by 'heart' Calvin means the mind" and to reduce the heart to "a fully persuaded mind" (R. T. Kendall, *Calvin and English Calvinism to 1649* [Oxford: Oxford University Press, 1979; repr., Carlisle, PA: Paternoster, 1997], 28). Cf. Graafland, *Zekerheid*, 22; Stuermann, *Critical Study*, 84–86, who follow the position taken here.
137. *Institutes*, 2.2.2, 12; *Comm.*, Phil. 4:7. Cf. the comments in the previous note. Cf. notes 145–49 below.
138. Kendall, *Calvin and English Calvinism*, 19–21, 29, 34, claims that Calvin held to an intellectualist view of faith as opposed to the voluntaristic view held by later Calvinism. He falls into the same mistake as Pighius of taking Calvin's talk of the effacing of the human will too literally. Cf. A. N. S. Lane, *John Calvin: Student of the Church Fathers* (Edinburgh: T&T Clark and Grand Rapids: Baker, 1999), 187–89. Bell, *Calvin and Scottish Theology*, 31, also denies that there is a voluntarist element to Calvin's doctrine of faith. On this, cf. Richard Alfred Muller, *The Unaccommodated Calvin* (New York and Oxford: Oxford University Press, 2000), 159–73, 255–62, who argues that Calvin "balances the functions of intellect and will in his conception of faith, rather than argue either a purely intellectualist or a purely voluntarist definition" (170).
139. *Institutes*, 3.2.2–5; *Comm.*, Isa. 52:15; *Comm.*, Rom. 10:17; *Comm.*, Gal. 1:8; *Comm.*, Titus 1:1; *Comm.*, 1 Peter 1:8.
140. *Institutes*, 3.2.8–10, 33.

veracity of the Gospel accounts.[141] It is more than sound doctrine.[142] All of these are important, but faith also includes the personal element. It is the knowledge of *my* salvation, not just the knowledge that Christ is the Savior of the world. It is the knowledge of God as *my* Father.[143] Faith is not just an opinion or a persuasion but rather a personal confidence in the mercy of God.[144] Faith involves not just the mind but also the heart.[145] It is not enough for the mind to be illumined; the heart must also be strengthened and supported. Faith is not just the assent of the mind but also confidence and security of heart. Indeed, the *chief* part of faith is firm and stable constancy of heart.[146] Calvin objects to the Roman idea of faith as mere intellectual assent by pointing out that assent "is more of the heart than of the brain, and more of the disposition than the understanding."[147] Calvin can even state that the seat of faith is not in the brain but in the heart.[148] Faith involves the feelings and affections of the heart as well as the intellect.[149] Faith does not just believe the promises of God but also relies on them, thus bringing confidence and boldness.[150]

At this point there is an ambiguity in Calvin's terminology.[151] Sometimes he uses *faith* to include both the knowledge of the mind and the

141. Ibid., 3.2.1, 9.
142. Ibid., 3.2.13.
143. Ibid., 3.2.2–3, 6–8, 12, 16, 19, 41–42.
144. Ibid., 3.2.1, 15–16, 29–30, 43; *Comm.*, Rom. 10:10; *Comm.*, Col. 2:2; *Comm.*, 2 Tim. 1:12; *Comm.*, Heb. 11:6. Kendall, *Calvin and English Calvinism*, 19, notes some of the terms used by Calvin for *faith*, including *certainty* (*certitudino*), *firm conviction* (*solida persuasio*), *firm assurance* (*solida securitas*), and *full assurance* (*plena securitas*), from *Institutes*, 3.2.6, 16, 22.
145. *Institutes*, 3.2.36; *Comm.*, John 2:23; 5:24; *Comm.*, Acts 16:14; *Comm.*, Heb. 11:6; *Comm.*, 1 Peter 1:8. Cf. Stuermann, *Critical Study*, 87–102, where faith is analyzed as the experience of certainty, the illumination of the mind, and the sealing of the heart. Letham, "Saving Faith and Assurance in Reformed Theology," 132, states that "the most crucial locus for faith is the heart."
146. *Institutes*, 3.2.33.
147. Ibid., 3.2.8.
148. *Comm.*, Rom. 10:10; cf. *Institutes*, 1.5.9; 3.2.36.
149. *Institutes*, 3.2.8; *Comm.*, Matt. 11:12; *Comm.*, John 2:23; *Comm.*, Acts 16:14; *Comm.*, Rom. 10:10; *Comm.*, Phil. 3:10.
150. *Comm.*, Eph. 3:12; cf. *Institutes*, 3.2.36.
151. For this paragraph, cf. Peter Brunner, *Vom Glauben bei Calvin* (Tübingen: J. C. B. Mohr, 1925), 142–43; Stuermann, *Critical Study*, 103–8. The position here adopted is that maintained by Graafland, *Zekerheid*, 20–28; Klaas Exalto, *De Zekerheid des Geloofs*

trust or confidence of the heart.[152] At other times he distinguishes *faith* (*fides*), which is knowledge, and *confidence* or *trust* (*fiducia*). The trust of the heart is then seen as the fruit or consequence of faith.[153] These two approaches are to be seen as complementary rather than contradictory. The distinction between faith and confidence shows the primacy of the mind over the will and the relation between knowledge and trust. Yet even when they are distinguished, the emphasis is on the close link between them. The inclusive definition shows clearly that faith is the function of the whole soul, including the will, not just of a part of it. Calvin calls faith knowledge not because it is restricted to the mind but to emphasize that it is based on God's Word, on the gospel. The trust of the heart is based on the knowledge of God in the mind. A "faith" that does not lead to the trust of the heart is not true saving faith.[154]

For Chalker, the crowning error of the English Calvinists was their concept of faith as the *appropriation* of salvation.[155] But it is equally true for Calvin that faith appropriates salvation. Faith does not simply recognize an existing situation; it changes the situation. Until God receives us into his favor, we are outside his kingdom and at deadly enmity with him.[156] It is by means of faith that we possess Christ and salvation in him.[157] Faith is receiving Christ, apprehending his righteousness, embracing Christ and the offer of the gospel.[158] Although faith may be passive in that it has nothing of its own to offer, it nonetheless appropriates salvation. Christ is set before us "that every one

---

bij Calvijn (Apeldoorn: Willem de Zwijgerstichting, 1978), esp. 7–8, 12, 36. Letham, "Saving Faith and Assurance in Reformed Theology," 128, also argues for faith as both including and distinct from *fiducia*. Letham notes the development in Calvin's view of faith from the 1536 to 1539 *Institutes* (128–30). This point is explored in detail by Geoffrey Michael Cooke, "Development of the Theme of Assurance between the 1536 and 1539 Editions of Calvin's *Institutes*" (PhD thesis, London School of Theology/ Brunel University, 2008).

152. *Institutes*, 3.2.15, 33; *Comm.*, Rom. 10:10; *Comm.*, Heb. 11:6.
153. *Institutes*, 3.2.15–16; *Comm.*, Eph. 1:13; 3:12; *Comm.*, Col. 2:2; *Comm.*, Heb. 3:6.
154. Cf. note 148 above.
155. Chalker, "Calvin," 37, 77, 294–95.
156. *Comm.*, Matt. 3:2.
157. Cf. notes 122–26 above.
158. *Institutes*, 3.1.1; 3.2.1; 3.3.2; 3.11.7; 3.14.17; 3.16.1; 3.24.6.

may appropriate the salvation which he procured."[159] The "chief hinge on which faith turns" is that "we make [the promises of mercy] ours by inwardly embracing them."[160]

There is a tension in Calvin between faith as knowledge and faith as appropriation. Faith is the knowledge of my salvation. But on what grounds can I know this? For the universalist, faith is simply the recognition that I (like all other people) will be saved. But for Calvin, with his doctrine of double predestination, this is not possible. Faith is the knowledge that I, *unlike* many others, will be saved. But on what grounds can I know this? It is not on the ground that I am elect, since that would be to pry into God's hidden counsel. For Calvin, faith is grounded on God's Word, on the promises of the gospel. But these promises, although given to all, benefit only those with faith. It therefore appears that Calvin is involved in a contradiction—faith is believing something (God is gracious to me *personally*) that does not become true until I believe it. The contradiction is not as serious as it appears, since faith is the knowledge primarily of God and only secondarily of my salvation. The gospel reveals the character of God and his offer of salvation. God's love for us is shown in his gift of his only Son to die for us. In the gospel all people without exception are invited to life.[161] Faith is the knowledge of this—of the character of God and the offer of the gospel. But faith does not stop in the mind. Being persuaded that God is good and merciful, we recline on him with sure confidence.[162] When the mind receives God's goodness, it is inflamed with love for him.[163] The heart and the will respond to the knowledge of the mind, but this does not happen automatically. As the illumination of the intellect is the work of the Spirit, so also it is the Holy Spirit who seals the heart and gives confidence and trust.[164] As the heart relies on the promises of God, so the knowledge of God's graciousness becomes the knowledge

---

159. *Antidote*, chap. 9 (127): "ut quisque sibi propriam, quae ab ipso parta est, salutem faciat" (CO, 7.457).

160. *Institutes*, 3.2.16.

161. *Comm.*, John 3:16; cf. *Institutes*, 3.2.6–7.

162. *Institutes*, 1.2.2; cf. *Comm.*, Heb. 6:4–5.

163. *Institutes*, 3.2.41; cf. *Comm.*, 1 Peter 1:8; *Comm.*, 1 John 2:3.

164. *Institutes*, 3.2.7, 33, 36; *Comm.*, Acts 16:14; *Comm.*, Rom. 8:16; *Comm.*, Eph. 1:13; *Comm.*, Heb. 10:29; *Comm.*, 1 John 2:3.

that this graciousness extends to me personally.[165] This does not happen by way of logical deduction (I am relying; therefore, I must be saved) but immediately. To rely on Christ *is* to trust him for my salvation and therefore to be confident and have assurance. Assurance is the fruit of trust in Christ, if not synonymous with it. It is not a logical deduction from the existence of trust.

Chalker criticizes the English Calvinists for teaching that one can know Christ as the Savior of believers but not of oneself, that one can know of a promise of salvation that one has not appropriated.[166] To this he contrasts Calvin's concept of faith as knowledge. There is some truth in this in that for Calvin the heart's trust flows from a knowledge of the character of God—but there is also another side to the picture. Calvin recognizes that many reject the gospel that is offered to them.[167] He charges unbelievers with ingratitude for rejecting Christ.[168] This clearly implies that they have some knowledge of that which they are rejecting. There is a bare, nonsaving knowledge of God outside of faith.[169] There is a partial faith that grasps only part of the gospel message and that can act as a preparation for true faith.[170] Clearly, those without true faith can have at least a partial but true (as far as it goes) knowledge of the gospel.

Those who have "temporary faith" go much further.[171] They can know the doctrine of the gospel.[172] They can believe that God is propitious to them and that he is their Father. But this belief is based on presumption and negligence, not on the promises of God.[173] Calvin normally teaches that such knowledge is found purely in the mind and does not reach the heart.[174] The sealing of the heart by the Spirit of adoption is the mark of

165. It is perhaps significant that the exhortations to appropriate salvation (notes 159–60) come in the context of an insistence that faith is a belief that God is gracious to *me*. A similar combination is found in *Comm.*, Matt. 21:21.

166. Cf. notes 79–82 above.

167. Cf. note 125 above.

168. *Comm.*, John 3:16–19.

169. *Comm.*, John 3:6; 17:3; *Comm.*, Eph. 3:12; *Comm.*, James 2:14, 19.

170. *Institutes*, 3.2.4–5; *Comm.*, John 2:23; 7:40.

171. Cf. section on "Perseverance and Temporary Faith" below.

172. *Comm.*, Acts 8:13. But Calvin also denies that the reprobate "proceed so far as to penetrate into that secret revelation which Scripture vouchsafes only to the elect" (*Institutes*, 3.2.12).

173. *Institutes*, 3.2.11; *Comm.*, Gal. 4:6; *Comm.*, Heb. 6:4–5. Cf. note 188 below.

174. *Institutes*, 3.2.10; *Comm.*, John 2:23.

the elect.[175] But at times Calvin can speak of the effect of this "faith" on the heart, although it is not deeply rooted and is not permanent.[176] The reprobate can be enlightened by the Spirit in their minds.[177] But their understanding is usually slight or confused.[178]

Calvin is not totally unambiguous about how much of the gospel the reprobate can know. But it is abundantly clear that they can know enough to be aware of what is offered to them. Thus it is possible, for Calvin as well as the English Calvinists cited by Chalker, to be aware of a salvation that one has not yet appropriated. Yet there is an important difference between them. For Calvin, the knowledge of God is primarily that which excites trust and confidence in our hearts, not that which presents our wills with an offer to accept or reject.

Perseverance and Temporary Faith[179]

Assurance, for Calvin, extends not simply to our present standing but to our future destiny. Faith is confident not just of God's present favor to us but of our final perseverance and eternal salvation.[180] Calvin was highly critical of Rome at this point:

> This passage [Rom. 8:38] clearly contradicts the schoolmen, who fool-ishly maintain that no one is certain of final perseverance, except by the favour of a special revelation, and this, they hold, is very rare. Such a dogma wholly destroys faith, and faith is certainly nothing if it does not extend to death and beyond.[181]

175. *Institutes*, 3.2.10–12; 3.24.8; *Comm.*, Matt. 13:21; *Comm.*, Luke 7:13; *Comm.*, John 6:69; *Comm.*, 2 Tim. 1:12; *Comm.*, Heb. 6:4–5; *Comm.*, 1 John 2:19; *Predestination*, 8.7 (131).

176. *Institutes*, 3.2.10, 12; *Comm.*, Luke 17:13; *Comm.*, Rom. 5:2; *Comm.*, Heb. 6:4–5.

177. *Institutes*, 3.2.11–12; *Comm.*, Heb. 6:4–5.

178. *Institutes*, 3.2.11–12; *Comm.*, Col. 2:2; *Comm.*, Heb. 6:4–5.

179. For a very helpful exposition of this topic, see David Foxgrover, "'Temporary Faith' and the Certainty of Salvation," *CTJ* 15 (1980): 220–32.

180. *Institutes*, 3.24.7; *Comm.*, Matt. 13:21; *Comm.*, Rom. 16:21; *Comm.*, 1 Thess. 5:24. Milner, *Calvin's Doctrine*, 64–65, makes assurance dependent on perseverance, contrary to Calvin. For the origin of this mistake, cf. note 185 below.

181. *Comm.*, Rom. 8:38; cf. *Institutes*, 3.2.40; *Comm.*, 1 Peter 1:5; *Predestination*, 8.6–8 (129–32).

Since, therefore, believers ascribe to God's grace the fact that, illumined by his Spirit, they enjoy through faith the contemplation of heavenly life, such glorying is so far from arrogance that if any man is ashamed to confess it, in that very act he betrays his extreme ungratefulness by wickedly suppressing God's goodness, more than he testifies to his modesty or submission.[182]

The elect will certainly continue to the end and receive eternal life, for their salvation is the work of God, who will not fail.[183] Thus assurance of salvation means assurance of final salvation.

But Calvin was aware that many who "believe" do not continue to the end. These, he argued, had a false or temporary faith. He distinguished between a true and lively faith that has its roots deeply fixed by the Spirit of God and the temporary faith that "many" have and that disappears. This should lead us to beware lest our own faith be extinguished.[184] For "experience shows that the reprobate are sometimes affected by almost the same feeling as the elect, so that even in their own judgment they do not in any way differ from the elect."[185]

The temporary faith of the reprobate is sincere, for they are self-deceived. They feel the divine power of the Word, undergoing an operation of the Holy Spirit inferior to the regeneration of the elect. They may believe the truth of the gospel history or even assent to the Scriptures as an infallible oracle. They can assent to the Word of God and be moved to action by its threats and promises, but this assent is not from the heart; they have roots but without life. They may have a sense of God's grace and believe that he is propitious to them, but they confusedly grasp the shadow, not the substance. They do not receive the sealing of the forgiveness of sins that the Spirit works in the elect alone. They are like a tree whose

---

182. *Institutes*, 3.2.40; cf. *Comm.*, 1 Cor. 10:12.

183. *Institutes*, 3.24.6; *Comm.*, John 10:28–29; *Comm.*, 1 Cor. 1:9; *Comm.*, Phil. 1:6; *Comm.*, Heb. 6:4–5.

184. *Comm.*, Luke 17:13; cf. *Institutes*, 3.24.6–7; *Comm.*, Ps. 106:12; *Comm.*, Matt. 13:21; 15:13; *Comm.*, John 8:31; *Comm.*, 1 John 2:19; 3:19.

185. *Institutes*, 3.2.11; cf. 3.24.8. But as the following will show, Milner is not correct in stating that the *only* difference between genuine and temporary faith is that the latter is temporary (*Calvin's Doctrine*, 63). This explains why he imagines that Calvin does not teach a real assurance of final salvation.

roots are not deep that may produce flowers and fruit for some years but will eventually wither away. They may have some "love" for God, but it is a mercenary affection, not a filial love.[186] Sometimes they receive a taste of God's grace, sparks of his light, and a perception of his goodness, having his Word engraved on their hearts. They have some knowledge, but it vanishes because its roots are not deep enough or because it is choked.[187] It is not surprising, therefore, that a false assurance can arise. But whereas true assurance rests on the promises of God and is a reliance on him with fear and humility, false assurance comes from pride and nonchalance.[188]

Three types of people profess the gospel. Some feign godliness even though a bad conscience inwardly reproves them. Others not only try to keep up a pretense before men but even manage to convince themselves that they are regenerate. Finally, those who are genuine have a living root of faith and carry the testimony of adoption firmly in their hearts.[189] The dangers of self-deception are very real. Simon Magus and others like him not only deceive others by their false semblance of faith but even deceive themselves. They think the reverence that they give to the Word is a genuine piety because they are unaware that impiety can be inward as well as outward.[190]

It does not follow that all assurance is invalid. The fact that some people may be falsely assured does not mean that no one else can have assurance—just as the fact that some people may be convinced that two plus two equals five does not shake my belief that two plus two equals four. The many examples of false faith are not to undermine the Christian's confidence in the promises of God, especially those relating to final perseverance. We are not to abandon all security but only a "crass and sheer confidence of the flesh, which bears in its train haughtiness, arrogance, and contempt of others, snuffs out humility and reverence for God, and makes one forget grace received." We are to have a fear that is not panic but that

186. *Institutes*, 3.2.9–12.
187. *Comm.*, Heb. 6:4–5; cf. *Comm.*, 1 John 2:19.
188. *Comm.*, 1 Cor. 10:12; cf. *Institutes*, 3.2.12; *Comm.*, Rom. 8:14; *Comm.*, Phil. 2:12–13; *Comm.*, 1 John 3:7.
189. *Comm.*, 1 John 2:19; cf. *Institutes*, 3.24.7. Calvin further distinguishes different types of hypocrites in *Comm.*, Matt. 6:2; *Comm.*, John 1:47, expounded in Foxgrover, "'Temporary Faith,'" 228–29.
190. *Institutes*, 3.2.10; cf. *Comm.*, John 2:23; *Comm.*, Acts 8:13; *Comm.*, James 2:14, 19.

teaches us to receive the grace of God in humility, *without* lessening our confidence.[191] Some might object that the wicked call God "Father" and have a greater confidence than the elect. But when Paul wrote of Christian confidence, he was referring not to idle boasting but to "the testimony of a godly conscience which follows the new regeneration."[192]

There remains the question of how to distinguish between a true and a false confidence. With others there is no sure way of doing this, and we are to rest content with a judgment of charity.[193] But no such uncertainty need cloud the individual's knowledge of his or her own state. The reprobate only appear to have the same signs as the elect.

> And I do not deny that they [who fall away] have signs of a call that are similar to those of the elect, but I by no means concede to them that sure establishment of election which I bid believers seek from the word of the gospel. So then, let not such instances induce us at all to abandon a quiet reliance upon the Lord's promise, where he declares that all by whom he is received in true faith have been given to him by the Father.[194]

But the description given above of the temporary faith of the reprobate might seem to indicate that they have as strong a testimony to their adoption by God as do the elect.

> I reply: although there is a great likeness and affinity between God's elect and those who are given a transitory faith, yet only in the elect does that confidence flourish which Paul extols, that they loudly proclaim Abba, Father.[195]

It is only in the elect that God effectually seals the grace of his adoption. But this does not obviate the need for careful self-examination.

The nature of this self-examination clearly separates Calvin from many of his would-be followers. It is not an introspective examination

191. *Institutes*, 3.24.7; cf. 3.2.22; *Comm.*, 1 Cor. 10:12; *Comm.*, Heb. 6:4–5; *Antidote*, chap. 13 (137).

192. *Comm.*, Gal. 4:6.

193. *Institutes*, 3.24.8; 4.1.7–9; *Comm.*, Matt. 13:24–30, 36–43; *Comm.*, 1 Cor. 1:9; *Comm.*, Phil. 1:6; 4:3; *Comm.*, 1 Peter 1:1–2.

194. *Institutes*, 3.24.7.

195. Ibid., 3.2.11; cf. *Predestination*, 8.7 (131).

of my faith to see whether it is genuine. This Calvin never recommends. It is not the testing of my faith by the fruit of the Spirit in my life. This is *a* test, but Calvin is emphatic that the basis of assurance must lie elsewhere.[196] Self-examination does not mean testing my works and deducing my election from them. It is not my faith that is examined but the *object* of my faith. Believers are to examine themselves to ensure that their trust is placed not in themselves but in Christ. They are to "examine themselves carefully and humbly, lest the confidence of the flesh creep in and replace assurance of faith."[197] Self-examination does not turn believers to themselves or to their faith but back to Christ and the gospel. Believers are not to compare their faith with that of the reprobate but to look to Christ and to place their trust in him.[198] It is not "am I *trusting* in Christ?" but "am I trusting in *Christ?*"[199]

Limited Atonement

When I wrote the original version of this essay, I had glanced only briefly at Robert T. Kendall's then-unpublished thesis on saving faith.[200] It makes two claims about Calvin's teaching on this topic. The first chapter provocatively begins with the claim that "fundamental to the doctrine of faith in John Calvin . . . is his belief that Christ died indiscriminately for all men."[201] The chapter goes on to argue that this belief is crucial for

196. Cf. section on "Works" above.
197. *Institutes*, 3.2.11; cf. 3.2.22. On this point, cf. Beeke, *Assurance of Faith*, 67–68.
198. *Institutes*, 3.24.7; *Comm.*, 1 Cor. 10:12.
199. In the first version of this article I wrote, "This subtle but vital distinction captures the whole essence of Calvin's doctrine of assurance." Joel Beeke rightly accuses me of exaggerating at this point (*Assurance of Faith*, 95).
200. The thesis was produced in 1976: "The Nature of Saving Faith from William Perkins (d. 1602) to the Westminster Assembly (1643–1649)" (DPhil thesis, Oxford University, 1976), but was not published until 1979. I managed to glance at the thesis for half an hour before publishing my article, and mentioned it in two footnotes. Bell, *Calvin and Scottish Theology*, 13, chides me for ignoring the issue of the extent of the atonement "even though fully aware of Kendall's work." I was fully aware of its existence, but only slightly aware of its contents. Bell is right that failure to tackle that topic was a serious weakness of the original article, which is one of the reasons for now revisiting the topic.
201. Kendall, *Calvin and English Calvinism*, 13. Kendall's further claim that (for Calvin) Christ died for all but intercedes only for the elect (17) has not met with approval.

Calvin's doctrine of assurance. "Had not Christ died for *all,* we could have no assurance that *our* sins have been expiated in God's sight."[202]

This is not the place to discuss at length the first of these claims. Kendall's thesis served to spark renewed interest in the topic and has helped to provoke a good number of books and articles. In my view, there is no doubt that the thrust of Calvin's teaching points in the direction of Christ's death for all without exception. Most persuasive of all is the structure of the *Institutes.* Having expounded the work of Christ at the end of book 2, Calvin begins book 3:

> We must now examine this question. How do we receive those benefits which the Father bestowed on his only-begotten Son—not for Christ's own private use, but that he might enrich poor and needy men? First, we must understand that as long as Christ remains outside of us, and we are separated from him, all that he has suffered and done for the salvation of the human race remains useless and of no value for us.[203]

Christ's death is for all, but it benefits us only when we are united to Christ by faith, through the work of the Spirit. It is the saving work of the Spirit that is restricted to the elect, not the death of Christ. Although this is the thrust of Calvin's teaching, it is not the whole picture. George Michael Thomas argues that when viewing the death of Christ from the perspective of God's promises, Calvin portrays it as universal; but when viewing it from the perspective of election, he can speak in more particular terms.[204] His exposition is a helpful corrective, but he exaggerates, giving the impression that Calvin was balanced between "universalism" and "particularism" *when speaking of the cross,* though there can be little doubt that the overwhelming emphasis in Calvin is that Christ died for all. The particularist passages to which Thomas points all come in Calvin's exegetical works where he is discussing the meaning of *all* in one specific biblical passage or another.

How relevant is this to assurance? Kendall sees it as crucial, but others have disagreed. In Calvin's thought, there is a tension between universal-

---

202. Ibid., 14.
203. *Institutes,* 3.1.1.
204. George Michael Thomas, *The Extent of the Atonement: A Dilemma for Reformed Theology from Calvin to the Consensus (1536–1675)* (Carlisle, PA: Paternoster, 1997), 12–40.

ism (the gospel is freely offered) and particularism (saving faith is given by the Holy Spirit to the elect alone). Assurance is arrived at by putting one's trust in the universal promises, and only then can be strengthened by knowledge of God's particular election.[205] Thus, for Calvin, faith initially engages with the universal promises of God without (at *that* point) any knowledge that one has been chosen. Although the universal offer of the gospel would logically suffice at this point, Calvin presents the fact that Christ has died for us as a significant part of the ground for faith. John 3:16 teaches us that faith is "placing Christ before one's eyes and beholding in Him the heart of God poured out in love. Our firm and substantial support is to rest on the death of Christ as its only pledge." "For men are not easily convinced that God loves them; and so, to remove all doubt, He has expressly stated that we are so very dear to God that for our sakes He did not spare even His only-begotten Son." It is not that we become convinced that Christ died for us when we become convinced that we are elect. Calvin draws attention to the words whosoever and world. The former serves "both to invite indiscriminately all to share in life and to cut off every excuse from unbelievers." By the latter God "shows He is favourable to the whole world when he calls all without exception to the faith of Christ, which is indeed an entry into life."[206] Thus, for Calvin, the death of Christ for all is an important aspect of the universal promise that is presented indiscriminately to all. It would be wrong, however, to deduce from this that Calvin's doctrine of assurance depends on the universality of the atonement. Bucer also taught that assurance is part of saving faith,[207] yet he also taught limited atonement.[208]

Calvin's Doctrine Compared with Others

A brief comparison of Calvin's doctrine of assurance with that of his Roman Catholic opponents and of some seventeenth-century

205. Cf. sections on "Predestination" and "Christ" above.
206. *Comm.*, John 3:16.
207. Letham, "Saving Faith and Assurance in Reformed Theology," 6, 77–86.
208. Jonathan Herbold Rainbow, *The Will of God and the Cross* (Allison Park, PA: Pickwick Publications, 1990), 49–60.

Calvinists will serve to focus more sharply the distinctive features of Calvin's teaching.

The Council of Trent

Assurance was discussed at the sixth session of the Council of Trent, and the doctrine is set out in the *Decree concerning Justification* of January 1547. Chapter 9 ("Against the Vain Confidence of Heretics") affirms that sins neither are nor have ever been remitted except freely, by God's mercy, for Christ's sake. But the mere possession of assurance is no guarantee of forgiveness because heretics have a vain and ungodly confidence. It is wrong to assert that those who are justified do, ought to, or must know the fact "without any doubt whatever." Although no Christian should doubt "the mercy of God, the merit of Christ and the virtue and efficacy of the sacraments," there is room for fear concerning one's own state, since "no one can know with the certainty of faith, which cannot be subject to error, that he has obtained the grace of God."[209] Chapter 12 ("Rash Presumption of Predestination Is to Be Avoided") affirms that it is not possible, except by special revelation, to know that one is elect.[210] The canons add that we cannot be sure of receiving the gift of perseverance "with an absolute and infallible certainty" except by special revelation.[211]

Calvin dissented, on four grounds.[212] First, to divorce faith from confidence and assurance is to undermine the New Testament concept of faith. "Faith is destroyed as soon as certainty is taken away." "Paul and John recognise none as the children of God but those who know it."[213] Second, to make assurance dependent on works undermines confidence and leads us to trust

---

209. John H. Leith, *Creeds of the Churches*, 2nd ed. (Richmond, VA: John Knox Press, 1973), 413–14. Cf. canons 13–14 (422).

210. Leith, *Creeds of the Churches*, 416. Cf. canon 15 (422).

211. Canon 16 (Leith, *Creeds of the Churches*, 422). Cf. canon 13 (416–17).

212. Calvin's response is found in *Antidote*. He also opposed the Roman Catholic position in the *Institutes* and his commentaries, before the Tridentine decree as well as after it.

213. *Antidote*, chap. 9 (125, 127); cf. canons 13–14 (154–55); *Institutes*, 3.2.15–16, 39; *Comm.*, Matt. 21:21; *Comm.*, Rom. 5:2; 8:16, 34; *Comm.*, 1 Cor. 2:12; 10:12; *Comm.*, 2 Cor. 13:5; *Comm.*, Gal. 4:6; *Comm.*, Eph. 3:12, 19; *Comm.*, Col. 2:2; *Comm.*, 1 Peter 1:8; *Comm.*, 1 John 5:19. Cf. sections on "The Necessity of Assurance" and "Justification by Faith" above.

in ourselves.[214] Third, the only "special revelation" needed for the assurance that we are elect is the witness of the Holy Spirit to our adoption, which is common to all believers.[215] Finally, faith in the New Testament extends to death and beyond and includes the assurance of final perseverance.[216]

Westminster Confession

Seventeenth-century English Calvinism diverged significantly from Calvin's doctrine of assurance, and this is reflected in the Westminster Confession.[217] Chapter 14 expounds "Saving Faith," and it is only after three further chapters, on repentance, works, and perseverance, that the confession turns to "Assurance of Grace and Salvation." There it is affirmed that "such as truly believe in the Lord Jesus, and love him in sincerity, endeavouring to walk in all good conscience before him, *may*, in this life, be certainly assured that they are in the state of grace."[218] In opposition to the Roman position, it is stated that "this certainty is not a bare conjectural and probable persuasion, grounded upon a fallible hope; but an infallible assurance of faith."[219] But "this infallible assurance doth not so belong to the essence of faith, but that a true believer may wait long, and conflict with many difficulties before he be partaker of it."[220] Contrary to Calvin, assurance and faith have been separated so that the latter is possible without the former. It is not beyond the reach of the ordinary

214. *Antidote*, chap. 16 (146–47); cf. *Institutes*, 3.2.38; *Comm.*, Isa. 59:20; *Comm.*, Heb. 11:6. Cf. sections on "Works" and "Justification by Faith" above.

215. *Antidote*, chap. 12 (135–36); cf. canon 15 (155). Cf. sections on "Predestination" and "Calvin's Doctrine Compared with Others" above.

216. *Antidote*, chap. 13 (136–38); cf. canons 15–16 (155); *Institutes*, 3.2.40; *Comm.*, Rom. 5:2; 8:38; *Comm.*, 1 Cor. 2:12; *Comm.*, Col. 1:23; *Comm.*, 1 Peter 1:5. Cf. section on "Perseverance and Temporary Faith" above.

217. Chalker, "Calvin"; Kendall, *Calvin and English Calvinism*, chap. 14; Beeke, *Assurance of Faith*, chap. 6. Quotations from the Westminster Confession follow the critical text of S. W. Carruthers (Manchester: R. Aikman [1937]), with one exception: *He*, *Him*, etc. revert to *he*, *him*, etc., as in the seventeenth-century originals. All emphases are mine.

218. WCF 18.1.

219. Ibid., 18.2.

220. Ibid., 18.3. Robert W. A. Letham points out that the Larger Catechism is more blunt, simply stating that assurance of grace and salvation is not of the essence of faith (*The Theology of the Westminster Assembly* [Phillipsburg, NJ: P&R Publishing/Craig Center for the Study of the Westminster Standards, forthcoming, 2009], chap. 12.

Christian "being enabled by the Spirit to know the things which are freely given him of God, he may without extraordinary revelation, in the right use of ordinary means, attain thereunto,"[221] but it is something extra, a "second blessing," that he is to seek, not part of saving faith itself. This is seen especially clearly in the statement that "it is the *duty* of everyone to give all diligence to make his calling and election sure."[222] True believers can lose their assurance, for a variety of reasons, although God does not abandon them totally and there remains a seed from which assurance may grow again.[223]

The shift of assurance from an aspect of faith to a subsequent achievement, from a privilege to a duty, has two roots. In the first place, saving faith is seen primarily in active rather than passive terms. The definition of saving faith is given in terms of its acts, in terms of what it does.[224] This contrasts with Calvin, who stressed the passivity of faith and saw it primarily as knowledge. The Westminster Confession does not totally distinguish assurance from saving faith in that strong faith "gets the victory; growing up in *many* to the attainment of a full assurance through Christ."[225] But it is clear that assurance is not of the essence of faith itself but accompanies the strong faith of many, not all, believers.

Second, there is a difference in the grounds of assurance. For the Westminster Confession, it is "founded upon the divine truth of the promises of salvation, the inward evidence of those graces unto which these promises are made, the testimony of the Spirit of adoption witnessing with our spirits that we are the children of God."[226] It is true that the promises of God are placed first, but we can be sure that they apply to us only if we have the inward evidence of certain graces.[227] The effect of this is to turn our attention from the promises themselves to the evidences that we have these graces. This, together with the reference to 2 Peter 1:10 both here

221. WCF 18:3.
222. Ibid., citing 2 Peter 1:10.
223. WCF 18:4.
224. Ibid., 14:2.
225. Ibid., 14:3.
226. Ibid., 18:2.
227. This is more explicit in the Larger Catechism, which states (Q. 80) that assurance is grounded on the promises but that we need the Spirit to enable us to discern within ourselves "those graces to which the promises of life are made."

(WCF 18:3) and elsewhere,[228] points clearly to the practical syllogism found in much of seventeenth-century English Calvinism. Assurance depends on the genuineness of my faith, and this is tested by the evidence of my sanctification.

Beeke makes a valiant attempt to harmonize Calvin with the Westminster Confession. He argues that the promises of God are the primary ground of assurance, the inward evidence and the testimony of the Spirit secondary grounds.[229] But this distinction is not made in the confession. Even if we accept that it is how the authors of the confession would have understood it, there remains a fundamental difference from Calvin. For Calvin, the primary ground suffices and the others serve simply to confirm and strengthen it. For the confession, the promises alone do *not* suffice without evidence that one is actually a partaker of them, and this point is established by the inward evidence and the testimony of the Spirit. This is clear from the way in which the practical syllogism operated.[230] Also, for the authors of the confession, the testimony of the Spirit either functioned through the practical syllogism or was seen as a special experience of the Spirit to be sought after conversion and given to only a few.[231] Neither of these agrees with Calvin.

Beeke also affirms the claim of Peter Lewis that the difference between Calvin and the confession was one of emphasis, on the ground that they did not have the same concern in view. Calvin was "defining what faith is in its assuring character"; chapter 18 of the confession was "describing what assurance is as a self-conscious experimental phenomenon."[232] Although there may be some element of truth in this, the contrast is not total, and it does not alter the fact that Calvin sees assurance very differently from the confession. What Beeke offers is a synthesis of the teaching of Calvin and the confession in which each is seen as emphasizing one side of a larger truth. This may be valid as an exercise in systematic theology, but it is dubious as an exercise in historical theology, especially where Calvin's

228. Cf. WCF 16.2: "good works . . . are the fruits and evidences of a true and lively faith: and by them believers . . . strengthen their assurance."
229. Beeke, *Assurance of Faith*, 152–72.
230. Ibid., 159–69.
231. Ibid., 169–72.
232. Ibid., 62 (his emphasis removed).

teaching is concerned. It should also be noted that Calvin's context was not as different from the following century as is sometimes implied. Randall Zachman notes (in response to those contrasting Calvin and Beza) that Calvin "consistently and explicitly" addresses the problem of "believers who have serious doubts about God's mercy, their faith, their adoption, and their election—in all aspects of his theological work, from the *Institutes* and commentaries to his sermons."[233]

Although Calvin was not aware of the developments that were to follow his death, he nonetheless managed to preempt them in his own teaching. Against the separation (by Rome) of faith and assurance he wrote:

> Also, there are very many who so conceive God's mercy that they receive almost no consolation from it. They are constrained with miserable anxiety at the same time as they are in doubt whether he will be merciful to them because they confine that very kindness of which they seem utterly persuaded within too narrow limits. For among themselves they ponder that it is indeed great and abundant, shed upon many, available and ready for all; but that it is uncertain whether it will even come to them, or rather, whether they will come to it. This reasoning, when it stops in midcourse, is only half. Therefore, it does not so much strengthen the spirit in secure tranquillity as trouble it with uneasy doubting. But there is a far different feeling of full assurance that in the Scriptures is always attributed to faith. It is this which puts beyond doubt God's goodness clearly manifested for us.[234]

It is ironic that these words, written against Calvin's opponents in his own time, should so accurately portray the situation of many Calvinists

233. Randall C. Zachman, "Crying to God on the Brink of Despair: The Assurance of Faith Revisited," in *Calvinus Praeceptor Ecclesiae*, ed. Herman J. Selderhuis (Geneva: Droz, 2004), 352–53. Beeke goes on to state that Calvin was addressing a situation in which people were searching for personal assurance of salvation (*Assurance of Faith*, 63–64)—an admission that weakens his earlier claim that Calvin and the Westminster Confession have different concerns.

234. *Institutes*, 3.2.15. There is, of course, the important difference between Trent and Westminster that the former denied the possibility of infallible assurance (apart from exceptional circumstances) while the latter affirmed it. Yet there remains the similarity that Westminster, like Trent, can lead believers to believe in God's mercy without the confidence that it applies to *them*.

in the following century. Against the search for evidence of election in good works he wrote:

> Indeed, if we should have to judge from our works how the Lord feels toward us, for my part, I grant that we can in no way attain it by conjecture. But since faith ought to correspond to a simple and free promise, no place for doubting is left.[235]

To those who, like many others in the seventeenth century, doubted whether they had truly appropriated salvation he counseled not an introspective self-examination but a turning to Christ:

> Therefore, if we desire to know whether God cares for our salvation, let us inquire whether he has entrusted us to Christ, whom he has established as the sole Savior of all his people. If we still doubt whether we have been received by Christ into his care and protection, he meets that doubt when he willingly offers himself as shepherd, and declares that we shall be numbered among his flock if we hear his voice. Let us therefore embrace Christ, who is graciously offered to us, and comes to meet us. He will reckon us in his flock and enclose us within his fold.[236]

For Calvin, the search for assurance leads believers not to a second stage beyond their acceptance of the gospel (looking within for faith and its evidences) but back to the gospel itself. Assurance is based not on anything in ourselves (whether faith, works, or the evidence of the Holy Spirit) but on Christ and the promises of God. Trust in Christ means trust that he is my Savior, both now and for eternity.

---

235. Ibid., 3.2.38.
236. Ibid., 3.2.46.

14

Calvin's Principles of Governance: Homology in Church and State

David W. Hall

ohn Calvin stood at the beginning of modernity, and his ideas and actions would change history forever. Others—today, though, mainly forgotten voices—have previously recognized the influence of Calvin in many areas, not the least of which is civil governance. The highly respected nineteenth-century Harvard historian George Bancroft was one of many who earlier asserted that Calvin's ideas buttressed liberty's cause. He and others noted the influence of this thought on the development of various freedoms in western Europe and America.[1] Writing in the middle

1. George Bancroft, "A Word on Calvin, the Reformer," in George Bancroft, *Literary and Historical Miscellanies* (New York, 1855), 405ff., cited in Philip Schaff, *History of the Christian Church* (New York: Charles Scribner's Sons, 1910; repr., Grand Rapids: Eerdmans, 1979), 8:264.

of the nineteenth century, Bancroft extolled Calvin as "the foremost of modern republican legislators," who was responsible for elevating the culture of Geneva into "the impregnable fortress of popular liberty, the fertile seed-plot of democracy."[2] Bancroft even credited the "free institutions of America" as derived "chiefly from Calvinism through the medium of Puritanism." Moreover, he traced the living legacy of Calvin among the Plymouth pilgrims, the Huguenot settlers of South Carolina, and the Dutch colonists in Manhattan, concluding: "He that will not honor the memory and respect the influence of Calvin knows but little of the origin of American liberty."

Bancroft esteemed Calvin as one of the premier republican pioneers, at one point writing, "The fanatic for Calvinism was a fanatic for liberty; and, in the moral warfare for freedom, his creed was his most faithful counselor and his never-failing support. The Puritans ... planted ... the undying principles of democratic liberty."[3]

John Calvin is known primarily as a churchman, pastor, and theologian, but he also contributed much to theories of societal governance. Numerous scholars have traced Calvin's civic contributions.[4] Among the various contributions, Douglas Kelly identifies the "sober Calvinian assessment of fallen man's propensity to seize, increase, and abuse power for personal ends rather than for the welfare of the many." He explains: "Governmental principles for consent of the governed, and separation and balance of powers are all logical consequences of a most serious and Calvinian view

2. Ibid., 8:522.

3. Robert M. Kingdon, *Calvin and Calvinism: Sources of Democracy* (Lexington, MA: D. C. Heath and Company, 1970), 8, quoting George Bancroft, *History of the United States of America* (Boston, 1853), 1:464.

4. Among the scholars who have explicated Calvin's political thought and impact are Harro Hopfl, *The Christian Polity of John Calvin* (Cambridge: Cambridge University Press, 1982); Quentin Skinner, *The Foundations of Modern Political Thought: The Age of Reformation*, vol. 2 (Cambridge: Cambridge University Press, 1978); Ralph C. Hancock, *Calvin and the Foundations of Modern Politics* (Ithaca, NY: Cornell University Press, 1989); John T. McNeill, "Calvin and Civil Government," in *Readings in Calvin's Theology*, ed. Donald McKim (Grand Rapids: Baker, 1984); *Collected Papers of Herbert D. Foster* (privately printed, 1929); Douglas Kelly, *The Emergence of Liberty in the Modern World* (Phillipsburg, NJ: P&R Publishing, 1992); Franklin Charles Palm, *Calvinism and the Religious Wars* (New York: Henry Holt and Company, 1932); Karl Holl, *The Cultural Significance of the Reformation* (Cleveland, OH: Meridian, 1959); and Keith L. Griffin, *Revolution and Religion: American Revolutionary War and the Reformed Clergy* (New York: Paragon House, 1994).

of the biblical doctrine of the fall of man."[5] Although historian Franklin Palm mistakenly classified Calvin as "wholly medieval" and as favoring an "aristocratic theocracy in which he was dictator," nevertheless, he recognized Calvin's contribution as "emphasizing the supremacy of God and the right of resistance to all other authority. . . . He did much to curb the powers of kings and to increase the authority of the elected representatives of the people."[6] Further, Palm noticed Calvin's belief in the "right of the individual to remove the magistrate who disobeys the word of God. . . . Consequently, he justified many revolutionary leaders in their belief that God gave them the right to oppose tyranny."

Recently, John Witte Jr. has noted how "Calvin developed arresting new teachings on authority and liberty, duties and rights, and church and state that have had an enduring influence on Protestant lands." As a result of its adaptability, this "rendered early modern Calvinism one of the driving engines of Western constitutionalism. A number of our bedrock Western understandings of civil and political rights, social and confessional pluralism, federalism and social contract, and more owe a great deal to Calvinist theological and political reforms."[7]

It is even possible in a culture that devalues the church to view Calvin's political contributions as his more enduring donation to society.[8] Moreover, there are some who persistently view a disconnect either between Calvin and his disciples or between Calvin's principles of government for the state compared to those for the church. With a little more care to detail, however, one will likely find an organic connection between Calvin's governmental principles in both areas. This essay seeks to elucidate Calvin's principles of government in both church and state and to illustrate how similar they are.

Methodologically, I will compare a *loci* that is sometimes viewed as peripheral to Calvin (politics) with a *loci* that is considered at the core (ecclesiology). To begin with some of his earliest pertinent writings (1536

5. Kelly, *The Emergence of Liberty in the Modern World*, 18.

6. Palm, *Calvinism and the Religious Wars*, 32.

7. John Witte Jr., *The Reformation of Rights: Law, Religion and Human Rights in Early Modern Calvinism* (Cambridge: Cambridge University Press, 2007), 2.

8. For my study of this, see *Calvin in the Public Square: Liberal Democracies, Rights, and Civil Liberties* (Phillipsburg, NJ: P&R Publishing, 2009).

Institutes and 1541, *Ecclesiastical Ordinances* [hereafter *EO*]) and to then compare those structural dynamics to a summary of Calvin's later work in civil governmental principles—indeed, some would argue that these principles were refined posthumously by Beza, Ponet, Daneau, Althusius, and others—is to see whether there is consistency both between the early Calvin (1536–41, the date of the *EO*) and between the later Calvin (1559 *Institutes*, 1561 revision of *EO*) and between disciplines. If such tenacity of principle is observed over that span of time and between differing disciplines, surely a core dogma is evidenced.

Survey of Calvin's Ecclesiastical Principles

Calvin's first theological publishing,[9] of course, was his shortened version of the *Institutes* in 1536, a work of approximately five hundred pages (octavo). Four years earlier, his earliest published work, a commentary on Seneca's *De Clementia* (1532), affirmed this radical notion: "The prince is not above the laws, but the laws above the prince."[10] After 1536 (except for catechisms and localized tracts), his publications were not resumed until 1539/1541 [Latin/French], perhaps because his Strasbourg exile provided him with slightly more time, research, and reflection than did his turbulent, initial residence in Geneva. By 1541, while in Strasbourg, he had published a revised French edition of the *Institutes*. In both of these early versions, Calvin included material on both church and state. Yet each was somewhat abbreviated when compared to the final edition.

To illustrate something of the emphasis, in 1536, Calvin devoted more pages (fifty) to his fifth chapter (on false sacraments) than he did to his exposition of the Apostles' Creed and the Lord's Prayer combined, or than to his exposition of the Ten Commandments *and* justification together.[11] In one of those sections in chapter 5, he devoted considerable critique to the Roman notion of ordination as a sacrament, including polemics

9. For more on Calvin's first publication, his Commentary on Seneca's *Soul Sleep*, see Ford Lewis Battles, *The Sources of Calvin's Commentary on Seneca's De Clementia: A Provisional Index* (Hartford: Hartford Seminary Foundation, 1962).

10. Hopfl, *The Christian Polity of John Calvin*, 16.

11. Source for the page references in parentheses in this section is Ford Lewis Battles' 1536 edition of Calvin's *Institutes of the Christian Religion* (Grand Rapids: Eerdmans, 1986).

against the Roman priesthood. The number of ecclesiastical orders as well as the laity-clergy distinction received customary criticism (161–62) in this early work. Calvin believed that the massive Roman infrastructure was more akin to pagan orders than to the simpler, biblical view. On one occasion, he even suggested that an accurate translation of the word for *acolyte* meant "lackey."[12] He also inferred that only gullibility (163) would lead to an embrace of the entire Romanist sacramental regimen for holy orders. Preferring "primitive church" order to the ever-blossoming tendrils of Roman ecclesiology, Calvin thought that the presbyterate and the priesthood were two names that "signify the same thing" (164).

Calvin's 1536 edition distinguished between the extraordinary offices (such as apostles) and ordinary offices (166). He then moved to explain what the office of presbyter meant, biblically speaking. He summarized it as "proclaiming the gospel and administering sacraments" (166). Calvin set forth a far less ornamented view of ministry than the received Roman view, which insisted on pomp and titles— or, as he provocatively called it, "the stews of Satan" (167). In another decentralizing step, he addressed the question of who had the lawful right to ordain ministers; and rather than lodging that power with a hierarchical bishop, Calvin spied the New Testament custom (which he also found in the Old Testament) of having the congregation elect a minister—certainly an early case of "consent of the governed." Citing historical precedents and the likes of Cyprian, Calvin went so far as early as 1536 as to assert that "an election is not properly made except by the common vote of all the people" (168). Calvin was also quick to deny a pure democracy, for he continues in the next section to opine that since crowds were so fickle, elders or senators should choose ministers (168). Thus Calvin's ecclesiastical republicanism is noted even before the publishing of his 1541 *EO* (below).

Calvin's early 1536 outline of ecclesiastical polity also included the diaconate (171), but distinguished this office from the Roman tradition, which primarily used deacons as liturgists. Yet he insisted that ordination to any office was not a sacrament.

12. Calvin also said that "bishoprics were rewards for panderings and adulteries" (168). He also railed against "pastors of the church" who never saw their flocks (169).

Calvin's sixth chapter in his original edition addressed three top-ics: Christian freedom, ecclesiastical power, and political administration (which we discuss below). His teaching on Christian liberty was one of the earliest features of his thought, and it is either an essential part of gospel teaching (176) or, as it would later become known, an "appendix to the doctrine of justification." Calvin's discussion of this topic, which was so important in his day, follows the same outline as his 1559 edition, albeit in slightly compressed form. The longest section in his sixth chapter is on ecclesiology proper. Calvin viewed this in his day as an extension of Christian freedom (184), for if church masters invaded the conscience, that tyranny threatened Christian liberty. It is worthy of note that Calvin viewed church government as important for spiritual liberty—thus the need to devote so much writing to that subject during the Reformation era. It is not too much to assert that Calvin viewed himself as setting forth an ecclesiology of liberty as opposed to the prevailing tyranny of "innu-merable," "limitless," and "entangling" church governance that he viewed as "traps to catch and ensnare souls" (185). In what would become associated with the customary Calvinistic ethos, Calvin expected that knowledge from the teaching of faithful pastors would "first assure that each one of us will keep his freedom in all these things; yet each one will voluntarily impose some necessity upon his freedom" (206).

Calvin, however, did not overreact and argue that all government was wrong simply because there were abuses of "tyrannical wickedness" (185). He viewed the New Testament (and the Old Testament) as exhibiting officeholders, given by God, and such officeholders must surely presup-pose governance (186). Early on in this subject, in expected form, Calvin also distinguished his views on governance by holding to *sola Scriptura* instead of relying on tradition or reason alone. His divine-right ecclesiology would later be extended by his disciples, but on the level of principle his advocacy of *sola Scriptura* in this topic is as clear as in other theological *loci*. With Scripture acknowledged as his authority even for ecclesiology, Calvin asserted that "if faith depends on God's word alone, if it looks to it and reposes in it alone, what place is now left for the word of men?" (189). Legislative power, thought Calvin, or the authority to "frame new laws" (189), was denied to the apostles; only ministerial power—the right to echo and assert what God had already declared—was given to the church. God, the sole ruler over souls, was the sole ruler over the church of all souls.

A comparison of Calvin's 1536 content with his 1559 edition shows perhaps the greatest single expansion of one 1536 chapter into parts of thirteen chapters in the final edition—mostly describing the historical evolution and abuses of the papacy. Calvin's vastly expanded 1559 edition is a fuller ecclesiology, detailing the marks of the church, the election of pastors, and how pastoral visitation should be practiced, along with a lengthy polemic against the primacy of Rome (4.6) and a lengthy chapter on the devolution of the Roman church (4.7). When one compares chapters 3–4 of book 4 of the 1559 *Institutes* to the first edition, it becomes clear that much of that latter content is drafted from the *EO* (below); thus, the final edition of the *Institutes* is more comprehensive of Calvin's wisdom on church governance, to be sure. Yet the cardinal principles of governance differ little.

Much of chapter 8 in book 4 is contained in abbreviated form in the 1536 edition, and the only major change between editions for chapter 9 is that the latter edition contains Calvin's rebuttals of criticisms leveled against him from the intervening years (e.g., "that I esteem the ancient councils less than I ought" [4.9.1—imagine!]); and of course, it is slightly more expansive. The final edition of the *Institutes* adds a middle section to chapter 10, exposing Roman constitutions as abuses that lead to tyranny (sections 10–18 of 4.10), and adds some scriptural data on the purity of worship along with the need to avoid pharisaism. Calvin's eleventh chapter in book 5 differs from the original in two respects: (1) by prefacing that discussion with a treatment of the "keys of the kingdom" (sections 1–3) and by delineating the difference of jurisdiction between bishops and civil magistrates; and (2) by supplementing with exposés of the Donation of Constantine, Hildebrand's many excesses (Gregory VII), and other Roman fraudulencies. Finally, Calvin's discussion of church discipline (4.12) in the final edition is material that is not included in his first primer. In these respects Calvin's earlier and later ecclesiology from the *Institutes* differs mainly in extent of discourse, not in major principles.

Although Calvin's discussion on "political administration" (or civil government) varies little over the years, to be sure, one of the largest changes in degree of content occurs in his ecclesiology, with the outline of the original version expanding significantly to the treatise that appears in the final edition. Calvin's experiences between 1536 and 1559 most likely colored this need for expansiveness. The raw amount of change over time was far greater in ecclesiology than in political theory. When one factors in how much of the 1541 *EO* was included in the final edition of the *Institutes*, however, it becomes clear that—other than extended history lessons—Calvin's ecclesiology was quite settled at an early date and consistent over time.

The Importance of the Ecclesiastical Ordinances

When urged by Louis Dufour to return to Geneva from Strasbourg in 1541, Calvin returned with one major demand, which was quickly consented to. In addition to this one major demand, Calvin was also offered a home near St. Pierre Cathedral, was given a salary that exceeded that of the aldermen, and was assigned to a committee that was revising the "Edicts" or city constitution of Geneva. Although he was not negotiating a raise, these plums—plus the agreement to his one major demand—indicated the degree to which the Genevans (or at least some political segments) yearned for a restoration of his leadership.

The major demand was that Calvin be supported in drafting and instituting the *EO*, the mother of Presbyterian books of order. Although modest in scope, and with detail that was contoured to a particular locale, this proto-governmental manual, if ever implemented, would break new ground in securing the freedom and independence of the church from state control. That principle, so taken for granted in the modern West, was no small achievement, nor was it easily obtained. In choosing this emphasis, however, Calvin let it be known that in order for Protestant ministry to be optimal, it must be free from external governmental control or incursion.

Accordingly, the *EO* chartered an essential Presbyterian government (likely copied in part from Calvin's Strasbourg experience) and was later copied by other ethnic branches of Calvinist ecclesiology, with certain cultural modifications (Belgic, 1561; Scots, 1579).

So important was this area to Calvin that it was a *sine qua non* for his return to Geneva. Thus, in sequence if not in importance, second after the 1536 *Institutes* (which would be revised until 1559) was Calvin's *EO*. He returned to Geneva on June 13, 1541, and began drafting a constitution for the church, assisted by other ministers. The *EO* was eventually approved on November 20, 1541, after first being approved by the Council of Sixty, then by the Council of Two Hundred.

Distilled Principles of the EO (1541, 1561)

This ecclesiological work provides many protocols for parish ministry. Admittedly, it does not have the feel of a document that is intended for all cultures, and it adapts certain habits of the Genevans, who were among the earliest to pioneer reformed polity. Notwithstanding, Calvin noted from the outset, "If we wish to see the Church well-ordered and maintained we ought to observe this form of government."

In this 1541 charter,[13] Calvin recognizes four separate offices for the church: minister, doctor, elder, and deacon. Included in the *EO* is a discussion of qualifications that were needed for pastors, as well as their primary responsibility, which was to preach, administer the sacraments, and fraternally join with other ministers to oversee and discipline the church. Heresies, personal failings, and crimes (including "intriguing to take over one another's position, leaving the Church without special permission") that disqualify from the ministry are also discussed in sections of the *EO*. Pastors were to be examined in both doctrine and habits. Doctors, ideally one Old Testament expert and one New Testament expert by 1561 (#44), were to teach and instruct, also establishing schools and colleges where possible. The elders, who were deputies to the pastors, were to assist the pastors and oversee the ministry of the parish. These were to "be chosen from each quarter of the city so that they can keep an eye on the whole of it." The deacons, which were discussed in great detail, were of two types: (1) one to oversee the finances, alms, and disbursements; and (2) "hospitalers," who were to see to the care of the ill in the parish.

13. A posted version from a translation by Robert M. Kingdon and Jean-François Bergier is available at http://www.cas.sc.edu/hist/faculty/edwardsk/hist310/reader/ecclesord.pdf.

Shrouded in this text was an orderly pattern of divided government, which was resistant to hierarchical patterns. It also lodged so much of the daily and weekly work of the church with her own ordained officers that there was no room left for statist incursions into the life of the church, nor was the Genevan church subordinate to any of the city councils. The process of calling and nominating her own ministers (although the Council wished to maintain some power of review) is provided in this manual, and processes for discipline are elucidated. The method for choosing elders was also contained as follows:

> Further we have decided upon the machinery for choosing them. The "council of 24" will be asked to nominate the most suitable and adequate men they can discover. In order to do this, they should discuss the matter with the ministers and then present their suggestion to the "council of 200" for approval. If they are found worthy [and approved], they must take an oath in the same form as it is presented to the ministers. At the end of the year and after the elections to the council, they should present themselves to the government so that a decision can be made as to whether they shall be re-appointed or not, but they should not be changed frequently and without good cause provided that they are doing their work faithfully.

A schedule for the sacraments was given, with baptism always to accompany the preaching of the Word. Concerning the frequency of the Lord's Table in 1541: "we have agreed and ordained that it should be administered four times a year, i.e., at Christmas, Easter, Pentecost and the first Sunday in September in the autumn." Protocols for offering the communion meal, including the positioning of the table, were included.

Finally, this 1541 work chartered a weekly meeting of the presbytery to oversee the ministry of the church and to resolve differences. Elementary steps for church discipline are also articulated, although with customary brevity. Lodging the power of excommunication exclusively with the church, prior to the 1550s anywhere within Protestantism, was a radical and unique governmental prerogative. This text concludes with a clearly anti-theocratic notion of jurisdiction:

All this must be done in such a way that the ministers have no civil jurisdiction nor use anything but the spiritual sword of the word of God as St Paul commands them; nor is the authority of the consistory to diminish in any way that of the magistrate or ordinary justice. The civil power must remain unimpaired. In cases where, in the future, there may be a need to impose punishments or constrain individuals, then the ministers and the consistory, having heard the case and used such admonitions and exhortations as are appropriate, should report the whole matter to the council which, in turn, will judge and sentence according to the needs of the case.

These powers of government, then, were unique to the church, diversified among various officers, collegial among one another, and decidedly anti-hierarchical.

Twenty years later, as the church matured, a 1561 version expanded on the themes of the pioneering 1541 *EO*. Greater clarity that the congregation was to participate in electing her ministers characterizes that later version. Moreover, ministerial visitation, the manner in which elders should be elected, matters pertaining to excommunication, communion regulations, and, most interestingly, the manner of treatment given to higher-class Genevan citizens are all treated in this document.[14]

Slight amendments to the 1561 document include amplifications or changes as follows:

1. A preamble states that this "ecclesiastical polity" is based on Scripture and is necessary for the territory.
2. Election of pastors originates with the area pastors, who are to inform the civil magistrate (as a courtesy), and then after confirmation by the Consistory, a man is elected "by the common consent of the company of the faithful." A process was specified (1561, #11) whereby the name of the pastoral candidate is to be publicly announced in advance, inviting objections, and if merited, another election is scheduled.

14. See the translation by Dr. Mary Crumpacker in *Paradigms in Polity*, ed. David W. Hall and Joseph H. Hall (Grand Rapids: Eerdmans, 1994), 140–55.

3. A similar process for electing, and objection from the church to electing, elders is specified (1561, #12). The same oath prescribed (#16–19) is then taken by elders and pastors.

4. A clear requirement for pastoral visitation is enunciated (#21, 31–37).

5. A longer list of intolerable crimes is detailed, this time including dancing, usury, evil cunning, both "avarice" and "too great niggardliness," inappropriate gestures or clothing, "tendency to seek out vain questions" (presumably in sermons), and "farfetched manner of treating Scripture, turning it into a stumblingblock."

6. Noon catechism for children and daily preaching in the four churches is prescribed.

7. Considerable developments for protocols and oversight in the hospital are outlined.

8. Attitudes and behaviors that disqualify one from receiving communion are also included.

In sum, we can highlight these features as signatures of Calvin's governing principles in the church:

1. Specific officers are ordained with authority to govern their sphere of governance.

2. Various officers are mandated, yielding a diversity of power.

3. Officers are collegial among one another, with no hierarchy.

4. Regular meetings are planned for ongoing government and oversight.

5. Election of local rulers cannot abridge the consent of the governed.

6. *Sola Scriptura* (or *jus divinum* in ecclesiology) constrains the information.

7. Governance is designed to oppose tyranny (*contra tyrannos*) and to maximize proper liberty.

Other than commentaries or sermons on specific texts, this 1561 manual was one of Calvin's final and most comprehensive statements of ecclesiastical polity, certainly exhibiting his refined principles of church government. Many of these specifics were also included in the final editions of the *Institutes*, supplementing the original 1536 content in this *loci*.

The Notion of Homology

At this point, one might legitimately raise the question "which came first, the chicken or the egg?" in terms of two spheres of government. Or pose the question in this fashion: Did Calvin first form ecclesiological principles that would later have application to the civil sphere? Or: Did Calvin import and revise principles from the civil sector and then tailor them to the church?

The latter seems improbable on a logical level, as well as historically. Calvin did not give great attention to civil governing principles until later in life. Thus, it is a distinct possibility that Calvin was a churchman first, par excellence, and that over time, some of the seven sturdy principles above were adapted to secular contexts. This seems to fit with both logic and the historical consideration mentioned above.

Yet it is also possible that Calvin developed both equally—albeit one *loci* was more pressingly urgent than the other in 1541—and that both flow from the same core principles. Such an idea is what Harro Hopfl cites as "homology"[15] or the sameness of principles between disciplines.

Hopfl identifies the following signatures of political Calvinism:

1. Calvin detested as much as anything rulers who acted as if their will made right (*sic volo sic iubeo*).
2. Because no single individual possessed "power and breadth of vision enough to govern" unilaterally, a council was needed.
3. Even in a monarchy, a council was required.
4. Tyranny was exhibited in a ruler's unwillingness to tolerate restraint or live within the law. Any ruler should be *sub Deo et sub lege* (under God and under law).[16]

15. Hopfl, *The Christian Polity of John Calvin*, 171.
16. Ibid., 112, 162, 164, 165, 166.

These limitations on the ruling class shaped the resulting political practices approved by Calvinists. Hopfl views Calvin's notion of order as necessitating law. Law next requires enforcement, and different agencies with differing gifts and tools must each "adhere to his station and perform its duties willingly." Hopfl's summary is worth repeating:

> There is an unmistakable preference for an aristocratic form with popular admixtures of sorts, and for small territorial units. Monarchy is explicitly rejected for ecclesiastical polity on scriptural grounds; in civil polity no such outright rejection was possible because of the earlier *parti pris* in favor of the divine authorization of all forms of government and Calvin's almost inflexible opposition to political resistance. Nonetheless, the animus against monarchs is clear enough, and civil monarchy remains a discrepant and disturbing element in an otherwise carefully synchronized arrangement of mutual constraints.[17]

Calvin was balanced in his views of government. He called for ethical and religious considerations to be included in good government, argued for republicanism on an authoritative basis, pleaded with believers to exemplify virtue and be submissive as a norm, and paved the way for later political developments by stating that the governor could be resisted under certain conditions. His disciples later augmented and expanded the conditions under which such revolution was acceptable.

Geneva's city government was patterned after a federal plan, with a gradation of governing judicatories. Ken Ristau has described it as follows:

> The government of Geneva in the time of Calvin consisted of three councils: the Small Council, the Council of Sixty and the Council of Two Hundred. The Small Council was the highest governing body, consisting of twenty-five members. These twenty-five members included four syndics (or chiefs of state), two secretaries and a treasurer. The Small Council maintained ultimate jurisdiction in all affairs of state. It supervised the conduct of all public officials. It also acted as the final appellate court in any disputes. Beneath the Small Council was the relatively

---

17. Ibid., 171. In this section and others, Hopfl notes "a very clear but imperfect homology" between church government and civil polity in Calvin.

obscure Council of Sixty. The primary responsibility of the Council of Sixty appears to have been to consider issues of an exceptional nature, particularly in the area of foreign affairs (Kingdon 1984:60). The largest official estate of Geneva was the Council of Two Hundred. This Council functioned primarily as an intermediary between the General Assembly, a commune of all eligible voters in Geneva, and the Small Council. Its primary role was to vote on legislation presented by the Small Council and each February, to elect members to that Council. They could also grant pardons to convicted criminals (Monter 1967:145).[18]

Political Principles

In his initial 1536 edition of the *Institutes*, Calvin's discussion is nearly as lengthy as, and virtually unchanged from, the final edition.[19] Using the same Scripture proofs in both editions, Calvin begins by affirming the distinction between civil power and spiritual power. He concludes that civil government is necessary and not "a thing polluted" (207), in contrast to the Anabaptist view of political involvement. This chapter may contain as much verbatim copying between the first and last editions as any other single *loci*. The main difference is that the final edition contains more polemic against the Anabaptists and those who deny the legitimacy of civil governance (e.g., 4.20.5).[20]

Calvin understood that the major role for civil governors (his references to "judges" and other inferior magistrates consistently betray his penchant for decentralized governing structures) was to serve the people. Such governors, already by 1536, were to be "protectors and vindicators of public innocence, modesty, decency," and their "sole endeavor" was to further and nurture the "common safety and peace of all," a notion not very different from "defending the common good" (212). Just as there was no room for tyranny in Calvin's thought, so there was no room for self-serving

18. Ken Ristau, *Politics and Polity* (November 22, 2000), available at http://anduril.ca/bible/essays/ce_his290.html.

19. Source for the page references in parentheses in this section is Ford Lewis Battles' 1536 edition of Calvin's *Institutes of the Christian Religion* (Grand Rapids: Eerdmans, 1986).

20. Although the 1536 Battles edition breaks sections slightly differently in some places compared to the 1559 edition, the content is almost identical to the 1559 edition.

aggrandizement among civil servants. Citing both Solon and Jeremiah, Calvin averred that magistrates could provide such protection only by prosecuting criminals and by rewarding the good (see Rom. 13:4–5).

In this early work, Calvin provided a brief (and probably not controversial) defense of the magistrate as having the authority to punish criminals and if need be to inflict capital punishment for the gravest of offenses. At the same time, while citing many Old Testament references, Calvin also recognized clemency as the "chief gift of princes" (213), realizing its place in moral government. Rulers were thus permitted to take up arms for public defense, either against crime or against external aggressors. Calvin considered mean criminals and invaders on the same ethical footing as "robbers to be punished accordingly" (214). This right to wage war or "civil defenses" (214) justified local militia and resistance against tyranny, ideas that would later blossom.

Although Calvin saw the magistrate as called to champion the law, with his high regard for the Old Testament, he still manifested the view now well attributed to him that distinguished the abiding validity of the moral law from that of the ceremonial and judicial (national) aspects of the law. Both ceremonial and judicial laws were designed to support piety in one case and neighbor-love in the other (216). Piety and love could both, the early Calvin argued, continue apart from either of those Israelite-specific codes. In fact, he viewed the judicial laws in the Pentateuch as given in order to incarnate specific acts of love, which was the goal of those laws. In this context, he supported constitutions as tools to assist in providing "equity." This equity was supported also by the moral law, which was a "testimony to natural law" (216), although each nation was not bound by all the Jewish particulars. Calvin thought that different crimes could receive differing punishments (217), but he saw an international commonality in societies that punished adultery, murder, and theft. He did not insist that all penology be the same, but certain violations of the moral law always undercut equity and love. "Agreement on the manner of punishment" was not required (217).

He also argued for the legitimacy of believers' using courts for lawsuits (217–19) and devoted considerable discussion to that issue, which is not as pressing for most today. Consistent with his other teachings, he also called on Christians to turn the other cheek and to be willing, for the sake of Christ's witness, to lose material goods on occasion (219).

Calvin concluded his first formal discussion of civil government by calling on believers to honor their leaders (as in Rom. 13:6–7) and to pay their taxes (220). Both attitude and action were summoned by Calvin. An honorable magistrate should always be obeyed, lest God avenge his order (220).

Calvin called for obedience to unjust magistrates (221–23) just as he did toward the end of his life. It was not "the men themselves" (224) but the office that was to be respected. Moreover, in his early edition, he evidenced his awareness of the claim that "rulers owe responsibilities in turn to their subjects" (224), which Calvin claimed to "have already admitted." Yet he labored to show that although submission to authorities was taught, authorities were not vindicated by acting unrighteously. Calvin both warned against "private individuals" taking matters into their own hands (225) and provided an early form of the later argument (see Beza, for example) that suggested that God did not wish men to disobey God in order to obey other human rulers. The Lord alone was "king of kings" (225), and "next to him we are subject to those men who are in authority over us, but only to him. If they command anything against him, let him go unesteemed. And here let us not be concerned about all that dignity that magistrates possess; for no harm is done to it when it is humbled before that singular and truly supreme power of God" (225). With a slight difference of degree, Calvin supplements in his final edition by referring to Daniel's resistance to an impious edict and refers to other prophets who disobeyed civil rulers: "As if God had made over his right to mortal men, giving them the rule over mankind! Or as if earthly power were diminished when it is subjected to its Author, in whose presence even the heavenly powers tremble as suppliants" (4.20.32). And in both editions, Calvin concludes with Peter (Acts 5:29) that we must obey God rather than men. Rather than becoming "enslaved" to wicked men or turning "aside from piety" (226), the life of the Christian man is to obey God above all others.

In sum, aside from some slight reorderings and supplements, Calvin's teaching on civil government changed very little between 1536 and 1559. His final edition (1559) contained a discussion of these topics:

20.1–2: Separation of Governments

20.3–8: Tasks of Magistrates, Ordination of Magistrates

20.9–13: The Magistrates' Prerogatives and Duties

20.14–16: The Rule of Law

20.17–21: Courts

20.22–29: Obedience and Deference from Citizens

20.30–32: Constitutional Mechanisms

Few political treatises by a theologian would even survive intact for such a tumultuous twenty-five-year period, much less serve to give guidance for centuries as this tractate did. It is little wonder in view of this that Calvin's ideas inspired a tradition led by his disciples. Thus, his contribution may be all the greater if dated as early as—and as mature at—1536. His primary axioms were that governors were legitimate and that they should govern *in loco Dei*.

I have summarized the five points of political Calvinism slightly differently from the TULIP of soteriology, referring to:

+ Depravity as a perennial human variable to be accommodated;
+ Accountability for leaders provided via a *collegium*;
+ Republicanism as the preferred form of government;
+ Constitutionalism needed to restrain both the rulers and the ruled; and
+ Limited government, beginning with the family, as foundational.

The resulting mnemonic device, DARCL (though not as convenient as TULIP), seems a more apt summary if placed in the context of the political writings of Calvin's disciples.

Later Calvinist Prime Minister of the Netherlands Abraham Kuyper distilled the essence of the impact of the Calvinistic emphasis on God's sovereignty vis-à-vis political and economical matters in modern Europe in 1900 as follows:[21]

21. Ralph C. Hancock, *Calvin and the Foundations of Modern Politics*, 61, asserts that the Protestant Reformation was "an essentially modern movement that in some way laid the foundations for our modern openness."

The Calvinistic confession of the sovereignty of God holds good for all the world, is true for all nations, and is of force in all authority which man exercises over man. . . . It is therefore a political faith which may be summarily expressed in these three theses: 1. God only, and never any creature, is possessed of sovereign rights, in the destiny of nations, because God alone created them, maintains them by his Almighty power, and rules them by his ordinances. 2. Sin has, in the realm of politics, broken down the direct government of God, and therefore the exercise of authority, for the purpose of government, has subsequently been invested in men, as a mechanical remedy. And 3. In whatever form this authority may reveal itself, man never possesses power over his fellow man in any other way than by the authority which descends upon him from the majesty of God.[22]

Calvinism, Kuyper continued, "protests against State omni-competence, against the horrible conception that no right exists above and beyond existing laws, and against the pride of absolutism, which recognizes no constitutional rights." Calvinism "built a dam across the absolutistic stream, not by appealing to popular force, nor to the hallucination of human greatness, but by deducing those rights and liberties of social life from the same source from which the high authority of government flows, even the absolute sovereignty of God."[23]

Analysis and Comparison

Below are several observations drawn from the foregoing comparisons.

Calvin's disciples certainly echoed these principles and, if anything, deepened them. Calvin's principles of governance may be seen, historically, as a jumping-off point; his disciples, however, channeled this into a potent political movement. As a result, a fairly coherent set of ideas becomes identified with Calvinistic thought.

Calvinists developed a knack for distilling and propagating theopolitical thought. Theodore Beza, for example, wrote widely on political

22. Abraham Kuyper, *Lectures on Calvinism* (1898; repr., Grand Rapids: Eerdmans, 1953), 85.
23. Ibid.

theory. His 1574 *The Right of Magistrates* became a classic supporting republicanism and limited submission to governors. Although Calvin and Beza had discouraged rebellion before Calvin's death, even recommending support of existing rulers if at all possible, with the treacherous slaughter and virtual extinction of Reformed religion in France, Beza led efforts to reassess that formulation. The result was a tradition that included the likes of Knox, Viret, and Ponet. Beza's argument to normalize resistance to evil governments on biblical bases transformed Calvinist political theory.[24]

After beginning with a historical review, his *The Right of Magistrates* argued for a circumscribed resistance to tyrannical rulers. Organizing his work around ten questions, he affirmed that scriptural obedience did not categorically deny revolution in some cases.

Toward the end of this tract, he articulated three "axioms" to clarify conditions warranting armed resistance: "(1) That the tyranny must be undisguised and notorious; (2) That the recourse should not be had to arms before all other remedies have been tried; (3) Nor yet before the question has been thoroughly examined, not only as to what is permissible, but also as to what is expedient, lest the remedies prove more hazardous than the very disease."[25]

From the Hebrew monarchy in the Old Testament, Beza, like Calvin, also induced the existence of popular election. Moreover, Beza championed a double-covenant idea, similar to later Protestant tracts. In what amounted to a sweeping survey of the history of Western civilization, Beza found support for resistance to tyranny not only in Swiss republicanism, but also in the political histories of Denmark, England, Scotland, Poland, Sweden, Venice, Spain, France, and the Roman empire itself. It is difficult to imagine a more informed or comprehensive history of resistance. The case Beza made was compelling.

Following Calvin's teaching but predating the final edition of the *Institutes*, in quintessential Calvinistic style, John Ponet delineated when

24. The summaries of Beza and Goodman below are taken, in part, from my *The Genevan Reformation and the American Founding* (Lanham, MD: Lexington Books, 2003), chaps. 4–5.

25. For a good summary of these ideas, see Patrick S. Poole, "The Development of the Reformational Doctrine of Resistance in the Sixteenth Century," available at http://fly. hiwaay.net;~pspoole/Defense.htm.

tyrannicide itself would be legitimate: either if the tyrant was an overt criminal or when lower-level political officials became involved. With a passionate style, Ponet's *Short Treatise* (1556) argued for the following (which tenets begin to exhibit the Calvinistic genome):

1. The people could hold a ruler, who was to be viewed as the servant of citizens, accountable.
2. Overthrow, even if forceful, was permitted under certain conditions.
3. The basis for just governance was transcendental as well as universal.
4. Government was to be limited in scope and in force.
5. Authority was to be diffused among various spheres, not concentrated in one office.
6. Checks and balances, via ephors or tribunes, were necessary.[26]

These and other tenets of Calvinism would become standard fare in lands where the Reformed faith spread.[27] The signature of Calvinism in political forums would be characterized by the following ideas: (1) that God is the Superior Governor, (2) that man is a fallen sinner, and (3) that law, fixed constitutions, and decentralization of power are all necessary to limit human aggression. Later, Hotman, Daneau, and Althusius expanded these themes as the tradition developed.

Most knowledgeable historians spot a definite evolution in political theology from Calvin's early disciples (Knox, Goodman, Ponet) to his later disciples (Beza, Hotman, Daneau). Two major linchpins, however, changed after the 1570s: (1) submission was *limited*, and (2) representation was *absolute*. These dynamics began to be publicized from pulpits and academies.

26. John Adams commended Calvinist theorist John Ponet for promulgating "all the essential principles of liberty, which were afterward dilated by Sidney and Locke" (John Adams, *Defence of the Constitutions of the Government of the United States of America*, available at http://www.constitution.org/primarysources/adams.html). Later Adams specifically endorsed several other Puritan classics, including those by Milton and the *Vindicae Contra Tyrannos*, among others.
27. Skinner, *The Foundations of Modern Political Thought*, 2:221–24, provides a helpful comparison of the thought of Ponet and Christopher Goodman.

By the early seventeenth century, a new tradition was congealing. A summary from Dartmouth historian Herbert Foster almost a century ago noted the following as hallmarks of Calvin's political legacy,[28] and most are exhibited by the works of his closest disciples referenced above:

* The absolute sovereignty of God entailed that universal human rights (or Beza's "fundamental law") should be protected and must not be surrendered to the whim of tyranny.
* These fundamental laws, which were always compatible with God's law, are the basis of whatever public liberties we enjoy.
* Mutual covenants, as taught by Beza, Hotman, and the *Vindiciae*, between rulers and God and between rulers and subjects were binding and necessary.
* As Ponet, Knox, and Goodman taught, the sovereignty of the people flows logically from the mutual obligations of the covenants referenced above.
* The representatives of the people, not the people themselves, are the first line of defense against tyranny.[29]

The evolution was real, it was philosophically significant, it was politically revolutionary, and it would last for centuries, providing a true turning point in history. Whether one agrees with all of Calvin's theology or not, the subsequent altered terrain is clear. And Calvin, whether it is in his *Institutes* or in his commentaries and sermons, stood at the font of a new, or renewed, political tradition.

There is abundant evidence that Goodman, Ponet, Beza, and Knox all had discussions with Viret, who also likely discussed these notions with Calvin. Noting that his *Remonstrances aux Fideles* (1547) was published a full generation before the St. Bartholomew's Day Massacre, and his 1561 *The World and the Empire* was available (and unrefuted by Calvin) more than a decade before that tragic event, it may be that an older theory was correct after all—namely, that the Calvinist and Huguenot resisters did

28. *Collected Papers of Herbert D. Foster*, 163–74.
29. Ibid., 174. Besides Calvin, this idea was reiterated in Buchanan, Beza, Peter Martyr, Althusius, Hotman, Daneau, *Vindiciae*, Ponet, William the Silent, and others (ibid.).

not merely react in the throes of crisis and then recast their theory after the fact. They had precedents and a history of understanding the propriety of resistance under certain conditions even before Calvin's death.

That being the case, Calvin's writings fit into a consistent paradigm, and the reason that Calvin devoted no more attention to explicit development of resistance theory is best understood as a combination of two important facts: (1) resistance theory based on priority of commandments was a philosophical given during Calvin's day, needing little further proof; and (2) with the tensions of the times, Calvin did not want to stoke revolutionary fervor unnecessarily, nor did he wish to attract royalist criticism from France and elsewhere for espousing anarchical views. The later works of Beza and Hotman, as well as the *Vindiciae Contra Tyrannos* in the 1570s, thus were not radical departures from the previous tradition that spanned from Farel to Viret to Calvin; rather, they were applications of the same seminal principles. Or as Robert Linder puts it: after 1547, anyone "looking for an ideology to justify revolution could have found many choice and useful ideas in the writings of Peter Viret."[30] The result, as one non-Protestant scholar put it, is that "in the political domain, Calvinist ideas are at the origin of the revolution which from the eighteenth to the nineteenth centuries gave birth and growth to the parliamentary democracies of Anglo-Saxon type."[31]

The ease with which Calvin goes back and forth between these disciplines in key texts suggests that he saw mutual applicability of his governing principles. For example, rather than commending either a democracy or a monarchy, Jethro advised Moses and the people to select a plurality of prudent representative leaders (Ex. 18:21).[32] Moses instituted a graduated series of administrations with greater and lesser magistrates, and Calvin

30. Robert Dean Linder, *The Political Ideas of Pierre Viret* (Geneva: Droz, 1964), 178.
31. Cited by Paul T. Fuhrmann, "Philip Mornay and the Huguenot Challenge to Absolutism," in *Calvinism and the Political Order*, ed. George L. Hunt (Philadelphia: Westminster Press, 1965), 50.
32. For an example of early American exposition on the character needed for officeholders, complete with a discussion similar to Calvin's on this Exodus passage, see Simeon Howard's 1780 Election Sermon (Boston: John Gill, 1780). Charles Chauncy addressed the requisite character of civil rulers in his 1747 election-day sermon (contained in *Election Day Sermons* [Oak Ridge, TN: Kuyper Institute, 1996], 143–68). T. H. Breen provides one of the most thorough studies of American expectations for civil rulers in *The Character of*

asserted that the earliest Hebrew republican government devolved from the divine mind long before the Golden Age of Greco-Roman governance, the Enlightenment, or modern revolutions.

The early federal scheme adopted in Exodus 18 seemed, at least to Calvin and his followers (as it had to Aquinas and Machiavelli), to be republicanism. Commenting on a similar passage in Deuteronomy 1:14–16, Calvin stated: "Hence it more plainly appears that those who were to preside in judgment were not appointed only by the will of Moses, but elected by the votes of the people. And this is the most desirable kind of liberty, that we should not be compelled to obey every person who may be tyrannically put over our heads; but which allows of election, so that no one should rule except he be approved by us. Moreover, this is further confirmed in the next verse, wherein Moses recounts that he awaited the consent of the people, and that nothing was attempted which did not please them all."[33] Thus, Calvin viewed Exodus 18 as a representative republican form.[34]

Later, Calvinist Johannes Althusius (1557–1638) agreed, writing: "I consider that no polity from the beginning of the world has been more wisely and perfectly constructed than the polity of the Jews." Part of what he believed was unimprovable was an early form of republican-federal government. As Doumergue noted, Calvin was the "founder of stable and powerful democracies, a defender not of 'egalitarianism,' but of 'equality before the law.'"[35] Whether Calvin was the founder of modern democratic governments or not, as Doumergue suggested, his sermons on these passages from the Pentateuch illustrated God's inestimable gift to the Jewish commonwealth, specifically the privilege of electing judges and magistrates by citizen vote.

A century after Calvin, Samuel Rutherford used this same Mosaic pattern in his 1644 *Lex Rex* to argue for a republican or at least an

---

the Good Ruler: A Study of Puritan Political Ideas in New England, 1630–1730 (New York: W. W. Norton & Company, 1970).

33. John Calvin, *Commentaries on the Four Last Books of Moses: A Harmony* (Grand Rapids: Baker, 1979), 1:310.

34. For more support, see my "Government by Moses and One Greater Than Moses," in *Election Day Sermons*, ed. David W. Hall (Oak Ridge, TN: Kuyper Institute, 1996), 109–21.

35. Quoted in Hancock, *Calvin and the Foundation of Modern Politics*, 66.

anti-monarchical form of civil polity. Indeed, most of the Reformation-era political tracts (by Calvin, Beza, Bucer, Knox, Buchanan, Ponet, Althusius, etc.) devoted extensive commentary to the Old Testament patterns of government. These Reformers viewed Old Testament precedents as applicable to the politics of their own settings, and these same ideas were drawn upon later by an American tradition that nourished its founders. Ideas such as those that Calvin espoused furthered these arguments and Western political discourse.

In another set of texts, one can almost hear Calvin railing against tyrannical prelates as much as civil tyrants. Calvin opposed similar notions in both church and state government. Calvin taught similarly that princes "who are not free agents through being under the tyranny of others, if they permit themselves to be overcome contrary to their conscience, lay aside all their authority and are drawn aside in all directions by the will of their subjects."[36] Calvin's frequent disparagement of ungodly kings in his sermons on Job and Deuteronomy in 1554 to 1955 and in his lectures on Daniel in 1561 indicates that he was not, in principle, a monarchist. Accordingly, the distinctive Calvinistic contribution was phrased: "Men's vices and inadequacies make it safer and better that the many hold sway. In this way may rulers help each other, teach and admonish one another, and if one asserts himself unfairly, they may act in concert to censure, repressing his willfulness."[37]

Calvin's commentary on Daniel 6[38] virtually enshrines all the major principles contained in the 1536 *Institutes*, yielding a consistency to be reckoned. Calvin displayed his suspicion of aggregate power in that commentary: "In the palaces of kings we often see men of brutal dispositions holding high rank, and we need not go back to history for this." Of the low and contemptible character of some rulers, he wrote, "But now kings think of nothing else than preferring their own panders, buffoons, and flatterers; while they praise none but men of low character."

36. John Calvin, "Commentaries on Daniel," in *On God and Political Duty*, ed. John T. McNeill (Indianapolis: Bobbs-Merrill, 1956), 100–101.

37. *Institutes*, 4.20.8.

38. Quotations are from John Calvin, *Calvin's Commentary on Daniel* (Grand Rapids: Baker, 1979), 12.350–87.

Rulers were to "avoid depraved counsels, since they are besieged on every side by perfidious men, whose only object is to gain by their false representations." The temptation of rulers to succumb to their own depravity necessitated strong constraints, for the examples of political self-indulgence were not rare in the world but recurred perennially. Calvin also diagnosed envy in magistrates, which enticed them to break the law, and if they fail to complete their crime, "they trample upon justice without modesty and without humanity."

Commenting on Micah 5:5, Calvin suggested that rulers should be elected, interpreting the Hebrew word for *shepherds* as synonymous with *rulers*. He asserted: "In this especially consists the best condition of the people, when they can choose, by common consent, their own shepherds; for when any one by force usurps the supreme power, it is tyranny. And when men become kings by hereditary right, it seems not consistent with liberty. *We shall then set up for ourselves princes,* says the Prophet: that is, the Lord will not only give breathing time to his Church, and will also cause that she may set up a fixed and well-ordered government, and that by the common consent of all."[39] This election by common suffrage is advocated elsewhere when Calvin recognized, "It is tyrannous if any one man appoint or make ministers at his pleasure." Election by members adequately balanced the mean between tyranny and chaotic liberty.[40]

These examples both illustrate the fullness of Calvin's commentary on political subjects and illuminate certain nuances of his theory that extend beyond the *Institutes.*

Nontheocratic. It is frequently though inappropriately implied that Calvin wished to unite church and state. If our study above accurately grasps parallel homology, then we might expect theocracy in civil governance to be as commonplace as ecclesiological papacy. In fact, Calvin persistently advocated a difference of jurisdiction, as noted above. François Wendel has corroborated that neither church nor state was to be formally annexed or collapsed into the other. This distinction or separation of jurisdictions "was the fountain of the entire edifice. Each of these autonomous powers, State and Church, was conceived as issuing from the Divine

39. John Calvin, *Calvin's Commentary on Micah* (Grand Rapids: Baker, 1979), 14.309–10.
40. John Calvin, *Calvin's Commentary on Acts* (Grand Rapids: Baker, 1979), 18.233.

Will."[41] Wendel recognized that Calvin advocated the complementarity of the civil and ecclesiastical powers, even if many modern interpreters do not sense his preservation of that key distinction. Moreover, Douglas Kelly suggests that this distinction, even with a close cooperation between church and state, was an important factor in the diffusion of Calvinism.[42] Calvin himself stated the relationship succinctly in a 1538 letter: "As the magistrate ought by punishment and physical restraint to cleanse the church of offenses, so the minister of the Word should help the magistrate in order that fewer may sin. Their responsibilities should be so joined that each helps rather than impedes the other."[43] Calvin did not merge church and state into a theocratic monster.[44] He had no desire to advance the Reformation's political tradition on the back of coercion. Instead, Calvin wished to energize the church to become a world-changing community.[45]

Sola Scriptura. Calvin, if either tempted to or willing to rely on secular wisdom, could certainly have been understood to have done so in the area of ecclesiology. Many are the pleas that claim that God's revelation is not sufficient for all areas or for only certain areas. Many traditions have been quite innovative in creating ecclesiological constructs. But Calvin wished to restrict himself—alas, against modernity's strong impulse against restraint in general—and set forth only the patterns of governance that were fully scriptural. Had he not held the highest regard for Scripture, then the temptation to formulate such constructs according to fallible knowledge, prevailing tradition, managerial efficiency, or human wisdom would have been irresistible. That Calvin held to a *jure divino* ecclesiology supports the conclusion that he held to *sola Scriptura*.

41. François Wendel, *Calvin*, trans. Philip Mairet (London: Collins, 1963), 79.
42. Kelly, *The Emergence of Liberty in the Modern World*, 14.
43. Quoted in ibid., 15.
44. William Naphy raises three key points to rebut the idea that Calvin was a repressive theocrat. First, he notes that the Genevan ministers focused on religious issues and did not seek to gain the civil magistrate's sword to punish crime. Second, the theoretical ideal for church government was not always followed, even at the height of Reformist zeal. Third, Naphy suggests that by the 1570s, the influence of the church had begun to wane. *Calvinism in Europe, 1540–1610: A Collection of Documents*, selected, trans., and ed. Alistair Duke, Gillian Lewis, and Andrew Pettegree (Manchester: Manchester University Press, 1992), 15.
45. See Kelly, *The Emergence of Liberty*, 23.

Indeed, he convinced future generations that one's view of Scripture affected many *loci*. Calvin's views of Scripture, of the church, and of its governance go hand in hand.

Summary and Conclusion

Calvin's essential principles of governance, then, are these:

1. A respect for God's revealed ways to supply transcultural guidance to various social spheres. Human reason, tradition, experience, and so forth are not the enduring bases for governing principles.
2. A distrust of human goodness that requires accountability. Governors, affected by depravity like anyone else, have standards, qualifications, and expectations to meet.
3. A multiplicity of counselors to make decisions; no single person atop a ruling triangle.
4. Local leaders elected with the consent of the governed; no external hierarchy or imposition of rulers without consent.
5. Diversified authority from representatives who act in accord with constitution.
6. The possibility of review from lower rungs of administration, providing checks and balances for governors.

These ideological hallmarks epitomize Calvinistic governance wherever it occurs.

This short study also yields a type of Calvin genome from this anatomy. It dissects a crucial strain that recurred often. One should expect the essential principles of Calvinism, if we have rightly spied a strain of thought, to appear in other *loci*.

Instead of the nineteenth-century search for one elusive, crucial gene that defines all of Calvinism (whether predestination, the Holy Spirit, Christocentricity, catholicity), it is probably best to understand Calvinism as a set of concepts. Its genomic mapping thus may not only exhibit the organic connections between various *loci*, but also more accurately reveal its true character. Where those beliefs are found gathered, since they are so contrary to the world's philosophy, most likely there is Calvinism.

One may wish to think of this as a corollary to the fine research by Professor Richard Muller on the continuity of thought between Calvin and the post-Reformation scholastics. Just as Muller has shown so well the strong continuity *between* Calvin and his Calvinistic disciples, so this approach sees the strong continuity *within* Calvin's thought on various topics.

15

PRAYER IN CALVIN'S SOTERIOLOGY

JAE SUNG KIM

The main focus of this study is the work of the Holy Spirit in prayer concerning John Calvin's soteriology. One of the distinctive contributions of John Calvin to Reformed theology is the firm establishment of the doctrine of the application of redemption. One can easily contrast Calvin's soteriology with that of the Roman Catholics by reviewing his book 3 of the *Institutes of the Christian Religion*. In this essay, we would like to expose a distinct aspect of Calvin's soteriology, which emphasizes that justification by faith should be complemented by prayer in the Holy Spirit.

Significant Aspects of Calvin's Soteriology

The focus of Calvin's doctrine of the application of redemption begins with recognizing faith as the primary gift and secret work of the Holy Spirit to unite us with Christ. The Holy Spirit recovers his deserved status and

343

authority in Calvin's soteriology by being compared with the sacraments of the Roman church. The chief role of the Holy Spirit in the application of redemption is to unite us with Christ. Calvin posed this question: "How do we receive those benefits which the Father bestowed on his only begotten Son[?] ... It is true that we obtain into the secret working of the Spirit, by which we come to enjoy Christ and all his benefits."[1] Calvin recognizes the nature and the effect of this union in gradual spiritual growth. He regards union with Christ as the goal of the Christian life. Without the power of the Holy Spirit, all human effort is a meaningless struggle, even if that struggle assumes a religious shape.[2]

Prayer and faith are both gifts of God. It is noteworthy that these two subjects are closely related in Calvin's biblical soteriology, especially in his numerous polemical arguments against the Roman Catholics and some radical Lutheran extremes. One of Calvin's controversial arguments on Reformed soteriology shows us a new understanding of justification by faith. The imputation of Christ's righteousness not only is alien but has been compared with the doctrine of infusion and self-attained righteousness of the Council of Trent. In this sense, Calvin's doctrine of prayer is also very different from that of the Roman Catholics.

Faith should be exercised throughout the Christian life, and prayer is essential to the manifestation of faith. From the very beginning of his 1536 edition of the *Institutes*, Calvin gives special attention to this subject in chapter 3, which he modified and expanded in later editions. Prayer was one of six topics that Calvin presented in the first edition. Calvin's treatise "On Prayer" includes a brief commentary on the Lord's Prayer as the perfect model for our praying. Calvin develops in detail six ways in which prayer strengthens our faith and four rules for biblical prayer in his lengthy exposition. Through continually revised editions of the *Institutes*, Calvin expanded the prayer section to over a hundred pages, so that the prayer section became the largest single subject among eighty chapters in the final edition (1559) of the *Institutes*.

1. John Calvin, *Institutes of the Christian Religion*, trans. Ford Lewis Battles (Philadelphia: Westminster Press, 1959), 3.1.1.

2. Sinclair B. Ferguson, *The Holy Spirit* (Downers Grove, IL: InterVarsity Press, 1996), 96–103; Jae Sung Kim, "*Unio cum Christo*: The Work of the Holy Spirit in Calvin's Theology" (PhD diss., Westminster Theological Seminary, 1998).

In that final edition, the doctrine of prayer links two important subjects: Christian liberty and predestination.[3] In chapter 19, Calvin expresses the relation that conscience bears to external obedience: first in things good and evil, and second in things indifferent. For refutation of errors in regard to Christian liberty, Christians need to pray in the fear of God. Christian freedom is within the boundary of relationship between Creator and creature. Calvin rejects any kind of perfectionism by human or autonomous efforts; rather, he clearly grounds our assurance of salvation in God's predestination. Following his chapter on prayer in the *Institutes*, the doctrines of election and predestination are useful, necessary, and most appealing, because these doctrines establish the certainty of salvation, peace of conscience, and the true comfort of the church. Consequently, prayer, like faith, is primarily a response to God's goodness and grace manifested in Christ. Calvin claims the importance of prayer that never disputes any kind of human efforts and emphasizes humble obedience.

From the very beginning of his ministry in Geneva, Calvin claimed the importance of prayer in the Christian life for recovering and sustaining true Christian piety.[4] Prayer is essentially intermingled with faith because a "man duly versed in true faith first readily recognizes how needy and empty of all goods he is and how all aids to salvation are lacking to him" (chap. 22). Calvin's doctrine of prayer has been revealed in two aspects (chap. 23). First, prayer means our obedience to God's commands; second, we will receive what we ask if we trust God according to his promise.

"Prayer" also is one of five topical headings, along with "Faith," "The Law," "The Word of God," and "The Sacraments," in the later edition of the Geneva Catechism (1541 in French and 1545 in Latin).[5] The proper mind and deep sense of full confidence of being heard through

3. *Institutes*, 3.20.1–52. Charles Partee presented insights on the relationship between prayer and the doctrine of predestination at a previous congress. Charles Partee, "Prayer as the Practice of Predestination," in *Calvinus Servus Christi*, ed. Wilhelm H. Neuser (Budapest: Presseabteilung des Raday-Kollegiums, 1988), 245–56.

4. Calvin's first catechism in the French language (1537) appears in *Instruction of Faith*, trans. Paul T. Fuhrmann (Philadelphia: Westminster Press, 1949), chaps. 22–25. ET from Latin (1538), trans. Ford Lewis Battles (Pittsburgh, 1972).

5. *Selected Works of John Calvin*, ed. Henry Beveridge, *Tracts and Letters*, vol. 2 (Edinburgh: Calvin Translation Society, 1849; repr., Grand Rapids: Baker, 1983), 33–94. Calvin revised this catechism for the youth.

the merits of Christ are considered with an exposition of the Lord's Prayer in order to pray aright.

Prayer in the Hand of God

In order to examine Calvin's doctrine of prayer properly, we should note what he intends to teach about the work of the Holy Spirit. If we were to miss his explanation of the secret work of the Spirit in chapter 20 of the *Institutes*, we would lose what he wants to emphasize about right prayer.

The Aid of the Holy Spirit

Calvin does not portray prayer as merely human action according to one's own deep spirituality and religious training but as the work of the Holy Spirit. The aid of the Spirit is not optional for our prayer. Only the Holy Spirit can open our heart for true prayer, just as he is the one who unites us with Christ by faith. The Spirit provides both the motive and the ground of our confidence in Christ. Calvin wrote:

> Hence the Apostle, to show that a faith unaccompanied with prayer to God cannot be genuine, states this to be the order: As faith springs from the Gospel, so by faith our hearts are framed to call upon the name of God, (Rom. 10: 14.) And this is the very thing which he had expressed some time before, viz., *that the Spirit of adoption,* which seals the testimony of the Gospel on our hearts, *gives us courage to make our requests known unto God,* calls forth groanings which cannot be uttered, and enables us to cry, Abba, Father, (Rom. 8: 26.) This last point, as we have hitherto only touched upon it slightly in passing, must now be treated more fully.[6]

In the *Institutes*, 3.1.3, Calvin already indicates that "Spirit of adoption" is the most important title of the Holy Spirit.[7] Again, we should be

6. *Institutes*, 3.20.1 (emphasis added).
7. "First, he is called the 'Spirit of adoption,' because he is witness to us of the free favor with which God the Father embraced us in his well-beloved and only-begotten Son, so as to become our Father and give us boldness of access to him; nay he dictates the very words, so that we can boldly cry, 'Abba, Father'" (ibid., 3.1.3).

346

aware of the same work of the Holy Spirit, "to pour out our prayers not in our own righteousness but in His great mercies, that He may answer us for His own sake, as His name is invoked upon us."[8]

Calvin frequently points out the Holy Spirit as our inner teacher.[9] One of the important works of the Spirit is to guide us in faithful prayer. Calvin rejects Roman Catholic doctrines on any forms of prayer that include free will, works-righteousness, or the treasury of merit laid up by the saints. As the hand of God, the Holy Spirit gives us the mighty power of our redemption in Christ. Here we look into two aspects of the work of the Spirit in prayer. On the one hand, the Spirit himself makes intercession for us; on the other hand, he strengthens us in our prayer life.

When we observe the title of the Holy Spirit as the "hand of God," we also conclude that the Holy Spirit exercises his might to help believers: "To prevent believers from objecting that they are too weak to be equal to bearing so many burdens ... the aid of the Spirit is abundantly sufficient to overcome all difficulties."[10] With our burdens and weaknesses, the Holy Spirit supports us by his mighty hand in prayer. Through prayer we receive power from heaven. Believers are encouraged to bear the cross by the Spirit; otherwise, the Christian life would be beyond our strength, knowledge, and efforts. Calvin points out the important points in Paul's letter: "unless we are supported by the hand of God, we are soon oppressed by innumerable evils ... [and because] we are weak in every part and various infirmities threaten our fall, there is sufficient protection in the Spirit of God to prevent us from ever being destroyed or being overwhelmed by any accumulation of evils."[11] The Holy Spirit groans for our salvation, and he instructs us with great certainty so that we can overcome any present difficulties.

Confidence and Testimony

Two aspects of the Spirit's work in a Christian's prayer characteristically distinguish Christian prayer from that of other religions. Calvin

8. Geneva Catechism (1538), chap. 23.
9. *Institutes*, 1.9.1; 3.1.4; 3.2.34; 4.14.9; 4.17.36.
10. *Comm.*, Rom. 8:26.
11. Ibid.

emphasizes, first, that the Spirit in our prayers gives the assurance of our salvation inwardly. Second, he also gives a testimony so that we may exercise an outward form of speech. Prayers in Christians' lives show both free confidence and testimony of their adoption as the children of God. Calvin understands that our minds are assured of the confidence, while the Holy Spirit is our "Guide and Teacher" and at the same time conveys the testimony of adoption:

> Our mind would not of its own accord convey this assurance to us, unless the testimony of the Spirit preceded it. While the Spirit testifies to us that we are the children of God, He at the same time pours this confidence into our hearts, so that we dare invoke God as our Father. And certainly, since the confidence of the heart alone opens our mouth, our tongues will be dumb to utter prayers, unless the Spirit bears testimony to our heart concerning the fatherly love of God.[12]

On the one hand, our prayer to "Abba, Father" (Rom. 8:15) is to express confidence and free conviction without fear within our hearts. On the other hand, the Spirit affords us such a testimony to the world through our faithful prayer about the fatherly caring and love of God.

Calvin comments on the first aspect of the work of the Holy Spirit, which is that of confidence:

> The word *cry* is used to express confidence, as if he said, "We do not pray in a doubtful way, but raise a loud voice to heaven without fear." Believers also called God Father under the law, but not with such free confidence, since the veil kept them far from the sanctuary. But now, when an entrance has been opened to us by the blood of Christ, we may glory with familiarity and in full voice that we are the sons of God. Hence arises this cry ... The more evident the promise is, the greater our freedom in prayer.[13]

The Spirit also provides us with a testimony in our prayer. By the testimony of the Holy Spirit we are assured of the adoption of God.

12. Ibid.
13. *Comm.*, Rom. 8:15.

The uncertainty and anxiety about the answer to our prayer can be fully assuaged by the power of the Spirit, who guides our prayer according to the will of God."This certainty, however, is not within the reach of man, but is the testimony of the Spirit of God."[14]

How can we pray according to the will of God? How does the Spirit lead us into God's will? The work of the Spirit in our prayer is closely related to the Word of God."Faith grounded upon the Word is the mother of right prayer; hence, as soon as it is deflected from the Word, prayer must needs be corrupted."[15] As the Holy Spirit gives us light for the understanding of Scripture, so also we need his help to pray rightly. If the Holy Spirit does not instruct us in the right pattern for prayer, we are confused. By the secret impulse of the Holy Spirit we desire to pray prayers that will be heard by God.

The Spirit's Intercession

According to Calvin, the role of the Holy Spirit in prayer is crucial. We do not know how to pray as we ought, so the Spirit comes to our help and intercedes for us with inexpressible groans (Rom. 8:26). Through the Holy Spirit we are convinced of the authority and divinity of the Scriptures,[16] so here by the prompting of the Spirit we are guided in prayer.[17] By the testimony of the Spirit we know that God is our Father. We are taught by the same Spirit how to pray and what to ask in our prayers. Calvin explains:

> The Spirit, therefore, must prescribe the manner of our praying. Paul calls the groans into which we break forth by the impulse of the Spirit *unutterable*, because they far exceed the capacity of our intellect (*ingenii nostri captum*). The Spirit of God is said to *intercede*, not

14. *Comm.*, Rom. 8:16.
15. *Institutes*, 3.20.27.
16. "The testimony of the Spirit is more excellent than all reason. For as God alone is a fit witness of himself in his Word, so also the Word will not find acceptance in men's hearts before it is sealed by the inward testimony of the Spirit" (ibid., 1.7.4). "The Holy Spirit has inwardly taught us to truly rest upon Scripture, and that Scripture indeed is self-authenticated; hence it is not right to subject it to proof and reasoning. And the certainty it deserves with us, it attains by the testimony of the Holy Spirit (*testimonium Spiritus sancti*)" (ibid., 1.7.5).
17. Ibid., 3.20.5n8.

because He in fact humbles Himself as suppliant to pray or groan, but because He stirs up in our hearts the prayers which it is proper for us to address to God.[18]

Paul calls those groans "inexpressible" that believers give forth under the guidance of the Spirit (*duce Spiritu*).[19]

When we try to pray, we are confused with dullness and need to seek this aid from the Spirit. It is dangerous, therefore, to open our lips before God "unless the Spirit instructs us in the right pattern for prayer."[20] God not only gives Christ as the pledge and guarantee of our adoption, but also gives the Spirit as a witness to the same adoption. The Spirit guides us to correct our fearfulness and to remove our hesitation whenever we ask him.[21]

How does the Spirit intercede for us? How does the Spirit manifest himself in our prayers? For Calvin, it is the "impulse of the Spirit" with which we break forth; therefore, we must pray "in the desire for prayer." This is the manner of prayer suggested by the Spirit: "The Spirit stirs up in our hearts those desires which we ought to entertain; and he also affects our hearts in such a way that these desires by their fervency penetrate into heaven itself."[22] By the "secret impulse" of the Spirit, which is the grace of the Spirit, God knocks at and opens our hearts.

Right Prayer

The focus of the whole chapter is on the discussion of right prayer. For Calvin, to pray rightly is a rare gift.[23] The prompting of the Spirit empowers us to compose prayers that by no means hinder or hold back our own effort, since in this matter God's will is to witness how effectually faith moves our hearts. Faith instructs us to recognize that whatever we need and lack is in God and in Jesus Christ. Because of his sote-

---

18. *Comm.*, Rom. 8:26.
19. *Institutes*, 3.20.5.
20. Ronald Wallace, *Calvin's Doctrine of the Christian Life* (Edinburgh: Oliver and Boyd, 1959), 287. See also *Institutes*, 3.20.34.
21. *Institutes*, 3.20.37.
22. *Comm.*, Rom. 8:26.
23. *Institutes*, 3.20.5.

riological concern, Calvin discusses "all aids to salvation" (*omnia salutis adiumenta*) in chapter 20 of the *Institutes*.[24] Through our communion with God, we invoke God's overarching providence, sustaining power, and merciful goodness.

Thus, we must pray to God in the presence of heavenly grace that already stirs up sincerity and seriousness by the Holy Spirit. Now we come to pray, but instead the Spirit himself prays. Calvin explains the Holy Spirit's intercession: "not because He in fact humbles Himself as a suppliant to pray or groan, but because He stirs up in our hearts the prayers which it is proper for us to address to God."[25]

Prayer is a most useful exercise, but we need guiding rules for right prayer. Its necessity and propriety perpetually remind us of our duty, and lead to meditation on divine providence. Calvin's four rules of prayer seek to reject any wrong guidance of prayer and to know the necessity of striving for holiness. These rules are: first, reverence to God; second, a sense of our want in repentance; third, the suppression of all pride; fourth, a sure confidence of being heard animating us to prayer.[26]

Calvin not only attacks the wrongly conceived prayers of the Roman Catholic, but also particularly points out the harmful effects of the intercession of saints.[27] Faith instructs us to recognize that whatever we need and lack (including forgiveness of sins) is available in God and in Jesus Christ. "Accordingly, in this prayer we are taught not to make any law of him, or impose any condition upon him, but leave to his decision to do what he is to do, in what way, at what time, and in what place it seems good to him."[28]

In the concluding part of the Geneva Catechism (1538), Calvin makes one more important point on right prayer. He recognizes that we are prone to impatience and skepticism as if God did not answer our prayers. It is important to keep in mind, therefore, that we should wait for his answer

24. Ibid., 3.20.1. In his first edition (1536), Calvin provided a useful summary and interpretation of the Lord's Prayer, and provided guidelines for right prayer. Ford Lewis Battles indicates how Calvin developed this section. See *Institutes* (1536), 268–69.

25. *Comm.*, Rom. 8:26.

26. *Institutes*, 3.20.4–16.

27. Ibid., 3.20.21–27.

28. Ibid., 3.20.50.

in its proper time, particularly if we believe the doctrine of the perseverance of saints as one of the principles of Reformed soteriology. We should be encouraged to pray by a sure hope that our prayers will be answered. Prayer relies on the promises of God and on Christ's covenant.[29] Christ has sealed the guarantee of the efficacy of our prayer upon himself and upon his command that we address ourselves to the fulfillment of his promises. Calvin rightly understood that our abilities cannot match such perfection, and we must seek a remedy to help us: "Therefore, in order to minister to this weakness, God gives us the Spirit as our teacher in prayer, to tell us what is right and temper our emotions."[30]

Historical Comparison

For the proper understanding of Calvin's perspective, we should examine this matter historically because prayer serves a different purpose in Calvin's theology, especially when contrasted with religious habits of the day. Among the first generation of Reformation leaders in the middle of the sixteenth century, Calvin sets the standards in establishing rules of prayer.[31] Ford Lewis Battles summarizes: "This thoughtful and ample chapter, with its tone of devout warmth, takes its place in the forefront of historically celebrated discussions of prayer."[32]

Calvin's treatise "On Prayer" in the *Institutes* is included in a brief commentary on the Lord's Prayer. It seems certain that Calvin used not only Martin Luther's Small Catechism, but also Martin Bucer's exposi-

29. Cf. Sinclair B. Ferguson, "Prayer: A Covenant Work," *The Banner of Truth* 137 (1975): 23–28; Douglas F. Kelly, "Prayer and Union with Christ," *Scottish Bulletin of Evangelical Theology* 8 (1990): 109–27.

30. Don B. Garlington, "Calvin's Doctrine of Prayer: An Examination of Book 3, Chapter 20 of the Institutes of the Christian Religion," *The Baptist Review of Theology* 1.1 (1991): 21–36; Robert D. Loggie, "Chief Exercise of Faith—An Exposition of Calvin's Doctrine of Prayer," *Hartford Quarterly* 5 (1964–65): 65–81; Bruce A. Ware, "The Role of Prayer and the Word in the Christian Life according to John Calvin," *Studia Biblica et Theologica* 12 (1982): 73–91; John Kelsay, "Prayer and Ethics: Reflections on Calvin and Barth," *Harvard Theological Review* 82 (1989): 169–84; Guy Anthony Chevreau, "A Pastoral Explication of John Calvin's Instruction on Private Prayer" (ThD diss., Wycliffe College and Toronto School of Theology, 1989).

31. *Institutes*, 3.20.5.

32. Ford Lewis Battles' comments in his translation of the *Institutes* (1559), 850.

tion of the Lord's Prayer found in Matthew 6.[33] Bucer's influence on the young Calvin's theology is verified by Alexandre Ganoczy and Thomas F. Torrance.[34] Bucer described prayer as a conversation with God in which "we give thanks to him for benefits received, [and] we pray as well for his blessings." Calvin agrees with Bucer that the true definition of prayer is to enter into "conversation with God (*colloquium*)."[35]

Ganoczy, however, compares the traditional contents of Roman prayer to Calvin only when he observes that "both Bucer and Calvin fail to mention the two other classical purposes of prayer: adoration and the request for forgiveness."[36] Calvin's intentional emphasis on two components of prayer, petition and thanksgiving, is seen from his comment: "But inasmuch as this goal of prayer has already been stated—namely, that hearts may be aroused and borne to God, whether to praise him or to beseech his help—from this we may understand that the essentials of prayer are set in the mind and heart."[37] Calvin repeatedly highlights the affinity between "petition and thanksgiving."[38] Regarding Ganoczy's issue of forgiveness, Calvin had already discussed the necessity of daily repentance. Our prayers are answered only through God's forgiveness, not because they conform to any rules of prayer. According to Calvin:

> With regard to seeking forgiveness of sins, although no believers neglect this topic, yet those truly versed in prayer know that they do not offer the tenth part of that sacrifice.... Accordingly, men should always seek a twofold pardon

33. There are interesting studies on prayer from Calvin's contemporaries. Martin Bucer's commentary on the Lord's Prayer and *Disputatio de Precatione* could be the chief source for Calvin (Ford Lewis Battles, "Calvin on Prayer," in *The Piety of John Calvin* [Grand Rapids: Baker, 1978; repr., Phillipsburg, NJ: P&R Publishing, 2009], 113; R. Gerald Hobbs, "In Introduction to the Psalms Commentary on Martin Bucer" [thesis, University of Strasbourg, 1971]).

34. Alexandre Ganoczy, *The Young Calvin*, trans. David Foxgrover and Wade Provo (Philadelphia: Westminster Press, 1987), 162–64; Thomas Forsyth Torrance, "Legal and Evangelical Priests: The Holy Ministry as Reflected in Calvin's Prayers," in *Calvin's Books: Festschrift Dedicated to Peter De Klerk on the Occasion of His Seventieth Birthday* (Heerenveen: J. J. Groen en Zoon, 1997), 63–74.

35. *Institutes*, 3.20.4. As John T. McNeill points out (note 6), Calvin is particularly careful to guard this conception from every element of irreverence, casualness, or levity.

36. Ganoczy, *The Young Calvin*, 162.

37. *Institutes*, 3.20.29.

38. Ibid., 3.20.28.

because they are aware of many offenses, the feeling of which still does not so touch them that they are as much displeased with themselves as they ought to be, but also because, in so far as it has been granted them to benefit by repentance and fear of God, stricken down with a just sorrow on account of their offenses, they pray that the wrath of the judge be averted.[39]

In order to escape from the errors of the Roman Catholics, Calvin attacks the practice of penance, especially the three steps of the scholastics: contrition of heart, confession of mouth, and satisfaction of works. For Calvin, God simply requires repentance and faith. Our sanctification is the object of regeneration, and our efforts strive to overcome bad habits. The first step in the Christian life is self-denial, which is the departure from self to thorough obedience to God. Then bearing the cross leads us to mature trust in God's will.

Conclusion

It is noteworthy that Calvin's doctrine of prayer contains a very practical perspective. This great man sought to pray "at all times, in every place, in all things, and under all circumstances."[40] After lectures and preaching, Calvin normally concluded with appropriate petitions. The prayers of Calvin have received little attention, as compared with the fame that crowns his theological writings.[41]

When we compare this with all the influential and well-known textbooks of systematic theology, modern Reformed doctrine often minimizes the role of prayer. Among many systematic theologians, even most Calvinists barely pay attention to prayer as a major component of soteriology.[42]

39. Ibid., 3.20.16.
40. Ibid., 3.20.28.
41. *Devotions and Prayers of John Calvin*, ed. Charles E. Edwards (Grand Rapids: Baker, 1976), 3.
42. Cf. the soteriology sections by well-known Calvinists, evangelicals, neo-orthodox, and modern theologians such as Louis Berkhof, Anthony Hoekema, Millard J. Erickson, Karl Barth, Carl F. H. Henry, Otto Weber, and Stanley Grenz. See, however, David Calhoun's recent chapter, "Prayer: 'The Chief Exercise of Faith,'" in *A Theological Guide to Calvin's Institutes: Essays and Analysis*, ed. David W. Hall and Peter A. Lillback (Phillipsburg, NJ: P&R Publishing, 2008), 347–67.

It seems to me that Calvin's doctrine of prayer has not been attractive to Calvin scholars; they typically tend to engage in heavy debates on the *ordo salutis* and other theoretical aspects of his soteriology. Yet Calvin himself admonishes: "To fail to take advantage of these rich resources available to us is like neglecting a great treasure buried and hidden in the earth even after we are aware of its existence."[43]

In summary, Calvin's perspective on the role of prayer is different from that of the Roman Catholics and others. For Calvin, it is the chief exercise of faith, by which we daily receive God's benefits.[44] "Christians may unburden themselves by prayer, and thus exercise their faith."[45] Calvin makes a connection between prayer and the believer's desire for piety. Our faith can be proved only by calling on God, and prayer is the most important exercise to embrace the promise of grace.

Calvin explains the aid of the Spirit that is sufficient to overcome all difficulties by the help of God's mighty hand, for bearing the cross is beyond our own strength. Calvin emphasizes that the Spirit not only shoulders the burden with us, but also protects us from evil whenever we need any help from our God. If we urgently need any help in our redemption, God holds us up by the groaning and sighing of the Holy Spirit's intercession. The Holy Spirit devotes himself to aiding the believer's efforts to keep a prayer life both in private and in public. Calvin prays:

> Grant, Almighty God, that since it is the principal part of our happiness that while we are absent from thee in this world there is yet open to us a familiar access to thee by faith, O Grant that we may be able to come with a pure heart to thy presence; and when our lips are polluted, O purify us by thy Spirit, so that we may not only pray to thee with mouth, but also prove that we do this sincerely, without any dissimulation, and that we earnestly seek to spend our whole life in glorifying thy name, until at length being gathered into thy celestial kingdom, we may be really and truly united to thee, and be made partakers of that glory which has been produced for us by the blood of thine only Son. Amen.[46]

43. Geneva Catechism (1538), chap. 22. See also I. John Hesselink, *Calvin's First Catechism: A Commentary* (Louisville: Westminster/John Knox Press, 1997).

44. *Institutes*, 3.20.1.

45. *Comm.*, Rom. 8:26.

46. *Comm.*, Zeph. 3:9.

16

JOHN CALVIN'S DOCTRINE
OF SCRIPTURE

A. T. B. MCGOWAN

I n a conference to mark the five hundredth anniversary of John Calvin's
birth, it is right that there should be a paper on Calvin's doctrine of
Scripture because unless we understand his attitude to Scripture, we
will not understand his theology as a whole. Calvin's approach to theological questions was determined by his view of Scripture.

There is, however, a problem. Scholars have been unable to agree on the
interpretation of Calvin's position. Some, such as Jack Rogers and Donald
McKim,[1] have argued that Calvin believed there to be errors in Scripture.
Others, such as John Murray,[2] John Woodbridge,[3] and Robert Reymond,[4]

---

1. Jack Bartlett Rogers and Donald K. McKim, *The Authority and Interpretation of the Bible: An Historical Approach* (San Francisco: Harper & Row, 1979).

2. John Murray, *Calvin on Scripture and Divine Sovereignty* (Grand Rapids: Baker, 1960).

3. John D. Woodbridge, *Biblical Authority: A Critique of the Rogers/McKim Proposal* (Grand Rapids: Zondervan, 1982).

4. Robert L. Reymond, "Calvin's Doctrine of Holy Scripture," in *A Theological Guide to Calvin's Institutes,* ed. David W. Hall and Peter A. Lillback (Phillipsburg, NJ: P&R Publishing, 2008), 44–64.

have argued that Calvin was an "inerrantist." It will be the argument of this essay that attempting to force Calvin into accepting one or the other of these two positions, the two most prevalent views among American evangelicals in the latter half of the twentieth century, has led to a distortion and misinterpretation of Calvin's own thinking. As Richard Muller has said, "Altogether too much of the discussion of the Reformation and Protestant orthodox doctrines of Scripture has approached the subject from theologically biased perspectives and with the specific intention of justifying one or another twentieth-century view of Scripture."[5]

In response to these attempts to claim Calvin for one side or the other, it will be argued that some of the scholars who engaged in this debate have been in danger of following the equivalent of a "proof-texting" method. That is to say, each side has found statements in Calvin that, interpreted in a certain way, support their position. If, however, we look carefully at the inner dogmatic structure of Calvin's *Institutes*, particularly the way in which he relates the knowledge of God with the person and work of the Holy Spirit, we can see that Calvin does not fit neatly into either of these warring camps of twentieth-century North America.

The essay will be structured as follows. First, we will make a number of introductory points concerning Calvin's overall approach to this doctrine. Second, we will briefly survey the battleground between the errantists and the inerrantists. Third, we will examine the inner dogmatic structure of the *Institutes*, with a view to establishing Calvin's understanding of the relationship between Word and Spirit. Fourth, we will present certain conclusions regarding Calvin's doctrine of Scripture and its authority.

Introductory Considerations

Five points ought to be made by way of introduction to this study. First, it is important to say at the beginning that Calvin had a high view of Scripture as the Word of God written and that this determined everything he wrote. Indeed, it was Calvin's high regard for Scripture and his concern that it be understood that led to the writing of his *Institutes of*

---

5. Richard A. Muller, *Post-Reformation Reformed Dogmatics*, vol. 2, *Holy Scripture: The Cognitive Foundation of Theology* (Grand Rapids: Baker, 1993), 4.

the Christian Religion.[6] More specifically, Calvin's purpose in writing the *Institutes* was to assist in the preparation of students for the ministry. It was written so that these "candidates in sacred theology" might properly understand the Scriptures.[7]

This is not to suggest that Calvin considered the *Institutes* to be necessary for a true reading of the Scriptures. He notes, "Holy Scripture contains a perfect doctrine, to which one can add nothing, since in it our Lord has meant to display the infinite treasures of his wisdom . . ." Nevertheless, "Perhaps the duty of those who have received from God fuller light than others is to help simple folk at this point, and as it were to lend them a hand, in order to guide them and help them to find the sum of what God meant to teach us in his Word."[8] In this vein, he sums up his intention in writing the book: "Nevertheless, I can at least promise that it can be a key to open a way for all children of God into a good and right understanding of Holy Scripture."[9] He does make it clear, however, that the reader must judge everything he says by the Scriptures. He notes that "all truth and sound doctrine proceed from God"[10] and therefore urges his reader "to have recourse to Scripture in order to weigh the testimonies that I adduce from it."[11]

Second, we should note that although his concern was for people to understand the Scriptures, this was not simply about obtaining knowledge. His concern was for godliness. As he writes in his Prefatory Address to King Francis I of France, "My purpose was solely to transmit certain rudiments by which those who are touched with any zeal for religion might be shaped to true godliness."[12] Calvin was supremely the pastor and doctor of Geneva, concerned that men and women and children should come to a true knowledge of God's Word so that they might live lives in accordance with God's will and truly follow Christ. It is this practical concern for godliness and right living that pervades all his preaching and

---

6. John Calvin, *Institutes of the Christian Religion*, ed. John T. McNeill, trans. Ford Lewis Battles, Library of Christian Classics vols. 20, 21 (Philadelphia: Westminster Press, 1977).
   7. *Institutes*, 1.1.4.
   8. Ibid., 1.6.
   9. Ibid., 1.7.
   10. Ibid.
   11. Ibid., 1.8.
   12. Ibid., 1.9.

writing. By contrast, the detachment of many modern theologians from the life of the church has led to the writing of some theology that is largely academic or even esoteric. Generations of theologians who were educated by these theologians have found themselves unprepared to be pastors and teachers in the church.

Third, it is clear from the beginning that Calvin, in writing his *Institutes*, is aware that he is speaking into a situation in which people have been taught that the church, in determining truth and defining doctrine, has a higher authority than the Scriptures themselves. He is thus writing with one eye on those who stand in opposition to his doctrine of Scripture. The battle lines are drawn even in his Prefatory Address. Calvin's view is that the authority of Scripture is to be derived from its essential nature, as that which has been breathed out by God, as that which came into existence when men spoke from God as they were carried along by the Holy Spirit. In speaking of his opponents, he says that "they do not hesitate to declare that the whole authority of Scripture depends entirely upon the judgment of the church."[13] As we will see later, this relationship between the Scripture and the church presents the crucial difference between the Reformed doctrine of Scripture and the Catholic doctrine of Scripture.

Fourth, we should note the significance of the *Institutes* in relation to his commentaries. Calvin notes that, having written the *Institutes*, he would not digress into major doctrinal sections in his commentaries:

> If, after this road has, as it were, been paved, I shall publish any interpretations of Scripture, I shall always condense them, because I shall have no need to undertake long doctrinal discussions, and to digress into commonplaces. In this way the godly reader will be spared great annoyance and boredom, provided he approach Scripture armed with a knowledge of the present work, as a necessary tool.[14]

This is important. When people use the commentaries to try to determine Calvin's doctrinal position, they are doing the reverse of what he himself

13. Ibid., 1.22.
14. Ibid., 1.4.

affirmed to be the proper method.[15] He then underlines this earlier comment: "Thus if henceforth our Lord gives me the means and opportunity of writing some commentaries, I shall use the greatest possible brevity, because there will be no need for long digressions, seeing that I have here treated at length almost all the articles pertaining to Christianity."[16]

Fifth, Calvin came to the Scriptures with certain principles and certain tools that he had acquired in his days as a humanist scholar. He was clear that he must work with the Hebrew and Greek texts, rather than depend on the translations and interpretations of those who had gone before him. He was clear that the Scriptures, like other ancient texts, must be allowed to speak for themselves, rather than have a structure forced upon them. He was also clear that they must be read and understood in their original context, where the *sitz im leben* of the original author is taken seriously. Finally, he was clear that the clear meaning of the text must be preferred to allegorical readings or to other interpretive grids.

Errantists and Inerrantists

For most of the period since the Reformation, it was taken for granted that Calvin held to a high view of verbal inspiration and did not believe that there were errors in Scripture. Only in the modern period has anyone seriously doubted this. John Murray identifies Charles A. Briggs as one who challenged this consensus.[17] Briggs was a professor at Union Theological Seminary who was charged with heresy by the Presbyterian Church for denying the inerrancy of Scripture. He did not believe that Calvin taught this doctrine. Murray, unlike others, does not brush aside the arguments of Briggs and others who questioned the traditional interpretation of Calvin. He takes their arguments seriously and recognizes that there is a case to be answered, given certain statements to be found in Calvin's writing. In particular, he identifies three passages in Calvin that are capable of being interpreted in ways that would support Briggs's position.

15. Cf. ibid., 1.7.
16. Ibid., 1.7.
17. Murray, *Calvin on Scripture and Divine Sovereignty*, 12.

The three passages concerned are Calvin's comments on Matthew 27:9, Acts 7:14–16, and Hebrews 11:21. The Matthew passage concerns the fact that a quotation from Zechariah is attributed to Jeremiah. Calvin comments, "How the name of Jeremiah crept in I cannot confess to know nor do I make much of it: obviously Jeremiah's name is put in error for Zechariah (13:7)."[18]

The Acts passage concerns a discrepancy between the number of people said by Moses to have left Egypt with Jacob (Gen. 46:27) and the number quoted by Stephen (Acts 7:14). Moses said seventy, but Stephen said seventy-five. Also, the name *Abraham* appears in Acts 7:16, which Calvin says is a mistake. On the first issue, Calvin argues that a mistake took place somewhere between the Hebrew and the Greek (Septuagint) texts. In Luke we have the (mistaken) Greek text instead of the (correct) Hebrew text. Calvin notes that "this was not such an important matter that Luke should have confused the Gentiles over it, when they were used to the Greek reading."[19] Calvin does allow that Luke might have quoted the correct number but that some copyist changed it to suit the Septuagint version, which was the common text in use. On the second issue, Calvin concludes that the name *Abraham* must be removed, saying, "This verse must be amended accordingly." In both cases, Calvin seems to be quite relaxed about these issues.

The Hebrews passage concerns the question whether Jacob worshiped "on the top of his staff" or "on the top of his bed." Calvin famously says, "We know that the apostles were not too particular in the matter of adjusting themselves to the ignorant who still had need of milk. There is no danger in this provided always that the readers are brought back to the pure original sense of Scripture."[20] The suggestion seems to be that the authors of Scripture were not concerned with precision in the details of their writing.

18. John Calvin, *A Harmony of the Gospels Matthew, Mark and Luke*, ed. David W. Torrance and Thomas F. Torrance, in *Calvin's Commentaries* (Edinburgh: St. Andrew Press, 1972), 177.

19. John Calvin, *The Acts of the Apostles 1–13*, ed. David W. Torrance and Thomas F. Torrance, in *Calvin's Commentaries* (Grand Rapids: Eerdmans, 1965), 181.

20. John Calvin, *The Epistles of Paul the Apostle to the Hebrews and the First and Second Epistles of St Peter*, ed. David W. Torrance and Thomas F. Torrance, in *Calvin's Commentaries* (Edinburgh: Oliver and Boyd, 1963), 175.

Murray is greatly concerned lest Calvin's remarks on these three passages be understood in such a way as to undermine the view that Calvin held to biblical inerrancy. Having surveyed Calvin's overall position, Murray concludes that Calvin could not possibly have conceived of errors in the *autographa* and that therefore these "mistakes" had "crept in" during the process of copying and transmission of the text.[21] He does say, however, that meticulous precision is not a requirement for belief in biblical inerrancy:

> Calvin does recognise that the writers of Scripture were not always meticulously precise on certain details such as those of number and incident. And this means that the Holy Spirit, by whom, in Calvin's esteem, they wrote, was not always meticulously precise on such matters. It must be emphatically stated that the doctrine of biblical inerrancy for which the church has contended throughout history and, for which a great many of us still contend, is not based on the assumption that the criterion of meticulous precision in every detail of record or history is the indispensable canon of biblical infallibility.[22]

Murray does not let Calvin off the hook entirely, however, saying, "We are not necessarily granting that Calvin's remarks are the best suited to the solution of the questions that arise in connection with Acts 7:14 and Heb. 11:21. We may even grant that the language used by Calvin in these connections is ill-advised and not in accord with Calvin's usual caution when reflecting on the divine origin and character of Scripture."[23]

The discussion on Calvin's doctrine of Scripture came to a head with the publication in 1979 of *The Authority and Interpretation of the Bible: An Historical Approach* by Jack Rogers and Donald McKim. The authors argue that Calvin's humanistic background and his training in "legal exegesis" mean that he "categorically rejected a narrow literalism" and instead focused on the intent of the author. They argue that he abhorred the legalism that came with literalism and regarded it as a sign of ignorance.[24] Rogers and McKim highlight Calvin's teaching on the divine "accommodation" as the

21. Murray, *Calvin on Scripture and Divine Sovereignty*, 29.
22. Ibid., 29–30.
23. Ibid., 31.
24. Rogers and McKim, *The Authority and Interpretation of the Bible*, 97.

key to understanding how Calvin dealt with difficulties in the Bible. They go so far as to say, "Given Calvin's understanding of the accommodated nature of God's communication in Scripture, it is not surprising that Calvin was unconcerned with normal, human inaccuracies in minor matters."[25] They go on to quote various examples, including the ones highlighted by Murray. Their view of these passages, however, is that they are indeed mistakes made by the original authors (rather than mistakes made by copyists) but that they do not matter and are to be expected:

> For Calvin, technical errors in the Bible that were the result of human slips of memory, limited knowledge, or the use of texts for different purposes than the original were all part of the normal human means of communication. They did not call into question the divine character of Scripture's message. Nor did they hinder the completely adequate communication of God's Word. In fact, they enhanced the telling of the Good News because they were part of God's gracious accommodation of himself to human means and thus made the message more persuasive to human beings. Scholars could and should deal openly and honestly with technical problems according to Calvin's theory and his own practice.[26]

Rogers and McKim go on to insist that Calvin did not necessarily expect Scripture to provide accuracy in matters of language, science, and history. These, they say, were all matters that Calvin dealt with under the rubric of accommodation.[27] Rogers and McKim thus reject the notion that Calvin held to biblical inerrancy and argue instead that he held to an "errantist" position, at least in respect to certain passages of Scripture. They continue to use the word *infallibility*, but with this defined limitation of its scope.

The most detailed response to Rogers and McKim was John Woodbridge's *Biblical Authority: A Critique of the Rogers/McKim Proposal*, in which he argued that Rogers and McKim had placed so much emphasis on the idea of "accommodation" that it had skewed their understanding of Calvin (and Martin Luther). He says that this "fallacious assumption" means that they "cannot adequately account for those many statements

25. Ibid., 109.
26. Ibid., 110–11.
27. Ibid., 111–14.

where Luther and Calvin affirm a commitment to complete biblical infallibility."[28] He argues that this is partly because they have based their interpretation on some studies that have a neo-orthodox origin.

Woodbridge goes through the various quotations from Calvin, which Rogers and McKim use to support their case, and demonstrates very persuasively that they have misunderstood what Calvin was saying.[29] He, in turn, amasses an impressive array of quotations from Calvin to justify his conclusion that Calvin did indeed hold to biblical inerrancy and did not believe there to be errors in Scripture, even in matters of history, science, and so on.

It seems, then, that no clear agreement can be reached on Calvin's teaching on Scripture. Was he an inerrantist as claimed by Murray and Woodbridge, or was he a semi-errantist as claimed by Rogers and McKim? To seek an answer to this problem, we must look at the inner dogmatic structure of Calvin's doctrine of Scripture as we find it presented in the *Institutes*.

Calvin on Word and Spirit

Given the many contradictory interpretations of Calvin's doctrine of Scripture, it will be our intention in what follows, as far as possible, to allow Calvin to speak for himself.

In order to draw out the core teaching of Calvin on the doctrine of Scripture, we follow the pattern of the *Institutes* and consider first the knowledge of God and second the person and work of the Holy Spirit. This will then enable us to open up the principal issue at stake in the Reformation, namely, the relationship between Scripture and tradition. It will also enable us to reach some conclusions regarding Calvin's doctrine of the authority of Scripture.

Scripture and the Knowledge of God

The immediate context for understanding Calvin's doctrine of Scripture is his teaching concerning the knowledge of God. The structure of

---

28. Woodbridge, *Biblical Authority*, 49–50.
29. Ibid., 59–63.

the early chapters of the *Institutes* clearly demonstrates the place given to Scripture in Calvin's systematic exposition of the knowledge of God.

He begins with this great affirmation: "Nearly all the wisdom we possess, that is to say, true and sound wisdom, consists of two parts: the knowledge of God and of ourselves."[30] Clearly, the knowledge of God is the more important element. Indeed, without the knowledge of God, we cannot have true knowledge of ourselves. If we compare ourselves with one another, we might reach the conclusion that we are doing quite well, better than some people, although perhaps worse than others. On this basis of comparison, we will undoubtedly reach a false judgment of our true condition. If, however, we first contemplate God in all his glory, majesty, and holiness and then turn to consider ourselves, a very different assessment will be reached. Calvin writes that "it is certain that man never achieves a clear knowledge of himself unless he has first looked upon God's face, and then descends from contemplating him to scrutinize himself."[31] On this basis of comparison, our sin and depravity will be clearly visible in contrast to God's holiness: "what in us seems perfection itself corresponds ill to the purity of God."[32] The knowledge of God, then, is fundamental for a true knowledge of self. Indeed, not only will this comparison enable a true evaluation of our human condition but it will also create in us a desire to be different: "we are prompted by our own ills to contemplate the good things of God; and we cannot seriously aspire to him before we begin to become displeased with ourselves."[33]

This, of course, leads to the important question as to the nature of this knowledge of God. Calvin makes it clear that true knowledge of God is not simply the conviction that God exists; it is rather a knowledge that is practical, a knowledge that makes a difference to our lives. Thus he can say, "Indeed, we shall not say that, properly speaking, God is known where there is no religion or piety."[34] Calvin should not be misunderstood here. He is not suggesting that only true believers can have this knowledge; rather, he insists that knowledge of God is possible even without salvation. He

30. *Institutes*, 1.1.1.
31. Ibid., 1.1.2.
32. Ibid.
33. Ibid., 1.1.1.
34. Ibid., 1.2.1.

writes, "Nevertheless, it is one thing to feel that God as our Maker supports us by his power, governs us by his providence, nourishes us by his goodness, and attends us with all sorts of blessings—and another thing to embrace the grace of reconciliation offered to us in Christ."[35]

In order to explain how it is possible to have true knowledge of God without being reconciled to God, Calvin introduces his notion of the twofold knowledge of God. In all that he has made, God reveals himself as Creator, and then "in the face of Christ," he reveals himself as Redeemer.[36] There is, then, knowledge of God in creation, which is accessible to all human beings, as well as a special knowledge of God accessible only to those who are in Christ. Calvin then widens the scope of this idea of a general knowledge of God by speaking also of a general grace of God, whereby gifts, benefits, and blessings from God come to all human beings. In this context Calvin gives the first indications of what would later come to be called the doctrine of common grace. He writes that "no drop will be found either of wisdom and light, or of righteousness or power or rectitude, or of genuine truth, which does not flow from him, and of which he is not the cause."[37] It must be stressed here that Calvin does not use this distinction to defend the idea of natural theology (which he rejects) but instead to defend a high view of general revelation.

In order to underline the nature of this general knowledge of God, Calvin teaches that all human beings, at some level of their being, have true knowledge of God: "There is within the human mind, and indeed by natural instinct, an awareness of divinity. This we take to be beyond controversy. To prevent anyone from taking refuge in the pretense of ignorance, God himself has implanted in all men a certain understanding of his divine majesty."[38] This innate knowledge of God is sufficient to render human beings without excuse before God. No one will be able to stand before God on the day of judgment and say that they did not know God. Rather, "Since, therefore, men one and all perceive that there is a God and that he is their Maker, they are condemned by their own testimony because they have failed to honor him and to consecrate their lives to his

35. Ibid.
36. Ibid.
37. Ibid.
38. Ibid., 1.3.1.

will."[39] To support this argument for the *divinitatis sensum,* Calvin quotes Cicero: "Yet there is, as the eminent pagan says, no nation so barbarous, no people so savage, that they have not a deep-seated conviction that there is a God."[40] He then adds, "Therefore, since from the beginning of the world there has been no region, no city, in short, no household, that could do without religion, there lies in this a tacit confession of a sense of deity inscribed in the hearts of all."[41] Calvin uses three significant phrases to describe this innate knowledge of the deity, translated as "awareness of divinity," "seed of religion," and "sense of deity."[42] He later adds a fourth, "sense of divinity."[43]

This innate knowledge of God explains why each human being has a natural desire to worship. Unfortunately, because of sin, the true God is not properly known; hence people worship gods of their own making or choosing. For this reason Calvin stresses the need for revelation, by referring to those who "do not therefore apprehend God as he offers himself but imagine him as they have fashioned him in their own presumption."[44] He goes so far as to say that "whatever they afterward bring by way of worship or service of God, they cannot bring as tribute to him, for they are worshiping not God but a figment and a dream of their own heart."[45]

Recognizing with the psalmist (Pss. 14:1; 53:1) that some say there is no God, he says that these are they "who, by extinguishing the light of nature, deliberately befuddle themselves. Accordingly, we see that many, after they have become hardened in insolent and habitual sinning, furiously repel all remembrance of God, although this is freely suggested to them inwardly from the feeling of nature."[46] This, of course, is Paul's argument in Romans 1, that human beings know God but deliberately suppress that knowledge because of their sin. Indeed, Calvin notes that sin and error so abound that human beings invent gods for themselves: "For as rashness and superficiality are joined to ignorance and darkness, scarcely

39. Ibid.
40. Ibid.
41. Ibid.
42. Ibid.
43. Ibid., 1.3.3.
44. Ibid., 1.4.1.
45. Ibid.
46. Ibid., 1.4.2.

a single person has ever been found who did not fashion for himself an idol or specter in place of God."[47]

Calvin insists that the evidence for God is all around us in the created order and is undeniable. This leads him to argue that the best way to know God is not ontological speculation but observation of his acts: "Consequently, we know the most perfect way of seeking God, and the most suitable order, is not for us to attempt with bold curiosity to penetrate to the investigation of his essence, which we ought more to adore than meticulously to search out, but for us to contemplate him in his works whereby he renders himself near and familiar to us, and in some manner communicates himself."[48]

The critical point in Calvin's argument about revelation and the knowledge of God, however, is his distinction between the two kinds of knowledge of God. Hence Calvin notes that despite the evidence of God in creation, in itself this is insufficient: "It is therefore in vain that so many burning lamps shine for us in the workmanship of the universe to show forth the glory of its Author. Although they bathe us wholly in their radiance, yet they can of themselves in no way lead us into the right path."[49] Calvin interprets Hebrews 11:3 to mean that although God's "invisible divinity" is clearly seen, "we have not the eyes to see this unless they be illumined by the inner revelation of God through faith." He goes on to quote Romans 1:19, noting that the clearly seen evidence of God in creation leaves human beings "inexcusable" but not reconciled to God.[50]

In this context and with this background, Calvin turns his attention to the doctrine of Scripture. Having established that neither God's general revelation of himself in creation nor the innate knowledge of God possessed by human beings (because they are made in the image of God) is sufficient to bring human beings to salvation, Calvin now explains the way of special revelation. Calvin states that God's Word is necessary because human beings, as a result of sin, are blind to the light of God given to them in their "sense of divinity" and in creation.[51]

47. Ibid., 1.5.12.
48. Ibid., 1.5.9.
49. Ibid., 1.5.14.
50. Ibid.
51. Ibid., 1.6.1.

Calvin uses a much-discussed simile[52] to explain the need for Scripture: "Just as old or bleary-eyed men and those with weak vision, if you thrust before them a most beautiful volume, even if they recognise it to be some sort of writing, yet can scarcely construe two words, but with the aid of spectacles will begin to read distinctly; so Scripture, gathering up the otherwise confused knowledge of God in our minds, having dispersed our dullness, clearly shows us the true God."[53]

Calvin expresses a very high view of the nature of Scripture in this context: "This, therefore, is a special gift, where God, to instruct the church, not merely uses mute teachers but also opens his own most hallowed lips." This revelation of himself in Scripture is for "the elect" or "his church."[54] Calvin understands, of course, that the actual revelation was separate from the Scriptures in its origin. That is to say, the revelation came to prophets and apostles, and only later was it written down. Calvin notes that when God's Word came to the patriarchs, they knew that what they had been given came from God. In order that this might become a permanent revelation, what God gave them was put into writing.[55]

Calvin also affirms a high view of the authority and sufficiency of Scripture. As to its authority, he writes, "When that which is set forth is acknowledged to be the Word of God, there is no one so deplorably insolent—unless devoid also both of common sense and of humanity itself—as to dare impugn the credibility of Him who speaks."[56] As to its sufficiency, he makes the point that "daily oracles are not sent from heaven, for it pleased the Lord to hallow his truth to everlasting remembrance in the Scriptures alone [cf. John 5:39]. Hence the Scriptures obtain full authority among believers only when men regard them as having sprung from heaven, as if there the living words of God were heard."[57]

Calvin deals with the claim that the Scriptures derive their authority from the church: "But a most pernicious error widely prevails that Scripture has only so much weight as is conceded to it by the consent of the

52. Ibid., 1.70n1 directs us to discussions of this simile in Calvin studies.
53. Ibid., 1.6.1.
54. Ibid.
55. Ibid., 1.6.2.
56. Ibid., 1.7.1; cf. ibid., 4.8.1ff.
57. Ibid., 1.7.1.

church. As if the eternal and inviolable truth of God depended upon the decision of men!" He then goes on to deal with the related argument that we are persuaded of the authority of the Bible only by the church. He says that those who argue in this way "mock the Holy Spirit."[58] Nevertheless, he does not undermine a proper understanding of the significance of the church in relation to the Scriptures. The church "receives and gives its seal of approval to the Scriptures, it does not thereby render authentic what is otherwise doubtful or controversial. But because the church recognises Scripture to be the truth of its own God, as a pious duty it unhesitatingly venerates Scripture."[59] In answer to the apologetic question as to how we can be sure that Scripture has come from God, if we do not accept it on the authority of the church, Calvin replies, "It is as if someone asked: Whence will we learn to distinguish light from darkness, white from black, sweet from bitter? Indeed, Scripture exhibits fully as clear evidence of its own truth as white and black things do of their color, or sweet and bitter things do of their taste."[60] In other words, Scripture is self-authenticating because God himself speaks in and through it. Indeed, Calvin goes so far as to say, "It is clear that the teaching of Scripture is from heaven."[61]

Scripture and the Holy Spirit

We must now move to a consideration of Calvin's teaching on the Holy Spirit because, having established his view that the Scriptures are necessary for a true knowledge of God, he goes on immediately to set this in the context of the person and work of the Holy Spirit. We might put it like this: if the knowledge of God is the immediate context for an understanding of Calvin's doctrine of Scripture, the wider context is his understanding of the person and work of the Holy Spirit.

Calvin speaks of the "inward testimony of the Holy Spirit." Perceptively, he points out that even if he were to destroy the arguments of those who argue against the authority of Scripture (and he believes he could!), it would ultimately make no difference:

58. Ibid.
59. Ibid., 1.7.2.
60. Ibid.
61. Ibid., 1.7.4.

But even if anyone clears God's Sacred Word from man's evil speaking, he will not at once imprint upon their hearts that certainty which piety requires. Since for unbelieving men religion seems to stand by opinion alone, they, in order not to believe anything foolishly or lightly, both wish and demand rational proof that Moses and the prophets spoke divinely. But I reply: the testimony of the Spirit is more excellent than all reason. For as God alone is a fit witness of himself in his Word, so also the Word will not find acceptance in men's hearts before it is sealed by the inward testimony of the Holy Spirit. The same Spirit, therefore, who has spoken through the mouths of the prophets must penetrate into our hearts to persuade us that they faithfully proclaimed what had been divinely commanded.[62]

This is a very important statement. Calvin is insisting that those who will not accept anything except on the basis of some rational proof will never be persuaded of the truth of Scripture because its truth is not established in that way. Rather, it requires an internal persuasion by the Holy Spirit. When this internal persuasion takes place, the believer no longer doubts the truth of Scripture but accepts it. To that extent, as Calvin argues, the Scripture is self-authenticating: "Let this point therefore stand: that those whom the Holy Spirit has inwardly taught truly rest upon Scripture, and that Scripture indeed is self-authenticated; hence, it is not right to subject it to proof and reasoning."[63] That is to say, since the authority of Scripture rests on the "testimony of the Spirit," "it seriously affects us only when it is sealed upon our hearts through the Spirit."[64]

Having been inwardly persuaded of the authority of Scripture by this testimony of the Spirit, the believer can have absolute certainty of both the origin and truth of Scripture. Its origin lies in God himself, as he spoke through the servants he had chosen. This certainty takes away the need to find rational proofs on which to base our view of Scripture. Calvin can say of Scripture that "we affirm with utter certainty . . . that it has flowed to us from the very mouth of God by the ministry of men.

62. Ibid.
63. Ibid., 1.7.5.
64. Ibid.

371

We seek no proofs, no marks of genuineness upon which our judgement may lean; but we subject our judgement and wit to it as to a thing far beyond any guesswork!"[65] Thus Calvin is "fully conscious that we hold the unassailable truth!" and can affirm that "the undoubted power of his divine majesty lives and breathes there."[66]

This should not be taken to mean that Calvin's view is based on some irrational fideism or that he cares nothing for evidence. Later in his work, Calvin defines the relationship between faith and the authority of Scripture, by insisting that faith rests on God's Word.[67] Like Cornelius Van Til in the twentieth century, Calvin argues that, having been convinced of the truth of Scripture by faith, a faith and conviction brought about in us by the work of the Holy Spirit, we can then see clearly all the evidence for the truth of Scripture. The evidence is not that which brings us to the conviction of Scripture's truth, but without that presuppositional stance, we would not see the evidence at all. To put it another way, if we begin with the presupposition that Scripture is the Word of God, a presupposition created in us by the Holy Spirit, everything else then begins to make sense. It is as if the lights have come on in a darkened room. If, however, we try to prove that Scripture is true, then ultimately we may fail. Calvin is thus able to say that his view of Scripture is "a conviction that requires no reasons" but yet is "a knowledge with which the best reason agrees," concluding that it is "a feeling that can be born only of heavenly revelation."[68]

Given that this conviction about Scripture can come only by revelation, Calvin's comment concerning the sovereign action of God is pertinent: "Whenever, then, the fewness of believers disturbs us, let the converse come to mind, that only those to whom it is given can comprehend the mysteries of God [cf. Matt. 13:11]."[69] In other words, we come to convictions about the truth of Scripture not by rational proofs and evidence but by the internal persuasion of the Holy Spirit, itself a strong function of the sovereign action of God in bringing sinners to himself.

65. Ibid.
66. Ibid.
67. Ibid., 3.2.1.
68. Ibid., 1.7.5.
69. Ibid.

Calvin goes on to underline the usefulness of various kinds of evidence for the authority of Scripture, but only when this evidence comes after (rather than before) the conviction that comes by the Spirit. He thus reaffirms his view of the self-authentication of Scripture through the testimony of the Holy Spirit:

> Unless this certainty, higher and stronger than any human judgement be present, it will be vain to fortify the authority of Scripture by arguments, to establish it by common agreement of the church, or to confirm it with other helps. For unless this foundation is laid, its authority will always remain in doubt. Conversely, once we have embraced it devoutly as its dignity deserves, and have recognised it to be above the common sort of things, those arguments—not strong enough before to engraft and fix the certainty of Scripture in our minds—become very useful aids.[70]

Calvin is also careful to emphasize that Scripture is not held in high regard because of the majesty of its language. Rather, it is expressed "in mean and lowly words."[71] Calvin notes that no matter how much one may be moved by great human writings, the profound effect of Scripture is such that "it is easy to see that the Sacred Scriptures, which so far surpass all gifts and graces of human endeavour, breathe something divine."[72] He points out that even in the most rustic writings of Scripture, the "majesty of the Spirit" is "evident everywhere."[73] He goes so far as to say that the sacred Scripture is "crammed with thoughts that could not be humanly conceived."[74] Such is its magnificence that its authors "must have been instructed by the Spirit."[75]

Calvin spends most of book 1, chapter 8 affirming the various evidences for the truth of Scripture: fulfilled prophecies, consent of the parts, inspiration, providential preservation of the Scriptures, death of the martyrs, and so forth. Yet at the end he repeats his main contention:

70. Ibid., 1.8.1.
71. Ibid.
72. Ibid.
73. Ibid., 1.8.2.
74. Ibid.
75. Ibid., 1.8.11.

There are other reasons, neither few nor weak, for which the dignity and majesty of Scripture are not only affirmed in godly hearts, but brilliantly vindicated against the wiles of its disparagers; yet of themselves these are not strong enough to provide a firm faith, until our Heavenly Father, revealing his majesty there, lifts reverence for Scripture beyond the realm of controversy. Therefore Scripture will ultimately suffice for a saving knowledge of God only when its certainty is founded upon the inward persuasion of the Holy Spirit. Indeed, these human testimonies which exist to confirm it will not be in vain if, as secondary aids to our feebleness, they follow that chief and highest testimony. But those who wish to prove to unbelievers that Scripture is the Word of God are acting foolishly, for only by faith can this be known. Augustine therefore justly warns that godliness and peace of mind ought to come first if a man is to understand anything of such great matters.[76]

All of this teaching about the work of the Holy Spirit in persuading us of the truth of Scripture does, however, leave Calvin with a problem. What about those who claim special insights or revelations from the Spirit, apart from Scripture? At the beginning of book 1, chapter 9, Calvin deals with those whose claimed direct revelations of the Spirit led them to disparage Scripture. He concludes, "Therefore the Spirit, promised to us, has not the task of inventing new and unheard-of revelations, or of forging a new kind of doctrine, to lead us away from the received doctrine of the gospel, but of sealing our minds with that very doctrine which is commended by the gospel."[77]

If we want to know what the Holy Spirit is saying, then, we must turn to the Scriptures because God has chosen to reveal himself in this particular way. "From this we readily understand that we ought zealously to apply ourselves both to read and to hearken to Scripture if indeed we want to receive any gain and benefit from the Spirit of God . . ."[78]

To those who argue that the Spirit cannot be subject to Scripture or tied to it, Calvin replies, "As if, indeed, this were ignominy for the Holy Spirit to be everywhere equal and in conformity with himself, to agree with

76. Ibid., 1.8.13.
77. Ibid., 1.9.1.
78. Ibid., 1.9.2.

himself in all things, and to vary in nothing!" and again, "But lest under his sign the spirit of Satan should creep in, he would have us recognize him in his own image, which he has stamped on the Scriptures. He is the Author of the Scriptures: he cannot vary and differ from himself. Hence he must ever remain just as he once revealed himself there."[79]

This unity of content and truth between the Word and the Spirit is vital for any true understanding of Calvin's position. He cannot conceive of any division between Word and Spirit, since this would undermine both:

> For by a kind of mutual bond the Lord has joined together the certainty of his Word and of his Spirit so that the perfect religion of the Word may abide in our minds when the Spirit, who causes us to contemplate God's face, shines; and that we in turn may embrace the Spirit with no fear of being deceived when we recognize him in his own image, namely, in the Word.[80]

Calvin is also firm in his response to those who suggest that when the Spirit came upon the church at Pentecost, revelation was no longer tied to the Scripture: "God did not bring forth his Word among men for the sake of a momentary display, intending at the coming of his Spirit to abolish it. Rather, he sent down the same Spirit by whose power he had dispensed the Word, to complete his work by the efficacious confirmation of the Word."[81] To put it another way, Scripture is itself the means by which we are enlightened by the Spirit. There is no separation of powers or division within God's revelation: "the Word is the instrument by which the Lord dispenses the illumination of his Spirit to believers. For they know no other Spirit than him who dwelt and spoke in the apostles, and by whose oracles they are continually recalled to the hearing of the Word."[82]

Throughout these early chapters of the *Institutes*, then, we see a clear and consistent picture emerging in Calvin's thought. God has chosen to

79. Ibid.
80. Ibid., 1.9.3.
81. Ibid.
82. Ibid.

make himself known. He did this through a general revelation, available to all human beings. This general revelation is sufficient to render human beings guilty before God for their failure to obey and serve him but insufficient to bring them to salvation. God has therefore also given a special revelation of himself by his Spirit. The Scriptures form part of this special revelation. They have come into existence through the work of the Holy Spirit acting upon men as they "spoke from God" (2 Peter 1:21).[83] They are "breathed out" by God (2 Tim. 3:16), and therefore we must affirm verbal inspiration. The Holy Spirit by his "internal testimony" persuades us that these writings, although written by men, are truly the Word of God. The same Holy Spirit enables us to understand their meaning and significance (1 Cor. 2:14).

Scripture and Tradition

A good deal of this teaching from Calvin was shared by his Catholic opponents. They too believed that the Scriptures were inspired by God and came into existence by the supernatural work of God's Spirit, they believed that Scripture is revelatory, and they taught that the Scriptures were the Word of God. We might put it like this: in the sixteenth century, there were many disputed issues between the church and the Reformers, but the nature and authority of Scripture was not one of them. Catholics and Reformers alike had a high view of Scripture. Indeed, as Richard Muller has shown, the medieval doctrine of the inspiration of Scripture "would pass over, virtually untouched by revision, into the sixteenth and seventeenth centuries."[84] Rather, the issue between Catholics and Reformers was the question of the relationship between this high view of Scripture and the doctrines of the church and of tradition. This issue can be expressed in the form of a question: Does Scripture have an innate authority because of its nature and form as a written text breathed out by God, or does its authority derive from the church?

Calvin's Catholic opponents argued that the church had decided which books should form the canon of Scripture and that therefore the Scriptures derived their authority from the church. Also, the church has a body

---

83. All quotations from the Bible in this chapter are from the ESV.
84. Muller, *Post-Reformation Reformed Dogmatics*, 2:49–50.

of tradition, separate from Scripture, given by the apostles and retained within the magisterium of the church, which has authority alongside Scripture. Indeed, when it comes to the interpretation of Scripture, the church has final authority to determine its meaning, using this "tradition" as a guide.

It is clear from the dogmatic structure outlined above that Calvin used his doctrine of the Holy Spirit as a means of answering these Catholic opponents. Scripture draws its authority not from the church, but from its nature as the Word of God, brought into being by the Holy Spirit. We recognize Scripture as the Word of God not because of the decision and testimony of the church, but because of the internal testimony of the Holy Spirit. We base our interpretation of Scripture not on what the church teaches, using its "tradition," but rather on the work of the Holy Spirit, who gives us the understanding. The church is to submit to Scripture, rather than Scripture's being a subordinate authority to that of the church.

Calvin and the Authority of Scripture

If we now return to the issue with which we began, namely, Calvin's view of the authority of Scripture, we are in a better position to deal with the question. Having seen the way in which Calvin related the knowledge of God with the person and work of the Holy Spirit, together with his application of this to a critique of the prevailing views of the authority of the church and of tradition, we can see more clearly to answer some of the difficult questions.

For example, why is it that Calvin can sometimes use language that appears to support a "dictation theory" of the origins of Scripture[85] and yet at other times (as we have seen) appear to be quite relaxed regarding apparent contradictions or other problems in the text? Murray and Woodbridge answer by focusing attention on the sections in Calvin that hold to a very "high" view of Scripture and arguing that the sections that

85. Calvin uses the expression "dictated by the Holy Spirit" in his commentary on 2 Timothy 3:16. See John Calvin, *The Second Epistle of Paul to the Corinthians, The Epistles of Paul to Timothy, Titus and Philemon*, ed. David W. Torrance and Thomas F. Torrance, in *Calvin's Commentaries* (Edinburgh: Oliver and Boyd, 1964), 330.

appear to take a different view must be interpreted in the light of these "clear" passages. Rogers and McKim solve the problem to their own satisfaction by arguing that Calvin regarded passages of Scripture that were dealing with "spiritual" matters to be inerrant, whereas passages dealing with such things as history, geography, and science could contain errors. Both Murray and Woodbridge on the one hand and Rogers and McKim on the other hand quote from Calvin to support their divergent views.

The problem with both of these positions is that there is too much focus on autographic text and its innate authority and not enough on the person and work of the Holy Spirit. Thus the argument revolves around which parts of Scripture are inerrant—all of it or only the spiritual parts? This is quite foreign to Calvin's own way of dealing with the problem. As we have seen, Calvin's emphasis on the work of the Holy Spirit shifts the argument away from autographic text and focuses instead on the relationship between Word and Spirit. As to its origins, the Scripture has come to us from God, through the work of the Holy Spirit in causing men to speak from God. As to its interpretation, we cannot understand it at all without the work of the Holy Spirit to give us understanding. In response to Rogers and McKim, then, Calvin is saying that one cannot distinguish between two types of Scripture (part inerrant and part errant) because all of it comes from God by his Spirit. In response to Murray and Woodbridge, Calvin is saying that the authority of Scripture does not depend on scientifically accurate autographic text but on the Spirit's inner persuasion that this text is the Word of God and therefore utterly reliable.

In other words, Calvin is arguing that God, speaking by his Spirit through his Word, is the final authority for Christians. Notice that the Scripture has authority only because it is the Word of God. The text itself is the vehicle through which God has chosen to speak, but it is not an end in itself. The relationship between Word and Spirit is critical. Without the Holy Spirit we would not have the Scriptures, we would not recognize Scripture as Scripture (the internal testimony), and we would not be able to understand the Scriptures.

Now, this should not be read in a neo-orthodox sense, as if somehow the actual text were not important but only the spiritual encounter between God and the believer occasioned by the text. For Calvin, the text of Scripture is vitally important, which is why he spends so much time discussing small details and seeking answers to difficult problems. In this respect, Murray and Woodbridge are far closer to Calvin's position than are Rogers and McKim. Nevertheless, Calvin is not as preoccupied with small textual matters as are many modern inerrantists, and he is quite comfortable with apparent contradictions and textual problems. The reason for this, as we have seen above, is that Calvin does not base his high view of the authority of Scripture on the edifice of a perfect autographic text but on the work of the Holy Spirit in the creation, recognition, and understanding of the Scriptures.

Conclusion

John Calvin, then, stands at the head of almost five hundred years of European Reformed theology in holding to the infallibility of Scripture. *Infallibility* means that Scripture is "un-fail-able," which agrees with the Hebrew prophet Isaiah, who said that God's Word does not fail to achieve the purposes for which it was given by God and that it does not return to him void (Isa. 55:11). Calvin, then, was strictly neither an "inerrantist" (the authority of Scripture is founded on an inerrant autographic text) nor an "errantist" (the authority of Scripture is founded on a partly errant and partly inerrant autographic text), but was instead an "infallibilist" (the authority of Scripture is based on the connection between Word and Spirit). This European Reformed doctrine of Scripture is to be seen in the Reformation and post-Reformation confessions of faith, almost all of which speak of the infallibility of Scripture, and was supremely expressed in the doctrine of organic inspiration as taught by Abraham Kuyper, Herman Bavinck, and others.

In practice, inerrantists and infallibilists are very close in their understanding of the authority of Scripture, but there are significant differences. Calvin could never be an "inerrantist" in the modern sense in which Baconian scientific method and rationalistic argument (Scripture came from God, God is perfect, therefore the autographa must have been perfect) play a very strong role in establishing the doctrinal position. Many inerrantists (especially those who are fundamentalists) seem to want all the benefits of dictation theory while denying that they believe in any such thing. This whole method was foreign to Calvin's own theological method and to his stated conclusions. He was quite clear that God is free to do as he pleases, and if he chose to use human beings to communicate his Word, then so be it, with all the consequences flowing from that.

Like Calvin, we can affirm that the Scriptures are God-breathed, having been written when men spoke from God, as they were carried along by the Holy Spirit. The Scriptures are infallible as originally given. This means that, on the one hand, there is a need for textual criticism (against fundamentalism), and on the other hand, we can affirm the utter reliability of God's Word (against all forms of liberal theology and its theological descendants). That is to say, the Scriptures are without error in all that they affirm. Since God superintended the work of writing the Scriptures, they are precisely as he intended them to be—although, having chosen to use human beings, he did not overrule their humanity or dictate the Scriptures to them. The Scriptures thus display the personal literary style of each author and the characteristics of the period in which they were written, while remaining in every respect the Word of God himself.

17

CALVIN'S EUCHARISTIC
ECCLESIOLOGY

MICHAEL HORTON

ommonplace now in ecclesiological discussions broadly is the
idea that the Eucharist *gives* the church. In other words, the
Lord's Supper is not simply something that the church does; it
is the source of its existence. Consequently, one's view of the Supper will
shape (or reveal) one's wider ecclesiological horizon.

Reformed Christians should have no reason to disagree with this
assumption, as long as it is qualified. I suggest these two qualifications:
First, Lutheran and Reformed theologies speak frequently of the church
as the "creation of the Word" (*creatura verbi*).[1] Therefore, it is not the
Eucharist by itself that gives the church, but the *Word* that is delivered
through preaching and baptism as well as through the Lord's Table. Properly speaking, it is the *Spirit* who gives (or creates) the church by his

---

1. On this point, see Michael Horton, *People and Place: A Covenant Ecclesiology* (Louisville: WJK, 2008), chap. 2. Many of the themes in this essay are explored more extensively
throughout this volume.

Word through the means of grace. Second, different understandings of the Eucharist "give" different ecclesiologies.

Generally speaking, a Roman Catholic formulation of the Supper as the *transubstantiation* of creatures (bread and wine) into the body and blood of Christ is formative in the development of an ecclesiology of the *totus Christus* that treats the visible church and Jesus Christ as virtually identical. On the other hand, a more characteristically "Zwinglian" eucharistic theology tends to separate the sign from the reality signified in such a way that whatever is creaturely, visible, and physical is incapable of being identified with God's saving activity. From Huldrych Zwingli to Karl Barth, this connection between a more Platonic dualism with respect to the means of grace is carried over into an explicit dualism between the visible and invisible church or the activity of believers (and the church) on one side and the activity of God on the other.

My argument in this essay is that John Calvin's controversial understanding of the Supper is an outworking of his broader theological emphases and offers a rich resource for contemporary ecclesiological reflection and practice. For Calvin, as we will see, creatures never become divine. Sin is not an ontological weakness, but ethical transgression. Therefore, sinners are not in need of being elevated by grace beyond nature toward the supernatural; rather, they are in need of being saved and sanctified in all their creatureliness. While remaining creatures, bread, wine, and the church are nevertheless sanctified by God for his use in his own saving action. Whereas Rome contends that God makes creatures divine and Zwinglianism contrasts divine action and creaturely means, Calvin held that the triune God works through creatures, liberating them to belong to him.

Owen F. Cummings suggests that humanity, for Calvin, is "eucharistic man."[2] And according to B. A. Gerrish, "the entire oeuvre of John Calvin may be described as a Eucharistic theology, shot through with the themes of grace and gratitude."[3] "The holy banquet is simply the liturgical enactment of the theme of grace and gratitude that lies at the heart of Calvin's entire

2. Owen F. Cummings, "The Reformers and Eucharistic Ecclesiology," *One in Christ* 33.1 (1997): 47–54.

3. B. A. Gerrish, *Grace and Gratitude: The Eucharistic Theology of John Calvin* (Minneapolis: Augsburg Fortress, 1993), 52.

theology, whether one chooses to call it a system or not ... It is this focal image of the banquet that made Calvin's doctrine (in his own estimate) simple, edifying, and irenic."[4] After summarizing the relationship of Eucharist and ecclesia in other traditions, I will focus on Calvin's contribution.

Confusing Christ with the Church: The Many as One

Formulated at the Fourth Lateran Council (1215) and refined in elaborate Aristotelian splendor by Thomas Aquinas, the dogma of transubstantiation was set forth in detail in Session 13 of the Council of Trent. The Supper is a memorial, an atoning sacrifice, and a thanksgiving (eucharist).[5] "As often as the sacrifice of the Cross by which 'Christ our Pasch has been sacrificed' is celebrated on the altar, the work of our redemption is carried out."[6] Thus, the sacrifice is ongoing. In fact, "The sacrifice of Christ and the sacrifice of the Eucharist are one single sacrifice," with Christ as the victim and the priest (on behalf of the worshipers) as the one who offers it to the Father.[7] In the consecration, the bread and the wine are converted into the body and blood of Christ, so that it is not only proper but required that believers offer adoration of the Host (i.e., the consecrated bread and wine).[8] At the eucharistic altar, "all laws of nature are suspended," wrote Pope Leo XIII, and "the whole substance of the bread and wine [is] changed into the Body and Blood of Christ," including his physical organs.[9]

The dogma of transubstantiation shapes Roman Catholic ecclesiology. In the wake of Trent, the church became understood as a legal institution with power over all souls and bodies.[10] The bodily absence

4. Ibid., 20, 13.

5. U.S. Catholic Church, *Catechism of the Catholic Church* (New York: Doubleday, 2003), 335, 342.

6. Ibid., 343, quoting "Lumen gentium," 3 (November 21, 1964), from the Second Vatican Council.

7. Ibid., 344, referring to the Council of Trent (1562): DS 1743.

8. Ibid., 346–47.

9. Pope Leo XIII, *Mirae Caritalis*, in *The Great Encyclical Letters of Pope Leo XIII* (Rockford, IL: TAN Books, 1995), 524.

10. Robert Bellarmine, *De controversies*, tom. 2, liber 3, *De ecclesia militante*, cap. 2, "De definitione Ecclesiae" (Naples: Giuliano, 1857), 75.

of Christ since his ascension is not a problem because he has returned in and as the church. Although he rules invisibly through his omnipresent divinity, his earthly-visible form is his body, the church. This is an implication of an extreme version of Augustine's *totus Christus* concept, according to which, as Augustine himself said, the church not only is one in Christ but is in fact made "Christ."[11] Kingdom and church, head and members, the work of Christ and the work of the church, eschatology and history began to merge. There is nothing questionable, ambiguous, or precarious about the church's location or identity in this age. It is simply the kingdom of God—the historical replacement for the natural body of Jesus Christ, with all visible power flowing from the visible head (the pope). "The Church is ordinated towards the invisible, spiritual and eternal. . . . But the Church is not only invisible. *Because she is the Kingdom of God*, she is not a haphazard collection of individuals, but an ordered system of regularly subordinated parts." Through this hierarchy, *"the divine is objectivised, is incarnated in the community*, and precisely and only in so far as it is a community. . . . So the Church possesses the Spirit of Christ, not as a many of single individuals, nor as a sum of spiritual personalities, but as the compact unity of the faithful, as a community that transcends the individual personalities . . . , *the many as one*." Christ's mission is "to reunite to God mankind as a unity, as a whole, *and not this or that individual man*."[12] Not only *unity* (common fellowship in Christ) but *unicity* (numerical oneness in a hierarchy with a papal head) is Karl Adam's understanding of the church.[13]

In a somewhat chilling illustration of his time and place, Adam passionately asserts, "One God, one faith, one love, one single man: that is the stirring thought which inspires the Church's pageantry and gives it artistic form."[14] Echoing Hegel, he declares, "For only in the whole can the divine realise itself, only in the totality of men and not in the individual."[15] As a

11. Augustine, *Confessions*, 13.28.

12. Karl Adam, *The Spirit of Catholicism* (New York: Crossroad, 1997), 31–32 (emphasis added).

13. Ibid., 38.

14. Ibid., 41. Like many other Catholic and Protestant theologians of his generation, Adam at first welcomed Hitler's ascendancy. According to Krieg, after declaring for Hitler, six months later Adam criticized the regime (xii).

15. Ibid., 53.

consequence, "the structural organs of the Body of Christ, as that is realised in space and time, are pope and bishops."[16] This empirical polity—the observable structure of the ecclesiastical hierarchy—*constitutes* the visibility of the church in the world. Where is the true church? The answer is obvious and unambiguous: the historical institution that possesses the apostolic succession of bishops under the primacy of the bishop of Rome. For all these reasons, says Adam, "the Catholic Church as the Body of Christ, as the realisation in the world of the Kingdom of God, is the Church of Humanity."[17]

The same view is taught by Joseph Cardinal Ratzinger, now Pope Benedict XVI, in his book *Called to Communion: Understanding the Church Today* (1996), where he wrote, "The temporal and ontological priority lies with the universal Church; a Church that was not catholic would not even have ecclesial reality."[18] Apart from papal primacy, not even a valid succession of bishops is adequate.[19]

> If Orthodoxy starts from the bishop and from the Eucharistic community over which he presides, the point on which the Reformed position is built is the Word: the Word of God gathers men and creates "community." The proclamation of the Gospel produces—so they say—congregation, and this congregation is the "Church."[20]

The marriage analogy often employed in Scripture suggests as much: the two become "one flesh," yet in such a way that they remain two people. Yet for Rome, the universal is ontologically supreme.[21] This is due in part to the difference between a Word-generated communion and a hierarchical unicity drawing its source from a single bishop. The former creates a community of hearers and heralds, while the latter engenders a "corporate personality" (Ratzinger's term, from German idealism). Ratzinger can go so far as to assert that the pope is "placed in direct responsibility to the

16. Ibid., 97.

17. Ibid., 159–65.

18. Joseph Cardinal Ratzinger, *Called to Communion: Understanding the Church Today*, trans. Adrian Walker (San Francisco: Ignatius Press, 1996), 44.

19. Ibid., 79–80.

20. Ibid., 80–81.

21. Ibid., 82.

Lord . . . to embody and secure the unity of Christ's word and work."[22] As a consequence, "Loss of this element of unity with the successors of Peter wounds the church 'in the essence of its being as church.' "[23]

Anglo-Catholic theologian Graham Ward goes so far as to suggest that the "displacement" of Jesus-in-the-flesh is not a loss, but a transubstantiation of his personal existence in and as the church. So once again we return to the basic substance of the "ascent of mind" that can be traced from Origen to Schleiermacher: the disappearance of Jesus is not a problem because he did not really disappear after all, but is just as present—or rather, more fully present—today in and as the church. Despite Ward's disclaimer that his "interpretation of the ascension is not in accord with Origen's 'ascension of the mind rather than of the body,' "[24] his arguments do little to allay the contrary judgment. According to this rather extreme version of the notion of Christ's ubiquity, "We have no access to the body of the gendered Jew . . . *It is pointless because the Church is now the body of Christ, so to understand the body of Jesus we can only examine what the Church is and what it has to say* concerning the nature of that body as scripture attests it."[25] "As Gregory of Nyssa points out, in his thirteenth sermon on Song," Ward quotes, " 'he who sees the Church looks directly at Christ.' "[26]

This emphasis on the church as the ongoing incarnation of Christ and the extension of his redeeming work in history is increasingly prominent in evangelical circles, especially in theologies of mission.[27] In this case, it

22. Quoted in Miroslav Volf, *After Our Likeness: The Church as the Image of the Trinity* (Grand Rapids: Eerdmans, 1997), 58.

23. Ibid., 59. Volf also notes on the same page that Ratzinger's claim, albeit before Vatican II, "The *sedes apostolica* as such is Rome, so that one can say that *communio catholica* = *communio Romana*; only those who commune with Rome are standing in the true, that is, catholic *communio*; whomever Rome excommunicates is no longer in the *communio catholica*, that is, in the unity of the church."

24. Graham Ward, *Cities of God* (London and New York: Routledge, 2000), 180.

25. Ibid. (emphasis added).

26. Ibid., 116.

27. Pioneers of a more explicitly "incarnational missiology" include Sherwood G. Lingenfelter and Marvin K. Mayer, *Ministering Cross-Culturally: An Incarnational Model for Personal Relationships* (Grand Rapids: Baker, 1986), and Charles van Engen and Jude Tiersma, *God So Loves the City: Seeking a Theology for Urban Mission* (Monrovia, CA: MARC, 1994). Latin American theologies of liberation have also shaped this emphasis, especially Orlando Costas, *Christ beyond the Gate* (Maryknoll, NY: Orbis, 1982). For a balanced theological analysis of

is not the church as an institution or its official ministry of preaching, sacrament, and discipline, but the church as a movement of disciples that is said to extend the incarnation—not principally by proclamation and sacrament, but by "living the gospel" among their neighbors. Especially in the emergent-church movement, the notion of the church as the ongoing incarnation merges with an essentially Anabaptist ecclesiology. God "creates the church as a missional community to join him in his mission of saving the world."[28] One often encounters the counsel attributed to Francis of Assisi: "Always preach the gospel, and when necessary use words." Although "living the gospel" has long been a familiar refrain in evangelical piety, this approach is increasingly radicalized, by relocating the church's identity and mission to its work in the world more than the means of grace in local churches.[29] Although the ecclesiology differs at important points with that of Rome, the tendency to collapse Christology into ecclesiology just as surely threatens the uniqueness of Christ's person and work as the head who saves his body and sends his Spirit to gather his body, build it up into him, and proclaim his completed work to the ends of the earth.

Separating Christ and the Church: The One as Many

If, according to Roman Catholic ecclesiology, the faith of the believer tends to be absorbed into the faith of the church, the obverse is evident in free-church ecclesiologies. The personal decision of each person to believe in Christ and to join a church actually constitutes ecclesial existence. In evangelical contexts, the church is often regarded chiefly as a resource

the concept, see J. Todd Billings, "'Incarnational Ministry': A Christological Evaluation and Proposal," *Missiology: An International Review* 32.2 (April 2004): 187–201.

28. Brian McLaren, *A Generous Orthodoxy* (Grand Rapids: Zondervan, 2004), 108. Drawing eclectically from ancient and medieval Christian mysticism, Anabaptism, Zen Buddhism, and liberation theology, McLaren even speaks of "The Great Chain of Being" (ibid., 279–80). This is only one of many instances that could be cited to indicate that the "overcoming estrangement" paradigm of Plato, Neoplatonism, Hegel, and New Age thought can find popular expression in evangelical "low-church" traditions as well as in others.

29. See, for example, I. Mosby, *Emerging and Fresh Expressions of Church* (London: Moot Community Publishing, 2007), 54–55; I. Mosby, *The Becoming of G-D* (Oxford: YTC Press, 2008).

for fellowship and a platform for individuals to serve the body and the world in various ministries.[30] Especially when wedded to an Arminian soteriology, a voluntaristic emphasis emerges, with human decision as the contractual basis for both conversion and ecclesial existence.[31] From this perspective, the church has come increasingly to be regarded primarily as a service provider for a personal (unique and individual) relationship with Christ. Actual membership in the visible church can be left to private judgment, and in some cases formal membership does not even exist. Taken to a radical extreme, it is now being argued that the visible church and its public ministry are even impediments to personal growth and Christian mission.[32]

Not all tendencies to set Christ in sharp contrast with the church fit neatly into the preceding description. For example, Karl Barth was a Swiss socialist, not an American individualist. Nevertheless, his "Zwinglian" emphases are shared by many contemporary evangelicals. His attraction to an independent ecclesiology, his rejection of the sacraments as means of grace, and his explicit rejection of infant baptism in 4.4 point up what seems to me to be the dominant tendency of his thought that is already discernible in the first edition of his *Römerbrief.*

Going beyond Zwingli (though, ironically, more closely echoing Martin Luther), Barth says that the true church belongs to the "submarine island of

30. At least in the history of pietism, the individual or circle of believers thought to be more truly earnest about the Christian life remained members of the wider church. In many forms of nondenominational evangelicalism, especially since the "Jesus movement" of the 1970s, church membership is optional or even eliminated. Seeking to replicate the worship of the first Christians (with dubious historical interpretations), the house-church movement is one of many examples of the "triumph of the laity," as it is sometimes called. In fact, as George Barna observes (and celebrates), the coming generation that he identifies as the "Revolutionaries" insists on finding alternative forms of spiritual edification and community to the organized church (*Revolution* [Wheaton, IL: Tyndale House, 2005]). Just how revolutionary this is may be open to debate, since pietism and revivalism have a long history of such experimentation.

31. See, for example, Stanley Grenz, *Theology for the Community of God* (Nashville: Broadman & Holman, 1997), 611.

32. The Willow Creek Association (led by Bill Hybels) concluded that as Christians mature, their dependence on the church diminishes and they need to become "self-feeders" (Greg Hawkins and Cally Parkinson, *Reveal: Where Are You?* [South Barrington, IL: Willow Creek Association, 2007]). George Barna (in *Revolution*) argues that most believers will increasingly abandon local churches and receive their spiritual resources from the Internet.

the 'Now' of divine revelation" that lies beneath observable reality.[33] In *Romans*, he speaks explicitly of "the *contrast* between the Gospel and the Church."[34] Christ is the only sacrament. In fact, not only is there a difference between the sign and its eschatological fullness, but the "invisible church" is taken to extreme limits when Barth writes, "In the heavenly Jerusalem of Revelation nothing is more finally significant than *the church's complete absence:* 'And I saw no temple therein.'"[35] Totalizing ecclesiologies may be faulted for an overrealized eschatology. Barth's dualistic ecclesiology is not underrealized, however; he simply does not have any place for the church even in the consummation. Therefore, "the activity of the community is related to the Gospel only in so far as it is no more than a crater formed by the explosion of a shell and seeks to be no more than a void in which the Gospel reveals itself."[36]

One of Barth's great achievements was to turn attention back to Jesus. He is properly concerned to see that Christ's reconciling work is in need of no further supplementation, no historical development, thus countering liberal historicism and synergism. The church is not an extension of Christ's person and work.[37] There is hardly a better statement of a covenantal ecclesiology than the following: "What constitutes the being of man in this [covenantal] sphere is not a *oneness* of being but a genuine *togetherness* of being with God."[38] Yet the same logic (actualism) that keeps Barth from identifying God's action directly with human words and deeds in his doctrine of revelation is also decisive for his ecclesiology.[39] Barth offers important warnings about collapsing Jesus Christ into

33. Karl Barth, *The Epistle to the Romans*, trans. Edwyn C. Hoskyns from the 6th ed. (London: Oxford University Press, 1933), 304; cf. 396 for the same analogy.

34. Ibid., 340 (emphasis added).

35. Ibid. (emphasis added). That this is the expression of 1920 should perhaps be taken into account here.

36. Ibid., 36.

37. CD, 4.3:7, 327; 4.2:132.

38. Ibid., 3.2:141 (emphasis added).

39. It is interesting that although Calvin rejects Erasmus's translations of *koinōnia* as *societas* and *communio*, in favor of stronger participationist language, Barth prefers *Gemeinde* (*community, society, fellowship*) to *Kirche* (*church*). To be sure, Barth affirms the New Testament motif of *koinōnia*, founded on Trinitarian presuppositions: the persons (modes of being) in communion with each other; the communion between God and human beings; the communion of believers with each other, and indeed with all creatures. Each communion is a different kind of *koinōnia*, but is ultimately grounded in this Trinitarian perichoresis (ibid., 256–60). There are more recent historical reasons,

the church.[40] In my view, however, it represents an overcorrection of the neo-Hegelian trajectory.

Superior to the contractual and existentialist-actualist versions we have considered is the revised free-church ecclesiology proposed by Miroslav Volf in his remarkable work *After Our Likeness*. He affirms the Reformers' view of the church as "mother" and distances himself from the counsel of Separatist leader John Smyth that those who are "born again . . . should no longer need means of grace," since the persons of the Godhead "are better than all scriptures, or creatures whatsoever."[41] Furthermore, Volf emphasizes the priority of God's gracious activity over human response in *salvation*. He wrestles honestly with the tendency of free-church ecclesiologies to become captive to modern individualism and consumerism and brings a richer eschatological and pneumatological perspective to bear.[42] Nevertheless, Volf's own ecclesiology remains rather subjective, with the faith of believers rather than the marks of preaching and sacrament as definitive of ecclesial existence. "That which the church *is*, namely, believing and confessing human beings, is precisely that which (as a rule) also constitutes it."[43] Not even the sacraments are ultimately constitutive, but "are a public representation of such confession."[44]

Evangelical theologian Stanley Grenz observes, "The post-Reformation discussion of the *vera ecclesia* [true church] formed the historical context

of course, for preferring *Gemeinde* to *Kirche*: namely, the way these are distinguished in German Protestantism.

40. Better than Barth's treatment, in my estimation, is John Webster's in *Word and Church* (Edinburgh: T&T Clark, 2001), 227ff.

41. Volf, *After Our Likeness*, 161–62.

42. Volf points out that the privatization of faith that warps ecclesiology also makes free-church ecclesiologies more effective in contemporary cultures. He recognizes that when decisions have been privatized, "the transmission of faith" is threatened (ibid., 16). Yet he also judges that this adaptability to a culture of personal choice renders such ecclesiologies especially effective in our day (17). "Whether they want to or not, Free Churches often function as 'homogeneous units' specializing in the specific needs of specific social classes and cultural circles, and then in mutual competition try to sell their commodity at dumping prices to the religious consumer in the supermarket of life projects; the customer is king and the one best suited to evaluate his or her own religious needs and from whom nothing more is required than a bit of loyalty and as much money as possible. If the Free Churches want to contribute to the salvation of Christendom, they themselves must first be healed" (18).

43. Ibid., 150nn93, 151.

44. Ibid., 153.

for the emergence of the covenant idea as the focal understanding of the nature of the church."[45] With their insistence on the marks of the church, "the Reformers shifted the focus to Word and Sacrament," but the Anabaptists and Baptists "took yet a further step," advocating a congregational ecclesiology. "This view asserts that the true church is essentially people standing in voluntary covenant with God."[46] The decision concerning baptism is decisive for this conception of the church. Especially in the context of Christendom, Baptist and free-church traditions have offered a powerful witness to the importance of personal faith. Yet there is an obvious connection between understanding the sacraments as symbols of human commitment rather than God's means of grace and the definition of the church as the aggregate of regenerate believers.

But the Lutheran and Reformed view that the visible church consists of believers *together with their children* violates the rule that is basic to an independent church polity: namely, a *voluntary* covenant, which entails not only the independence of local churches but the independence of individuals within them until they mutually agree on the terms of that relationship. "No longer did the corporate whole take precedence over the individual as in the medieval model," notes Grenz. Rather, individuals formed the church, rather than vice versa. "As a result, in the order of salvation the believer—and not the church—stands first in priority."[47] "Because the coming together of believers in mutual covenant constitutes the church, it is the covenant community of individuals," although it has a history as well.[48]

One *and* Many: A Covenantal Interpretation of Unity and Catholicity

I have defended the Reformation claim that the church is the creation of the Word. What constitutes the unity and catholicity of the church? As Paul Avis has observed, "Reformation theology is largely dominated

45. Grenz, *Theology for the Community of God*, 609.
46. Ibid., 610–11.
47. Ibid.
48. Ibid., 614.

by two questions: 'How can I obtain a gracious God?' and 'Where can I find the true Church?' The two questions are inseparably related . . ."[49] The Lutheran and Reformed confessions offer the same response to both questions: wherever God's Word is truly preached and the sacraments are administered according to Christ's command.[50] The unity of the church arises from its origin, and since the canon (even before its formal inscripturation) created and still creates the church, this unity cannot be lodged either in a historical office or in personal experience. For the remainder of this essay, I hope to show the vital connection between Calvin's understanding of the Supper and his eucharistic ecclesiology.

The Reformation Debate

As Douglas Farrow has argued, Christ's ascension is one of the most significant and neglected topics in ecclesiological reflection.[51] For Origen, it was "more of an ascent of mind than of body," and even Augustine thought that the absence of Christ in the flesh was not a real problem, since his divinity is omnipresent and his humanity is visible in and as the church.[52] Luther had no illusions of grandeur when it came to identifying the church as a substitute for Jesus, but his own view of the Supper failed to reckon fully with the ascension and therefore with the absence of Christ on the earth in the flesh until his return. Zwingli's separation of sign and reality revealed a nearly Nestorian separation of Christ's two natures. Although the ascension played an important role in his polemic against Luther, Zwingli left the matter there. Christ's bodily absence is not a loss for the church in the present, because he saved us by his divine nature and Christ is omnipresent in power according to his divinity. Farrow judges that Calvin's unique contribution was to turn the spotlight back onto the ascension and the real absence as well as the real presence of Christ in this present age, through the power of the Holy Spirit. In this time

49. Paul D. L. Avis, *The Church in the Theology of the Reformers* (Atlanta: John Knox Press, 1981), 1.
50. The Reformed confessions added discipline, which I discuss below.
51. Douglas Farrow, *Ascension and Ecclesia* (Edinburgh: T&T Clark, 1999).
52. Ibid., 97, 119–20.

between Christ's advents, the question is not how to bring Christ down to us. "It is *we* who require eucharistic relocation."[53]

The Lutheran Position

Just as the water of baptism cleaves to the Word and Christ is present according to both natures, the bread and wine, consecrated by the words of institution, communicate the whole Christ to believers and unbelievers alike (though, in the latter case, in judgment). God's Word alone makes these ordinary elements bearers of Christ (Large Catechism 5.9, 14). The Word brings forgiveness through the sacrament (Large Catechism 5.32–33, 35). Therefore, the bread and wine are only secondarily "signs by which people might be identified outwardly as Christians"; they are primarily "signs and testimonies of God's will toward us" (Augsburg Confession 13.1; Epitome 7.27; Solid Declaration 7.115).

Luther strongly rejected the Roman Catholic doctrine of transubstantiation (that is, that the bread and wine become the body and blood of Christ), declaring, "We do not make Christ's body out of the bread ... Nor do we say that his body comes into existence out of the bread [i.e., impanation]. We say that his body, which long ago was made and came into existence, is present when we say, 'This is my body.' For Christ commands us to say not, 'Let this become my body,' or, 'Make my body there,' but, 'This is my body.'"[54] Instead of saying that the bread and wine *become* the body and blood of Christ, Christ comes *to* the bread and wine *with* his body and blood. The sign and the signified become "coupled," according to Luther's Large Catechism (5.18).

Luther's view is sometimes identified as "consubstantiation" because of the belief that Christ's body is present "in," "with," and "under" the consecrated bread and wine. Lutherans, however, generally eschew this term because it suggests a local (circumscribed) presence of Christ's body, which the Formula of Concord rejects as "gross, carnal, and Capernaitic."[55]

---

53. Ibid., 176–77.
54. Martin Luther, *Luther's Works*, American ed., ed. Jaroslav Pelikan and Helmut Lehmann, 55 vols. (St. Louis and Philadelphia: CPH and Fortress Press, 1955–86), 37.187; cf. Formula of Concord, Solid Declaration 7.59.
55. Formula of Concord, Epitome 7.42; Solid Declaration 7.127; Triglot Concordia 817, 1015.

Nevertheless, with the bread and the wine Christ's body and blood are physically received by all who partake, with the mouth, and not simply through faith. This feeding is just as true for the unworthy (*manducatio indignorum*). The Lutheran view emphasizes that the words of institution, "This is my body" and "This is my blood," are not figurative (Solid Declaration 7.59) and also stresses the importance of the words "given for you" and "shed for you" (Shorter Catechism 6.6). Edmund Schlink explains, "When the Sacrament of the Altar is defined as 'the true body and blood of our Lord Jesus Christ, under the bread and wine' (SC VI, 2),'"the true body" is to be understood as the body crucified and now glorified.[56] Believers have life from Christ and in Christ not merely according to his divinity or spirituality but in his flesh (Apology 10.3). Therefore, in the Supper Christ's body and blood are present "in, with, and under the bread and wine," and thereby Christ himself is "offered and orally received."[57] Or, in the words of the Formula of Concord (Solid Declaration 7.35, 37), the body of Christ is given "under the bread, with the bread, in the bread."

Therefore, everyone who communicates receives Christ's body and blood, but "the promise is useless unless faith accepts it" (Apology 13). According to the Formula of Concord (7.7), even "the unworthy and unbelieving receive the true body and blood of Christ," but their "receiving turns to their judgment and condemnation, unless they be converted and repent (1 Cor. 11:27, 29)." The Supper communicates the benefits not only of justification but of sanctification as well, "for the strengthening and encouragement of the sinner in the battle against sin."[58] In this view, the Supper is emphatically not a sacrifice that we offer to God (which vitiates its character as a means of grace), but is God's gift of his Son for us and to us.

How can Christ be present bodily at every eucharistic celebration, in, with, and under the bread and the wine? In other words, is his bodily presence affirmed at the expense of having a real body? At this point, arguments broke out among Lutherans themselves, and according to Schlink,

56. Edmund Schlink, *Theology of the Lutheran Confessions* (Philadelphia: Fortress Press, 1975), 161–62.
57. Ibid., 169.
58. Ibid., 163.

they were not fully resolved even in the Formula of Concord.[59] Ultimately, this is a Christological issue, treated in chapter 13. To avoid a Nestorian separation of Christ's natures, for Lutherans (and the Reformed agree with this point) the real presence of Christ can mean only the presence of the *whole* Christ. Yet to affirm the presence of the whole Christ at every eucharistic celebration, Lutherans offered the novel argument that Christ is omnipresent in the flesh because his divine attributes penetrate his humanity. Christ's exaltation to the right hand of the Father refers not to a place but to a position (Solid Declaration 8.28). This view came to be known as *ubiquity* (ability to be omnipresent).

The Zwinglian Position

Among others, Geoffrey W. Bromiley points out that not even Zwingli was a "Zwinglian," since this position has come to be identified with a "real absence" position.[60] Zwingli did believe that Christ was present in the Supper. Nevertheless, Zwingli's own writing makes it clear that this was only according to his divinity and power. For Zwingli (like Augustine), it did not seem to matter as much that Christ had bodily ascended, since he is omnipresent in his divinity.

Crucial in Zwingli's conception was a dualistic view of spirit and matter. "For faith springs not from things accessible to sense nor are they objects of faith," he insists.[61] Of course, if this view is followed consistently (which, happily, he did not do), one wonders how faith could come by *hearing* (Rom. 10:17). To suggest that in the sacrament one fed on the true body of Christ but in a spiritual manner (which became the confessional Reformed position) was, to Zwingli, as ludicrous as saying that he was chewed with the teeth.[62] In fact, Zwingli concludes, faith "draws us to the invisible and fixes all our hopes on that. For it dwelleth not amidst the sensible and bodily, and hath nothing

59. Ibid., 189–93.

60. Geoffrey W. Bromiley, *Zwingli and Bullinger*, Library of Christian Classics, vol. 24 (Philadelphia: Westminster Press, 1953), 179–84.

61. Huldrych Zwingli, *Commentary on True and False Religion*, ed. Samuel Macauley Jackson and Clarence Nevin Heller, trans. Samuel Macauley Jackson (Durham, NC: Labyrinth Press, 1981), 214.

62. Ibid.

in common therewith."[63] In fact, this dualistic ontology underwrites a not-so-subtle Nestorianizing Christology, as in Zwingli's remark, "We must note in passing that Christ is our salvation by virtue of that part of his nature by which he came down from heaven, not of that by which he was born of an immaculate virgin, though he had to suffer and die by this part."[64] Luther and Zwingli realized that they were working with different conceptions not only of the Supper, but of Christology and even of cosmology.

The Reformed Position

Although Martin Bucer and other Reformed leaders had already reached a certain agreement with Luther (especially in the Wittenberg Concord), Calvin filled in the arguments for a Reformed consensus. Affirming with Luther the maxim *distinctio sed non separatio*, Calvin refused to separate the sign (bread and wine) from the signified (body and blood of Christ). Yet with Zwingli he held that the doctrine of ubiquity (Christ's omnipresence even in the flesh) led to a "monstrous phantasm" rather than an actual (albeit glorified) human person. Calvin recognized that the question about *where* Christ is was decisive for *who* Christ is in his post-resurrection existence, but it was the latter that most concerned him. Consequently, he kept his focus on the economy of grace: descent, ascent, and parousia *in the flesh.*[65]

So whereas Rome, Luther, and Zwingli concentrated on how Christ was or was not present *in the bread and the wine*, Calvin directed his atten-

63. Ibid.

64. Ibid., 204. Besides Gerrish's work, a growing number of helpful studies have appeared, including Ronald S. Wallace, *Calvin's Doctrine of Word and Sacrament* (Grand Rapids: Baker, 1988); Jill Rait, *The Eucharistic Theology of Theodore Beza: Development of the Reformed Doctrine*, AAR Studies in Religion (Chambersburg, PA: American Academy of Religion, 1972); Keith Mathison, *Given for You: Reclaiming Calvin's Doctrine of the Lord's Supper* (Phillipsburg, NJ: P&R Publishing, 2002); and Leonard J. Vander Zee, *Christ, Baptism and the Lord's Supper: Recovering the Sacraments for Evangelical Worship* (Downers Grove, IL: InterVarsity Press, 2004). Where Reformed theology has attracted a growing following among evangelicals, the Reformed understanding of the church and sacraments has been often treated as nonessential to the system or a Zwinglian interpretation is regarded as an adequate Reformed option.

65. Farrow, *Ascension and Ecclesia*, 204, points out that Calvin—especially in the eucharistic debate—picked up on the historical economy and reckoned with the real absence and real presence of Christ in ways that had been blocked by the medieval "ascent of mind."

tion to how Christ is present *in action* in the sacrament even though he is absent from earth in the flesh until his return. This required a robustly pneumatological understanding of the sacrament that had been more fully developed in the East but was lacking in Western debates. Reckoning more resolutely with the bodily ascension of Jesus Christ in the flesh than Rome or Luther, Calvin nevertheless affirmed, against Zwingli, a true feeding on the very body and blood of Christ in the sacrament. As strongly as Calvin rejected the Lutheran doctrine of ubiquity, he and his Reformed colleagues (other than those in Zurich) were convinced that they did not disagree with Wittenberg over the question of *what* was received in the Supper.[66]

Even Zwingli's successor, Heinrich Bullinger, distanced himself from the view of the sacraments as "bare and naked signs," both in the Second Helvetic Confession and in his consensus statement with Calvin.[67] Calvin could assert regarding their consensus, "Although we distinguish, as is proper, between the signs and the things signified, yet we do not sever the reality from the signs."[68] After affirming the sacramental union of sign and signified, the Second Helvetic Confession rejects "the doctrine of those who speak of the sacraments just as common signs, not sanctified and effectual. Nor do we approve of those who despise the visible aspect of the sacraments because of the invisible, and so believe the signs to be superfluous because they think they already enjoy the things themselves, as the Messalians are said to have held."[69] It is difficult to imagine that Bullinger did not know that he was rejecting a prominent line of his predecessor's argument.

66. "Later, after Marburg," as B. A. Gerrish points out, "it was repeatedly argued that the point at issue between the Lutherans and the Reformed was no longer whether, but only how, the body and blood of Christ were present in the Sacrament. Calvin himself so argued" (*Grace and Gratitude*, 8). Since even Bullinger (Zwingli's successor) came to embrace the sacramental union of sign and signified, the focus was on *what* is received (Christ and all his benefits) in the Supper, rather than on the *manner* of eating—in other words, presence as such.

67. The *Consensus Tigurinus* can be found in *CO*, 35.733, and in ET in John Calvin, *Tracts and Treatises*, trans. Henry Beveridge (Grand Rapids: Eerdmans, 1958), 2:212–20. See Timothy George, "John Calvin and the Agreement of Zurich (1549)," in *John Calvin and the Church: A Prism of Reform*, ed. Timothy George (Louisville: WJK, 1990), 42–58.

68. *Consensus Tigurinus*, OS, 2.249.

69. The Second Helvetic Confession, chap. 19, in PCUSA, *The Book of Confessions* (Louisville: Office of the General Assembly, 1991), 5:180–81.

Calvin on the Supper

"From the very first," notes Gerrish, Calvin "was convinced that Zwingli was wrong about the principal agent in both Baptism and the Lord's Supper. A sacrament is first and foremost an act of God or Christ rather than of the candidate, the communicant, or the church."[70] Whereas Zwingli can only force a choice between God's action and creaturely action, Calvin says, "Whatever implements God employs, they detract nothing from his primary operation."[71]

The Nature of the Supper

First of all, "*The Lord's Supper is a gift.* This is fundamental to the whole orientation of Calvin's thinking on the Sacrament," and signals a decisive departure from a Zwinglian conception, which Calvin found to be "scarcely less defective than the Roman Catholic." Especially in the *Institutes*, 4.17.6, Calvin underscores this point that "the Supper is a gift; it does not merely remind us of a gift." As with receiving the gospel through the preached Word, in the sacrament we are receivers: it is "an *actio mere passiva* (a 'purely passive action')."[72] The human response to a gift is thanksgiving, says Calvin, which is why it is called the Eucharist, in opposition to the Mass, which instead is an atoning sacrifice that the people pay. "The sacrifice differs from the Sacrament of the Supper as widely as giving differs from receiving."[73] Second, "*The gift is Jesus Christ himself,*" not only his divinity but the whole Christ.[74] Third, "*The gift is given with the signs.* Once again a criticism of both Zwingli and Rome is implied."[75] Fourth, "*The gift is given by the Holy Spirit,*" which Calvin goes on to detail in *Institutes*, 4.14.9 and 12.[76] Fifth, "*The gift is given to all who communicate, pious and impious, believers and unbelievers.*"[77] One

---

70. Gerrish, *Grace and Gratitude*, 204.

71. *Institutes*, 4.14.17.

72. Gerrish, *Grace and Gratitude*, 150, from *Institutes*, 4.14.26.

73. *Institutes*, 4.18.7.

74. Gerrish, *Grace and Gratitude*, 136, citing Calvin, De la Cene, OS, 1.508; cf. *Confessio fidei de eucharistia* (1537), OS, 1.435–36 (*Institutes*, 4.17.7, 9).

75. Gerrish, *Grace and Gratitude*, 137.

76. Ibid.

77. Ibid., 138.

may refuse the gift, but this does not negate the sacrament any more than the preaching of the gospel is invalidated by unbelief. "The integrity of the Sacrament, which the whole world cannot violate," says Calvin, "lies in this: that the flesh and blood of Christ are no less truly given to the unworthy than to God's elect believers."[78] At the same time, the reality is embraced only through faith. "The sacramental word is not an incantation," Gerrish summarizes, "but a promise." "The eucharistic gift therefore benefits those only who respond with the faith that the proclamation itself generates."[79]

When we receive the bread and the wine, says Calvin, "let us no less surely trust that the body itself is also given to us."[80] Rather than transform the sign into the signified (Rome), confuse the sign and the signified (Luther), or separate the sign and the signified (Zwingli), Calvin affirmed that signs were "guarantees of a present reality: the believer's feeding on the body and blood of Christ."[81] In explicit contrast with Zwingli, Calvin held that the reality—Christ and his benefits—could be truly communicated to believers through earthly means. Otherwise, he says (appealing to Chrysostom), faith becomes a "mere imagining" of Christ's presence.[82]

Although Calvin's formative influence cannot be denied, it is important to recognize that he was articulating a view that was also taught by his Reformed peers (such as Bucer, Vermigli, Musculus, Knox, and the later Cranmer) and their confessional successors. Therefore, with respect to *what* is received in the sacrament, the Reformed unanimously answered, in the words of the Belgic Confession, that it is nothing less than "the proper and natural body and the proper blood of Christ."[83] Reflecting Calvin's

78. *Institutes*, 4.17.33.
79. Gerrish, *Grace and Gratitude*, 139; see *Institutes*, 4.14.4; 4.17.15.
80. *Institutes*, 4.17.10.
81. Gerrish, *Grace and Gratitude*, 165.
82. *Institutes*, 4.17.5–6.
83. For the Reformed, as Louis Berkhof summarizes in his *Systematic Theology* (Grand Rapids: Eerdmans, 1996), the Supper gives the believing sinner assurance "that he personally was the object of that incomparable love" in Christ's sacrifice, "the personal assurance that all the promises of the covenant and all the riches of the gospel offer are his by a divine donation, so that he has a personal claim on them," and assurance "that the blessings of salvation are his in actual possession." Secondarily, and as a consequence, it is a profession of allegiance to Christ as King (651). For Zwingli, although it is not entirely clear what he believed about the Supper consistently throughout his life, "for him the emphasis falls on what the believer, rather than on what God, pledges in the sacrament. . . . He denied the

contention that there is no communication of Christ's benefits apart from his person, the confession adds that "Christ communicates *himself* to us *with all his benefits*. At that table he makes us enjoy *himself as much as the merits of his suffering and death*, as he nourishes, strengthens, and comforts our poor, desolate souls by the eating of his flesh, and relieves and renews them by the drinking of his blood."[84]

How Is Christ Given in the Supper?

Whereas rival views turned to the mechanics of substantial presence, Calvin turned to the Spirit's mediation. Calvin firmly rejected any rationalizing of the Eucharist, insisting that Christ is not received "only by understanding and imagination."[85] The Supper, according to Calvin, is the assurance of our own participation in what Luther described as the *mirifica commutatio* ("marvelous exchange").[86] If, unlike Zwingli, we affirm that the substance of the sacrament is Christ's true and natural body, Calvin wondered, "What could be more ridiculous than to split the churches and stir up frightful commotions" over *how* this happens?[87] The only pious conclusion, he says, is "to break forth in wonder at this mystery, which plainly neither the mind is able to conceive nor the tongue to express."[88] Calvin writes, "Inquisitive persons have wanted to define

bodily presence of Christ in the Lord's Supper, but did not deny that Christ is present there in a spiritual manner to the faith of the believer. Christ is present only in His divine nature and in the *apprehension* of the believing communicant" (653). The Reformed view followed Calvin, who rejected Zwingli's view on several counts: "(a) that it allows the idea of what the believer does in the sacrament to eclipse the gift of God in it; and (b) that it sees in the eating of the body of Christ nothing more nor higher than faith in His name and reliance on His death." For Calvin, the Supper has to do not only with Christ's work in the past, but his work in the present. Although not present locally in the bread and wine, Christ nevertheless gives "His entire person, both body and blood," through the meal (653). The efficient agent of this sacramental union is the author of the mystical union itself: namely, the Holy Spirit. "This view of Calvin is that found in our confessional standards" (654, citing Belgic art. 35; Heidelberg, Q. 75–76, and the Communion Form).

84. Belgic Confession of Faith, art. 35, in *Psalter Hymnal, Doctrinal Standards and Liturgy of the Christian Reformed Church* (Grand Rapids: Board of Publications of the CRC, 1976), 87–88.

85. *Institutes*, 4.17.9.

86. Ibid., 4.17.2.

87. John Calvin, *Defensio doctrinae de sacramentis*, OS, 2.287.

88. Ibid.

how the body of Christ is present in the bread." After summarizing the rival theories, he urges, "But the primary question to be put was how the body of Christ, as it was given for us, became ours; and how the blood, as it was shed for us, became ours. What matters is how we possess the whole Christ crucified, to become partakers of all his blessings."[89] The point is to assure trembling consciences that it is "not a bare figure, but is joined with the reality and substance."[90] Typical of Reformed confessions, the Westminster Larger Catechism points out that the *mode*, not the *substance*, is spiritual.[91]

Although Christ is not present on earth in the flesh until his return in glory, he is active in grace from his heavenly throne through the agency of his Spirit. Therefore, he can make himself the substance of the sacrament without bodily descending to the bread and the wine. Because of the agency of the Spirit, who unites us to the whole Christ in the first place, there can be a real communication of Christ's person and work to the church. It is not simply Christ's divinity but the Spirit who makes Christ's reign universally present, so that even Christ's true and natural body and blood can be communicated to believers.

"When this perichoretically trinitarian framework is recognized," Philip Butin observes, "Christ's ascension is no longer a 'problem' for Calvin."

> To the contrary, it contributes a distinctively positive and "upward" emphasis to his entire theology of the eucharist. Calvin's approach at this point thus complements and completes the "downward" Lutheran emphasis on incarnation with an equal "upward" emphasis on resurrection and ascension. There is "a manner of descent by which he lifts us up to himself." Not only does Christ (in the Spirit) condescend to manifest himself to believers by means of visible, tangible, created elements; at the same time by the Spirit, the worshiping church is drawn into the heavenly worship of the Father through the mediation of the ascended Christ, who is seated

---

89. John Calvin, 1536 *Institutes*, in *OS*, 1.139.

90. Ibid., 1.508–9.

91. See, for example, WLC 170, which underscores this point by confessing that believers truly "feed upon the body and blood of Christ" (the substance of the sacrament), "not after a corporal and carnal, but in a spiritual manner; yet truly and really, while by faith they receive and apply to themselves Christ crucified, and all the benefits of his death."

with the Father in the heavenlies. For Calvin, this accentuates, rather than diminishes, the true humanity of Christ.

Hence the emphasis in the eucharistic liturgy on the *sursum corda* ("We lift up our hearts to the Lord") and *epiclesis* (calling upon the Spirit).[92] By the effective working of the Spirit, says Calvin, "the flesh of Christ is like a rich and inexhaustible fountain that pours into us the life springing forth from the Godhead into itself."[93] We are related to Christ not only generically as fellow humans, but eschatologically, pneumatologically, mystically, and soteriologically.[94] Thus, "The Spirit makes things which are widely separated by space to be united with each other, and accordingly causes life from the flesh of Christ to reach us from heaven."[95]

So the question for Calvin is not how to relate spirit and matter, but how Christ, being glorified in heaven, can be related to us in our present condition. As the work of the Spirit, the precise mode of this feeding remains mysterious—something to be marveled at and enjoyed rather than explained. Similarly, the Belgic Confession declares that while the mode "cannot be comprehended by us, as the operations of the Holy Spirit are hidden and incomprehensible, ... we nevertheless do not err when we say that what is eaten and drunk by us is the proper and natural body and the proper blood of Christ."[96] The Spirit, in this view, is not a substitute for Christ, but is the agent who unites us to Christ and therefore communicates Christ and his benefits to believers.

Where Is Christ Received in the Supper?

Reformed theologians were unfairly criticized by their Lutheran interlocutors as holding a crude literalism with respect to Christ's whereabouts, as if he were confined to an actual chair in heaven. The Reformed con-

---

92. Philip Walker Butin, *Revelation, Redemption and Response: Calvin's Trinitarian Understanding of the Divine-Human Relationship* (NY: Oxford University Press, 1995), 118.

93. *Institutes*, 4.17.8.

94. John Calvin, *Commentary on Paul's Epistle to the Ephesians* (Grand Rapids: Baker, 1979), commenting on Ephesians 5:30–31.

95. John Calvin, "The Best Method of Obtaining Concord," in *Selected Works of John Calvin: Tracts and Letters*, repr. ed., vol. 2, ed. Henry Beveridge and Jules Bonnet, trans. Henry Beveridge (Grand Rapids: Baker, 1983), 578.

96. Belgic Confession of Faith, art. 35, in *Psalter Hymnal*, 87–88.

cern, however, was simply to point out the contradiction between Jesus'
own promise that he would depart in the flesh and not return until the
last day—and yet that he would be with them by his Word and Spirit.
This follows the coming-and-going pattern of the Son and Spirit in Jesus'
upper-room discourse (John 14–16). Even Lutheran theologian Robert
Jenson remarks, "But if there is no place for Jesus' risen body, how is it a
body at all. For John Calvin was surely right: '. . . this is the eternal truth
of any body, that it is contained in its place.'"[97]

Not only does a sacrament exhibit the signs, but also the reality
signified is joined to them. Therefore, the Reformed argued, the whole
Christ may be said to be present and to offer himself in the sacrament
without being enclosed in the elements. "It is one thing to say that
Christ is present in the bread, another to assert the presence in the
Holy Supper," says Wollebius.[98] Zwingli's argument seemed to stop at
the ascension, whereas Calvin's equally emphatic affirmation of a true
feeding on Christ drew his attention to the activity of the Spirit in this
time between the two advents.

Reformed theologians were only extrapolating from the doctrine of
union with Christ in their view of the Supper. Although Christ has not
yet returned bodily to earth, we are seated with Christ in heavenly places
(Col. 3:1–4; Eph. 1:20; 2:6). Christ is not seated with us on earth, but we
are seated with him in the heavenlies—in a semi-realized manner now,
but one day face to face. Even now, the Spirit takes that which is Christ's
and makes both him and his gifts our own. Calvin found ample evidence
for this eschatological, heavenly feeding also in the church fathers. In fact,
his positive statement of his view of this true feeding (4.17.8–39) is basically a gloss on a host of passages drawn from Scripture and the church
fathers. Integrating comments from Cyril, Chrysostom, and Augustine,
Calvin concludes that although Christ has been bodily raised to the right
hand of God, "this Kingdom is neither bounded by location in space nor
circumscribed by any limits. Thus Christ is not prevented from exerting
his power wherever he pleases, in heaven and on earth." But right where

97. Robert W. Jenson, *Systematic Theology* (New York: Oxford University Press, 1997),
1:202, quoting 1536 *Institutes*, 4.122. See his excellent treatment at 202ff.
98. Quoted in Heinrich Heppe, *Reformed Dogmatics*, rev. and ed. Ernst Bizer, trans.
G. T. Thomson (London: Allen & Unwin, 1950), 642.

one might have expected him to correlate this unbounded extension of Christ's reign with his omnipresent *deity* (as in Augustine and Zwingli), Calvin says, "In short, he feeds his people with his own body, the communion of which he bestows upon them *by the power of his Spirit*."[99] We need not transform Christ's natural substance into a divine substance in order to affirm that his personal agency is omnipresent.

Calvin complains that his critics seem to think that "Christ does not seem present unless he comes down to us." But how is Christ less present "if he should lift us to himself"? Why must he be present in the bread and the wine in order to be present in the sacrament? Is this not the point of the Holy Spirit's work of uniting us to Christ in heaven?[100] "Shall we therefore, someone will say, assign to Christ a definite region of heaven?" Again Calvin eschews speculation: "But I reply with Augustine that this is a very prying and superfluous question; for us it is enough to believe that he is in heaven."[101]

As Calvin and the Reformed tradition emphasized, the prospective aspect, "until he comes again," is meaningless if in fact Christ returns bodily to earth in order to be present at every altar or table. Calvin thus interprets the copula (*is*) in the words of institution ("This *is* my body") in the light of Paul's elaboration. Paul says neither that the bread and cup are mere *symbols* nor that they *are* Christ's body and blood, much less that Christ's body and blood are *in, with, and under* the bread and cup. Rather, he says that the bread and wine are "*a participation in*" the body and blood of Christ (1 Cor. 10:16).[102] Instead of saying that because Christ is Lord over time and space and therefore does not conform to the rules of ordinary bodies, we should say that because Christ is Lord over time and space *in the power of his Spirit*, his past work in the flesh for our salvation and the future consummation converge in a semi-realized manner at the Lord's Table.

If Christ's bodily return occurs at every Eucharist, what is the significance of his return at the end of the age? It is significant that the angel comforts the disciples at Jesus' ascension by saying, "This Jesus, who was taken

---

99. *Institutes*, 4.17.18 (emphasis added).
100. Ibid., 4.17.31.
101. Ibid., 4.17.26.
102. Ibid., 4.17.22. All quotations from the Bible in this chapter are from the ESV.

up from you into heaven, will come in the same way as you saw him go into heaven" (Acts 1:11). This eschatological tension is *accentuated* rather than *resolved* by the Supper, which is why the memory of his redeeming work (anamnesis) and its effects in the present (epiclesis) necessarily engenders a longing for his appearing in the future (epektasis). The eucharistic event occurs here—and places us here—in this nexus where the powers of the age to come penetrate this present age. A qualitatively different presence will occur in the parousia: "When Christ who is your life appears, then you also will appear with him in glory" (Col. 3:4). Nevertheless, even now, he "is [our] life." The Spirit communicates the energies of Christ's life-giving flesh. "If the sun sheds its beams upon the earth and casts its substance in some measure upon it in order to beget, nourish, and give growth to its offspring—why should the radiance of Christ's Spirit be less in order to impart to us the communion of his flesh and blood?"[103]

Here, I suggest, we detect the East's essence-energies distinction, including the usual analogy of the sun and rays. Such statements have sometimes been regarded (especially in American Presbyterian circles) as an odd inconsistency in Calvin's sacramental teaching.[104] But this is largely because Calvin appropriates the critical Eastern distinction between essence and energies. Athanasius affirmed that God "is outside all things according to his essence, but he is in all things through his acts of power."[105] This distinction provides the context for Calvin's (and broader Reformed) reflection on everything from how we know God to union with Christ

103. *Institutes*, 4.17.12.

104. Charles Hodge, "Doctrine of the Reformed Church on the Lord's Supper," selected from *The Princeton Review* in Charles Hodge, *Essays and Reviews* (New York: Robert Carter & Brothers, 1957), 363–66. With John Williamson Nevin in his sights, Hodge characterizes even Calvin's understanding of Christ's whole vivifying person being communicated in the Supper (which he acknowledges to be taught in some of the Reformed confessions) as "an uncongenial foreign element" drawn from patristic sources, a too-literal reading of John 6, and a desire to placate the Lutherans (363–66). Even sharper views were expressed by James Henley Thornwell, Robert Lewis Dabney, and William G. T. Shedd, the last of whom attempted to assimilate Calvin's view into his own Zwinglian conception (*Dogmatic Theology*, 3rd ed., ed. Alan W. Gomes [Phillipsburg, NJ: P&R Publishing, 2003], 814–15). Otto Ritschl expresses the same frustration with Calvin's Cyrillian interpretation of the sacrament in *Die reformierte Theologie* (1926).

105. St. Athanasius, *On the Incarnation* 17, trans. R. W. Thomson, *Athanasius: Contra Gentes and De Incarnatione* (Oxford: Clarendon Press, 1971), 174.

to sacramental theology. Regardless of one's conclusions concerning this perspective, it is not an odd inconsistency but is deeply embedded in Calvin's doctrine of union with Christ.[106] His eucharistic view at this point did not run counter to his forensic understanding of justification, as Bruce McCormack suggests, because he saw justification as the basis but not the sole aspect of the mystical union.[107] Furthermore, if we interpret the "energies" as "the powers [*dunameis*] of the age to come" (Heb. 6:5), which Christ fully possesses as the firstfruits of the whole harvest, then the same pneumatological mediation that is the hallmark of a Reformed doctrine of mystical union is at work in its sacramental theology. Recent scholarship has confirmed that Calvin's formulations at this point reflect his reading of patristic sources, especially Irenaeus and Chrysostom, but also Cyril of Alexandria.[108] Yet Calvin was hardly alone, his theological contemporaries and heirs reflecting similar views, including the essence (sun) and energies (rays) analogy.[109]

106. Calvin explicitly connects his view of union with Christ to the Supper (*Institutes*, 4.17.9). In a letter to Peter Martyr Vermigli (August 8, 1555), Calvin writes:
What I say is that the moment we receive Christ by faith as he offers himself in the gospel, we become truly members of his body, and life flows into us from him as from the head. . . . That is how I interpret the passage in which Paul says that believers are called into the *koinōnia* of Christ (1 Cor. 1:9). The words "company" or "fellowship" do not seem adequate to convey his thought: it suggests to me the sacred unity by which the Son of God engrafts us into his body, so as to communicate to us all that is his. Thus we draw life from his flesh and blood, so that they are not undeservedly called our "food." How it happens, I confess, is far above the measure of my intelligence. Hence I adore the mystery rather than labor to understand it.
CO, 15.722–23.
107. Bruce McCormack, "What's at Stake in Current Debates over Justification?" in *Justification: What's at Stake in the Current Debates?* ed. Mark Husbands and Daniel J. Treier (Downers Grove, IL: InterVarsity Press, 2004), 104–5.
108. See Irena Backus, "Calvin and the Greek Fathers," in *Continuity and Change: The Harvest of Later Medieval and Reformation History*, ed. Robert J. Bast and Andrew C. Gow (Leiden: Brill, 2000), 253–76; cf. Johannes Van Oort, "John Calvin and the Church Fathers," in *The Reception of the Church Fathers in the West: From the Carolingians to the Maurists*, ed. Irena Backus (Leiden: Brill, 1997). See also Anthony Lane, *John Calvin: Student of the Church Fathers* (Edinburgh: T&T Clark, 1999), 41–42. Especially in Oort, Calvin is cited as estimating that Cyril is next to Chrysostom in depth of insight ("John Calvin and the Church Fathers," 693).
109. Heppe, *Reformed Dogmatics*, 641, offers a number of pertinent quotations. Like many other early Reformed theologians, Wollebius explicitly appeals to the category of energies in discussing the Supper, including the usual analogy of the sun and its rays, so that

Calvin's view of the Supper as communicating Christ's flesh for our immortality is not a slip of the pen. Only with the Eastern category of God's energies, distinct from his essence and a created thing, was Calvin able to affirm that Christ is an inexhaustible life-giving fountain communicated in the Supper (4.17.9), without suggesting any more than Cyril that the essence of Christ—either divinity or humanity—was poured into creatures. After all, he added a section to the 1559 *Institutes* in refutation of Osiander's formulation of that view. Interpreted eschatologically, this does not mean a fusion of essences, as if our personal identity were assimilated to Jesus' or vice versa. Nevertheless, it does mean that the efficacy (energy) of the sun is communicated to us, so that even now Christ's exalted flesh as well as divine power reach us and renew us with their vigor. The branches share in the life, not simply the effects, of the vine; the relation of Christ to his body is that of the firstfruits to the harvest.

What Is the Effect of the Supper?

Calvin could affirm the efficacy of the Supper in no less realistic terms than his critics. First, with respect to his person, Calvin's Christology was free of Zwingli's nearly Nestorian emphasis on the distinction between the two natures. Whereas Zwingli seems to assume that Christ's deity does all the work of redemption, Calvin writes:

> The situation would surely have been hopeless had the very majesty of God not descended to us, since it was not in our power to ascend

---

"what is remote spatially is present in efficacy." He adds, "The presence is opposed not to distance but to absence." The eating and drinking of Christ's body and blood in John 6:51–56 cannot be reduced to believing or "simple cognition," adds Bucannus; rather, it teaches that "by true participation in himself we should be quickened." His whole life becomes the food that quenches our starvation, according to Olevianus. "Is our soul merely without the body, united to Christ's soul only, or our flesh also with Christ's flesh?" asks Bucannus. "Indeed the whole person of each believer, in soul and body, is truly joined to the whole person of Christ." As he assumed our mortal flesh, so we participate in his immortal flesh. How else, he asks, could we be assured of our own glorification and resurrection? Martin Bucer, Peter Martyr Vermigli, Wolfgang Musculus, and other prominent Reformed leaders (seniors and contemporaries of Calvin) occupied essentially the same eucharistic terrain. The fact that Reformed and Presbyterian confessions (as Charles Hodge concedes) reflect these views further challenges the notion that Calvin introduced an "uncongenial foreign element" into the tradition's eucharistic teaching.

to him. Hence, it was necessary for the Son of God to become for us "Immanuel, that is, God with us," and in such a way that his divinity and human nature might by mutual conjunction coalesce with each other [*ut mutual coniunctione eius divinitatas et hominum natura inter se coalescerent*]. Otherwise, the nearness would not have been enough, nor the affinity sufficiently firm, for us to hope that God might dwell with us [*Deum nobiscum habitare*].[110]

If the whole Christ—as human no less than as divine—secured our redemption, then our communion must be with the whole Christ. Second, if we cannot receive the benefits of Christ apart from his person, then the Supper must communicate Christ's person as well as his work.[111]

The Frequency of Communion

One's view of the efficacy of communion largely determines one's views concerning frequency. It has often been noted that the confessional theology of Reformed and Presbyterian churches often differs from their practice, with long seasons of preparation for communion. Against the traditional medieval practice of infrequent communion Calvin offered a

110. *Institutes*, 2.12.1.

111. In the light of this retrieval of Eastern patristic emphases, it is interesting to compare Calvin with contemporary Orthodox theologian Alexander Schmemann: "Like the entire eucharist, the remembrance is not a repetition. It is the manifestation, gift and experience, in 'this world' and therefore again and again, of the eucharist offered by Christ once and for all, and of our ascension to it." The Supper does not complete or extend Christ's redemptive work, adds Schmemann. "No—in Christ all is already accomplished, all is real, all is granted. In him we have obtained access to the Father and communion in the Holy Spirit and anticipation of the new life in his kingdom." He adds:

The purpose of the eucharist lies not in the change of the bread and wine, but in our partaking of Christ, who has become our food, our life, the manifestation of the Church as the body of Christ. This is why the holy gifts themselves never became in the Orthodox East an object of special reverence, contemplation and adoration, and likewise an object of special theological "problematics": how, when, in what manner their change is accomplished. . . . Nothing is explained, nothing is defined, nothing has changed in 'this world.' But then whence comes this light, this joy that overflows the heart, this feeling of fullness and of touching the "other world"? We find the answer to these questions in the epiclesis. But the answer is not "rational," built upon the laws of our "one-storied" logic; it is disclosed to us by the Holy Spirit.

Alexander Schmemann, *The Eucharist: Sacraments of the Kingdom* (Crestwood, NY: St. Vladimir's Seminary Press, 1988), 224–27.

sustained plea that the Supper should be celebrated whenever the Word is preached "or at least once a week."[112] "The Eucharist is the communion of the body and blood of the Lord," so infrequent communion is in effect, says Calvin, a withholding of Christ and his benefits from the covenant assembly.[113] In fact, only a year after the city of Geneva officially embraced the Reformation, Calvin's Articles for Organization of the Church and Worship at Geneva (1537) stated, "It is certain that a Church cannot be said to be well ordered and regulated unless in it the Holy Supper of our Lord is always being celebrated and frequented. . . ."[114] From the beginning Reformed and Presbyterian church orders and directories called for "frequent" observance. Calvin articulated a new conceptualization of "liturgy" itself, according to Lee Palmer Wandel: "For him, certainly, the Supper was a drama, but the source of that drama was God. No human movement could add to that meaning in any way, no crafted object could draw greater attention to those earthly elements." She adds, "Perhaps most important of all, however, was Calvin's insistence on frequency. Most evangelicals condemned the medieval requirement of annual communion as nonscriptural. . . . But no other evangelical so explicitly situated the Eucharist within a dialogic process not simply of deepening faith, but of the increasing capacity to read the signs of the Supper itself, and by extension, of God, in the world."[115] In both Roman Catholic and Zwinglian conceptions, the Eucharist was chiefly a human work, either of offering Christ again for sacrifice or of remembering and pledging. And yet, says Wandel, "The Supper, for Calvin, was not 'external'—a ceremony . . . nor even 'worship' in the sense that other evangelicals, such as Zwingli and Luther, used: a mode of honoring God." Rather, it is a means of binding us together more and more with

112. *Institutes*, 4.17.44–46.
113. Mary Beaty and Benjamin W. Farley, eds., *Calvin's Ecclesiastical Advice* (Louisville: WJK, 1991), 165.
114. John Calvin, "Articles concerning the Organization of the Church and of Worship at Geneva Proposed by the Ministers at the Council, January 16, 1537," in *Calvin: Theological Treatises*, ed. and trans. J. K. L. Reid, Library of Christian Classics (Philadelphia: Westminster Press, 1954), 48.
115. Lee Palmer Wandel, *The Eucharist in the Reformation: Incarnation and Liturgy* (Cambridge: Cambridge University Press, 2006), 171.

Christ in an ongoing relationship in which "Christ 'is made completely one with us and we with him.' "[116]

Although Reformed theology emphasizes the priority of God's action in the Supper, it also recognizes a broader efficacy, which underscores the importance of its frequent celebration. The forensic yields the effective; justification yields sanctification; the vertical, disrupting, objective work of God *extra nos* issues in a new system of horizontal, ordered, and subjective relationships between human beings. Like the Word, the sacraments draw us out of our private rooms into the public dining room. Here we are co-heirs at the family table, not consumers of exotic or meaningful religious experiences. Christ gives his body, and we thereby become "one body by such participation."[117]

No part of the body can be injured without pain to the whole body; and the Supper not only illustrates or represents this point, but is a means through which Christ actually effects ecclesial unity. "Accordingly, Augustine with good reason frequently calls this Sacrament 'the bond of love.' "[118] In this sacrament, Christ makes himself the common property of all believers, Calvin insists, no believer possessing any greater or lesser participation in Christ or any of his benefits than the others.[119] Again, Calvin is not alone, but in many ways is simply echoing Bucer, among others.[120] Most importantly, this view originates with Jesus' institution of the meal and with Paul's instruction. There can be no participation in Christ that is not simultaneously a participation in each other.

In this vein, Dutch pastor Karl Deddens has remarked:

> Here we have the very root of diaconal work. The festive spirit in which we celebrate the Lord's Supper is also an occasion for us, in accordance with Lord's Day 38 of the Heidelberg Catechism, to show compassion for the poor ... And this ideal would become reality if the festive character of the Lord's Supper came to full expression in our services.[121]

116. Ibid.
117. *Institutes*, 4.17.38.
118. Ibid.
119. Ibid.
120. See Martin Bucer, "The Reign of Christ," in *Melanchthon and Bucer*, ed. Wilhelm Pauck, Library of Christian Classics (Philadelphia: Westminster Press, 1969), 182, 236–59.
121. Karl Deddens, *Where Everything Points to Him*, trans. Theodore Plantinga (Neerlandia, Alberta: Inheritance Publications, 1993), 93.

Eucharist and Ecclesia

Although important differences remain with respect to the Eucharist, recent ecumenical conversations have yielded impressive areas of consensus.[122] I will conclude this essay, however, by indicating the significance of our sacramental theology for ecclesiology more generally.

Separating the Sign from the Signified

As we saw previously, Karl Barth lamented the "sacramentalism" of the confessional Reformed position.[123] This is consistent, however, with his view that these are strictly human acts of obedience rather than God's means of grace. For Zwingli, spiritual blessings do not come through material means. The Spirit does not need "a channel or vehicle."[124] For Barth as well, divine and creaturely agency run on parallel tracks, never truly intersecting on an extended horizontal plane. Throughout the last fragment of the *Church Dogmatics* that he was able to complete, Barth repeats his sharp distinction between God's work of salvation and water baptism

122. On the Lutheran-Reformed consensus, see Keith F. Nickle and Timothy F. Lull, *A Common Calling: The Witness of Our Reformation Churches in North America Today; The Report of the Lutheran-Reformed Committee for Theological Conversations, 1988–1992* (Minneapolis: Augsburg Fortress, 1993), 37–49. See also "Lutheran-Reformed Dialogue," in *Growth in Agreement II: Reports and Agreed Statements of Ecumenical Conversations on a World Level, 1982–1998*, ed. Jeffrey Gros, Harding Meyer, William G. Rusch (Geneva: World Council of Churches; Grand Rapids: Eerdmans, 2000), 230–47, esp. 242. It is important to point out, however, that significant branches of Lutheran and Reformed families have not participated in these discussions and would not endorse their conclusions or consensus. On the Reformed-Roman Catholic discussions, see *Growth in Agreement II*, 815. For a general consensus among member bodies of the World Council of Churches, see *Baptism, Eucharist & Ministry 1982–1990: Report on the Process and Responses, Faith and Order Paper No. 149* (Geneva: WCC Publications, 1990), 115–16.

123. CD, 4.4:128–30. Under a discussion of how the Spirit works in the life of the believer and the community to direct them to Christ (ibid., 4.2:360–77), baptism and the Supper do not even receive mention.

124. Quoted from "An Account of the Faith," in W. P. Stephens, *The Theology of Huldrych Zwingli* (Oxford: Clarendon, 1986), 186. Cf. Huldrych Zwingli, *Commentary on True and False Religion*, ed. Samuel Macauley Jackson and Clarence Nevin Heller (Durham, NC: Labyrinth Press, 1981), 214–15, 204–5, 239.

and the Supper as the purely human work of liturgical obedience.[125] "He is He, and His work is His work, *standing over against all Christian action, including Christian faith and Christian baptism.*"[126] Whereas the Reformed and Lutherans appealed to Augustine's definition of the sacraments as "the visible Word" (*verbum visibile*), Barth writes, "The *verbum visibile*, the objectively clarified preaching of the Word, is the only sacrament left to us."[127] Here Barth's understandable wariness of Roman Catholic and neo-Protestant tendencies to "enclose" Christ and his saving work, bringing them under the auspices of human control, motivates an overreaction.[128] The Supper, for Barth, is concerned with "the action of *the community*, and indeed with the action by which *it* establishes fellowship."[129]

The separation of the sign and thing signified opens a fissure in ecclesiology from top to bottom between the visible church as a historical institution with its structure, offices, order, and sacraments on one side and the invisible church as a relatively unknown and unknowable community of believers on the other side. As has frequently been observed, a weak pneumatology is one reason for (and perhaps result of) this divide.[130] As that which Barth calls "the subjective side in the event of revelation," the Spirit's work consists entirely of awakening people to that which has already happened rather than contributing in his own distinct manner to our salvation.[131]

The dominant view of the Supper in contemporary evangelical theology may even go beyond a Zwinglian conception, with the efficacy of the sacrament lodged entirely in its symbolic role of testifying to the believer's "act

125. CD, 4.4. Titled *The Christian Life*, this volume is a fragment that Barth developed and published as part of his unfinished dogmatics. See CD, 4.3.2:756, 783, 790, 843–901.
126. Ibid., 88 (emphasis added).
127. Karl Barth, *The Word of God and the Word of Man*, trans. Douglas Horton (New York: Harper Torchbooks, 1957), 114. He adds cheerfully, though erroneously from a historical perspective, "The Reformers sternly took from us everything but the Bible."
128. See David Allen, "A Tale of Two Roads: Homiletics and Biblical Authority," *JETS* 43.3 (September 2000): 492. Cf. CD, 1.1:127.
129. CD, 4.3.2:901 (emphasis added).
130. Among the many criticisms of Barth in this connection, see especially Robert Jenson, "You Wonder Where the Spirit Went," *Pro Ecclesia* 2 (1993): 296–304; Wolfhart Pannenberg, *Systematic Theology*, vol. 3, trans. G. W. Bromiley (Grand Rapids: Eerdmans, 1998), 1–27.
131. CD, 1.1:449.

of commitment."[132] Sacramental theology shapes ecclesiology, regardless of the perspective. When the main goal of preaching is to motivate our decision and action and the main goal of baptism and the Supper is to testify to our decision and action, the church is most likely to be conceived as a voluntary association of like-minded individuals but hardly "the mother of the faithful." A personal relationship with Jesus Christ may then easily be set over against church membership and covenantal nurture.

Confusing Sign and Signified

With the doctrine of transubstantiation the sign is absorbed (hence, lost) in the reality signified. Rather than natural creatures penetrated by the *energies* of God (while remaining what they are), the bread and wine are simply obliterated and converted into a supernatural *essence*. But in this case, neither remains what it is. The natural body of Jesus Christ becomes identified as the church as his ongoing incarnation, and the natural signs are no longer consecrated creatures but elevated to become something else. This tendency is evident in a variety of contemporary theologies.[133]

According to Graham Ward, Calvin seems fixated on the body of the "gendered Jew," but Ward's own solution is to regard this body as infinitely expanded—"transcorporeal"—so that he "returns" in and as the church.[134]

132. Interestingly, something close to this interpretation is also articulated as "transsignification" by some Roman Catholic theologians today. For the most thorough development and defense of transsignification, see Edward Schillebeeckx, *The Eucharist* (London: Sheed & Ward, 1968), 108–19.

133. One indicator of this trend is the movement known as Radical Orthodoxy, led by John Milbank, Graham Ward, and Catherine Pickstock. On this point especially, see John Milbank, "Alternative Protestantism," in *Radical Orthodoxy and the Reformed Tradition: Creation, Covenant, and Participation*, ed. J. K. A. Smith and James H. Olthuis (Grand Rapids: Baker Academic, 2005), 31. For lengthy interaction with some of these trends, see Michael Horton, *People and Place*, 146–50, 163–64. Milbank writes that "Calvin's sacramental theology is not really coherent. In relation to the Eucharist he is indeed to be thoroughly commended for his strong pneumatological emphasis—reminiscent of Greek views and perhaps superior to some Catholic treatments. . . . But the idea of the spiritual participation in a body that is in heaven makes very little sense." Better is the doctrine of transubstantiation, which avoids a local presence of Christ's body and blood either in heaven or in the bread and the wine by suggesting instead "that participation in a physical—albeit mysteriously physical—reality is itself mysteriously physical" ("Alternative Protestantism," 35). The other essays in this volume (*Radical Orthodoxy and the Reformed Tradition*) offer tremendous insights and responses.

134. Ward, *Cities of God*, 154–72.

413

This spiritual body is *"more real than any physical body."*[135] The assimilation of the natural body of Jesus to the ecclesial body (the church) represents "the spiritual incorporation par excellence."[136] Matter is at last transcended. The body and blood of Christ are the sign (*sacramentum*); the church is the reality (*res*)—*"only this ecclesiastical Body should be called purely res."*[137]

A more complete substitution of the church for Christ is difficult to conceive. There is therefore nothing left for the Spirit to mediate, since the church itself *is* the expanded Christ. Ironically, what gets lost in the process is the one who has died, is risen, and will come again just as the disciples saw him leave. Given the correlation of head and members, is it any wonder that in the displacement-as-expansion of Jesus' natural body, the eschatological hope, according to Milbank and Pickstock, is not the resurrection of the body but a transcorporeal existence?[138] Since Christ is the firstfruits, if his natural body has vanished, so too has our resurrection hope. If he is "transcorporeal," so will we be but so many drops in an ocean of spirit. As goes the head, so go the members. A docetic Eucharist means a docetic consummation. Avoiding the reality of the ascension, which keeps us praying, "Amen. Come, Lord Jesus," the church substitutes itself as the real and only true body of its absent Lord.

Sign and Signified: Union without Confusion

Only the communication of Christ himself with all his benefits is sufficient to generate an ecclesial body. But the church is not Jesus Christ. It does not extend his incarnation or complete his saving work, but receives the benefits of this work and shares it with others.

It is properly said that the Eucharist gives the church. There is not first of all a church and then certain practices, such as preaching, baptism, and the Supper. Together with the first two, the Supper identifies the true church because it is through these means of grace that the Spirit is at work

135. Ibid. (emphasis added).
136. Ibid.
137. Ibid., 180 (emphasis added).
138. John Milbank and Catherine Pickstock, *Truth in Aquinas* (London: Routledge, 2001), 37. I am grateful to James K. A. Smith for pointing to this reference in his carefully nuanced interpretation in "Will the Real Plato Please Stand Up?" in *Radical Orthodoxy and the Reformed Tradition*, 70.

creating a communion for the Father in the Son. Paul asks, "The cup of blessing that we bless, is it not a participation in the blood of Christ? The bread that we break, is it not a participation in the body of Christ? *Because there is one bread,* we who are many are one body, *for we all partake of the one bread*" (1 Cor. 10:16–17 [emphasis added]). But unless the matter of the Eucharist remains the *natural* body of Jesus Christ, the *ecclesial* body will also be a docetic illusion.

A eucharistic theology that confuses the sign and the signified and collapses the eschatological "not yet" into an overrealized "already" makes the church a substitute for Jesus Christ and the Holy Spirit. And a eucharistic theology that separates the sign and the signified as well as this age from the penetrating powers of the age to come already breaking in on us will likely yield an association of choosers rather than a communion of saints. The first error leads to a triumphalistic ecclesiology, while the latter leads to a weak one. Whatever our view of the Supper, it must be one, as Douglas Farrow suggests, that places the church in the precarious collision of the powers of death and life, in complete dependence on the Spirit. "The comfort of the *Christus praesens* is clearly grounded in the stubborn and troubling fact of the *Christus absens*," Farrow notes.

> Covenant history and world history have divided at this departure, for in and with Jesus the former has already reached its goal. In the resulting gap a place has opened up for the eucharistic community as a genuinely new entity within world history, albeit a peculiar one with its own peculiar view of the way things are. . . . It is the divergence of Jesus-history from our own that calls for a specifically eucharistic link: for the breaking and remoulding . . . of worldly reality to bring it into conjunction with the lordly reality of Jesus Christ.[139]

Taking our coordinates from the redemptive economy of Christ's descent, ascent, and parousia—concretely manifested and in fact constituted by the Spirit through Word and sacrament—this covenantal ecclesiology locates the church's identity at this unsettling, strange, and even dangerous, yet wonderful intersection between the two ages.

139. Farrow, *Ascension and Ecclesia*, 37, 40, 10.

PART 3

CALVIN TODAY
AND
TOMORROW

18

CALVIN BIBLIOGRAPHY

RICHARD C. GAMBLE

This chapter will present broad strokes of Calvin interpretation, focusing only on books published on John Calvin from the year 2000 to the present. The chapter does not intend to cover all the topics of the thousands of pages written during this partial decade! In fact, the choice of texts was based in part on personal acquaintance with the various authors.

The method employed is a quick look at the overall flow of Calvin's life, followed by topical analysis of Calvin as theologian, social reformer, and churchman.

Biographical Analysis[1]

Calvin's Life to 1538

Calvin was a trained humanist scholar whose first interest lay primarily in the world of printed books.[2] Of course, Calvin's own plans for a life of quiet scholarship did not match up with God's intentions for him. The Lord, using Guillaume Farel, wanted Calvin to work for reform in the important city of Geneva.[3]

Calvin's beginnings in Geneva in the summer of 1536 were quite small, and his position was not powerful.[4] His first sojourn in Geneva included some disputations and rather frustrating attempts at reform. The flash point of controversy between the ministers and city leaders focused on who would wield the power of excommunication.[5]

Calvin Expelled: Ministry in Strasbourg and Return (1538–41)

Having been released from labors in Geneva, Calvin had hoped to pick up his beloved scholarship again.[6] Although that was not to be the case

1. An outstanding biography was written in French by Bernard Cottret, and translated into English by M. Wallace McDonald, *Calvin: A Biography* (Grand Rapids: Eerdmans, 2000). For a short and very readable account of Calvin's life and work, see Lester De Koster, *Light for the City: Calvin's Preaching, Source of Life and Liberty* (Grand Rapids: Eerdmans, 2004). Another biography is Robert Reymond, *John Calvin: His Life and Influence* (Fearn, Ross-shire, UK: Christian Focus, 2004). Most recent is Herman J. Selderhuis, *John Calvin: A Pilgrim's Life* (Downers Grove, IL: InterVarsity Press, 2009).

2. "In Basel he followed with interest his cousin Olivetan's production of the first French version of the Bible, based on the original Hebrew and Greek. Calvin wrote two short pieces for that Bible, which were published in June 1535: a fictitious privilege in Latin and the preface to the New Testament. . . . Calvin saw himself as a man who would spread his ideas via books and correspondence, without having active pastoral responsibilities" (Jean François Gilmont, *John Calvin and the Printed Book*, trans. Karin Maag [Kirksville, MO: Truman State University Press, 2005], 11).

3. "The city of Geneva began to support the Reformation in 1534, following Bern's strong support for Farel's actions" (ibid., 12).

4. "At first, he took on the role of *Sacarum litterarum* professor, limiting himself to his beloved academic pursuits. At this time he was only a minor figure. The registers of the Small Council, when discussing payment for his lectures in Saint-Pierre, refer to him as a little-known man, calling him *ille gallus,* 'that Frenchman'" (ibid.).

5. "The debate over excommunication led to defeat in April 1538." "The Genevan Council played their trump card to ensure their hold on power by sending Farel and Calvin into exile" (ibid., 12–13).

6. "'Because of what happened [that is, the departure into exile], since I am free and released from my vocation, I intend to live peacefully and not take up any public responsi-

in light of further pastoral duty, nevertheless Calvin continued a strong writing ministry while in Strasbourg. While there he learned much from older colleague Martin Bucer.[7]

Calvin was in financial trouble during these early years in Strasbourg.[8] But life was much improved in every way after his marriage to Idelette in 1540.[9]

While Calvin was absent, a tract was written to the city of Geneva (March 1539), attempting to persuade the city to return to the Roman Catholic Church. From Strasbourg, Calvin wrote a response on the city's behalf entitled *Reply to Sadolet*.[10]

Calvin's Return and Ministry in Geneva

Calvin demanded certain changes in the way the city was run as a condition of his return. It was debatable, however, whether Calvin's changes were really accomplished at the beginning of his ministry; the situation on his return may have been different *de jure* and not *de facto*.[11] Upon his return to Geneva, Calvin mounted the pulpit and simply began preaching from where he had stopped at the time of the first sojourn.

The first period of Calvin's ministry encompasses the years 1541–47. The city was governed by four bodies—a Great Council, a General

---

bilities.' . . . His arrival in Strasbourg in the summer of 1538 marked the beginning of the French church in that city" (ibid., 13, quoting Calvin).

7. "Calvin lived in Strasbourg, from 1538 to 1541, while this struggle was going on, and he established close contacts with Bucer. In effect Calvin did in Geneva what Bucer wanted to do in Strasbourg" (Robert M. Kingdon, "Calvin and Church Discipline," in *John Calvin Rediscovered*, ed. Edward Dommen and James D. Bratt [Louisville: Westminster/John Knox Press, 2007], 30).

8. "Beginning in May 1539, the situation improved a little. At this time, the city began paying him the same amount that deacons received, fifty-two florins a year. But he did not obtain an increase to a hundred florins as had been projected in July 1540. Hence, to make ends meet, he took up some bread-and-butter work by writing political pamphlets for the Count of Furstenberg" (Gilmont, *Calvin and the Printed Book*, 13–14).

9. "And with her help he ran his household more effectively and rented rooms to wealthy students" (ibid., 14).

10. "The Bernese suggested asking Calvin for a response and he agreed to help his former church at the end of August 1539" (ibid.).

11. "The Reformer actually obtained only an ambiguous text that gave the spiritual sword to the Consistory and refused to give any civil jurisdiction to the pastors. This undoubtedly deliberate equivocation merely deferred the problem until later, and the clash between the pastors and the Council over conflicting interpretations of the rules occurred in 1553" (ibid., 15).

Council, a Small Council, and four syndics. During the fall and winter of 1542–43, Calvin worked on composing the constitution of the city-state.[12] At this time Calvin also wrote commentaries as well as many polemical tracts.[13]

The second stage of reform lasted between the years 1548 and 1555. That season of Calvin's ministry saw difficulties on at least two fronts: a rise of political opposition and a deep theological controversy over predestination. The political opposition focused on the "foreigners" who wanted to deny the Genevans their entitled worldly pleasures.[14] The period ended with the defeat of the enemies of the reform movement. Calvin's controversy with Jerome Bolsec over predestination was also hard.[15] Sadly, Gilmont interprets this period of ministry in an unsympathetic fashion.[16]

Yet there were high points—such as when Calvin worked with the ministers of Zurich and a consensus was reached between them on the Lord's Supper in 1549.[17] Furthermore, Calvin's preaching was loved by the people, and his commentaries saw wide distribution. Contemporary research has demonstrated more clearly the close relationship between the publication of Calvin's commentaries and his work with the other ministers in the congregations.[18]

12. Ibid., 16–17, 24.

13. See Richard C. Gamble, "Calvin's Controversies," in *The Cambridge Companion to John Calvin*, ed. Donald K. McKim (Cambridge: Cambridge University Press, 2004), 188–203.

14. "First, they objected to his overly harsh moral rigor that led him to ban all of life's pleasures. Second, out of anger at the growing tide of French exiles in Geneva, his detractors stated that Calvin was himself a foreigner and had no right to intervene in the city's affairs" (Gilmont, *Calvin and the Printed Book*, 15).

15. "The conflict led to a trial that lasted from October 1551 to February 1552 and resulted in Bolsec's banishment, as well as division among Calvin's friends" (ibid.). "Among the friends Calvin lost, the most distinguished was Jacques de Bourgogne, seigneur de Falais, the highest-ranking nobleman of the Low Countries who had accepted the Reformation" (ibid.).

16. "This period ended in the spring of 1555, when the Perrinist opposition was ruthlessly crushed" (ibid., 16). "We have already discussed Calvin's debate with Bolsec over predestination. Clearly, Calvin hardened his position in order to crush his opponent and thus prove the truth of his cause. If he had admitted that he was in the wrong, Calvin would have put his position as a Reformer in jeopardy" (ibid., 286).

17. For more information on sacramental discussions, see Richard C. Gamble, "Sacramental Continuity among Reformed Refugees: Peter Martyr Vermigli and John Calvin," in *Peter Martyr Vermigli and the European Reformations*, ed. Frank A. James III (Leiden: Brill, 2004), 97–112.

18. Gilmont, *Calvin and the Printed Book*, 49–59.

The final stage of ministry lasted between the years 1555 and 1564.[19] During that phase the final edition of the *Institutes*, as well as a number of commentaries, including the *Harmony of the Pentateuch*, appeared. Throughout his ministry, Calvin recognized important differences between his commentaries and his preaching and was reluctant to have his sermons published.[20]

Calvin as Theologian[21]

Important analysis of various parts of Calvin's theology has recently been published under the direction of Hall and Lillback. A few of the topics discussed include Clark on predestination[22] and Lillback on Calvin's understanding of the covenant.[23] Gaffin gave valuable insight to Calvin's view of justification.[24]

A unique recent publication by Paul Helm digs deeply into the nature and structure of Calvin's thought. He addresses the commonly held assumption that Calvin was a "practical" theologian.[25] Helm com-

19. See Robert M. Kingdon, "Calvin's Last Years," in *Calvinus Praeceptor Ecclesiae*, ed. Herman J. Selderhuis (Geneva: Droz, 2004), 179–88.

20. "One particular aspect of the sermon style increased Calvin's reluctance, namely, that the sermons were too long-winded. Brevity was one of the hallmarks of Calvin's written style, while the persuasive aim of sermons meant that they made use of repetitions" (Gilmont, *Calvin and the Printed Book*, 78).

21. For more on Calvin as theologian, see David C. Steinmetz, "The Theology of John Calvin," in *The Cambridge Companion to Reformation Theology*, ed. David C. Steinmetz and David Bagchi (Cambridge: Cambridge University Press, 2004), 113–29. See also Randall Zachman, *John Calvin as Teacher, Pastor, and Theologian* (Grand Rapids: Baker, 2006), 173–260. An interesting analysis of Calvin's view of the human will is found in Dewey J. Hoitenga Jr., *John Calvin and the Will* (Grand Rapids: Baker, 1997). The most recent work to date is Charles Partee, *The Theology of John Calvin* (Louisville: Westminster/John Knox Press, 2008).

22. R. Scott Clark analyzed Calvin's views of election and predestination in the Romans commentary (chap. 9), the sermons on Ephesians, and the *Institutes*. See "Election and Predestination: The Sovereign Expressions of God," in *A Theological Guide to Calvin's Institutes*, ed. David W. Hall and Peter A. Lillback (Phillipsburg, NJ: P&R Publishing, 2008), 98–120.

23. Peter A. Lillback, "Calvin's Interpretation of the History of Salvation," in *A Theological Guide to Calvin's Institutes*, 168–204.

24. Richard B. Gaffin Jr., "Justification and Union with Christ," in David W. Hall and Peter A. Lillback, *A Theological Guide to Calvin's Institutes* (Phillipsburg, NJ: P&R Publishing, 2008), 248–69.

25. "Calvin is not a philosopher; he is a very practical theologian who bases knowledge of God on the gift of faith, not independent reason" (Elsie A. McKee, "The Character and

pares Calvin to his theological/philosophical predecessors as well as his "Calvinist" successors.[26]

Thus, to make a short presentation on this massive subject can best be approached from specific textual analysis as well as thematic analysis. First, Calvin's early work called the *Psychopannychia* and, of course, the development of the *Institutes* will be explored. From there we address Calvin's theological method.

Calvin's Earlier Writing: The Psychopannychia

This early tract was drafted in 1534, revised in Basel in 1536, and finally published in 1542. Thus, Calvin worked on both the *Institutes* and the *Psychopannychia* while in Basel. The state of the soul at death was certainly what most of us would call an "interesting" topic for analysis by a theologian who was still in his mid-twenties—and he already had contemporary critics for such a beginning.[27]

Connected to later analysis of Calvin's theological method, Tavard argues that Calvin's method in this treatise is not different from that of other theological writings of the time—it is in basic continuity with medieval theology.[28] Specifically, it is argued that Calvin is in fundamental

---

Significance of John Calvin's Teaching on Social and Economic Issues," in *John Calvin Rediscovered*, ed. Edward Dommen and James D. Bratt [Louisville: Westminster/John Knox Press, 2007], 5).

26. Paul Helm, *John Calvin's Ideas* (Oxford: Oxford University Press, 2004).

27. "Although his still unpublished writing on the soul has been seen by few readers, the rumor is already abroad that Calvin is about to publish an attack on the catabaptist, for there are those, as Calvin says, 'who criticize my project (consilium),' who blame him for making a mountain out of a mole-hill, 'starting huge fights about nothing.' It is not nothing, however, he responds, 'to see the light of God extinguished by the devil's darkness.' And in any case, 'this question'—the matter of the soul's sleep, death, or awakened survival—'is more important than is believed by many.' At this point, Calvin does not explain the importance of it, since this should be made obvious by the argumentation of the book. As to himself, he has attempted to defend the truth. He nonetheless remains quite modest as to the outcome of his endeavors" (George H. Tavard, *The Starting Point of Calvin's Theology* [Grand Rapids: Eerdmans, 2000], 45).

28. "Calvin outlines the theological method that he intends to use . . . explanation of a thesis, analysis of the state of the question, presentation of arguments, refutation of counterarguments" (ibid., 46). "Nothing has been said in this that would distinguish Calvin's theological method from the general approach of medieval theology" (ibid., 47). "A long presentation of patristic doctrine is introduced with the sentence, 'Thus also did those who treated of God's mysteries with moderation and reverence transmit them to us by hand' " (ibid.).

accord with Thomas Aquinas—and that by the time of the work's publication in 1542, Calvin had not yet even embraced the Protestant notion of *sola Scriptura*.[29] Furthermore, Calvin also had a Platonic conception of the soul.[30] Thus, the *Psychopannychia* is supposedly the writing of a theological scholastic—not one who has embraced Protestant theological methods, and perhaps hardly even Protestant theology.[31]

Calvin and the Institutes[32]

Richard Muller's monumental work, *The Unaccommodated Calvin*, dominates most recent English-language analysis of Calvin's *Institutes*. Agreeing with earlier scholars, Muller holds that Calvin's *Institutes* was written in a sixteenth-century context.[33]

The first edition of the *Institutes* had a different structure and intention in comparison to the later editions, and from the Latin the work was quickly translated into French.[34] The work of the early *Institutes* was translated

29. "I do not find any evidence in *Psychopannychia* that by the time it was published Calvin had endorsed a reformed conception of reliance on scripture alone" (ibid., 47). "The Angelic Doctor had explicitly taught that only 'authorities' taken from Scripture can provide apodictic arguments in theology, and furthermore that only from the literal sense of Scripture, expressing the author's intention, and not from allegorical sense, can valid arguments be drawn" (ibid.).

30. "The proposed outline is subordinated to the central thesis that Calvin the humanist entertained a thoroughly Platonic conception of the soul, in keeping with a fairly general trend in the Renaissance" (ibid., 53).

31. "In the second part of his demonstration—from page 61 to the end—Calvin refutes his adversaries' arguments in scholastic fashion" (ibid., 51).

32. The best overall introduction to the *Institutes* was written by William S. Barker, "The Historical Context of the *Institutes* as a Work in Theology," in *A Theological Guide to Calvin's Institutes*, 1–15.

33. "This historical problem of the term, however, ought not to stand in the way of an examination of the substance of the issue—the place of Calvin's *Institutes* within the sixteenth-century forms of the historical discipline that has come to be known as 'systematic theology'" (Richard A. Muller, *The Unaccommodated Calvin* [New York: Oxford University Press, 2000], 102). Melanchthon was an important model for Calvin, but Erasmus was not: "Hovering somewhere in the background of Calvin's desire, in 1539, to establish an *ordo recte docendi* or 'correct order of teaching' according to the various *loci* of theology that might be presented was Erasmus's *Ratio seu methodus compendio perveniendi ad veram theologiam*" (ibid., 124). "Yet it is clear from a comparative examination of the structure and order of Erasmus's *Ratio* and Calvin's *Institutes* that the two documents present widely different conceptions both of the order and arrangement of the topics and of the specific topics to be identified" (ibid.).

34. "The 1539 edition of Calvin's *Institutes* marks a crucial solidification of purpose and yet a significant alteration of direction" (ibid., 102). "Much of the original title, and, to

into Geneva's catechisms.[35] Muller argues, however, that the *Institutes* soon outgrew the notion of a catechism or something that could be grasped in the memory.[36] Calvin was convinced that the 1539 (second) edition was a "true" *Institute*.[37] Nevertheless, the definitive text was written after 1558.[38]

Calvin's Theological Method[39]

There is a consensus in contemporary Calvin scholarship that Calvin had certain axioms about God's nature and truth that were simply unquestioned— for example, that the Bible has revealed all of God's will for our lives.[40]

---

that extent, of the original intention also, carried over in the first French edition (1541), the title of which deleted only the final clause of the 1536 version, namely 'a work most worthy to be read by all those zealous for piety'" (ibid.).

35. "The 1536 edition was conceived in some relationship to the early catechism, written shortly afterward for use in Geneva, also called an 'institution' or 'instruction': the first edition of the *Institutes* followed the order of Luther's *Small Catechism*, and Calvin's *Catechismus, sive christianae religionis institutio* of 1538 paralleled the 1536 *Institutes*, albeit with significant addition of topics, adumbrating the new materials of the 1539 *Institutes*" (ibid., 103–4).

36. "Thus, as of 1539/41, Calvin ceased to identify catechetical works by the term *institutio* and reserved it for his ever-expanding theological 'summa'" (ibid., 104). "Third among the grounds for Calvin's alteration and development of his text, therefore, is the negative aspect of Calvin's 1539 editorial decision. In the midst of his work of writing the Romans commentary and editing the *Institutes*, Calvin was also involved in the composition and reworking of a series of catechisms for Geneva and Strasbourg: in part the recasting of the *Institutes* involved a decision concerning what it was not to be—namely, a catechetical instruction" (ibid., 123).

37. "At a third and even more profound level, the continuity between the 1536 and the 1539 titles is found principally in the identification of the work as an *Institutio* and the claim of the 1539 that now, presumably, the work for the first time has become an *Institutio*—a profound issue for Calvin, given his attention to precise literary genre" (ibid., 103). "We can conclude from Calvin's carefully phrased letter to the reader of 1539, from the related 'argument' prefaced to the 1541 French translation of the *Institutes*, and from the rather pointed editing of the title of the work that Calvin understood the transition from 1536 to 1539 as a major shift in the genre of the document" (ibid., 122–23).

38. "From October 1558 to June 1559, he essentially never left his room. In spite of these problems, he continued to write, but much more slowly. It was in this period that he established the definitive text of the *Institutes*, both in Latin and in French" (Gilmont, *Calvin and the Printed Book*, 17).

39. The best concise introduction to Calvin's theological method is K. Scott Oliphint, "A Primal and Simple Knowledge," in *A Theological Guide to Calvin's Institutes*, 16–43.

40. "A third axiom is that the Bible is the sole and sufficient revelation of God's will; nothing can be added or ignored, and no speculation may fill in what look to us like gaps. More significantly, this revelation is unified because God is the one original Author" (McKee, "The Character and Significance of John Calvin's Teaching," 4).

From those axioms Calvin taught that the Bible revealed various "types" of theology: there were eternal truths that could not be doubted, principles for life and worship, and practical instruction.[41]

On top of that, Muller sees an intimate relationship between Calvin's exegetical work (seen in the commentaries) and the development of the *Institutes*.[42] In light of his work, much earlier scholarship has to be modified.[43] Prior scholars did not appreciate the relationship between the *Institutes* and Calvin's other writings.[44] They had also not sufficiently wrestled with how humanism influenced Calvin.[45] In the last decade, other scholars have provided information that supports Muller's thesis. For example, it is noted that Theodore Beza made a clear distinction between Calvin's various literary genres.[46]

41. "Calvin operates with certain axioms, assumptions about truth that require no proof. (This is true for all people, whether they recognize it or not.) One of Calvin's axioms is the conviction that God is good and just and that what God wills is good and right by definition." "No evidence is necessary, but explanations may be given so that what is believed may be understood and practiced" (ibid., 4–5).

42. "Once it is recognized that the *Institutes* must be read in a developmental relationship with Calvin's exegetical and interpretive work, the issue of Calvin's relationship to the history of exegesis rises in importance as a key to the understanding of his theology" (Muller, *The Unaccommodated Calvin*, 116). "Calvin's own theological development, particularly as it took place in his work preaching, lecturing, and commenting on Scripture, is the one basis for the development and expansion of the *Institutes* that was mentioned explicitly by Calvin. It was in the *Institutes*, as he declared in his preface to the 1539 edition, that he would place the theological *loci* that arose out of the work of exegesis" (ibid., 122).

43. "We rule out as untenable both the denial that the *Institutes* is a theological system and the modern dogmatic or systematic reading of the text of the *Institutes* without reference to the highly contextual character of its contents and the ongoing dialogue—recorded only in part in its pages!—between Calvin's ample exegetical and dogmatic labors" (ibid., 117).

44. "The express intention of the *Institutes* was to state only one part of Calvin's doctrine" (ibid., 116). "This type of exposition of Calvin's thought—once quite prevalent—ignores the very nature of the *Institutes* and disregards Calvin's division of labor" (ibid.).

45. "The basic work of this rhetorical logic, 'invention,' was defined by Agricola as the location of proof or grounds of argument in and through the identification of the *loci*, which is to say the 'places' or *topoi* in which they might be found" (ibid., 109). "In view of Calvin's methodological statements and the nature of *loci communes* as theological topics related to particular texts, not only must the *Institutes* be understood as a gathering of *loci*, but the contents of these *loci* must also be regarded as primarily exegetical *both* in origin *and* in their continuing frame of reference" (ibid., 112).

46. "Beza made clear distinctions between Calvin's different literary genres, including his commentaries, lectures, and sermons, noting in particular that the sermons only partly filled the gap filled by missing commentaries" (Gilmont, *Calvin and the Printed Book*, 61).

Calvin as Social Reformer[47]

A full analysis of Calvin as social reformer should include analysis of the important topic of Calvin's views on science and the natural world.[48] With that limitation, contemporary readers must remember that Calvin's work in the city was done in the context of the many problems connected to religious persecution: in France especially, but also throughout Europe.[49] Calvin's contemporaries noted the great changes that came about in the city even with those challenges.[50]

Life and Religion

The "religious" work of reformation—specifically, men and women coming from the kingdom of Satan and entering into the kingdom of God—was never abstracted from all of life.[51] For Calvin, religious worship and religious life always went hand in hand. Correct worship required correct living.[52] The twenty-first-century separation of the two was foreign

47. A good introduction to Calvin on the Christian life is by William Edgar, "Ethics: The Christian Life and Good Works according to Calvin," in *A Theological Guide to Calvin's Institutes*, 320–46.

48. Culminating many years of research and thought, see the work of Davis A. Young, *John Calvin and the Natural World* (Lanham, MD: University Press of America, 2007).

49. "When the court of Francis I was devastating villages of evangelical believers in southeastern France in 1544–45, Calvin encouraged the Genevan government to welcome the refugees, care for their sick, and employ the healthy" (McKee, "The Character and Significance of John Calvin's Teaching," 20).

50. "John Knox's letter to Mrs. Locke of 1556 . . . [informed] her that he had found in Geneva 'the most perfect school of Christ that ever was in the earth since the days of the Apostles. In other places, I confess Christ to be truly preached, but manners and religion to be so sincerely reformed, I have not yet seen in any other place'" (Kingdon, "Calvin and Church Discipline," 28).

51. "No sixteenth-century persons who followed Calvin's theology would ever be able to separate how they ruled their subjects, nursed their sick neighbors, priced the goods in their shops, or obeyed their parents or disciplined their children from their relationship to God" (McKee, "The Character and Significance of John Calvin's Teaching," 21).

52. "Right worship should be expressed in prayer and praise—hearing God's word, receiving the gift of the sacraments, and giving material aid for the needy. It should also be expressed in the home and the marketplace, in city council and business activities, in care for the refugee and the poor and afflicted, in fair working conditions and just wages and conscientious labor" (ibid.). "What would have been distinctive in Calvin's version of the common biblical teaching was the constructive character and intensity with which he insisted

to Calvin's thinking as well as to his culture.[53] Correct belief and correct life were intertwined because Calvin was convinced that God saw and judged all human thoughts and actions.[54]

Christian "Service"

Calvin redefined the nature of what is thought of as "pleasing service" to God. No longer did one have to become a monk. But one also did not have to become a minister! Calvin had a high view of godly human government and the state.[55]

There was a connection in Calvin's mind between the work of the believer's hands and God's blessing. Even humble service, when offered with a pure heart, was pleasing to God.[56] Being united to Christ was the highest sign of "success."[57]

Business, Finance, and Education

The financial principle of "equity" was important.[58] With that notion in mind, Calvin argued that interest could be charged on

on the indivisible connection between right worship of God and right living as a social and economic being" (ibid., 22).

53. "To the sixteenth-century European this necessary interrelationship of theology and ethics, of love for God and for the neighbor would not have appeared strange" (ibid., 22).

54. "One of his recurrent phrases is *negotium cum Deo,* 'in every detail of life it is with God that we have to do' (e.g., 1.17.2; 3.3.6, 16; 3.7.2). The quasi-economic language is notable, though Calvin does *not* mean bargaining with God. In effect, what he is saying is that there is no moment or facet of believers' existence that is not present to God's sight" (ibid.).

55. For insightful analysis of Calvin on civil government, see David W. Hall, "Calvin on Human Government and the State," in *A Theological Guide to Calvin's Institutes,* 411–40.

56. "The Calvinist conviction that the action of the smallest child or humblest servant, prompted by faith and expressing love, is counted a worthwhile contribution to God's service, resulted in a dynamic sense of personal and corporate responsibility and power" (McKee, "The Character and Significance of John Calvin's Teaching," 22).

57. "For Calvin, having God's goodwill and being engrafted into Christ (his earthly cross as well as his final resurrection) *is* success for the Christian, and all material wealth and human relationships must be lived in accordance with criterion of what is good and right and desirable" (ibid., 22–23).

58. "Calvin the trained lawyer does not regard the judicial laws of ancient Israel to be obligatory for other societies, but the fundamental principles of equity these Old

loans.[59] Surprisingly for many evangelicals, the Genevan Consistory regulated business practice.[60]

They participated in that practice because Calvin was convinced that the church had social obligations.[61] Another of those social obligations concerned education.[62] During Calvin's time, there were great educational changes in Geneva.[63]

Calvin as Churchman[64]

Often people view Calvin as either a great theologian or a solid exegete. Although both views are correct, Calvin saw his life defined

Testament laws express are universal, and those principles must always be maintained (4.20.15–16)" (ibid., 10).

59. "Calvin allows the legitimacy of a 5 percent interest rate in particular business projects where no one's livelihood is endangered; however, no loans at interest may be charged to poor people who must borrow to live" (ibid.).

60. "These deals amount to usury, since they permitted a rate of return on a loan well in excess of the rates permitted by city ordinances. Businessmen found guilty of these deals were subject to harsh penalties. So were people charged with other deviations from ethical business practice" (Kingdon, "Calvin and Church Discipline," 27).

61. "What is significant here is that these two offices, the eldership and the deaconate, demonstrate Calvin's conviction that the church as an earthly institution has corporate responsibility for social and economic issues" (McKee, "The Character and Significance of John Calvin's Teaching," 18).

62. "The founding of the Genevan Academy was an important part of creating an international network of European leaders, which helped shape a new kind of religious (confessional) connectionalism" (ibid., 19).

63. "In Calvin's day the educational system was confusing: primary and secondary education was available both from public schools and private instructors, while university studies provided a basic grounding as well as a smattering of liberal arts to boys around thirteen or fourteen years old. In this context, the creation of colleges modeled on the Strasbourg Academy was profoundly innovative. Inspired by the teachings of the Brethren of the Common Life, this school offered a more structured curriculum, bringing in humanistic values and thus breaking free from scholasticism. In the Reformed world, theological training was added to the curriculum and the whole institution became similar to a university, whether in Geneva or in the United Provinces and the Rhineland. These changes marked more than a break with the practices of scholasticism. Instead, new institutions were established beyond the confines of the old ones" (Gilmont, *Calvin and the Printed Book*, 27). "Following the establishment of the Genevan Academy in 1559, the lectures were intended first and foremost for theology students and were always done in Latin" (ibid., 29).

64. For details on Calvin's life and ministry in Geneva, see the twenty volumes published in French and then translated into English in the United States. See, e.g., Paule Dubuis Hochuli, ed., *Registres du Conseil de Genève à l'époque de Calvin* (Geneva: Droz, 2003).

around his work as a teacher, preacher, and pastor.[65] He maintained a very rigorous preaching schedule.[66] The preached Word was very important to him.[67] Calvin's vision for *lectio continua* differentiated him from Lutheranism.[68] It is sometimes forgotten that Calvin, as a very busy churchman, also had to attend a lot of meetings![69] His life was also a life of prayer.[70]

Calvin defined the church in a way that was different from his contemporaries, both Lutheran (with only two marks of the church in their

65. For more on Calvin as teacher and pastor, see Randall C. Zachman, *John Calvin as Teacher, Pastor, and Theologian* (Grand Rapids: Baker Academic, 2006), 11–172. For Calvin on the sacraments, see Keith Mathison, *Given for You: Reclaiming Calvin's Doctrine of the Lord's Supper* (Phillipsburg, NJ: P&R Publishing, 2002). Hughes Oliphant Old gives a good overview in "Calvin's Theology of Worship," in *Give Praise to God: A Vision for Reforming Worship*, ed. Philip Graham Ryken (Phillipsburg, NJ: P&R Publishing, 2003), 412–35. See also W. Robert Godfrey, "Calvin, Worship and the Sacraments," in *A Theological Guide to Calvin's Institutes*, 368–89.

66. "Indeed, in 1541, Calvin probably preached twice on Sundays and three times during the week, one week out of two" (Gilmont, *Calvin and the Printed Book*, 30). "In that year, Calvin was preaching daily every second week. He also preached twice on Sundays every week, once in the morning and once in the afternoon. In his sermons he worked his way through entire books of the Bible. On Sundays he preached on the New Testament or Psalms, and during the week, he did the same for books of the Old Testament. In 1549, Calvin preached on three different books simultaneously, one on Sunday mornings, another on Sunday afternoons, and a third during the week. From 1554 onwards, he only dealt with one book of the Bible on Sundays" (ibid., 31). "Calvin's work as an author was one task among many for a very busy man. His regular schedule in Geneva included two sermons on Sundays, morning sermons on weekdays every second week, and exegetical lectures on the first three days of alternate weeks" (ibid., 277). For an excellent focused study, see Derek W. H. Thomas, *Proclaiming the Incomprehensible God: Calvin's Teaching on Job* (Fearn, Ross-shire, UK: Mentor, 2004).

67. "Everything Calvin did was underpinned by his sense of calling" (Gilmont, *Calvin and the Printed Book*, 285). "Calvin saw himself as a servant of the truth" (ibid.). When Calvin preached, "he believed that he was the conduit of God's word" (ibid.). In a sermon on Genesis, Calvin said: "And we should not consider sermons as coming from mortal men, but instead we should raise our eyes higher, so that we receive with reverence that which we know has come from on high, namely, from God" (ibid.).

68. "While Lutheran churches maintained the practice of preaching from set texts spread through the liturgical year, the Reformed preferred the *lectio continua*, and this principle prevailed in Geneva" (ibid., 27).

69. "Sermons and lectures each lasted an hour. Beyond that, he attended the Consistory meetings on Thursday and the *congregations* on Fridays" (ibid., 277).

70. See the fine work by Jae Sung Kim, "Prayer in Calvin's Soteriology," in *Calvinus Praeceptor Ecclesiae*, ed. Herman J. Selderhuis (Geneva: Droz, 2004), 265–74.

Confession of Augsburg) and other Reformed.[71] Those differences, and
the struggles that came with them, continued after Calvin's death.[72]

Development of Church Offices[73]

The offices of elder and deacon, which are the norm for Presbyterian
and Reformed believers today, were enhanced in Calvin's order.[74] Calvin
actually held to four church offices: elder, deacon, teacher, and pastor. The
work of the deacons was very important.[75] But Calvin also worked hard
to establish the "company of pastors" in the city and surrounding countryside.[76] Similar in structure to what had been done in Zurich before Calvin,

71. "The Zurichers, now led by Henry Bullinger, were terribly afraid of the Anabaptists
who had disrupted their program of reform, and they would thus have nothing to do with
formulas that to them smacked of Anabaptism. They supported discipline, but they wanted it
to be enforced by Christian governments" (Kingdon, "Calvin and Church Discipline," 30).

72. "That difference continued to fester, however, and broke out into the open after Calvin's
death as the Erastian quarrel in the Palatinate. There the theologian Olevianus, in close touch
with Geneva's Beza, pushed for discipline of a consistorial type, and the physician Erastus,
in close touch with Zurich's Bullinger, opposed it. That quarrel led to similar arguments
in England between Calvinist Puritans and Erastian Anglicans" (ibid.). The issue is three
marks for the church. "But the confessions adopted by churches outside of Switzerland that
were purely Calvinist did add discipline as a necessary mark and thus advanced a three-mark
definition of the true church" (ibid.).

73. For an insightful article, see Joseph H. Hall, "John Calvin's View of Church Government," in *A Theological Guide to Calvin's Institutes*, 393–96.

74. See McKee, "The Character and Significance of John Calvin's Teaching," 17–23;
Kingdon, "Calvin and Church Discipline," 25.

75. "The deaconate['s] . . . responsibility was to care for all those who could not care for
themselves, such as orphans, widows, and the handicapped. Calvin's sermons clearly demonstrate his conviction that this office is biblical and normative" (McKee, "The Character
and Significance of John Calvin's Teaching," 17).

76. Gilmont provides some interesting details: "The 1541 ordinances called for eight city
pastors. By 1544, there was already a total of eighteen, counting the pastors from rural areas.
From 1559 onwards, the Company of Pastors also included the professors of the Genevan
Academy" (Gilmont, *Calvin and the Printed Book*, 25). "The Company was led by a moderator, a post held by Calvin from 1541 until his death" (ibid.). "Thus the body of the faithful
had no say in the choice of their pastor, and civil authorities had at most the opportunity to
approve of the Company's choice" (ibid.). "The Company of Pastors was completely finan-
cially dependent on the Council" (ibid.). See also Erik A. deBoer, "Calvin and Colleagues:
Propositions and Disputations in the Context of the Congregations in Geneva," in *Calvinus
Praeceptor Ecclesiae*, 331–42; Elsie Anne McKee, "Calvin and His Colleagues as Pastors: Some
New Insights into the Collegial Ministry of Word and Sacraments," in *Calvinus Praeceptor
Ecclesiae*, 9–42.

there were regular meetings (held on Fridays) called the *congregations*. The number of men who attended these meetings reached sixty.[77]

The Work of the Consistory

The Consistory was a great benefit to the body of believers in Geneva.[78] There was, in Calvin's thought and practice, a relationship between the Genevan catechism and the work of the Consistory.[79]

The Consistory was an ecclesiastical body, but was closely related to civic power.[80] This work was important enough for Calvin to make its establishment a condition of his return from Strasbourg. He wanted the church to be able to excommunicate—without the possibility of that ecclesiastical judgment's being overturned by the (political) City Council.[81]

This court judged all manner of issues related to marriage.[82] The Consistory also prohibited prostitution and extramarital sexual activity.[83] But

77. Gilmont, *Calvin and the Printed Book*, 31.

78. "This discipline was not the harsh series of continual excommunications often caricatured in older accounts of Calvin's Geneva. The consistory was rather what he deftly calls a 'compulsory counseling service,' which worked diligently to correct and reconcile those who were at odds, for the sake of God's honor and building up the Christian community" (McKee, "The Character and Significance of John Calvin's Teaching," 17). See also Kingdon, "Calvin and Church Discipline," 26.

79. "He insisted that Geneva must institute a form of catechism to be sure that the entire community could understand Christian doctrine. And he insisted that Geneva must establish a form of discipline to be sure that the entire community behaves in a Christian way" (Kingdon, "Calvin and Church Discipline," 25).

80. "The Consistory was the main control mechanism over the moral and social life of the entire population of Geneva. It met on Thursdays and was chaired by a syndic. It included all the city pastors and twelve elders" (Gilmont, *Calvin and the Printed Book*, 25). "From the judicial point of view, therefore, the Consistory was a commission subject to the civil powers. For instance, it could call on the services of a court usher from the Council to summon perpetrators or witness. Nonetheless, the Consistory remained an ecclesiastical body, since the 1541 ordinances stated that elders were one of four categories of office-bearers in the church" (ibid.).

81. "Calvin insisted that a sentence of excommunication could be levied and lifted only by the Consistory, that it could not be appealed to the city government or overruled by the city's councils" (Kingdon, "Calvin and Church Discipline," 26).

82. Ibid., 26–27.

83. "It no longer permitted prostitution under careful controls as had the earlier government. It tried to eliminate all forms of sexual activity outside of marriage" (ibid., 27). See John Witte Jr. and Robert M. Kingdon, *Sex Marriage, and Family in John Calvin's Geneva* (Grand Rapids: Eerdmans, 2005).

the Consistory did more than work with matters of marriage—its labors included all manner of disputes.[84] The Consistory had a specifically "religious" work in regulating religious behavior at home.[85]

Indeed, "discipline" had become well established in Geneva by the end of Calvin's ministry.[86]

Church Finances

The church in the city and Genevan countryside was related both geographically (covering the same territory) and financially to the state.[87] Calvin had a lot to say about giving to Christ through the church. Those who were well off had significant financial responsibilities, since Christ has given every good gift. Calvin was very concerned for the Genevan poor.[88]

In conclusion, Calvin research continues strong and will develop in the future as more students analyze the minutes published by Droz in Geneva and Eerdmans in the United States.

84. "But the Consistory in actual fact went well beyond cases of this sort. A great deal of its time was devoted to resolving disputes—within families, as between parents and children or between brothers and sisters, among neighbors, and among business associates" (Kingdon, "Calvin and Church Discipline," 27).

85. "The Consistory also tried to discover and suppress devotional practices regarded as 'papist,' leftovers from Roman Catholic times" (ibid.). "Cases of this type were most common in the early years of the Consistory's operation and more often than not involved women rather than men, including many elderly women, some of them no doubt illiterate" (ibid.).

86. "Controlling all these types of misbehavior is what the Consistory meant by discipline, and by the end of Calvin's ministry the Consistory had become remarkably successful in establishing it" (ibid., 28).

87. "Calvin always thought of the church as a territorial institution, responsible for all the inhabitants of an area. This is why he saw the need for links between church and state. Furthermore, the pastors' salaries were paid by the state, and the Consistory, while an ecclesiastical institution, still exercised state control over all inhabitants without leaving room for rival confessional groups, or even worse, for atheism" (Gilmont, *Calvin and the Printed Book*, 26).

88. "Calvin deals with the cavil that what we have earned is our own possession, as if we had not received it" (McKee, "The Character and Significance of John Calvin's Teaching," 8). "Calvin believes that giving is not limited to sharing our profits or what is superfluous for our own needs: 'We are not to spare our capital funds, if the interest available from these fails to meet the necessities [of the poor]. In other words, your liberality has to go as far as the diminution of your patrimony, and the disposal of your estates'" (ibid., 9). "Implicit here is the idea that one cannot give a certain amount and wash his or her hands of the poor. The rule of love must be held constantly in mind; in each new situation, one must assess what the loving response to the neighbor should be in this concrete time and place" (ibid.).

19

CONSISTENTLY CONTESTED: CALVIN AMONG NINETEENTH-CENTURY REFORMED PROTESTANTS IN THE UNITED STATES

DARRYL G. HART

John Calvin cast a long shadow over theology in North America. According to E. Brooks Holifield, most of the history of theology in early America was "an extended debate, stretching over more than two centuries, about the meaning and truth of Calvinism." He adds that in New England among Congregationalists, and elsewhere among the Presbyterians and ethnic Reformed communions, Calvinism "attained to such a position of dominance in highly respected institutions"—from churches to schools and seminaries—"that most subsequent theological movements had to define themselves in relation to the Calvinist traditions."[1] In his

---

1. E. Brooks Holifield, *Theology in America: Christian Thought from the Age of the Puritans to the Civil War* (New Haven: Yale University Press, 2003), 10.

own history of American philosophy, Bruce Kuklick confirmed Holifield's argument and even furthered it by noting that Calvinism in its New England form did not finally decline until after the publication of Darwin's *Origin of Species* (1859). Until the 1870s, Kuklick explains, when social transformations made social science and pragmatism more plausible than theology, Calvinism dominated intellectual life in the northeastern United States and every academic institution that Congregationalists and Presbyterians founded. "Orthodox" theologians, rather than religious modernists such as the Unitarians or Transcendentalists, were "at the heart" of the nation's intellectual life.[2]

As accurate as these assessments are for recognizing the dynamics of elite discourse among professors responsible for undergraduate and seminary, the health of Calvinist theology among nineteenth-century American Protestants looks less rosy in other contexts. In fact, the rise of the appeal of popular sovereignty, combined with the political philosophy that informed a substantial part of the American founding, contributed greatly to ecclesiastical conditions and popular notions of autonomy that made Calvinism implausible. As Nathan O. Hatch demonstrates in his book on antebellum American religion, *The Democratization of American Christianity*, the new political and cultural changes wrought by revolution unleashed a religious populism that thrived in an environment of religious disestablishment. Freed from the restraints of state-controlled churches and polite learning, Methodists and Baptists not only grew faster than all other Protestant denominations but also inverted "the traditional modes of religious authority." Rather than "revering tradition, learning, solemnity, and decorum," as Calvinist clergy did, according to Hatch, "a diverse array of populist preachers exalted youth, free expression, and religious ecstasy." These religious upstarts assumed that "divine insight was reserved for the poor and humble rather than the proud and learned."[3]

On one level, such antagonism to Calvinism stemmed directly from the seemingly hierarchical plan of salvation involved in the doctrines of divine sovereignty and election. Men and women who had won their political

2. Bruce Kuklick, *Churchmen and Philosophers: From Jonathan Edwards to John Dewey* (New Haven: Yale University Press, 1985), xvi–xvii.
3. Nathan O. Hatch, *The Democratization of American Christianity* (New Haven: Yale University Press, 1989), 35.

freedoms must also have their soteriological liberty. But the disagreement with Calvinism went deeper to involve outright disdain for tradition. As one Protestant on the Kentucky frontier put it, "we are not personally acquainted with the writings of John Calvin, nor are we certain how nearly we agree with his views of divine truth; neither do we care."[4] The sentiments that Hatch records of one Kentucky Baptist, Daniel Parker, were likely typical of the sort of reception that graduates from the Northeast's colleges and seminaries received outside the relative civilization of the eastern seaboard. "The preaching manufactories of the east appear to be engaged in sending hirelings to the west," Parker groused, "and should any of those *man-made, devil sent,* place-hunting gentry come into our country, and read in our places, we shall likely raise against *them* seven shepards [*sic*], and eight principle [*sic*] men."[5]

From a different angle but a similar impulse came adjustments to Reformed theology that stemmed from the overwhelming support that Congregationalists in New England and Presbyterians in the middle states gave to the War for Independence. Mark A. Noll's *America's God: From Jonathan Edwards to Abraham Lincoln* (2002) argues thoroughly that the eighteenth-century Protestants who embraced republicanism—and Reformed Christians bulked exceedingly large in this group—did so in a manner that at once baptized the nation and secularized theology. Noll writes that the particular combination of Christian theology and republican political theory forced theologians to translate the historic Christian message into the dominant cultural languages of politics and intellectual life "so successfully that these languages were themselves converted and then enlisted for the decidedly religious purposes of evangelism, church formation, moral reform, and theological construction."[6]

But the price of this success was high and had significant consequences for the vitality of Calvinism. According to Noll, the lure of republicanism tempted Calvinists after Edwards to abandon the genius of Reformed theology for the dilemma of trying to justify civil war as an expression of God's just rule. Noll concedes that America's theologians in the early

4. Robert Marshall, quoted in ibid., 174.
5. Quoted in ibid., 178.
6. Mark A. Noll, *America's God: From Jonathan Edwards to Abraham Lincoln* (New York: Oxford University Press, 2002), 444.

nineteenth century still professed much that Edwards had. "Almost all still maintained that humans were sinners in need of salvation, and they continued, with only isolated exceptions like Ralph Waldo Emerson, to think that salvation was provided by God in Jesus Christ." Even so, America's Calvinists were "much more likely than before to hold that the human will was an active, necessary, and determinative participant in the reception of divine grace, that the human mind played a decisive role in determining the reality of both natural and supernatural phenomena, and that personal apprehension and action were more important than traditional, mediated, or historic authorities in determining the nature of Christian truth."[7] Consequently, for Noll the key moves in the creation of evangelical America were also the same moves that established a secular society. "If in a great surge of evangelization and moral reform, American Protestants almost converted the nation, so too did the nation mold the Christian gospel in the contours of its own shape."[8]

As much as these recent assessments by distinguished historians appear to yield two different verdicts about nineteenth-century Calvinism, both perspectives share the view that Reformed theology during the century after the American Revolutionary War was on the decline. The main point of disagreement is timing—whether it occurred before or after the United States' Civil War. What most of these books fail to examine is the actual content of Calvinism in relationship to the main outlines of John Calvin's own teaching and ministry. More often than not, the interest in Reformed theology is less about Calvinist teaching itself and more in Reformed and Presbyterian thinkers' thought about other subjects—such as philosophy, political theory, and educational philosophy.

What follows is an examination of three important debates among nineteenth-century American Calvinists over bragging rights on being followers of Calvin. These disagreements—two between Congregationalists and Old School Presbyterians, and one between German Reformed and American Calvinists—demonstrate that Calvin mattered less to would-be Calvinists than either their own originality or Reformed voices from the seventeenth century. The result is an isolation of parts

7. Ibid., 231.
8. Ibid., 444.

of Calvin's teaching and practice that the Frenchman himself had held together in the context of active ministry within the church. In that case, the decline of American Calvinism during the course of the nineteenth century may have less to do with external threats from American intellectual or sociopolitical circumstances than with the misappropriation of Calvin by Calvinists themselves.[9]

Consistent versus Federal Calvinism

Church life in the newly established United States presented an unusual set of circumstances for most Protestants. The disestablishment of religion that the Constitution's First Amendment codified set most communions on a voluntaristic footing. Unlike previous arrangements whereby churches received subsidies from the state as part of the official apparatus of the nation, disestablishment in principle leveled all churches, made them dependent on their own followers for financial support, and freed each denomination to regulate its own affairs independent from the oversight of government. To be sure, at the state level ecclesiastical establishments remained in place after 1789, and those legal arrangements lasted the longest in New England, thanks to the Standing Order among Congregationalists in Connecticut and Massachusetts. But despite the longevity of state churches in various places, the First Amendment signaled the future of church life: denominations would not receive state subsidies and in turn would be free to pursue their ministries as they deemed best.[10]

The new political context for the churches gave an advantage to denominations that were either independent of tax support or less particular about a learned ministry. Baptists and Methodists expanded dramatically during the first half of the nineteenth century, while Episcopalians and Congregationalists lagged behind. Because Presbyterians had never

9. An older but still useful and original contribution to the study of Calvinism's demise is Daniel Walker Howe, "The Decline of Calvinism: An Approach to Its Study," *Comparative Studies in Society and History* 14.3 (June 1972): 306–27.

10. Mark A. Noll, *A History of Christianity in the United States and Canada* (Grand Rapids: Eerdmans, 1992), 143–53, provides a helpful overview of the new American environment for church life.

enjoyed an establishment status in any of the American colonies or states, they had figured out ways to minister without the support that their counterparts in such places as Scotland possessed. Even so, demands for pastors who knew Greek and Hebrew, not to mention a prior training in the liberal arts, put Presbyterians at a disadvantage in American church life—perhaps not as great as that experienced by Episcopalians and Congregationalists, but sufficiently burdensome to prevent Presbyterians from competing with Baptists and Methodists as the most popular and rapidly growing Protestant denominations in the new nation.[11]

The Calvinist remedy to this predicament was the 1801 Plan of Union between Congregationalists and Presbyterians. Since they engaged in regular fraternal relations during the Revolutionary War and its aftermath, an effort to cooperate in church planting in the recently acquired Northwest Territory made a lot of sense for denominations hoping to keep up with congregants who were migrating westward in search of cheap land and economic health. The plan itself raised a number of awkward procedures, such as what to do in the case of a Congregationalist minister functioning in a Presbyterian congregation and where to resolve disputes should they arise. But aside from ecclesiastical anomalies, the Plan of Union was about the best that Calvinists could do to try to keep up with the expansion of the new nation.[12]

One wrinkle that the Plan's designers did not foresee was the friction that might ensue from the different trajectories of New England and Presbyterian Calvinism. As much as Jonathan Edwards may have been an inspiration for Calvinists in both communions, the Northampton minister's speculative theology, at least in the hands of his most admiring followers, was not a stable basis either for denominational cooperation or for maintaining and defending Reformed orthodoxy. As early as the late 1760s, when John Witherspoon arrived in North America to preside over the College of New Jersey, the philosophical tensions between Edwards's

11. See Roger Finke and Rodney Stark, *The Churching of America, 1776–2005: Winners and Losers in Our Religious Economy*, 2nd ed. (New Brunswick, NJ: Rutgers University Press, 2005), for a provocative study of Protestants in America's religious free market.

12. On the Plan of Union and its context, see D. G. Hart and John R. Muether, *Seeking A Better Country: 300 Years of American Presbyterianism* (Phillipsburg, NJ: P&R Publishing, 2007), chap. 5.

version of idealism and Scottish Common Sense Realism surfaced, with the new college president excluding the curriculum and many of the tutors that Edwards had established in his brief tenure at the college before succumbing to smallpox in 1758. Meanwhile, Edwards's successors in the Connecticut River Valley, the New Divinity men, emphasized pieces of their mentor's philosophical system that seriously diminished the contours of Reformed teaching on the nature of original sin, the efficacy of the atonement, and man's capacity for virtue.[13]

The theological tensions that had been percolating beneath the surface in American Calvinism did not finally come out in the open between Congregationalists and Presbyterians until the 1820s. Contrary to the Plan of Union's intention, the mingling of these two Calvinistic bodies actually brought these potential antagonisms out into the open, thanks to the regular deliberations of and interactions between each communion. The occasion for these disagreements among Calvinists was the popularity of Charles G. Finney's revivals along with the gradual infiltration of the New England theology into the center of Presbyterian strength through the ministry of Albert Barnes. Finney entered the ranks of Presbyterians in 1824 when the Oneida Presbytery of western New York ordained the former attorney to be an evangelist. Barnes's preaching caused agitation a few years later when he was pastor of First Presbyterian Church in New York City and preached a provocative revival sermon in nearby New Jersey, entitled "The Way of Salvation." In 1830 when Barnes became the pastor of First Presbyterian Church in Philadelphia, he left the orbit of New England and entered a region where an Old School Presbyterian Calvinism was beginning to assume its own identity. As George Marsden well explains, the revivals that both Finney and Barnes advocated and led presumed a theology that sounded strikingly different from the Calvinism of the Westminster Confession of Faith and catechisms, the theological standard of the Presbyterian Church. According to Marsden, the views of Finney and Barnes "denied that men were held guilty for Adam's sin; . . .

---

13. For a useful overview of tensions between Presbyterians and Congregationalists in which Edwards was an authoritative guide for both sides, see Mark A. Noll, "Jonathan Edwards and Nineteenth-Century Theology," in *Jonathan Edwards and the American Experience*, ed. Nathan O. Hatch and Harry S. Stout (New York: Oxford University Press, 1988), 260–87.

rejected the doctrine that the atonement was a substitutionary sacrifice for the elect only"; and held that "the inability of sinners was limited to the will, implying . . . that the unregenerate had the ability to contribute to their own salvation."[14]

Even if the differences between the Calvinism taught and defended among middle-state and Southern Presbyterians and the version promulgated in New York and New England did not take shape until the division between Old School and New School Presbyterians in the 1830s, they did tap theological developments that had been taking shape for several decades. A particularly revealing aspect of these different conceptions of Calvinism was the doctrine of the atonement. The New School party of Presbyterians followed the trajectory of New England theology by advocating a governmental theory of the atonement along with other modifications of Calvinist teaching on sin and human capacity for virtue, while the Old School wing held on to constructions from the era of Reformed scholasticism and related notions of federal headship, original sin, and total depravity.[15]

Since the late eighteenth century, the adherents of the New Divinity in New England had generally adopted the governmental theory of the atonement, partly because of theological developments among Edwardseans and partly to counter charges against Calvinism for rendering God vindictive and arbitrary.[16] For instance, Jonathan Edwards Jr. in 1785 articulated the governmental theory of the atonement in a series of sermons. In order to affirm the authority of divine law, Edwards believed that an atonement was necessary. Without the atonement, the law and the Lawgiver would fall into contempt. Of course, God could "uphold

14. George M. Marsden, *The Evangelical Mind and the New School Presbyterian Experience: A Case Study of Thought and Theology in Nineteenth-Century America* (New Haven: Yale University Press, 1970), 53. Marsden's book remains the standard account of New School Presbyterianism, a version of Calvinism that adhered more to New England conversations than to the Reformed teaching propagated at Princeton Seminary and Presbyterians in the South.

15. For an overview of these developments, see Noll, "Jonathan Edwards and Nineteenth-Century Theology"; Hart and Muether, *Seeking a Better Country*, chaps. 5–7.

16. The following several paragraphs are adapted from D. G. Hart, "Princeton and the Law: Enlightened and Reformed," in *The Law Is Not of Faith: Essays on Works and Grace in the Mosaic Covenant*, ed. Bryan D. Estelle, J. V. Fesko, and David VanDrunen (Phillipsburg, NJ: P&R Publishing, 2009), 59–74.

his moral government over intelligent creatures once his law hath fallen into contempt." He could simply use "irresistible force." But this would be a different kind of government from a moral one that needed to have a scheme of "rewards and punishments." In this way, the atonement supported the various ends of "the authority of the law, the dignity of the divine moral government, and the consistency of the divine conduct in legislation and execution."[17]

Behind this understanding of the atonement stood a view of law and grace that was essentially antithetical. According to Edwards, "grace is ever so opposed to justice that they mutually limit each other. Wherever grace begins, justice ends; and wherever justice begins, grace ends." This antagonistic relationship led him to render the atonement not as a "payment of our debt." "If it had been," Edwards explained, "our discharge would have been an act of mere justice, and not of grace." To avoid the implication that the atonement lacked a display of divine grace, he appealed to the idea of general or public justice. "Whatever is right is said to be just, or an act of justice; and whatever is wrong or improper to be done, is said to be unjust, or an act of injustice." General or public justice followed from the Edwardsean notion of virtue, or disinterested benevolence. To act in conformity to the "dictates of general benevolence, or to see the glory of God and the good of the universe," was to practice general justice.[18] Rather than seeing grace as flip sides of the same coin stemming from the covenant of works, the Edwardsean idea of virtue severed grace from law and set into motion the governmental view of the atonement.

From the late eighteenth century down to the middle decades of the nineteenth century, the governmental theory of the atonement became the dominant teaching among New England's theologians. According to Frank Hugh Foster, "the New England writers emphasized the divine government as the sphere within which the atonement was wrought." In so doing, they "all with increasing clearness founded that government upon an ethical idea, a conception of the character of God as love, which redeems the theory from the charge of artificiality and superficiality."[19]

17. Jonathan Edwards Jr., quoted in Frank Hugh Foster, *A Genetic History of the New England Theology* (Chicago: University of Chicago Press, 1907), 201–2.

18. Ibid., 202–3.

19. Ibid., 215–16.

This was as true for the orthodox at Andover Seminary as it was for Connecticut peers at Yale. Edward D. Griffin, for instance, who taught at Andover Seminary before presiding over Williams College, asserted that a moral government was the fundamental rule of "motives" because "these are the instruments by which it works." Moral government undergirded the entirety of God's revelation and dealings with man and comprehended "the atonement, and all the covenants made with man, and all the institutions of religion, with the whole train of means and privileges." For Griffin, the moral government and its vindication by the atonement turned men from "passive receivers of sovereign impressions" into responsible active moral agents.[20] So too did Nathaniel W. Taylor argue from his lectern at Yale Divinity School when he taught that moral government was the fundamental aspect of God's rule and the chief influence in cultivating genuine human virtue. A moral governor who was "truly and perfectly benevolent, must feel the highest approbation of right moral action and the highest disapprobation of wrong moral action on the part of his subjects." To display such approval and disapproval, and to reestablish the original pattern of laws, rewards, and punishments for his subjects, Taylor reasoned, God needed an atonement for sin.[21] In the hands of Calvinists in New England, the atonement had lost its significance as an instance of divine mercy that accorded with the just demands of the law but had become instead an iteration and vindication of the universal standard of benevolence.

To the south the Presbyterians connected to Princeton Seminary articulated a markedly different understanding of Calvinism, one that drew directly on categories supplied by seventeenth-century Reformed orthodoxy through the likes of Francis Turretin and the Westminster Confession of Faith and catechisms. Again, teaching on the atonement is instructive for the differences between Congregationalists and Presbyterians. For instance, Charles Hodge's statement was straightforward even if predictable. "The work of Christ," he wrote, "is a real satisfaction, of infinite merit, to the vindicatory justice of God; so that He saves His people by doing for them, and in their stead, what they were unable to

20. Griffin, quoted in ibid., 212.
21. Taylor, quoted in ibid., 214.

do for themselves, satisfying the demands of the law in their behalf, and bearing its penalty in their stead . . ."[22]

The brevity of Hodge's statement misses lengthy explanations that linked the atonement to a federal theology that drew on prior under-standings of the covenant of works, the moral law, and the law's require-ments and penalties. For instance, on the topic of Christ's satisfaction, Hodge insisted that the Savior's work satisfied the justice of God. This justice was not vindictive but "vindicatory." About the justice of God Hodge was adamant:

> This is the corner-stone, and the whole fabric falls into ruin if that stone be removed. That God cannot pardon sin without a satisfaction to jus-tice, and that He cannot have fellowship with the unholy, are the two great truths which are revealed in the constitution of our nature as well as in the Scriptures, and which are recognized in all forms of religion, human or divine. It is because the demands of justice are met by the work of Christ, that His gospel is the power of God unto salvation, and that it is so unspeakably precious to those whom the Spirit of God have convinced of sin.[23]

Hodge drew the implication that the chief design of Christ's satisfac-tion "is neither to make a moral impression upon the offenders them-selves, nor to operate didactically on other intelligent creatures, but to satisfy the demands of justice; so that God can be just in justifying the ungodly."[24]

Also important to Hodge's understanding of the Reformed doctrine of the atonement was a distinction between the satisfaction of divine justice and meeting the "demands of the law." The law demanded far more than punishment of sin. It also required God's creatures to be holy. For man "to love and obey God" could never cease to be obligatory. But Christ's work on the cross delivered man from his "federal relation" to the law. "We are no longer bound to be free from all sin," Hodge wrote: "We are not under

22. Charles Hodge, *Systematic Theology* (New York: Scribner's, 1871–73; repr., Grand Rapids: Eerdmans, 1979), 563.
23. Ibid., 492.
24. Ibid., 493.

law but under grace." But this deliverance did not stem from the abroga-
tion of the law or from "lowering its demands." Through Christ's passive
and active obedience, "he endured all that the law demands."[25] Unlike the
New England Calvinists, who saw a tension between the law and grace,
Hodge contended that a proper understanding of grace depended on
prior understanding of the law's demands as comprehended in the covenant of works.

This understanding of the atonement led directly to critiques from
Hodge of New England Calvinism and its offshoots infiltrating the Pres-
byterian Church. One of his most sustained critiques of New School
Presbyterian theology in general and the New England view of the atone-
ment particularly appeared in a review of *Christ, the Only Sacrifice*, a pamphlet by the New School Presbyterian minister Nathan S. Beman. A
graduate of Middlebury College in Vermont and widely regarded as a
New School leader, Beman was in the estimation of Holifield simply a
"Presbyterian Edwardsean."[26] Although he was by no means hostile to
Edwards and had in fact received his own theological instruction from
Archibald Alexander, a reluctant Old School Presbyterian who harbored
affection for the experimental Calvinism that Edwards defended and
embodied, Hodge gave no room to Beman and showed the extent of the
differences between Calvinism above and below New York City. Again,
Hodge criticized Beman's neglect of the federal scheme that made sense
of Calvinism's soteriology.

On the one hand, Hodge's concern stemmed from a view of salvation
that seemed to stop with a general offer of the gospel but that overlooked
"that Christ came into the world and accomplished the work of redemption, in execution of the covenant of grace."[27] Beman's teaching only
made "the pardon of all men possible," as if Christ's work only brought
"the sinner within the reach of mercy."[28] This notion clearly left aside any
consideration of either the covenant of redemption or the covenant of
works. "If Christ suffered by covenant," Hodge explained, "if that covenant

25. Ibid.
26. Holifield, *Theology in America*, 374.
27. Charles Hodge, "Beman on the Atonement," reprinted in Charles Hodge, *Essays and Reviews Selected from the Princeton Review* (New York: Robert Carter & Bros., 1879), 175.
28. Ibid., 176.

promised to him his people as his reward and inheritance, on condition of his obedience and death, then assuredly, when he performed that condition, the salvation of all whom the Father had given to him was rendered absolutely certain."[29] On the other hand, Hodge believed that in treating the atonement as merely a symbolical display of moral instruction, New England Calvinism and its progeny vitiated "the essential nature of the atonement."[30] According to Hodge, who believed that he was simply following the pattern of sound doctrine handed down by Reformed orthodoxy, the Calvinist understanding of the atonement taught

> that Christ, by really obeying the law, and really bearing its penalty in the place of his people, and according to the stipulations of the covenant of grace, secured the salvation of all whom the Father had given him, and at the same time throws open the door of mercy to all who choose to enter it . . .[31]

Hodge understood that either from the direction of Finney's free-will theology or from the Unitarians' critique of Calvinism as making grace arbitrary, the classic Reformed view looked incompatible with American ideas about the virtuous capacity of human nature. But he countered that by treating the atonement as if it only made mercy possible, New Schoolers were the ones who were really restricting the gracious provision of Christ's sacrifice. Beman had in effect left out "the very soul of the doctrine."[32]

These rival versions of Calvinism were a major source of the break in 1837 between the Old School and New School Presbyterians, a division that would eventually also lead to a breach between even the New School Presbyterians and Congregationalists. Throughout the 1830s Presbyterian conservatives through a variety of mechanisms attempted to shut down the influence of New England Calvinism within the PCUSA. None of these efforts were successful until the 1837 General Assembly convening in Philadelphia yielded a clear majority for the Old School. By a vote of 143 to 110, the Assembly ratified a motion to abrogate the

29. Ibid., 179.
30. Ibid., 183.
31. Ibid.
32. Ibid.

1801 Plan of Union. The logical extension of this action was a decision to exscind four synods that had come to the PCUSA through cooperation with Congregationalists—those of Western Reserve (Ohio), Utica (New York), Geneva (New York), and Genesee (New York), areas where the New England presence was strongest. With one vote, the Presbyterian Church excluded 28 presbyteries, 509 ministers, and close to 60,000 communicant members. In addition, the Assembly adopted a statement that specified sixteen doctrinal errors that had been agitating the church for the past two decades, thus finally achieving the theological clarity that the New Englanders had obscured. Among those errors enumerated were the assertions that Adam was not the federal representative of the human race, that Christ did not become the legal substitute for sinners, that the atonement was merely an exhibition of divine wrath, and that the atonement applied equally to the elect and nonelect.[33]

Although the break between New School and Old School Presbyterians essentially brought the dispute between New England and Old School Calvinism to an end, both sides continued to monitor each other, and rivalry between these camps resurfaced under other topics. One of the most heated exchanges took place more than a decade after the Old School–New School split, when again Charles Hodge engaged in a protracted debate with Edwards Amasa Park over the nature of theological language. As much as this dispute involved the question whether theology resembled literature more than science, it also tapped the older controversy over the nature of Calvinism because it concerned a proposal for putting that older contest behind and chalking it up to a misuse of theological terminology.[34]

33. On the Old School–New School Presbyterian division, see Hart and Muether, *Seeking a Better Country*, chap. 6.
34. The debate between Park and Hodge ran as follows: Park, "The Theology of the Intellect and That of the Feelings," *Bibliotheca Sacra* 7 (1850): 533–69; Hodge, "The Theology of the Intellect and That of the Feelings," *Biblical Repertory and Princeton Review* 22 (1850): 642–74; Park, "Remarks on the Princeton Review," *Bibliotheca Sacra* 8 (1851): 135–80; Hodge, "Prof. Park's Remarks on the Princeton Review," *Biblical Repertory and Princeton Review* 23 (1851): 306–47; Park, "Unity and Diversities of Belief Even on Imputed and Involuntary Sin: With Comments on a Second Article in the Princeton Review," *Bibliotheca Sacra* 8 (1851): 594–647; Hodge, "Prof. Park and the Princeton Review," *Biblical Repertory and Princeton Review* 23 (1851): 674–95; Park, "New England Theology," *Bibliotheca Sacra* 9 (1852): 170–220.

Park was arguably the last proponent and defender of Edwardsean Calvinism in a line of theological development that lasted over a century and that seeped from its home in the Connecticut River Valley to central New England. Park himself taught theology at Andover Seminary for close to half a century, and by the end of his life in 1900 was the last advocate of New England's Consistent Calvinism. He acquired what Bruce Kuklick has called "arguably the most important post in American divinity"[35] by route of studies at Brown University, Andover, and Yale Divinity School, experience in the pulpit, and success as a revivalist. Before teaching theology, Park taught sacred rhetoric also at Andover, duties that in 1836 persuaded him to leave the pastorate. His awareness of the power of language both as a pastor and as a professor of homiletics likely inclined him to hear Horace Bushnell's provocative 1848 lecture "Dogma and Spirit," delivered before students and faculty at Andover with a measure of sympathy. Bushnell, a Congregationalist minister in Hartford, Connecticut, had read in English Romanticism and believed that an impasse in doctrinal wrangling might have been on the horizon if theologians could simply acknowledge the metaphorical or figurative nature of language. But the advent of theological peace came with a price in Bushnell's argument. Not only was language inherently incapable of bearing the weight of literalism; doctrinal expressions as well were inadequate for capturing religious truth.[36]

Park was apparently intrigued by the potential of this proposal, and although he defended the ability of systematic theology to articulate essential Christian truths, he still believed that Bushnell's point could be useful for harmonizing the antagonisms among American Calvinists. In an essay published two years after Bushnell's lecture, Park expressed his belief that doctrinal propositions could be classified as belonging to either the "theology of the intellect" or the "theology of the feelings." Accordingly, Park distinguished between rational and figurative doctrinal expressions, the former satisfying the criteria of the inquiring mind, the latter moving the devout heart. The theology of the intellect, in other words, was the

---

35. Kuklick, *Churchmen and Philosophers*, 205.

36. Horace Bushnell, "Dogma and Spirit," in *God in Christ* (New York: Charles Scribner's Sons, 1876), 277–356. On reactions to and fallout from Bushnell's address for American Protestant theology, see D. G. Hart, "Divided between Heart and Mind: The Critical Period for Protestant Thought in America," *Journal of Ecclesiastical History* 38 (April 1987): 254–70.

product of all the faculties essential to reason and took shape in precise, logical, and well-proportioned propositions. In contrast, the theology of the feelings was characterized by vagueness, metaphor, and vivid language that was designed to move the affections. This distinction allowed Park to propose a remedy for the apparent contradictions that afflicted systematic theology. Not only would the distinction between theologies of intellect and feeling provide a way to overcome theological quarrels, but it also accounted for the discrepancies within a theological system. Many tensions within Christian theology could be resolved if theologians simply recognized that certain doctrines were products not of the intellect but of the feelings.[37]

Park was responding to Bushnell in the context of New England Calvinism and probably did not realize how provocative his argument was for Calvinists in other parts of the country. Charles Hodge, who by 1850 had established a reputation for sniffing out any form of theological novelty through the pages of the *Biblical Repertory and Princeton Review*, a journal that he founded and chiefly edited, quickly turned the tables on Park. The exchange between the two foremost American Calvinists would last eighteen months and consume 250 pages of theological journal format.

Hodge had already reviewed Bushnell's discourse on theological language, and because he found the Hartford pastor's views wanting, he was not inclined to appreciate Park's generous reading of Bushnell. The Princeton professor judged Bushnell's theory of language to be a fast track to skepticism and unbelief. Hodge complained that Bushnell had relegated the knowledge of God to the subjective realm of the feelings, and transformed the Bible into little more than cunningly devised fables. Hodge countered that the Bible was principally didactic in nature, and that it was addressed not only to the feelings but also to the intellect and the imagination. As much as religious truths resonated with all of man's faculties, for knowledge of God to be real, it needed to be comprehended with man's reason.[38]

37. Park, "The Theology of the Intellect and That of the Feelings," 535–40, 545–51, 558–61.

38. Hodge, "God in Christ," reprinted in *Essays and Reviews*, ed. Arnold S. Nash (New York: Robert Carter, 1856), 453–71.

Hodge registered similar criticisms against Park, and faulted the Andover theologian for not erecting adequate barriers against Bushnell's inherent anti-intellectualism. The Princetonian was willing to concede that theology relied on metaphorical expressions and that figurative language sometimes helped with comprehension. But these less-than-literal aspects of systematic theology did not make the study of Scripture and God any less intelligible or rational. Figurative constructions either in the creeds or in the Bible were addressed to the intellect as much as to the feelings, and it was an intellectual dodge to relegate some to the former and others to the latter. Thus, a figurative expression in Scripture or theology was not to be evaluated as if either beautiful or ugly, or as either moving or dull; metaphors and figures of speech needed to be judged as either true or false, as either describing religious reality or failing to do so. Hodge particularly faulted both Bushnell and Park for failing to take a proposition in its original context. When properly situated, a metaphorical expression was capable of communicating the full range of ideas, from abstract concepts to simple notions.[39]

Beyond problems in an impoverished understanding of theological language, Hodge detected in both Bushnell and Park a presumption in favor of reason over special revelation. Consequently, when Bushnell appealed to figurative language to raise questions about the Trinity and the incarnation, or when Park resorted to metaphor to question older teachings about the bondage of the will and the atonement, they were basically raising objections from their own intellects about Christian teaching and trying to camouflage such dissent with a theory about the limits of human communication. The fundamental error in both cases was to chalk up to incomprehensibility or irrationality whatever was objectionable to man's intellect apart from Scripture's teaching. The effect of Bushnell and Park's proposal was to hold that certain doctrines made sense only if they could be comprehended—a conclusion that jeopardized a whole range of doctrinal truths. Hodge countered that although the Bible and the creeds contained ideas that could not be grasped intellectually in all their complexity or significance, these

39. Hodge, "Theology of the Intellect and That of the Feelings, Article I," reprinted in *Essays and Reviews*, 548–49.

ideas were still capable of being expressed in rational categories and judged as either true or false.[40]

Aside from a debate about the nature of theological language, also at issue in this contest was a question of Calvinism's intellectual coherence. Particularly in Park's essay, Hodge detected an abandonment of the main contours of Reformed orthodoxy—and this is why the exchange between Princeton and Andover was so extensive. Until Bushnell's proposal, the problem that Old School Presbyterians had with New England Calvinism was its rejection of federal theology and the covenantal context for Reformed soteriology. Throughout the 1820s and 1830s, the doctrines of the imputation of Adam's sin, the vicarious atonement, and the imputation of Christ's righteousness had been the main issues separating New School and Old School Presbyterians. But with Bushnell's theory appropriated by Park came an attempt to relegate the federal theology of the Old School to the realm of metaphor and human subjectivity, and to claim for New England's Calvinism the honor of a properly intellectual or reasonable theology. Hodge rejected Park's attempt to place Reformed teaching about original sin, the bondage of the will, and the atonement in the category of the theology of the feelings, as well as its corollary that the Consistent Calvinism of New England was a rationally coherent system that put the abrasive metaphors of the old orthodoxy in a new precise and didactic form. For the Princeton professor, Park's effort was a clever attempt to reconceptualize the arguments between Presbyterians and Congregationalists, but it was essentially one more sign of New England's break with historically Reformed teaching.[41]

The tussle between America's two greatest Calvinist theologians did indeed come down to each man's understanding of the Reformed tradition and his respective school's place in it. Park and Hodge disagreed vigorously on the theology of Jonathan Edwards. Late in the exchange, Hodge threw a significant uppercut:

> We apprize Professor Park that if he hopes to succeed in his present course, or to carry with him the sympathy and confidence of New England,

40. Hodge, "God in Christ," 443–47; Hodge, "Theology of the Intellect and That of the Feelings, Article II," in *Essays and Reviews*, 607–11.
41. Hodge, "Theology of the Intellect . . . Article I," 545.

the first thing he has to do is answer Edwards on the Will, Edwards on the Affections, and Edwards on Original Sin. When he has done this, it will be time enough to come all the way down to us. In the meanwhile, we think it best to step aside, and let him face his real antagonist.[42]

These were indeed fighting words to a theologian who had written extensively on the New England theologians, considered himself one of its loyal followers, and for good measure was named after Edwards. Despite his own investment in the tradition that followed in the wake of Edwards's theology and ministry, Park responded by correcting Hodge on the nature of the New England theology. "It includes not the peculiarities in which Edwards differed, as he is known to have differed, from the larger part of his most eminent followers," Park clarified, "nor the peculiarities in which any one of his followers differed, as some of them did, from the larger part of the others." Instead, the New England theology comprehended "the principles, with their logical sequences, which the greater number of our most celebrated divines have approved expressly or by implication."[43] After explaining the various tenets and methods that distinguished the New England school from others and as the superior form of Calvinism, Park summarized the chief achievement of Edwards and his followers as theological comprehension. It "unites a high, but not an ultra Calvinism, on the decrees and agency of God, with a philosophical, but not an Arminian theory, on the freedom and worth of the human soul." In other words, Edwards and his followers united the apparently antagonistic elements of "certainty and spontaneous choice."[44]

The question, then, that had animated Presbyterians and Congregationalists for half a century was the degree of continuity between Edwards and later New England developments. For Hodge, the movement was all downhill after Edwards. He believed that Edwards refuted the major tenets of Park's theology, and the New Haven theology of Taylor was a major turning point in moving Congregationalists away from colonial Calvinism. So thorough was the demise of Edwards's orthodoxy that

42. Hodge, "Theology of the Intellect and That of the Feelings, Article III," in *Essays and Reviews*, 624.
43. Park, "New England Theology," 174.
44. Ibid., 212.

Hodge could assert that "old-school theology" was foreign language to Park. Endeavoring to teach "Old-school men Old-school theology ... is very much like a Frenchman teaching an Englishman how to pronounce English." Like the "amiable Gaul," Park was sure "to make sad work with the dental aspirations."[45] In contrast, Park viewed the entire New England theological enterprise as trying to work out the tensions within Edwards's Calvinism that Edwards himself was at pains to explain. Edwards's followers may have differed with him on the particulars, but the unity within the New England theology was the theological project itself. According to Park, New England's Calvinism was "the only system of speculative orthodoxy which will endure examination; and it is, therefore, destined to prevail." Park added that "the spirit and plain import of the Bible, are in favor of it. The moral instincts of the race are in favor of it. The common sense of common men is in favor of it. They can be kept back from it, only by the incessant roll of a polemic drum, which alarms them by its discordant sounds."[46]

Mark Noll's evaluation of this debate captures well the difference between Hodge and Park regarding their distinct understandings of continuity and discontinuity of American Calvinism after Edwards. Noll argues that Park perceived "the intellectual spirit of Edwards more accurately than did Princeton." The New Englanders, according to Noll, were "bold and original thinkers who ... wished to be known as Calvinists while calling no man 'father.'" In contrast, Old School Presbyterian theology was singular in its self-understanding as a conserving effort. Hodge was "willing to say 'father' to a whole host of orthodox divines."[47]

British Calvinism Is Not the Only Option

While New England Congregationalists, their New School Presbyterian cousins, and Old School Presbyterians were debating the legitimacy of rival claims to the mantle of American Calvinism, an ethnic strain of Reformed theology outside the northeastern axis of elite seminaries

45. Hodge, "Theology of the Intellect ... Article III," 633.
46. Park, "New England Theology," 214, 219.
47. Noll, "Jonathan Edwards and Nineteenth-Century Theology," 268–69.

and divinity schools was becoming frustrated by the narrowness of Calvinist expression in the United States. At Mercersburg Seminary in the relative isolation of central Pennsylvania, John Williamson Nevin and Philip Schaff were training ministers for the German Reformed Church, an ethnic communion that had developed more or less independently of Presbyterian or Congregationalist influence. To be sure, the German Reformed were experiencing the difficulties that followed any non-English-speaking church in the United States that tried to hold on to the best of its own traditions while adapting them to a new ecclesiastical and cultural environment. During the early nineteenth century, the German Reformed Church experienced specific difficulties from two directions, thanks to its hyphenated status—one came from American revivalism, the other from intellectual developments in Germany that were foreign to the United States' Anglo-American philosophical and educational patterns. To complicate matters even more, the German Reformed's senior theologian at Mercersburg, Nevin, was a Scotch-Irish Presbyterian in background who had studied first in the New England Puritan tradition at Union College in New York State, and then at Princeton Seminary.[48]

German Reformed Calvinism may have assimilated more organically if not for the presence of Nevin, who kept tabs on American and German theological developments. Thanks to his own experiences, during the 1840s Nevin developed a significant critique of American Calvinism, whether the New England variety represented by Park or the Old School Presbyterian version promoted by Hodge. Nevin took issue most directly with the Puritan tradition and accused it of functioning with an inappropriately low view of the church, an illegitimately high view of the individual and his experience of conversion, and a strangely exalted view of the Bible over against the creeds of the church, especially the Apostles' Creed. Although Nevin was by no means the purest of theological founts— at one point he contemplated joining the Roman Catholic Church before experiencing physical, mental, and spiritual exhaustion—he did register an incisive critique of Anglo-American Calvinism that revealed the ways

48. For an overview of the German Reformed tradition in America and Nevin's place in it, see D. G. Hart, *John Williamson Nevin: High Church Calvinist* (Phillipsburg, NJ: P&R Publishing, 2005), chaps. 1–2.

in which Congregationalists and Presbyterians had lost touch with the liturgical and sacramental theology of Calvin and other sixteenth-century Reformed theologians. The import of Nevin's critique became especially evident in a lengthy debate he had with Hodge over Christ's presence in the Lord's Supper. In fact, at roughly the same time that Hodge was feuding with Park, he was also responding to another Calvinist rival from a different geographical direction.

When Nevin wrote *The Mystical Presence: A Vindication of the Reformed or Calvinistic Doctrine of the Holy Eucharist* (1846), he had his sights less on American Calvinists than on debates within his own communion. In *The Anxious Bench* (1844), he had objected to the reception of revivalist practices among the German Reformed. He and Schaff had also been the object of attacks from German Reformed pastors who were more friendly to revivalism and believed Mercersburg's high view of the church was little more than warmed-over Roman Catholicism. Nevin's book on the Lord's Supper drew directly upon the church piety that Nevin had used to criticize revivalism, while also trying to defend the Mercersburg theology as genuinely Calvinistic from German Reformed critics.

In order to contrast the views of historic Calvinism with those of its German-American proponents, Nevin appealed directly to Calvin. According to Nevin, "To obtain a proper view of the original doctrine of the Reformed Church on the subject of the eucharist, we must have recourse particularly to Calvin." The French Reformer was nothing less than "the accredited interpreter and expounder of the article for all later times." By appealing to Calvin, Nevin was implicitly denouncing the Zwinglian views on the sacrament that he believed were legion among the German Reformed. But Nevin did not simply cast Zwingli or a symbolic understanding of the Lord's Supper aside. Instead, he used an understanding of historical development that he shared with Schaff—that even though Calvin was younger, he was more authoritative for the Reformed tradition than Zwingli because the Geneva pastor had benefited from debates in which Zwingli could not participate because of his premature death in 1531. For Nevin, Calvin's doctrine was the mature reflection of the original Reformed church, thus making him the "theological organ" of the Reformed doctrine of the mystical presence.[49] The Lord's Supper for Calvin, then, according to Nevin, was more than a pledge of "our own consecration to the service of Christ, or of the faithfulness of God as engaged to make good to us in a general way the grace of the new covenant." If the Supper were no more than a sign, then, it would "carry with it no virtue or force, more than might be put into it in every case by the spirit of the worshipper himself." Instead, it embodied "the actual presence of the grace it represents in its own constitution." This grace was not merely the promise of God to encourage troubled souls but "the very life of the Lord Jesus Christ himself."[50] Throughout, Nevin based his own high-church view of the Supper on a profound difference between the teaching of sixteenth- and seventeenth-century Reformed theologians and creeds on the Supper on the one side, and Puritans and modern Reformed theologians on the other.

Nevin's argument about the Lord's Supper relied on more than just history. It also involved an understanding of the incarnation and the believer's union with Christ that drew on German philosophy and theology. When Hodge reviewed *Mystical Presence*, he aimed precisely at what he believed were errors in Nevin's Christology and the doctrine of union. At this point in the exchange that would develop between Princeton and Mercersburg, Hodge and Nevin were talking past each other by using different sources. But when the debate turned to history and the old view of the Supper among Calvinists prior to the piety encouraged by modern revivalism, Hodge and Nevin revealed a fundamental disagreement. Nevin rested his case on Calvin's teaching on a real spiritual presence of Christ in the Lord's Supper, while Hodge sided much more with Zwingli's symbolic view. Hodge even resorted to calling Calvin's views "extreme," "peculiar," and "dubious."[51] The Princetonian believed that Calvin was an aberration that the Reformed tradition corrected by the end of the sixteenth century. In that case, Hodge was disputing more than Nevin's reading of Reformed history. He was debating what was tolerable within Reformed

49. John Williamson Nevin, *The Mystical Presence: A Vindication of the Reformed or Calvinistic Doctrine of the Holy Eucharist* (Philadelphia: J. B. Lippincott, 1846), 54.
50. Ibid., 56–57.
51. Charles Hodge, "Doctrine of the Reformed Church on the Lord's Supper," *Biblical Repertory and Princeton Review* 20 (1848): 234, 241, 251.

circles on the Lord's Supper, with Calvin left on the outside of the acceptable positions.

The debate between Nevin and Hodge went on for another round and almost grew to the length of the Park-Hodge exchange. What the contest between Princeton and Mercersburg showed was a different side of vulnerability for American Calvinism. If the Park-Hodge dispute revealed the difficulties inherent in trying to straighten out the paradoxes of Reformed teaching on salvation, the Nevin-Hodge exchange revealed the challenge of trying to maintain an old-world conception of the corporate character of the church in a new-world environment that exalted the individual. Although Hodge was one of the few theologians of note to take pride in being conservative, in Nevin the Princeton theologian had found someone who may very well have stood to his sacramental right, a theologian who believed that Princeton's conservative Calvinism had capitulated to modern conceptions of piety and faith. Hodge may not have followed Park or Finney with modifications of Calvinist theology, but if Nevin was right, even the most Calvinistic of American theologians was following fellow Americans in leaving behind the liturgical and sacramental aspects of historic Calvinism.

Where's Calvin?

John Calvin was not the founder of a tradition in the way that Martin Luther was. Even if the word *Calvinism* functions as a handy synonym for *Reformed Protantism*, the teachings and practices of Reformed and Presbyterian churches were never bound by Calvin's writings in the manner that Lutheranism attached great significance to Luther's ideas and texts—especially his Large and Small Catechisms. To assess nineteenth-century American Calvinist theologians, then, according to their appeal to Calvin's own example and writings is for most intents and purposes to hold them to a standard that has rarely been applied to other Reformed churchmen and thinkers in the history of Calvinism. Because Calvinism developed from the sixteenth century in a variety of circumstances, Reformed churches grew with distinct trajectories that were by no means copies of the specific context in which Calvin's own theology and ministry took root.[52]

What was happening to nineteenth-century American Calvinism, consequently, was not at all different from what had been occurring among Reformed and Presbyterian churches and institutions since the 1530s. Calvinists adapted to their own settings, and those adaptations did not refer directly to John Calvin. The new nation of the United States provided circumstances that created significant challenges for Calvinism. Aside from the new voluntarism that made churches independent from the state for both oversight and finances, America presented a cultural style that was new for most Reformed churches. Whereas Calvinism was selectively hierarchical, corporate, and systematic, America was increasingly becoming egalitarian, individualistic, and intuitive. Particularly challenging for Reformed theology was the American ideal of human autonomy that would eventually jettison the founders' recognition of human depravity and embrace notions of human nature that were far removed from an Augustinian framework, let alone the Calvinist idea of total depravity.[53]

The debates among New England Calvinists, American Presbyterians, and German Reformed between roughly 1830 and 1850 reveal the ways in which Reformed theology in the United States was adapting to the new political and cultural environment. Arguably, the greatest adaptations taking place were those in New England that strained the very idea of Reformed orthodoxy. Unable to reconcile the antimonies of divine sovereignty and human freedom, of election and damnation, of human responsibility and original sin, New England Calvinists generally adopted strategies that softened the hard edges of Reformed theology in order to

52. A stunning account of Calvinism's varied and highly situated origin and development comes from Philip Benedict, *Christ's Churches Purely Reformed: A Social History of Calvinism* (New Haven: Yale University Press, 2002).

53. For an overview of these tensions for European Protestants, see Mark A. Noll, *The Old Religion in the New World: A History of North American Christianity* (Grand Rapids: Eerdmans, 2001). For particular instances of the difficulties of the American context for historic Protestant communions, see, e.g., Robert Bruce Mullin, *Episcopal Vision/American Reality: High Church Theology and Social Thought in Antebellum America* (New Haven: Yale University Press, 1986); Allen C. Guelzo, *For the Union of Evangelical Christendom: The Irony of Reformed Episcopalians* (University Park, PA: Pennsylvania State University Press, 1994); David A. Gustafson, *Lutherans in Crisis: The Question of Identity in the American Republic* (Minneapolis: Fortress Press, 1993).

preserve its relevance in America. The Old School Presbyterians at Princeton, where Charles Hodge emerged as the chief spokesman, did better than the New Englanders in preserving the main contours of Reformed soteriology and defending an account of human sinfulness and divine mercy that were increasingly implausible in the American setting. An important reason for Princeton's resourceful defense of Calvinism was the ongoing relevance of covenant theology for Old School Presbyterians. The federal headship of Adam and Christ and the related doctrine of imputation enabled Hodge and others to see intellectual consistency where often New Englanders saw contradiction. At the same time, as upholders of the Calvinistic revivals of the colonial era, the Princetonians tried to vindicate their own teaching by appealing not only to the Reformed orthodoxy of the Westminster Standards and Francis Turretin but also to Jonathan Edwards. The attempt to appropriate Edwards not only provoked contemporary New Englanders, but also revealed a tendency to regard the Reformed tradition as more monolithic than it really was.

From the perspective of the German Reformed as embodied in the teaching of Nevin, the debates between Presbyterians and Congregationalists were disembodied intellectual struggles too far removed from the sacramental life of the church. Nevin's own attempt to see within the ethnic conclave of congregations in Pennsylvania and Ohio the fruition of the mystical body of Christ may have suffered from its own abstractions of German philosophy. Certainly, his biggest critics within the German Reformed Church often wondered exactly what Nevin was writing about. Yet if Nevin's theories about the Lord's Supper and the presence of Christ within the body of the church posed obstacles to those less philosophically inclined, his attention to the nature of Reformed piety and what individualism and scholastic theology were doing to the lives of Christians and the work of pastors was a concern that usually escaped the interest of other American Calvinists. Nevin's liturgical project made little impact on Congregationalists and Presbyterians, but his arguments did register an important caution about the ways in which the American experience was altering the character of congregational life among Reformed Protestants.

Interestingly enough, Nevin was the rare nineteenth-century American Calvinist to appeal directly to Calvin. Indeed, the premodern conceptions of church membership and sacramental theology that Calvin taught were the same ideas that struck Nevin's critics as sounding the most Roman Catholic. For Old School Presbyterians and New England Calvinists, the question about Calvin's teaching, as much as it came up (which was seldom), had less to do with Christian ministry, church membership, and the sacraments than it did with doctrines about the fall, free will, virtue, and the atonement. In this respect, as much as the Calvinism taught by New England and Presbyterians differed in substance, for both sides Calvinism was a system of thought that could be appropriated by the individual mind. Whereas for Nevin Calvinism's great appeal was in its corporate (and therefore mystical) dimensions in the body of Christ, for Congregationalists and Presbyterians Calvinism's significance was its capacity to achieve coherence or power as an intellectual system. If Park's "consistent Calvinism" could sound old-fashioned because of its reliance on New Divinity habits of mind, and if Hodge's Reformed orthodoxy could sound even more old-fashioned and therefore un-American in its reliance on seventeenth-century modes of expression, Nevin's sacramental Calvinism was the most glaring because its appeal to sixteenth-century notions of the church and sacraments sounded not only un-American but also Roman Catholic.

The outcome of these debates among some of the United States' most important Reformed theologians was to stamp American Calvinism in ways that would still be discernible 150 years later. George Marsden has distinguished three branches of Calvinism in the United States. One of the dominant tendencies of American Reformed theology was to stress the importance of correct doctrine. Marsden detected this feature in the denomination of his upbringing, the Orthodox Presbyterian Church, a communion that was and remains an important successor to theological methods and themes practiced and maintained by Charles Hodge and the Old School Presbyterian tradition. Another Reformed strand was culture engagement, which Marsden witnessed firsthand among Dutch Calvinists in the Christian Reformed Church, and which was arguably an important piece of Edwards Amasa Park's effort to retain for New England Calvinism a voice within America's cultural establishment. The last strain of Reformed theology that Marsden delineated was a pietistic or experimental version, kept alive at institutions such as Fuller Seminary and Trinity Evangelical Divinity School, which juggled the compatibility of Calvinism and revivalism. To the degree that Hodge and Park were both claiming to be the rightful heirs of Jonathan Edwards, both the Old School and New England strands of Calvinism represented this experiential form of Reformed theology in America, while also contributing to the distinct brands of doctrinalism and culturalism.[54]

The odd man out in this map of American Reformed theology, obviously, is Nevin. The reasons are many, spanning from his own isolation in an ethnic communion that did not establish a presence within the American Protestant mainstream to the verdicts of his contemporaries that found incredible his own reading of Calvin and the Reformed tradition. As much as Nevin did employ nineteenth-century philosophical idioms that hurt the reception of his arguments, and as unstable as he could be in his own theological reflection, he may have been closer to Calvin than any of his Reformed contemporaries and their successors. The reason for this suggestion is that Nevin recognized, as few other American Calvinists have, the importance of the church and the sacraments to Calvin's theology and ministry.[55] Whether Nevin appropriated Calvin's liturgical and sacramental concerns with the attention to precise theology and to individual devotion that the Geneva pastor achieved is open to debate. Even so, reading basic summaries of the Christian faith that Calvin put in catechetical form leaves the distinct impression that the leading proponents of Calvinism in the United States were essentially indifferent to the churchly and sacramental features of Calvin's own ministry and theology. When, for instance, Calvin discussed the Apostles' Creed's phrase "forgiveness of sins," and linked it directly to membership in the church, he made an assertion that even the most conservative of American Calvinists would be loath to affirm: "no man obtains pardon for his sins without being previously incorporated into the people of God, persevering in unity and communion with the Body of

54. George M. Marsden, "Reformed and American," in *Reformed Theology in America: A History of Its Modern Development*, ed. David F. Wells (Grand Rapids: Eerdmans, 1985), 1–12, esp. 2–3.
55. See B. A. Gerrish, *Tradition and the Modern World: Reformed Theology in the Nineteenth Century* (Chicago: University of Chicago Press, 1978).

Christ in such a way as to be a true member of the Church."[56] And when Calvin wrote of the Lord's Supper that it was a mode of being united to Christ such that "He dwells in us, and conjoined with us in a union as the Head with the members, that by virtue of this conjunction He may make us partakers of all His grace,"[57] Calvin was affirming truths about mystical presence and sacramental efficacy that spooked most American Calvinists, who preferred a Zwinglian understanding of the sacraments and an individualistic conception of the church.

If Nevin did understand the sacramental side of Calvin in ways that his Reformed peers did not, then not only was the Mercersburg theologian an unfortunate loser in the nineteenth-century debates over Calvinism, but so was Calvin. Recognizing this loss need not detract from the valuable contributions made by other keepers of Calvin's flame. But it does point to important tensions within the Reformed tradition as well as to the need for more work than historians have yet accomplished on the reasons for the turn by modern Calvinists away from the churchly, corporate, and sacramental features of the original Reformed impulse.[58]

56. "Catechism of the Church of Geneva," in John Calvin and Theodore Beza, *Tracts Relating to the Reformation*, trans. Henry Beveridge (Edinburgh: Calvin Translation Society, 1849), 52.

57. Ibid., 90.

58. For one attempt to account for this anomaly, see D. G. Hart, "Jonathan Edwards and the Origins of Experimental Calvinism," in *The Legacy of Jonathan Edwards: American Religion and the Evangelical Tradition*, ed. D. G. Hart, Sean Michael Lucas, and Stephen J. Nichols (Grand Rapids: Baker Academic, 2003), 161–80.

20

CALVIN'S IMPACT ON THE ARTS

WILLIAM EDGAR

Against Calvin

Opinions stating that John Calvin and Calvinism degrade the arts abound. Voltaire said that Calvin was responsible for the city of Geneva's being dour, hostile to the pleasures of theater and the arts.[1] Ferdinand Brunetière, literary critic in France's Third Republic, equated Calvinism with the horror of art. We can add Orentin Douen, who is unrelenting in his criticism of Calvin, whom he deems the "ennemi de tout plaisir et de toute distraction, même des arts et de la musique."[2] For the Roman Catholic historian Louis Réau, Calvinist iconoclasm belongs quite simply to the "history of vandalism."[3]

1. See also Graham Garget, "Goldsmith as Translator of Voltaire," *The Modern Language Review* 98 (October 2003): 842–56. In fairness, Voltaire would later become a defender of the Huguenots and would praise the city of Geneva for its industriousness.
2. The "enemy of all pleasure and of all diversion, even of the arts and music" (Orentin Douen, *Clément Marot et le psautier Huguenot*, vol. 1 [Paris: Imprimerie Nationale, 1878], 377).
3. Louis Réau, *Les monuments détruits de l'art français. Histoire du vandalisme* (Paris: Hachette, 1959; repr., Paris: Robert Laffont, 1995 [orig. 1959]).

These critiques carry a certain plausibility. In a letter to a young student, written in 1540, Calvin encourages greater devotion to religion. He makes the following comparison: "Those who seek in scholarship more than an honored occupation with which to beguile the tedium of idleness I would compare to those who pass their lives looking at paintings."[4]

Rehabilitations

Does this settle the case? Hardly, although achieving clarity about Calvin and his legacy on the arts is fraught with pitfalls. At least two major types of rehabilitation have been attempted. They are based on two historiographies. The first is represented by Abraham Kuyper (1837–1920), Émile Doumergue (1844–1937), and their heirs. Kuyper's approach to Calvinism and the arts is best ascertained from the fifth lecture, "Calvinism and Art," in the celebrated *Lectures on Calvinism* sponsored by the L. P. Stone Foundation at Princeton University in 1898.[5] Not surprisingly, Kuyper's thoughts, while emanating from a Reformed heritage, carry a decidedly nineteenth-century ethos. His orientation is theological and apologetical. The arts exist, he says, to elevate "the Beautiful and the Sublime in its eternal significance." They are one of God's richest gifts to mankind. Kuyper believes they have a role to foster a "proper mysticism" that helps recognize the benefits of true religion, although he also rails against the current tendency to abandon such mysticism for an "art-intoxication."[6] One senses an affinity with Matthew Arnold here as well (whether or not Kuyper ever read him). According to this influential British thinker, culture is "the best that has been thought and said in the world." Furthermore, culture exists "to make reason and the will of God prevail."[7]

As he had done throughout, Kuyper here defends Calvinism's role in moving in an evolutionary way into a "multiformity of life-tendencies,"

4. CR, 11.56.
5. I am using the edition copyrighted in 1931, Grand Rapids: Eerdmans, 142–70.
6. Ibid., 143.
7. Matthew Arnold, *Culture and Anarchy* (London: Smith, Elder and Company, 1869; repr., Cambridge: Cambridge University Press, 1960), 6, 42.

over against putting everything under the tutelage of the state or other established institutions. The effect of this is to free the arts from merely functioning in the context of worship. However closely they are aligned in the "lower stage of human development," it is now time to evolve away from such a congruence and, in effect, send the arts out of the church.[8] He adds that since art is "incapable of expressing the very essence of Religion," it must live in a sphere of its own. Calvinism, he says, released art from the guardianship of the church and so, even more than the Renaissance, was the first to recognize its maturity.[9]

This does not mean that *religion* cannot generate an art style. On the contrary, Kuyper argues that, unlike the rationalist Enlightenment, Calvinism has generated a rich heritage in the arts.[10] Calvinism did this not by reaching some higher stage that forbids the symbolical expression of religion in visual terms, but by setting forth a world and life view that in turn inspires the artists to interpret the world and represent it in a certain way.[11] To defend Calvin against the charge of Philistinism, Kuyper cites many passages in which the Reformer shows approval of the arts. But his central argument is that Calvinism promotes a good aesthetic principle, derived from his view of the creation. Accordingly, the artist's calling is "to discover in those natural forms the order of the beautiful, and, enriched by this higher knowledge, to produce a beautiful world that transcends the beautiful of nature." Thus, the arts should remind us of what was lost through the curse and what is to be hoped for in the creation's "perfect coming luster."[12]

So what does all this look like in the actual visual arts? Through Calvinism, and also by God's common grace, much fruit has been borne. Kuyper finds important examples in the Netherlands, where, he says, poetry and, more especially, music and painting flowed out of a "reformational" orientation. He cites Rembrandt (and other painters) and argues that they began from the doctrine of election by free grace, which led to the implication of giving special importance to simple people and ordinary events in the eyes

8. Kuyper, "Calvinism and Art," 146–47.
9. Ibid., 157.
10. Ibid., 148, 151–52.
11. Ibid., 152.
12. Ibid., 154–55.

of God. Consequently, he argues, the arts could focus on the seemingly small and insignificant, and elevate *real* people, as opposed to high-placed people—more so than had ever been the case.[13] Using decidedly populist and romantic rhetoric, Kuyper declares, "Ecclesiastical power no longer restrained the artist, and princely gold no longer chained him in fetters. If artist, he also was man, mingling freely among the people, and discovering in and behind their human life, something quite different from what palace and castle had hitherto afforded him . . ."[14] In music, the same evolution occurred. No longer attached to the church, composers were free from Gregory's chant, and now "selected their melodies from the free world of music."[15]

Émile Doumergue takes a similar approach. Although French, he too goes from Calvin to the golden age of Dutch art, and particularly Rembrandt.[16] The Calvinists not only freed the arts, but made them relevant to the people and stressed the possibility of psychological and spiritual interiority. We should include among the heirs to these views Léon Wencélius, whose classic work, *L'esthétique de Calvin*, similarly defends the Reformed worldview as a generator of the arts.[17]

Interestingly, Hans Rookmaaker would echo these views a generation later. Rookmaaker was an art historian, so that one would expect him to go into much more detail than Kuyper or Doumergue, which he most certainly did. His essays on individual artists such as Dürer, Bruegel, and Rubens introduce us to the ways in which a world and life view inform paintings.[18] Of course, Rookmaaker's best-known work is a critique of the contemporary world, through the lens of the arts. *Modern Art and the Death of a Culture* is a fascinating journey through art history with a historiography of decline, based on the epistemology of the artists within their different epochs.[19]

13. Ibid., 165–66.
14. Ibid., 167.
15. Ibid., 168.
16. Émile Doumergue, *L'art et le sentiment dans l'oeuvre de Calvin* (Genève: Société Genevoise d'Edition, 1902; repr., Genève: Slatkine Reprints, 1970), 13–14, 36–40.
17. Léon Wencélius, *L'esthétique de Calvin* (Paris: Belles Lettres, 1937).
18. See, for example, his articles on Western art history, collected in *Western Art and the Meanderings of a Culture*, vol. 4 of the *Complete Works* (Carlisle, PA: Piquant, 2002), 1–187.
19. Downers Grove, IL: InterVarsity Press, 1974; latest ed., Wheaton, IL: Crossway Books, 1994. It is not only these generalists who connect Calvinism to, say, the seventeenth-century

In addition to the brilliant appreciation of the way in which a world-view enlightens history and culture in these thinkers, one cannot miss the romantic and even Hegelian spirit that informs the approach of Kuyper and Doumergue, although the approach of Rookmaaker is more complex. The idea that culture and everything related to it emanates from a "worldview"—a religious consciousness that then characterizes all of human activity in a given period—is, we believe, a biblical idea, at least in part. But the broad periodization, the search for an ethos or a *zeitgeist* that characterizes a given era, can lead to anachronisms and oversimplifications when we are not careful to honor the details. At worst, this approach can lead to an unhealthy endorsement of culture wars.

Nuance and Context

Reactions were to be expected, and they have been plentiful. But with them, a door has been opened for a second historiography of how Calvinism relates to the arts. One of the first to put into question the first historiography is Ernst Gombrich. His major contribution to the discussion is his *In Search of Cultural History*.[20] He questions whether different epochs are really held together by a single *zeitgeist*. As he looks at the arts, he notes the many rival schools and approaches within each period. Each of these has its own coherency, but also shares, unwittingly or not, with the others, making somewhat problematic the idea of a worldview governing a movement that affects the way artists work.

Besides Gombrich, all kinds of other culture critiques have arisen, challenging the Hegelian model. One can think of schools such as culturalism, structuralism and post-structuralism, the Frankfurt School, feminism, Foucaultian views, and many others. The extreme version of this new direction must be in the various approaches known as postmodernism.[21]

Dutch landscapists. Maarten de Klijn and other contemporary art historians make such connections as well, as we will see below.

20. New York: Oxford University Press, 1969. Interestingly, Rookmaaker reviews this book very favorably (*Modern Art and the Death of a Culture*, 275–77). My guess is that he was moving in the direction of this second historiography.

21. This elusive term refers to at least several tendencies that oppose "metanarrative" historiographies. Jean-François Lyotard famously called for the suspicion of the *grand*

These schools, decidedly anti-Hegelian, bring needed correctives and modesty to the enterprise of culture studies. Yet it is clear that they are not without their own agendas, some of which make almost any generalization difficult. For example, the very thoughtful culture analyst Pierre Bourdieu seeks to locate value and meaning in the world of everyday experience.[22] He helpfully guides us through various cultural tastes, to unveil the many layers of lifestyles and habits. Still, his purpose is to identify the relations of power and economic dominance of one group over another. The unintended result may be, in Storey's words, that "the much heralded collapse of standards rehearsed (almost weekly) in the so-called 'quality' media of our postmodern new times, may be nothing more than a perceived sense that the opportunities to use culture and to make and mark social distinction are becoming more and more difficult to find."[23] What has happened here is that cultural impact and cultural differences are simply more complex to identify. The tools given us by the second historiographers are most useful, as long as one is able to discern the ideologies behind their not-so-innocent approaches.

Applied to the question of Calvinism and the arts, this second historiography brings helpful clarifications. It not only guides us in answering the larger question "does Calvinism in fact form a cultural sensibility that is coherent?" but also helps us be more empirically responsible. And in the bargain, it reminds us how culture works. The question remains whether his aesthetic ideals could crystallize into a movement so deeply rooted that it could eventually give rise to such fruits as the Dutch landscapists of the seventeenth century, as was claimed by Kuyper and Doumergue.

---

récit, particularly as proffered by science and education. For him and many others, knowledge is not an end in itself, but cultural capital, power to arrive at a particular end. See Jean-François Lyotard, *The Postmodern Condition: A Report on Knowledge* (Minneapolis: University of Minnesota Press, 1984), 46. For an excellent summary of these and other schools in relation to culture studies, see John Storey, *An Introduction to Culture Theory and Popular Culture*, 2nd ed. (Athens, GA: University of Georgia Press, 1998).

22. See, for example, Pierre Bourdieu, *Distinction: A Social Critique of the Judgment of Taste*, trans. Richard Nice (Cambridge, MA: Harvard University Press, 1984).

23. Storey, *Introduction to Culture Theory and Popular Culture*, 198.

In Search of a Middle Ground

Philip Benedict is also skeptical about the claims of the first historiography. He shares some of the doubts of the second. But he is unwilling to abandon the quest for some kind of connection between Calvinism and the arts.[24] He points out that careful studies of particular regions and particular epochs reveal that Calvinism could not quite achieve a total recasting of artistic or musical culture and remake it into a new image. He compares claims of such reformation to the reality on the ground. For example, Emmanuel LeRoy Ladurie's *The Peasants of Languedoc*[25] affirms that the Cévennes were so steeped in Calvinist culture that even lullabies were taken from the psalms and no local or traditional songs were used. But he based his conclusions on the work of nineteenth-century folklorists. More modern studies show something different. For example, the Huguenot minister Pierre Jurieu had wished to train the heart, "so that it conceives its thoughts and forms its meditations only in the terms of the Holy Spirit as expressed in the Psalm."[26] But Benedict argues that such an aspiration was quite impossible on the ground, because "the Bible always had to make its peace with beliefs, motifs, and genres derived from nonbiblical sources, even in the greatest strongholds of Calvinist fidelity."[27] He cites other examples, such as the folk belief that May was an unlucky month in which to get married, and found that the Huguenots of the Cévennes abstained from marriage in May just as readily as did Roman Catholics, despite their rhetoric against superstitious religion. Benedict further argues that sometimes the circles of those given to literary, artistic, scientific, or antiquarian interests were in locales where the confessional differences of the era were easily overcome. In such cases, religious differences were not measurably different in practice. Benedict argues that Catholics and Huguenots gathered in such places in order to cultivate their common interests, in ways in which their religious views may not

---

24. Philip Benedict, "Calvinism as a Culture?" in *Seeing beyond the Word: Visual Arts and the Calvinist Tradition*, ed. Paul Corby Finney (Grand Rapids: Eerdmans, 1999), 1–45.

25. Emmanuel Le Roy Ladurie, *The Peasants of Languedoc* (Champaign, IL: University of Illinois Press, 1977), 172ff.

26. Pierre Jurieu, *Traité de la devotion* (Rouen, 1675), 184.

27. Benedict, "Calvinism as a Culture?" 25.

have been particularly inflected.[28] As Ernst Walter Zeeden and others have shown, there could even have been overlap in popular devotional literature from the two traditions.[29]

We have recently traveled in central Europe, and whatever else one might want to say about the newfound freedoms of democracy, it is hard to deny the influence of such a bureaucratic system on communications, architecture, religious life, and simply the ethos still hanging over many of the newborn democracies. Yet one could also argue that Communism itself depended in part for its success on previous models of tyranny. So then, to take Benedict's point, we should not give up trying to find connections between Calvinism and the arts, but we should do so by giving attention to various layers of cultural indicators, rather than the grand schemes that Kuyper and Doumergue seem to allow.

How, for example, did theological sensibilities affect the place of the arts in church and in life? How much were artists affected with the religious beliefs, the permissions and prohibitions connected with Calvinism? An obvious place to focus on is the whole issue of iconoclasm. Let us look first at the general background of iconoclasm, then Calvin's specific views, and then his own statements about the visual arts. After that, we can attempt to move on to larger questions about Calvinist impact on the arts.

The Background of Iconoclasm

It is a given that John Calvin strongly preached and practiced the reformation of worship. One of his consistent polemics was against idolatry, and particularly the use of images as aids for the cult. Most often his invectives are labeled *iconoclasm*. His views were not developed in a vacuum. The cult of images was quite widespread in the Middle Ages and became particularly strong in the fifteenth century. Practices included devotion to relics, pilgrimages to shrines and other symbolic places, the cult of

28. Ibid., 26.
29. Ibid. See Ernst Walter Zeeden, *Die Entstehung der Konfessionen* (München: Oldenbourg, 1965); Quentin Skinner, "The Origins of the Calvinist Theory of Revolution," in *After the Reformation*, ed. Barbara C. Malament (Philadelphia: University of Pennsylvania Press, 1980), 309–30.

the saints, and the externalization of the Mass, including bleeding hosts and the full development of the feast of Corpus Christi.[30] And already there were critiques of this popular piety well before the Reformation, even in the West, which had generally resisted the *iconodules* of the Byzantine Church. Although Pope Gregory I and even Thomas Aquinas had defended the use of imagery for the education of the illiterate, various preachers and movements had warned against it. One may think of the Cistercians and the Franciscans, who cautioned against the use of symbols to adorn places of worship. One can also think of the precursors of the Reformation, men such as John Wycliffe and Jan Hus, who made moderate criticisms of images, particularly those used to elevate the Virgin Mary in near-competition with Christ.

Certainly the most systematic of the critics in the late fifteenth and early sixteenth centuries was Erasmus of Rotterdam (c. 1466–1536). His widely read *Enchiridion Militis Christiani* (1503) is a strong tract against the corruption of the church.[31] In it Erasmus lamented the formalism and materialism of current practice, and affirmed the inward, spiritual nature of worship. Clearly influenced by Plato, it nevertheless pleaded for an intimate relation between God and the human soul. Venerating images was accordingly condemned, with the exception of those who "from weakness of mind" could worship only according to the flesh.[32] Still, he argued, there could be nothing more "disgusting" than the cult of relics or other so-called blessed objects, since Christ himself eschewed all use of divine power, and instructed his followers to go straight to him in heaven, without intermediaries.[33] Erasmus's views were enormously influential on the Reformers, even those who thought his overall theology lacking consistency.

Switzerland in general and the town of Geneva in particular were profoundly marked by the Reformers' iconoclasm. Merle d'Aubigné's

30. See, e.g., Herman Heimpel, "Characteristics of the Late Middle Ages in Germany," in *Pre-Reformation Germany*, ed. Gerald Strauss (New York: Macmillan, 1972), 68.

31. W. Welzing, ed., *Erasmus von Rotterdam Ausgewählte Schriften*, vol. 1 (Darmstadt: Wissenschaftlichen Buchgesellschaft, 1968). For an English edition, see *Enchiridion, or The Manual of the Christian Knight*, trans. Raymond Himelink (London: Kessinger, 2003).

32. Ibid., 90–91.

33. Ibid., 204.

Histoire de la Réformation au XVIème siècle tracks the story of the Protestant movement in Switzerland largely through the story of acts of iconoclasm.[34] His assessment is that "in the times of the Reformation, the doctors attacked the Pope and the people the images."[35] He is not far off. According to Carlos M. N. Eire, although iconoclasm varied in place and intensity, in the Reformation it was prominent because it meant publicly testing whether or not Roman Catholic worship was legal, and set forth how the Mass could be replaced by a spiritual and Word-based religion.[36] Switzerland became a crucial place for this pattern to be displayed, he argues, for at least three reasons: (1) it is where Huldrych Zwingli was able to produce what is the most consistent and influential iconoclastic theology;[37] (2) Switzerland was the first area, far more than Germany, where iconoclasm became a consistent policy, particularly in the patterns established whereby its cities became officially Protestant; and (3) because the towns had a republican structure, the people were better able to participate and use iconoclasm as a political tactic.

Geneva, in the years before Calvin arrived (particularly 1530–36), experienced this process intensely. Its alliance with Bern meant that it had important encouragements to reform, particularly in its struggle to become independent both from the House of Savoy and from the prince-bishop of Geneva.[38] The Bernese council had staged a disputation in 1527 in which the Protestant faith triumphed over Roman beliefs and practices such as the merits of Christ, tradition, transubstantiation, the Mass, and the cult of images. The Reformation triumphed from then on. Geneva fell under the sway of Bern at first through a military alliance with its armies against the Savoy. As the Bernese army marched down through

34. Paris: Firmin Didot Frères, 1938.

35. Ibid., 767.

36. Carlos M. N. Eire, *War against the Idols: The Reformation of Worship from Erasmus to Calvin* (Cambridge: Cambridge University Press, 1986), 107.

37. His *De vera et falsa religione* had a direct influence on Calvin (compare Samuel Macauley Jackson, ed., *The Latin Works and the Correspondence of Huldreich Zwingli, etc.*, vol. 3 [New York: Putnam's Sons, 1912], 332, to Calvin's *Institutes*, 1.11.9).

38. One can date this struggle from 1519, when Genevan patriots followed Besançon Hughes, the "oath-fellow" who led the Genevans in their fight. He eventually signed treaties with Bern and Fribourg, and may have given the Swiss Confederates the name of *Eidgenossen*, from which we derive the term *Huguenot*.

the southern territories, they destroyed images, quartered their horses in churches, and generally imposed their own services, including preachers, on the city. Although these armies left, they had begun to stir the people into anti-Catholic behavior. Then in 1532 Pope Clement VII proclaimed a general indulgence in Geneva. The Protestant sympathizers rose up and posted placards all over the city, mocking the indulgence system and proclaiming that forgiveness was available by praying directly to Christ.

After these incidents, the Reformation began to take root in the city for theological reasons. Guillaume Farel, Pierre Olivetan, and others began to arrive there in 1532, and preached clandestinely. When opposed, they said they were preaching "in God's authority," accusing the priests of foisting human traditions and inventions on the people.[39] Although expelled, Farel and Olivetan would return, with their friend Antoine Froment, in 1533, to continue preaching Reformation principles. Preaching was followed by rioting, and many church ornaments and statues were destroyed. Disputations and revolts accumulated, and finally, after a message preached by Farel in the cathedral in August 1535, a serious revolt occurred, destroying most of the icons, including the Foyseau altarpiece. Although there were laws forbidding, or at least curtailing, this activity, the sympathies of the Town Council were clearly with the iconoclasts. On May 25, 1536, the Council voted unanimously to "Live according to the Holy Gospel Law and the Word of God, according as it is preached, wanting to abandon all Masses and other Papal ceremonies and abuses, images and idols."[40]

Iconoclasm in Geneva was both a revolutionary act and a theological statement. Obviously, it carried mixed motives. But the central concern was truly a religious conviction.[41] As Oecolampadius put it, describing the religious conflicts in Basel, the hesitancy of the government was a "hard knot" to untangle, but iconoclasm represented "the wedge of the Lord" that simply split the knot.[42] Here we have a combination of political action that concretizes theological conviction.

---

39. See Provana di Collegno, "Rapports de Guillaume Farel avec les Vaudois du Piémont," *Bulletin de la Société d'Études des Hautes-Alpes* 10 (1891): 257–78.

40. *Registres du Conseil de Genève*, ed. Émile Rivoire and Victor van Bercham, vol. 13 (Genève: H. Künding, 1940), 576, my translation.

41. Eire, *War against the Idols*, 155.

42. Quoted in ibid., 156.

Thus, iconoclasm was never pure vandalism but always intended as reform. Such was the case for Geneva.

Calvin and Icons

When Calvin arrived in the city, he found a magistracy freshly committed to this approach. Although he never advocated tyrannicide, he favored iconoclasm. As with the earlier Reformers, his views must be seen within the overall context of his theology. Calvin's own spiritual journey must have played a part in his convictions. Although we know little about his conversion, we do have the oft-quoted testimony in his commentary on the Psalms, where he spoke of God "by a sudden conversion" pulling him out from "so profound an abyss of mire" as the "superstitions of Popery."[43] In the *Institutes*, from the earliest edition until the final one, he develops extended arguments against images in worship. By the 1559 edition the discussion is robust, especially in the relevant section on the knowledge of God (1.11.12) and in the portion on the second commandment (2.8.17–21).

The foundation for Calvin's theology of worship, hence his attacks on idolatry, is the doctrine of life's central purpose, the glory of God. In the powerful words of the Geneva Catechism:

8.1 Quelle est la principale fin de la vie humaine?
    C'est de connaître Dieu.
8.2 Pourquoi dis-tu cela?
    Parce qu'il nous a créés et mis au monde pour être glorifié en nous. Et c'est bien raison que nous rapportions notre vie à sa gloire puisqu'il en est le commencement.
8.3 Quel est le souverain bien des hommes?
    Cela même.[44]

43. CR, 31.22.
44. "1. What is the chief end of human life? It is to know God. 2. Why do you say this? Because he created us and placed us in the world to be glorified in us. And this is surely the reason to connect our life to his glory, since he is its beginning. 3. And what is the supreme good of men? The same."

Further into the catechism, in the section regarding the Ten Commandments, the following reasons are given as an explication of the second commandment:

+ Veut-il du tout défendre de faire aucune image?
  Non, mais il défend de faire aucune image, ou pour figurer Dieu, ou pour adorer.
+ Pourquoi est-ce qu'il n'est point licite de représenter Dieu visiblement?
  Parce qu'il n'y a nulle convenance entre lui, qui est Esprit éternel, incompréhensible, et une matière corporelle, morte, corruptible et visible.[45]

We should note here in passing what we will soon discover: that Calvin forbids not any image whatsoever, but images of God.

Throughout his preaching and his writing, Calvin insisted that only God was worthy of all glory. Any use of images leads to idolatry, he argues. In book 1 of the *Institutes*, he takes on a number of papal abuses by citing the fathers. For example, he refutes the "papist" argument that images are to help the unlearned develop a better idea of theology by citing Augustine and others who say that statues are a way to "remove fear and add error."[46] Teachers in the church lapsed into the veneration of images because "they themselves were mute." Imagining there being some divinity in the image, "therefore, when you prostrate yourself in veneration, representing to yourself in an image either a god or a creature, you are already ensnared in some superstition."[47] His frequent attacks on Roman Catholic "idolatry" center on robbing God of his due.

At the heart of Calvin's opposition to images in worship is a concern for the spiritual nature of truth. Indeed, because God is for him the end point of all human acts and aspirations, and because he is a pure spirit,

45. "144. Do it forbid any image at all? No, but it forbids making any image either to portray God, or to worship. 145. Why is it illicit to represent God visibly? Because there is no conformity between him, who is an eternal, incomprehensible Spirit, and a physical, dead, corruptible and visible object."
46. *Institutes*, 1.11.6–7.
47. Ibid., 1.11.7.

one should never attempt to form any earthly replica of him. For Calvin, the worship of God must be spiritual, so that it may correspond to his nature. A further level that leads Calvin to banish images from worship is his understanding of the fulfillment of all the Old Testament figures that announced him. He recognized the propriety of images in the age of preparation. But once Christ had come, and the church was founded, all images, except the representations in the two sacraments, are abolished.

Thus, images were often destroyed. Sculpture was particularly targeted, paintings somewhat less. And stained glass was often preserved. A constant call to vigilance was characteristic of the Reformers. Sometimes this could be quite extreme, as it was in Puritan England.[48] At the same time, it must not be forgotten that never did the magisterial Reformers issue blanket condemnations of visual imagery or forbid the proper enjoyment of the arts.

Music

Calvin's approach to music is the same. As Charles Garside has demonstrated, Calvin's preference for singing mostly the psalms, unaccompanied, in the worship comes from the same conviction. When he came to Geneva, he found the people still "ignorant" because of the troubles the city had experienced. So one of the very first actions Calvin pleaded for was a combination of church discipline, including excommunication in order to safeguard the Lord's Supper, the singing of the psalms, catechism, and marriage licenses. Without these there could not be a well-ordered or "regulated" church life, according to the Word of God.[49] Why the psalms? They were prayers given by God himself. Following Augustine, Calvin insisted that worshipers sing with intelligence, so the psalms were to be sung in French.[50]

What about the music? Less the musician than Martin Luther, Calvin nevertheless developed a theology of music that separated what was sung

---

48. See Patrick Collinson, *From Iconoclasm to Iconophobia* (Reading, PA: University of Reading, 1986).

49. *CR*, 10.7.

50. Ibid., 2.17.

in church and outside of church. Still, wherever it was practiced, music needed to be appropriately unassuming. He did strongly believe that music can lift the soul to heavenly joy. Therefore, music is the gift of God. At the same time (echoing Plato), he cautioned against immoderate music that could lead to "immodesty" [*impudicité*] and "effeminacy by disordered delights" [*de nous effeminer en délices désordonnées*].[51] Further, he required the entire congregation to sing, and thus forbade the use of choirs. Accordingly, the psalms were to be rendered in music that had both gravity and majesty. Here is not the place to develop Calvin's appropriation of Louis Bourgeois and Claude Goudimel, who wrote simple but elegant melodies for the declamation of the sacred text. Musical instruments in worship were frowned upon, on the grounds that they belonged to the Old Testament times, when people were less spiritually mature: "while they were yet tender and like children, by such rudiments until the coming of Christ. But now, when the clear light of the gospel has dissipated the *shadows* of the law and taught us that God is to be served in a simpler form, it would be to act a foolish and mistaken part to imitate that which the prophet enjoined only upon those of his own time."[52]

Anti-art?

The impression may be given that Calvin's strong views against images came from his opposition to the arts in general. Despite statements such as the one above to his student, it is unjust to cast Calvin as against the arts. Although he strongly denounced images of sacred subjects, because they would stand as open invitations to idolatry, he nevertheless acknowledged the place for artistic expression in life. In the *Institutes* we find several cases where he approves the legitimacy of the visual arts. For example, alongside the condemnation of altars and "votive pilgrimages to see images," he goes on to add, "and yet I am not gripped by the superstition of thinking absolutely no image permissible." "But," he adds, "because sculpture and painting are gifts of God, I seek a pure and legitimate use of each." Although it is wrong to represent God, because he is invisible, it is fine

51. Ibid., 2.16.
52. *Comm.*, Ps. 81:3.

to sculpt or paint things that the eye can see. This particular reference is admittedly somewhat grudging.[53]

But there are others. His most comprehensive statement about the arts in general is found in the *Institutes*, 2.2.12–16. The discussion is embedded within the larger question of the vestiges of gifts and the freedom of the will. Calvin affirms that our natural gifts have been corrupted, including reason, or the power of understanding, and the will. Still, there exists what we might anachronistically call common grace. Calvin notes that we may still operate within the realms of government, household management, all mechanical skills, and the liberal arts. Despite the fall, we still know about the need for law to run human organizations. In section 14 he specifically discusses the arts, both liberal and manual. He notes that hardly anyone can be found who has no talent in some art. He disagrees with Plato, who said that the ability to perfect the arts is merely from memory. Rather, it is inborn. In sections 15 and 16 he celebrates the gifts that God's Spirit gives to those who do not necessarily confess the name of Christ. These gifts include discernment of civic order, equity, the art of disputation, physics, mathematics, and also poetry and "the useful arts."[54]

Where and What Kinds?

It is clear, then, that Calvin is not set against the arts in general, nor does his kind of iconoclasm or restrictions on music in worship indicate a total horror of the arts, as Brunetière, Douen, Réau, and others maintain. To be sure, one cannot miss the power of the iconoclastic arguments from Calvin and the other Reformers. More than most other polemics, it struck at the very heart of medieval piety. Still, there was legitimate room for a reasonable appreciation of the arts. Zwingli, very much the iconoclast in matters of worship, wrote in 1525, "No one is a greater admirer than I of painting and statuary." He allowed freedom for imagery to adorn the

---

53. *Institutes*, 1.11.12.

54. No doubt he is mindful of Cicero, who cites Plato's *Timaeus* in his *Tusculan Disputations* (1.26.64). Léon Wencélius presents an extensive discussion of this passage and others in various parts of Calvin's writings (*L'esthétique de Calvin*, 97–126).

home, even though he was careful to limit the visual arts in church.[55] Examples of this balance abound. A bit later, early in the seventeenth century, a polemic developed in Holland between Jacob Trigland, a Reformed believer, who defended the propriety of paintings (except nudes), and the Quakers, who prohibited the possession of any painting whatsoever.[56]

Beyond such statements and polemics, this question must be raised: are there specific ways in which a Calvinist sensibility can be said to be represented in particular art forms? To answer that, we should look at the actual practice. Some connections are simply obvious. We might think of the devotional works or the polemics that had illustrations to make the point. Graphic satire was particularly popular. Lucas Cranach (the Elder), famous for his portrait of Martin Luther, was a favorite cartoonist against the Roman Catholic Church. His *Antichristus* was so popular in Geneva, it saw nine editions published. Indeed, the arts were regularly used to foster all the Reformation ideas. Illustrated Bibles were produced by Reformed artists. Interestingly, the biblical illustrations from Strasbourg and Zurich were richer and more original than those coming out of Wittenberg.[57]

When we move up to Holland, later in the century, we find Jan Swart van Groningen (1500–c. 1560), a prolific engraver and illustrator, whose works were often based on biblical passages teaching a Protestant view. For example, his pair of drawings *The Broad Way* and *The Narrow Way*, based on Matthew 7:13–14, clearly contrast the high and mighty on their way to destruction with the humbler folks, able to trust in simple faith, on their way to heaven.[58] One could also think of Dirck P. Crabeth (1501–77) from Gouda, whose drawings and stained-glass windows carried distinctively Reformed ideas. Crabeth was often fascinated by the need for the new birth in the journey to heaven, rather than good works.[59]

---

55. See his *Commentary on True and False Religion*, ed. Samuel Macauley Jackson and Clarence Nevin Heller (Durham, NC: Labyrinth Press, 1981).

56. Cited in Benedict, "Calvinism as a Culture?" 32.

57. After 1566, illustrated Bibles would be discouraged in Geneva because the artists were becoming too creative (ibid., 33)!

58. See Max J. Friedländer, "Zu Jan Swart van Groningen," *Oud Holland* 63 (1948): 1–6.

59. J. Q. Van Regteren Altena, "Teekeningen van Dirck Crabeth," *Oud Holland* 55 (1938): 1–6.

Connections between Calvinism and the arts, again, are obvious in certain art forms, particularly those directly connected with worship. For example, communion tokens, known as *méreaux*, carried designs such as a shepherd, an open Bible, a communion cup, and the like. And of course, there is a clear connection between Calvinist principles and church architecture and furnishings. Architectural issues generated less controversy, since in many cases Protestants often simply took over existing Catholic churches and modified them in order to conform to Reformed principles of worship. For example, replacing the altar with a pulpit as a focal point was a typical statement of Word-centered worship.[60] In other cases, new buildings were constructed, and various patterns were gradually adopted. In France before the Revocation of the Edict of Nantes, a good number of churches accommodated the Word-centered principles of the Reformation. The disposition of the chairs around the pulpit signaled not only a listening assembly but also a closer fellowship.[61] Often they were notable for their extreme simplicity.[62] Touches such as a weathervane in the form of a rooster were often found, to signify the preaching of the Word.[63]

Dutch Landscape Art

How much carryover of such aesthetic principles was there to the rest of the arts, particularly those not meant for the churches? Here is where matters become interesting, and complex. Let us focus briefly on the issue of landscape art from the Dutch seventeenth century. Hans Rookmaaker argues that a problem was raised with the Renaissance, namely, that historical scenes or, for that matter, natural scenes require

60. Article 22 of the Second Helvetic Confession required that when buildings are chosen, they are "to be purged of everything that is not fitting for the church," and to be banished are "luxurious attire, all pride, and everything unbecoming to Christian humility, discipline and modesty."

61. See André Biéler, *Liturgie et architecture: Le temple des chrétiens* (Geneva: Labor et Fides, 1961), 64–65.

62. For example, the barnlike design using long beams derived from rural structures in the Cévennes. See Hélène Guicharnaud, "An Introduction to the Architecture of Protestant Temples," in *Seeing beyond the Word*, 141.

63. Or, according to some, to remind a Roman Catholic onlooker that Peter (whom they consider the first pope) betrayed Christ three times before the cock crew.

481

realism and interpretation.[64] That is, should the artist show what the eye could see (which might end up in what we now call positivism, or simply acknowledging raw data), or should he depict interpretation (which might require departing from the literal scene and highlighting interpretation)? This problem was especially present in the portrayal of biblical narrative. If the picture was made to be historically exact, it would resemble a photograph, but would not be capable of theological interpretation. According to Rookmaaker this dilemma led many seventeenth-century painters in Reformation countries to simply abandon painting biblical scenes altogether.

Then two possibilities arose. The first is represented in Rembrandt. According to Rookmaaker, he alone really overcame this problem. He did so by using compositional and psychological means to render meaning. For example, in his drawing *Christ on the Road to Emmaus*, we see three men walking down a path. Although they look like real persons, it becomes clear that the one in the middle, who is Jesus, is the most important. Rembrandt achieves this by drawing a house on the right side of the canvas, thus "creating a rhythm, man-Christ-man-house, with the downbeat on Christ and the house."[65] No halo is needed because one of the trees silhouetted in the background is halo-like.[66]

These observations are confirmed by art historian Christian Tümpel, who has persuasively argued that the Dutch tradition of biblical histories rendered in such a psychological or compositional way represents "a fundamental Protestant contribution to art." He does recognize that Rembrandt had a Catholic teacher (Pieter Lastman), yet believes the entire genre was developed in a Calvinist culture.[67] Whether Rembrandt was alone in this achievement, as Rookmaaker maintained, the view that his Calvinism informed these kinds of choices does make sense.

64. The following discussion is taken from Rookmaaker, *Modern Art and the Death of a Culture*, 16ff.

65. Ibid., 18.

66. See H.-M. Rotermund, "The Motif of Radiance in Rembrandt's Biblical Drawings," *Journal of the Warburg and Courtland Institutes* 15.3–4 (1952): 101–21.

67. Christian Tümpel, "Die reformation und die Kunst der Niederlande," in *Luther und die Folgen für die Kunst*, ed. Werner Hoffman (Munich: Prestel, 1983), 314–15.

The second approach was to paint landscapes in ways that celebrate the creation, and God the Creator. Rookmaaker gives an interesting example. Jan Van Goyen's *Landscape* (1646) is a depiction of the world, not as it could be photographed as one thin slice, but as it is in all its beauty, its complexity, and its fragility. Such paintings are so real, we imagine we could see just such a sight or catch it with photography. Yet that is impossible, since this is highly thought-out *composition*, not reproduction. In contrast, say, to Poussin's often nostalgic or idealist landscapes, Van Goyen "sings his song in praise of the beauty of the world here and now, the world God created, the fullness of reality in which we live—if we only open our eyes."[68] In other words, although they are landscapes, they are pregnant with theistic meaning, simply by the way in which each motif is displayed, their "musicality," and the underlying assumption that we are living in God's world—one that is fallen, yet being redeemed. (Here, then, Kuyper and Doumergue had a point: Calvinism contributed to uncoupling the arts from only the church, and helped free the arts to depict all of life, including landscapes.)

Can this view be sustained today, particularly in light of the challenges of the second historiography? Here are the elements of the discussion. Rookmaaker shares what we might call the standard view, put forth by the received art historical wisdom, tailored by his Christian interpretive grid. Basically, this view states that from 1615 to 1630, in places such as Haarlem, a new style developed that was generally more realistic and "secular" than the traditional "mosaic-like" Flemish landscape art. For some historians, this was a reaction to mythology, leaning toward a sort of "art for art's sake," or simply an attention to personal feelings or moods. As recently as 1982, art historian Maarten de Klijn argued that, in keeping with Francis Bacon, Calvinism saw nature as God's "second book," the first being the Bible. Thus, depictions of the creation should show forth God's power and the loveliness of a divine order, without recourse to keys, halos, or the like. This mentality also explains the move from a more mannerist to a more realistic kind of picture.[69]

68. Rookmaaker, *Modern Art and the Death of a Culture*, 23.
69. Maarten de Klijn, *De invloed van het Calvinisme op de Noord-Nederlandse landscap-schilderkunst, 1570–1630* (Apeldoorn: Willem de Zwijgerstichting, 1982).

Other art historians find similar connections between the enjoyment of the world and the Calvinist view of the creation. Boudewijn Bakker argues that the Reformed artist Claes Jansz Visscher's paintings are songs of praise to God the Creator. He examines an interesting print series, called *Plaisante plaetsen* (c. 1612). One of them features a woman paging through a travel book, and lines in Latin and Dutch explain that even if a viewer has no time to actually go to the "pleasant places" in the environs of Haarlem, it is possible to enjoy the sights through the pictures. Bakker suggests that the enjoyment of such scenes is motivated by the Christian worldview, whereby we understand nature to be a "proper song in praise of God."[70]

That was the received view. Now, though, in keeping with the critique of Hegelian approaches, various art historians are putting these connections into question. For example, Reindert L. Falkenburg asks that we take a closer look at the Visscher series.[71] He agrees that the sequence is meant to please the eyes of the viewer, particularly since it recalls a favorite pastime, to take walks outside the city walls and enjoy the stimuli of the senses. But he questions whether there is a clear connection to a Calvinist worldview. Indeed, he even questions whether these sensuous pleasures are not in some important ways opposed to the Calvinist view. He wonders whether a Calvinist ethic might even associate these pleasures with the fall, not the "second book of God."

Falkenburg is not opposed to finding any Calvinist element in the series. He simply asks us to weigh the complexity of such associations. He cites Huygen Leeflang, who argues that that the viewers may have attached a multiplicity of semantic relations to landscape images, rather than setting forth a single, overarching meaning. These might include an Enlightenment secularism, pride in the new Republic, particularly because of its economic prosperity, or, indeed, the praise of the Creator.[72] Nevertheless, Falkenburg does argue that Calvinism was not likely in the

70. Boudewijn Bakker, "Levenspelgrimage of vrome wandeling? Claes Janszoon Visscher en zijn serie 'Plaisante Plaetsen,'" *Oud Holland* 107 (1993): 1.
71. See, for example, his "Landschapschilderkunst en doperse spiritualiteit in de 17de eeuw—enn connectie?" *Doopsgezinde Bijdragen* 16 (1990): 129–53.
72. Huygen Leeflang: "Het landschap in boek en prent . . . ," in *Nederland naar't leven: Landschapsprenten uit de Gouden Eeuw* (Zwolle/Amsterdam: Waanders, 1993), 18–32.

purview. He thinks that "the development toward a realistic idiom and secular staffage in early seventeenth-century Dutch landscape is, as a general principle, not likely connected with a religious, and more specifically Calvinist, view of nature."[73]

Perhaps. But I have my doubts about overcomplicating things. It appears to me that Bakker's view, echoing Rookmaaker's, is defensible, whatever other influences there might have been on these seventeenth-century landscapists. They are not mutually exclusive. This approach is confirmed by E. John Walford in his remarkable study of Jacob van Ruisdael.[74] This preeminent Dutch landscapist celebrates the majesty of God's creation, while fully recognizing the threat of the fall.

Back to the Question

In the end, I do side with Philip Benedict and others who have critiqued the sweeping associations of Kuyper, Doumergue, and the like, on the one hand, and opened up doors for significant research into the connections between Calvinism and choices made by painters, on the other hand. There is much work to be done, on various levels. A closer look at the historical, religious, and cultural contexts will help advance our studies. For example, more comparative work should be done on the similarities of and differences between art done in a primarily Protestant context and a Roman Catholic context. In the former case, for example, we know that it took a bit of time for the arts to return into full favor after the constrictions of iconoclasm. Often the very numbers of artists declined until a better balance could be restored.[75] Ecclesiastical patronage waned considerably in these countries. Eventually, however, things went better. Individuals began to want to own paintings. In the case of primarily Catholic areas, the arts continued to flourish, but were affected by factors such as the Counter-Reformation and the Enlightenment. The

73. Reindert L. Falkenburg, "Calvinism and the Emergence of Dutch Seventeenth-Century Landscape Art," in *Seeing beyond the Word*, 364.

74. E. John Walford, *Jacob Van Ruisdael and the Perception of Landscape* (New Haven: Yale University Press, 1992).

75. See Carl C. Christensen, "The Reformation and the Decline of German Art," *Central European History* 6 (1973): 207–32.

case was different again when Protestants and Catholics lived more or less side by side.

Related to this, what choices of subject matter were made by Protestant and Catholic artists or patrons? In seventeenth-century Amsterdam, for example, although the contrast was not sharp, yet one can note that Catholics tended to own more paintings with directly religious subjects than did Protestants. And when the subject was religious, Calvinists preferred stories from the Old Testament, then the New, and then Nativity scenes, whereas Catholics preferred the crucifixion, the Virgin, and saints.[76] As Philip Benedict demonstrates, these choices clearly reflect the differences in sensibilities of the two groups, particularly in that Protestant polemics required true, biblical histories, or landscapes that showed God's creation, rather deliberately rejecting crucifixions and other motifs associated with Catholic piety. At the same time there was common property, which meant that the different sensibilities were not always so manifest as we might think.

There is also fruit to be borne in the study of what we call cultural appropriations. A pioneer in this research is Roger Chartier, who has extensively studied the numerous ways in which one group will appropriate materials found in the surrounding environment for its own purposes.[77] They may be as seemingly modest as the choice of a painting about an Old Testament story over one depicting a crucifixion. Or they may be as large as the "secularization" of art, in the sense that it leaves the church in order to live more fully in God's world.

Therefore, in order to study the relation of Calvin, Calvinism, and the arts, while more cautious than the grand generalizers, we still can say that something significant did change because of the man's theology and its trajectory in the decades after his revolution in Geneva. So there is plenty of work to be done here, in the year of Calvin's five hundredth birthday! May it be to the greater glory of God.

76. John Michael Montias, "Works of Art in Seventeenth-Century Amsterdam: An Analysis of Subjects and Attributions," in *Art in History/History in Art: Studies in Seventeenth-Century Dutch Culture*, ed. David Freedberg and Jan de Vries (Santa Monica, CA: Getty Center for the History of Art and the Humanities, 1991), table 5.

77. Roger Chartier, *On the Edge of the Cliff: History, Language and Practices* (Baltimore: Johns Hopkins University Press, 1996).

21

CALVINISM IN ASIA

JAE SUNG KIM

Prolegomena

Generally speaking, the influence of Calvinism on Asian people would
barely be noticeable to Western Christians except in Presbyterian churches.
Indeed, Calvinism spread to Asia indirectly in many ways. First of all, Asian
Christians opened their eyes as to how to serve God's glory biblically, not
only through Protestant worship at church and Christian academics, but
also through daily works during radical changes of whole social systems.
Calvinism aided the rise and development of democracy and capitalism in
the social history of Europe by promoting godliness and the "reformation
of life" in all activities.[1]

Moreover, Calvinism contributed to the shaping of biblical worship,
prayer life, and the visible organization of Protestant churches. Both *sola*

---

1. Philip Benedict, *Christ's Churches Purely Reformed: A Social History of Calvinism*
(New Haven: Yale University Press, 2002), xvii.

Scriptura and *tota Scriptura* are the most important subjects for pastors and serious Christian leaders in Asia.[2] Many Reformed missionaries joined the laborious work of translation into Asian languages. Most Asian people would learn the worship of God and his sovereignty from nineteenth-century missionaries who had grown up knowing the Bible as John Calvin's exegesis of "promise and fulfillment."[3]

Particularly, Calvinism powerfully advanced in Korea more than any other Asian country during the twentieth century. Calvinism supports the idea of modernization through various kinds of social and political reformation, for example, in Christian education, public charity ministry, book publication, and mass media. All aspects of Dr. Abraham Kuyper's Neo-Calvinism have been successfully flowering in Korea during the past century. The Presbyterian Church is not the state church, but Presbyterian churches make up 50 percent of all Korean churches. From the very beginning of Korea's mission history in 1884, Calvinism has spread the best theology and orthodox Christianity.

Specifically, the President of Korea, Mr. Lee Myung Bak, is an active session member of the Somang Church in Seoul, a pietistic Presbyterian church that had a wonderful celebration on Calvin's five hundredth birthday. His mother was a very diligent woman devoted to early-morning prayer meetings every day at Po-hang Presbyterian Church. She raised her first son to be National Senator (now sixth elected!), the second to be President of Korea, and her fifth daughter to be a missionary who graduated from Chong-Shin Presbyterian Seminary.

Again, Calvinism provided theological standards for Presbyterian churches, and it maintained doctrinal consistency in Korea during heavy debates on modern liberal theology in the 1950s and on MinJung theology in the 1970s. More recently, many different types of lay ministries for charity have been developing among Calvinists,

---

2. "Calvin's concern was to show that the biblical writers did not commit error. In conclusion, we must in fairness to Calvin declare that he stood with the church of all ages and did in fact believe that the Bible's original autographs were inerrant" (Robert L. Reymond, "Calvin's Doctrine of Holy Scripture," in *A Theological Guide to Calvin's Institutes*, ed. David W. Hall and Peter A. Lillback [Phillipsburg, NJ: P&R Publishing, 2008], 63).

3. Richard A. Muller, "The Hermeneutic Promise and Fulfillment in Calvin's Exegesis of Old Testament Prophecies of the Kingdom," in *The Bible in the Sixteenth Century*, ed. David C. Steinmetz (Durham, NC: Duke University Press, 1990), 70.

such as shelters for the homeless, orphanages, foreign workers, and international marriage.

In 2009, many festivals and conferences on Calvin's legacy and theology were held in Korean churches. More than fifty Christian colleges, seminaries, and institutions gave new attention to the heritage of Calvinism. Of special note, the Calvin quincentenary was recognized by the Korean Evangelical Theological Society in October 2009. I presented "Calvin and Renewal of Church" as the keynote lecture at this largest association of theologians in Korea. I presented a "warm Calvin" and emphasized that Korean churches must retain a "balanced faith" from the rise and decline of Calvinism in Western church history until the postmodern era.[4]

Asian Calvin scholars have met together every two years since 1987. Dr. Han Chul Ha (Korean) and Dr. Watanabe (Japan) were the pioneers of this organization for studying and discussing Calvin and Calvinism. Thus far, the Asian Calvin Society has finished its tenth conference. It is growing with the participation of Taiwanese and Indonesian members.

Calvin and his legacy, however, are not as popular in other areas of Asia, even though Calvinism used to be a popular subject for Japanese scholars in academic institutions. Even many young Korean seminary students, who were thirsting for new education, went to Japan and learned about Calvin from Japanese professors in the 1940s when Korean seminaries were closed by Japan's national worship of Shintoism. It is interesting that modern Japanese churches seek other solutions, just as those in European countries do. Many modern intellectuals in Japan and other parts of Asia are not interested in Calvin because of their postmodern philosophy. It seems to me that the Japanese church is looking for sensational experiences. Many Japanese Christians visit Korean churches for their strong spiritual experiences. Those who want to have the healing of the Holy Spirit go to the Full Gospel Church (General Assembly of God), and those who want to taste exciting experiences rush to the contemporary style of worship in Seoul.

---

4. I have published one book on Calvin's life and three books of history of Calvinism in the Korean language: Jae Sung Kim, *Life of Calvin and the Reformation* (Seoul: Jireh, 2001); *The Heritage of Reformed Theology*, vol. 1, *Confessional Calvinism* (Seoul: Jireh, 2003); *The Marrow of Reformed Theology* (Seoul: Jireh, 2004); *The Perspective of Reformed Theology* (2005).

For Asian pastors and theologians who read English, Calvin's *Institutes* and commentaries are subjects for high-level group study in Hong Kong, Singapore, the Philippines, Taiwan, India, and Indonesia. But except for these distinguished, well-educated pastors and scholars, most Asians do not know the importance of Calvin and Calvinism, mainly because they lack historical knowledge and are influenced by the cheap gospel.

In the case of China, Calvinism as a sound model of Christianity is competing with very clever Communists who do not like to teach the core doctrines of Calvin, such as total depravity and justification by faith for our union with Christ.[5] In contrast, Martin Luther's teachings were welcomed by Communists in East Germany because of a perceived similar revolutionary reaction to the old government. God asks for our painful efforts in order to persuade people of this world who are looking for the triumph of materialism and socialism.

I would like to draw your attention to the hard work of Korean missionaries who are establishing Bible colleges and seminaries and teaching Calvin's Reformed faith and Calvinism. Korean missionaries introduced the dynamic world of the sixteenth-century Reformation in Europe and Calvin's monumental writings, along with those of his successors. The influence of Calvinism is growing in many Asian countries, where it is now shielded from our eyes. But for young pastors, evangelists, and missionaries, Asia is the land of future hope.

The Beginning of Calvinism in China

Studying European history and the Reformation will bring Calvinism to the attention of more Asian students. My generation, including my children who were born in America, heard about Calvinism in their high school years as a part of world history. But the essence and character of Calvinism is not important to Asian people because of their limited

---

5. Richard Gaffin Jr., "Union with Christ: Some Biblical and Theological Reflections," in *Always Reforming: Explorations in Systematic Theology*, ed. A. T. B. McGowan (Downers Grove, IL: InterVarsity Press, 2006), 271–88; Mark A. Garcia, *Life in Christ: Union with Christ and Twofold Grace in Calvin's Theology* (Milton Keynes, UK: Paternoster, 2008).

knowledge of the five hundred years of Calvinism. Calvinism and the Reformed faith were largely unknown to Asian people until the late eighteenth century. Most Asians were living in remote areas, far away from the Holy Land, the Christianity of Constantine's Roman empire, and the church of Europe, as well as North American Christianity.

Furthermore, most Asian countries were blocked by the persecution of old kingdoms whose interests in solidarity and ethnic exclusivity or localism prevailed in the nineteenth century. Indeed, the good news of Christianity competed with Confucianism, Taoism, Buddhism, animism, Islam, and Communism in the past and still does today. The patriotism of royal native religion was ensconced with strong power. It is hard to change the tradition of these nations' ancestors; they not only have to geographically stick together but also must physically maintain all kinds of relationships.

We should think about the reason for failure in China. For the connection between Calvinism and the mind and soil of Asia, we need a very careful approach. When we consider Asian church history from the mission perspective of the West, it is clear that we have been striving not to be a European religion. Dr. Neil's criticism was as follows:

> The European nations, with their loud-voiced claims to a monopoly of Christianity and civilization, had rushed blindly and confusedly into a civil war which was to leave them economically impoverished and without a shred of virtue. The Boer war, by a tacit agreement between the combatants, had been fought as a white man's war; others had not been armed. In the First World War it was otherwise; Indian, African, and Japanese troops took part, with great distinction, against white men. On the whole, they dutifully followed the behests of their rulers; but here and there, there was lingering resentment that so many thousands of Indians and Africans had been drawn into quarrels which were not theirs. The Second World War only finished off what the first had already accomplished. The moral pretensions of the West were shown to be a sham; "Christiandem" was exposed as being no more than a myth; it was no longer possible to speak of "The Christian West."[6]

6. Stephen Neil, *A History of Christian Missions* (Baltimore: Penguin Books, 1963), 452. Dr. Ralph D. Winter (William Carey International University, USA) expressed the same point as one of ten mistakes of Western missions at the Asian Society of Missiology,

Introducing Calvinism through missionaries took a long time and many sacrifices for both Calvinists from outside and new Calvinists who live in Asian countries. If you look at the brief history of Christian missions in Asia, the mainland of India as a British colony was the first country to hear the gospel of Jesus. It was British missionaries who tried to evangelize in the early nineteenth century through the East Indian Company. William Carey (1761–1834), known as the father of modern missions and a Baptist missionary, was a thorough Calvinist and a postmillennialist.[7] In 1785, during his first experience with full-time ministry, Carey read Jonathan Edwards's *Account of the Life of the Late Rev. David Brainerd* and the journals of the explorer James Cook, and became deeply concerned with propagating the Christian gospel throughout the world. His friend Andrew Fuller had previously written an influential pamphlet in 1781, titled "The Gospel Worthy of All Acceptation," answering the hyper-Calvinist belief, then prevalent in the Baptist churches, that not all men were responsible to believe the gospel. At a ministers' meeting in 1786, Carey raised the question whether it was the duty of all Christians to spread the gospel throughout the world. J. R. Ryland, the father of John Ryland, is said to have retorted: "Young man, sit down; when God pleases to convert the heathen, he will do it without your aid and mine." The younger Ryland, however, disputes his father's statement.[8]

The first Protestant missionary to China came out of a revival movement in an English Methodist church and later a Presbyterian church. In April 1799, British churches made great advances for their foreign missions board, The Church Missionary Society for Africa and the East. In 1807, the London Missionary Society sent Robert Morrison (1782–1834) to China at the age of twenty-five. Even though political tension was dangerous and terrible, he provided grand projects for the future of the Chinese church and its mission. He published a Chinese translation of the New Testament in 1811. With the help of William Milne, he finished translat-

---

Bangkok Forum, in 2007: "The Mistake of Insisting That Devout Followers of Jesus Call Themselves 'Christians' and Identify with the Western Church."

7. Brian Stanley, *The History of the Baptist Missionary Society 1792–1992* (Edinburgh: T&T Clark, 1992), 6–7.

8. See Carey's postmillennial eschatology as expressed in his major missionary manifesto: Iain Murray, *The Puritan Hope* (Carlisle, PA: Banner of Truth, 1975); cf. Bruce J. Nichols's article "The Theology of William Carey," *Evangelical Review of Theology* 17 (1993): 372.

ing the Bible in 1823. Then he edited a Chinese-English dictionary with more than ten books of Chinese translation. Morrison, in twenty-seven years, until his death (August 1, 1834), baptized about ten members and prepared medical missions.

James Hudson Taylor (1832–1905) was a successful British Protestant Christian missionary to China and founder of the China Inland Mission (CIM, now OMF International). Taylor spent fifty-one years in China. He brought over eight hundred missionaries to the country, who began 125 schools and were instrumental in eighteen thousand Christian conversions, as well as the establishment of more than three hundred stations of work with more than five hundred local helpers in all eighteen provinces.

After Communism took over, Chinese authorities persistently targeted Christian leaders who did not conform to the state-run Three-Self Patriotic Church (TSPC). Nowadays, the official church of China is one registered with and controlled by the government. There is a significant conflict and confusion between the kingdom of God and the authority of the People's Party in China. It is not easy to discern the Reformed faith even in the TSPC.

There are two opposing shadows in the history of the Christian church and Protestant missions in China. On the dark side, the superiority of foreign missionaries was not sensitive to the ethos of the Chinese people, who were under pressure to open the whole country. For some hundred years beginning in 1724, evangelism by missionaries was prohibited by the emperor. This policy was completely changed by the Opium War, with British and peasant riots against heavy taxes. Anti-Westerner movements were growing during the first Opium War with the British navy (1839–42), during the Taiping Uprising by peasants (1851–64), and during the Second Opium War in 1856–60. Under heavy pressure from Western powers for having provoked British military retaliation in the First Opium War, the Chinese people looked for a hero who would stand against European imperialism. The Boxer Rebellion (1899–1901) and the downfall of the Qing Dynasty in 1912 put an end to a dynastic China's spreading of an anti-Christian movement.[9] From his five years' experience in China after 1941, Dr. Arthur

9. Cf. Diana L. Ahmad, *The Opium Debate and Chinese Exclusion Laws in the Nineteenth-Century American West* (Reno: University of Nevada Press, 2007); Timothy Brook

Glasser points out what they could not see about intercultural respect dur-ing the early days of the missionary movement in China.[10]

The establishment of the NCC in 1922 echoes the independent spirit of the Chinese people's nationalism. Sixteen Christian denominations united China's Christian church under a three-self policy: self-government, self-supporting, self-propagation.

In October 1949, Communists took over the power, and they allowed only one system of Christianity under the three-self patriotic principles. After 1954, Communist governments registered only one church society, which was required to follow the policy of the government and the People's Party. Against Western missionaries, Communists pushed the Three-Self Patriotic Movement (TSPM): "all Christians must support Security of Nation's Law and maintain three principles, such as Self-Government, Self-Support, Self-Propaganda under the leadership of China Commu-nism and Peoples' government." The TSPM emphasizes a theology of love rather than justification by faith. Churches cannot teach the resurrection, the hope of eschatology, or saving faith in Jesus Christ exclusively. The TSPC must preach the possibility of nonbelievers' salvation.[11]

We must remember what happened in the last century (1944–89) concerning Russian Communism throughout eastern European countries. After their revolution, Christians in Russia created an underground church because of the rising power of Communism and the betrayal by many official church leaders that likewise compelled us to create in China many house churches to evangelize and preach the gospel. The Communists forbade all this to children under the age of eighteen. Just as in eastern Europe under the Soviet Communists, the "deputy bishop of the Lutheran church in Romania, began to teach in the theological seminary that God had given three revelations: one through Moses, one through Jesus, and the third through Stalin, the last superseding the one before."[12]

and Bob Tadashi Wakabayashi, eds., *Opium Regimes: China, Britain, and Japan, 1839–1952* (Berkeley: University of California Press, 2000).

10. Arthur F. Glasser, "Timeless Lesson from Western Missionary Penetration of China," in *New Forces in Missions*, ed. David J. Cho (Seoul: East-West Center for Missionary Research & Development, 1976).

11. *The Voice of the Martyrs*, February 2006, 6.

12. Richard Wurmbrand, *Tortured for Christ* (Bartlesville, OK: Living Sacrifice Book Company, 1967), 16.

The influence of Calvinism in China started with the Rev. Robert Morrison, who arrived in Macao in the southeast in October 1807, following a two-hundred-day journey from London. Morrison with his son spread out his Scottish Calvinism, mostly through a Bible-centered life. Morrison's work was so wonderful that later Korean missionaries looked to him as the most patient model in the field.[13]

No one knows exactly how many Chinese have been converted to Christianity. We assume hundreds of millions, perhaps around 10 percent of the whole 1.3 billion population. Since 1995, we have noticed the rapidly growing numbers of confessing Christians. Membership of official churches in the totalitarian systems has approached over thirty-three million Christians, twenty thousand churches, and seventeen seminaries with a thousand students. Lay leadership in the "house church," however, focuses on a hundred million members in its movement, and most of these underground church members are rural farmers and low-income workers in the cities. Almost 90 percent of the Christians among house-church members are illiterate people who need basic Christianity. Both house churches and TSPS are urgently seeking the training of biblical knowledge and sound doctrines.

In order to grasp the direct impact of Calvinism in China, it is necessary to understand the importance of sanctification and prayer life in house-church leadership. These leaders have long prayer times in worship, and they respect the simple life of Jesus. They love to listen to the Puritans' story. In limited areas and time, we could handle the continuing education for lay leadership in many ways, such as short-term training courses, remote study through computers, and written materials.

There is a Chinese translation of Calvin's *Institutes* by Mr. Suh and Mr. Sa (exact date unknown). In 1992, Mr. Wang Ji Young added chapter 7 of book 2, and chapter 16 of book 4, and then completed the whole translation from John T. McNeill and Ford Lewis Battles' English version. Calvinism can be tasted through the Chinese translation of Louis Berkhof's *Manual of Christian Doctrines* (translator and publisher unknown).

13. At the sixth Korean International Mission Conference in Chicago, which was held at Wheaton College in the summer of 2008, Morrison was a popular figure who left the Chinese people with effective ways of doing ministry.

There are three million Korean-Chinese just north of Korea. Calvinism is the driving force of many channels of close relationships with Korean churches, such as the building of new businesses, schools, and hospitals. The Reformed faith and Presbyterian confessions have been transferred to them, and these are primary transmitters of the theology of John Calvin. I had the chance to translate the core doctrines of the Geneva Confession (1537) into Korean. When I introduced Dr. James Boice's *Foundations of the Christian Faith* at a ministers' seminar in Manchuria (in the far northeast of China), I received sincere appreciation from all the participants.[14]

Expansion of Calvinism in Asia

Japan is the most difficult nation in the world in terms of Christian missions. Today, about one to two million Japanese are Christians, only 1 percent of Japan's population. The modern economic goals and the ethos of national culture do not give much chance to Christianity in Japan, where the missionaries' activities were greatest during the sixteenth century. We have received some discouraging reports from contemporary missionaries there. Still, about four hundred Korean missionaries are doing marvelous work in Japan. National pride of Shintoism as the traditional religion and local animism cover the Japanese mind with strong iron clothes. But Korean missionaries and Korean-American missionaries seek to replace economic desires with God's love.

According to Operation World, Japan has 15,594 churches, although this number includes Catholics, Mormons, the Unification Church, and others. Operation World lists 144 Reformed churches in Japan and does not even list Presbyterian as a category. But a more in-depth assessment shows that there are 7,987 Protestant churches in Japan; and 237 churches are Reformed and Presbyterian among those.[15]

14. James Montgomery Boice, *Foundations of the Christian Faith: A Comprehensive and Readable Theology* (Leicester: IVP, 1978), 11–12. This four-book, sixteen-part work corresponds more or less to the ground covered by Calvin's four-book *Institutes*.

15. Thanks to Dr. Michael Oh, missionary and professor from the Presbyterian Church in America at Nagoya Seminary since 2001.

To consider the influence of Calvinism in Japan, Calvinism among all models of theology is famous for intellectual groups who are reading theological materials seriously. It is easy to make contact with Calvinism in Japan. Good translations of John Calvin's corpus are available. The first translation of Calvin's *Institutes* was made by Masaki Nakayama in 1937, according to the *Dictionary of the History of Christianity in Japan*. But according to another publication, the first publication of the Japanese *Institutes* was on June, 21, 1939, and the publisher was Shinkyou Shuppansha (Protestant Publications).

The second translation was made by Nobuo Watanabe, published by the same publisher at a later date. This was begun in 1962. The project was probably started to commemorate the 450th anniversary of the *Institutes*. Nobuo Watanabe completely retranslated and published books 1 and 2 in 2007, books 3 and 4 in 2008. There is a translation of the abridged version by H. Carr. The translation of the *Institutes* from the 1536 edition was by Atsumi Kume. There is also a translation of "The Golden Booklet of the True Christian Walk" by Shigeru Yoshioka. A translation of the commentaries was started after 1945. The comprehensive translation of the New Testament series is a work in progress and is near completion.

The Transformation of Calvinism in Korea

Calvinism and the Reformed faith were nonexistent in Korea until 1884, when the first missionary arrived. Within one hundred years, however, it had become a major religious trend. From the very beginning of the Presbyterian mission, in God's providence, Christianity was competing with Japanese colonialism. During that time Korean people looked at missionaries as preferable to Japan's military dictatorship; thus, little by little, they became more open toward the gospel. Through modern education, private Christian schools, dramatic health care by the hospitals, and social organizations such as the YMCA, missionaries wonderfully worked together in the hermit land.

The first seminary in Korea, Pyung Yang Seminary, was opened by an American Presbyterian mission in 1901. The first generation of seminary faculty members were conservative Presbyterians from America,

Canada, and Australia.[16] Dr. Samuel A. Moffet, who graduated from McComick Theological Seminary, one of the American Calvinist schools in the nineteenth century, led a strong team at the seminary. He and other missionaries, the Revs. Clark, Reynolds, and R. L. Roberts, taught a Confessions class, emphasizing continuity with the apostolic fathers. At the age of twenty-nine, three years after landing in Korea, Dr. Moffet earned new converts through street evangelism in Pyung Yang.

The authority of the Bible was at the core of Dr. Moffet's presidency. Dr. Moffet's first seven alumni who received ordination established the General Assembly in 1907. Fifty years later, Dr. Moffet proudly characterized the triumph of Bible-centered ministry in Korea. Dr. Clark also pointed out that all the Korean churches focused on the study of the Bible at their initial stages.[17] The Bible was "the Book of Korea." Dr. Moffet emphasized the power and authority of the Bible: "The Bible has certainly occupied a rather unique position in the work in Korea, and the Korean Church derives its power, its spirituality, its great faith in prayer, its liberality, from the fact that the whole Church has been, as it were, saturated with a knowledge of the Bible."[18]

William Davis Reynolds, who came from a Southern Presbyterian church in America, was the first chair of systematic theology at Pyung Yang Seminary (1917–37). As an alumnus of Union Seminary in Richmond, he taught a strong Southern Presbyterianism and used Robert Lewis Dabney's book as the text. Before his teaching at Pyung Yang, Reynolds had been involved in the crucial work on a Korean Bible translation since 1895. For three and a half years (from October 1902 to March 1906) Reynolds spent most of his time with Drs. Underwood (the first missionary to Korea in 1884, a Presbyterian, who graduated from New Brunswick Seminary in New Jersey) and Gale (Canada, and Northern Presbyterian

16. H. M. Conn, "Studies in the Theology of the Korean Presbyterian Church, Part I," *WTJ* 29 (November 1966): 53.
17. Charles A. Clark, "Fifty Years of Mission Organization Principle and Practice," in *The Fiftieth Anniversary Celebration of the Korea Mission of the Presbyterian Church in the U.S.A. June 30–July 3, 1934*, ed. Harry A. Rhodes and Richard H. Baird (Seoul: YMCA Press, 1934), 56.
18. Samuel A. Moffet, "Evangelical Work," in Quarto Centennial Papers Read before the Korean Mission of the Presbyterian Church in the U.S.A. at the Annual Meeting in Pyung Yang, August 17, 1909 (Seoul: Korea Mission of the PCUSA, 1909), 17.

Church of America) to finish the Bible translation.[19] First, the New Testament translation was completed in 1900, and then the Old Testament was finished in 1910. But Reynolds was the most crucial person associated with the project because of his thorough knowledge of Hebrew. For such a sound Korean Bible translation, all Koreans are indebted to these three Presbyterian missionaries, who published their work in 1937, around the time of Reynolds's retirement.

In addition to Bible study, consecutive revival meetings became the typical program of the Korean church with the extraordinary outpouring of the Holy Spirit in 1907 at Pyung Yang.[20] The Korean church has preserved the legacy of confessional Calvinism as the best religion. I experienced the revival of prayer life in Korea through my parents at home. In 1974, Korean churches gathered one million souls in Seoul for Billy Graham's revival. With the broadening of modern theology in the West and in America, the rapidly growing Korean church also divided into some major Presbyterian denominations. I would like to categorize seven groups in the Korean Presbyterian church:[21]

+ Separate fundamentalist Presbyterian church: a small but very strong church that claims historic orthodoxy and purity. Founders of this group were against the idol worship of Japanese Shintoism. This church comprises Koshin University and its related denominations.
+ Classical/Puritan conservative Presbyterian church: Chongshin University and its many related schools and denominations.
+ Pragmatic evangelical Presbyterian church: This church focuses on mass evangelism and the emotional revival movement.
+ Regional Presbyterian churches: Localism combines with the spirit of orthodoxy.

19. James Scrath Gale, *Korea in Transition* (New York: Young People's Missionary Movement of the United States and Canada, 1909), 138.

20. William Newton Blair and Bruce F. Hunt, *The Korean Pentecost and the Sufferings Which Followed* (Edinburgh: Banner of Truth, 1977).

21. Jae Sung Kim, *Understanding and Task of Reformed Theology* (Suwon: Hapdong Seminary Press, 2004), 233–36. Cf. George M. Marsden, "Fundamentalism and American Evangelicalism," in *The Variety of American Evangelism*, ed. Donald W. Dayton and Robert K. Johnson (Downers Grove, IL: InterVarsity Press, 2001), 23.

+ Inclusive/ecumenical Presbyterian church: Dr. Han Kyung Jik and Korea Presbyterian University and its denomination. Neo-orthodox theology is predominant.
+ Contemporary Presbyterian church: Cultural contextualization and modern worship.
+ Progressive Presbyterian church: MinJung theologians; its denomination prefers to adopt all kinds of modern theology.

Recent statistics show Christians in Korea to number approximately 20 percent of the whole population, with 94,615 pastors, 58,404 churches in 124 denominations, and 11,944,000 Christians in Korea. We must count about 19,413 Korean missionaries in 168 countries out of 232 all over the world and 250 missionaries from the Korean American Church to the world.[22] Also, 5,174 Korean churches are outside of Korea, most of them in America (3,933), with 377 churches in Canada, 214 in Japan, 114 in Germany, 54 in England, and 53 in Argentina. Some 192 churches were added in 2009 (an increase of 3.8 percent).[23]

Why is Presbyterianism so popular among the Korean people? My simple answer is this: From very miserable circumstances, the Korean people found hope of survival in Christianity. One only needs to think, for example, about the Korean War, Japanese occupation for thirty-six years, involvement in the Vietnam War, and so on. In America, as new immigrants, Koreans are drawn to the new hope in Christianity, particularly in the stories of the sufferings and accomplishments of the Puritans. Just like Koreans, almost all other Asians endure extremely severe sufferings in their lifetimes.

Koreans respect the authority and principle of classical traditions. Presbyterian confessions, as exemplars of standard and orthodox Christianity, are perfect matches for this mind-set. Confucianism was the only belief system for five hundred years of the Lee Dynasty. It was the only ethical standard for young students. Korean people love to say with great pride, "These are the original principles." The Presbyterian church, how-

22. Sources: Korea World Missions Association, http://www.kwmc.org; *Koreatimes*, January 23, 2009, section A23 (Religion), http://www.koreatimes.com.
23. Sources: http://www.koreanchurchyp.com; http://www.christiantoday.us/data/.

ever, is the oldest church system in western Europe. Buddhism was the second-largest religion in Korea at that time, and it still has the largest membership. Although Confucianism provides benefits only for the upper classes, Buddhism offers unknown training. These religions were shown to be powerless, however, when the Logos of God came into Korea. For example, when Western medical hospital systems started their marvelous healing in Korea, average people admired modern science and the hospitality of missionaries who could touch all patients. They could build such good schools and an oasis for sick people alongside the gospel.

The New World came to Korea with missionaries. Most national leaders of the Republic of Korea who had the chance to study abroad wished to transform the old social systems according to that of the Western commonwealth. First President Dr. Lee Seung Man, who studied in America, could build his leadership by combatting the Communism of North Korea. He was a thorough Methodist Christian. Later generations of Korean leaders, around the time of the Korean War, had favorable experiences of the church from very young ages because the church was the only place to get supplies for the poor. American brothers and sisters sent food, money, and love for the neglected. My parents prayed for a good education for their two sons. And they believed this came from God as the reward of their sorrowful prayers.

Three different translations of the *Institutes* in Korean languages have been published, full sets of Calvin's commentaries and sermons are also available, and the Calvin Studies Society of Korea has a good body of professors.

Calvinism in Southeast Asia

Christianity is not popular at all in southeast Asia. Indonesia has 230 million people, which is the fourth-largest population in the world. Islam is the predominant religion, comprising nearly 87 percent of the entire nation. Protestants make up 6 percent. It is very hard to reach 330 tribes in many islands.

In Bangladesh, Christians of all flavors account for less than 1 percent of Bangladesh's 138 million people. Some 87 percent are Muslim,

12 percent Hindu, 0.6 percent Buddhist. Thailand's Christian population is estimated at 0.5 percent of the total population.

Presbyterian and Reformed churches are very few, and Calvin's *Institutes* has not yet been translated into the Thai language. In Thailand, Baptists are fairly healthy, but only two schools teach Reformed theology, and each school has fewer than two hundred students.

Burma, officially the Union of Myanmar, is the largest country by geographical area in mainland southeast Asia, or Indochina. But as in Thailand, the Reformed faith is very weak there.

The Presbyterian church in Singapore associates with the National Council of Churches of Singapore. It used to be called "Antioch of Asia," with the hope of evangelizing Asia. The Christian population is not small—14.6 percent of the country's population.

In Malaysia, about 9.8 percent of the whole population attends five thousand churches. Christianity is a minority among the religions practiced, and most Christians live in East Malaysia. Christian books cannot be purchased, and they are available only secretly from Indonesia. The major Christian denominations in Malaysia are Anglican, Baptist, Brethren, nondenominational churches, independent charismatic churches, Lutheran, Methodist, Presbyterian, and other Protestant denominations. Presbyterians are in very small numbers, so no translation of Calvin's writings exists in the local languages. It is almost impossible to read Calvin's *Institutes* in English. Three seminaries are located in West Malaysia and two in East Malaysia.

Conclusion: Hope in Taking New Calvinism to the World

Embracing the Reformed faith and Calvinism as the best form of biblical Christianity is the only answer for Asians, as well as everyone else in the world. In this season of global economic crisis, *Time* magazine has paid attention to "the new Calvinism" that is welcomed by a new generation. Just as Calvinist beliefs rescued European people in the sixteenth century, the same spirit could have a great impact on those in this century. "It will be interesting," as that *Time* article opines, "to see whether Calvin's legacy will be classic Protestant backing or whether, during these hard times, more Christians searching for security will submit their wills to the austerely demanding God of their country's infancy."[24] New strategies are needed for Asian countries where Calvinism has not been successful.

Finally, I would like to point to very positive aspects of Calvinism in our days. I claim these seven characteristics of Calvinism as the basis for a new hope for the people of Asia:

1. The Reformed faith can provide a high level of moral, ethical criteria for the Asian people. Puritan revival, Asian style, is needed.
2. As Calvin and his successors offered academic excellence for all Europeans, Asian people would benefit from the best Reformed teachers in developed countries. The practice of godliness at Reformed University could be a useful channel for producing teachers.
3. All Asian countries are struggling with corruption and the private use of power by the upper class. The Calvinistic idea of public service in all areas of life should be proclaimed, especially to officers of the government.
4. All kinds of secular hedonism must be revoked, in order to promote a clean society and home by living a holy life.
5. Calvinism recognizes human beings as being created in the image of God. The Reformed church should be instrumental in promoting the respect especially of men and women who are uneducated, neglected, and disabled.
6. Seasonable reading and thinking as part of the Reformed lifestyle would result in the enjoyment of God and recognition of his sovereignty.
7. Only from a true knowledge of God and his Word can one discern the foolish syncretism of Taoism, Buddhism, and Confucianism.

With Calvinism's short past and, Lord willing, long future ahead in Asia, we offer these Calvinistic contributions to a culture that we pray will be more and more open to its timeless truths.

24. David Van Bierma, "The New Calvinism," *Time*, March 12, 2009, available at http://www.time.com/time/specials/packages/article.

22

UNION WITH CHRIST IN CALVIN'S THEOLOGY: GROUNDS FOR A DIVINIZATION THEORY?

BRUCE L. MCCORMACK

I
t is becoming increasingly popular among interpreters of John Calvin's theology to treat his soteriology as in some way akin to the divinization (*theosis* or deification) theories of the Eastern Orthodox.[1] In many ways, this development comes as no surprise. The Finnish school of

1. The literature includes the following: Joseph C. McClelland, "Sailing to Byzantium," in *The New Man: An Orthodox and Reformed Dialogue*, ed. John Meyendorff and Joseph C. McClelland (New Brunswick, NJ: Agora Books, 1973); Carl Mosser, "The Greatest Possible Blessing: Calvin and Deification," *Scottish Journal of Theology* 55 (2002): 36–57; Julie Canlis, "Calvin, Osiander and Participation in God," *International Journal of Systematic Theology* 6 (2004): 169–84; Todd Billings, "John Calvin: United to God through Christ," in *Partakers of the Divine Nature: The History and Development of Deification in the Christian Traditions*, ed. Michael J. Christensen and Jeffrey A. Wittung (Grand Rapids: Baker Academic, 2007), 200–18. Also relevant to the issues surrounding Calvin and divinization are Wilhelm Kolfhaus, *Christusgemeinschaft bei Johannes Calvin* (Neukirchen-Vluyn: Buchhandlung der Erziehungsvereins, 1938); Dennis E. Tamburello, *Union with Christ: John Calvin and the Mysticism of St. Bernard* (Louisville: Westminster John Knox, 1994); Philip Walker Butin,

research on Martin Luther has led a fair number of Lutheran theologians to the conclusion that forensicism did not play as large a role in Luther's thinking as was once thought by late nineteenth- and early twentieth-century German researchers especially. The "Joint Declaration on the Doctrine of Justification" provides official ecclesiastical support for that point of view. Where the Reformed are concerned, the point of entry into this conversation lies in Calvin's understanding of union with Christ and especially with the (allegedly) prominent position that doctrine is given in book 3 of the 1559 *Institutes*. Indeed, some Calvin scholars seem to labor under the impression that Calvin is an even better candidate for revisionist reading than is Luther. It is this conviction that I would like to contest in this essay.

Before turning to Calvin, however, I would like to begin by registering a critical observation that will hover in the background of all my reflections in this essay. It is rarely if ever the case that the meaning of *divinization* is set forth in anything like a clear and consistent manner that would allow for meaningful discussion and debate. What finally is meant by the well-worn phrase *participation in the life of God?* The phrase is ambiguous on the face of it. Does it mean "participation in the life that is God's own, the life that is proper to him as God, that life that is his *essentially?*" If so, how then is it possible to participate in it without participating in the divine essence? Or does the phrase envision participation in a life that is called "God's" only because he has made it? Is it called "his" only because it belongs to him (as is the case with all that he has made)? To put a finer point on it: is the "life of God" in which we are said to participate *uncreated* life or *created* life?

The distinction that is typically adduced as a way of warding off the more questionable elements in "divinization" theories—that is, the distinction between divine essence and divine energies—does not give us a direct answer to this question. To the extent that this distinction is used to say that we do not participate in the divine essence (but only in the energies), then surely the life in which we participate would have to be *created* life. But most Orthodox or Orthodox-leaning theologians today do

Revelation, Redemption and Response: Calvin's Trinitarian Understanding of the Divine-Human Relationship (New York: Oxford University Press, 1995).

not seem to be satisfied with this conception because they are convinced (on metaphysical grounds) that immortality must be *uncreated*; the idea of a *created immortality*, eternal life as a created gift of grace, would seem to be an unthinkable possibility for them. But of course, once you say that human beings are granted, by God's grace, a share in the uncreated life that is proper to God as God, then the distinction between the divine essence and the divine energies is fatally eroded. For surely participation in the uncreated life of God is, by definition, a participation in something that is essential to God. My point is this: those who wish to find a "divinization" theory in Calvin must be more clear than they have been up to this point with regard to what they mean. I will try to set a good example in what follows by being very clear with regard to what I mean when I speak of "union with Christ" in Calvin's theology, what it implies for the overall shape of his soteriology, and so on.

In what follows, I am going to reflect on the doctrine that, more than any other, has led to the thesis that Calvin taught a version of a divinization theory, the doctrine of union with Christ or participation in him. The essay will comprise three major sections. In the first section, I will seek to locate Calvin's thinking about union with Christ in its material (rather than its literary) context. My focus here will be on those doctrinal commitments that impinge directly on Calvin's understanding of union. What web of doctrines, if you will, control Calvin's thinking about *this* doctrine? That is my question. The result of this investigation will be a delimitation; it will tell us what Calvin could not have had in mind in speaking of union with Christ. I will then turn in a second section to a more positive description of what I think Calvin did understand by union. A third section will consider residual problems, specifically, whether an alternative conception to the one laid out in the second section is to be found in other writings of Calvin.

Material Dogmatic Commitments Impinging on Calvin's Treatment of the Theme of Union

John Calvin's mature theology was forged in the crossfire of debates that took place at decisive moments in his theological development. In

1540, he wrote a treatise on the Lord's Supper whose express purpose was to find a "middle way" between the extremes offered by Martin Luther and Huldrych Zwingli. Calvin was at his most ecumenical in this stage of his thinking. The signing of the Consensus Tigurinus in 1549, however, earned him the enmity of Lutheran theologians such as Joachim Westphal, which led to a fiery debate over Christology and the nature of the real presence of Christ in the Lord's Supper. At much the same time, the emergence of the teaching of Andreas Osiander led Calvin to give a degree of precision to his teaching on justification that it had not possessed to this point.

I would now like to consider the doctrines under discussion in each of these debates in turn, for Calvin's conclusions with regard to each of them render him a most unpromising candidate for inclusion in the new orthodoxy of the twenty-first century. I will begin with the problem of the real presence, turning then to Christology and finally to justification.

Participation in the Humanity of Christ in the Lord's Supper

In his "Short Treatise on the Holy Supper," Calvin had already laid down the main lines of his concept of "participation" that would control his thinking about union with Christ through the remainder of his life. The question that Calvin seeks to address here is this: How does it come about that believers "are truly made partakers of the real substance of the body and blood of Jesus Christ"?[2] It should be noted that the concept of participation that Calvin here envisions is strictly delimited to a participation in the "substance" of Christ's body and blood. No participation in the "substance" of Christ's divine nature is envisioned. That possibility is simply not on the table. Calvin is careful to speak only of a participation in Christ's *humanity*: "if the reason for communicating with Jesus Christ is in order that we have part and portion in all the gifts which he has procured for us by his death, it is not only a matter of being partakers of his Spirit; it is necessary also to partake of his *humanity*, in which he rendered

---

2. John Calvin, "Short Treatise on the Holy Supper of Our Lord and Only Savior Jesus Christ," in *Calvin: Theological Treatises*, ed. J. K. S. Reid (Philadelphia: Westminster Press, 1954), 166.

complete obedience to God his Father, to satisfy our debts . . ."[3] How then does Calvin explain this?

Calvin defines his position over against what he takes to be the Catholic view of the real presence on the one side and the Zwinglian understanding on the other side. As he understands the Catholic position, the transubstantiation of bread and wine into body and blood yields a "local" presence. This he rejects, on the grounds that a local presence would require that the body of Christ be "without limit," i.e., "that it can be in different places" at the same time.[4] Calvin agrees with Zwingli that the gift of immortality bestowed on Christ's body in the resurrection does not change its "nature."[5] A body that could be in more than one place at a time is but a "phantom"[6]—not a real body at all. After the ascension, Christ's body is to be found "locally" in heaven, and there alone. To fall down in adoration before him would require that we lift up our hearts to heaven rather than fall down before the visible signs of bread and wine.[7] On the other hand, Calvin also makes it clear that the visible signs are not "bare" signs, but "joined" to their "reality and substance."[8] So Zwingli's view does not satisfy Calvin either.

Calvin's solution to the problem of the real presence is well known. His solution is to say that "the Spirit of God is the bond of participation" that joins "the internal substance of the sacrament . . . with the visible signs."[9] At this stage certainly (if not so clearly later), Calvin's account of the real presence is rightly described, in the language of Brian A. Gerrish, as "symbolic instrumentalism."[10] The substance of the sacrament is joined by the Holy Spirit to the elements rather than to the communicant. Therefore, the communicant participates in the substance of the body and blood *indirectly*, not directly.

3. Ibid., 146 (emphasis added).
4. Ibid., 158.
5. Ibid., 159.
6. Ibid., 158.
7. Ibid., 159.
8. Ibid., 147.
9. Ibid., 148.
10. Brian A. Gerrish, "The Lord's Supper in the Reformed Confessions," in *Major Themes in the Reformed Tradition*, ed. Donald K. McKim (Grand Rapids: Eerdmans, 1992), 253.

This answer to the fundamental question of the nature of the real presence of Christ in the Supper undergoes no substantive change in the definitive edition of the *Institutes*. There Calvin writes, "Even though it seems unbelievable that Christ's flesh, separated from us by such great distance, penetrates to us, so that it becomes our food, let us remember how far the secret power of the Holy Spirit towers above all our senses, and how foolish it is to wish to measure his immeasurableness by our measure. What, then, our mind does not comprehend, let faith conceive: that the Spirit truly unites things separated in space."[11] Again, the visible signs are not "empty." The reality that is signified is also presented to us. What Calvin sets forth, then, is the idea of a *spiritual* real presence, as opposed to a local or physical real presence.

As I say, all of this is well known. But its significance for an understanding of the nature of our union with Christ has rarely been appreciated. First, we need to underscore once again that the participation of which Calvin speaks—and hence, the union that he contemplates—is a participation in the humanity of Christ, a participation in the "substance" of a body that remains separated from us in space even as we participate in it. Thus far, what Calvin has said is completely congruent with the thought that bodies individuate—that it is our bodies that secure and guarantee our *ontological otherness* from one another as human beings. Christ's body is not here physically. It is not present in, with, or under the elements. It remains other even as we participate in its "substance" spiritually.

Second, the power that joins to the "substance" of bread and wine is the Holy Spirit. Now, this claim is very important, especially if we are seeking to supply what is largely lacking in Calvin, that is, an ontology of the Supper. Calvin is well aware that the New Testament regularly depicts the Holy Spirit as indwelling the believer. But what kind of "indwelling" is this? Certainly, the idea of "indwelling" sets forth the thought that the Holy Spirit is causally effective in us. But the Holy Spirit is not hypostatically united to us. We are not incarnations of the third person of the Trinity. The Holy Spirit remains ontologically other than ourselves even as he

11. *Institutes*, 4.17.10.

509

indwells us. It would seem to follow quite naturally that the "substance" of Christ's body and blood to which the ontologically other Spirit joins us remains, in the joining, ontologically other as well. Or, to change the metaphor: if the "bridge" leading us to the body and blood is other, then that to which it leads must also be other. Ontological differentiation on the creaturely plane (our humanity in relation to the humanity of Christ) is not set aside.

Third, the element of indirection in the "joining" of the "substance" of body and blood to the visible signs also serves to secure and protect the ontological otherness of that humanity of Christ in which we participate in the Supper. Our "contact" with Christ's humanity is a mediated contact, mediated through the instruments of bread and wine. Even if we set aside the consideration just mentioned—that the Holy Spirit who makes the signs to be "effective" in us remains other than ourselves in all his activity—we would still have this element of indirection to deal with. We do not come into direct contact with the body and blood; that thought is an unthinkable one for Calvin.

It is in the light of these considerations, then, that we should understand the more florid language of Calvin so beloved by those who subscribe to the new orthodoxy. That Christ is made "one substance with us"[12] in the Supper means simply that we participate in the "substance" of body and blood *spiritually*. Calvin is not speaking of the kind of union that is made possible by substance metaphysics. And he is certainly not speaking of a participation in Christ's divine nature.

If, however, there is a set of passages in which Calvin seems to contradict the picture I have been drawing here, a passage or set of passages in which he certainly seems to teach a participation in the divine life, they are the following (which are all taken from two small subsections): "we are taught from the Scriptures that Christ was from the beginning that life-giving Word of the Father [John 1:1], the spring and source of life, from which all things have always received their capacity to live."[13] Clearly, Calvin is speaking here of the divine Word, the Logos, the Son of God. And he goes on to say:

12. Ibid., 4.17.3.
13. Ibid., 4.17.8.

The same John afterwards adds that life was manifested only when, having taken on our flesh, the Son of God gave himself for our eyes to see and our hands to touch [1 John 1:2]. For even though he previously poured out his power upon the creatures, still, because man (estranged from God through sin and having lost participation in life) saw death threatening from every side, he had to be received into communion of the Word in order to receive hope of immortality. For how little assurance would you grasp, if you heard that the Word of God (from which you are far removed) contains in itself fullness of life, but in and round about yourself nothing but death meets you and moves before your eyes? But when the Source of life begins to abide in our flesh, he no longer lies hidden far from us, but shows that we are to partake of him. But he also quickens our very flesh in which he abides, that by partaking of him we may be fed unto immortality. "I am," he says, "the bread of life come down from heaven. And the bread which I shall give is my flesh, which I shall give for the life of the world." [John 6:48, 51; cf. 6:51–52, Vg.] By these words he teaches us not only that he is life since he is the eternal Word of God, who came down from heaven to us, but also that by coming down he poured that power upon the flesh which he took in order that from it participation in life might flow unto us.[14]

This passage is then followed by an even more extravagant one: "the flesh of Christ is like a rich and inexhaustible fountain that pours into us the life springing forth from the Godhead into itself. Now who does not see that communion with Christ's flesh and blood is necessary for all who aspire to heavenly life?"[15] Here Calvin makes the life that is proper to the Word of God as God to be mediated to us through our feeding on the flesh of Christ. The question is: how can he say this? Can he say it with any consistency at all? The problem that surrounds Calvin's language here lies in the fact that it seems to demand something more than a participation in the humanity of Christ: a participation in his divine nature as well. And as I will now try to show, Calvin's own Christology will not allow for such a participation. In any event, such passages work exceptionally in Calvin's writings; they are not the norm.

14. Ibid.
15. Ibid., 4.17.9.

Calvin's Christology

Calvin's worry that the Catholic doctrine of transubstantiation would yield a "local" presence of the physical body and blood of Christ was actually unfounded—at least if one had recourse to the best and brightest of medieval Catholic theologians, Thomas Aquinas. For Thomas, "locality" or extension in space was clearly an "accident" (in Aristotle's sense). Transubstantiation—the great miracle of the replacement of the substance of bread and wine by the "substance" of body and blood—cannot yield a local presence, except by concomitance, as Thomas would put it. And the Christology that would support this understanding of the real presence is not one that entails that the physical body of Christ be rendered without limit. To get to that notion, one would have to embrace the so-called genus of majesty of the Lutherans: that version of the traditional doctrine of the "communication of attributes" in accordance with which the human nature of Christ was given a share in the divine attributes of omniscience, omnipotence, and (most importantly for sixteenth-century debates over the real presence) omnipresence (or ubiquity). This is a move that Thomas did not make. In truth, the genus of majesty was a novum in the history of Christian theology when it was first advanced by the Lutherans. The fact is that Calvin stood much closer to Thomas's version of transubstantiation with his concept of a *spiritual* real presence than he could have imagined.

Be that as it may, Calvin's Christology was designed from the beginning to overcome the defects that he mistakenly perceived to follow from the idea of transubstantiation and then (in the 1550s) rightly found in the Lutheran doctrine of ubiquity. And that is a point of no small importance for our theme.

There can be no question but that Calvin intended to be faithful to the Chalcedonian Formula. But his primary goal was to overcome the concept of a direct communion of the natures, that interpenetration of the natures that made possible the Lutheran genus of majesty. To achieve this, he did two things. First, he understood the "person of the union" to be a "compound person" in John of Damascus's sense. To put it this way is not to suggest a literary dependence on John; in truth, Calvin does not seem to have known John's *De Fide Orthodoxa*, even though a new Latin translation by Léfèvre (Faber Stapulensis) had appeared in the early sixteenth century. But Zwingli left behind a well-marked copy of the new translation,[16] and if Zwingli knew it, then its central ideas might well have spread to other Reformed theologians. In any event, Calvin says that it was necessary for our salvation for "the Son of God to become for us, 'Immanuel, that is, God with us' [Isa. 7:14; Matt. 1:23], and in such a way that his divinity and our human nature might by mutual connection *grow together.*"[17] Such language is, of course, also reminiscent of a phrase found in the Chalcedonian Formula that was admirably suited to Calvin's purposes: "at no point was the difference between the natures taken away through the union, but rather the property of both natures is preserved and comes together into a single person and a single subsistent being."[18] Calvin's concern throughout is to preserve the two natures in their original

16. See Alfred Schindler, "Zwingli als Leser von Johannes Damascenus," in *Auctoritas Patrum: zur Rezeption der Kirchenväter in 15. Und 16. Jahrhundert*, ed. Leif Grane, Alfred Schindler, and Markus Wriedt (Mainz: Verlag Philipp von Zabern, 1993), 185–95. Thanks are due here to the late David Wright, who first put me on to this essay.

17. *Institutes*, 2.12.1. Since Philip Butin rests the whole of his case for Calvin's alleged belief in an interpenetration of natures on this single sentence, this is the right place to make a comment on his thesis. The Latin text that lies behind the Battles translation that I have reproduced here reads: "ut mutua coniunctione eius divinitas et hominum natura inter se coalescerent." Butin translates this phrase "in such a way that divinity and human nature might by mutual conjunction coalesce with each other." On the face of it, such a translation might seem unquestionably correct. Certainly, it is more literally correct than what Battles has in the sentence quoted in the text above. Moreover, the word *coalesce* might well seem to require an *interpenetration* of the natures, rather than simply a coming together. Battles has certainly made an effort to expand on the meaning of *conjunction* by adding "grow together" so that the two words *coniunctione* and *coalescerent* are not simply identical in meaning. The problem with Butin's translation—and the idea of an interpenetration of the natures that he uses to justify it—is that he leaves entirely out of account any elements in Calvin's thinking that would render impossible the thought of an interpenetration. He never considers, for example, the significance of Calvin's treatment of the *communicatio idiomatum*. In my view, the material that follows in my text above offers sufficient reason to believe that Calvin did not intend to teach an interpenetration of natures. And if that is the case, then a literal translation of *coalescerent* would fail to grasp the significance of this statement in the context of Calvin's treatment of Christology when seen as a whole. In truth, Battles' translation "grow together" is most apt. Todd Billings, too, subscribes to an "interpenetration of natures" view, but with even less textual evidence than Butin managed to adduce. See Billings, "John Calvin: United to God through Christ," 202.

18. Norman P. Tanner, ed., *Decrees of the Ecumenical Councils*, vol. 1 (Washington, DC: Sheed & Ward and Georgetown University Press, 1990), 86.

integrity subsequent to the union.[19] So the "growing together" of which
he speaks refers *not* to a direct communion of the natures but to a living
communication of the natures to the person by means of which the person
itself is constituted. Such a reading is completely congruent with Calvin's
treatment of the "communication of attributes," the second move to which I
alluded earlier. Like John of Damascus before him, Calvin treats the communication as occurring not directly (between the natures) but indirectly
(from the natures to the person). In fact, it is precisely this rendering of
the "communication" that *requires* the supposition of a "compound person,"
for only the latter can make sense of the former.

Calvin finds three kinds of predication in Holy Scripture. First, he tells
us, there are predications made of the divine nature alone—such as "before
Abraham was, I am" in John 8:58[20] and the depiction of Christ as "the
firstborn of all creation" who was "before all things, and in him all things
hold together" in Colossians 1:15, 17.[21] The second class of predications
has reference to the human nature alone. These include statements such
as "And Jesus increased in wisdom and in stature and in favor with God
and man" (Luke 2:52); Jesus' claim not to know the Last Day in Matthew
24:36 and Mark 13:32 also belongs to this class. "All of these refer solely
to Christ's humanity. Insofar as he is God, he cannot increase in anything,
and . . . nothing is hidden from Him . . ."[22]

The third class of statements is the class judged by Calvin to consist in
a "communication of attributes," properly speaking. Such a "communication"
is to be found in those cases in which a New Testament writer explicitly
turns language on its head, so to speak, ascribing to God what is proper
only to the human or to the human that which is proper only to God.
Examples include God's purchasing the church "with his own blood" (Acts
20:28); "the Lord of glory" being crucified (1 Cor. 2:8); and "the word of
life" being handled (1 John 1:1). Of these, Calvin says, "Surely God does

19. "He who was Son of God became the Son of man—not by confusion of substance
but by unity of person. For we affirm his divinity so joined and united with his humanity
that each retains its distinctive nature unimpaired, and yet these two natures constitute one
person" (*Institutes*, 2.14.1).

20. All quotations from the Bible in this chapter are from the ESV.

21. *Institutes*, 2.14.2.

22. Ibid.

not have blood, does not suffer, cannot be touched with hands. But since Christ, who was true God and also true man, was crucified and shed his blood for us, the things that he carried out in his human nature are transferred *improperly*, although not without reason, to his divinity."[23] If such predication is finally improper, how is it that it occurs "not without reason"? The reason is that "because the selfsame one was both God and man, for the sake of the union of both natures he gave to the one what belonged to the other."[24] It is of the utmost importance to see what is happening here. When Scripture says that God purchased the church with his blood, it speaks not of the divine nature but of the *One who possesses both divine and human natures*. In other words, the attribution is being made to the person of the union, not to the divine nature. And the person of the union is both divine and human at the same time, which allows predication of what is proper only to a part to be made to the whole. Presumed throughout is the notion of a "compound person"; that is, what makes the predication possible is that the one *person* is both divine and human. Human attributes can be ascribed to the divine-human person *with respect to his humanity* just as divine attributes can be ascribed to the divine-human person *with respect to his divinity*. What Calvin has done is to read the logic of the distinction of natures into the person itself.

But that then also means that the communication of attributes never rises above the level of a figure of speech. In Calvin's hands, the ascription of human predicates to the divine or divine predicates to the human entails a use of synecdoche—the ascription of a part to the whole of which it is a part.[25]

23. Ibid.
24. Ibid.
25. Carl Mosser asserts that Calvin taught "a communication of properties between Christ's divinity and his humanity." On the basis of this claim, he then adds, "Christ unites believers to God because God and humanity are already united. Significantly, this distinction is the very heart of patristic and Orthodox notions of deification. In patristic terms, individual believers can be deified because the incarnation of Christ deified human nature" (Mosser, "The Greatest Possible Blessing," 46). Given that he thinks the hypostatic union resulted in a deification of Christ's humanity for Calvin, Mosser has to intend his first statement to be taken realistically. That is to say, he thinks Calvin holds to a realistically conceived communication of attributes, not a merely figural communication. But he only asserts this as true. He does not bother even to engage the first sentence of Calvin's treatment of the problem of the communication.

How is this relevant to the issues surrounding participation, union with Christ, and divinization theories? Calvin has retained the later orthodox idea of a "compound person" and the later orthodox treatment of the communication of attributes. *But he has dispensed completely with that which made divinization theories possible: the idea of an interpenetration of the natures.* And this only serves to underscore what we saw earlier. The believer participates only in the human nature of Christ. And since there can be no interpenetration of the natures in Christ, participation in the human nature of Christ cannot result in a participation in the divine nature. The end result is that you simply cannot find the ontological ground needed for a divinization theory in Calvin's Christology. If there is no interpenetration of the natures, there can be no divinization.

But then, of course, that raises the question of how Calvin could speak in book 4 of life springing forth from the Godhead into the flesh of Christ.[26] The language, as I said earlier, is extravagant. Like the early fathers, Calvin is seeking (in the context in which this image is employed) to solve the problem of mortality by means of an appeal to the immortality of the divine Word, which is infused into the flesh of Christ, presumably in the resurrection. But Calvin has no license to say what he does here once he has abandoned the thought of interpenetration of the natures in Christ. His Christology simply will not allow him to get there. Even more: preoccupation with the dialectic of mortality and immortality collides sharply with Calvin's forensic thinking in his doctrines of the atonement and justification. I turn then to Calvin's doctrine of justification.

Calvin's Doctrine of Justification (the Role of "Acquired Righteousness")

No one contributed more to the final clarification of the (shared) Protestant understanding of justification than did Calvin. He did this in his definitive edition of the *Institutes*, largely in response to the Osiandrian controversy. The material directed to the refutation of the views of Andreas Osiander is new to the 1559 edition. And it is striking that this material is located immediately after Calvin's definition of justification and before he turns to the Roman Catholic conception, which seems to indicate that addressing Osiander had become for Calvin, by this point in

26. See note 13 above.

time, an even more important task than that of addressing the Catholics (which he had already done many times).

Calvin's basic definition of justification is as follows. "Therefore, we explain justification simply as the acceptance with which God receives us into his favor as righteous men. And we say that it consists in the remission of sins and the imputation of Christ's righteousness."[27] God accepts us as righteous men and women: the basic idea here is not that of pardon but of acquittal: "'to justify' means nothing else than to acquit of guilt him who was accused as if his innocence were confirmed."[28] The setting is that of a courtroom. The question is one of guilt or innocence. And the divine verdict is one of innocence. How can this be? Because the guilt for our sins was imputed to Christ, who then suffered the legal penalty that our guilt required. "This is our acquittal: the guilt that held us liable for punishment has been transferred to the head of the Son of God [Isa. 53:12]."[29]

Let me pause here for just a moment to make an observation about this concept of acquittal. A judgment of acquittal would require that the righteousness on which it is based be complete. That is to say, the acquitted person must be completely innocent of the charge against him or her. But complete innocence is found in Christ alone. He alone was sinless. His obedience alone is perfect. But that, then, means that the ground of our justification must lie, at every moment of the Christian life, outside of ourselves. It is not just that our works do not justify us. For Calvin, it is not even God's work *in us* that justifies us. For God's work in us is never complete in this life. Outside of us, Christ's righteousness is complete; in us, it is not.[30] Therefore, if justification does indeed consist in acquittal, then the ground of our justification must be found to lie in the alien righteousness of Christ and in it alone.

We return then to Calvin's definition to notice a second point. The mechanism by means of which Christ's perfect righteousness is made

27. *Institutes*, 3.11.2.
28. Ibid., 3.11.3.
29. Ibid., 2.16.5.
30. "This is a wonderful plan of justification that, covered by the righteousness of Christ, they should not tremble at the judgment they deserve, and that while they rightly condemn themselves, they should be accounted righteous outside themselves" (ibid., 3.11.11).

517

to be ours is that of imputation. Imputation is a concept drawn from the realm of accounting (of bookkeeping). Guilt is not credited to the account of the sinner; Christ's righteousness is. The same mechanism is employed by Calvin to explain how our guilt is made to be Christ's—in other words, how he who knew no sin was made sin on our behalf (2 Cor. 5:21). "'The Lord has laid on him the iniquity of us all' [Isa. 53:6]. That is, he who was about to cleanse the filth of those iniquities was covered with them by transferred imputation."[31] Clearly, the idea of "cleansing" here is intended metaphorically. Christ had no sin nature that could be "cleansed" or "healed" in a more literal sense. Our guilt was made his by imputation. The "cleansing" spoken of in this context refers to the fact that a debt of penalty was removed from us and taken out of the way. It is that of which we have been healed by the atoning death of Christ. In any event, atonement and justification are twin doctrines for Calvin. Both are construed in strictly forensic terms.

We may now look with profit at Calvin's refutation of Osiander. As Calvin understands it, Osiander's view is that the union with Christ spoken of in the New Testament is a union with him in his divine as well as his human essence. To be united with Christ is to be united with what Osiander calls the "essential righteousness" of Christ, that which is proper to him as God. Against this conception, Calvin says that Osiander ought to have been "content with that righteousness which has been acquired for us by Christ's obedience and sacrificial death."[32] The *acquired* righteousness of Christ: by this phrase Calvin clearly means to refer to the righteousness that accrues to Christ's sinless obedience in life and in death—in other words, to his *human* righteousness, that which is added to his divine righteousness.[33] The care taken by Calvin to render impossible a mixture of natures in Christ himself is now playing itself out in his conception

31. Ibid., 2.16.6.

32. Ibid., 3.11.5.

33. Todd Billings acknowledges Calvin's rejection of Osiander's concept of "essential righteousness" but makes no mention whatsoever of his alternative: the *acquired* righteousness of Christ. Moreover, he replaces Calvin's concept of acquittal with the concept of pardon. See Billings, "John Calvin: United to God through Christ," 206. The attempt to find a union with God in Calvin's thinking is certainly made easier by these moves. But one has to ask whether it is still Calvin's theology that is being set forth once these moves have been made.

of justification. It is the human righteousness of Christ that is made ours. And no mixture of the divine and the human (either in Christ or in ourselves) is necessary to explain this, since the human righteousness of Christ is made ours by means of imputation.[34]

34. Julie Canlis does very well, in my view, to recognize that *participatio Christi* means a participation in Christ's humanity, in his *"human* righteousness." See Canlis, "Calvin, Osiander and Participation in God," 174. She is even willing to grant that Calvin's appeal to the Spirit as the bond of participation in Christ is the move that allows Calvin to posit a union that preserves the ontological distinction between God and ourselves, which again is the right move to make: "the Holy Spirit allows us to remain *other"* (ibid.). And yet she also thinks that participation in Christ's humanity yields a "participation in the Trinity" (172). This result is achieved by a twofold movement in thought, both steps of which entail dubious assumptions. The first is that she flattens out the "wondrous exchange" so as to make it consist solely in "an exchange of sonship"; the second is that she unpacks the meaning of this exchange by reference to Calvin's doctrine of adoption that she construes in ontological terms that violate her earlier contrast of the ontological with the spiritual. First, on the "wondrous exchange": Calvin's principal way of explaining the "mechanism" of the "exchange" is, as we have just seen, by means of the imputation of our guilt to Christ and the imputation of his acquired righteousness to us. That is how the "exchange" takes place. That Calvin can also speak of the "exchange" in the context of sonship only shows how closely related the themes of justification and adoption are in Calvin's mind. In awakening faith in us (the faith that receives the promise of justification), the Spirit is, at the very same time, creating a spirit in us that cries out "Abba, Father." But then that leads to a further point with respect to the nature of adoption—a point that impinges directly on Canlis's claim that adoption yields participation in the Trinity. If it is the Spirit who enables the elect to cry out "Abba, Father" in a spirit of sonship and the Spirit remains ontologically other than the person in whom he creates the faith that has this cry as one of its principal effects, how then can participation in sonship be a participation in an inter-Trinitarian relation? No doubt: Calvin can speak, from time to time, of adoption in ways that suggest an incorporation into the relation of a natural-born Son to his Father, which leads us quite naturally to think along the lines of a participation in Trinity. But that, I suggest, is not Calvin's primary way of thinking about adoption. Calvin's primary way of thinking of adoption is simply in terms of that regeneration that accompanies justification. Justification is basic: "Whomever, therefore, God receives into grace, on them he at the same time bestows the spirit of adoption [Rom. 8:15], by whose power he remakes them to his own image. . . . Osiander mixes that gift of regeneration with this free acceptance and contends that they are one and the same" (*Institutes*, 3.11.6). Moreover (and this is the decisive point), Calvin typically associates adoption with the reception of *created* goods, gifts given to Christ by the Father not for himself but to be handed on to us (see *Institutes*, 3.1.1). The gifts of the Spirit that are made to be the "inheritance" of believers through adoption are the everlasting glory and the everlasting blessedness that they will enjoy in the kingdom of heaven (see *Institutes*, 3.18.2). Such gifts are created because they are finally understood by Calvin to be the fruit of the divine-*human* work of the Mediator, not a participation in that which is proper to the divine nature as such. The bottom line is this: I do not believe that Calvin understands adoption to result in participation in an inter-Trinitarian relation. I would say that we would come closer to Calvin's view if we said that we are adopted into the relation of the Mediator (i.e., the God-*human*) to his Father—a relation that can be characterized as a participation in the "natural" relation of the Son to the Father only by synecdoche (because

What troubles Calvin about Osiander's view is that participation in the righteousness that is "essential" to God would require that God's essence be somehow infused into the believer. Osiander "throws in a mixture of substances, by which God, transfusing himself into us, as it were—makes us part of himself. . . . The fact that it comes about through the power of the Holy Spirit that we grow together with Christ . . . he reckons of almost no importance unless Christ's essence be mingled with ours." Osiander's view is that "we are made partakers in God's righteousness when God is united to us in essence."[35]

The root of Osiander's errors lies, for Calvin, in the fact that he has failed to understand the nature of "the bond" of our unity with Christ; he has mistaken "the manner of the indwelling."[36] Clearly, then, when Calvin explains union with Christ by means of an appeal to the Holy Spirit, he is doing so *as a hedge against* the idea of a "mixture of substances." It will not do, at this point, to say, "Well, if Osiander really did hold to a mixture of substances, then he spoke incautiously," on the grounds that the orthodox conception does not require or even allow for a participation in the divine *essence* but only in the divine *energies*. One will not, through this device, have delivered Calvin safely into the hands of the orthodox. For Calvin is clearly talking about the power of the Holy Spirit to unite us to Christ in his acquired (human) righteousness only, not in the righteousness that is proper to him as God. Moreover, the ontological distinction we observed earlier between Holy Spirit and human spirit even in the indwelling of the believer is of great significance here. It is precisely that ontological distinction that requires that participation in the acquired righteousness of Christ—a righteousness, mind you, that must be complete and perfect if acquittal is to be a just verdict—be accomplished through imputation. For again: the Spirit's work in us (in regeneration and sanctification) is not complete in this life.

Union with Christ, on this showing, is a mediated union with the humanity of Christ (and all the gifts given to it). It is a participation in

---

the human work of mediation is done by One who is *also* God). What we really participate in are the benefits of that human work, which is why Calvin regularly refers to a participation in the humanity, rather than in the divinity, of Christ.

35. *Institutes*, 3.11.5.
36. Ibid.

created righteousness, not the uncreated righteousness proper to God. And if this be so, then it lies close to hand to say that participation in the "life of God" must surely be limited to a participation in the life that belongs to God because he has *created* it—to be sure, a life that is characterized by the gift of immortality, but a life that is *created* and, as such, appropriate to the creature as creature.

The fact that Calvin himself transgressed the delimitation to which I have just referred, that he on occasion spoke of a participation in a life of God that is God's own life, I would put down to a failure to see that a *principled* refusal of participation in the essential righteousness of God (based on his Christology and his emphasis on the acquired righteousness of Christ) demands an equally principled refusal of the idea that believers participate in the essential (uncreated) life of God. After all, the life of God is no less essential to him than are his other predicates. To refuse a participation in *any* of those predicates on the grounds that we humans do not participate in the divine essence would require a refusal of the thought of a participation in *all* the predicates proper to that essence, including life.

United by Faith: Calvin's Positive Treatment of the Theme of Union with Christ

Calvin takes up the theme of union with Christ in the first chapter of book 3 of his 1559 *Institutes*. He begins with a statement much loved of the divinization crowd:

> As long as Christ remains outside of us, and we are separated from him, all that he has suffered and done for the salvation of the human race remains useless and of no value to us. Therefore, to share with us what he has received from the Father, he had first to become ours and to dwell within us. For this reason, he is called "our Head" [Eph. 4:15], and "the first-born among many brethren" [Rom. 8:29]. We also, in turn are said to be "engrafted into him" [Rom. 11:17], and to "put on Christ" [Gal. 3:27]; for, as I have said, all that he possesses is nothing to us until we grow into one body with him.[37]

37. Ibid., 3.1.1.

The first half of this statement reaches back to Calvin's Christology. That Christ had first to "dwell within us" means that the eternal Son took on our "flesh." In this way, he was made our head, the firstborn, and so on. And then we must also be "engrafted into him."

Now, the meaning of this phrase "engrafted into him" is anything but perspicuous in Calvin or in the New Testament. How does Calvin understand this "engrafting" to take place? The passage just quoted continues as follows: "It is true that we obtain this [the engrafting] by faith. Yet since we see that not all indiscriminately embrace that communion with Christ that is offered through the gospel, reason itself teaches us to climb higher and to examine into the secret energy of the Spirit, by which we come to enjoy Christ and all his benefits."[38] Now, at first glance it might appear as though the reference to "the secret energy of the Spirit" were intended to *add something to* the faith spoken of in the previous sentence. But I doubt that this was Calvin's intention at all. In his magnificent treatise on faith in chapter 2, Calvin will go on to distinguish the faith as mere assent to the truth of propositions from a faith that engages mind and heart: "Now we shall possess a right definition of faith if we call it a firm and certain knowledge of God's benevolence toward us, founded upon the truth of the freely given promise in Christ, both revealed to our minds and sealed upon our hearts through the Holy Spirit."[39] Calvin then goes on to distinguish the knowledge of faith from that which counts as knowledge in other spheres of inquiry:

> When we call faith "knowledge" we do not mean comprehension of the sort that is commonly concerned with those things which fall under human sense perception. For faith is so far above sense that man's mind has to go beyond and rise above itself in order to attain it. Even where the mind has attained, it does not comprehend what it feels. But while it is persuaded of what it does not grasp, by the very certainty of its persuasion it understands more than if it perceived anything human by its own capacity.... For very good reason, then, faith is frequently called "recognition."... The knowledge of faith consists in assurance rather than in comprehension.[40]

38. Ibid.
39. Ibid., 3.2.7.
40. Ibid., 3.2.14.

I submit that when Calvin speaks of "climbing higher," he is attempting to say something about the *nature* of faith as the mechanism by which our engrafting into Christ occurs. He is not referring to something that is added to faith—a *substantial* indwelling of his historical humanity, for example. He is simply suggesting that the faith that is indeed the mechanism by means of which engrafting is accomplished is a faith that can be wrought in us only by the Holy Spirit. That is why he says we need to "climb higher and to examine into the secret energy of the Spirit." And that is also why he concludes his brief treatment of the subject of union with Christ with a section on faith as the "principal work" of the Holy Spirit. The Spirit, he says,

> is the inner teacher by whose effort the promise of salvation penetrates into our minds, a promise that would otherwise only strike the air or beat upon our ears.... Perfect salvation is found in the person of Christ. Accordingly, that we may become partakers of it "he baptizes us in the Holy Spirit and fire" [Luke 3:16], bringing us into the light of faith in his gospel and so regenerating us that we become new creatures [2 Cor. 5:17]; and he consecrates us, purged of worldly uncleanness, as temples holy to God [cf. 1 Cor. 3:16–17; 6:19; 2 Cor. 6:16; Eph. 2:21].[41]

Faith is the mechanism which joins us to Christ. It is effected in us by the Holy Spirit; it is not a gift we could give ourselves. By it, we trust in Christ, surrender ourselves to him, and rest in him alone. We need look no further for any other conceivable mechanism or mode of explanation. Faith when understood rightly in its most Christian sense simply *is* communion with Christ.

Now, I also think this explanation sheds light on the question of why Calvin treats regeneration/sanctification prior to justification and why he treats union with Christ prior to both. It is not simply because, as Wilhelm Niesel long ago observed, he wants to take the ground out from beneath the Catholic argument that the Protestant conception of faith is devoid of good works.[42] That is also true, but that is not the whole

41. Ibid., 3.1.4.
42. Wilhelm Niesel, *The Theology of Calvin* (Philadelphia: Westminster Press, 1956), 130.

story. For Calvin, the faith that receives the divine acquittal in justification must first be in us before it can receive anything. Thus, he treats regeneration—as the explanation of how faith is awakened in us by the Spirit—prior to justification.

Now, I immediately grant that it is questionable whether this was a wise move. Calvin clearly did not wish to make anything God does in us to be the ground of our justification. In placing regeneration prior to justification, he ran the risk that he might be understood as doing precisely this. It would have been better by far to think about the divine verdict in justification as itself an effective word that creates the faith in us that receives the truth of that verdict.[43] Had Calvin made this move, he could have treated justification first, which would have been far more consistent with the definition of justification as acquittal that he then proceeds to offer. But this is not what he does.

Still, I do not think there can be any question but that faith, in the 1559 *Institutes*, is understood to be the mechanism by means of which the Holy Spirit unites us to Christ. The only remaining question is this: are there grounds in the *Institutes* or in other writings for thinking otherwise—grounds, perhaps, for constructing a different account of union with Christ?

Residual Questions

Dennis Tamburello thinks himself to find evidence of a "twofold communion" with Christ in Calvin's writings—one of which corresponds to justification and one to sanctification.[44] His primary sources for this claim are Calvin's commentary on Galatians 2:20 (published in 1548) and a letter written to Peter Martyr Vermigli (in 1555). In the first, he says, "Christ lives in us in two ways. The one consists in his governing us

43. Julie Canlis thinks herself to find such a view in Calvin, although she offers no evidence for it. She says that "this forensic Word does not remain outside of us, but by its very creative nature, transforms us" (Canlis, "Calvin, Osiander and Participation in God," 176n26). That, I think, is a very good way to redeem Calvin's teaching on imputation. The problem is that it is a twentieth-century idea, found in theologians ranging from Karl Holl to Eberhard Jüngel. In fact, Canlis appeals to Jüngel at this point to support her idea, not to Calvin's writings (see ibid.).

44. Tamburello, *Union with Christ*, 86.

by his Spirit and directing all our actions. The other is what He grants to us by participation in His righteousness, that, since we can do nothing of ourselves, we are accepted in Him by God. The first relates to regeneration, the second to the free acceptance of righteousness."[45] It is surely not without significance that this work was published before the onset of the Osiandrian controversy, and therefore before Calvin had given his doctrine of justification its final form. Be that as it may, it is conceptually odd to treat justification as a form of communion *if* one understands justification along the lines of the imputation of an alien righteousness. One could say that it is still necessary for faith to be awakened in the individual who would receive the promise of imputed righteousness—and that therefore union with Christ must logically precede justification. All of that would make sense, though it would be strange to describe it in terms of a twofold *communion*.

In the letter to Peter Martyr Vermigli, Calvin again refers to two kinds of communion. But here, the meaning assigned is somewhat different. This is not the two kinds found in the Galatians commentary. Here the focus is on an initial engrafting into Christ and his church (perhaps in infant baptism?) and a subsequent growth through the bestowal of gifts by the Spirit. And so Calvin says of the first that it is a communion "which flows from His heavenly majesty and breathes life into us, and makes us grow together into one body with Him." Calvin then goes on to say that he has no idea *how* this takes place: "How this is done, is, I confess, far deeper than the measure of my understanding. And, therefore, I rather receive this mystery, than labor to comprehend it." What is clear is simply the fact that it is the Holy Spirit who effects this union: "I only know that it is through the divine power of the Spirit that life flows down from heaven to earth because the flesh of Christ is neither life-giving in itself nor can its effect reach us without the immeasurable work of the Spirit. It is the Spirit, therefore, who makes Christ live in us, who sustains and nourishes us, who accomplishes everything on behalf of our Head."[46] Over against this first communion, Calvin then goes on to elaborate a second:

45. John Calvin, *The Epistle of Paul the Apostle to the Galatians, Ephesians, Philippians and Colossians*, trans. T. H. L. Parker (Grand Rapids: Eerdmans, 1974), 43.

46. "An Pietro Martire Vermigli in Straßburg," in *Johannes Calvins Lebenswerk in seinen Briefen: Eine Auswahl von Briefen Calvins in deutscher Übersetzung*, vol. 2, *Die*

After Christ has, by the inner working of the Spirit, bound us to Himself and has taken us into His body, He makes yet another work of the Spirit visible in that He enriches us with gifts of the Spirit. That we are, therefore, strong in hope and patience, that we are sober and keep ourselves from worldly lusts, that we exert ourselves zealously to control the passions of the flesh, that the striving after righteousness and piety lives powerfully in us, that we are ardent in prayer, that the thought of eternal life draws us forward—all of that flows, I say, from this second communion, in that Christ, in order not to dwell idly in us, shows the power of His Spirit in clear gifts.[47]

So the first union is a union that makes us one with Christ and members of his body, which I take to mean members of the church. The second union refers to a subsequent (at least in the case of baptized infants) work of the Holy Spirit in giving to us spiritual gifts. In any event, we have before us not a communion that corresponds to justification and a communion that corresponds to sanctification but rather a communion that corresponds to regeneration and a communion that corresponds to sanctification. Dennis Tamburello was misled into thinking the former was the case by Calvin's treatment of the first communion as "total" and the second as one that "grows."[48] But it is not just justification that is "total" for Calvin; regeneration, too, as the initial act in which the Spirit awakens us to faith and obedience and in this way unites us to God, is a definitive act that admits of no advance or loss. We are spiritually alive, or we are not. Sanctification, on the other hand, most certainly does know of an ebb and flow, of advance and decline. It is my view that what Calvin says in this letter about union with Christ is completely congruent with what he says in his 1559 *Institutes*, whereas what he says in the Galatians commentary is not.

What is said here does pose a difficulty, however. If the content assigned to union with Christ is made to be regeneration, then how can union with Christ be treated as the source from which both regeneration

Briefe der Jahre (1548–55), trans. Rudolf Schwarz (Neukirchen-Vluyn: Neukirchener Verlag, 1962), 794.

47. Ibid.

48. Tamburello, *Union with Christ*, 87.

and justification flow?[49] How can regeneration be both the source and the effect of itself? And even more ominously (since it is not simply a logical conundrum), how can regeneration be made the source of justification without undermining Calvin's belief that the ground of justification is to be found in the alien righteousness of Christ alone? Surely, to make regeneration the source of justification is to make a work of God *in us* the ground of justification—in spite of Calvin's express teaching to the contrary. How are we to understand this?

My own answer is that Calvin is anything but sure-footed here. He is feeling his way toward what was termed by the later Reformed *effectual calling.* Calvin characterizes the notion as an initial (definitive) union. He would have been better off to have thought about this initial moment solely in terms of the divine activity itself, in its objective character, rather than in terms of its effect *in us* (that is, regeneration). Expressed in a more complete form: Calvin would have been on safer ground—and more consistent with his Christology and his forensic treatment of the themes of atonement and justification—had he treated justification and adoption as descriptions of the *objective side* of God's saving work, the Spirit's work when considered solely from the standpoint of its ground in Christ, and then treated regeneration and sanctification as the *subjective* effects of that work. "Union with Christ," when seen in the light of this set of distinctions, would then be an omnibus term, descriptive of the whole saving work from the standpoint of its eschatological fulfillment.

Be that as it may, Calvin's treatment of the theme of union in the letter to Peter Martyr gives us no reason to correct or further embellish the model of union that was elaborated in a previous section of this essay.

No treatment of Calvin's teaching on the themes of union and participation would be complete without attention to that biblical passage that, more than any other, has been appealed to by proponents of divinization as the key that unlocks all the other organological passages found in John's writings and those of Paul. I refer, of course, to 2 Peter 1:4. In his com-

---

49. "By partaking of him, we principally receive a double grace: namely, that being reconciled to God through Christ's blamelessness, we may have in heaven instead of a Judge a gracious Father; and secondly, that sanctified by Christ's spirit we may cultivate blamelessness and purity of life" (*Institutes*, 3.11.1). Calvin goes on to denominate these two gifts *justification* and *regeneration*.

mentary on that passage, Calvin does indeed say that it teaches "a kind of deification." But he then defines what he means as follows:

> The word *nature* does not denote essence but kind. The Manichaeans used to dream that we took our roots from the stem of God and that when we have finished the course of our life we shall revert to our original state. Likewise today, there are fanatics who imagine that we shall cross over into God's nature so that His nature absorbs ours.... This kind of madness never occurred to the minds of the holy apostles. They were simply concerned to say that when we have put off all the vices of the flesh we shall be partakers of divine immortality and the glory of blessedness, and thus we shall be in a way one with God so far as our capacity allows.[50]

"In a way . . . so far as our capacity allows," the limit placed by Calvin on "oneness" with God, is precisely the limit of our finitude—that which remains after the "vices of the flesh" have been set aside. At the end of the day, to be "one" with God is to be made like him in *kind*—a term I take to be referring to a kinship in purity. Certainly, Calvin's teaching on union with Christ authorizes nothing more than this.

Conclusion

In this essay, I have argued that the complex of doctrines immediately adjacent to Calvin's treatment of union with Christ make the assimilation of his teaching on union to the Eastern conception of divinization (or *theosis*) impossible. His treatment of the Lord's Supper makes the "bridge" joining us to Christ to be One who remains ontologically other than ourselves in the act of joining. His treatment of Christology takes the ground out from beneath the concept of an interpenetration of natures— an absolutely crucial building block in the construction of *theosis* theories. His treatment of justification makes it clear that our union with Christ is a union with his human righteousness, not with his divine nature. And the content that he assigns to the theme of union itself (that is, regenera-

50. John Calvin, *The Epistle of Paul the Apostle to the Hebrews and the First and Second Letters of St. Peter* (Grand Rapids: Eerdmans, 1974), 330.

tion) allows us to say no more than that we are united to Christ in that we are awakened to the faith that lays hold of Christ and his promises and the obedience that, in conforming us to him, makes us *like* him. For all these reasons, I say that Calvin makes a poor candidate for inclusion in the new orthodoxy of the twenty-first century.

I should add, by way of conclusion, that I do not say these things out of a desire to undermine faith-and-order ecumenism. I am a firm believer in the importance of visible unity among the churches. The division of the churches is indeed a scandal. For if it is true that the world knows we are Christ's disciples by the love we have for one another (John 13:35), then faith-and-order dialogue is not an option we can take or leave; it belongs to the very heart of the church's mission to the world. All this I believe.

But I also believe that attempts to find a divinization theory in Calvin short-circuit the very valuable contribution that Calvin could make to faith-and-order discussions. Where the representatives of the Reformed churches in official dialogues or unofficial discussions and debates loosen their grasp on Calvin's teaching so as to find in him nothing that can offend other churches, it is no longer Calvin's voice that is heard in those dialogues and debates. And that, I think, is a great pity—and one of the contributing factors in the erosion of a genuinely *theological existence* in the Reformed churches. For the sake of a better ecumenical future, I hope we will seek to do justice to the *full dimensions* of Calvin's soteriology and cease and desist from offering truncated and forced readings of it. That, it seems to me, is a reasonable thing to ask in this year of Calvin celebrations.

23

SEE YOU IN HEAVEN: CALVIN'S VIEW OF LIFE, DEATH, AND ETERNAL LIFE

HERMAN J. SELDERHUIS

Quite a few people in this world think that Calvinists have no fear of death, are unconcerned about whatever happens to them in life, and are brought up with the warning that any tear over grief, pain, or loss may be a sign of protest against God's providence and that when it comes to going to heaven, any longing to see loved ones would take away from the longing for Christ. Of course, the father of all these unattractive ideas is supposedly John Calvin, the man with no heart, no feelings, but full of doctrines. Now, it might be interesting to read what the man himself said about all this. Listening to Calvin himself might demonstrate the relevance of Calvin's thought for today, and it might also correct some views that Calvinists have or that some have of Calvinists.

530

The first part of this essay will give a more theological analysis on this topic based on Calvin's letters and on his commentary on Psalms, his favorite book in the Bible. The second part deals with more biographical aspects and with the way in which Calvin's theology became practice.[1]

Theological

Death and Eternal Life

The fact that the faithful remain living even after the death of the body is assured, argues Calvin, through God's divine nature—especially his immutability. "The faithful are born again from imperishable seed and will survive death because God always remains the same."[2] God will thus save our lives even from death itself, since when one dies, the Lord will keep him or her from being destroyed.[3] Calvin claims that the grace of God would be grossly underestimated if he were able to take care of us only in life.[4] Appealing to Scripture, he asserts that "death for God's servants does not mean destruction, and they are not wiped out when they depart from this world, but they keep on existing."[5] Although it seems that our soul disappears when it leaves the body, in fact "it is gathered in God's bosom in such a way that it is faithfully preserved there until the day of resurrection."[6] Consequently, it is a serious heresy to believe that everything just ends upon death.[7] On the contrary, God protects us throughout our lives and then finally takes us to be with him.

Therefore, the faithful have no need to fear death, Calvin writes, since death is the destruction of the flesh but not of the soul.[8] Indeed, he says that the one who truly trusts in God scorns death.[9] This is

1. All references are from CO.
2. CO, 32.74.
3. "Ut ab interitu vindicet in ipsa morte" (ibid., 31.303).
4. Ibid., 31.157.
5. Ibid., 31.259.
6. Ibid., 31.491.
7. Ibid., 31.809.
8. "Quae licet carnis sit interitus, animas tamen non exstinguit" (ibid., 31.303).
9. "Unde sequitur, neminem vere Deo fidere, nisi qui salutem sibi a Deo promissam ita apprehendit ut mortem despiciat" (ibid., 31.156).

something that only those who direct themselves toward Christ can do. David already knows that Christ would rise from the dead, and from this he derives the assurance that he himself will also be resurrected. But we share in this imperishability only if we have become subject to what is perishable. This means that the fullness of life that is in Christ, our head, filters down to the members of his body "only in drops."[10] By this Calvin means that through justification the faithful do not also directly begin to participate in the resurrection and the glorification of Christ. The faithful will first have to make their way through death and the grave. In the burial of people God does indeed want something to be evident of the resurrection on the last day,[11] and therefore, it is entirely grievous when circumstances prevent the faithful from being buried. Burial is an aid to the living[12]— suggesting something almost sacramental for Calvin, but that is not absolutely required. Faith looks toward immortality even without an actual burial.

As far as any communication with God after death is concerned, Psalm 88:5 makes the troubling statement that God no longer remembers those who are in the grave. Calvin solves this matter by interpreting that here the author has let go of himself, being so overwhelmed by his cares that he does not express himself as thoughtfully as he should. Calvin even speculates that the light of faith may have been momentarily dimmed in the author of the psalm.[13]

When David says that in death there is no consideration of God, this is no proof that the dead are aware of nothing. Rather, David here points out in prayer to God that a dead David has no opportunity anymore to praise God among the living. Meanwhile, God's consideration will indeed be considerable if it is God who keeps him alive.[14] Calvin emphatically rejects the interpretation of those who conclude from this verse that the dead no longer feel or realize anything. Death does indeed put an end to

10. Ibid., 31.157.
11. "Porro quum in hominem sepultura Deus aliquod testimonium exstare voluerit ultimae resurrectionis" (ibid., 31.747).
12. "Media adminicula . . ." (ibid., 31.748).
13. "Quia suffocatur erat lumen fidei, quod statim emicuit" (ibid., 31.807).
14. Ibid., 31.76.

our praise of God,[15] but that does not imply that "when the souls of the faithful have discarded their bodies," they no longer have any knowledge of God or any sentiment toward him.[16]

Calvin describes how even after death we continue existing before God. Those who no longer exist bodily are yet kept safe in his embrace.[17] This formulation begs the question, though, as to the way in which deceased believers continue existing—a question that is not answered by Calvin's observation that although the faithful are indeed resting in the grave, they are nevertheless in hope in heaven.[18] The faithful do descend into the grave, but they do so with the hope that they will also once again emerge. To questions about the mode of existence for the faithful after death, Calvin's commentary on the Psalms gives no answer. He does address, however, another question often asked. According to Calvin, there is no wine in heaven, nor will other means of living be found there, since these are matters that are required only for this earthly life.[19] As to wine, by the way, Calvin does certainly appreciate it, and even encourages his readers to drink it.

Judgment

Calvin states that there is a clear difference between the faithful and the unfaithful where their eternal existence is concerned.[20] It is noteworthy that although saying that believers have eternal life with God, in the commentary on the Psalter Calvin says nothing about the continued existence of the unfaithful. Also, he says that there is such a continued existence for the unfaithful, but he offers no details about the end that awaits the godless. In only a single instance does he speak of hell as the eternal fire that has been prepared for the outcast—the place into which Christ will throw his enemies.[21] In a different passage, he does not go any further than to say that those who reject Christ will have to deal with the majesty of God.[22] He

15. Ibid., 31.298.
16. Ibid., 31.76.
17. "In suo sinu et custodia qui videntur secundum carnem exstincti" (ibid., 31.103).
18. "Quin potius in sepulchro reconditi, spe tamen in coelo habitant" (ibid., 31.106).
19. Ibid., 32.190.
20. Ibid., 31.157.
21. "Aeternae gehennae quae reprobis parata est" (ibid., 31.217).
22. Ibid., 32.44.

also dismisses as too harsh the common interpretation he has encountered that, in Christ's victory over his enemies, so much blood will flow that it will form a stream from which Christ will drink.[23] He states that it is sufficient to know that the end will result in the damnation of the unfaithful and that their lives here on earth have been of no consequence.[24] He often points out the contrast between the faithful, who find themselves in an abyss of adversity but also come out of it again, and the unfaithful, who ultimately find themselves in eternal ruin.[25] The blame for their destruction lies within themselves, Calvin declares, since God's vengeance is a response to their depravity.[26] God hates transgressions, and therefore he casts out those who commit them.[27] He who does not voluntarily honor God now will in the end be forced by God to humble himself before God.[28] When God approaches us in a friendly manner and we do not respect him or receive him in sincerity, destruction awaits us.

Calvin sets forth the cities of Jerusalem and Nazareth as illustrations of God's judgment. The desolate state in which these cities find themselves in Calvin's time is "a showcase of God's wrath."[29] These cities prove that it is not sufficient to have God in one's midst if one does not also receive him in faith. Christ grew up in Nazareth, and he lived and preached in Jerusalem, yet both cities were nevertheless ruined.

Calvin thus devotes relatively little attention to the end that awaits the godless. His primary concern is not the question of how the wicked perish but rather how the faithful persist when it seems as though God does not concern himself with the things that are done to his children.[30] This is precisely why he points out that it is God's duty to reject the godless and not our duty.[31]

It is, however, the duty of the faithful to warn the godless. Calvin interprets Psalm 21:8 ("Your hand will find out all your enemies . . ." [ESV]) as

23. "Verum hunc nimis dure, meo iudicio, exponunt multi interpretes" (ibid., 32.166).
24. "Quum eorum vita nihil sit" (ibid., 31.683).
25. Ibid., 31.546.
26. Ibid., 31.376.
27. "Cuius officium est improbos omnes perdere, quia odio habet omne scelus" (ibid., 31.68).
28. Ibid., 31.611.
29. Ibid., 31.741.
30. Ibid., 31.217.
31. Ibid., 31.68.

a prophecy of Christ's final judgment. The purpose in speaking so clearly about the horror of the judgment is to wake up those people who mock God's judgments. Since Christ is the one who carries out the judgment, believers themselves should not take up the sword, but they should instead patiently bear their cross.[32] Although it is Christ who will judge and his judgment is terrifying, Calvin reminds his readers that this truth is not in opposition to Bible passages that say that Jesus is gentle. A shepherd is, after all, kind to his flock, but he takes energetic action against wolves and thieves.[33]

Life in This World

Given that the world is in constant change, there is no stability in it. Calvin brought up the topic of the uncertainty of this existence and of the chaos in this world numerous times in his Psalms commentary alone. Heaven may offer stability and rest, but the world is characterized by upheaval and instability.[34] The whole world has been turned on its head.[35] Calvin refers to the abhorrent disorder that overshadows the order of God's providence.[36] But God himself is hard at work in that disorder, "since God everywhere lays traps for us, digs pits, throws all kinds of obstacles in our way, and finally encloses us in the abyss."[37] It is as if God were toying with us and our life were little more than a plaything. God puts us on a track and makes us run a small obstacle course. It is a short race, for he soon takes us back to himself again.[38] Life is short and means very little. Wherever we look, there is despair. Our very insides are spoiled, and we are but mirrors of death. And are not all the events of this life nothing but a prelude to the final destruction?[39] "We as humans are like dry grass, we can wither away at any moment, are never far from death, indeed it is as if we are already living in the grave."[40] Our life "hangs as if from a silk

---

32. Ibid., 31.217.
33. Ibid., 32.166.
34. Ibid., 32.13.
35. Ibid., 31.461.
36. Ibid., 32.11.
37. Ibid., 32.234.
38. "Quod brevis quaedam versatio sit in qua celeriter gyrum implemus" (ibid., 31.834).
39. "Praeludium interitus ..." (ibid., 32.73).
40. Ibid., 32.66.

thread," and we are "surrounded by a thousand deaths."[41] This begins right at birth: "leaving the womb is the entrance to a thousand deaths."[42] Life just flies by, and it is as if we have hardly been born before we die again.[43] There are dangers everywhere.

If only you look up, how many dangers threaten us from there? But if you look down at the ground, how many poisons do you find there? How many wild beasts that can tear you to pieces? How many snakes? How many swords, pits, stumbling blocks, ravines, caved-in buildings, stones, and thrown spears? In short, we cannot take a single step without encountering ten deaths.[44]

Many accidents are but waiting to happen in the city, but if you go out into a forest without knowing the way, you soon run the risk of becoming prey to lions or wolves.[45] According to Calvin, our bodies are in themselves already full of all kinds of maladies, and think then of all those threats from outside!

If you step onto a ship, you are only one step away from death. If you climb onto a horse, your foot only needs to slip and your life is in danger. Just walk through the city streets one time, and there are as many dangers as there are tiles on the rooftops. If you or your friend is carrying a weapon, injury lies in wait.[46]

Thus Calvin could come up with a virtually endless list of dangers to show that human life is in constant threat, and amounts to little.

Nothing is certain, everything is in danger, and "it appears as if the heavens are crashing down, the earth is being moved, and the mountains rooted up."[47] Calvin calls life "a churning river,"[48] and finds the human condition "as desperate as that of someone in the grave or of those who met their end in a labyrinth."[49] One is even "in an ominous labyrinth"[50]

41. Ibid., 31.302.
42. "Imo exitus ab utero, ingressus est in mille mortus" (ibid., 31.656).
43. Ibid., 32.73.
44. Ibid., 40.135–36.
45. Ibid., 32.136.
46. *Institutes*, 1.17.10.
47. CO, 31.460–61.
48. Ibid., 31.834.
49. Ibid., 32.308.
50. Ibid., 31.368.

and escapes only by turning to God's providence. Those who do not are in hell already now—for Calvin, hell is the agony of fear and uncertainty, "since there is no more terrifying agony than to tremble from fear and uncertainty."[51] Seeing human existence as he did, it is no wonder Calvin sought refuge in providence and predestination.

Predestination

Now that predestination has been mentioned, it seems best to treat this complicated issue here, since it directly relates to Calvin's view of life and death. As the mother of election, the doctrine of providence belongs to this discussion as well. Predestination is but a small part of the whole that is providence, but has all the same specifically drawn all the attention. The image of an arbitrary, merciless God as tyrannical as Calvin himself, of a theological system that filled psychiatric wards and led people to commit suicide, cannot be left unmentioned in this context. Unfortunately, many who came after Calvin did indeed make a real mess of things, whether it be the deliberate misrepresentations by his opponents, or the foolish way in which many of his followers brought their church members to a state of mental despair through their preaching and pastoral work.

Needless to say, Calvin himself saw things very differently. Through the fall into sin in Paradise, humanity broke with God, is now excluded from life, and is under judgment. All are fallen. Yet God came with a plan of salvation, and this means that whoever believes in Christ is freed from judgment and receives eternal life. But, asks Calvin, how is it that one does believe and another does not? It must depend on God's choice, for if the choice were made by humans, God would be dependent on what they do. That only leaves us with a weak God, and—what may be worse—with believers who lack certainty. If, on the other hand, you make the choice to depend fully on God, he receives all glory and the believer all certainty— this is the doctrine of election! That God decided not to lead all people to faith implies that there were people he did not choose, whom he left under judgment and thus actually condemned. For this exact reason Calvin speaks of a *decretum horribile*. This term has nothing to do with horror, but everything to do with the shivers. It is not a "horrible decree," but all

51. Ibid., 32.144.

the same a decision that causes one to tremble and shiver, if not rightly embraced. And it humbles us. Calvin spoke of a *humilitas*, and did so often, expecting this of everyone as their basic attitude before God.

Calvin himself found that the notion of an electing God left people not only humble, but also at peace. The same with the idea that he works in all things, that nothing happens by chance, and that everything rather comes from his fatherly hand. But if things are like that, you must also be willing to learn something from that hand of God. If, for example, terrible things happen to you in this life, you can learn that this world is passing away, that we must seek true rest elsewhere, that with God even setbacks aim at the good, that we must be humble, that we need forgiveness of sins—and the list goes on. If God does nothing randomly, there must always be something to learn. God works with a goal, and so all Calvinists do so as well. As Calvin sees it, something must always come of it.

Biographical

We now come to see how this doctrine fitted into Calvin's life and the lives of those around him.

Death

It is true that his only comfort was "that even death could not be an unhappy circumstance for a Christian,"[52] but Calvin's letters are at the same time full of tears over loved ones who had died. He thought that this grief did not conflict with the belief that God was in control over all things. When he heard of the persecutions suffered by the Waldenses, he wrote to Guillaume Farel: "I am writing in tears, and worn out with grief I sometimes burst out in tears so that I have to stop writing."[53] And when his friend Guillaume de Trie, lord of Varennes, passed away, Calvin became sick with grief: "I have to dictate this letter from my bed in great grief, for my dear Varennes has been taken away from me."[54]

52. Ibid., 6.631.
53. Ibid., 12.76.
54. Ibid., 18.649.

Calvin alluded to a well-known medieval song when he wrote that we are surrounded by death in the middle of this life, but that we can be convinced we will in death be surrounded by life.[55] But in such situations, Calvin always explained God's life direction in such a way to make it constantly clear that God intends these things for some good. When Claude Féray, a deacon to whom he had become very close, died from the plague, Calvin wrote that he was a complete wreck. When he realized how much this man had meant to him and had been his support and refuge in all circumstances, he could only conclude that God was gravely pointing him to his sins by taking this friend away.[56] He said the same when Jacques, his own child, was taken. Calvin thanked Farel for the letter of comfort he had written to Idelette. She herself was unable to respond because of her grief, and Calvin wrote: "The LORD has dealt us a heavy stroke in the death of our little son. But He is our Father. He knows what is good for his children."[57]

These are beautiful words, and yet we find other things in Calvin's writings as well. He expresses his fear of death, fear of having to appear before God as a sinful person, a fear that for Calvin only increases as one better comes to know God and desires more and more to live for him.[58] It is the realization that "a sinner is confronted here with a judge whose wrath and severity count many deaths besides the eternal death."[59] Yet what dominated was the conviction that believers ought to have no fear of death.[60]

Idelette

The death of Calvin's wife was also not just a remote possibility, and Idelette's already rather weak health was further assaulted by her inability to get over the death of Jacques. Calvin's letters are full of references to her illnesses, and he often writes that she was confined to bed because of them. "My wife is recovering slowly. Now she also has hemorrhoids. Added

55. Ibid., 14.561–62.
56. Ibid., 11.213.
57. Ibid., 11.430.
58. Ibid., 31.77.
59. Ibid., 31.318.
60. Ibid., 31.303.

to that are her coughing fits that increase her pain. Nor has she shaken her fever."[61] Once she traveled to Lausanne to help Viret's wife, who had just given birth, but Calvin had to offer apologies upon her return. "I am very sorry that my wife was such a burden on you and, I suspect, was not able to help your wife that much, since she herself constantly needs to be helped by others because of her own illness."[62]

How serious her health problems were is clear from a letter from 1545 in which Calvin wrote that she had recovered a little, and that he had as it were received her back from the dead.[63] This went on for years, but around eight o'clock in the morning of March 29, 1549, death would no longer give her up. Several months before, Calvin had already written that Idelette was once again confined to her bed because of a long-lasting sickness, and it appears that she never recovered. "She was no longer able to speak, but could still indicate how she was doing. I spoke to her of the grace of Christ and the hope of eternal life . . . And I withdrew to pray. With a quiet heart she listened to the prayers and clearly heard the words of comfort."

Calvin's announcement to Farel of the death of his wife speaks of his great love, care, and grief. Because she never spoke of her children, Calvin was afraid that she worried about them in her heart but did not really dare to say this even though this worry tormented her more than her illness did. When he told her in the presence of the brothers that he would care for her children as if they were his own, she answered, "I have already committed them to God." When Calvin said, "But that does not mean that I am not ready to do my part for them," she responded, "If God cares for them, then I know that they are commended to you as well." Her willpower was so strong that she already appeared to be beyond this world.[64]

The fact that Calvin related the same story to Viret some five days later attests to his great concern for Idelette's worry about her children. Calvin described Idelette's last hours to Farel, how he had time and again come back to her throughout the night to encourage her with God's grace,

61. Ibid., 12.241.
62. Ibid., 12.732.
63. Ibid., 12.202.
64. Ibid., 13.228–29.

and then would withdraw to pray. In the morning the end came: "Shortly before eight she quietly breathed her last, so that those who were present barely noticed her passage from life to death."[65]

Half a Man

Concerning Idelette's passing, Calvin claimed that he had lost his best friend, adding that she had been extremely faithful in helping him in his ministry.[66] These are nice testimonies, but Calvin felt the need to add that she never hindered him in his work. For one who was so afraid of such a thing in a marriage as Calvin was, this is of course a positive observation. Still, although we wish that everyone could claim that his or her partner was no hindrance, we may also wish that Calvin had simply dropped this remark. But here he was as open as he was everywhere else—for example, his remark that he tried to deal with his grief in such a way "that I continue my ministry without a break."[67] Work comes before the woman, work also continues without that woman, and indeed working hard helps him overcome his grief over her. But Calvin would have to continue life as "no more than half a man, since God recently took my wife home to Himself."[68] That Idelette was more to him than just a helper and no hindrance is clear, for example, from the letter of comfort he sent several years later to a colleague at a French church in Frankfurt when he also lost his wife: "What a terrible injury, what a pain the death of your wife has caused you, and I speak from my own experience. For even now I fully know how difficult it was, seven years ago now, to deal with such grief."[69]

Gladness

Amid all the sadness, Calvin could still also rejoice over the death of some. At the passing of the sister of de Fallais, whose husband had become lukewarm to the Reformed cause although she remained such

65. Ibid., 13.229.
66. Ibid., 13.230, 228–29.
67. Ibid., 13.229.
68. Ibid., 20.394.
69. Ibid., 15.867.

an ardent supporter, Calvin remarked that she could be glad to be freed
from this life, that is, from this man. "The woman would have had to
live in an unhappy captivity had she been forced to continue to live on
this world."[70] Now she was free of it, and her brother could think of her
without continually worrying.

Well known and typical is the letter Calvin wrote to the lord of
Richebourg to comfort him when his son Louis died from the plague.[71]
It reveals everything about how Calvin viewed life, and how he saw God's
guidance. Anyone who wants to know what Lord's Day Question 10 of
the Heidelberg Catechism, both greatly despised and much loved, looks
like in practice needs to read this letter.

Calvin begins by telling of his own sorrow over the death of his friend
Claude Féray, who had been Louis's teacher, and about his worries for his
own family when the plague raged in Strasbourg.

> When I received the message about the death of master Claude and of
> your son Louis, I was so shocked and so despondent that for several days
> I could only cry. And although I tried to find strength in the presence of
> God and wanted to comfort myself with the refuge he grants us in time
> of need, I still felt as if I was not at all myself. Really, I was no longer able
> to do the normal things, as if I myself were half dead.[72]

There is no such thing here as a hardened Calvin who, rooted in
God's almighty power, undauntedly and emotionlessly lets all things
pass over him. Rather, we see a Calvin who is at his wits' end, overwhelmed by grief. He spoke of these things so as not to give the
impression that it was easy for him to talk when offering comfort to
de Richebourg, and exhorting him to stand firm. He knew the pain
of losing a child, he knew the pain of that hole, and he knew the
burden of the "Why?" question. But that was exactly why he pointed
de Richebourg to God's providence.

There is nothing that robs us more of our power, nothing that dejects
us more, than when we let ourselves fall into such complaints and ques-

70. Ibid., 12.423.
71. Ibid., 11.188–94.
72. Ibid., 11.188.

tions as: Why did things go like this? Why not another way? Why like that just here? There would be reason to utter such words if we on our part had made a mistake and if we had neglected our duty, but if we have done nothing wrong in this matter, there is also no place for these types of complaints.

In this way Calvin tried to set this father free from such endless questioning as well as from self-reproach, and guided him to the only conclusion that Calvin thought could offer comfort: "And so it is God who has reclaimed your son, that son whom he entrusted to us to care for him under the condition that he ever remain his possession."[73]

For that reason, Calvin contrasts the present life with the life to come: "If in your pondering over your son you were to consider how difficult it is in these dark times to bring our life in a pure manner to a good end, you would surely consider happy one who has been delivered from this at an early age."[74] Calvin in this context used the image of our life as a journey through stormy seas, and spoke of what a blessing it was to arrive at a safe haven earlier than expected. Calvin also praised the boy for his conduct and faith, and for the good things that were expected of him. But he immediately anticipated the objection he thought de Richebourg would raise, namely, that he knows his son is now in heaven, but that the reality remains that he has lost a child. It is clear that Calvin himself knew the questions and the difficulties that could take the wind out of the sails of any form of comfort. But the fact that this is God's way does not mean we may not grieve over it:

> You will say that all of this is too heavy to drive away or suppress the grief of a father so as to suffer no more pain at the death of your son. But I am not asking you to suffer no more pain. For this is not the life-view that we are taught in the school of Christ, that we lay aside the God-given human emotions and that we turn from people into stones.[75]

Calvin was not of stone, and if there are Reformed people who are, they are poor Calvinists.

73. Ibid., 11.190.
74. Ibid., 11.191.
75. Ibid., 11.194.

Dying

In order to understand Calvin, one should actually begin with the end, when he died still dressed in full armor. On Wednesday, February 2, 1564, he gave his last lecture on a passage from Ezekiel, and he preached his last sermon the following Sunday, when he was carried to the pulpit on a bed. On Easter Sunday, April 2, he was once again carried to church, this time to participate in the Lord's Supper. Calvin then turned his deathbed into a pulpit when he invited first the Little Council (April 27) and then the Consistory (April 28) for one final discussion. Even when facing death, he wanted to see the politicians and church officers one last time—and above all to speak to them. He did this as a patriarch, but without making a scripted scene of it. Calvin was a lawyer, not an actor, and he did not speak dramatically but in a businesslike and pastoral manner. He made use of the fact that he did not die suddenly, and—according to himself—until his dying day remained clear in spirit, so as to give a clear testimony. In this way, he continued to work until the very end.

See You!

Yet this is not the end of the story. Calvin assumed that people would recognize each other in heaven, and went rather far in his descriptions thereof. Richard Vauvill, pastor to the refugee church in Frankfurt, received a letter from Calvin on the death of his wife with the comfort "that you were able to live with a woman to whom you would gladly return in order to reunite with her when you depart from this world."[76] If Calvin's plans have indeed become a reality, he himself will already have had many discussions and conversations in heaven. In his letter to Martin Luther, which Luther never received, Calvin wrote that they would soon be together in heaven, where they could continue their discussion in quiet. He wrote the same to Philipp Melanchthon, with whom he also wanted to feast in heaven, even though neither of them was much of a partyer.

Anyway, Calvin, if anyone at all, cannot be behind the image of Calvinists who show no emotion at death, bury their loved ones without

76. Ibid., 15.867.

shedding even a tear, and thereby purportedly show that they are ready to receive whatever comes from God's fatherly hand. Calvin was a man with a heart, with emotions, a man who knew how troublesome life can be and how much grief death can bring. He was also a man who knew that the God of the Scriptures is the God who desires to be a gracious Father to sinners, and who guides them through the storms of life into the safe haven where, together with all his children, we will feast forever.

Appendix: Original Schedule of Calvin500 Tribute Conference[1]

July 5, 2009 (Sunday): All services this day at St. Pierre Cathedral

11:30   Greetings for Opening Convocation of Calvin500 in St. Pierre Cathedral

Worship and Sermon by Dr. Sinclair Ferguson: "In Christ Alone," Philippians 3:8–12

18:00   Joint Worship, with Sermon by the Rt. Rev. Henry Orombi, Archbishop of Uganda: "Who Is the Faithful and Wise Servant?" Matthew 24:45–51

19:00   Reception

19:45   Psalm Sing and Worship

20:00   Sermon by Dr. Bryan Chapell: "In Praise of Predestination," Ephesians 1:3–6

July 6, 2009 (Monday)

9:00   Paper: Dr. Douglas Kelly: "The Catholicity of the Theology of John Calvin"

9:40   Paper: Dr. Richard Gamble: "Recent Research in Calvin Studies"

10:20   Paper: Dr. Darryl Hart: "Calvin among Nineteenth-Century Reformed Protestants in the United States"

1. St. Pierre Cathedral (PM) and The Auditoire (AM), Geneva, July 5–9, 2009.

11:00 Break

11:15 Paper by Dr. Robert M. Kingdon, "Calvin and Ecclesiastical Discipline" (read by Dr. William McComish), and Lifetime Achievement Award to Dr. Robert M. Kingdon

12:00 *Keynote Address:* Dr. John Witte: "Reading Calvin as a Lawyer"

19:00 Sermon by Dr. Philip Ryken: "A Wide Door for Spreading the Gospel," 1 Corinthians 16:5–11

19:45 Psalm Sing

20:00 Sermon by Dr. Peter Lillback, "All the Glorious Offices of Christ," 1 Corinthians 1:29–31

20:45 Break

21:00 Sermon by Dr. Robert Godfrey, "Calvin's Cherished Text," John 17:1–5

July 7, 2009 (Tuesday)

9:00 Paper: Dr. Richard Burnett: "Calvin on Secular and Sacred History"

9:40 Paper: Dr. William Edgar: "Calvin's Impact on the Arts"

10:20 Paper: Dr. Anthony Lane: "Calvin's Doctrine of Assurance Revisited"

11:00 Break

11:15 Paper: Dr. Isabelle Graesslé: "Calvin and Women: Between Irritation and Admiration"

12:00 *Keynote Address:* Dr. Herman Selderhuis: "See You in Heaven: Calvin's View of Life and Death"

19:00 Sermon by Dr. Steven Lawson: "John Calvin and Guarding the Gospel," Galatians 1:6–10

19:45 Psalm Sing

20:00 Sermon by Dr. Iain D. Campbell: "Three Great Intercessions," Romans 8:26, 34

20:45   Break

21:00   Sermon by Dr. J. Ligon Duncan: "The Christian Life," Philippians 2:12–13

July 8, 2009 (Wednesday)

9:00   Paper: Dr. George Knight: "Calvin as New Testament Exegete"

9:40   Paper: Dr. R. Scott Clark: "Calvin's Principle of Worship"

10:20   Paper: Dr. Hughes Old/Dr. Terry Johnson: "Calvin's Worship Reforms"

11:00   Break

11:15   Paper: Dr. Henri Blocher: "Calvin the Frenchman"

12.00   *Keynote Address:* Dr. William McComish, "Calvin's Children"

14:30   *Young Calvin Scholars Symposium* (The Auditoire): Papers to Be Announced

19:00   Sermon by the Rev. Geoffrey Thomas: "Election," Ephesians 1:3–14

19:45   Break

20:00   Sermon by Dr. Joel Beeke: "Cherishing the Church," Matthew 16:18b

20:45   Psalm Sing

21:00   Sermon by Dr. Martin Holdt: "Psalm 110 Then and Now," Psalm 110

July 9, 2009 (Thursday)

9:00   Paper: Dr. Andrew McGowan: "John Calvin's Doctrine of Scripture"

9:40   Paper: Dr. Michael Horton: "Union and Communion: Rediscovering Calvin's Eucharistic Theology"

10:20   Paper: Dr. Henri Blocher: "Calvin on Divine Election"

11:00   Break

11:15   Paper: Dr. Jae Sung Kim, "Calvinism in Asia"

12:00   ***Keynote Address:*** Dr. Bruce McCormack: "Union with Christ in Calvin's Theology: Grounds for a Divinization Theory?"

        Catered Commemorative Luncheon in the Old Town

16:30   Address: Dr. Henry Krabbendam: "Reformation and Revival"

19:00   Sermon by the Rev. Ted Donnelly: "More Than Conquerors," Romans 8:37

19:45   Psalm Sing

20:00   Sermon by Dr. Hywel Jones: "One of a Thousand," Job 36:1–4

21:00   Sermon by Dr. Derek Thomas: "Adoring the Majesty of God," Romans 11:33–36

INDEX OF SCRIPTURE

INDEX OF SUBJECTS AND NAMES

Carruthers, S. W., 309n217
Cassius, Dio, 221
Catechism
  Geneva, 288, 345, 351, 410, 425–26,
    433, 475–76
  Heidelberg, 250, 267, 268n116,
    542
  Large, 178, 180, 184, 279n43, 393,
    458
  Shorter, 394
  Small, 184, 206, 352, 426n35, 458
  Westminster Larger, 309n220,
    310n227, 401
Catholicity, 151–52, 190–95, 198–201,
    203–4, 206–9, 211, 213, 215–16,
    265, 341, 391
Cauvin, Gérard, 60
Cauvin, Jeanne Le France (or Lefranc),
    60, 86
Chalcedonian Formula, 512–13
Chalker, William H., 283–95, 283n71,
    286n88, 287n96, 289n102,
    290n108, 298, 300–1
Chartier, Roger, 486
Chauncy, Charles, 336n32
Chaunu, Pierre, 62n9, 63–64
Chesterton, G. K., xvi
Church and State, 34–37. 43, 52–54,
    56, 58, 314, 316–17, 338–40,
    434n87
Churches, World Alliance of Reformed,
    20
Churchill, Winston, 11
Civil Government, 4, 53, 207, 317, 321,
    328, 330
Clark, Charles A., 498
Clark, R. Scott, 249n11, 423
Colladon, Nicolas, 27, 157n11, 198
Comenius, Czech Calvinist, 10
Commentaries of Calvin, xviiin6, 32,
    35, 38, 63, 79, 89, 98–102, 105,
    114, 116, 153–58, 161–65,
    196–97, 202, 206, 209–10, 215,

  218, 221–23, 225n32, 226n35,
  227, 233–35, 237–38, 241, 260,
  269, 271–72, 312, 317, 325, 335,
  338–39, 344, 352–53, 359–61,
  422–23, 426n36, 427, 475, 490,
  497, 501, 524–26, 531, 533, 535
Communes, Loci, 32, 81, 427n45
Communication of Attributes, 395, 512,
  514–16
Communion
  Easter, 113–14
  Frequency of, 25, 28–29, 122, 142,
    146, 247, 263, 323, 408–9
Confession, Confessions
  Augsburg, 32, 167–68, 174–78, 393
  Belgic, 393, 402
  Confessio gallicana/Confession de
    La Rochelle, 66
  Formula of Concord, 168
  Geneva, 496
  Lutheran, 32, 392
  Reformed, 91, 392, 400n83, 401,
    405n104, 407n109, 444, 496
  Scots, 33, 122
  Second Helvetic, 193, 397, 481n60
  Westminster, 124n20, 274, 309,
    312n223, 441
  The Book of (Harmony of),
    167–68
Conseil, Petit, 7, 28
Consistoire, Registres du . . . de Geneve, 208
Consistory
  Geneva, 22–31, 35, 88, 208–9, 430,
    433–34, 544
  Reformed, 50–55, 324, 421n11
Consubstantiation, 393
Cook, James, 492
Cooke, Geoffrey Michael, 298n151
Cop, Nicholas, 136–38, 223n22
Cordier, Mathurin, 73, 223n72
Cornwall Alliance for the Stewardship
  of Creation, 216n80
Cottret, Bernard, 201, 248, 420n1

Council, Councils
  Bernese, 473
  City, 263, 323, 433
  Ecumenical, 204
  Fourth Lateran, 383
  General, 421
  Genevan, 22, 51–52, 55, 60, 141–42,
    247, 322–24, 327–28, 47
  Great, 421
  Lateran, 17
  Little, 544
  National Council of Churches of
    Singapore, 502
  Reformed Ecumenical, 20
  Second Vatican, 104
  Small/*Petit Conseil*, 28–29, 327–28,
    420n4, 421
  Supreme, 8
  Town, 141–42, 191, 474
  Trent, 254n40, 272n8, 308, 312n234,
    344, 383
Courthial, Pierre, 191–94, 211, 215
Crabeth, Dirck P., 480
Cranach, Lucas (the Elder), 480
Cranmer, Thomas, 79, 122, 132, 184, 399
Croce, Benedetto, 229n45
Crodel, Marcus, 171
Cummings, Owen F., 382
Cyprian, 191, 200, 203–4, 215, 318
Cyril of Alexandria, 403, 405n104, 406–7

Dabney, Robert L., xvii, 498
Damascus, John of, 512–14
Daneau, Lambert, 317, 334
Danes, Pierre, 196, 223n22
Dantzig, Charles, 73
Darlow, Thomas H., 5n2
Darwin, Charles, 436
De Bovelles, Charles, 73
De Clementia (Seneca), 196, 221–23,
    224n31, 225n32, 238, 240n95, 317
De France, Renée, 67, 91–94
De Koster, Lester, 420n1

Deacons, 31, 49, 54–55, 318, 322,
    421n8, 430n61, 432, 432n75
Deddens, Karl, 410
Democracy, 2, 7, 9–11, 13, 45, 54, 315,
    318, 336, 471, 487
Dentière, Marie, 90–91
Depravity, 178, 180–81, 288, 331, 339,
    341, 465, 442, 459, 490, 534
Descartes, 70–73, 76
Devereux, George, 69
Diodati, Giovanni, 6, 17
Discipline, Church, 21–33, 44–46,
    49–50, 52–53, 55, 58, 60, 81,
    85, 146, 248, 320, 322–23, 387,
    428n51, 430n60, 432nn71, 72,
    433nn78, 79, 81, 434, 434nn84,
    86, 477, 481n60
Divinization, 504–6, 516, 521, 527–29
Divines, Westminster, 123, 130, 136–37,
    267–68, 453–54
Divinitatis, Sensus/Sensum, 367
Divorce, 24, 51, 88–89
Dolet, Etienne, 74, 230n50
Dooyeweerd, Herman, 215
Dort, Synod of, 5–6, 19, 269
Douen, Orentin, 464, 479
Doumergue, Émile, xviii, 75, 75n49, 78,
    81–82, 337, 465, 467–69, 471,
    483, 485
Dreyfus Affair, 77
Dufour, Louis, 321
Duke, Alistair, 263n100
Dulles, John Foster, 13
Dunant, Henry, 14–15
Duncan, J. Ligon, 152
Dunlap, John, 11
Dupré, Louis, 229n46
Durand, Marie, 18
Dürer, Albrecht, 75, 467

Ecclesiastical Ordinances of Geneva,
    22–23, 34, 316–19, 321

Contributors

Henri A. G. Blocher is Professor of Systematic Theology at Faculte Libre de Theologie Evangelique, Vaux-sur-Seine, France.

Richard Burnett is Professor of Systematic Theology at Erskine Theological Seminary in Due West, South Carolina.

R. Scott Clark is Professor of Church History and Historical Theology at Westminster Seminary in Escondido, California.

William Edgar is Professor of Apologetics at Westminster Theological Seminary in Philadelphia, Pennsylvania.

Richard C. Gamble is Professor of Systematic Theology at Reformed Presbyterian Theological Seminary in Pittsburgh, Pennsylvania.

Isabelle Graesslé is the Director of the International Museum of the Reformation in Geneva, Switzerland.

David W. Hall is the Senior Pastor of Midway Presbyterian Church in Powder Springs, Georgia.

Darryl G. Hart is Adjunct Professor of Church History at Westminster Seminary in Escondido, California.

Michael Horton is the J. Gresham Machen Professor of Systematic Theology and Apologetics at Westminster Seminary in Escondido, California.

Terry L. Johnson is the Senior Pastor of the Independent Presbyterian Church in Savannah, Georgia.

Douglas F. Kelly is Professor of Systematic Theology at Reformed Theological Seminary in Charlotte, North Carolina.

Jae Sung Kim is the Senior Pastor of Korean United Church in Philadelphia, Pennsylvania.

Robert M. Kingdon is Emeritus Professor of History at the University of Wisconsin in Madison, Wisconsin.

George W. Knight III is Professor of New Testament at Greenville Presbyterian Theological Seminary in Greenville, South Carolina.

Anthony N. S. Lane is Professor of Historical Theology at the London School of Theology in London, England.

William A. McComish is the Dean Emeritus of St. Pierre Cathedral in Geneva, Switzerland.

Bruce L. McCormack is the Frederick and Margaret L. Weyerhaeuser Professor of Systematic Theology at Princeton Theological Seminary in Princeton, New Jersey.

James Edward McGoldrick is Professor of Church History at Greenville Presbyterian Theological Seminary in Greenville, South Carolina.

A. T. B. McGowan is Minister of the Inverness East Church in Inverness, Scotland; Professor of Theology at UHI Millennium Institute; and Honorary Professor of Reformed Doctrine at the University of Aberdeen.

Albert Mohler is President of the Southern Baptist Theological Seminary in Louisville, Kentucky.

Hughes Oliphant Old is the John H. Leith Professor of Reformed Theology and Worship at Erskine Theological Seminary in Due West, South Carolina.

Herman J. Selderhuis is Professor of Church History and Church Polity at the Theological University of Apeldoorn in the Netherlands.

John Witte Jr. is the Jonas Robitscher Professor of Law at Emory University School of Law in Atlanta, Georgia.